ALI

ALI

A Life

JONATHAN EIG

**SIMON &
SCHUSTER**

London · New York · Sydney · Toronto · New Delhi

A CBS COMPANY

First published in the US by Houghton Mifflin Harcourt, 2017
First published in Great Britain by Simon & Schuster UK Ltd, 2017
A CBS COMPANY

1 3 5 7 9 10 8 6 4 2

Simon & Schuster UK Ltd
1st Floor
222 Gray's Inn Road
London WC1X 8HB

www.simonandschuster.co.uk

Simon & Schuster Australia, Sydney
Simon & Schuster India, New Delhi

The author and publishers have made all reasonable efforts
to contact copyright-holders for permission, and apologise
for any omissions or errors in the form of credits given.
Corrections may be made to future printings.

A CIP catalogue record for this book
is available from the British Library.

ISBN: 978-1-4711-5593-2
Trade paperback ISBN: 978-1-4711-5594-9
Ebook ISBN: 978-1-4711-5595-6

Quotations from the conversation between Muhammad Ali and Joe Frazier
appearing in Chapter 29 are from *The Greatest: My Own Story* by Muhammad Ali,
with Richard Durham. Copyright © 1975 by Muhammad Ali, Herbert Muhammad,
Richard Durham. Permission arranged with Graymalkin Media, LLC.

Book design by Chloe Foster
Endpapers © Peter Angelo Simon. This photo was first published in
Muhammad Ali: Fighter's Heaven 1974: Photographs by Peter Angelo Simon
(Reel Art Press, 2016) and is reprinted with permission

Printed and bound by CPI Group (UK) Ltd, Croydon, CR0 4YY

Simon & Schuster UK Ltd are committed to sourcing paper
that is made from wood grown in sustainable forests and support the Forest
Stewardship Council, the leading international forest certification organisation.
Our books displaying the FSC logo are printed on FSC certified paper.

For Lola

CONTENTS

PREFACE

Miami, 1964

ROUND 1. THE CHALLENGER: CASSIUS CLAY

A long, black Cadillac glides past waving palm trees and stops in front of the Surfside Community Center. The afternoon sun flashes off the car's chrome bumpers. Cassius Clay gets out. He's dressed in a custom-made denim jacket and swinging a dandyish walking stick.

He checks to see if anyone has noticed him.

Not yet.

He shouts, "I'm the biggest thing in history! I'm the king!"

Clay is tall and stunningly handsome, with an irresistible smile. He's a force of gravity, quickly pulling people into his orbit. Horns honk. Cars on Collins Avenue stop. Women lean out of hotel windows and shout his name. Men in shorts and girls in tight pants gather around to see the boastful boxer they've been hearing so much about.

"Float like a butterfly! Sting like a bee!" he yells. "Rumble, young man, rumble! Ahhhh!"

As the crowd grows, the chief of police arrives and tries to move Clay off the street and into a parking lot where he might cause less trouble. A newspaper photographer points his camera, but instead of smiling Clay opens his mouth wide in a pantomime scream. He throws a left jab that stops inches short of the camera.

"I'm pretty and move as fast as lightning," he says in his sweet Kentucky accent. "I'm just twenty-two and I'm gonna make a million dollars!"

ROUND 2. THE CHAMPION: SONNY LISTON

Sonny Liston's left hand is a battering ram, his right a sledgehammer. *Bom!*
Boom! Bom! Boom! He pounds the heavy bag so hard the walls shake and
sportswriters' hands jump as they scribble ornate synonyms for "scary."

Liston is the most punishing boxer in more than a generation, with fists
each measuring fifteen inches around and a chest jutting forth like the front
end of an M4 Sherman tank. He is fearless and vicious. How vicious? Once,
he started a fight with a cop, beat the cop senseless, snatched his gun, picked
him up and dumped him in an alley, and then walked away smiling, wearing
the cop's hat.

Liston does not merely defeat his opponents; he breaks them, shames
them, haunts them, leaves them flinching from his punches in their dreams.
Sonny Liston is America's curse. He is the black menace sprung from white
racist stereotypes. And he likes it that way.

"There's got to be good guys, and there's got to be bad guys," he says, comparing the world to a cowboy movie. "Bad guys are supposed to lose. I change
that. I win."

When he learns that the young man he will soon fight for boxing's world
heavyweight championship is outside the community center where he trains,
Liston steps into the sun to meet the troublemaker. He swats away the out-
stretched hands of fans and marches until he's nearly within punching distance of Cassius Clay.

Liston stops and smiles.

"Clay," he tells a reporter, "is just a little kid who needs a spanking."

ROUND 3. THE MINISTER: MALCOLM X

In a cramped hotel room near John F. Kennedy Airport in New York, thirty-eight-year-old Malcolm X talks into the night, telling his life story to a
reporter. Malcolm is a tall, lean man with a strong jaw and horn-rimmed
glasses. Even smiling, he bears a stern expression.

Malcolm paces as he dictates, sitting only to scribble notes on napkins.
He can't wait until old age to produce his autobiography. He's recently been
suspended from the Nation of Islam for disobeying the radical group's leader,

Elijah Muhammad, and doesn't know if he'll ever go back. A few months earlier, Elijah Muhammad had ordered his ministers not to comment on the assassination of President Kennedy, out of respect for a nation in mourning, but Malcolm had spoken out anyway, saying the killing was an outgrowth of the violence sown by America in Vietnam, the Congo, and Cuba. "Being an old farm boy myself," Malcolm had said, "chickens coming home to roost never did make me sad; they've always made me glad." There are other issues, other forces driving a wedge between Malcolm and his teacher. Malcolm has learned that Elijah Muhammad had fathered numerous children with young women employed by the Nation of Islam. Malcolm has been telling others in the organization about their leader's disappointing behavior. Now, Elijah Muhammad is furious, and rumors have made their way to New York that Muhammad wants Malcolm X dead.

All his life Malcolm has survived. He's survived poverty, prison, and knife fights. He plans to survive this, too.

This is where his struggle for survival starts: in a hotel room by the airport, working on his autobiography, because words give power. And Malcolm isn't going to let Elijah Muhammad or J. Edgar Hoover's Federal Bureau of Investigation or the white news media or anyone else define him with *their* words. He will define himself with his own words, his own new credo, on his own terms. A great revolution is building in America. The prevailing racial order is under attack with a fury not seen since the Civil War. Black men and women are awakening and fighting for power. Change is coming, finally, and Malcolm is determined to push it — force it, if need be — regardless of what Elijah Muhammad or anyone else has to say.

It's 2 in the morning when Malcolm leaves the hotel and drives to his home in Queens. An FBI agent monitors his every move. Later the same day, Malcolm, his wife, and three daughters board a plane for the family's first vacation ever. This, too, is part of Malcolm's plan. He wants the world to see that he's not a bomb-throwing lunatic but a father, a husband, a minister of God who believes America can and must reform. He plans to take pictures and jot notes for a newspaper feature story he's calling "Malcolm X, the Family Man."

When the plane touches down in Miami, a car waits to carry Malcolm and his family to their blacks-only motel on Miami Beach. According to an FBI informant, the driver is Cassius Clay.

ROUND 4. THE CHALLENGER: CASSIUS CLAY

Clay shouts like he's possessed by demons: "You ain't got a chance, ain't no way you gonna beat me and you know it!"

It's the morning of the fight, time for the combatants to meet the press, show off their powerful bodies, and step on the scales to check their weights. The room reeks of cigarette smoke, body odor, and cheap cologne. The reporters have never seen a professional athlete behave so unprofessionally. Some say Clay has lost his mind, that fear of Sonny Liston has made him snap.

Everyone in the room is talking, but Clay is talking loudest of all.

"No chance! No chance!" he hollers, ignoring the boxing officials threatening to fine him if he doesn't shut up. Like Malcolm X, Clay won't be told what to do. He'll beat the odds and defy the expectations of any who would seek to control or exploit him.

Clay points at Liston, saying he's ready to fight the champ now, this very instant, without gloves, without a referee, without a paying audience, man against man. His face shows no trace of humor. He yanks off his white robe, revealing a long, lean, brown physique, his stomach and chest muscles rippled. He lunges at Liston as members of his entourage grab hold and restrain him.

Maybe Clay's not crazy. Maybe he knows instinctively, or from the experience of growing up with a bullying, violent father, that the worst thing a threatened man can do is show fear.

"I am the *GREATEST!*" Clay shouts. "I am the *CHAMP!*"

ROUND 5. THE CHAMPION: SONNY LISTON

Liston warns opponents about the power of his punch, both its short- and long-term effects. Explaining the dangers to a reporter, he slides the knuckles of one enormous hand into the grooves between the knuckles of the other enormous hand, and he lectures: "See, the different parts of the brain set in little cups like this. When you get hit a terrible shot — *pop!* — the brain flops out of them cups and you're knocked out. Then the brain settles back in the cups and you come to. But after this happens enough times, or sometimes even once if the shot's hard enough, the brain don't settle back right in them cups, and that's when you start needin' other people to help you get around."

Cassius Clay might run away for a round or two, but Liston promises he will catch his young opponent sooner or later, and, when he does, he will hit Clay so hard his brain will flop out of its cups.

ROUND 6. IN THE RING

Gray smoke hangs under brilliant white ring lights, obfuscating everything in sight. Reporters peck their portable typewriters and brush cigarette ash from their neckties. There's little debate among the men in the press corps about who will win tonight. The question — the only question, in most minds — is whether Cassius Clay leaves the ring unconscious or dead.

This is more than a boxing match, and at least a small percentage of the people in the Miami Beach Convention Center understand that. They sense there are brutal, romantic forces building beneath the placid surface of American life, and that Cassius Clay is a messenger for the change to come, a radical in the guise of a traditional American athlete. "He fools them," Malcolm X says of Clay before the fight. "One forgets that though a clown never imitates a wise man, the wise man can imitate the clown."

Malcolm gazes up into the ring lights from the front row, where he sits with the singer Sam Cooke and the boxer Sugar Ray Robinson. Rumors swirl that Malcolm plans to bring Cassius Clay into the Black Muslim fold.

Retired heavyweight champ Joe Louis sits ringside too, leaning into a microphone and describing the action for fans preparing to watch the fight in black and white on movie-theater screens across the country. Louis, known as the "Brown Bomber" during his boxing days, was the greatest heavyweight of his generation, a black man who earned the admiration of white Americans for his service in World War II, for defeating German boxer Max Schmeling in 1938, and for showing humility: accepting that even a black champion should never behave as if he were the equal of an ordinary white man.

Clay enters the ring and removes his robe to reveal white satin shorts with red stripes. He dances on long, lean legs and flicks jabs at the air to stay loose. Liston makes Clay wait and then lumbers slowly and silently through the arena and into the ring.

The men exchange glares.

The bell rings.

"That's the only time I was ever scared in the ring," Clay will say years later, after he has won and lost the heavyweight championship three times; after he has declared his loyalty to the Nation of Islam and taken the name Muhammad Ali; after he has become one of the most despised men in America and then, presto-change-o, one of the most beloved; after he has become everything from a draft dodger to an American hero; after he has established himself as one of the greatest heavyweight boxers of all time: a fighter with an unmatched combination of speed, power, and stamina, with a freakish ability to absorb punishment and remain standing; after he has become the most famous human being on the planet, "the very spirit of the 20th Century," as one writer called him; after Parkinson's disease and somewhere around 200,000 blows to the body and head have robbed him of the very things that made him astonishing: the swiftness, the strength, the charm, the arrogance, the wordplay, the grace, the force-of-nature masculinity, and the boyish twinkle in his eyes that said he wanted to be loved no matter how outrageously he behaved.

Cassius Clay's celebrity will carry through the civil rights era, the Cold War, the Vietnam War, the terrorist attacks of September 11, 2001, and well into the twenty-first century. He will live to see his boyhood home in Louisville turned into a museum, and, across town, yet another, bigger museum built to honor his legacy. The arc of his life will inspire millions, even if it ignites adoration in some and revulsion in others.

Much of Clay's life will be spent in the throes of a social revolution, one he will help to propel, as black Americans force white Americans to rewrite the terms of citizenship. Clay will win fame as words and images travel more quickly around the globe, allowing individuals to be seen and heard as never before. People will sing songs and compose poems and make movies and plays about him, telling the story of his life in a strange blend of truth and fiction rather than as a real mirror of the complicated and yearning soul who seemed to hide in plain sight. His appetite for affection will prove insatiable, opening him to relations with countless girls and women, including four wives. He will earn the kind of money once reserved for oil barons and real-estate tycoons, and his extraordinary wealth and trusting nature will make him an easy mark for hustlers. He will make his living by cruelly taunting opponents before beating them bloody, yet he will become a lasting worldwide symbol of tolerance, benevolence, and pacifism.

"I am America," Clay will proudly declare. "I am the part you won't recognize. But get used to me. Black, confident, cocky; my name, not yours; my religion, not yours; my goals, my own; get used to me."

His extraordinary gift for boxing will cement his greatness and make the many contradictions of his life possible. Yet this will be the bitterest irony in a lifetime full of them: his great gift will also instigate his downfall.

In the fight's opening seconds, Liston throws big lefts and rights, going for one of the quick knockouts he has come to expect, to depend on. Clay dodges and ducks and bends backward like he has a rubber spine. Liston clomps forward, forcing Clay into the ropes, where big hitters usually destroy fancy-footed opponents. But just as Liston's eyes go wide in anticipation of murder, Clay slips sideways, and a left hook by Liston whistles past, hitting only air.

Clay dances in a circle, fast and light as a hummingbird, and then, suddenly, flicks a left jab at Liston's face. It lands. Thousands of voices scream as one. Liston unleashes another powerful right, but Clay ducks and slides left, entirely avoiding the blow. He straightens and flicks another jab that meets its mark, and then another.

There's less than a minute left in the round when Clay throws a hard right that thuds solidly against Liston's head. Clay dances, then plants his feet ever so briefly and unleashes a machine-gun-fast flurry of punches, right-left-right-left-left-right. Every shot connects.

Suddenly, everything changes.

The crowd is roaring. Liston is ducking for cover.

Clay is finally showing what he's known all along: that what he can do is more important than what he says.

And what Clay can do is fight.

PART I

1

Cassius Marcellus Clay

His great-grandfather was a slave. His grandfather was a convicted murderer who shot a man through the heart in a quarrel over a quarter. His father was a drinker, a bar fighter, a womanizer, and a wife beater who once in a drunken rage slashed his eldest son with a knife. These are the roots of Muhammad Ali, who was born with what he called the slave name Cassius Marcellus Clay Jr. and who ultimately became one of the most famous and influential men of his time.

John Henry Clay, the great-grandfather of Muhammad Ali, was counted as a piece of property by his owner and by the government of the United States. He was tall, strong, and handsome. His skin was creamy brown. He had a sturdy chest, broad shoulders, high cheekbones, and warmly expressive eyes. He belonged to the family of Henry Clay, the U.S. senator from Kentucky, one of the most hot-headed and controversial politicians of his era, a man who called slavery a national disgrace, an abomination that corrupted the souls of masters and slaves, a "great evil . . . the darkest spot in the map of our country."

Senator Clay spoke out boldly against slavery. He founded the American Colonization Society with the goal of shipping America's slaves back to Africa. At the same time, he and most of his Kentucky family members continued to own scores of men, women, and children of African heritage.

When Senator Clay's son, Henry Jr., traveled to Mexico in 1846 to fight in the Mexican-American War, he took with him a young slave named John. According to members of Muhammad Ali's family, that slave was John Henry

Clay, Ali's great-grandfather. Muhammad Ali's descendants also maintain that John Henry Clay was the illegitimate son of Henry Clay or Henry Clay Jr. It's possible to look at photos of the white Henry Clay Sr. and the black John Henry Clay and see a resemblance, but there has been no attempt so far to prove the connection with genetic tests. Marriages, births, and deaths were seldom carefully recorded among slaves. It was even more rare for white men to acknowledge the children they sired with black women, many of those children the product of rape. Names proved nothing. Names were the property of masters, not slaves, and they were adhered like cattle brands. Slave names changed on a whim or on an auction block. Often, when a slave was freed or when he escaped from bondage, he celebrated by choosing his own, new name. "For it is through our names that we first place ourselves in the world," Ralph Ellison wrote.

On January 1, 1847, Henry Clay Jr. sent a letter from Mexico to his son in Kentucky. It read, in part, "John asks me to give his Xmas compliments to you. He is still with me and has turned out on the whole a very good boy. He thanks God that he is still safe as several of his black companions have been killed by the Mexicans." Soon after writing the letter, while leading a charge of his regiment, Henry Clay Jr. was killed. John Henry Clay returned to Kentucky, still a slave.

It's not clear when he was emancipated, but the 1870 U.S. Census shows John Clay as a married man, a laborer, father of four children, and the owner of property valued at $2,500. With his wife, Sallie, he would go on to have nine children, including Herman Heaton Clay, the grandfather of Muhammad Ali, born in 1876 in Louisville.

Herman Heaton Clay quit school after the third grade. He grew into a handsome man, strong and tall. In 1898, he married a woman named Priscilla Nather. They had a baby boy, but the marriage didn't last. On November 4, 1900, while playing craps in an alley in Louisville, Herman Clay snatched a quarter from a man and refused to give it back. Later the same day, Herman presciently told his brother Cassius that anyone who bothered him about the money "was going to get hurt." Herman and his brother were standing beside a telephone pole on the corner of 16th and Harney when they spotted Charles Dickey, a friend of the man who'd been robbed of the quarter. Dickey was twenty-five years old, an illiterate day laborer. He carried a cane with a heavily weighted handle as he approached the Clay brothers. Herman Clay had a gun. Cassius clutched a knife so Dickey could see it.

Dickey asked why Cassius had the knife.

"I had this knife before you came down here," Herman's brother said.

"You must have intended doing something with it . . . ," Dickey replied.

According to witnesses, no further words were exchanged. Herman Clay turned, pulled his .38, and fired once, striking Dickey in the heart. "Death was instantaneous," the *Louisville Courier-Journal* reported.

Herman ran from the scene of the crime but was quickly captured. He was convicted of murder and sentenced to life in prison. Shortly after his conviction, he and Priscilla divorced. After six years in the state penitentiary in Frankfort, Kentucky, Clay was paroled. Three years later, on December 30, 1909, he married Edith Greathouse. They went on to raise twelve children. Their first child, Everett Clay, went to prison for killing his wife with a razor and died behind bars. Their second child, Cassius Marcellus Clay, born November 11, 1912, became the father of Muhammad Ali.

Slavery was no abstraction to the black Clay family of the twentieth century. It had specific people attached to it. It had details. Cassius Marcellus Clay Sr. inherited his name from two people, one black, one white. The black Cassius Clay was his uncle, who had stood by his brother Herman's side the day Herman shot and killed a man. The white Cassius Clay was Senator Henry Clay's cousin, born in 1810. The white Cassius Clay was a lawyer, soldier, publisher, politician, and critic of slavery. "For those who have respect for the laws of God, I have this argument," he once said, presenting a leather-bound copy of the Holy Bible. "For those who believe in the laws of man, I have this argument." He set down a copy of the state constitution. "And for those who believe neither in the laws of God nor of man, I have this argument." He set down a Bowie knife and two pistols. On another occasion, Clay was stabbed in the chest during a debate with a proslavery candidate for state office, but he survived the attack and stabbed the rival back.

The white Cassius Clay believed that enslavement was a moral evil, and he called for the gradual freeing of all slaves. Although he did not free all the slaves who belonged to his estate, his outspoken views made him a hero to many black men, enough so that a former slave named John Henry Clay would name one of his sons Cassius; Herman Heaton Clay, born a decade after slavery's end, would do the same; and Cassius Marcellus Clay, born in 1912, would pass along the name one more time to his son born in 1942, the name enduring as the effects of slavery and racism continued to resound across the country, through Reconstruction, separate-but-equal, the birth of the National Association for the Advancement of Colored People (NAACP), Jack Johnson, the Great Migration, Joe Louis, Marcus Garvey's fight for black independence, World War II, Jackie Robinson, and the birth of the twentieth-century civil rights movement.

2

The Loudest Child

Muhammad Ali's father fought only when he was drunk.

Cassius Marcellus Clay Sr. was a man well known and not particularly well respected among his neighbors in the all-black West End section of Louisville. Cash, as everyone called him, dropped out of school after the eighth grade. He made a modest living as a sign painter.

At an age when most men settled down and started families, Cash wore shiny white shoes and tight pants and danced all night and deep into the morning at smoky jazz clubs and juke joints in the West End and Little Africa neighborhoods. He was six feet tall, muscular, and dark skinned, with a pencil-thin mustache. The women of the West End called him "Dark Gable," only half-jokingly. Cash Clay boasted about his good looks, his powerful physique, the luxurious vibrato of his singing voice, and the beautiful billboards and signs he painted for local businesses, most of them black owned. There was KING KARL'S THREE ROOMS OF FURNITURE on Market Street; A. B. HARRIS, M.D., DELIVERIES AND FEMALE DISORDERS on Dumesnil Street; and JOYCE'S BARBER SHOP on 13th Street. He painted Bible scenes on church walls, too. Compensation for a church job might be twenty-five dollars and a free chicken dinner, hardly enough to call a living, but there was something to be said for a black man in the South who could make his own way in the world, with his own hands and his own talent, without the permission or approbation of a white man. Cash had heard his father, Herman, preach about the dangers and indignities of working for the white man. A black man was better off on his own, Herman had always said.

Cash was far from famous, and even further from wealthy, but those painted signs provided independence as well as a degree of public recognition that he loved. People hired him not only for his excellent work but also for his gregariousness. "When Cassius is working on a sign, he has to stop a hundred times a day to talk to people he knows who were just passing by," said Mel Davis, who hired Cash to paint a sign for his pawnbroker shop on Market Street. "You don't want anybody else to do your sign painting for you, but you sure don't want to pay Cassius by the hour."

Cash insisted it wasn't lack of talent or training that prevented him from gaining fame and fortune as a serious artist; it was Jim Crow America keeping him down, he said, referring to the so-called Jim Crow laws that enforced racial segregation in the southern United States.

When sober, Cash was enormously entertaining, liable to burst out in laughter or a few stanzas of Nat King Cole. When he drank — gin was his usual — he grew loud, obnoxiously opinionated, and frequently violent. "He couldn't fight a lick," one of his friends said. "But as soon as he'd have too many drinks, he'd take on anybody."

Cash was in no hurry to settle down, and, given that his personality and income were both unsteady, women were not exactly begging him for commitment. Clay never would settle down — he would drink and chase women all his life — but he did eventually marry. He was walking home from work one day when he spotted a girl across the street. "You're a beautiful lady!" he shouted, according to the story he would later tell his children.

Odessa Lee Grady was light skinned, round, and giggly, still enrolled at Central High School in Louisville. She was the granddaughter of Tom Morehead, a light-skinned black man who fought for the Union in the Civil War, rising from private to sergeant in one year of service. Morehead was the son of a white Kentuckian who married a slave named Dinah. Her other grandfather may also have been a white man — an Irish immigrant named Abe Grady — but the evidence supporting her Irish ancestry is shaky.

As a mere teenager, Odessa was probably unaware of Cash Clay's reputation when the older man called to her from across the street. Odessa was a churchgoer and a conscientious student, never the sort of girl who hung around nightclubs.

She was widely admired for her hard work and sunny demeanor. She grew up in Earlington, a small town in western Kentucky. When her coalminer father abandoned the family, Odessa was shipped off to Louisville to live with one of her aunts. To pay for clothes, Odessa worked after school as a cook for white families. No one recalled hearing her complain. Even so, for a teenaged girl living in the big city, away from her mother and father during the depths of the Great Depression, an early marriage to a handsome, confident older man who earned a decent income must have been tempting. After Odessa became pregnant, marriage probably seemed compulsory.

Cash and Odessa were opposites in many ways. He was rambunctious; she was gentle. He was tall and lean; she was short and plump. He railed against the injustices of racial discrimination; she smiled and suffered quietly. He was a Methodist who seldom worshiped; she was a Baptist who never missed a Sunday service at Mount Zion Church. He drank and stayed out late; she stayed home and cooked and cleaned. Yet for all their differences, Cash and Odessa both loved to laugh, and when Cash teased her or told her stories or burst into song, Odessa would release herself completely in a beautiful, high-pitched ripple that helped inspire her nickname: Bird.

They probably met in 1933 or 1934, given that Odessa said she was sixteen at the time of their introduction, but they didn't marry until 1941. The wedding took place on June 25 in St. Louis, when Odessa was already about three months pregnant. On January 17, 1942, she delivered her first son. The six-pound, seven-ounce baby was born at Louisville City Hospital, well after the anticipated due date. Odessa said she endured a painful and protracted labor, which concluded only after a doctor used forceps to grab the baby boy by his big head and extract it from her womb. The forceps left a small rectangular mark on the boy's right cheek that would remain throughout his life.

Cash favored the name Rudolph, for the Hollywood actor Rudolph Valentino, but Odessa insisted that the child should have his father's name, "the most beautiful name for a man I ever heard," she said, a name rooted in the nation's and family's tortured history, and so they called him Cassius Marcellus Clay Jr. On his birth certificate, the name was misspelled as "Cassuis," but his parents either didn't notice or didn't care enough to have it corrected.

Cash and Odessa lived at 1121 West Oak Street, a block from the home where Odessa had been living, in an apartment that probably rented for six or seven dollars a month. The baby's birth certificate indicated that Cash

Clay worked for Southern Bell Telephone and Telegraph, a suggestion that he was concerned enough about starting a family to secure a steady paycheck for the first and last time in his life.

Cassius Jr. was the loudest child in the hospital, his mother told journalists years later. "He cried so much he could touch off all the other babies in the ward," Odessa said. "They would all be sleeping nice and quiet, and then Cassius would start screaming and hollering. And the next thing every baby in the ward would be screaming."

Less than two years after the birth of Cassius Jr., Odessa and Cassius Sr. had another son. This time Cash got his way, and they named the baby Rudolph Arnett Clay. The Clay family purchased a cottage at 3302 Grand Avenue, in Louisville's West End. It was a tiny box of a house, no more than eight hundred square feet, with two bedrooms and one bathroom. At one point, Cash painted the cottage pink—Odessa's favorite color. Cash also built a goldfish pond and dug a vegetable garden in the backyard. Later, he constructed a small addition to the rear of the house so the boys could have more room to play. Cassius Jr. and little Rudy shared a room that was about twelve feet wide and twenty feet long, the wallpaper white with red roses. The boys slept side by side in twin beds. Cassius had the bed by the window, where the view was of the neighbor's house, seventy-two inches away.

Their accommodations were modest, and most of their clothes came from Goodwill, including shoes that Cash would reinforce with cardboard linings. Even so, the Clay boys never set out to school haggard or hungry. The house smelled of paint from Cash's large supply of paint cans and brushes. But the aroma of Odessa's fine cooking often overwhelmed the paint fumes. Odessa cooked chili. She made fried chicken with green beans and potatoes. She mixed cabbage with carrots and onions and fried it up in oil until the aroma filled the house and floated out the windows so the boys could smell it in the yard. She baked chocolate cakes and made banana pudding. At one point, the family owned a pet chicken, and at another a black dog with a white tail named Rusty. As they got older, Cassius and Rudy would have electric train sets, motorized scooters, and bicycles.

Some of the roads in the West End were crudely paved, and some of the houses near the Clays' cottage were mere shacks. But it was a far better neighborhood than nearby Little Africa, where outhouses and unpaved streets remained well into the middle of the twentieth century. Most of the Clays' neighbors in the 1940s were solid earners: plumbers, schoolteachers, chauffeurs, Pullman porters, auto mechanics, and shop owners. "Of course, we knew everyone who lived in every house on the block," recalled Georgia Powers, who grew up on Grand Avenue with the Clays and went on to become the first African American and first woman elected to the Kentucky State Senate. "There were thirteen teachers and three doctors — one was an M.D., one was a dentist, and one was a Ph.D. Joseph Ray was a banker, and he'd drive by in his black Cadillac and tip his hat and say, 'Hello, Miss Georgia.' It sent a message to all of us in the community."

Black children from the West End were warned about venturing into poorer, more dangerous black neighborhoods, such as Little Africa or Smoketown. They didn't have to be warned about avoiding white neighborhoods. The West End offered a sense of security. "Our childhood was not difficult," recalled Alice Kean Houston, who grew up two doors down from the Clays. "We had businesses and banks and movies. It wasn't until we went outside that world that we recognized our world really was different."

Odessa Clay recalled her first son's early years in a biography written in pen on lined notebook paper, with fine penmanship but many errors in spelling, capitalization, and punctuation. She composed the biography at the request of a magazine writer in 1966. "Cassius Jr's life to me was an unusual one from other Children, and he is still unusual today," Odessa wrote. "When a baby he would never sit down. When I would take him for a stroll in his stroller, he would always stand up and try to see everything. He tried to talk at a very early age. He tried so hard he learned to walk at 10 months old. When he was one year old he would love for some One to rock him to sleep, if not he would sit in a Chair and keep bomping his head on the back of the Chair until he would go to sleep. He did not want you to dress him or undress him. He would always crie. He wanted to feed himself when he was very young. At the age of 2 years old he always got up at 5 in the morning and throw everything Out of the Dresser's drawer and leave the things in the middle of the floor. He loved to play in water. He loved to talks a lot and he love to eat, loved to climb up on things. He would not play with his toyes. He would take all the Puts and pan Out of the Cabienet and beat on them. He Could beat on anything and get rhythm. When a very small Child he walked upon his toes, By doing this he has Well developed Arch's, and that is why he is so fast on his feet."

As a baby, Cassius loved to eat but hated being fed. He insisted on handling the food himself, the bigger the mess he made the better. He had a massive appetite and grew big and strong and endlessly playful. He never walked when he could run and, in Odessa's words, was in such a hurry that he contracted chicken pox and measles at the same time. His first word — and his only word, for many months — was "Gee." He would look at his mother and say, "Gee! Gee!" He would look at his father and say, "Gee! Gee!" He would point to food and say, "Gee! Gee!" When he needed a new diaper, he announced it by declaring "Gee! Gee!" Naturally, Odessa and Cash began calling their little boy "Gee," or sometimes "Gee-Gee." Odessa also called her son "Woody Baby," a derivation of "Little Baby." But "Gee-Gee" was the tag that really stuck, not only in the house and not only throughout his childhood, but all over the West End and throughout his life.

Cassius craved adventure. He crawled into the laundry machine, climbed into the sink, and chased the chicken around the yard. When he was one or two years old, he threw his first hard punch, accidentally hitting his mother in the mouth and knocking loose a tooth that her dentist would later remove. By the time he was three, Cassius was too big for his baby bed. Bus drivers would insist that Odessa pay a fare for the child, assuming the boy was at least five or six when he was only three or four and still eligible to ride for free. Never one to challenge authority, Odessa paid the driver without argument.

Odessa knew from the beginning that both her boys were precocious, but Cassius more so, with little regard for rules and no concern for punishment. His rebelliousness and swagger came from his father, just as much as his warmth and generosity came from his mother. When Rudy got in trouble, Cassius would warn his parents that Rudy was *his* baby and that no one was going to spank *his* baby. With that he would grab Rudy by the arm and hustle his brother off to their room.

Patience was not his strength. When Cassius started attending the blacksonly Virginia Street Elementary School, Odessa would send him every day with lunch. He would eat it on the way to school, even though he'd already consumed a big breakfast at home. Some children would have worried that if they ate their lunch before school they'd be hungry later but not Cassius. He assumed he would improvise a solution, and he usually did, cajoling friends at lunchtime to share their food. To address the problem, Odessa stopped packing Cassius a meal and instead gave him money to buy a hot lunch in the school cafeteria. Cassius was not to be denied, though. He used his mother's money to buy his friend Tuddie's bagged lunch and ate *that* on the way to school.

By the time he was seven or eight, Cassius was the leader of a pack of boys ever on the lookout for action. Odessa would look through the screen door and see her eldest son standing on the concrete porch, like a politician on a platform, addressing his youthful followers about what he had planned for them. As soon as he was old enough to keep up, Rudy Clay became his brother's shadow and chief competitor. "We were like twins," Rudy recalled years later. For fun, Cassius would stand in the seventy-two-inch gap between his house and the neighbor's and let Rudy throw rocks at him. Rudy threw as hard as he could while his older brother jumped, ducked, and darted. The boys played marbles and jacks and hide-and-seek, with Cassius almost never letting his younger brother win. When they played cowboys and Indians, Cassius was the cowboy — every time.

The boys were teased and picked on, not only because they were loud and called attention to themselves but also because they had unusually big heads. "Honey," recalled their aunt Mary Turner, "those kids had some large heads, let me tell you. They'd be sitting on the edge of the curb, shooting marbles or playing some kind of street game, when one or two kids would sneak up behind them and bump their heads together, *pop!* Then the kids would scamper off, with Rudy and Cassius at their heels. They thought that was great fun. But after the boys grew up a little, that kind of thing stopped. Cassius and Rudy could handle most all the boys on the block, because they were very quick and very big. Eventually their bodies grew enough so their heads weren't too big."

Before long, it was Cassius and Rudy who were teasing and torturing smaller children. They would borrow bicycles from smaller children and keep them for hours. "They weren't being mean," their aunt said, "but they just thought they were the greatest little things around. Cassius thought nobody had a brother as good as Rudy, and Rudy thought the same way about Cassius."

Friends who grew up with the Clay boys in the West End recalled Cassius as a fast runner and a good but not especially gifted athlete. He couldn't swim at all. He would agree to play softball or touch football, but he had little passion for those sports.

"That Gee would run around and get me in trouble all the time," recalled his classmate and neighbor Owen Sitgraves. "We used to hide in the alley behind Kinslow's flower shop and roll old tires in the street in front of cars and make 'em stop. Once, the tire got stuck under a car, and we ran out the other end of the alley and around some houses and came around to look at it. The lady got out of the car. She said, 'Boys, I'll pay y'all two dollars to get that tire out from under my car.' So we got the jack out of her trunk and we got that tire out for her." On another occasion, Owen and Cassius found an old shirt in an alley and filled it with dirt, then flung the shirt in an open window of a passing bus. "This guy in a white panama suit — he must've been on a date — he got out and chased us all the way from 34th and Virginia to the Cotter Homes, but we were too fast . . . I still feel bad about that. He was really clean."

Cassius would always love the playfulness and cruelty of pranks. He once cut down his father's plum tree. He imitated a siren's sound so well that drivers pulled to the side of the road and craned their necks looking for the police car. He plucked tomatoes from the family's garden and lobbed them over the fence of a teacher's house, splattering guests at the teacher's backyard party. He tied a string to the curtains in his parents' bedroom, ran the string across the hall to his own room, then waited until his parents were in bed to rustle the curtain. He covered himself in sheets and sprang from dark corners of the house to scare his mother. No amount of scolding or punishment would inhibit him.

"I would make 'em take naps every day," Odessa recalled, "and one day he said to Rudy, 'You know what, Rudy? We too big to be in here taking naps.' And they never did take another one."

When the boys' disobedience went too far, Odessa would send them to the bathroom, where Cash would bend Cassius and Rudy over his knee one at a time and spank them. These punishments did nothing to make Cassius more cautious. "Cassius Jr. would always go in first and get his spanking and go right out and do something else!" Odessa paused to laugh as she told the story to Jack Olsen, who interviewed her for a series of stories in *Sports Illustrated* in 1966. "He was a very unusual child."

When Cassius's friends described the fun they had as children, they sometimes failed to mention the myriad ways that racial discrimination and prejudice hung over their lives. In part, that may be because Cassius Clay's friends and neighbors took discrimination for granted, so deeply was it ingrained in their daily activities. It may also have been because black people in Louisville in the late 1940s and early 1950s believed they were better off than other black Americans, that they were fortunate to live in a city that exhibited "a more polite racism," as Louisville historian Tom Owen put it.

Although the majority of Kentuckians sympathized with the Confederacy, Kentucky did not secede from the Union during the Civil War. No race riots or lynchings occurred in Louisville between 1865 and 1930. Unlike most of their southern counterparts, black Louisvillians had been granted the right to vote beginning in the 1870s and had never lost it. Louisville's white civic leaders expressed frequent and seemingly genuine concern for the living conditions of their black neighbors and gave generously of their own money to support black causes. In return, of course, these white civic leaders, like the slave owners from whom some of them were descended, expected blacks to be passive and accept their second-class status without fuss or fury.

Some white community leaders were patronizing, proclaiming that without proper guidance and support, the Negroes of Louisville would return to their barbaric African ways. Many white Louisvillians deemed segregation intrinsic, natural, and inevitable. Others were more progressive and genuine in their desire to help. Robert W. Bingham, owner of the *Louisville Courier-Journal*, served on local branches of the Urban League and the Commission on Interracial Cooperation. Jewish leaders, including the family of Supreme Court justice Louis Brandeis, worked with volunteer organizations serving black neighborhoods. Prominent local white attorneys fought against housing discrimination.

Black and white journalists who visited the city in the 1940s and 1950s stated almost unanimously that black people in Louisville were treated better than those in the Deep South and in many northern cities. They usually neglected to mention, because it was taken for granted, that black people still lacked equal access to housing, schools, employment, and healthcare. They didn't point out, because it was standard treatment, that while black customers were allowed to buy clothes in the city's big department stores, they couldn't try on the clothes first. They also failed to say, because it was so obvious, that many of the wealthy white people helping black causes were motivated by the desire to keep the black community from rising in protest.

For young Cassius Clay, it would have been impossible not to notice that there were, in essence, two Louisvilles: one for blacks and one for whites. For blacks, the best schools, best stores, and best hospitals were off limits. So were most country clubs and banks. Black moviegoers were permitted in only a handful of the big downtown movie theaters, and even then only in the balcony.

"Bird," Cassius would ask his mother when they went downtown, "where do the colored people work? Bird, what did they do with the colored people?"

The answer was clear, if not necessarily easy to explain to a child. Louisville's economy was booming in the years after World War II, with thousands of new manufacturing jobs. Tobacco plants, distilleries, and tire factories offered steady employment, although black workers were routinely paid less than white workers and routinely denied promotions. In 1949, the annual median income for black workers in Louisville was $1,251, while the median income for white workers was almost twice that, at $2,202. Black workers got the dirtier and more dangerous jobs, not only the lower-paying ones. Often, black men worked in the service of white men as waiters, caddies, and shoeshine boys, where docility was not just a job requirement but also necessary for survival. For black women, prospects were even worse. A handful worked as secretaries, hairdressers, or schoolteachers, but 45 percent of all black women who worked in Louisville did the same thing as Odessa Clay — they walked or rode buses to well-to-do neighborhoods, where they spent their days cooking and cleaning for white families, carving their identities from the stone slab of white supremacy. The scraps of leftover food they were permitted to take home helped feed their families, and the money they earned not only paid the household bills but purchased prayer books for their churches.

According to his mother's recollections, Cassius quickly made a merciless judgment: that the world was for white people. He recognized it long before he could have understood it as he watched his mother return home, exhausted after caring for white families, then summoning energy to care for her own.

Sometimes, when he was a child and still learning how society made distinctions about race and how much those distinctions mattered, Cassius Jr. would ask his mother whether she was black or white. She was, after all, much fairer than her husband. But Odessa wasn't light enough to pass for white, nor did she try. The shade of her skin and the genetic influence of her white ancestors mattered little in her day-to-day life. As far as the laws and customs of Kentucky and the United States of America were concerned, the Clays were black—or "colored," to use the term more commonly applied at the time—and that racial designation determined where they could eat, where they could shop, where they could work, where they could send their children to school, where they could live, how they would be treated if they broke the law or were accused of doing so, whom they married, how they would be cared for if they got sick, and where they would be buried when they died. Cassius knew that he was permitted to play in Chickasaw Park, Ballard Park, and Baxter Square but not in Iroquois Park, Shawnee Park, Cherokee Park, Triangle Park, Victory Park, or Boone Square.

Signs of inequality were everywhere. The homicide rate for black people in Louisville was about fifty-six per thousand in the mid-1950s, compared to three per thousand for white people. The death rate from natural causes was 50 percent higher for blacks than whites. But if those signs didn't register for a young, energetic boy growing up in the West End, a more glaring one did. It was called Fontaine Ferry Park, the city's most popular amusement park. It was within walking distance of the Clay house on Grand Avenue, and only whites were allowed. On summer weekends, thousands of Louisville residents would arrive by car, ferry, or trolley. To the black children who lived in nearby neighborhoods, it was more than tantalizing to have it out of reach; it was torturous. The black neighbors of Fontaine Ferry Park could hear the rattle of the rollercoaster cars and the frightened screams of the riders. They could smell the overcooked grease and fried dough and smoking beef. They could watch the parade of sunburned families in station wagons leaving each night. They could hardly miss the message as to whose fun mattered and whose did not.

"We'd stand by the fence," Rudy Clay said, "but we couldn't go in."

As a little boy, Cassius Clay Jr. lay in bed crying, asking why colored people had to suffer so. He asked why everyone at his church was black but all the portraits of Jesus were white, including the portraits painted by his father.

Young Cassius Clay also learned about discrimination from his grandfather Herman Heaton Clay, the man who had gone to prison for murder at the turn of the century. Herman boasted that he had been a talented baseball player in his youth—so talented that he might have played professionally if big-league baseball hadn't been off limits to black men at the time. Herman

Heaton Clay, Cash Clay, and Cassius Clay Jr. all understood that they had to live with the effects of slavery, that the country had been built by slave labor, that their work and even their identities had been stolen from them, and that slavery had left behind a caste system that relegated black and white Americans to dramatically different lives, at least for the foreseeable future.

Herman died in 1954, when his grandson was twelve. The same year, the Supreme Court of the United States ruled in *Brown v. Board of Education* that the U.S. Constitution prohibited segregation in public schools. Reaction in the South was swift and brutally negative. Some states began maneuvering to deny funding to integrated schools. In Mississippi, white business leaders and politicians organized the White Citizens Council to resist integration and defend white supremacy. Leaders of the Ku Klux Klan urged supporters to resist the "mongrelization" of the white race that integration would bring. The summer after *Brown,* fourteen-year-old Emmett Till traveled from his home in Chicago to spend time with relatives in the small Delta town of Money, Mississippi, population fifty-five. More than five hundred black people had been lynched in Mississippi since officials began keeping count in 1882. The state's governor had recently declared black people unfit to vote. Till's mother, anxious about sending her son to the South in the summer of 1955, warned him that it was important to behave in the manner that white Mississippians expected of young black men. He was to answer them with "yassuh" and "nawsuh" and to humble himself if necessary to avoid confrontation.

But, like Cassius Clay Jr., who was only six months younger, Emmett Till could be feisty. He ignored his mother's warning. One day in Money, Emmett was standing outside a grocery store, showing friends a picture of his white girlfriend from Chicago. One of the kids dared Emmett to go into the store and talk to the white cashier. Emmett accepted the challenge. On his way out of the store, he reportedly told the cashier, "Bye, baby." A few days later, the cashier's husband and another man broke into the house of Till's uncle and dragged Emmett out of his bed. He was pistol-whipped and ordered to beg forgiveness. When Emmett refused to beg, he was shot in the head. His killers used barbed wire to tie a heavy cotton-gin fan around the boy's neck and then threw his body into the Tallahatchie River. An all-white jury needed only sixty-seven minutes to acquit the accused men. "If we hadn't stopped to drink pop," one juror said, "it wouldn't have taken that long."

Till's mother insisted on an open casket so the world would see her young son's mutilated face, and *Jet* magazine published photos from the funeral that became seared in the consciousness of many black Americans. Till became a martyr for civil rights and inspiration to countless activists. Soon after the trial of Till's killers, Rosa Parks refused to give up her seat on an Alabama bus, setting off waves of protest.

Cash Clay showed his sons photos of Emmett Till's disfigured face. The message was clear: This is what the white man will do. This is what can happen to an innocent black person, an innocent child, whose only crime is the color of his skin. America, according to Cash Clay, wasn't fair and never would be. His own career was proof. He had the talent to be a great artist, didn't he? Yet he was almost forty years old and painting store signs for meager pay, with almost no chance of earning his way out of the cramped, four-room cottage where his family lived. Only money would give the black man a shot at equality and respect, Cash told his boys.

Cassius Clay Jr. absorbed his father's words. At age thirteen, he didn't talk about changing the world or improving the plight of his people. He didn't talk about getting an education and striving to do something meaningful with his life. He talked, as his father did, about making money.

"Why can't I be rich?" the son asked his father once.

"Look there," his father said, touching the boy's walnut-colored hand. "That's why you can't be rich."

But every son comes to believe he can be more than his father, that he is not beholden to his position in the line of his ancestors, not tethered to that soul-crushing concatenation formed in a past beyond his control, and Cassius Marcellus Clay Jr. was no exception. At an early age, he talked about owning a hundred-thousand-dollar house on a hill with fancy cars in the garage, with a chauffeur to drive him around, with a chef to prepare his meals. He vowed to buy one house for his parents and another for his brother. He would keep a quarter of a million dollars in the bank for emergencies.

By the summer of 1955, the summer of Emmett Till, he had an idea of how he might make that money.

3

The Bicycle

Late one afternoon in October 1954, twelve-year-old Cassius pedaled his bike through downtown Louisville, his brother perched on the handlebars, a friend riding alongside, when a sudden rain forced the boys to seek shelter. They scrambled into the Columbia Auditorium, at 324 South 4th Street.

The *Louisville Defender*, the city's black newspaper, was sponsoring a Home Service Exposition at the auditorium. It was a hall of wonders, packed with displays of the latest innovations in housewares. Visitors registered to win prizes, including a Magic Chef Range, a Hoover Steam Iron, and an RCA Victor Record Player. In the 1950s, as the economy boomed and new technology made household jobs like ironing and vacuuming a little less onerous, black families strove to acquire the same wondrous devices they saw white families demonstrating on television and in magazine advertisements. Cassius wasn't interested in the latest kitchen gadgets, but the exposition offered refuge from the storm, and the boys happily gobbled up the free popcorn and candy.

It rained all afternoon, and it was still pouring at around 7 p.m. when Cassius, Rudy, and their friend finally left the auditorium. But when they got outside, they discovered their bicycles gone. They ran up and down the block, searching for the thieves. Cassius began to cry, "frightened," he said, "of what my father would do."

Cassius's bicycle had been a Christmas present: a Schwinn Cruiser Deluxe, red and white, with chrome fenders, chrome rims, whitewall tires, and a big, red, rocket-shaped headlight. It retailed for sixty dollars, the equivalent of about five hundred today. The Clays couldn't afford new bicycles for both their boys, so Cassius and Rudy were supposed to share this one, an agreement that Cassius did his best to ignore. For a boy who lived in one of the smallest houses on his block, who wore secondhand clothes, who received some of the lowest grades in his class, and who had thus far not established himself as one of his community's brighter sports stars, the bicycle was a rare and wonderful gift: it was a status symbol, probably his only one.

Someone told the distraught boys to report the stolen bicycle to the police officer who happened to be in the basement of the auditorium. They flew back into the building and down the stairs. There they met Joe Elsby Martin, a white-skinned, bald-headed, big-nosed Louisville patrolman and part-time boxing coach. Martin was off duty. He was in the basement training a group of amateur boxers, black and white, mostly teenagers. For young Cassius, the gymnasium opened a world and contented a need. The large, low room; the smell of heavy sweat; the pounding of gloves against bags, gloves against bodies; a place where young men could act out violently and under the approval of a caring adult, where the well-ordered and unjust structure of the outside world disappeared. These things mesmerized Cassius Clay. He became so overwhelmed, he recalled, "I almost forgot about the bike."

Cassius was angry — "hotter'n a firecracker," as Joe Martin put it — saying he wanted to find the person who stole his bicycle and give him a good whupping.

Martin listened calmly. He was an easygoing man who spent most of his time on the job emptying coins from parking meters. In jest, his fellow cops called him "Sergeant," because, in twenty-five years on the job, Martin had never bothered to take the sergeant's exam. He was content to walk his beat by day and train young fighters by night. Martin also produced a local television program for amateur boxers called *Tomorrow's Champions,* which was broadcast Saturday afternoons on WAVE-TV in Louisville.

Martin looked at Cassius, all eighty-nine pounds of him, and asked, "Do you know how to fight?"

No, Cassius said. He'd fought with his brother and engaged in occasional scraps with kids on the street, but he'd never laced on a pair of boxing gloves.

"Well," Martin said, "Why don't you come down here and start training?"

Destiny is a function of chance and choice. Chance delivered young Cassius Clay to Joe Martin's boxing gym, but choice would bring him back. It wasn't just the sport that captivated Cassius. He had always been confident in his strength and in his good looks. He had always craved attention. He had already figured out that school was not going to propel him to wealth and fame. But boxing? Boxing had always been a sport that appealed to people looking to make a way out of no way.

Cassius never recovered his bicycle, nor did he get another one. Instead, his parents bought him a motorized scooter, which he proceeded to ride everywhere at high speed, zipping in and out of traffic. With no pedaling required, it was better than a bike. Years later, when the story was told of how the young boxer got his start, the replacement scooter was a lost detail. The lost bike resonated most strongly, but the scooter told a story, too. The scooter meant young Cassius wasn't punished for losing his bike, wasn't made to get a job and earn money until he could purchase a replacement. Instead, his parents rewarded him with an upgrade, perhaps suggesting that accountability was not the most heavily stressed value in the Clay household.

Soon after losing the bicycle, Cassius was at home watching TV when Joe Martin's face flickered across the screen, standing in the corner with one of his amateur boxers on *Tomorrow's Champions*. It was all the prompting Cassius needed to go back to the gym. On his second visit, he climbed into the ring "with some older boxer," as he recalled in his 1975 autobiography, and got hammered. "In a minute my nose started bleeding. My mouth hurt. My head was dizzy. Finally someone pulled me out of the ring."

When his head cleared, Cassius went to work with Martin, learning how to set his feet, how to turn his body at an angle to his opponent, where to hold his hands to protect his head from damage, how to duck a punch, how to throw the left jab and the right cross, the uppercut, the hook.

About a month later, on November 12, 1954, he stepped into the ring for his first amateur fight, a three-round bout, two minutes per round, against a white boy roughly his own age named Ronnie O'Keefe. The fight was televised on *Tomorrow's Champions*. Each boy was paid three dollars. The boxers wore fourteen-ounce gloves and no headgear, "and those boys really went at it," Joe Martin recalled. Cassius won by a split decision.

Nothing in the young fighter's performance suggested that a prodigy had stepped into the ring. "He was just ordinary," Martin said. But soon after,

Martin began to see things he liked, things a trainer can't teach. Cassius was quick, for one thing, with fast hands and feet and excellent reflexes that helped him avoid punches. He never seemed to tire. When a shot to the head scrambled his senses, he recovered quickly. When he might have fled out of pain or panic, he fought back instead, exerting will over impulse.

But boxing triggered something wholly new in Cassius: ambition. His father had taken him along on jobs, teaching his son how to mix paint and draw neat letters, making sure each word was spaced precisely, but the boy had no patience for such work, nor did he inherit from his father even the modest ability to render a landscape or portrait. Cassius Jr. was good at shooting marbles and dodging rocks in rock fights, but those were not skills likely to take him far. School had certainly never lit a fire in him. Now, for the first time, he had found something he wanted to do other than mischief-making, something for which he was willing to labor and sacrifice, something that would put him on TV for Lord knows how many people to see.

The story of Cassius Clay's lost bicycle would later be told as an indication of the boxer's determination and the wonders of accidental encounters, but it carries broader meaning, too. If Cassius Clay had been a white boy, the theft of his bicycle and an introduction to Joe Martin might have led as easily to an interest in a career in law enforcement as boxing. But Cassius, who had already developed a keen understanding of America's racial striation, knew that law enforcement wasn't a promising option. This subject — what white America allowed and expected of black people — would intrigue him all his life.

"At twelve years old I wanted to be a big celebrity," he said years later. "I wanted to be world famous." The interviewer pushed him: *Why* did he want to be famous? Upon reflection he answered from a more adult perspective: "So that I could rebel and be different from all the rest of them and show everyone behind me that you don't have to Uncle Tom, you don't have to kiss you-know-what to make it . . . I wanted to be free. I wanted to say what I wanna say . . . Go where I wanna go. Do what I wanna do."

For young Cassius, what mattered was that boxing was permitted, even encouraged, and that it gave him more or less equal status to the white boys who trained with him. Every day, on his way to the gym, Cassius passed a Cadillac dealership. Boxing wasn't the only way for him to acquire one of those big, beautiful cars in the showroom window, but it might have seemed that way at the time. Boxing suggested a path to prosperity that did not require reading and writing. It came with the authorization of a white man in Joe Martin. It offered respect, visibility, power, and money.

Boxing transcended race in ways that were highly unusual in the 1950s, when black Americans had limited control of their economic and political lives. Boxing more than most other sports allowed black athletes to compete on level ground with white athletes, to openly display their strength and even superiority, and to earn money on a relatively equal scale. As James Baldwin wrote in *The Fire Next Time,* many black people of Clay's generation believed that getting an education and saving money would never be enough to earn respect. "One needed a handle, a lever, a means of inspiring fear," Baldwin wrote. "It was absolutely clear the police would whip you and take you in as long as they could get away with it, and that everyone else — housewives, taxi drivers, elevator boys, dishwashers, bartenders, lawyers, judges, doctors, and grocers — would never, by the operation of any generous feeling, cease to use you as an outlet for their frustrations and hostilities. Neither civilized reason nor Christian love would cause any of those people to treat you as they presumably wanted to be treated; only the fear of your power to retaliate would cause them to do that, or seem to do it, which was (and is) good enough." A handle. A lever. A means of inspiring fear. For young Cassius Clay, boxing proved just the thing.

He took up running for exercise. He could have run before school, or after, but he didn't. He ran *to* school. In his autobiography years later, he described his routine as "racing the bus." But he had a peculiar way of racing. First, he waited with the other children from his neighborhood for the Greenwood Avenue bus to arrive. Then, when the other children boarded and the bus started to grind its way east on Greenwood, Cassius, wearing his school clothes and school shoes, ran alongside, sun assaulting his eyes. When the bus stopped for a traffic light or to pick up passengers, Cassius stopped, too. He stopped again when his friends got off at 28th Street, where he waited with them for the Chestnut Street bus. When that bus arrived, he took off running again. He ran fast, over well-worn roads that buckled and cracked, past houses that looked like only the peeling paint held them together, until the promise of downtown Louisville came into sight, with its big banks and glittering car dealerships and neon-lit movie houses. By that time, Cassius was hot, his shirt suckered to his back. But the kids on the bus knew that Cassius ran for attention as well as exercise. He wasn't running full speed, and he wasn't really racing, because he could have won the race handily if he hadn't stopped to entertain friends every time the bus stopped. "Sometimes he would hop on and hold on to the window and ride for free for a block or two," Owen Sitgraves recalled. With his fingers clutching the window frame and his legs dangling inches off the road, Cassius would look up at his friends' faces and smile. "You had to worry about the bus driver looking out the window and catching you though," Sitgraves said, laughing.

Cassius looked like a colt, long-limbed and knock-kneed, with a slender frame. But he was determined to get bigger and stronger. For breakfast he guzzled a quart of milk mixed with two raw eggs. Soda pop, he declared, was as bad as alcohol or cigarettes for an athlete, and he vowed never to touch them. Perhaps in his declaration of asceticism he was trying to prove his superiority to his father, who drank almost every day and had a reputation for laziness. Perhaps he recognized that discipline offered a source of power lacking in Cassius Sr. Or, perhaps, as his brother Rudy recalled, he simply liked looking in the mirror at his muscles.

"It was almost impossible to discourage him," Joe Martin said. "He was easily the hardest worker of any kid I ever taught."

Cassius enjoyed the attention that came with his pursuit of boxing. Suddenly, he had an identity. He had something to brag about. He was an athlete. He was the kid who raced the bus, the one gulping down garlic water because he said it would help him keep his blood pressure low, and it wasn't long before he began telling strangers (because his friends already knew) that he intended to be not merely a professional boxer but the heavyweight champion of the world, an avowal that must have sounded as ridiculous as that of a child who said he intended to become president of the United States.

He began knocking on doors before his Friday night fights to stir up interest and boost attendance. No one told him to do it, and it was completely unheard of at the time.

"I'm Cassius Clay," he'd say, "and I'm having a fight on television. I hope you'll watch me." Once, canvassing a neighborhood halfway across town, he knocked on a door only to be greeted by Joe Martin. The two laughed about it, but Martin also recognized it as a sign of the kid's dedication.

"It's safe to say that Cassius believed in himself," Martin said.

• • •

In 1954, boxing was a central part of American culture. For sports fans, no single event mattered as much as a heavyweight championship fight, and no individual athlete earned the respect of the heavyweight division's top boxer. Only boxing's top competitors were referred to everywhere they went for the rest of their lives as "Champ." Boxing's heavyweight champ was godlike, fearsome, a figure of manliness and courage upon whom all the world gazed in admiration and respect — unless he was black, in which case the matter became more complicated.

Rocky Marciano was the heavyweight champ at this moment in Cassius Clay's youth. Marciano was flat-nosed, bull-necked, and broad-shouldered, with a face shaped as much by pugilistic demolition as DNA. Standing a shade over five-foot-ten and weighing 188 pounds, Marciano was not especially big. Nor was he especially quick. But he charged his opponents relentlessly and hit them hard, knocking out almost nine of every ten he faced. Marciano, born Rocco Francis Marchegiano, was the kind of boxer Americans loved to cheer, a son of Italian immigrants who had built his muscles digging ditches and hauling ice and had served his country for two years in the army during World War II.

Before Marciano, black men had held the heavyweight title for fifteen years. Marciano took the championship by beating Jersey Joe Walcott, who had taken it from Ezzard Charles, who claimed it after the retirement of Joe Louis and cemented that claim by beating Louis when Louis had come out of retirement in 1950.

Joe Louis had reigned as heavyweight champion for twelve years, longer than any champ in the history of the sport, and in that twelve years' time he became the most popular black man in the history of America. When he first came to the attention of boxing fans in 1934 at the age of twenty, he was handsome, light-skinned, and quiet, and promoters went out of their way to present him as wholesome, the polite sort of Negro who evinced proper respect for whites. Louis loved his mother and loved the Bible: that's what his publicists said, and that's what white newspapermen wrote. To make sure that this mighty fighter maintained an unthreatening image outside the ring, Louis lived under strict rules imposed by his managers: he was never to be photographed with a white woman; he was never to enter a nightclub alone; he was never to gloat over a fallen opponent, never to raise his arms in victory or brag of his talent in interviews. He wasn't Sambo, the smiling, shuffling, buffoon of minstrel shows, but he wasn't fully a man of free will, either. He was Good Joe, the Negro who knew his place and appreciated the opportunities White America had granted him.

The U.S. economy then had been deep in depression. Fascism was stirring in Europe. America needed a new boxing hero, and Louis had the strength and talent. His only sin was in his skin, to paraphrase the song made popular by Louis Armstrong, another black man who won the approval of white Americans in part because he appeared not to hate them. More than anything, that's what white Americans expected of Joe Louis. They would let him fight, let him be champ, even let him knock white men bloody and senseless, so long as he remembered that whites were superior and always would be; so long as he remembered that his position as an American hero was provisional. Black men like Joe Louis and Louis Armstrong were expected to be representatives of their people, although the role placed an impossible burden on them. What traits of blackness were they supposed to portray? Only the ones that white people wanted? How were they supposed to serve as symbols while maintaining their individuality and the freedom to speak their minds? Before Joe Louis, another black boxer, Jack Johnson, had failed as black ambassador to the white world. When Jack Johnson had begun fighting and winning in the late 1890s, there had never been a black heavyweight champion. The mere idea of it offended many whites. "Any fighter who'd get in the same ring with a nigger loses my respect," said John L. Sullivan, the last heavyweight champion of the bare-knuckled era.

As Jack Johnson and other black fighters emerged, they not only posed a threat to white champions; they posed a threat to firmly held attitudes about race. "We are in the midst of a growing menace," Charles A. Dana, the editor of the *New York Sun*, wrote in 1895. "The black man is rapidly forging to the front ranks in athletics, especially in the field of fisticuffs. We are in the midst of a black rise against white supremacy."

Jack Johnson was the nightmare that woke white supremacists in a cold sweat. He was big, black, and belligerent. When taunted, he taunted back. He challenged the natural order, and he was smart enough to recognize how much that disturbed people in power. He predicted the outcomes of his fights. He mocked his opponents. Somehow, in spite of everything American history had taught to that point, Johnson concluded that his skin color and ancestry did not require him to kowtow and cringe before the white master.

In 1908, after a string of convincing victories, Johnson earned the right to challenge the champion, a white German-Canadian named Tommy Burns. Johnson taunted Burns before knocking him out in the fourteenth round. Almost immediately, the search began for a white boxer who would restore the natural order. But Johnson was difficult to beat. In 1910, when he defeated Jim Jeffries, the so-called Great White Hope, celebrations erupted in black communities followed by reprisal attacks from white gangs.

Johnson held the title nearly seven years, and the more he won, the more boldly he behaved, as if being heavyweight champion of the world actually proved his superiority. He wore expensive jewels and long fur coats. He performed in vaudeville routines. He sassed his critics. He openly consorted with white women, from prostitutes to well-off married women, and he would eventually marry three. Johnson became the most celebrated and most despised Negro of his time. He was hounded out of the country, and when he returned he was jailed on trumped up charges of transporting a woman across state lines for "immoral purposes."

Jack Johnson showed that the boxing ring existed in a special place in American society — as an altar of sorts, where normal rules and beliefs did not always hold. In a boxing ring, during a regulated match, a black man in 1910 could pound in the skull of a white man and not go to jail or get lynched for it. In a boxing ring, one man could kill another and not face a murder charge. And it was in that space that Jack Johnson flashed America's future.

In the years to come, black Americans would grow more openly militant in their opposition to southern segregation and northern discrimination and the seemingly endless insults and hypocrisies contained in the American credo that all men are created equal. It would take roughly half a century, though, for another black boxer to boldly challenge America's racial codes. When his time finally came, that fighter, too, would be criticized for his disrespectful behavior and lack of humility. That fighter, too, would face punishment from his government and an outpouring of rage from his white countrymen.

"I grew to love the Jack Johnson image," Cassius Clay would say. "I wanted to be rough, tough, arrogant, the nigger white folks didn't like."

4

"Every Day Was Heaven"

One hot August night in the summer of 1957, Officer Charles Kalbfleisch of the Louisville police department responded to a domestic disturbance at 3302 Grand Avenue in the West End neighborhood of Louisville. When Kalbfleisch arrived, he found Cassius Clay Jr. with blood dripping from his leg. The lanky fifteen-year-old said his father had cut him with a knife. His mother confirmed the boy's account.

When interviewed years later about the domestic disturbance, Kalbfleisch did not say what had provoked the attack. He couldn't remember if the cut was to the calf or thigh, the left leg or right, only that it was a minor wound, not requiring stitches. Given that domestic violence cases almost never resulted in convictions when black families were involved, the white police officer decided that arresting Cassius Clay Sr. would be a waste of time. "They'll kill each other," Kalbfleisch said, referring to black men and women involved in domestic disputes, "and when you go to court two or three months later, they've forgotten."

Louisville police knew Cash Clay well by that time. Over the years, they'd responded to several complaints from Odessa that her husband had struck her, usually after he'd been drinking. They had arrested Cash a number of times for drunk driving and disorderly conduct after nights of revelry at the Dreamland or Club 36. He never did jail time, thanks largely to the work of his lawyer, a white man named Henry Sadlo, who also happened to be the state's boxing commissioner. There were other brushes with the police that stopped short of arrest, and further signs of troubling behavior that escaped attention altogether. But most of all Cash Clay was a heavy drinker and a wolf. "He used to go with my aunt," said Howard Breckenridge, who grew up in the Little Africa neighborhood of Louisville. "Matter of fact, he went with two of my aunts." Cash Clay liked to hit on the plumpest woman in the bar, but all too often he wound up brawling with the biggest, strongest man.

For three days after suffering the gash on his leg, young Cassius failed to show up at the boxing gym where he trained. His instructor, Joe Martin, grew concerned. "Finally," Martin said, "he came in and he was all patched up where he'd been cut. I asked him how he hurt himself, and he said he fell on a milk bottle." That didn't fool Martin, the cop. Later that year, Clay told Martin the truth: he'd been cut by his father while trying to break up a fight between his parents. "It wasn't long before I knew the kid was scared to death of his old man," Martin said.

In later years, Cassius and Rudy would tell interviewers that they had been happy children in a happy home, not rich but never hungry, all too aware of their father's unpredictable outbursts but not afraid of him. They would say their parents had fought at times, and that their father had taken them into the bathroom and "strapped" them for assorted misdeeds, but that they didn't consider such spankings out of the ordinary. Rudy would also admit that their father had sired at least two children out of wedlock and that Odessa had known about the children. Rudy said the most violent act he'd ever witnessed at home was Odessa striking Cash after she had discovered one of his sexual affairs; he said he didn't remember his father ever striking his mother.

"Every day was heaven," Rudy Clay said years later. "Heaven!"

Brother Cassius, who would talk about almost everything else with reporters throughout his life, would never go into detail about his relationship with his father. Did he stay away from alcohol because his father drank? Did boxing appeal to him because he felt threatened at home? He never discussed such things.

"I just know I had a nice time as a kid," he said, and left it at that.

The *Centralian,* Central High School's yearbook, did not select Cassius Clay as the school's best athlete in 1959. That honor went to Cassius's friend Vic Bender, star of the basketball team. That was fine with Clay. Although he was taller and faster afoot than most of his classmates, he showed little interest in team sports, joining none of the popular squads at Central. As he explained it years later, "About the onliest other sport I ever thought about was football, but I didn't like it because there was no personal publicity in it: you have to wear too much equipment and people can't see you." Boxing had become his life, his religion, his reason to get up in the morning. He shadowboxed in the halls between classes, throwing punches that stopped inches shy of the lockers that lined the hallways. As his teachers lectured, he doodled pictures of boxing rings and boxing gloves and jackets like the ones the football players at Central High wore — only the jackets he drew were emblazoned with the words "National Golden Gloves Champion" or "World Heavyweight Champ." He offered classmates autographs and signed them "Cassius Clay, World Heavyweight Champion."

One day, when Cassius was daydreaming, his teacher called on him to answer a question he hadn't heard.

"Cassius," she said, "are you listening to what's going on in class?"

He lied and said he was.

"Then answer the question," the teacher said.

Nothing.

"Cassius, what are you going to do with your life?" the teacher asked.

Cassius still had no reply. But three boys in the class raised their hands and one of them blurted out: "Teacher, Cassius can fight!"

After the Supreme Court's decision in *Brown v. Board of Education,* governors in some southern states declared that they would avoid or subvert the integration of public schools. The rebellion grew stronger as President Dwight Eisenhower stood silent on the issue. With local white leaders controlling the process, integration stalled, tensions mounted, protests erupted, and violence exploded in many communities.

But Louisville was not one of them.

In the fall of 1956, the year before Cassius Clay entered Central High, Louisville's schools were integrated without violent protest. The superintendent ordered that the city's 46,000 public school students (27% of whom were black) should attend the schools closest to their homes, regardless of whether the school had previously been all black or all white. That meant most schools would remain segregated because most neighborhoods were segregated. The rules also contained an escape clause: if parents didn't want their children attending schools where the children would be in the minority, the parents were permitted to request a transfer. In other words, no one would be forced to attend a school populated predominantly by another race. Black leaders objected to the transfer option, but the superintendent refused to budge, and no serious protest emerged from the black community. The integration process moved on, imperfectly, but as smoothly as could have been expected.

After the first day of school in September 1956, a day that saw fifty-four of the city's seventy-three schools integrated, the *New York Times* reported from Louisville: "White and Negro children walked through the school corridors together. They solemnly recited the Pledge of Allegiance in unison. Pupils sat side by side in the classroom. And they rushed gaily down the steps together when the first day had ended. Color differences seemed forgotten."

A year later, in the fall of 1957 at the all-white Central High School in Little Rock, Arkansas, members of the Arkansas National Guard drew bayonets to turn away a fifteen-year-old black girl who sought to attend classes, motioning her in the direction of an angry mob of white men threatening to kill her. After a three-week standoff, heavily armed federal troops arrived to escort the girl and eight other black students, known as the Little Rock Nine, to their classes. The crisis made international headlines. Still, calm prevailed in Louisville.

Louisville's early efforts at integration were not perfect. While white parents didn't seem to mind sending their children to school with black children, they didn't want their children educated by black teachers. Black community leaders protested, but the superintendent held the line, insisting that being taught by Negroes would likely prove harmful to white children. One of Cassius Clay's history teachers, a black man named Lyman Johnson, launched a campaign to pressure the school district to change its policy and integrate school faculties. After two years of protest, the district agreed to choose ten black teachers who possessed "good poise" and who were not "too aggressive on the race question" to begin working in predominantly white schools.

Even in Louisville, white civic leaders recognized that they could no longer count on black men and women remaining submissive or indifferent. The victims of slavery and Jim Crow were growing more confident now that they had the law on their side. In 1955, the NAACP filed petitions for desegregation with 170 school boards in seventeen states. In some communities, white resistance hardened and relations between the races cracked. Openly racist white Citizens' Councils gained in popularity. Black men and women used boycotts as weapons to push for equal rights. Still, Cassius Clay's junior high and high school remained all black and would remain predominantly black for decades to come.

Since its creation in 1882, when it was known as Central Colored High School, the school had been a source of pride in Louisville's black community. The building Cassius attended was new, completed and opened in 1952 at a cost of almost $4 million. The massive red brick structure — with 111 rooms, including a swimming pool, radio station, and twelve-thousand-book library — would not have looked out of place on a college campus. In addition to math, science, and English, students could take classes in dry-cleaning, sheet-metal work, radio, electrical repair, plumbing, upholstery, cosmetology, tea-room service, commercial food preparation, and cafeteria management.

None of those subjects interested Cassius Clay.

"He was dumb as a box of rocks," Marjorie Mimmes, one of his class-mates, recalled years later. Mimmes was one year behind Cassius in school and dated him briefly.

"Not the sharpest tack," said his friend Owen Sitgraves.

"I sat next to the skinny kid with glasses in school and copied his answers," Cassius himself acknowledged years later, explaining his approach to aca-demic work.

In January 1957, while enrolled at DuValle Junior High School, Cassius took the Standard California Intelligence Quotient Test and scored a be-low-average eighty-three. In his first year at Central, he earned a sixty-five in English, a sixty-five in American history, a seventy in biology, and a seventy in general art. On March 31, 1958, before completing his tenth-grade classes, Clay left school. His academic records don't indicate a reason, although poor grades and a busy boxing schedule were likely factors. A grade of seventy was required to pass a class at Central, which meant he was failing two and barely passing two others. He enrolled again the following fall. The poor grades might have been explained in part by his active boxing schedule. In 1957, Cassius fought at least twelve amateur bouts. Although he lost three fights that year, it was becoming clear to everyone who followed the sport in Lou-isville that he possessed great potential as a boxer.

While his spelling and punctuation were better than his parents', Cassius was a slow reader and hesitant writer. The written word frustrated him and would for much of his life. Years later, family members would say that Cassius was dyslexic — "very dyslexic," according to his fourth wife, Lonnie — but the diagnosis was little known and infrequently applied when he was young. Even getting through a simple article in a newspaper's sports section proved a chore, taking him two or three times longer than it should have. Math problems befuddled him too, especially if they contained words *and* numbers. The only thing about school he seemed to like was the audience it provided. Attention was what he craved most, and he earned it with irre-pressible exuberance as well as with boxing.

Boxing, he said, "made me feel like something different. The kids used to make fun of me. 'He thinks he's gonna be a fighter. He ain't never gonna be nothin'.' But I always liked attention and publicity . . . Attracting attention, showmanship, I liked that the most. And pretty soon I was the popularest kid in school."

He arrived at Central High in lipstick one day and pretended he was a girl. He pretended to bash a friend's head into a locker, over and over, until the other kids in the hall realized it was a stunt and no one was getting hurt. He carried his money in a change purse, the bills folded up tidily, at a time when no boy in his right mind would carry any kind of purse. He referred to himself as pretty, a word boys almost never used to describe themselves. When he wasn't running alongside the bus to get to school, he rode his motorized scooter, and if there were girls watching him when he arrived in the driveway, he would take the final turns at speeds designed to make them scream and cover their eyes in anticipation of crashes that never came. It was immature behavior, perhaps, but not inconsequential to Clay, who cared about winning his fellow students' esteem more than his teachers' praise.

"I don't know anybody who didn't like Cassius Clay," said his classmate Vic Bender.

Ali's attention-getting ploys may have been compensation for his deficiencies with the written word. In addition to playing for laughs, he learned to listen well, to read people's moods, to charm, to defuse difficult situations with humor, and, when all else failed, to fight. Scientists don't fully understand the reasons, but dyslexia can be an advantage for some people. Studies show that learning to read rewires the brain. Reading teaches us to block out the world, and in the process certain kinds of visual processing skills get lost. That may be why some dyslexics exhibit exceptional visual talents, helping them to understand shapes and movements in faster and more nuanced ways than others. It may be why Cassius Clay had a gift for anticipating a punch and backing or sliding out of its way. His brain didn't focus well on words and sentences that needed to be processed in precise order, but he was extraordinarily good at the opposite: being alert to all things at once and spotting things that looked odd or out of place. A raised eyebrow, a shift in the angle of a fighter's shoulder, a twitch of a muscle — these were all potential clues as he faced another boxer, mind racing to help him keep a safe distance away. Dyslexics might make lousy bookkeepers but excellent security guards; they can read the mood of a crowded room even if they struggle to concentrate on what the person in front of them is saying. They assimilate patterns and see opportunities others can't detect. Scientists believe dyslexia is relatively common among entrepreneurs and other leaders — especially people who show a knack for creative thinking, for veering from the mainstream, and for seeing the big picture.

In July 1958, when he was sixteen, Cassius began boasting of his intention to fight the toughest young man in all of the West End, perhaps the toughest in all of Louisville. His name was Corky Baker. While Cassius was already a well-established amateur boxer, Baker was a legend — the strongest, meanest young man around. His was a name to be whispered, in case he happened to be nearby and looking for a fight. Corky Baker wore leather jackets and snarled and made even grown men step off the sidewalk to get out of his way. "He was inhuman," recalled Howard Breckenridge, a neighbor of roughly the same age as Baker. "I seen him pick up a car once."

Cassius Clay knew how to box, but Corky Baker knew how to fight, and he outweighed Cassius by at least twenty pounds.

"You're crazy if you get in the ring with him," Cassius's friend John Powell Jr. told the teenaged boxer in 1958.

"I'm gonna whip him," Cassius replied.

The buildup to the fight was tremendous. The West End was abuzz. "It created as much stir in the little town as a big fight did years later between Joe Frazier and me," Clay said years later, "and in its way it was just as important to me."

When the bout began, Baker set out like a man bent on murder, swinging wildly and bulling forward with his head down. Cassius pounded him with long left jabs and skipped away from punches until Baker was exhausted, his nose bloodied and one eye blackened. "This ain't fair!" Baker shouted in the middle of the second round before staggering out of the ring and out of the gym.

"Man," John Powell told Cassius after the fight, "you are the baddest dude I know, now."

Between November 1954, when he had his first amateur bout, and the summer of 1960, from ages twelve to eighteen, Cassius Clay would fight 106 times as an amateur, according to the records kept by Joe Martin. Some researchers have disputed those numbers. Years later, in his autobiography, the boxer said he fought 167 amateur bouts. The best estimate compiled in recent years found the boxer had a record of 82–8, with twenty-five knockouts, although it's likely that at least a few bouts were missed in that count.

Regardless of the precise number, it's clear that Cassius Clay fought often — an average of about once every three weeks — and won much more often than he lost. It's also clear he would have fought more frequently if not for a four-month respite imposed by a doctor who thought he detected a heart murmur in the boxer. In addition to his organized bouts, Cassius sparred at least three or four times a week as he prepared for competition.

Rudy boxed too, and on many occasions the brothers appeared on the same card, although they never fought each other. "To tell you the truth," said Vic Bender, a fellow boxer and friend to both of the Clay boys, "Rudy had more potential [than Cassius], we thought. He was a little bit stronger." Cash and Odessa Clay attended almost all of their boys' bouts. There's something unnerving for an adult in the sight of a boy boxer, scrawny, loose-limbed, awkward, transformed at the clang of a bell into a hard-breathing, wild-eyed attacker, fueled by hormones he didn't know he had. On fight nights, Cash would hoot and holler and punch the air as his sons threw lefts and rights while Odessa moaned and covered her eyes. After the fights, the Clays would go home and eat meatloaf or big bowls of Odessa's homemade chili served over spaghetti, followed by bigger bowls of store-bought vanilla ice cream.

The more he fought, the more Cassius began to develop a style of his own. Some fighters like to move forward, to step in for big punches, but Cassius preferred to circle his opponent clockwise, to punch and move away, to pull his head back from blows rather than duck them. Bobbing and weaving won't work when an opponent gets in close. But Cassius learned that if he could keep his distance and keep circling, sticking, and moving, he would absorb less punishment. His greatest talent may have been measurement; he had a brilliant knack for staying just beyond the reach of his opponents and, then, getting just close enough to throw punches that hurt. He possessed a "built-in radar," as he said years later. "I know how far I can go back, when it's time to duck or tie my man up. I learn there is a science to making your opponent wear down. I learn to put my head within hitting range, force my opponent to throw blows, then lean back and away, keeping my eyes wide open so I can see everything, then sidestep, move to the right, or to the left, jab him again, then again, put my head back in hitting range. It takes a lot out of a fighter to throw punches that land in the thin air. When his best punches hit nothing but space, it saps him."

There was danger in such an approach. Fighters are taught to keep their hands up near their heads to block punches, but Cassius dropped his gloves, tempting his opponents to go for his face and counting on his reflexes to get him out of the way in time. Also, by keeping his distance, Cassius all but abandoned the body blow as a weapon. He seldom got inside and pounded a fighter's ribs. He seldom launched punches with the full force of his own body behind them. He fought like a bomber jet rather than a tank, counting on speed, agility, and good aim.

Although he was exceptionally fast and probably absorbed fewer punches than most young fighters, Cassius Clay wasn't fast enough to avoid all the hard shots launched in his direction. On February 4, 1955, just three months after his first amateur bout and three weeks after his thirteenth birthday, Cassius was beaten by a young fighter named James Davis. In the summer of the same year, he beat John Hampton one week and lost to him the next. On August 30, 1957, fifteen-year-old Cassius beat a seventeen-year-old Louisville fighter named Jimmy Ellis, who would go on to become, briefly, the World Boxing Association's heavyweight champion. Fighting eight days later, Clay lost in the first round when he suffered a cut over his eye against a fighter named Terry Hodge. A month after that, Cassius fought Jimmy Ellis again, losing this time in a split decision.

As his skills improved and he challenged older boxers, as his television appearances brought him a measure of local celebrity, Cassius grew more confident than ever, predicting he would win the national Golden Gloves boxing championship, then turn professional and become the heavyweight champion of the world. Some of his fellow fighters tired of Clay's rap. Clay didn't care. In the school cafeteria he needed two trays to carry his lunch, which included half a dozen bottles of milk and tilting towers of sandwiches, and if anyone accused him of gluttony, he reminded them that he was in training.

"I started boxing because I thought it was the fastest way for a black person to make it in this country," he once said. "I was not that bright and quick in school, couldn't be a football or a basketball player, 'cause you have to go to college and get all kinds of degrees and pass examinations. A boxer can just go into a gym, jump around, turn professional, win a fight, get a break, and he's in the ring. If he's good enough he makes more money than ballplayers make all their lives."

Cassius continued to attend classes at Central, although his absences must have mounted given his schedule of boxing tournaments. He also hustled for money, working as a babysitter for some of his neighbors and doing light janitorial work in the library of Louisville's Nazareth College, where the nun who supervised Cassius once found him sleeping deep in the library's stacks when he was supposed to be dusting.

Joe Martin and his wife, Christine, drove their team of young boxers to tournaments in Chicago, Indianapolis, and Toledo. "In those days the black boys couldn't go in the restaurants, so I didn't take *any* of the boys in," Christine Martin told a reporter. "I'd just go in myself and get what they wanted, however many hamburgers per boy, and bring it back to the car. Cassius was a very easy-to-get-along-with fellow. Very easy to handle. Very polite."

Cassius was not merely polite; he was genuinely shy in small groups, and especially around girls. But when it came to boxing, he had a sure sense of his talent. He sensed early on that confidence could be a weapon; it made him seem bigger and tougher than he was, and sometimes it rattled opponents. At a tournament in Louisville when he was only twelve, he walked into the visiting team's locker room and started sassing a fighter named George King, who was twenty-one years old and married with a child. "I'm taller than you," Cassius said. "Do you think you could beat me?" Cassius threw two quick punches at the air. "Think you could stop this jab?"

He composed the kind of poems that would later become his trademark, this one for the *Louisville Courier-Journal*:

This guy must be done.
I'll stop him in one.

In February 1957, when Cassius was fifteen, the well-regarded light-heavy-weight Willie Pastrano came to Louisville from Miami for a fight with John Holman at the State Fairgrounds. One night, when Pastrano was in his hotel room, Cassius phoned Pastrano from the lobby. Pastrano's trainer, Angelo Dundee, answered.

"Hello," Cassius told Dundee. "My name is Cassius Marcellus Clay. I am the Golden Gloves champion of Louisville . . . I'm gonna be the Olympic champion, and then I'm gonna be the champion of the whole world. I'd like to meet you."

There was nothing on TV, so Dundee and Pastrano told Cassius to come up to their room. Cassius asked if his brother could come, too.

Cassius and Rudy spent four hours in the company of Pastrano and Dundee, with Cassius asking questions about training and boxing technique. Later, Cassius asked if he could work out with Pastrano in the ring, and Pastrano and Dundee consented. Pastrano, from New Orleans, had more than five years of experience as a professional fighter and would go on to win the world light-heavyweight championship a few years later. But he would regret the decision to get in the ring with the teenaged Cassius Clay.

"He hit me many times, and I didn't like being made to look bad by an amateur," Pastrano said. "He didn't look so good from outside the ring, but when he's up there in front of you he throws them long jabs. They come out so easy and so fast."

A year later, on February 25, 1958, Cassius Clay was in Chicago for the biggest fight of his life, in the Golden Gloves Tournament of Champions. More than 250 of the best fighters from twenty states competed in a series of bouts that stretched for ten days. The fights were held at Chicago Stadium, home of hockey's Chicago Black Hawks and once the world's largest indoor arena. Cassius had fought before big crowds in Louisville. His fights had been televised. But never before had he witnessed a scene like this. For a fighter, there is no drama like that of an important bout in a big arena, the cigarette and cigar smoke draping the air, the shouts, the moans, the voices screaming for holy blood.

After winning his first-round fight, sixteen-year-old Cassius faced Francis Turley, a young rancher from Roundup, Montana. Turley was short, at five-foot-eight, but he was rugged. In his first fight of the tournament, Turley had bloodied his opponent's nose in the first round with a left jab before pummeling him through the ropes and out of the ring in the third round. Turley and Cassius traded punches more or less evenly in the first round, but in the second Turley noticed that Cassius was keeping his distance, putting all his weight on his right leg, and stepping in to punch. Turley timed it right, closed the gap quickly, and unleashed a furious flurry of punches that set the crowd roaring and Cassius tumbling to the mat.

Still, Cassius got up, overcoming the noise of the crowd and whatever buzzing he might have had in his head, and floored Turley with a right, demonstrating for one of the first times his ability to shake off damage and continue fighting. In the final round, Cassius danced away, avoiding Turley altogether, and the judges awarded the victory to the young fighter from Louisville.

With one more win, Cassius would fight for the light-heavyweight championship. But his opponent in the semifinal match was another strong one: Kent Green, who was not only two-and-a-half years older but also nine pounds heavier than Cassius.

The night before the fight against Green, Cassius and another Louisville fighter stepped out of the St. Clair Hotel, hailed a taxi on Michigan Avenue, and asked the driver to take them to a place where they could purchase prostitutes. The driver took them to 47th Street and Calumet Avenue on the South Side, where the boys were quickly approached by two women, one black and one white, who said they could each be had for "seven and two" — seven dollars for the sex and two for the room. Cassius picked the black woman, who looked in his young eyes to be about thirty years old. The women escorted the teenaged boys inside a nearby building, up rickety wooden stairs, and past graffiti-covered walls.

"Do you want a trip around the world?" the prostitute asked Cassius as she led him to bed.

"What's a trip around the world?"

"Well, that's some of everything."

As he recalled years later: "She grabbed me with both her hands, pulling me to her. 'Just push,' she said. The panic left and all of a sudden I felt like a man. In a man's position. 'Just go up and down,' she said. So I went up and down, up and down, until finally she asked, 'Aren't you through? Hurry up. Aren't you through?' But I just kept on going up and down. She said something like 'Did you? Did you reach your climax?' I didn't know what she was talking about. 'Didn't you get a ticklish feeling? A sensation? I said, 'No.' There was nothing else to say.

"She pushed me off, and I got up right away and started to put on my pants. She stood up and cut the lights on.

"I hollered, 'Hold it! Hold it!' And I cut the lights right back off.

"'What's the matter with you?' she shouted.

"'I haven't got my clothes on yet,' I explained. I couldn't look at her."

The next day, as the tournament resumed at Chicago Stadium, Cassius used his most effective punch — the jab — to keep Kent Green from attacking. The jabs landed, and landed hard, but they weren't enough. Green took the punches and moved forward, getting in close to Cassius's body, turning the fight into a slugging match that favored the bigger, stronger man. By the second round, Cassius had abandoned his jab completely and tried to match Green with hooks and uppercuts, going toe to toe, power punch for power punch. Cassius soon tired while Green continued throwing and landing big punches. Finally, the referee stopped the fight, scoring it a technical knockout for Green.

The kid was "getting shellacked pretty good," Martin recalled.

In the dressing room after the fight, Clay cried.

The following year, Cassius returned to Chicago to fight in the intercity Golden Gloves tournament. At seventeen he was still slender — all elbows and knees, with a flat chest and rippled stomach — but he had grown to six feet in height and weighed more than 170 pounds.

Cassius, fighting for the Chicago team, which included boxers from twenty states, fought his way to the finals of the light-heavyweight division where he was matched against the New York team's most accomplished light-heavyweight, Tony Madigan, a twenty-nine-year-old who had represented Australia in the 1952 and 1956 Olympics before moving to New York. Despite his advanced age and experience, Madigan remained an amateur. Their fight — on March 25, 1959 — would be held before a crowd of more than seven thousand fans and televised nationally on ABC. Madigan was the heavy favorite to win.

Even in the 175-pound-and-under light-heavyweight division, boxers tended to be sluggers. Madigan certainly fit the bill. He had a strong right hand, and he often tussled like a barroom brawler, lowering his head and swinging away until someone fell. It usually wasn't him. Madigan had won ninety-four of ninety-nine bouts.

From the opening bell, however, it was clear that this fight was not going to be the usual for Madigan, nor was it the kind of fight that boxing fans, gathered around black-and-white TVs or crowded into smoky arenas, were accustomed to seeing big men fight. Clay flicked jabs and flitted around the ring, moving so quickly that the shorter-armed Madigan couldn't reach him. When Madigan tried to fight his way inside, Clay popped a left to the top of Madigan's head and bounced away. After three or four left jabs, with Madigan still forcing himself forward, Cassius would throw a right with real power that stopped the veteran fighter's progress. Soon, Madigan's eyes were swollen, his face red.

As the older fighter weakened and slowed, blinking away pain, Cassius began setting his feet and throwing more thumping rights. A year ago, he had lacked the power to stop Kent Green from muscling his way inside, but Cassius was stronger now. Madigan's only hope was a knockout punch, but every time he loaded up to throw one, Cassius disappeared out of range.

In the end, Cassius won convincingly.

By the 1950s, boxing's popularity was in steep decline. As the U.S. economy improved, young men had better options for work. Millions of World War II veterans were enrolled in college or job-training courses. As population shifted from the cities to the suburbs, neighborhood fight clubs began to fail and boxing matches grew less numerous. Black and Latino fighters started taking the place of the sport's Irish, Jewish, and Italian boxers. Overall, the number of professional boxers in the United States fell by 50 percent. If not for television, the sport's decline would have been more precipitous. In the mid-1950s, boxing could still be seen on TV almost every night of the week, and it rivaled *I Love Lucy* in the ratings.

Of all the fights televised March 25, 1959, Cassius Clay's was the most exciting. Fans who had expected to see the younger, lighter boxer take a beating instead caught a glimpse of boxing's future. The next day, in hundreds of newspapers nationwide, this report from the Associated Press appeared:

> New York won an unprecedented second straight intercity Golden Gloves team title over Chicago Wednesday night, but the individual spotlight was turned on the Windy City's Cassius Clay.
>
> Clay, a 17-year-old high school student from Louisville, Ky., proved he was quite advanced for his age and a sharp counter puncher in taking a three-round decision.

The world was beginning to take notice, just as he had always said it would.

5

The Prophet

Before fights, when other boxers were usually conserving their energy, focusing their thoughts, receiving last-minute counsel from trainers, praying, or throwing up, Cassius Clay was on his feet, shadowboxing, telling jokes, bragging, and checking his reflection in the mirror, as if idle time were the only challenger he feared. Years later, he would admit to friends that he had been frightened before every one of his fights. But he hid it beautifully. And once the bell rang, his fears vanished.

In 1959, before his nationally televised fight with Tony Madigan, Clay couldn't sit still, driving the other fighters to distraction with his nervous energy. He was in Chicago, three hundred miles from home. He wanted to *do* something. Didn't anyone else want to *do* something? He kept asking until he got the answer he wanted.

"We trained together," said Wilbert "Skeeter" McClure, a teenage boxer from Toledo, "and I remember Cassius kept bugging everybody on the team, saying, 'Man, there are all these pretty girls on the streets, all these pretty girls walking around; we got to meet some of these girls.'" Some of the young men were afraid to explore Chicago on their own. Others wanted to rest for their upcoming fights. But Clay persisted: "Come on, let's put on our [Golden Gloves] jackets and go someplace to impress the girls." Eventually, the adult chaperones for the boxers relented and organized an outing to Marshall High School on the city's West Side.

"We had pretty girls as hostesses to show us around," McClure said. "Then we went into the cafeteria for lunch, which was filled with more pretty girls.

There were pretty girls sitting everywhere. And the guy who'd been agitating just sat there, staring at the food on his tray the whole time. He didn't say a word."

Some of the young men who met Clay at these boxing tournaments found him irresistibly fun; they took his boastfulness as an act and weren't put off by it. Others found his self-absorption repulsive. None recalled conversations on politics, world affairs, race, or culture. He wanted to fight. He wanted to be great. He wanted to be famous and wealthy. He wanted to have a good time. That was all.

Beginning in 1958, Clay would make three trips to Chicago in three years. More than any other city, Chicago provided him a pathway not only to adulthood and big-city life but also to new complexities defined by race and its consequences. Chicago was not the Promised Land, not for Clay nor for new arrivals from the South who had come to the city on Lake Michigan expecting something better than they'd left behind. Wages and living conditions for black families were far from equal to those of white families. Blacks were still not welcome in many jobs, unions, clubs, and neighborhoods. In the North, as sociologist Gunnar Myrdal wrote in 1944, "almost everybody is against discrimination in general but, at the same time, almost everybody practices discrimination in his own personal affairs." Nonetheless, Chicago offered Clay his first sexual experience and his first national media exposure. Chicago showed him that his confidence in the boxing ring was justified, that he really could compete against the best fighters in the country, which in turn made him more confident than ever. The city, while still deeply segregated, offered a greater sense of freedom than Louisville ever had. Not only was Clay away from his parents; he was in the North, in a city where many southern blacks had discovered that they could more openly express their opinions, where they could stroll the sidewalks without stepping aside for white men, and where they could sit beside a white woman at a lunch counter without fear of a violent reaction, where a young man like Cassius Clay could behave mischievously with only a moderate fear of reprisal.

It was also in Chicago that Cassius Clay discovered a man who would change his life perhaps more than any other.

Elijah Muhammad referred to himself as the Prophet of the Nation of Islam, a religious group dedicated to black separatism and empowerment. The

Nation of Islam made its home on Chicago's South Side, where most of the city's black residents lived. On street corners and in mosques, followers of Elijah Muhammad preached a message of black strength that was beginning to resonate with young black men in the 1950s as outrage grew over segregation and violent attacks like the one on Emmett Till. If Europeans and white Americans worshipped a white Christ and if Buddhists in China worshipped a Buddha who looked Chinese, Elijah Muhammad asked, why didn't Negroes worship a Negro god? And if Europeans and Chinese had names rooted in their ancestries and cultures, why were Negro men and women in America still referred to by names they'd been assigned by slave owners in much the same way ranchers branded their cattle? These were conditions imposed by white men, without the consent of those affected, conditions that relegated black men and women to a seemingly permanent position of inferiority, conditions that would change only when black men demanded they change.

To the Nation of Islam, it wasn't enough that courts were ordering the integration of schools, trains, buses, and beaches. Integration would never suffice so long as Americans of African ancestry were treated as second-class citizens, more likely than their white neighbors to be incarcerated, unemployed, underemployed, homeless, or hungry; more likely to die young; more likely to be shot by police; more likely to be lynched.

In Africa, black people in the 1950s were finally breaking free of colonialism. Were black Americans going to be the last surviving symbols of racial inferiority and submission? Not if Elijah Muhammad was to be believed. If Muhammad's prophecies came to pass, a new nation of freed black Americans would soon be established, occupying as much as one-fifth of the territory currently belonging to the United States. To thousands of black Americans — especially those who felt most disenfranchised, including prison inmates and the unemployed, who made up the core of the Nation of Islam's following — Elijah Muhammad's message proved alluring. Muhammad rejected the pacifism of civil rights leaders such as the Rev. Martin Luther King Jr. and rejected the efforts of the NAACP to bring gradual change through the American judicial system.

Before he changed his name, Elijah Muhammad was Elijah Poole, a sharecropper's son, born in 1897 in rural Georgia. In 1923, Poole, like so many others, migrated north, settling in a poor section of downtown Detroit, where economic conditions were not much better than those he'd left behind in Georgia. Poole drank heavily and relied on government relief to get by, but he eventually fell under the teachings of a mysterious preacher named W. D. Fard, a light-skinned black man who went door to door in Detroit selling garments he said were similar to those worn by the black people of the Middle East. Fard claimed to be from Mecca though in fact he had never been there. He referred to himself by an assortment of exotic names, including Mr. Farrad Mohammad, Mr. F. Mohammad Ali, Professor Ford, and Mr. Wali Farrad. Regardless of which name he used, Fard found customers eager to hear more about the places he claimed to have been, about the places where black people had roots; where they were proud members of the majority; where they prayed to a god called Allah, not Jesus; where they had pride in the color of their skin and the history of their lineage.

Fard began holding meetings throughout the community, referring to himself as a prophet and offering suggestions to his audiences about how they could improve their health by avoiding certain foods. As his popularity grew, Fard became increasingly critical of the Christian Bible and the "blue-eyed devils" comprising the white race. Fard promised his followers a way out of their misery: by returning to their ancient Islamic heritage and embracing a philosophy of cleanliness, independence, and hard work, he said, black people would rise up. They would form their own, independent nation. A "Mother Plane" hovering in space, controlled telepathically by black pilots, would destroy the earth, and only believers in his message would survive. This cataclysmic event would most likely take place in 1966, according to Fard.

This philosophy, though unusual, was not entirely new. Booker T. Washington and countless other black leaders had long ago preached the importance of morality and hard work. In the 1920s, Noble Drew Ali (born Timothy Drew in North Carolina) had founded the Moorish Science Temple of America, which taught that all people of color were originally Moorish, or Muslim. And Marcus Garvey had stoked the imaginations of countless men and women by preaching Negro pride and urging his people to leave America and return to Africa.

Fard called his new religious group the Nation of Islam. Within a few years, he had established a Temple of Islam and a University of Islam, both in

Detroit. He built a base of about eight thousand followers. Elijah Muhammad became one of the group's first officers. In 1934, Fard appointed Muhammad the chief Minister of Islam and gave him power to run the organization. Soon after Elijah Muhammad's appointment, Fard disappeared and was never heard from again. Elijah Muhammad would go on almost singlehandedly to perpetuate Fard's teaching, to deify his mentor, and to vastly expand the Nation of Islam's reach. In an ironic way, Elijah Muhammad's views included strands that were both genuinely American and fundamentally conservative, even if they did include spaceships. He urged black people to quit waiting for white America to help them. The only way forward, Muhammad said, was for black people to separate themselves — by starting their own businesses, buying from those black-owned business, and, eventually, forming their own nation.

By 1955, the Nation of Islam was enough of a force to attract the attention of the Federal Bureau of Investigation, which referred to the organization as the Muslim Cult of Islam, or MCI, calling it "an especially anti-American and violent cult." In a document intended to serve as a guide to field agents, the bureau concluded:

1. The MCI is a fanatic Negro organization purporting to be motivated by the religious principles of Islam, but actually dedicated to the propagation of hatred against the white race. The services conducted tl. oughout the temples are bereft of any semblance of religious exercises.

2. Organizationally, the MCI is a collection of autonomous temples bound by a tremulous personal relationship between the heads of the temples and the headquarters of the Cult in Chicago, Illinois.

3. The MCI, although an extremely anti-American organization, is not at the present time either large enough or powerful enough to inflict any serious damage to the country; however, its members are capable of committing individual acts of violence.

4. The aims and purposes of the MCI are directed at the overthrow of our constitutional government, inasmuch as the Cult members regard it as an instrument of the white race; therefore, it is obvious that this group, as long as it retains the ideas now motivating it, will remain an investigative problem to the FBI.

The Nation of Islam's growth was not all the work of Elijah Muhammad. It was also a product of rising discontent among black Americans. "Without the failings of Western society," wrote Louis E. Lomax, one of the first authors to document the history of the Nation, "the Black Muslims could not have come into being." And without the racism he experienced growing up, without the angry voice of his father reverberating through his family's small home, without the image of Elijah Muhammad as a wise and powerful and sober alternative to his father, and without the shocking death of Emmett Till, young Cassius Clay might not have been so captivated by the message of the Black Muslims, as they were known.

Cassius Clay would fall under the spell of two great influences in his life: The first was boxing, which was violent at its core but offered the promise of fame, riches, and glory. The second was the philosophy of Elijah Muhammad, who said a black man should take pride in his color, and that black men would soon rule the world, that they would use violence if necessary to come to power, and that there was nothing white America could do about it.

After his trip to Chicago for the Golden Gloves in 1959, Cassius returned home with a recording. Some journalists have said it was a recording of Elijah Muhammad's speeches, but it was more than likely a recording of a song: "A White Man's Heaven Is a Black Man's Hell," written and performed by Minister Louis X, formerly known as Louis Eugene Walcott and later known as Minister Louis Farrakhan. The recording was more than ten minutes long, split over two sides of a 45-rpm record. Over a subdued calypso beat, Minister Louis X delivered something like a sermon, speaking more than singing:

> Why are we called Negroes?
> Why are we deaf, dumb, and blind?

The song went on with a list of questions: Why was everyone else making progress while black people were left behind? Why were black people treated so poorly? Why were they stripped of their names, their languages, their religion?

"White Man's Heaven" served as an introduction to the Nation of Islam for many black Americans. It could be heard on jukeboxes in black-owned cafes and restaurants and purchased in black-owned record stores. For centuries, the white man had imposed his religion on Africans, often in the name of liberation. Now, the song urged the children of slavery to rethink their relationship with the Christian church and reframe their identities. Its lyrics were a reflection of the philosophy of Elijah Muhammad, who taught young men like Louis X that they possessed characteristics beyond the ones imposed by the white men who had enslaved their ancestors; that they had a history and a religion of their own; that they could break free of the systems and rituals that rendered them first as slaves and then as second-class citizens.

Clay listened to the recording repeatedly, as his aunt once told a reporter, until everyone else in the house was sick of it and until Clay himself was completely "brainwashed, hypnotized," his life irrevocably altered.

After beating Tony Madigan for the national Golden Gloves light-heavyweight championship in March 1959, Clay became something close to a full-time amateur boxer. In April, he won the National Amateur Athletic Union (AAU) championship with a unanimous victory over Johnny Powell.

In May, he suffered the biggest loss of his amateur career — a split decision to left-handed fighter Amos Johnson — a defeat that kept him out of the Pan-American Games finals. Although Clay took a pounding from Johnson, Joe Martin continued to be impressed by his young fighter's ability to stay on his feet and keep calm when hurt.

"Cassius really knew how to fight when he got in trouble," Martin told a reporter. "He never panicked or forgot what I'd taught him. When he'd get hit, he wouldn't get mad and wade in, the way some boys do. He'd take a good punch and then he'd go back to boxing, box his way out of it . . . Only once did I ever see him knocked out, knocked cold, and that was in the gymnasium, working out with an amateur named Willy Moran. Moran was a good hitter . . . Anyway, he really flattened Cassius that day. Cassius had been talking to me about wanting a scooter, and when he regained consciousness he said to me, 'Mr. Martin, which way was the scooter going that hit me?' The scooter was on his mind. That was the only time I ever saw him knocked cold. He was about sixteen then, and it didn't faze him. He was back working out with Moran again the next day."

In 1959, though everyone knew that the skull was a container for the brain, little thought was paid to the damage done by the bashing of one's cranium;

quite the contrary, the ability to take a punch was considered a totem of manliness and, for a young fighter like Clay, an indication of a bright future.

During the spring of 1959, Clay was boxing almost constantly, with an average of about three fights a month. Most of the contests were on weekends, but he nevertheless must have missed many days of school. No longer did friends see Cassius running alongside the bus on the way to Central High. Now Cassius and Rudy ran almost exclusively at Chickasaw Park and on a nearby track. The brothers remained almost inseparable. They shared a bedroom, meals, and a training regimen. Rudy boxed in tournaments almost as often as his older brother. While Rudy fared well, it was clear to the brothers as well as to their coaches that Cassius was the more promising fighter. It was a matter of talent, not effort or strength. Cassius had the gift, and his brother didn't. "My mind was not as quick as his," Rudy said. "Boxing is a thinking man's game."

Being the younger brother of Cassius Clay was not easy. Cassius was the finer athlete and the more popular, more entertaining, more charismatic of the two. Rudy Clay seemed to accept his status in much the way a straight man accepts that his comedy partner gets the laughs. Rudy knew his limitations and enjoyed having an all-access pass to the carnival that was his brother's life. Rudy was his brother's most trusted companion. Cassius never wore a watch because he had Rudy there to tell him the time. And Cassius made his brother a promise: whatever came along — money, women, travel, glory — they would share every bit of it, forever, together.

By 1960, Cassius was six-foot-one and weighed about 180 pounds. In March, he returned to Chicago to fight again in the Golden Gloves tournament. This time he competed as a heavyweight, not a light-heavyweight, in order to avoid a possible showdown with Rudy, who had also entered the competition. After winning in Chicago, Cassius traveled to New York to fight the Golden Gloves champion of the east, Gary Jawish, who outweighed Clay by about forty pounds. Clay started by measuring Jawish with jabs, then began throwing quick hooks. He kept them coming so swiftly and with such forward momentum that Jawish lost the ability to hit back. Soon he lost the ability to stand up straight, and by the third round the referee decided that Jawish was in danger of serious injury, declaring Clay the winner by a technical knockout.

Throughout the first half of 1960, Clay fought on a schedule that might have suited a hungry young professional. In April, he once again won the National AAU light-heavyweight title and took home a trophy as the tournament's outstanding boxer. "WATCH CLAY in the future," wrote the boxing promoter and journalist Hank Kaplan after the AAU tournament. "Best amateur prospect in the country. Not a hard hitter, but is fast, throws fast combinations."

The AAU championship assured Clay of a chance to compete in the upcoming Olympic trials. But instead of resting, he returned to Louisville, where he continued to fight and win.

"Let's forget the Olympics," he told Joe Martin. "I'm ready to turn pro."

6

"I'm Just Young and Don't Give a Damn"

Years later, historians would say that 1959 marked the end of a decade of American innocence. It was an age when image trumped substance, an era remembered for pink Cadillacs, drive-in movies, drive-in restaurants, slick-haired rock 'n' rollers, daylight baseball, and fraternity-house panty raids, all of it flashing in bright colors as if it were a Hollywood-made tribute to youth.

For Clay, in his last year of high school, the rumors of distant wars meant nothing. Neither did the actions of four black college freshmen at the Agricultural and Technical College in Greensboro, North Carolina, who asked politely for coffee at a Woolworth's lunch counter and sat in silent protest when they were refused service, their actions setting off a wave of "sit-ins" in seven other southern states. Soon after, in April 1960, a group of young, militant black men formed the Student Nonviolent Coordinating Committee (SNCC). They would go on to participate in Freedom Rides, aimed at desegregating busing, and countless other civil rights protests. The self-discipline and courage of these young rebels might have struck a chord with Cassius Clay. But, for the time being, he was not engaged with politics. He was young. He was handsome. He was talented. His attention was focused on boxing, girls, cars, money, and mirrors.

When a reporter suggested he was conceited, Clay seemed hurt.

"No," he said, "I'm just young and don't give a damn about anything."

One day during his senior year of high school, Cassius Clay attended a school talent show. When the show ended, he spotted a former classmate named Areatha Swint and stopped her to say hello. Areatha had dropped out of school the year prior after becoming pregnant and having a baby boy. She had left the baby home with her mother so she could attend the talent show and see some of her old friends at Central High. When the show was over, Clay offered to walk her home.

Some boys weren't interested in dating a young woman with a baby, even a beautiful young woman like Swint. The boys tended to become even more leery when they learned that the father of Swint's child was doing time in jail. Clay didn't care. He'd always had a crush on Swint, and he was not the sort to worry about minor details. After the talent show, Clay walked Swint back to her home in the Beecher Terrace apartments. Swint enjoyed Clay's company. She liked his infectious laugh. She liked the fact that, despite all the bragging, he seemed nervous and humble. Swint knew that Clay was a celebrity at Central High. All the girls knew about his athletic success, and they all admired his striking features and long, muscular arms, which he went out of his way to show off by wearing tight, white, short-sleeved shirts. He had beautiful skin and dark brown eyes and a small gap between his two upper front teeth, an imperfection that made him even more desirable. "He was like a live chick walking through Colonel Sanders," recalled Swint, who later changed her name to Jamillah Muhammad. "He drew them like a magnet." But it was his personality even more than his looks that attracted Swint.

"The thing I liked about him," she said, "I don't care what kind of mood you were in, being around him one hour could make you forget everything. He was always positive, always funny. He had a sense of humor like you wouldn't believe."

That night, when Clay and Swint reached Beecher Terrace, they walked together up the stairs to Swint's second-floor apartment. When they reached her door, Clay leaned in for a kiss, and Swint closed her eyes to give him one back. Then came a series of loud thudding sounds — and no kiss. When Swint opened her eyes, Clay was lying on the ground at the foot of the stairs in a tangle of long arms and legs.

Clay had fainted.

From the bottom of the stairs, he looked up sheepishly at Swint. "Ain't nobody gonna believe this," he said.

Throughout the spring and summer of 1960, Clay and Swint dated, although Clay was too busy boxing and Swint too busy raising her baby for the relationship to get serious. Clay loved playing with Swint's little boy, Alan. The baby had a stuffed Collie, and Clay would tie a string around the toy dog's neck, hide the string under the rug, and make the dog move around the room.

"Every minute I ever spent with him was fun," she said. "That's just the kind of man he was."

Although he had talked about turning professional, Clay remained an amateur, and in May 1960, he traveled to San Francisco to fight for a spot on America's Olympic boxing team. Eighty young men would compete. Ten of them — one from each weight division — would make the team and go on to the Olympics in Rome. But before he could participate in the trials, Clay had to overcome his fear of flying.

Cassius Clay Sr. was afraid of air travel, and his son had developed much the same phobia after an early flight from Louisville to Chicago in 1958 or 1959. Clay, in his 1975 autobiography, wrote that the turbulence was so severe, "some of the seats were torn from their bolts on the floor." Joe Martin remembered much the same: "I mean, we was doing all kinds of flips and things were falling out on the floor, you know? And that plane started slipping down thataway and them motors just a-screaming and a-squalling. I really thought it was our last ride . . . We hit bottom so hard it pulled the screws right out of the floor where my seat was, and I had a black mark across my stomach where my seatbelt was. And I mean Cassius was praying and hollering! Oh, man, he was scared to death."

Now, a year or so after that traumatic flight, Clay told Martin he would skip the Olympic trials in San Francisco if flying were the only way to get there. If he won in San Francisco, after all, it would only mean another flight to Rome, followed by *another* flight back to the United States. He would be better off turning pro now, he argued, and scheduling fights in cities he could reach by car, bus, and train. His goal, he said, was to be the youngest heavyweight champion in the history of boxing. Clay was only eighteen, which meant he had three years to break the record of Floyd Patterson, who had become champ at the age of twenty-one years and ten months.

But Joe Martin wanted Clay to fight in San Francisco and win a spot on the team. He told his protégé that nothing would get him a quicker shot at the heavyweight championship than an Olympic gold medal.

"The decision by Clay is a big one," wrote Dean Eagle, a sports columnist for one of the boxer's hometown newspapers, the *Louisville Times*. "If he doesn't fly now he might have to ride a lot of buses before he gets anywhere in professional boxing." Eagle went on to point out that baseball, basketball, and football teams had all recently begun flying, and that the price of airline insurance indicated the low risk. A flier could purchase $7,500 of insurance for only 25 cents, Eagle wrote, which put the odds of death by plane crash at about thirty thousand to one.

Eventually, Martin persuaded Clay to fly. "But then he went to an army supply store and bought a parachute and actually wore it on the plane," said Martin's son, Joe Martin Jr. When the flight to San Francisco hit turbulence over Indiana, Clay bent over his seat and prayed.

Clay moved easily through the early rounds of the qualifying competition. But in the final round, he faced an opponent who had left behind a trail of knocked-out fighters en route to San Francisco. Allen "Junebug" Hudson, an army veteran from Long Island, New York, who usually fought as a heavyweight, had one of the meanest left hooks anyone in the tournament had seen, and a personality to match. His previous opponent had lasted only thirty-two seconds.

Hudson intimidated in and out of the ring. But if he made Clay nervous, Clay had a funny way of showing it. Before the fight, the two young men were playing cards. Some gentle teasing became less gentle, and soon Clay and Hudson were barking at each other across the table. Chairs scraped the floor, chests puffed, and fists rose, according to one witness, Tommy Gallagher, an amateur fighter who would go on to become a trainer. According to Gallagher, Clay started the trouble. "He was the most obnoxious guy you ever met," Gallagher recalled. "Obnoxious! Obnoxious! He came from this middle-class family. He wasn't no ghetto black guy, and he just had this way about him that was fucking obnoxious. Actually, I think he was just scared to death and he had no idea how to act."

Julius "Julie" Menendez, head coach of the 1960 Olympic boxing team, stepped in and broke up the fracas, telling the young men to put on gloves and get in the ring if they wanted to fight. They did. The day before their sanctioned fight, Clay and Hudson boxed before a handful of their peers and coaches, a fight in which only pride was at stake.

"I hate to say it," Gallagher recalled, "but [Clay] kicked the shit out of him."

The next night, when their official fight began at the Cow Palace, with a trip to Rome on the line, Hudson and Clay barked at each other in a manner seldom seen in the polite world of amateur boxing. It was a foreboding moment for Clay, who would go on hectoring opponents throughout his career, convinced that his braggadocio and ill manners unnerved them. It was also a good reminder that boxing — even amateur boxing — ran on anger, that it was combat, that every boxer who ever stepped into a ring was looking to assert his superiority, to exploit a rival's weakness, to knock loose a jawbone, fracture a nose, bloody an eye socket, rattle a skull, turn out the lights.

Despite the animosity between these two fighters, Clay kept calm in the early minutes of the bout, jabbing and moving, as if scouting the terrain before launching an attack. With nimble dancing he rendered Hudson's looping punches ineffective. Clay, his left hand snapping forward and back, stayed out of range of Hudson's fearsome left hook. Hudson got hit but seemed unhurt, powering his way past Clay's jabs and pounding the young fighter's body. After two rounds, the fight was close, but Clay had the lead on points, which meant Hudson probably needed a knockout in the third and final round to make the Olympic team.

The bell rang and the fighters met at the center of the square ring, no longer jawing at each other. The pace quickened. Hudson fired two left jabs. Clay ducked both and hit Hudson with a soft right. Hudson followed with a hard right to Clay's body. Clay threw more jabs. Hudson nearly tagged Clay with a left hook, but the punch merely grazed Clay's face. The fighters clinched and shoved. The referee separated them, and then it happened — the thing Hudson had been counting on but for which Clay was entirely unprepared. Hudson bullied his way past a weak Clay jab and let fly another left hook — one that thudded Clay's chin and spun his head and neck. Clay probably never saw the punch. He hit the canvas rear end first. It was a quick, thunderous blow, followed by a roar of the crowd. But Clay was popping back up before the referee could begin to count him out, talking to the ref, nodding, clearing the haze from his head, insisting he was okay, ready to fight, not beaten.

The referee grabbed Clay's gloves, looked him in the eyes for signs of damage, and signaled for the fight to go on.

Hudson moved in, trying to finish his younger opponent, and landed two hard punches. But now Clay was through dancing, through trying to score points. He was on the attack, possibly angry, adrenaline surging. After ducking a punch, Clay leaned back and launched a huge right hook — the sort he seldom threw because it left him open to retaliatory blows. But here it was, and it not only landed; it staggered Hudson, who momentarily lost his balance. While Hudson tried to set his feet, Clay leapt forward and threw another big right, this one square on Hudson's jaw. The punch spun Hudson 180 degrees, casting him face-first into the ropes in a corner of the ring.

Hudson stumbled to his feet but couldn't stop wobbling. The referee ended the fight. Clay, arms thrust high above his head in a V, bounced around the ring in celebration as Hudson slumped in his corner and cried.

It was as vicious a contest as anyone had seen that week in San Francisco. Young Cassius Clay had emerged as a winner and, perhaps, as America's top contender for a gold medal in Rome.

When the Olympic trials were over, Clay asked Joe Martin to lend him money for a train ticket. When Martin refused, saying he had already paid his plane fare, Clay pawned a gold watch that had been one of his prizes for winning the tournament. He traveled home by rail, alone.

Clay arrived in time for graduation ceremonies at Central High. But in the weeks leading up to commencement, it was unclear whether he would receive a diploma. He had spent much of his senior year out of school, boxing in tournaments nationwide. Even when he had attended classes, his academic performance had been desultory, as usual.

Some members of the faculty at Central High School complained that Clay didn't deserve to graduate. "He was not a good student," said Bettie Johnson, one of the counselors at Central. "School was something he did because he was supposed to." During his senior year, Clay submitted a paper to his English teacher about Elijah Muhammad and the Nation of Islam. Any submission of work by Clay should have been cause for celebration among the faculty, but this teacher was "a very conforming Christian," Johnson recalled, "and just the mention of separatism or of blacks being super-assertive frightened her." The English teacher intended to flunk Clay. But the school's courtly and respected principal, Atwood Wilson, stood up at a faculty meeting and made a speech that would be remembered in Central High lore as the

"Claim to Fame" address. Wilson said he understood that some members of the faculty believed that granting Clay a diploma would send the wrong message to young athletes, giving them cause to believe that schoolwork didn't matter if they could run quickly, throw a ball accurately, or land a sharp punch to another man's head. On the other hand, Wilson said, Cassius Clay might one day be famous, making more money than all the school's faculty combined. If that were to happen, Wilson said, every member of the faculty and administration would boast about having known him and having taught him. It would be their greatest claim to fame. That's how Wilson preferred to be remembered, not as the man who flunked Cassius Clay.

Clay received his diploma. He graduated 376th out of 391 in his senior class, receiving a "certificate of attendance," the lowest degree granted by the school but good enough to make him a high-school graduate.

7

America's Hero

Before leaving for Rome, Cassius Clay and the rest of the Olympic boxing team spent a few days in New York City. One afternoon, Dick Schaap, a reporter for *Newsweek* magazine, showed up at the midtown hotel where the boxers were staying and invited Clay and three of his teammates to join him for dinner. Schaap, who knew everybody in town, suggested they go up to Harlem to meet Sugar Ray Robinson.

Clay was thrilled. He idolized Robinson, and he had modeled his boxing style on Sugar Ray's. Even though he was bigger than Robinson, Clay was convinced he could fight with the same speed and flair. He also admired Sugar Ray's showmanship, the way he traveled with a giant entourage and ordered new Cadillacs each year in outrageous colors. There were no more than a few black men in America who flaunted their wealth and fame as outrageously as Robinson. Clay was intent on adding to that number, and so he and Schaap and three more boxers squeezed into a taxi for the ride to Sugar Ray's restaurant at the corner of Seventh Avenue and 124th Street. When they arrived, Robinson wasn't there, so Schaap and the young men strolled around Harlem. At the corner of Seventh Avenue and 125th Street, a member of Elijah Muhammad's Nation of Islam, dressed in suit and tie, was standing atop a soapbox, urging black men and women to buy from black merchants, to remember who they were, and to be proud of it.

"Ain't he gonna get in trouble?" Clay asked Schaap.

Clay picked up on an important element of the Nation of Islam's appeal. There had long been soapbox speakers in Harlem, many of them standing on the very same corner, and many of them had made similar pronouncements about the need for a separate black nation with a separate black economy. What struck newcomers like Clay most about the Nation of Islam's soapbox orators was the restrained reaction of police, who had been known to drag speakers off their podiums and arrest them for saying things far less virulent than the Nation of Islam's speakers did.

The Nation of Islam orators spoke of power. They offered proof, divine and historical, that white people were devils and destined to fall. Allah Himself had revealed this to His prophet, the Honorable Elijah Muhammad. The crowds gazed attentively and hopefully.

To Schaap, it was a sign of the young boxer's gullibility. Clay, he said, was so "malleable . . . I could've converted him to Judaism." But Schaap, as a white man, could not have understood why a young black man from the South might be excited to have divine confirmation of his experiences, to learn that there was a reason black people had been mistreated for so long, and that their suffering would soon end. As James Baldwin wrote, Elijah Muhammad's messages had power because they articulated the historical suffering of black people and offered a way to end it, investing followers "with a pride and serenity that hang about them like an unfailing light."

But Clay hadn't come to Harlem to hear the word of the Honorable Elijah Muhammad. He had come to meet a prophet of a different order. When Sugar Ray Robinson finally pulled up in his purple Lincoln Continental, Schaap introduced the young Olympians to the man considered by many to be the greatest and flashiest pound-for-pound fighter of all time. For Clay, there would be no bragging for once. He stepped humbly before his hero.

Robinson autographed a photo for one of the young boxers, muttered vaguely in the direction of the others, and then wandered off. "His usual haughty, disdainful self," Schaap said. Clay got little more than a nod.

"I was so hurt," he recalled years later. "If Sugar Ray only knew how much I loved him and how long I'd followed him, maybe he wouldn't have done that . . . I said to myself right then, 'If I ever get great and famous and people want my autograph enough to wait all day to see me, I'm sure goin' to treat 'em different.'"

Clay arrived in Rome with a crown atop his head and a choir singing behind him everywhere he went — or so it seemed from the way he comported himself. He strode into the Olympic Village as if he had been named its king and everyone else had come to celebrate his coronation and gaze upon his beauty and grace.

He introduced himself to one journalist as Cassius Marcellus Clay VII, perhaps hoping that his lineage might be traced back to a Roman gladiator or king. With a camera hanging from his neck, Clay flitted about the village, "friendly and frisky as a puppy" according to the same reporter, snapping pictures and then handing off the camera so he could be included in group photos.

"Took forty-eight pictures today," he said before hopping away to photograph a group of foreigners. He used hand gestures to pose the men and then returned to the interview. He corralled a group of Russians and quickly had them all smiling and hugging.

"Gotta study the language," he said. "I'm just lost here. All I know in Italian is *bambino*."

He made eyes at a lot of pretty young women — "foxes," he called them — and seemed particularly enamored with the great American sprinter Wilma Rudolph. He met the singer and actor Bing Crosby, striding with him arm in arm, and then found himself posing for pictures with Floyd Patterson, boxing's heavyweight champion and an Olympic gold medalist from 1952. Clay noticed — and pointed out to a reporter — that he stood a little bit taller than Patterson and had longer arms.

"Be seeing you in about two more years," Clay said, implying that he would be ready then to fight and beat the champ. If Patterson answered Clay, reporters didn't mention it. But it's safe to say the kid's swagger displeased at least a portion of his audience. In part, it was Clay's delivery that hurt him. When other great athletes bragged, they usually did so with a touch of slyness. But Clay's face seldom showed humor. He seldom softened his affect.

Clay had never been outside the United States and never been surrounded by so many world-class athletes and celebrities. Now, as he went out into the world, he used his new experiences to distance himself from his upbringing. One night he went dancing with athletes from other nations. On another day he joined a group of young men and women who went to see and hear Pope John XXIII in St. Peter's Square. Why not? No one cared that he was black, that he could scarcely read, that he was young, that he didn't come from a wealthy, well-educated family. No one knew him yet. He would write his own life story, starting now.

"Wouldn't it be wonderful if people could be this friendly all the time?" he asked a reporter from his hometown.

For newspapermen, the Olympic games offered a special opportunity, and not just to pad their expense accounts. The Olympics gave pencil pushers who seldom strayed from the nuts and bolts of competitive sport the opportunity to write about something grander. The Olympics provided the best place in the world to witness the interaction of nations, races, religions, and ideologies. In 1960, with Cold War tensions running high, it was impossible to watch men and women compete in Rome without considering the global, potentially apocalyptic struggle between communism and capitalism raging across the globe.

American women took a newly prominent role in the 1960 Olympics — in part because women were fighting for equal rights but also because the U.S. team thought women might give America the edge over the Soviets when it came to the final medal count. The Rome Olympics foretold other cultural shifts. There was the first doping scandal, the first commercial television broadcast, and the first runner paid to wear a brand of track shoes.

When the American decathlete Rafer Johnson led the U.S. delegation at the Parade of Nations at Stadio Olimpico, it marked the first time a black athlete carried the American flag in an Olympic competition. With the selection of Johnson, the Americans meant to send a message that America was a land of freedom and opportunity, although it also afforded America's critics the opportunity to point out that Johnson and other black Americans still faced discrimination at home. European reporters were surprised to see so many black athletes on the American squad. Twelve percent of the men and twenty-five percent of the women on the American team were black. In the Olympic village, American mess halls and dormitories were fully integrated, although white athletes who requested white roommates were usually accommodated.

Twenty-four years earlier, Hitler's propaganda machine had accused the United States of using subhuman "black auxiliaries" like Jesse Owens to compete with Hitler's so-called master race. Now, the comingling of white and black athletes on the U.S. team was something Americans bragged about.

The press glommed on to Clay not only because he entertained them but also because he seemed to represent much of what was new in the 1960 games. He was cocky and opinionated, which was unusual for a young, black athlete. He spoke openly about his eagerness to turn pro and get rich, which was also fairly novel and refreshing. And he wasn't afraid to talk about politics, even if he scarcely knew what he was talking about.

"Is there a crisis for Negroes in the United States?" a foreign reporter asked Clay before the start of the competition.

"Oh, I guess there are some troubles," he said. "But nothing you can't fix. And the United States is still the greatest country in the world."

When a Russian reporter pushed him, asking if it was true that Negroes couldn't eat in the same restaurants as whites back in the States, Clay was honest. He said, yes, there were times when it was difficult for a black person to get a meal in an American restaurant, but that wasn't the only indicator of a nation's greatness. Life in America was still wonderful. After all, he said, "I ain't fighting off alligators and living in a mud hut."

Clay had tried all his life to be noticed, to find the tallest pedestal and to stand on it and shout as loudly as he could, to tell the world he was different and special and they had better pay attention. Had he found himself at age eighteen in the military or enrolled in college or working in a factory, no one would have cared about his views of the racial crisis in America; his cockiness might have earned him a reprimand — or worse — from a drill sergeant, a teacher, a factory foreman, or an angry white law enforcement officer. Had he not been a celebrated athlete, he might have been forced to civilize the unruliness within.

It was the right place at the right time for a young man in a hurry to become a star. Of course, to complete the journey to stardom, he still had to fight and win, and the boxers lined up to face Clay were not likely to be as submissive as the reporters.

Before the competition began, writers were naming Clay the best boxer on a mediocre American team. Dan Daniel, the legendary sports columnist for the *New York World-Telegram*, predicted that in all likelihood none of the nine Americans would make it as a professional fighter. "If there is a Rome winner and potential money-making star among our boxers," Daniel wrote, "he is the 175-pounder Cassius Clay, from Louisville . . . Some say Clay is a better boxer than [Floyd] Patterson was when he won the middleweight medal in the 1952 Olympics at Helsinki . . . However, Clay finds himself in the toughest of the 10 classes to be contested in Italy."

The three best amateur fighters in the world, according to many reporters, were all in Clay's light-heavyweight division. They were Tony Madigan, the Australian whom Clay had faced a year and a half earlier in New York; Russia's Gennadiy Shatkov, winner of a gold medal as a middleweight in the 1956 Melbourne Olympics; and a left-handed Polish fighter named Zbiegniew Pietrzykowski ("Some guy with fifteen letters in his name," Clay called Pietrzykowski), who had fought more than 230 bouts, winning three European championships, and was considered a heavy favorite to take the gold medal.

In his first fight, Clay, wearing a white tank top with the number 272 on his back, came out of his corner jabbing and dancing, zipping in and out so quickly that his twenty-four-year-old Belgian opponent, Yvon Becot, looked like a man trying to hit smoke rings. He punched, missed, looked up to see where Clay had gone, and punched and missed again. When Becot poked his head up, Clay popped him with a left jab. At the end of round one, a stiff jab from Clay rattled the Belgian. In the second round, Clay came out slugging and knocked Becot down with a left hook that traveled so quickly few in the audience could have seen it. Before the second round was over, Becot was too damaged to go on. The referee stopped the bout.

In his next fight, Clay blackened both eyes of the Russian gold medalist Shatkov and scored an easy win. That set up a rematch with Tony Madigan. After their fight in New York, Madigan had complained that Clay was the sort of fighter he dreaded. "He's very tall and has a very fast left hand and he continually moves away," Madigan said, "and I haven't got the flexibility to fight those fighters the way they should be fought. Unfortunately, I can't vary my style — as I should be able — to meet that contingency."

Now, in Rome, Madigan didn't try to vary his style. He lowered his shoulders and prowled, letting Clay hit him with those long, quick jabs, and throwing heavy hooks to Clay's body and head. The fight was close, but the judges gave the unanimous decision to Clay, sending him on to meet Pietrzykowski for the gold medal.

Clay must have been thinking of the left-handed Amos Johnson when he learned he'd be facing Pietrzykowski in the finals. A year earlier in Wisconsin, at the Pan American trials, Johnson had given Clay the worst beating of his life. Since then, Clay had won forty-two consecutive fights. Now he not only faced another lefty; he faced one of the best in the world in Pietrzykowski.

"Do southpaws bother other fellows?" Clay asked sports columnist Red Smith. Smith assured him that all fighters believed that southpaws should be drowned at birth.

If he was worried, though, Clay didn't show it. His coaches begged him to spend more time in the gym, but Clay was too busy signing autographs and taking pictures. He ran a mile or two most mornings, but otherwise he saw little need for training. Either he was ready or he wasn't.

The bell rang and Clay went to work. To enter a boxing ring is to willingly lose control. You train, you study, you commit yourself fully, perhaps you make up your mind on a strategy, a plan of attack, perhaps you pray, and then you step through the ropes and face an opponent who has also trained, studied, committed himself fully, possibly prayed, and who has adopted a strategy meant to render yours null and void. The fight starts and all is irresolution. Anything can happen — victory, defeat, even death. The great fighters lose themselves in the void. They don't think about it. They ride the rush.

Clay stepped in and met Pietrzykowski with his usual speed and high energy, but he didn't look like the same fighter spectators in Italy had been watching all week. Whether he had made up his mind before the bout to change his style or whether he arrived at the decision spontaneously upon seeing his opponent's style, Clay didn't say, but it was clear that he was treating this opponent differently. He wasn't dancing much, for one thing. And instead of using his left jab to wear down his foe, he mixed left jabs with right leads.

At the end of the first round, Pietrzykowski landed two hard lefts, but they didn't faze Clay. Clay had thrown more punches than his opponent, but most of Clay's punches had missed. When the bell rang to end the round, Clay could not have been sure if he had won it.

In the second round, Pietrzykowski lowered his head and fought more aggressively. He landed two big left hands, but neither seemed to bother Clay. Again in round two, Clay used his right hand more than usual. When Pietrzykowski went into a crouch to defend himself, Clay pounded the Pole's ribcage with left hooks.

Going into the third round, the fight remained close. Clay probably had the edge, but neither fighter wanted to take the chance of letting the judges determine the winner. Clay came out hitting faster and harder. He used body punches to set up head shots. He shuffled his feet with lightning speed before unleashing a flurry of hooks. In the final minute, Clay punched and punched. For every punch Pietrzykowski landed, Clay landed three. Blood gushed from the Pole's mouth and nose, staining his white shirt. Clay kept coming, like a beast who tastes blood, eyes locked on his opponent's head, arms flying without pause, the look on his face saying *this is mine*. He surged forward and slugged until the bell's clang called him off.

Moments later, a three-tiered podium was lifted into the ring and Clay climbed to the center and highest step. An Olympic official stood before him, offering the gold medal, the greatest honor available to an amateur boxer. Clay waved modestly to the crowd as his name was announced, said something to the Olympic official, and bent over as the medal was draped around his neck.

Then, in a rare moment of silence, he stood to full height and gently smiled.

8

Dreamer

Oh, he was *something* now. The wittiest, the prettiest, the brashest, the rashest. A picture of life's promises. The embodiment of confidence. Sunshine with a snappy left jab.

"Man," he said, "it's gonna be great to be great."

Clay flew from Rome, stopping in New York before returning to Louisville, and he could hardly pass a stranger without looking to see if they recognized him or walk by a storefront window without pausing to admire his reflection. He was tall and slender, with skin the color of chocolate milk and eyes slightly darker. The terrain of his face was gentle, with no hard lines or unexpected angles, everything in lovely proportion — too lovely, if anything, for a boxer. His youthful grin shone brighter than the glittering medal that hung around his neck.

"Look at me! I'm beautiful," he said, aloud, not to himself, because seldom did a thought pass from his mind unexpressed. "And I'm gonna stay pretty 'cause there ain't a fighter on earth fast enough to hit me!"

He wore his medal everywhere, even to bed. He slept on his back so it wouldn't cut his chest.

His trainer, Joe Martin, met him at Idlewild Airport in New York, along with William Reynolds, who, as vice president of the Reynolds Metal Co., was one of Louisville's wealthiest and best-known citizens. The men drove Clay to the Waldorf Towers Hotel and ensconced him in a suite next to one occupied at the time by the Duke and Duchess of Windsor. Reynolds gave Clay a pile of cash and told him to buy presents for his mother and father.

The boxer selected a $250 watch for his mother and a pair of $100 watches for his father and brother. He dined at the Waldorf, Olympic medal still draped from his neck, and ordered two steaks at $7.95 each.

Everywhere he went in New York, Clay was asked if he intended to turn pro. The answer was a certain yes. "I want money, plenty of it," he said. He noted that he might eventually become a pop singer, "like Elvis Presley," but boxing would come first. He vowed that within three years he would be the world heavyweight champion. In a sign of impatience, he stepped into a Times Square arcade and bought a mock newspaper with a banner headline of his own construction: "Cassius Signs for Patterson Fight."

"Back home they'll think it's real," he said.

Once again, Dick Schaap served as Clay's tour guide. The sidewalks of New York in the fall of 1960 were filled with men in fedoras and women in mink. Jazz fans squeezed in to the Village Vanguard to hear Miles Davis. Billboards advertised Rheingold beer and Kent cigarettes. The boxer marveled at many things, including the steep $2.50 check for a roast beef sandwich and a slice of cheesecake from Jack Dempsey's restaurant.

Clay told Schaap he dreamed of having a hundred-thousand-dollar home, a beautiful wife, two Cadillacs — plus a Ford, "for just getting around in." There was another dream, he said: "I dream I'm running down Broadway — that's the main street in Louisville — and all of a sudden there's a truck coming at me. I run at the truck and then I take off and I'm flying. I go right up over the truck, and all the people are standing around and cheering and waving at me. And I wave back and I keep on flying. I dream that all the time."

In New York, he thrilled with delight whenever he was recognized, never mind that he was doing everything he could to call attention to himself, wearing both his Olympic jacket and his gold medal.

"Really? You really know who I am?" he asked. "That's wonderful!"

The city rolled before the young champion like an overladen dessert cart. It was the new and exciting 1960s; young John F. Kennedy was the Democratic nominee for president; girls were letting their skirts inch up to their kneecaps with the promise of more to come; the birth-control pill had hit the market, and everything and everyone offered the promise of a sexy new order. Cassius Clay acted as if he intended to conquer it all, as if the city lights shined just for him.

At two in the morning, when Schaap was ready to end their adventure and go home, Clay would not yet dismiss his audience; he invited the reporter back to his suite at the Waldorf to look at his scrapbook from Rome. Schaap accepted the invitation, but he told Clay the boxer would have to explain to Mrs. Schaap why her husband was out so late.

"You mean your wife know who I am, too?" Clay asked, excitedly.

And then the young hero stretched out on the bed and went to sleep, perhaps to dream of flying.

Billy Reynolds had made the trip to welcome Clay home and to make the young boxer an offer. The men already knew each other. That summer, Reynolds had offered Clay a job doing yard work at his estate. Clay had shown up every day and splashed in the pool with Reynolds' children, not doing a lick of work but still getting paid. Reynolds didn't mind. He was more interested in helping a promising athlete and securing the trust of a boxer with potential to earn a great deal of money; he had other people to trim his hedges.

Now, Reynolds wanted to put together a deal to launch Clay's professional career. Joe Martin would be hired as Clay's trainer, and a group of white Louisville executives would manage the fighter's business interests. The white Louisville businessmen, along with Martin, would select the boxer's opponents, guiding him toward a shot at the championship. They would pay Clay a straight salary plus a percentage of his earnings, and they would cover all of the expenses associated with his training and his work. They would set aside money for taxes to make sure he never got in trouble with the Internal Revenue Service. And they would create a trust fund so that some of the boxer's income would be saved for his retirement.

Reynolds didn't come to New York to pressure Clay to sign right away, but he did want to show the young fighter he was eager to help. As Clay already knew, most professional fighters were managed by gym rats and mobsters, which left young and often uneducated athletes vulnerable to all sorts of dirty dealings and helped explain why so many fighters ended their careers broke, broken down, and badgered by the tax collector.

Reynolds and his friends were all so wealthy they would never dream of cheating Clay. That was a big part of their pitch. They didn't need his money. Rather, they said, they saw their role as civic boosters. They came from Kentucky, a peculiar and abundant place where fortunes were made on stallions that ran in the mud and whiskeys that came from corn mash. With Clay, these men saw the opportunity to take a Negro from the West End and give him a shot at fame and fortune while possibly turning a profit at the same time. Of course, they may also have been interested in staking Clay for the same reason certain underworld figures and frustrated former jocks got behind boxers — because watching a professional fight is more fun when you've got a front-row seat and a piece of the action.

Reynolds intended to wait until he and Clay were back in Louisville, and then he would make his pitch to the boxer and his parents. For now, the businessman wanted merely to congratulate the Olympic champion, to make his return to the United States more memorable, and, of course, to impress Clay with his wealth.

For his arrival in Louisville, Clay recited a poem.

> *To make America the greatest is my goal,*
> *So I beat the Russian, and I beat the Pole*
> *And for the USA won the Medal of Gold.*
> *Italians said, "You're greater than the Cassius of old."*

The refrain was not good enough to make former teachers reconsider Clay's poor grades, but that hardly mattered to the three hundred fans cheering his arrival on the tarmac at Standiford Field Airport in Louisville. Clay's parents and his brother were there to greet him, of course, along with Mayor Bruce Hoblitzell, six cheerleaders, and a city-furnished twenty-five-car motorcade, which carried the gold medalist to Central High for a pep rally.

Atwood Wilson, the principal who had so generously granted Clay his diploma, stepped to a microphone and said, "When we consider all the efforts that are being made to undermine the prestige of America, we can be grateful we had such a fine ambassador as Cassius to send over to Italy." The mayor called him a "credit to Louisville" and "an inspiration to the young people of this city." Clay addressed the students. He joked that along the way to winning the gold medal, he'd fought and defeated several fighters who were members of the U.S. military, and that if a high-school student could beat the nation's toughest soldiers, "then Uncle Sam's defenses are down and he had better do something." His speech caught some old friends by surprise. "I thought, 'Is that the same Cassius Clay I know?'" asked his classmate

Vic Bender. "Where'd he get that confidence from? I think it came from the Olympics, being able to stand up to all those foreigners. Before that he was always kind of shy."

Back home on Grand Avenue, Odessa Clay baked a turkey for dinner, Cassius Clay Sr. sang "God Bless America," and a steady stream of neighbors arrived at the house and walked up the front steps, which Cash had recently painted with red, white, and blue stripes.

In the fall of 1960, boxing royalty lined up with offers to handle Clay's career. Cus D'Amato, who managed the heavyweight champ Floyd Patterson, expressed interest in nurturing the new gold medalist, as did the 1956 Olympic champion Pete Rademacher, former heavyweight champion Rocky Marciano, and light-heavyweight champ Archie Moore. But Billy Reynolds had the inside track, and he quickly offered Clay a ten-year contract containing terms far more generous than those usually extended to young fighters. The deal offered Clay 50 percent of all the money generated by his fights. His managers would cover all of his training and travel costs. Reynolds also said he would deposit 25 percent of Clay's earnings in a trust that Clay would gain access to when he reached age thirty-five or retired from boxing.

Gordon Davidson, Reynolds's lawyer, drew up the contract. "I did some research and I found out most boxing contracts were very one-sided to the owners," Davidson said. But Davidson was operating on orders from Reynolds that said the contract should be tilted strongly in Clay's favor.

That's why Davidson was surprised when Alberta Jones, a lawyer representing the Clay family, called to say her client had decided to reject the deal. It turned out that Cassius Clay Sr. didn't want Joe Martin as his son's trainer. Cash said he wanted a more experienced trainer, someone who had worked with professional fighters, although the fact that Martin was a white police officer also may have been a factor.

Cash Clay was enjoying his son's success. Cash was a local celebrity in his own right now, with a remarkable new line of dialogue available in his pursuit of free drinks and fast women. His behavior, always somewhat erratic, now became unabashedly bizarre. He would wander the neighborhood in a sombrero, pretending to be a Mexican, showing up uninvited at backyard barbecues and helping himself to beer. If he wasn't feeling Mexican that day, he would insist that he was an Arab sheik, pointing out that his dark color and wide, flat nose proved it. He would remove from his pockets ticket stubs from prizefights and newspaper articles and point out that the name on the tickets and in the newspapers — Cassius Clay — was his name. He would sing in nightclubs if the bandleaders would let him, and he would sing even louder as he stumbled home drunk.

"Oh, my, he was so proud he could hardly stand it," recalled one of the Clays' neighbors, Dora Jean Malachi, who went by Dora Jean Phillips at the time. "You couldn't do nothing but laugh."

With his sense of importance inflated, Cash Clay felt entitled to guide his son's career, and that meant Joe Martin had to go. The rejection bruised the Louisville police officer. "The old man, he don't care no more about that boy than the man in the moon," Martin said.

Once Martin was dumped, Reynolds quit too, out of loyalty to his friend. Almost immediately, though, Gordon Davidson received a call from another wealthy Louisville business executive, William Faversham Jr., a big, gravelly voiced man, vice president at one of Louisville's biggest distilleries, Brown-Forman. Faversham, a former investment advisor, actor, college boxer, and son of a British-born matinee idol, put together a syndicate of eleven of Kentucky's wealthiest men to back Cassius Clay. He asked Davidson if he would use the Reynolds contract as the basis of a new agreement, and that's exactly what Davidson did. The contract was for six years, with an option for Clay to break the deal after three. The boxer would receive a $10,000 signing bonus, $4,800 a year in guaranteed income for the first two years, and $6,000 a year in guaranteed income for the remaining four, in addition to the same promise to pay the boxer 50 percent of the money generated from his activities in and out of the ring. Clay and the syndicate would split gross earnings evenly, and the group would underwrite all of Clay's training expenses, including travel, housing, and food. Fifteen percent of Clay's money would go into a trust fund until he turned thirty-five or retired from boxing. And to reduce the boxer's tax liability, Clay was made an employee of the syndicate and paid a monthly salary and a year-end bonus based on his earnings. Clay and his father would both have a say in choosing the boxer's next trainer.

The members of Faversham's syndicate were among the city's mightiest business executives, men who played pool at the Pendennis Club and chewed mint leaves on the veranda at Churchill Downs. Seven were millionaires. All were white and male. They were William Lee Lyons Brown, chairman of the Brown-Forman distillery, where Faversham worked, and a great southern charmer ("Ah wonder if you realize," he once told *Sports Illustrated,* "that Cassius Clay's aunt cooks for my double-first cousin?"); James Ross Todd, the youngest member of the group at twenty-six and the descendent of an old-line Kentucky family, who said he got involved with Cassius Clay instead of his father "because Daddy had enough on his mind"; Vernter DeGarmo Smith, former sales manager for Brown-Forman and a former executive of the state's horse-racing commission; Ross Worth Bingham, assistant to the publisher (the publisher being his father) at the *Louisville Courier-Journal* and the *Louisville Times;* George Washington Norton IV, known as Possum to his friends, a distant relative of Martha Washington and secretary-treasurer of WAVE-TV, the local NBC affiliate that broadcast *Tomorrow's Champions;* Patrick Calhoun Jr., a horse breeder who admitted, "What I know about boxing you can put in your eye"; Elbert Gary Sutcliffe, grandson of the first chairman of U.S. Steel, who liked to call himself a "retired farmer"; J. D. Stetson Coleman, who had his hands in a Florida bus company, an Oklahoma oil operation, an Illinois candy firm, and a Georgia drug company; William Sol Cutchins, president of the Brown & Williamson tobacco company, makers of Viceroy and Raleigh cigarettes; and Archibald McGhee Foster, senior vice president of a New York–based ad agency that handled the lucrative Brown & Williamson account.

Most of the members of the group espoused the official line: they were in it to "to do something nice for a deserving, well-behaved Louisville boy," as one put it, and to "improve the breed of boxing." Each member of the Louisville Sponsoring Group invested $2,800, tax deductible. Although they hoped to see a return, they weren't counting on it. In fact, the group's treasurer warned members that in the first six months of 1961, he expected expenses of $9,015.86 with little or no income. Cassius Clay was the recipient of the greatest contract ever extended to a boxer with no professional experience, but to the men backing him, he was little more than an amusement. Such was the state of race relations in 1960. The white business leaders assumed that Cassius Clay would consider himself fortunate to have such privileged and unselfish white men guiding his career, and, at least for the time being, they were right.

· · ·

Clay's dreams were coming true. First the gold medal, followed by a check for $10,000, followed soon after by the pink Cadillac, which cost $4,450 — paid with $1,100 down and installments of $120 a month.

When people saw Clay driving his new car, rumors spread around the West End that he had already spent his bonus, which prompted Clay to hand one reporter his bankbook, revealing a balance of $6,217.12. "I may be only eighteen years old," he said. "But I'm not that silly." After the car, he said, his only big expense had been his lawyer's fees, which had come to $2,500.

Clay told the reporter that the Cadillac was a gift for his parents, but he was the one who did most of the driving. With the Caddy, every day was a cavalcade, every trip a chance for a handsome young champion to soak up public adoration, every encounter with a neighbor an opportunity to revel in his marvelous accomplishments, past and future. No one seemed to mind that Clay had not yet bothered to get a driver's license. When Wilma Rudolph visited from Tennessee, the two Olympic champions rolled slowly through the streets, with Clay shouting out the car window to announce their royal presence and Rudolph squirming in her seat, embarrassed by the attention. "The only difference between me and the Pied Piper," Clay once said, "is he didn't have no Cadillac."

According to some of Clay's friends, the young boxer proposed marriage to Rudolph during that visit, only to be rejected. He also proposed a race, Clay v. Rudolph, the gold-medal boxer versus the gold-medal sprinter, running along a stretch of Grand Avenue. Men, women, boys, and girls lined the street to watch the contest. A great cheer went up as the two fine athletes took off sprinting, and a greater cheer rose as Rudolph pulled away to win by a more than comfortable distance.

On October 29, 1960, Clay began his professional career with a thorough beating of Tunney Hunsaker, the thirty-one-year-old chief of police of Fayetteville, West Virginia, who had lost six fights in a row before facing Clay. When it was over, Hunsaker was impressed. The kid had potential. "He's six-three, for one thing," Hunsaker said. "He has long arms and is fast on his feet . . . He backpedals and counterpunches a lot like Willie Pastrano. He's a very good boxer for a kid; best I've met for a boy just starting out."

Hunsaker's only complaint was Clay's attitude. "Perhaps spoiled," he said, referring to Clay's ten-thousand-dollar bonus and pink Cadillac. Clay would have to settle down and work hard if he wanted to be a champion. "I could have helped him with some good punches on the nose," the police chief said, "but he was too tough to catch."

Although Clay had no trouble with Hunsaker, sportswriters were unimpressed with Clay's debut, saying that if he intended to compete with the best heavyweights in the nation, he ought to be able to knock out a galoot like Hunsaker. A. J. Liebling, who wrote about boxing with florid language and cutting attention to detail in *The New Yorker,* described Clay's early fights as "attractive but not probative," adding that the Olympic champion had a "skittering style, like a pebble scaled over water. He was good to watch, but he seemed to make only glancing contact."

In preparation for his fight with Hunsaker, Clay had run through Chickasaw Park and sparred with his brother Rudy. He had also worked out with a trainer named Fred Stoner, whom Cash Clay preferred to Joe Martin largely because Stoner was black and not a police officer. That training regimen had been good enough to beat the Fayetteville chief of police, but members of the Louisville Sponsoring Group were still searching for a real trainer, one who would teach Clay what it took to battle legitimate heavyweight contenders, and one who would know how to choose the best opponents for Clay. One of a trainer's most important jobs is to educate his fighter by exposing him to different challenges in the ring, building both his body and his body of experience, slowly, step by step, without getting his man killed. Ideally, the trainer chooses opponents his fighter can beat even as he absorbs his lessons. There's a catch, of course. If the trainer overestimates his fighter's readiness or underestimates an opponent, a young boxer's career can crash to a halt. And that's exactly what happens to all but a small handful of fighters. If he's lucky, over the course of his career, a trainer might find one fighter whose flaws are never exposed, who fixes his mistakes and makes steady progress, racking up one win after another against increasingly difficult opponents on his way to a championship.

Archie Moore, still the light-heavyweight champion at age forty-four, ran a training camp near San Diego. Moore had sent Clay a telegram after his victory in Rome offering his services as trainer. Clay and Moore seemed like a suitable match. Like Clay, Moore was a showoff. He was a native Mississippian who liked to speak in a fake British accent. Moore was also a smart fighter who relied on more than power, especially as he got older, to defeat stronger opponents. If any trainer was likely to appreciate Clay's unorthodox style and unrestrained personality, it was Archie Moore.

The Louisville Sponsoring Group had another reason to choose Moore as trainer. If Clay established residency in California, his contract with the group would be legally binding. California had a law, written to protect child actors, that said minors could sign contracts and have the state watch over their earnings until they reached majority age. The law was intended to prevent greedy parents from making off with their children's money.

Days after beating Hunsaker, Clay was on his way to Ramona, California. Moore called his training camp the Salt Mine, and it was an ideal place for a young boxer in need of discipline. The property was adorned with boulders painted with the names of great fighters of the past, including Joe Louis, Jack Johnson, and Ray Robinson. Fighters chopped wood, cooked their own meals, and washed their own dishes. They ran four or more miles a day and sparred under the watch of one of the greatest fighters of the era. Clay had no desire for such discipline, even though he may have needed it. He had his Cadillac, a gold medal, and a monthly base salary of $363.63 (at a time when a starting police patrolman would earn about the same).

"Archie," he said, "I didn't come here to be a dishwasher. I ain't gonna wash dishes like a woman."

After a few weeks, Moore telephoned Bill Faversham to say the arrangement wasn't working. The Louisville Sponsoring Group was paying two hundred dollars a week for Clay's training, but Moore couldn't take their money if the boxer wasn't going to cooperate.

"I think the boy needs a good spanking," Faversham said.

"So do I," said Moore, "but who's going to give it to him?"

In choosing a new trainer, Faversham turned to a man who might have been Archie Moore's opposite. Angelo Dundee was soft-spoken. He had black hair, thick forearms, and a face that might have been called handsome were it not so heavily dominated by his nose. He was thirty-nine years old, Italian, the father of two, and when he wasn't working he liked to fish or take his wife square dancing. During a big fight, Dundee would stand calmly in his boxer's corner, his jaw chewing tirelessly on a wad of adhesive tape, his expression a blank.

Dundee was the son of illiterate immigrants from Calabria, the fifth of seven children. The family name was originally Mirena, but one of his brothers changed his name to Joe Dundee in honor of an Italian featherweight champion, Johnny Dundee, from the 1920s, and brothers Angelo and Chris took the name, too. Angelo Dundee inspected planes during World War II and afterward took a job in a missile factory. In 1948, he went to work with his brother Chris, who managed a stable of fifteen boxers in New York. Soon the brothers relocated to Miami, where they operated the Fifth Street Gym, a rat- and termite-infested second-story space above a drug store at the corner of Washington Avenue and Fifth Street in Miami Beach.

The gym was a dump. It wasn't old but it looked old. It smelled of wood and leather. It smelled of rubbing alcohol and liniment and cigarette and cigar smoke. But mostly it smelled of perspiration, because boxers came to the gym to work themselves to the point of exhaustion under the watch of curmudgeonly trainers who looked at a sweat-soaked floor at the end of the day with the same satisfaction a grocer gazed upon empty shelves.

The Fifth Street Gym had the nonchalance of having been decorated and designed by men who cared nothing for style. Busted chairs from an old movie theater surrounded the boxing ring. Speed bags, heavy bags, jump ropes, jock straps, rubdown tables, medicine balls, punch mitts, headgear, and yellowed fight posters, all lit by a couple of bare bulbs, were the notable decor. The floor was splintered, with patches of plywood where the worn-out planks had given way. Sunlight slanted through grimy windows. On one of the windows, someone had painted a picture of a boxing glove and the word "GYM" in yellow letters stacked one atop another. It was the kind of place that made a man feel like a fighting man.

While Angelo Dundee worked more closely with fighters, Chris Dundee was the man who built and managed the gym. He had a desk in the corner he never used because he was always on his feet, always hustling, always reaching into the pocket of his baggy pants to pull out a wad of business cards and bills wrapped in a rubber band, always making friends and making connections. The sportswriter Edwin Pope of the *Miami Herald* called Chris Dundee "the most engaging person" he ever met in sports. After starting his career as a candy butcher, a ten-year-old selling Baby Ruth bars on the trains running between Philadelphia and New York, Chris got into the fight business. He had a gift for functionality. He got things done. And he worked well with everyone, regardless of race, ethnicity, or criminal tendencies.

In a file cabinet, Chris Dundee kept a record of every fight he'd ever worked and every payoff he'd made, from thirty to three hundred dollars. He used initials only — no names — to indicate the sportswriters and gossip columnists who'd been greased in exchange for good publicity. The larger payoffs to mafia bosses like Frankie Carbo and Blinky Palermo, presumably, were not kept on file. Neither did Chris Dundee make a record of his routine acts of generosity. He welcomed men with no means of visible support — men like Mumblin' Sam Sobel and Ben "Evil Eye" Finkel — to the Fifth Street Gym and found work for them. With the help of the great Cuban trainer Luis Sarria, he recruited some of the sport's best Cuban fighters to the gym. Chris Dundee operated under the philosophy that drunks would be drunks, thieves would be thieves, idiots would be idiots, and they were all entitled to make a living.

Clay arrived in Miami on December 19, 1960, in time to prepare for his second pro fight — against Herb Siler, who, like Clay, had only one professional bout to his name. On his first day in Miami, Clay insisted that Angelo Dundee take him to the gym so he could do some sparring. He carried his Olympic gold medal with him everywhere he went and insisted that strangers try it on until the gold began to wear off from being handled so much.

Clay lived on his own now for the first time. Dundee rented his young fighter a room at the Mary Elizabeth Hotel in Miami's Overtown neighborhood. The Mary Elizabeth and its neighbor, the Sir John Hotel, were hot spots for visiting black entertainers. Sammy Davis Jr., Redd Foxx, Nat King Cole, Ella Fitzgerald, and Cab Calloway came to town to perform in posh hotels for white crowds on Miami Beach, but those posh hotels refused black guests, so the celebrities retired after their shows to the Mary Elizabeth and Sir John Hotels, where they would often hold after-hour parties far more entertaining than their earlier performances. Pimps and prostitutes plied the lobbies, but Clay avoided them. Each morning he ran along Biscayne Boulevard, watching the day break orange and yellow. He would run until he burned and his gray sweatshirt turned black under the arms and across his chest.

"Training him was like jet propulsion," said Angelo Dundee, the former airplane inspector. "You just touched him and he took off."

And take off he did. Clay fought four times in less than two months after his arrival in Miami. On December 27, 1960, he beat Siler with a four-round technical knockout. Three weeks later, on his nineteenth birthday (and three days prior to the inauguration of the new president, John F. Kennedy), Clay needed only three rounds to beat Tony Esperti, who soon after retired to become a shakedown artist for the mob. Three weeks after that, Clay defeated Jimmy Robinson, a last-minute replacement for Willie Gulatt, who had failed to show up for the fight; and two weeks later, Clay wore out Donnie Fleeman — "a pork and beaner," as the *Louisville Times* called him — who abandoned his boxing career after the loss.

In these early fights, Clay fought the same way he did as an amateur: dancing, bobbing, and snapping back his head to avoid punches. Sportswriters sniffed. His technique was a mess, they said, and while it might be effective against bums like Jimmy Robinson, it would never be good enough to beat a talented fighter. Interestingly, though Dundee was a boxing traditionalist, the trainer made no attempt to change Clay's style. Dundee even tolerated the young man's big mouth. No doubt he had heard that Clay had butted heads with Archie Moore. Perhaps the experienced trainer recognized that Clay would not respond well to lectures. Perhaps he knew that the best way to hang on to his two-hundred-dollar-a-week job was to keep his fighter happy. Or perhaps he recognized that Ali was like a gifted singer who couldn't read music, one whose natural gifts might be diminished by excessive education.

Dundee proved to be a smart psychologist. Recognizing that Clay possessed an extraordinarily healthy ego, the trainer kept feeding it. "There's only one way to handle a kid like this," he said. "Reverse psychology. If you want to teach him something, you pretend it was his idea in the first place . . . After a workout I'll walk up to him and say, 'Hey, that was really some uppercut you threw in there. That's one of the best I've ever seen.' Of course, he never threw any uppercut, but I'm dying for him to work on one. Next day he's in there throwing uppercuts."

Nothing in Clay's early experience as a professional fighter dissuaded him of his own greatness. He began wearing white T-shirts with his name printed in red script, perhaps inspired by the Coca-Cola logo. Fighters always wore their own names on the backs of their robes, but that was only on fight nights, when there were fans and TV cameras focused in. It may have been the first time an American athlete devised his own name-brand apparel for daily wear. Already, he was emerging as one of the most adept self-promoters in all of sport.

After beating Donnie Fleeman, Clay was invited to spar for three rounds with Ingemar Johansson, a heavyweight with a punishing right hand and a lifetime record of twenty-two wins and only one loss. At the time, Johansson was preparing for a third fight with heavyweight champ Floyd Patterson. Johansson had beaten Patterson in 1959 to win the heavyweight championship before losing a rematch in 1960. Although it was only an exhibition, Clay must have been excited to step into a ring for the first time with a heavyweight who ranked near the top of the sport. Better yet, he did so in front of about one thousand paying customers. To Johansson, it may have been just another workout, but Clay took the chance seriously. He moved quickly across the ring to engage Johansson, flicking jab after jab and skipping out of reach. Johansson stumbled clumsily in pursuit. After only two rounds, the Swede's manager put an end to the performance.

When he was told he would get twenty-five dollars for the sparring session, Clay cheekily said he ought to get a split of the gate.

Weeks later, Johansson twice floored Patterson in the first round of their title fight, but Patterson came back to win with a sixth-round knockout. Clay's conclusion was perhaps predictable: he boasted that he could beat either fighter.

Still, boxing was a hierarchy, and Clay would have to work his way up to a shot at the championship. His first tough opponent was LaMar Clark, a slugger from Utah who had beaten forty-three of his first forty-five opponents, knocking out forty-two and dispensing with twenty-eight in the first round. The fight took place in Louisville, before a crowd of more than five thousand, including many of Clay's friends and relatives.

While Clay had been training in Miami, there had been drama back home. His father had been carrying on recklessly — drinking, bragging, and fighting with his wife even more than usual, according to a family friend who gave an interview to Jack Olsen of *Sports Illustrated*. "The old man teed off on the old lady right after the Olympics," the family friend said, "and Rudy damn near killed [Cash] . . . Rudy said he wasn't gonna have it anymore." Rudy moved out of his childhood home after the incident. At one point, the fighting grew so intense that Odessa threatened to divorce her husband, and Cassius Jr. made an emergency trip from Miami to urge his parents to work out their differences.

At about the same time, in what most young American men at the time accepted as a formality, Clay registered for military service with the Selective Service System. In a form signed March 1, 1961, he described his eyes as dark brown, his skin light brown, his height six-foot-three-and-a-half, his weight

195 pounds, his occupation "professional boxer," his pay three hundred dollars a month, his employer the "Louisville Sponsoring Groupe [*sic*]," and his prior work experience as "Winning the World Light heavy Weight Olympic Boxing Champion at Rome."

The fight against Clark was held April 19, 1961, at Freedom Hall in Louisville. In the first round, Clark almost embarrassed the local hero. A right to the jaw and a left to the chest staggered Clay, but the young boxer slipped away and kept his distance until he recovered, and in the second round he broke Clark's nose and left him lying in a heap on the mat.

After Clark, Clay faced and defeated tougher and tougher opponents, but his performances continued to raise doubts among sportswriters.

"The world of the squared circle is not quite sure whether Cassius is a wonder boy or just another windbag putting his mouth where his gloves should be," the *New York Times* said. Certain prejudices were hard for writers to overcome: A ballerina was supposed to be lithe and light on her feet, a blues singer was supposed to wail with sorrow in his voice, and a heavyweight boxer was supposed to act more like King Kong than Fred Astaire.

Clay's next fight was against a big Hawaiian named Duke Sabedong. How big was Sabedong? "Six-foot-twenty," Angelo Dundee joked. "Big, tall sucker."

It was Clay's first bout in Las Vegas.

"I'm not afraid of the fight; I'm afraid of the flight," he said.

Once again, Clay won, but his victory did nothing to sway the skeptics. The fight went ten rounds, and Clay never came close to a knockout. "He punches like a middleweight," said Sabedong, thus landing one of his better shots.

Before the Sabedong fight, Clay appeared on a local radio show with Gorgeous George, the most famous professional wrestler of his day, who wore his blond hair long and showed up for his matches with the hair still in curlers, waiting until moments before the start of each fight before allowing one of his handlers to brush out his wavy locks. He painted his fingernails and wore a silver lamé robe. "The Human Orchid," as Gorgeous George called himself, was one of the most famous entertainers of his time. In 1950, he made $100,000 — the same as Joe DiMaggio got for playing center field for the Yankees. Gorgeous George spent more time working the news media than battling opponents in the ring, and he knew perhaps better than any per-

former in America that infuriating fans could be more lucrative than charming them. People paid because they wanted to see George get his beautifully
coifed head knocked off. In later years, Bob Dylan, James Brown, and John
Waters would all say they took inspiration from Gorgeous George.

After his radio appearance, Clay watched Gorgeous George wrestle in a
sold-out arena. "I saw fifteen thousand people coming to see this man get
beat," he said. "And his talking did it. I said, 'This is a gooood idea!'"

Clay was already an accomplished showman, but he redoubled his efforts
after meeting the perfumed wrestler. As he prepared for the toughest opponent he'd ever met, Alonzo Johnson, Clay told anyone who would listen that
he was ready for Floyd Patterson, that he, Clay, was the greatest, the soon-
to-be youngest champ in history, a fighter like no other the heavyweight division had seen, too fast to be hit, too strong to be hurt. Reporters didn't
buy it. Neither did Alonzo Johnson, loser of six of eight previous fights but
once a highly rated contender. Johnson managed to go the distance with Clay
and made the young fighter look bad at times before losing on points. "He
knocked me down once but I wasn't hurt," Johnson said years later, reclining
in a chair in his basement, where fight posters and old black-and-white photos filled the walls.

Clay's victory over Johnson was so uninspiring that the crowd booed him
in the later rounds. This was not the sort of booing Gorgeous George had
in mind; these were paying customers voicing their dissatisfaction with the
quality of the boxing match they were witnessing. Their disapproval was all
the more troubling given that the fight took place in Louisville.

After the fight, Clay took a six-week vacation in Louisville, indulged heavily in his mother's cooking, and gained fifteen pounds. He returned to Miami, where he stayed in an un-air-conditioned room to begin getting back
in shape. "I just sit here like a little animal in a box at night," he said. "I can't
go out in the street and mix with the folks out there 'cause they wouldn't be
out there if they was up to any good. I can't do anything except sit . . . It's
something to think about. Here I am, just nineteen, surrounded by show-
girls, whiskey, and sissies, and nobody watching me. All this temptation and
me trying to train to be a boxer . . . But it takes a mind to do right. It's like I
told myself when I was little. I said, 'Cassius, you going to win the Olympics
some day, and then you're going to buy yourself a Cadillac, and then you're

going to be the world champ.' Now I got the gold medal, and I got the car. I'd be plain silly to give in to temptation now when I'm just about to reach out and get that world title."

Before his next fight, with an overweight Argentinian boxer named Alex Miteff, Clay not only guaranteed a win but also predicted the round in which the bout would end. "Miteff must fall in six," he said. In the opening rounds, Clay clobbered Miteff's head. Miteff hammered Clay's body. By the fourth round, Miteff's face was puffed like a dinner roll, but Clay was losing speed as Miteff's body blows wore him down. Clay quit bouncing. He set his feet and put more weight behind his punches. In the fifth, he threw machine-gun-fast combinations at Miteff's head, and in the sixth one of those combinations — a light left jab and a whopping, compact right — sent the big Argentine tumbling to the mat. Miteff got up, but he was too wobbly to continue.

It was, without a doubt, the best performance of Clay's professional career — so good, in fact, that Dundee told him after the fight he could beat anybody if he continued fighting so well.

Most fighters at this point in their careers began to understand the near impossibility of their mission. They lived in poverty, fighting every three or four weeks for purses so small they could barely pay rent on their gym lockers, struggling to get enough food to replace the thousands of calories they were burning every day in training, knowing each time they stepped in the ring that a single injury or a single defeat might end their careers and send them back to the assembly line or truck-driving jobs they had been sacrificing time, money, and brain cells in order to escape. But Clay was the Golden Boy. He was a boxer on a salary, something almost unheard of in the sport, which meant he had no financial worries. If his special treatment wasn't enough to make him feel superior, his success in the ring surely did. He predicted a seventh-round knockout of Willie Besmanoff, and when the German appeared ready to fall in the fifth, Clay backed off, circled, and tossed jabs through the sixth, then made good on his prediction, finishing off his opponent in the next round. Once again, reporters griped. It was bad etiquette — and dangerous — to coast for a round so that a prediction might be fulfilled, they said. Once again, Clay didn't care what his critics thought. He liked his new gimmick, liked the extra attention that came with his increasingly bold behavior, and he was convinced that publicity would help him get a quicker shot at the championship.

"I'm tired of being fed on set-ups," he said. "I can't get a title shot by knocking out a bunch of has-beens or novices."

Clay surely knew there was one big difference between his act and Gorgeous George's: Clay was black, which meant that every time he bragged and acted up, he was playing the part of the sassy Negro and risking a backlash from white writers and fans.

Clay was a young man in a hurry. But was he trying to make a larger point? Was he subversively and subtly making the kind of argument that Elijah Muhammad might — that a black man was better off going his own way than attempting to play by the white man's rules?

He never said.

9

"Twentieth-Century Exuberance"

One December afternoon in 1961, Cassius Clay went roller-skating with friends at the Broadway Roller Rink, a blacks-only establishment on Broadway and Ninth Street in Louisville. Despite his growing fame, he was still a few weeks shy of his twentieth birthday, still a playful kid, and he still enjoyed the company of old friends from the West End and Central High.

When he left the rink at about 6 p.m., it was already dark. Streetlights guided men and women on their way home from work. Across the street from the roller rink, Clay spotted a crowd on the sidewalk and decided to check it out, hoping to find "a pretty girl to say something to," as he recalled years later in a letter. By the time he got across the street, Clay recognized what was happening. The crowd was listening to a black man in a dark suit preaching on the wisdom of the Honorable Elijah Muhammad, leader of the Nation of Islam.

"My brother," the man in the suit said, turning to Clay, "do you want to buy a *Muhammad Speaks* newspaper, so that you can read about your own kind, read the real truth of your history, your true religion, your true name before you were given the White Man's name in slavery?"

Clay knew about the Nation of Islam. He could recite lyrics from Minister Louis X's song, "The White Man's Heaven Is the Black Man's Hell," and he had heard a similar street-corner speech in Harlem before his trip to Rome. But the newspaper was probably new to him; this was only the second issue of *Muhammad Speaks*. Clay accepted a copy, and the man in the dark suit invited him to attend a meeting at eight o'clock that evening at 27th and Chestnut Streets.

"OK, I'll be there," Clay said.

He took the newspaper and walked away, with no intention of attending the meeting. Later, though, as he thumbed the pages of *Muhammad Speaks,* a cartoon at the top of page thirty-two caught his eye. About ten years later, he described the impact of that cartoon in a handwritten letter. The letter, which survives only in fragment, is revealing for its earnestness and naiveté. Rather than exploring some of the deeper reasons the Nation of Islam appealed to him, Clay explained step by step how Elijah Muhammad's message began to take hold of him. With unsteady spelling, capitalization, and punctuation, he wrote,

> The Cartoon was about the first slaves that arrived in america, and the Cartone was showing how Black Slaves were slipping off of the Plantaintion to pray in the arabic Language facing East, and the White slave Master would Run up Behind the slave with a wip and hit the poor little [slave] on the Back with the Wip and say What are you doing praying in the Languid, you know what I told you to speak to, and the slave said yes sir yes sir Master, I will pray to Jesus, sir Jesus, and I liked that cartoon, it did something to me.

He was on the brink of independence, moving beyond Louisville and beyond his parents, and he was exploring what else the world had to offer. Clay had encountered the Nation of Islam at least three times by 1961, which offered a solid indication about the speed with which Elijah Muhammad's message was spreading across America. If you were a black man in an American prison, or in a major American city, the Nation of Islam was becoming all but unavoidable. With the advent of the newspaper, Elijah Muhammad was building a broader and more mainstream audience, as well as a new source of income.

Despite his earlier exposure, nothing had yet moved Clay to consider joining the Nation of Islam. Boxing, not race or religion, was foremost on his mind. Cash Clay had hired a black lawyer to review his son's first professional contract, and the elder Clay had also pushed his son to choose a black trainer in Fred Stoner. But those choices proved inconsequential. Cassius Clay the boxer had been interested in the shortest path to fame and glory, not in philosophical or political gestures, which is why he trusted his career to the all-white Louisville Sponsoring Group and why he chose a white man for a trainer. In his dozens of interviews with reporters in 1960 and 1961, Clay never discussed or expressed solidarity with the Freedom Riders who were touring the South by bus and facing arrest and violent attack as they tested a recent Supreme Court ruling that had desegregated interstate transport. Neither did he voice support for students engaged in sit-ins at lunch counters or for Rev. Martin Luther King Jr., who was assaulted by rock-throwing crowds of white men when he spoke at a church in Montgomery, Alabama. If Clay knew about these events, he either didn't consider them important or didn't know what to say about them. But as he found himself exposed repeatedly to the Nation of Islam, Elijah Muhammad's message began to shape his view of what it meant to be a black man in America in 1961. As Rudy Clay put it, "It gave him confidence in being black."

The front page of the issue of *Muhammad Speaks* that Clay held in his hand that December day included an article written by Elijah Muhammad, whose byline identified him as "MESSENGER OF ALLAH." The article began, "My followers and I are being accused of being un-American. We actually do not know what is American and what is un-American, as the United States of America has not instructed us as to what constitutes an American or an un-American." Muhammad's column referred to a subcommittee report from the California State Senate that labeled "Negro Muslims" unpatriotic and accused the Nation of Islam of using its schools to teach racial hatred. "This is untrue," Muhammad wrote, "for we only teach them who YOU really are. They can hate or love you, it is up to them." He went on to write that white people were clearly using their schools to instruct white children in the hatred of black people, and that white people were "the number one murderers of Negroes."

Many of the articles in the second edition of *Muhammad Speaks* reinforced the central philosophy of the Nation of Islam: a "war of Armageddon" was approaching. Allah had permitted America and other Christian nations to enslave Africans — "chewing on men's bones for three hundred years," as Elijah Muhammad put it. The suffering had been a test, Muhammad said, and those black men and women who were ready to take responsibility and embrace Islam would be rewarded when the white man was vanquished and the black man ruled the earth. Muhammad scolded his black followers: "You are the man that is asleep," he wrote in another issue of the newspaper. "The white man is wide awake. He is not a dummy by any means. He has built a world. His knowledge and wisdom is now reaching out through space."

Clay was not a pensive person. He had not led a life of poverty and suffering. Nor had he been exposed through books or teachers to the world of ideas. But Elijah Muhammad's call for discipline and self-improvement struck a chord for a young man who drank garlic water, ran alongside buses to school, and avoided alcohol-fueled late nights with friends. And Muhammad's proclamation that the so-called Negroes were God's chosen people surely resonated with someone who already called himself "The Greatest." The cartoon resonated, too; it was easy to understand why Africans forcibly transported across the ocean might be suspicious of the religion thrust upon them by the men who had enslaved them and labeled them subhuman. Finally, though he had not been the victim of any violent racial attacks, Clay understood that the white man had the authority to inflict all manner of suffering on him. He'd heard his father say it countless times. The white man had the power, and as long as that remained the case, every black person would live in fear. Survival was the black man's goal — not enlightenment, not enrichment. Survival was the best he could hope for, because around every corner and in every contact with white society, the black man faced the possibility of financial ruin, imprisonment, and death.

That vulnerability strengthened some black men and women; it reminded them they were engaged in an eternal struggle. Now, as he grew more comfortable and confident in his role as a public figure, Clay may have been trying to take a stand in solidarity with suffering black Americans, taking on the burden of his father. If power is the currency of human existence, Cassius Clay was flexing his muscles in the broadest possible sense, exploring his capacity to influence others and shape the world around him.

Elijah Muhammad's philosophy offered a black man the possibility of dignity and power. It offered him a sense of self. And the white man's approval was not required. "The mind is its own place," says Lucifer in Milton's *Paradise Lost*, "and in itself can make a Heav'n of Hell, a Hell of Heav'n." The black man didn't have to remain in hell just because the white man relegated him to it, Muhammad said. He had the power to forge his own identity, to transform the conditions imposed upon him, and he needed no one's permission, no Supreme Court order. He could do it through the power of his own thoughts, through his own might, his own actions. Cassius Clay wasn't terribly interested in religion, but Elijah Muhammad's message was not strictly religious. Islam was a "facade," said Bennett Johnson, who worked for the Nation of Islam and met Clay in the early 1960s, "a structure." It was a story that gave Elijah Muhammad a way to teach black Americans how they might liberate themselves.

It resonated with Clay, Johnson said, because Clay was a fighter above all else.

Clay was splitting his time between Louisville and Miami as 1961 turned to 1962. In Miami one day, at the corner of Second Avenue and Sixth Street, he saw a black man in a seersucker suit selling copies of *Muhammad Speaks*. This time, before the newspaper salesman could make his pitch, Clay shouted across the street: "Why are we called Negroes? Why are we deaf, dumb, and blind?" Clay was quoting the lyrics from the Louis X song, "The White Man's Heaven Is the Black Man's Hell."

The newspaper salesman was a boxing fan and recognized Clay. He introduced himself as Captain Sam, though his real name was Sam Saxon and he would later change it to Abdul Rahman. Saxon was a high-school dropout, drug user, and everyday gambler — "the third best pool shooter in Atlanta," he said — before the Nation of Islam straightened him out. When he wasn't peddling copies of *Muhammad Speaks*, Saxon worked at Miami's racetracks — Hialeah, Gulfstream, and Tropical Park — where he spent his shifts in the men's rooms, handing out towels, shining shoes, and hoping for tips from the white clientele.

Clay was eager to show Saxon his scrapbook, so the men got into Captain Sam's old Ford and drove to the fighter's hotel. Along the way, Clay went into his usual routine, describing how he intended to fight Ingemar Johansson first and then Floyd Patterson to become the youngest heavyweight champion in the history of boxing. Saxon loved the young man's energy and confidence: "I thought, 'Yeah, that man *is* gonna be champ. He believe!'"

A friendship sprung quickly, and Saxon decided that he would bring Clay into the Nation of Islam. "He knew about it, but he wasn't in yet," Saxon said. They talked about Elijah Muhammad's message, about slave names, and about the meaning of the word *Negro,* which had been the term many black men and women had preferred through most of the twentieth century, a term used with pride to refer to men who had flown fighter planes in World War II, started businesses, integrated baseball leagues, and founded universities, but also a term that seemed to be losing its power in the early part of the 1960, running its course, a word that felt inadequate to men like Captain Sam who were striving to define themselves on their own conditions.

"I pulled him in to what we call a registered Muslim," Saxon said, recalling that the conversion involved no twisting of arms or subtle psychological ploys. "It ain't hard for a black man to come out of the Christian religion when there's nothing there for black folks. The white Christian people had enslaved us and given us their names and he saw all that. It ain't hard for any black man to be convinced. Most people who don't come over have fear in their hearts. He was fearless. I was fearless . . . Wasn't nothing slow about him believing. He started coming to the meetings and participating like everybody else, thinking the right way, eating the right way."

In Louisville, Clay hadn't been ready to attend a Nation of Islam meeting, but now, perhaps because of the independence offered with a little distance from his hometown and his parents, he visited Temple No. 29, a vacant storefront converted into a mosque—and he was hooked by what he heard.

"This minister started teaching, and the things he said really shook me up," he told the writer Alex Haley years later. "Things like that we twenty million black people in America didn't know our true identities, or even our true family names. And we were the direct descendants of black men and women stolen from a rich black continent and brought here and stripped of all knowledge of themselves and taught to hate themselves and their kind. And that's how us so-called 'Negroes' had come to be the only race among mankind that loved its enemies. Now, I'm the kind that catches on quick. I said to myself, listen here, this man's *saying* something!"

As his twentieth birthday approached, Clay was preparing for his first pro fight in Madison Square Garden, the nation's high temple of boxing. His opponent, Sonny Banks, wasn't much of a fighter, owner of a record of ten wins and two losses against a string of mediocre opponents. But Clay nonetheless saw this as a big moment, not only because he would be fighting in the Garden but because he would get the chance to promote himself in New York

City, the nation's media capital. On his first trip to New York since his return from the Olympics, Clay was at his brashest and most ebullient. Reporters ate it up. The journalists didn't know, of course, that there was one thing about which Clay never spoke: his recent immersion into the Nation of Islam.

On February 6, 1962, Clay was the featured speaker at a luncheon for the Metropolitan Boxing Writers' Association. "Boxing is not as colorful as it was in the past," he said. "We need more guys to liven it up and I think I can help." He predicted that he would knock out Sonny Banks in the fourth round.

A cold wind whipped Manhattan on fight night, and many fans decided to stay home to watch on TV. Paying customers at Madison Square Garden booed when Clay was introduced, although these were not the lusty, full-throated, out-for-blood screams that greeted Gorgeous George. Spectators who came to see if Banks would shut Clay's ever-running trap enjoyed a moment of excitement in the first round as Banks sprung from a crouch and hit Clay with a short left hook. Clay fell, landing on his bottom. He practically bounced back up, spending less than a second on the mat. Still, it was the first time he'd been knocked down as a pro. Banks threw more left hooks as the round continued, hoping he'd discovered Clay's weakness, but Clay caught on quickly and resisted. Sam Langford — one of boxing's wise men and mighty punchers — once proffered this advice to fellow fighters: "Whatever the other man want to do, don't let him." Clay punched back and scooted away, and Banks never hurt him again. By the second round, Clay was calmly in control, the moment spent on his backside seemingly forgotten, and by the third he was using Banks as his punching bag. Banks flopped and staggered until the referee stopped the fight in the opening seconds of the fourth round. When it was over, Banks's corner man, Harry Wiley, explained, "Things just went sour gradually all at once."

It was no clash of titans. Clay, after all, was ranked only ninth among heavyweight contenders, and Banks was unranked. But by surviving a knockdown and bouncing back to knock his opponent stupid, Clay had at least earned points with the reporters who considered him "of feeble constitution," as A. J. Liebling put it. A few boxing writers made what might have seemed an obvious observation — that for all the talk of Clay's incredible speed and reflexes, he was, in fact, bigger and stronger than most of his opponents.

Clay kept winning throughout 1962, mostly against solid but unspectacular fighters such as George Logan and Don Warner, men who were in it for the payday, mostly, not to fulfill promises of glory; men who were happy to fight a loudmouth because the loudmouth's growing celebrity meant bigger than usual crowds. The only fighter who gave Clay trouble was a twenty-four-year-old New Yorker named Billy "The Barber" Daniels, who bobbed and jabbed and forced Clay to backpedal. Daniels, who came into the fight with a 16–0 record, landed big, heavy punches. He seemed to be in control until he suffered two cuts to the left eye, prompting the referee to stop the action in the seventh round out of concern for the damaged fighter's health. The referee awarded Clay the technical knockout.

Finally, in July, Clay stepped into the ring against a top-ten fighter, the Argentinian Alejandro Lavorante, who had knocked out Zora Folley a year earlier. In front of twelve thousand fans at the Los Angeles Sports Arena, Clay came out jabbing against his bigger, stronger opponent, and needed only about two minutes to open a cut under Lavorante's left eye. In the second round, Clay threw so many punches Lavorante scarcely had time to hit back. One of Clay's punches — a straight right hand — landed flush on the Argentinian's jaw and wobbled the big man's legs. In the fifth, another right hand flattened the left side of Lavorante's face. Lavorante fell hard. When the wounded boxer staggered to his feet, Clay threw a furious left hook and knocked him back down. Lavorante fell so suddenly his head bounced off the top rope and came to rest on the bottom strand, as if it were his pillow. The referee, concerned for the fallen boxer's condition, didn't even count Lavorante out. He waved his hands in the air, declaring the match over and signaling for a trainer or doctor to tend to the injured man at once. (Two months later, Lavorante fought again, got knocked out again, and slipped into a coma from which he never woke.)

Four months after beating Lavorante, on November 15, 1962, Clay faced Archie Moore, the man who had briefly served as his trainer. Moore was a month shy of his forty-sixth birthday (or his forty-ninth, by some accounts), a boxing ancient, with a mind-boggling professional record of 185 wins, 22 losses, and 10 draws, a record running all the way back to 1935, when Babe Ruth played baseball and Franklin Delano Roosevelt pitched his Social Security Act. Moore also owned the all-time record for wins by knockout with 132.

"I view this man with mixed emotions," Moore said of Clay. "He's like a man that can write beautifully but doesn't know how to punctuate. He has this twentieth century exuberance, but there's a bitterness in him some-where . . . He is certainly coming along at a time when a new face is needed on the boxing scene, on the fistic horizon. But in his anxiousness to be this person, he may be over-playing his hand by belittling people. He wants to show off regardless of whose feet he's stepping on."

Moore said he would hit Clay with a new punch called "the lip-buttoner," a reference to the nickname recently bestowed on Clay by the press: "The Louisville Lip."

Clay answered with the easy rhyme: "Moore must fall in four."

Clay enjoyed himself as he looked forward to the biggest payday and the biggest audience of his career. Hardly an interview went by in which he failed to describe the luxurious manner in which he would soon be living — dressed in $55 alligator shoes, with $500 cash in his pocket, a "fox" on each arm, driving a brand-new red Fleetwood Cadillac with a built-in telephone, and living in a $175,000 house. Clay spoke of these things romantically, the way a painter talks of capturing the perfect light at sunset. Asked once if he fought for money or glory, he replied without hesitation: "The money comes with the glory." The more audaciously he spoke, the more unpopular he grew. One day, while training at the Main Street Gym in Los Angeles, Clay was booed so lustily that police were summoned to prevent a riot. Jim Murray, the *Los Angeles Times* columnist, complained that "Cassius' love affair with himself is so classic in proportion if Shakespeare were alive he would write a play about it. It is one of history's great passions and the love of Cassius for Clay is so rapturous no girl could come between them. Marriage would almost be bigamy."

Before the fight, Angelo Dundee told reporters that Moore was too old to backpedal, that he would only move forward. Clay's jabs would stop Moore from getting in close, the trainer predicted, and then Moore would be help-less, all but immobilized. Dundee had it right. Moore crouched. Clay circled and jabbed. Moore resembled a turtle, ducking for cover, looking around for his attacker before ducking again. Within minutes, the older fighter's face was swollen. By the middle of the third round, Moore looked like a man desper-ate to be somewhere, anywhere else, at one point cringing in anticipation of a blow. Finally, in the fourth round, Clay knocked him down. Moore got up, then fell again, then got up one more time and fell for the last time.

"I'll take Sonny Liston right now," Clay said after the fight, "and I'll finish him in eight rounds."

This was the same Sonny Liston who had just humiliated the heavyweight champion, Floyd Patterson, knocking him out in only 126 seconds; the same Sonny Liston who had beaten Wayne Bethea so badly that after the fight his corner men had removed seven teeth from the losing fighter's mouthpiece and spotted blood dripping from his ear.

That night, as it happened, Clay ran into Liston in a downtown Los Angeles ballroom.

"You're next!" Clay said.

The champion did not appear concerned.

10

"It's Show Business"

Cassius Clay was a contender now, ranked fourth in the world among heavyweights, his fame spreading fast, his path to the championship clear. All he had to do was keep talking and keep winning.

He celebrated his twenty-first birthday with a luncheon at the Sherwyn Hotel in Pittsburgh, along with his mother, father, brother, and dozens of local news reporters from print, radio, and television. He was in Pittsburgh to prepare for his next bout, against Charlie Powell, a giant of a man who not only boxed but had also played defensive end for the Oakland Raiders and San Francisco Forty-Niners of the National Football League. Powell was bigger and more experienced than Clay, but Clay, of course, expressed his usual outsized confidence to the lunch crowd. After his defeat of Archie Moore, Clay had initially said he would not fight again until either Floyd Patterson or Sonny Liston agreed to face him. What would he prove by "knocking out some bums," he had asked. But he had changed his mind and agreed to fight Powell, he said, because it sounded like easy money, and he wanted to keep sharp while waiting for his shot at the championship. He prophesied an early knockout.

Clay said he was worried about the weather keeping fans away, and he was aware that some of the proceeds for the fight were going to help the families of thirty-seven miners who had died the month prior in a disaster in Greene County. "I heard all about that mine explosion," he said. "I'd like to draw a big crowd for that reason. And that's another reason that I'll let it go five. I don't want anyone to miss the fight, so it will not be an early knockout."

A cake and ice cream were presented. Clay blew out the candles.

"They come to see Cassius fall," he continued, referring to himself now in the third person, perhaps a sign of narcissism or merely a suggestion that Clay thought of himself as a product to be shilled. "But Cassius won't fall 'cause boxing needs him." He was right. Or at least the members of the press corps had reason to hope he was right. The boxing game had grown dull since the retirement of Rocky Marciano, the hairy-chested, hard-punching all-American. Mobsters ran the sport, and too many fighters seemed like hoods, not heroes. Liston had the great misfortune of being both a hood and a black man, which made him the most unpopular heavyweight champion since Jack Johnson. His biography, published in 1963, had the title *The Champ Nobody Wanted.*

Clay had youth, personality, and a million-dollar smile on his side. He was a gust of fresh air in a dank, sweaty room. His success had raised an already impressive high spirit. With any high spirit, there is always a danger of inconsistency. But there were not obvious contradictions in Clay. He was what he appeared — fresh and natural, always eager for more, more of everything. The boxing writers would have liked him better if he had been white, of course, but he was still far and away the most interesting and entertaining figure to grace the sport in years. Some reporters started calling him "Cassius the Gaseous," and some considered him lacking in grace, but almost everyone who covered the sport admitted that he was making boxing more interesting. As the former champ Jack Dempsey put it: "I don't care if this kid can fight a lick. I'm for him. Things are live again."

Among the celebrities taking in Clay's Pittsburgh performance were Len Dawson, quarterback of the Dallas Texans; Pie Traynor, the retired baseball player; and TV actor Sebastian Cabot. Clay doodled and jotted notes on napkins and handed them to anyone who wanted one.

A week later, on the morning of the fight, Clay revised his prediction, saying he was sorry but he really didn't think he could let Charlie Powell last five rounds. He would end it in three, he said. "I got a headline for you," he said. "'Beauty Beats Beast.'"

Powell was a grown man, age thirty, and he'd spent most of his adult life among professional athletes, where younger men usually showed respect for their elders, and where smaller men, if they were smart, didn't start trouble. At the weigh-in, Powell, not clowning, clenched a fist and shoved it under

Clay's nose. Then Powell's brother, Art, also a pro football player, taunted Clay: "Fight me, boy! Fight me and I'll kill you!"

Clay stormed out of the room.

The fight set a Pittsburgh record, with revenue of about $56,000 on 11,000 tickets sold. The crowd pulled for Powell, roaring wildly in the second round when he sunk a gloved fist deep into Clay's ribs. Powell followed the body blow by pushing Clay to the ropes and rocking him with a right to the chin. Clay, hurt, had to grab Powell to get his bearings, but he quickly straightened up and launched a counterattack that "had Charlie's head bouncing to and fro like a punchball," as one writer put it.

The bell rang and Powell glared at Clay: "C'mon sissy, pretty boy. Is that as hard as you can hit?"

To open the third round, Clay didn't necessarily hit harder, but he hit more often, bashing Powell's head with forty unanswered punches. Powell looked like a man caught in a nightmare that had him spinning and opening his mouth to scream. Blood gushed from his left eye and drained into his mouth. Finally, from the cumulative effect more than from any one punch, Powell slid slowly to the canvas, eyes closed, crawling on all fours, as the referee counted ten.

Later, Powell would offer this assessment: "When he first hit me, I thought to myself, I can take two of those to get in one of my own. But in a little while I was getting dizzier and dizzier every time he hit me, and he hurt. Clay throws punches so easily you don't realize how much they shock you until it's too late."

In the dressing room after the fight, Clay, surrounded by reporters, slid out of warrior mode and back to entertainer.

"I'm so pretty," he said. "Let me get dressed. I have so many pretty girls waiting for me outside."

Had he been an ordinary fighter with a record of seventeen wins and no losses against less than top competition, Clay would not have been in contention for a shot at the title. His lip helped, as did his accurate predictions and good looks. He evoked a sense of merriment and mystery, an irresistible combination for the media. He figured it out by himself, it seems, and he became a sophisticated pitchman during a new age in marketing, when advertising agencies on Madison Avenue found stylish new ways to build brands, boost celebrities, and generate wealth. The sales pitch was no longer just a means to an end — it was a work of art, a product of its own, and a reflection of the nation's consumer-oriented society. No athlete in American history had ever been so conscious of the power of brand building as this young boxer, and Clay was doing it without the help of one of those Madison Avenue agencies or even a promoter or full-time business manager. The image he fashioned was both romantic and thrilling: a young man who believed that if he worked hard enough he could become the world's heavyweight champ, that he could have it all, the wealth, the fame, the women, the cars — all without compromise, without getting bloodied, without getting hurt.

While lying in bed one day, Clay explained his media strategy to a reporter from the *Miami News*. "Now take those Associated Press reporters," he said. "I always talk to them. I don't let them get away. Some of them send to thirty-eight papers. *Ebony* and *Jet* come around; I see them. Negroes want to know about me . . . Now take *Time* . . . that magazine goes to intelligent people. People who don't go to fights much. They read about me and want to go to fights. They talk about me. And your paper. Cover all of Miami and Florida. Lots of people down there . . . Networks come around, I'm glad to see them. Millions of people watching. Only ones I had to send away is those little radio stations that put you on at 4:30 in the afternoon and nobody's listening." He even began the process of building his own mythology: "I was marked," he told one reporter. "I had a big head and I looked like Joe Louis in the cradle. People said so. One day I threw my first punch and hit my mother right in the teeth and knocked one out."

In another interview, a reporter asked just how much of his bragging was genuine and how much was hype? How much of his "I-am-the-greatest-and-gee-ain't-I-pretty" routine did he believe?

He answered precisely and without hesitation: "Seventy-five percent."

It must have been refreshing for the public to know that there were limits to his self-love. Was it possible he possessed a trace of humility?

Before going out to greet the pretty girls in Pittsburgh, Clay sat in his dressing room with William Faversham, the leader of the Louisville Sponsoring Group. Faversham told Clay his next fight might be against Doug Jones — ranked third among heavyweight contenders — at Madison Square Garden in March.

"What are we gonna get?" Clay asked.

Faversham said they'd probably get $35,000 guaranteed, or 25 percent of the gross from ticket sales, whichever was the larger amount.

When Clay asked how much of the $35,000 would be his, Faversham was surprised. Clay knew that his contract called for him to receive 50 percent. Then it hit him: "He couldn't divide 35,000 by two," Faversham said in an interview several years later. "This went on all the time," he continued. "What month is this? How many months away is February? And you take a column in a newspaper, like Red Smith's. You and I can read it in four, five minutes. He'll take twenty minutes, half an hour. In my opinion he has no formal education regardless of what the Louisville school system says."

Clay also had a strange relationship with money. He would stop at a gas station and put fifty cents' worth of gas in the tank, apparently convinced he was saving money, and untroubled an hour or two later when the needle on his gas gauge touched E again and he had to buy fifty cents more.

Fortunately, the members of Louisville Sponsoring Group weren't counting on Clay for spelling bees or math tests. They invested in a boxer, and so far they had reason to be pleased.

At the end of 1962, the financial ledger for the group looked like this:

Gross revenues: $88,855.76.
Clay compensation: $44,933.
Business expenses: $2,287.14
Legal expenses: $1,867.16
Manager's compensation: $950.00
Transportation: $970.60
Telephone: $1,319.83
Training: $17,989.76
Bad debt expenses: $250.00

That left a net profit of $18,287.77, or 20.7 percent of income, which meant that each member of the Louisville group earned $1,828.78. At that rate, members of the group would probably see their initial investment repaid before the end of 1963, according to an internal memo. In a private meeting, the investors discussed renewing the boxer's contract and purchasing insurance in case Clay was injured or killed. Everyone in the group agreed that their investment had been a wise one, and no one had anything unkind to say about Clay. He'd piled up a few speeding tickets and lost his driver's license, and he'd occasionally asked for cash advances on his salary, but such behavior was to be expected of a twenty-one-year-old, the men agreed.

Members of the Louisville Sponsoring Group had modest expectations when they initially backed Clay, but now they recognized that if he beat Jones, he might start earning significant sums of money. They were already discussing the possibility that they could supplement Clay's fight income by arranging for TV and movie appearances. Clay was less than three years out of high school and still hadn't fought for a championship, but he was easily the most exciting young boxer in the country, and if there was any doubt about his growing celebrity, it was erased on March 22, 1963, when *Time* magazine, circulation 10 million, put the young fighter on its cover. Boris Chaliapin painted Clay's portrait for the magazine and showed him with his head cocked and mouth open; over Clay's head, a pair of boxing gloves clutched a book of poetry. The article inside, written by Nick Thimmesch, declared, "Cassius Clay is Hercules, struggling through the twelve labors. He is Jason chasing the Golden Fleece. He is Galahad, Cyrano, D'Artagnan. When he scowls, strong men shudder, and when he smiles, women swoon. The mysteries of the universe are his Tinker Toys. He rattles the thunder and looses the lightning."

In the early 1960s, magazine journalism was soaring to new heights of creativity. Feature writers borrowed from the novelist's toolbox, immersing themselves in their subjects, using dramatic dialogue and elaborate descriptions to bring their characters and stories to life. But this wasn't one of those stories. Either Thimmesch failed to get beneath the surface of Clay's personality or else got there and found it dull stuff. In this profile, which stretched for four densely packed pages of type, Clay had nothing to say about race, almost nothing to say about women, and little to say about what motivated him beyond the obvious quest for fame and fortune. Clay recited his usual clunky poems, boasted of his intention to buy a "tomato-red Cadillac" with white leather upholstery after his fight with Jones, and offered the usual mockery of his opponents' looks. Of Sonny Liston, he said, "That big, ugly bear. I hate him because he's so ugly." Of Jones: "That ugly little man! I'll annihilate him!"

In *Esquire* soon after, Tom Wolfe fared better, but only because Wolfe seemed to conclude that Clay's superficiality *was* the story, that outside the ring this boxer was nothing but an actor putting on a performance. Clay told him as much. "I don't feel like I'm in boxing anymore," he said. "It's show business." With that in mind, Wolfe produced an artful series of vignettes that showed the young celebrity in action: Clay dazzled by the view out the window of his room on the forty-second floor of the Americana Hotel in New York; Clay rehearsing new poems for a session at Columbia Records studio; Clay leading a parade of foxes to the Metropole Café; Clay taunting a man in the nightclub who asked for an autograph but failed to produce a pen; Clay predicting an eight-round victory over Sonny Liston but adding, "If he gives me any jive, he goes in five"; Clay mimicking white southern accents; Clay growing jealous upon spotting a trio of street musicians attracting attention that should have been his; and Clay finally stealing the spotlight from the trio by going into another one of his routines about the big, ugly bear.

Years later, Wolfe said he felt like he "never got through" to Clay. But that was likely because Clay wasn't letting him. At the Metropole, when a white man with a southern accent asked for an autograph and referred to Clay as "boy" ("Here you are, boy, put your name right there"), Clay let it go. He certainly wasn't behaving like a man already fallen under the spell of Elijah Muhammad.

There were many subjects Clay could have discussed, had he been interested, or had journalists asked him. In April 1962, a police officer in Los Angeles had shot and killed an unarmed member of the Nation of Islam even as the man raised his hands in compliance with the officer's direction. The shooting set off huge waves of protests and earned nationwide headlines for the Nation of Islam, whose leaders raised angry voices in rallying the city's black population. Nation of Islam officials called Martin Luther King Jr. a "traitor to the Negro people" for insisting on a nonviolent approach to the fight for equality, saying a movement based on sit-ins and Freedom Rides would never suffice. Real action was required — perhaps even violent action, they insisted.

The writer James Baldwin made no threats, but he too warned that black men and women would have to fight for justice. "The Negroes of this country may never be able to rise to power," Baldwin wrote in *The New Yorker,* "but they are very well placed indeed to precipitate chaos and ring down the curtain on the American dream."

Clay, publicly, offered no comment on any of it. And the writers spending time with him, almost all of them white, seldom pressed. To those reporters, Clay seemed to be following in the footsteps of Sugar Ray Robinson. The young boxer loved his fine cars and fine clothes and spoke of a future filled with even finer cars and clothes. His biggest gripe with the American system of government seemed to be with the Louisville Department of Safety for taking away his driver's license. He made a rare statement on race when a photographer tried to take his picture with a young white woman. Clay objected, reminding the photographer of the trouble that befell Jack Johnson for cavorting with white women.

In the buildup to the Jones fight at Madison Square Garden, Clay had to work overtime to generate publicity. Printers had gone on strike, shutting down seven New York newspapers (and eventually helping to kill four of them). Boxing, with no fixed schedules, relied more than most sports on newspaper coverage. But Clay didn't mind. Driving through Manhattan, he would stop his car at random and get out and talk to his fans. He joshed and joked with Johnny Carson on NBC's *Tonight Show,* no doubt shocking television viewers who expected boxers to be big, grunting, crooked-nosed thugs, not slick and Hollywood-handsome like Clay. He wandered down to Greenwich Village and recited poetry — an ode to himself, of course — at the Bitter End, a beatnik coffeehouse where folk singers such as Bob Dylan and Joan Baez usually commanded the stage.

"How tall are you?" he asked Jones one day as they came together to promote their bout.

"Why do you ask that?" said Jones.

"So's I can know in advance how far to step back when you fall in four," Clay said.

His material was improving, thanks to steady practice, and he was growing more confident in his give-and-take with interviewers.

"The Garden is too small for me," he complained. "Where are the big places? That's what I need. Maybe the Los Angeles Coliseum . . . You know what this fight means to me? A tomato-red Cadillac Eldorado convertible with white leather upholstery, air-conditioning and hi-fi. That's what the [Louisville Sponsoring Group] is giving me for a victory present. Can you picture me losing to this ugly bum Jones with that kind of swinging car waiting for me?"

This was his finest performance in salesmanship to date. In thirty-eight years of boxing at Madison Square Garden, there had never been a sellout in advance of a fight, and there had been no sellouts of any kind for six years . . . until Clay v. Jones, March 13, 1963. The top ticket price for the event was twelve dollars, but scalpers outside the Garden were getting one hundred dollars and more. Almost 19,000 fans crowded the arena, thousands more were turned away, and 150,000 watched on TV in thirty-three cities.

"I can't believe it," said Harry Markson, the Garden's boxing director. Given the newspaper strike, given that the fight was not for the championship, and given that Jones, with a record of 21–3–1, was hardly Joe Louis, there was only one explanation for this kind of demand; Clay offered it in verse:

> *People come to see me from all around*
> *To see Cassius hit the ground.*
> *Some get mad, some lose their money,*
> *But Cassius is still as sweet as honey.*

A big part of boxing's attraction had always been primal. In this case, there was no question which boxer the crowd wanted to see suffer. They were coming to see Cassius Clay, a cocky young black man, get his mouth shut and pretty face disfigured.

On the morning of the fight, Clay couldn't sleep. At 6:30 a.m., he slipped out of his hotel to gape at his name on the billboards outside Madison Square Garden, then went back to his room and slept until 10. He showed up for the weigh-in with masking tape covering his mouth, a gag that made even Jones smile.

When it was 9:47 p.m., time to fight, Clay climbed into the ring and whirled his arms like windmills. The crowd booed loudly. Jones, a Harlem native, entered to cheers. In attendance were former boxing champs Gene Tunney, Jack Dempsey, Sugar Ray Robinson, Rocky Graziano, Barney Ross, and Dick Tiger. Also on hand were Jackie Robinson, Althea Gibson, Ralph Bunche, Malcolm X, Toots Shor, and Lauren Bacall.

The bell rang, the men measured each other and jabbed lightly for a minute or so, and then Jones bashed Clay's head with a right hook that sent Cassius toppling into the ropes. The crowd screamed in chorus, eager to see if he would fall. But, somehow, Clay bounced off the ropes, regained his balance, and continued fighting. He jabbed to keep the smaller, lighter man away.

By the second round, Clay was Clay again, seemingly undamaged, mixing jabs and hooks, inflicting more damage than he received. Clay's body language was by now familiar to boxing fans. He stayed on the balls of his feet, bouncing like a big ball, bouncing, bouncing, shifting side to side, moving his wide, chiseled shoulders left and right, always moving, making it all but impossible to predict when he would pop a quick jab. His eyes went wide as he moved away from an opponent's punch and his cheeks puffed and blew air when he launched one of his own. In the fourth, the round in which Clay had promised to end the fight, Jones had other ideas, letting loose big left hooks that spun Clay around. From ringside Clay heard jeering: "Get that loudmouth!"

It looked as if Jones had a chance. For the first time, Clay's bad boxing habits made him vulnerable. With his hands down by his sides, Clay couldn't stop Jones from throwing hooks to the head. And Clay's attempts to lean away from punches rather than ducking left him off balance and vulnerable to Jones's surging body blows. Still, Jones couldn't finish the job. Every time he was struck, Clay hit back, sometimes two punches for one, and by the sixth round both men looked ragged.

By the end of the seventh, Angelo Dundee was convinced that his fighter was behind on points, although the trainer may have been influenced by the crowd, which screamed more lustily for Jones's punches than for Clay's.

"You can kiss that tomato-red Cadillac goodbye!" Dundee yelled at Clay.

Maybe that's what did it. In the eighth round, Clay kept his hands high and attacked, landing 21 punches, which was more than he'd landed in any other round. In the ninth round, he did even better, landing 22 punches, and in the final round he exploded, throwing an overwhelming 101 punches and landing 42 of them. Jones threw only 51 punches and landed 19 in the same round. Once threatened, Clay had committed to full-scale war, using his size, strength, and speed in an onslaught that should have left the crowd in awe. But it didn't.

When the final bell rang, the audience exploded with approval, happy to have seen such intense combat and convinced that their man Jones had won. TV announcers said they thought the fight might have been a draw.

Clay went to his corner, ignoring Jones, and awaited the judges' decision.

But to the judges and referees, the fight wasn't close. They awarded Clay the victory in a unanimous decision.

"Fix!" the crowd chanted "Fix! Fix! Fix!"

The crowd's passion, however, had clouded its judgment. Clay threw more punches than Jones, landed more punches than Jones, and landed more power punches than Jones. He also dominated the last two rounds. It was a tough fight, a good fight, and Clay had won it impressively in spite of the audience's hostility.

As angry fans hurled beer cups, programs, and peanuts, Clay raised his arms, opened his mouth, and walked to all four sides of the ring, roaring back at the crowd.

Then he picked up a peanut and ate it.

A TV announcer reached Clay, pointed him toward the camera, and asked if he would consider giving Jones a rematch.

Clay said no.

"I am gunning for Sonny Liston. I want that big bear bad."

More than a hundred reporters crowded Clay's dressing room, along with old friends from Louisville, Sugar Ray Robinson, the Olympian Don Bragg, and football star Jim Brown. The skin under Clay's left eye was swollen, and he was uncharacteristically surly. "I ain't Superman," he said. "If the fans think I can do everything I say I can do, then they're crazier than I am."

Charles "Sonny" Liston may have been the most unpopular man in all of America. Now, however, as a match between Liston and Clay drew nearer, many sports fans were reconsidering the champion, wondering if maybe they'd been too hard on him, asking themselves if they might be better off with Liston than Clay. Black fans, in particular, seemed wary of Clay, who came across as an oddball and not the kind of proud, strong, black man who would represent them well.

Writing in the *Chicago Defender*, the nation's most influential black newspaper, columnist Al Monroe tried to rally support for Liston, saying that the prejudice of white reporters contributed to the champ's reputation as a menace to society. Monroe offered examples of Liston's sharp wit and intelligent answers to questions. In another column, Monroe wrote that Liston should be credited for improving himself and leaving his criminal past behind.

"What fans want is a champion they can look up to," wrote Monroe. "Will

Cassius Clay prove to be such a man outside the ring?" Clay's taunting of Liston was "most unbecoming of a champion," Monroe continued. "Would Clay hold the title with dignity or would he be merely a king's jester and not a crowned head with the sovereignty that the position calls for?"

The lofty language suggested that the heavyweight title still mattered to Americans. And to black Americans, who saw few of their own in positions of power in 1963, it mattered perhaps more than it did to whites. All over America, black activists were organizing voter-registration drives, marches, and sit-ins to improve living conditions and promote equality. The unemployment rate for black men was double the rate for whites, these activists reminded people. School integration was still being impeded in many southern states. In the fall of 1962, James Meredith needed a force of 320 federal marshals to reach his dormitory as he enrolled as the first black student at the University of Mississippi. President Kennedy called for calm but didn't get much as armed mobs attacked the federal troops in what historian C. Vann Woodward called "an insurrectionary assault on officers and soldiers of the United States government and the most serious challenge to the Union since the Civil War." Riots broke out in Birmingham, Alabama, where police used attack dogs and fire hoses to turn back protesters. Martin Luther King Jr. and his allies made plans for a massive rally in Washington called "The March for Jobs and Freedom." Other black leaders, including ministers within the Nation of Islam, were calling for more than marches. They said white America would never give up power unless black America *made* them do it.

Young activists spoke of Black Pride. It wasn't enough for them to find a place within the confines of white America; they wanted people to take pride in their skin, the darker the better. Cassius Clay disappointed some of these radical young leaders. Liston had been a disappointment too, but civil rights activists hadn't expected much from Liston. Clay, on the other hand, was young, clever, and outspoken. Leaders in the movement would have been thrilled if he had taken a stand, but they were puzzled as to why he seemed uninterested in civil rights, and they were angry at his habit of speaking condescendingly toward other black boxers. In a letter to the *Defender*, Cecil Brathwaite, president of the African Jazz-Art Society in New York, complained that Clay was turning his back on the movement and feeding racial stereotypes by calling Liston a big, ugly bear. Brathwaite addressed Clay with a poem that read, in part:

Sonny Liston is the standard,
And that you should respect,
We are the racial vanguard,
Our image, we shall protect.

Why try to rate his comeliness
Before the whole wide world,
You proclaim him in homeliness
And you "pretty as a girl."

And did you really tell the press,
"Jones is an ugly little man?"
But when he put you to the test,
You turned around and ran.

Jones also bears the standard,
An African for sure.
No one yet, has said the bard,
Is anything but pure.

And of Mother Africa — mine an' yours
Were you in the same old rut?
"I ain't fighting off no alligators
and living in a mud hut!"

Why you would gladly turn your back,
Is to us, a mystery . . .
For a Tomato Red Cadillac,
With its white upholstery?

From now on, think before you speak,
You've got a lot to learn,
'Cause you may never reach your peak,
Then, to whom shall you turn?

• • •

After the Jones fight, Clay attended a victory party in the basement of Small's Paradise, a nightclub in Harlem. The guest of honor was presented with a victory cake dotted in strawberries that sagged in the heat and humidity of the crowded room. Clay sagged too, exhausted from his fight and shortage of sleep. He slumped down at the table and struggled to keep his eyes open.

After a few minutes, he told the party guests he was feeling sick and excused himself.

The next day, he was still dragging. "I got a little headache," he said, as he prepared to leave New York. The knuckles on his right hand were swollen and his ribs were bruised, too. "I'll be glad to get back to Louisville . . . I don't like that big city. Louisville, my home . . . Can relax in Louisville."

Outside the Plymouth Hotel, beautiful young women asked for his autograph. He obliged, and then climbed into a black chauffeured limousine with two members of the Louisville Sponsoring Group, Sol Cutchins, the president of Brown & Williamson tobacco, and attorney Gordon Davidson. A reporter from *Time* magazine joined them. As the limousine went through the Lincoln Tunnel en route to Newark Airport, Davidson showed Clay an inch-thick contract from the William Morris Agency, which wanted to represent Clay as an entertainer, helping him make deals in TV and film.

Clay seemed skeptical. "You mean it's a 50–50 split with us?" he asked.

"No," Davidson said. "It's just ten percent. You pay five, we pay five."

Cutchins piped in: "Cassius, this is a good organization."

Clay was not satisfied with 90 percent, or else he didn't understand. He said his father taught him that promises were worthless — up-front pay was the only kind of pay a man could count on. And then he was back on the subject of Sonny Liston. "I want some money," he said. "We should go for the big money now. We should go for the big one. We don't need that buildup anymore. We're big now. We go for Liston and the money . . . Let's go for the big monkey, that big, ugly Liston."

He paused, as if the conversation about TV and movie appearances had begun to sink in — along with his recollection of the pounding he had taken the night prior — and he began to speak again, softly.

"Maybe if we make enough personal appearances, we don't have to fight so much and get banged around. We should make it while we're hot."

Here was Clay, in the privacy of his own limousine, at the age of twen-ty-one, in the rarest of moments, speaking about the risks of boxing, about the damage his sport did to body and mind, about quitting while he was still healthy enough to enjoy life after boxing. He could sing! He could tell jokes! He could act on TV and in movies! But soon his focus shifted to the more immediate concern of airplane travel, and in particular that afternoon's flight to Louisville.

"When was the last crash?" he asked as they sat in the airport lobby, wait-ing to board. "When was the last crash?" He said it so loudly that one of his traveling companions had to hush him, afraid that he would frighten other passengers and get his whole party barred from the flight.

After an uneventful trip, Clay landed in Louisville, rented a car, and drove to the new house he had recently purchased for his parents, at 7307 Verona Way, about eighteen miles from the family's former home on Grand Ave-nue, in a predominantly black suburban neighborhood known as Montclair Villa. He paid $10,956, agreeing to monthly installments of $93.75. Cash and Odessa Clay were in Florida on vacation, so Rudy and Cassius stayed by themselves in the new house. They hired a cook — paid for by the Louisville Sponsoring Group — to keep them fed until their mother returned.

The next day, his energy and good spirits restored, Clay visited Cutchins at his office to further discuss the William Morris contract. Clay agreed to sign. "With all this here," Clay said, waving around at Cutchins' lavishly decorated office, "you can't be a crook. I know you fair with me."

Then Cutchins said he had a surprise for Clay: the tomato-red Cadillac would be a gift to the boxer from members of the Sponsoring Group (or from Cutchins personally, if the group didn't approve the expense), and Clay would only have to pay the sales tax on the purchase. Cutchins asked Clay if he wanted his name inscribed on the side of the car in gold lettering. Clay said no, expressing concern that one of his enemies or jealous rivals might see his name and scratch up the car. Clay's driver's license was suspended, but such small details were no bother. Soon, he was on his way to the Cadillac dealership in downtown Louisville.

"Tomato-red Cadillac convertible, I am here!" he shouted, throwing his arms in the air as he pushed open the glass door.

But when he saw the car Cutchins had ordered, Clay was crestfallen.

"It ain't no Eldorado," he said. "It ain't no Eldorado at all. I don't want it. I was supposed to get Eldorado. Call up Cutchins and tell him I don't want it."

This Cadillac was one notch below an Eldorado, with a bit less chrome and absent some of the Eldorado's trim. The manager of the showroom said he could get the Eldorado, but it would take a month. Clay, cooling off, said he would wait.

In his rented Chevy, driven by Nick Thimmesch, the reporter from *Time*, Clay spent the rest of the day touring Louisville, soaking up adulation, and complaining to Thimmesch that the adulation wasn't *quite* as strong as it ought to have been. "I won so many amateur fights, and now I win all these professional fights, that people around here used to me winning," he said. "It don't make much difference to them anymore."

That night, exhausted, he changed into a set of thermal underwear that he used for pajamas, stretched out on the living room floor in front of the big TV he'd bought for his parents, and turned the dial until he found the Andy Williams Show. He proceeded to give a speech that may have been a thoughtful reflection but was more likely a performance for the sake of Thimmesch, his amanuensis: "My parents fed me good," he said. "My daddy always told me I'd be world champ. Reading the rules of athletes made me learn clean living. My mother was always humble and helpless and she was always for me. She taught me good. She is a good woman. I try to treat everybody right and try to live right, and when I die, I go to the best place." Cassius continued to describe his life story, leading up to the heroics of his Olympic journey and quoting his best lines to those Russian reporters about the glories of America. "It's economical jealousy that causes wars," he said. "If the world was all sports, there would be no guns and no wars."

Then he described what he saw in his own future.

"There ain't no such thing as love for me," he said. "Not while I'm goin' on to that championship. But when I get that championship, then I'm goin' to put on my old jeans and get an old hat and grow a beard. And I'm goin' walk down the road until I find a little fox who just loves me for who I am. And then I'll take her back to my $250,000 house overlooking my $1 million housing development, and I'll show her the Cadillac and the patio and the indoor pool in case it rains. And I'll tell her, 'This is all yours, honey, 'cause you love me for what I am.'"

Then he slept.

The next morning, Clay summoned his brother with a clucking of his tongue. It was a private signal they used, and Rudy responded as if a servant's bell had been rung. Ordered to make breakfast, Rudy dutifully went to the store to buy eggs, milk, and whole-wheat bread. While his brother was gone, Cassius, restless, took off his shirt and checked his reflection in every mirror in the house, feinting, snapping jabs, pausing only to admire his profile.

"Mmmh, mmmh," he said, the sound of pure satisfaction. "Mmmh, mmmh . . . Oh, if we were only in a tomato-red convertible today! Would they be lookin'!"

11

Float Like a Butterfly, Sting Like a Bee

Sooner or later, just about every great fighter attracts an entourage. At first, the athlete is flattered by the attention of people who want to be near him. He thinks the sycophants might be fun and perhaps even useful to keep around. Before he knows it, he's traveling in a crowd with a bunch of men in possession of vague titles and even vaguer job descriptions, men who expect first-class hotels, fine food, beautiful women, and payment in cash.

In the prime of his career, Sugar Ray Robinson's entourage included a barber, a golf instructor, a masseuse, a voice coach, a drama coach, a secretary, and a dwarf who served as a mascot. Frank Sinatra tagged along too, sometimes.

Cassius Clay had always had his brother, Rudy, his one-man cheering section, best friend, sparring partner, time teller, and errand boy. But now, as Clay's fame spread, he attracted more followers, and he seldom turned anyone away. His life was a traveling circus, the more the merrier as far as he was concerned. Captain Sam Saxon, the Muslim street-corner preacher from Miami, became one of the first to join the Clay show. Saxon brought on a cook to make food according to the dietary laws of the Nation of Islam. In Los Angeles in 1962, before the George Logan fight, Clay befriended a *Los Angeles Sentinel* photographer named Howard Bingham. Soon after, Clay invited Bingham to join his crew, because the only thing the boxer loved more than a mirror was a camera. Archie Robinson, a portly man in a chauffeur's uniform, became Clay's personal secretary. Then there was Ferdie Pacheco, a doctor who worked in a medical clinic in Miami's poverty-stricken Over-town neighborhood and hung around the Fifth Street Gym until he became the unofficial physician for Chris and Angelo Dundee's fighters; "the clap doctor," the boxing men called Pacheco, because much of his work was de-voted to clearing up the boxers' sexually transmitted diseases. What was in it for the doctor? "I got to go to the fights for nothing," Pacheco said.

One of the most important new people in Clay's life in 1963 was Drew Brown Jr., also known as Bundini Brown (or *Bodini*, as Clay and others pro-nounced it), a ghetto poet and shaman who was sent to Clay by Sugar Ray Robinson or by a member of Robinson's entourage.

Clay met Brown in New York before the Jones fight. The men seemed mis-matched in many ways. Clay was still nervous around women, while Brown was a great philanderer. Clay never drank alcohol, while Brown drank heav-ily at times and used recreational drugs, too. Clay was a product of the black working class who seldom expressed opinions on matters concerning politics and race, while Brown had grown up in Harlem and spoke loudly and fre-quently about the black man's struggles and strife. Brown — who referred to God as "Shorty" — wore a Jewish star around his neck in tribute to the white Jewish woman to whom he was married. He talked about a God who encom-passed all religions, and he described race as a misguided human concept, not a heavenly or a natural one. "Blue eyes and brown eyes see grass green," was Bundini Brown's favorite expression.

Brown challenged Clay like no one else, telling him Elijah Muhammad was wrong, that white people were not devils, that God didn't care a thing about a person's color. He sometimes berated the fighter, sometimes coddled him, but almost always made him smile. Like Don Quixote, Cassius Clay was a man of desire who often mistook passion for truth, and now, in Bundini Brown, Clay had found his Sancho Panza.

"He was not an admirable character; he was a funny character," Gor-don Davidson of the Louisville Sponsoring Group said of Bundini. "And he pleased the king."

Brown served another, more specific role in the Clay camp: he helped boost and improve the boxer's poetic output, which to that point had mostly been confined to short lyrics ending in the numbers one through ten. But Brown was a devoted reader and fancied himself a writer. He also had deeper roots than Clay in the ghetto, and gave the boxer's rhymes a grittier, jazzier feel.

In a 1962 *New Yorker* article, A. J. Liebling had written of the "butterfly Cassius" who boxed with "busy hands stinging like bees." No one knows if Bundini Brown read Liebling's descriptions or if he arrived independently at the idea that Clay's style bore comparison to butterflies and bees, but one thing is clear: it was Bundini who invented and trademarked the refrain that would become the boxer's best-known slogan, an eight-word motto that first appeared in American newspapers in February 1964, and one that Clay would go on to utter thousands of times until the contributions of Liebling and Brown were entirely forgotten and it belonged only to the fighter whose style it so deftly captured: "Float like a butterfly, sting like a bee!"

While Clay was building his following, he also became a follower. The man he had come to admire and to emulate was Malcolm X, or Malcolm Little as he had been known before joining the Nation of Islam. Elijah Muhammad was the Nation's leader and its guiding spiritual force, but Malcolm X was the movement's fiery young prince. Wiry, stern, and burning with passion, Malcolm was the man who truly made whites uncomfortable. Malcolm was the man who spoke and acted as if he really were free. "If he hated," as the writer Ta-Nehisi Coates later said, "he hated because it was human for the enslaved to hate the enslaver, natural as Prometheus hating the birds."

Malcolm's life story served as a minor-key variation on the American Dream. He was born in Omaha and grew up mostly in Michigan, near Lansing. His father was an itinerant Baptist preacher with a driving interest in Marcus Garvey's Universal Negro Improvement Association. Earl Little's activism brought death threats from the Black Legion, a white supremacist organization, and twice forced the family to flee its home. In 1929, the Little family's Lansing home burned to the ground, and two years later, Earl Little was found dead along a set of trolley tracks. Police ruled both incidents accidental. When Malcolm's mother was institutionalized for mental illness, her children were split up. Malcolm drifted into a life of crime and drugs and spent about seven years in prison for burglary. By the time he was paroled in 1952, he had become a follower of the Nation of Islam, abandoned his so-called slave name, and replaced it with the letter X to represent the lost name

of his African tribe. He proved to be a dynamic speaker, attracting a large following, helping to establish new mosques, and quickly becoming the second
most powerful force in the organization.

Clay met Malcolm X for the first time in June 1962 before a Nation of Islam
rally in Detroit. Malcolm was eating at the Student's Luncheonette next to the
Detroit Mosque when Cassius and Rudy entered. Like most people, Malcolm
was struck first by the Clay brothers' size and good looks. He described the
moment years later in his autobiography: "Cassius came up and pumped my
hand. . . . He acted as if I was supposed to know who he was. So I acted as
though I did. Up to that moment, though, I had never heard of him. Ours
were two entirely different worlds. In fact, Elijah Muhammad instructed us
Muslims against all forms of sports."

Later that day, Cassius and Rudy Clay attended Elijah Muhammad's sermon and "practically led the applause," as Malcolm put it. In his travels across
the country, Malcolm would occasionally hear that the Clay brothers had visited mosques and Muslim restaurants, and if Malcolm found himself in the
same place at the same time, he would call on the Clays. Rudy was the more
passionate disciple of Elijah Muhammad in those days, according to several
people who knew the brothers at the time, but it was Cassius who intrigued
Malcolm. "I liked him," Malcolm wrote. "Some contagious quality about him
made him one of the very few people I ever invited to my home." Cassius also
charmed Malcolm's wife and children. He became part of the family, like a
playful uncle to the kids and a younger brother to Malcolm.

Malcolm must have recognized that Clay's friendliness and naiveté might
make him vulnerable to con men and crooks, because he made it his responsibility to teach Clay that "a public figure's success depends upon on how alert
and knowledgeable he is to the true natures and to the true motives of all the
people who flock around him."

That included women.

"I warned him about the 'foxes,'" Malcolm wrote. "I told Cassius that instead of 'foxes,' they really were wolves." Clay ignored that advice.

Malcolm, of course, had his own reasons to be concerned with the "true
motives" of people around him. He also had reason to cling to this blos-
soming friendship with Cassius Clay, a man whose sunny personality melted
away worries. In 1963, Malcolm's life was in turmoil. He had discovered that

his great mentor, the Honorable Elijah Muhammad, was an adulterer who had been having sex, perhaps for more than a decade, with some of the young secretaries who worked with him in the offices of the Nation of Islam in Chicago. Muhammad had been telling the young women that his wife was dead to him and that he had a duty to spread his holy seed among virgins. Eventually, seven women who had been his personal secretaries would claim to have given birth to a total of thirteen children fathered by the Nation of Islam leader. As stipulated by Nation of Islam code, the women were punished for having children out of wedlock; they were forced into isolation and banned from participating in activities at local mosques. Elijah Muhammad, however, faced no such punishment, and by 1963 his affairs were well known within the hierarchy of his organization and the offices of the FBI.

The behavior did not damage Muhammad's reputation among his disciples, at least not right away. Women had always been treated as an inferior class in the sect (even more so than in society as a whole), subject to the control of men, barred from using birth control, and, of course, discouraged from fraternizing with white men.

Those closest to Elijah Muhammad had known for years about his sexual affairs, but no one had dared complain. The culture within the Chicago headquarters of the Nation of Islam had always been one that gave unchecked power to the organization's leader. High-paying jobs were awarded to Muhammad's relatives, and Nation of Islam funds supported the Messenger's comfortable lifestyle. These conditions help explain why Muhammad, like so many other men in positions of power, felt comfortable indulging in behavior discouraged among his followers. There was little risk of harm, unless the stories of his sexual behavior became so widely known that they damaged the image of the Nation of Islam and, in turn, the organization's recruiting and fundraising.

When Malcolm X first heard the rumors, he dismissed them as lies. But by 1962, as the stories persisted and as members of the Chicago mosque defected, Malcolm had concluded the allegations were true. "I felt like something in *nature* had failed," he wrote, "like the sun, or the stars."

Did Malcolm talk to Clay about his growing concerns about Elijah Muhammad? He doesn't say in his autobiography. If Clay had misgivings about Muhammad or the Nation of Islam, he didn't show it. In August 1962, he and his brother attended a Nation of Islam rally in St. Louis. A year later, a reporter for the *Chicago Sun-Times* spotted Clay's red Cadillac in an alley behind the University of Islam at 5335 South Greenwood Avenue in Chicago. When Clay walked out of the school, which was founded to provide education to young members of the Nation, he got into the back seat of the car while his brother drove. Two other cars full of Muslims joined Clay's caravan, with the *Sun-Times* reporter following close behind. At 54th Street and Lake Park Avenue, the reporter's car pulled up alongside Clay's Caddy, with the vehicles moving "at a speed that might have been disapproved by Police Supt. Orlando W. Wilson," an interview commenced, questions and answers shouted from open windows.

"What are you doing in Chicago?"

"I just happened to be here. I'm sure glad I was. That session I attended tonight was the greatest I've ever attended in my whole life."

"Are you a Black Muslim?"

Clay thought about it for half a block.

"No," he said, and then added. "I don't know." He paused again before continuing: "I'm for the Black Muslims."

"Do you believe in everything they advocate?"

"Listen," Clay said. "I've looked real hard at every organization that's for the black man. This is the greatest one that I've found. The Black Muslims are the sweetest thing next to God." He raised his voice to overcome a swell of traffic noise and offer a poem. "The sweetest thing that would keep you clean — the greatest thing I've ever seen."

The reporter asked if Clay planned to attend one of the upcoming civil rights demonstrations in the South.

"I'm for integration," he said, smiling. "Sure I'm for integration. I've got ten white managers."

"Are you planning to go down there like Dick Gregory did?"

Clay stopped smiling.

"I'm for everything good that can happen to the black man. But I'm not going down there. I don't want anybody to sic dogs on me."

When Clay's car veered onto the Chicago Skyway, headed for Indiana, the interview ended.

Two days later, in a report published by the *Louisville Times,* Clay denied having declared allegiance with the Nation of Islam. He said he had been reading a lot about the group and had indeed attended a banquet but insisted that "I don't really know much about them." He continued, "I was surprised to see that there are hundreds of thousands of Negroes who don't want to integrate. And the whites seem more worried about them than they are about those who do want to integrate." Finally, he said he had refrained from joining the Nation of Islam or any other civil rights group because he hadn't found a group that offered "an eternal solution" and because he didn't want to be "made into a politician."

As he liked to do in the ring, Clay dodged.

As Clay's chance to fight Liston drew nearer, members of the Louisville group began discussing ways in which their fighter might make money outside the ring — not only to supplement his income but also to prepare him in case he should lose or find his boxing career shortened by injury. The businessmen believed that Clay might thrive as an entertainer. Already, the Jack Benny variety show had offered Clay $7,500 for an appearance. Producers of the TV show *Mr. Ed,* a comedy about a talking horse, wanted Clay to film an episode. And Frank Sinatra inquired as to whether the boxer might be available to act in a movie with a cast expected to include Sinatra, Dean Martin, Bette Davis, and Jack Palance.

But Clay's management team didn't know what to make of the boxer's rumored connections to Elijah Muhammad and Malcolm X, and they were worried. Malcolm was "a charming sumbitch," said Gordon B. Davidson, lawyer for the Louisville Sponsoring Group, but Malcolm's link to the young boxer posed a danger. If Clay really had fallen in with the Black Muslims, it was hard to imagine that those offers from Jack Benny and *Mr. Ed* would stand. Clay was still young, still becoming a man, but now, for the first time, two of his strongest impulses conflicted: his lust for fame and his itch to rebel. He was not a deliberate person, but he surely knew his association with the Nation of Islam would complicate his relationships with his white backers, his white trainer, and the white news reporters whose attention he so craved. Clay probably understood that his public image would be forever altered if he allied himself publicly with Elijah Muhammad, bringing a degree of animosity that might make even Gorgeous George shrink away. It was one thing for a man to wear rollers in his hair and feign homosexuality, and quite another to advocate the destruction of all white people.

In his public pronouncements, Clay focused on Liston. He talked about no other boxer but Liston. Only by beating the unbeatable Liston, Clay believed, would he prove his talent and fulfill his destiny.

But Liston had signed to fight Patterson again, and Clay needed money and needed to stay sharp. He would have to face at least one more opponent before getting a shot at the title. By the middle of 1963, Clay was ranked third among heavyweights, after Liston and Patterson. Doug Jones was fourth, but Clay was determined to avoid a rematch with the dangerous Jones. And so he settled for a bout against the fifth-ranked fighter in the world, an Englishman named Henry Cooper, twenty-nine years old, winner of twenty-seven, loser of eight, with one draw. Cooper had a reputation as a quick bleeder, with skin around his eyes said to be as brittle as an antique porcelain doll's. Jimmy Cannon wrote that it took a hiccup to reopen the scars on Cooper's face. But Cooper also possessed one of the best left hooks in the business—'Enry's 'Ammer, the punch was called—which meant his challenge would be landing a few of those good 'ammers before Clay hiccupped.

The fight was set for June 18, 1963, at London's Wembley Stadium. If Clay felt disappointed by having to wait for Liston, he consoled himself with the knowledge that a fight in England would expose a whole new country to his wondrous charm.

He still didn't like flying, but he had little choice, and upon arrival in London, Clay wasted no time offending.

"There has never been anything quite like it," wrote Peter Wilson in the *Daily Mirror*. "He came, he saw . . . and he talked."

Clay began by referring to Buckingham Palace as a "swell pad" and followed by insulting the country's greatest boxer. "Henry Cooper is nothing to me," he announced. "If this bum goes over five rounds I won't return to the United States for thirty days, and that's final! I'm not even worried about this big bum. Cooper will only be a warm-up until I get that big, ugly bear, Sonny Liston." At the weigh-in for the fight, Clay pointed out that England had a queen, but it ought to have a king. He then produced a cardboard crown, placed it on his head, and declared the solution: "I am the king!"

The king weighed in at 207 pounds, the heaviest of his career so far, and 21½ pounds heavier than Cooper.

As he entered the ring, ready to fight, Clay once more wore the crown, as well as a red and white satin robe he'd had specially made for the occasion at a cost of twenty pounds. The audience of 35,000 cursed and hollered insults. Elizabeth Taylor and Richard Burton sat ringside, she in a long coat, turquoise dress, and white gloves; he in a conservative suit and tie.

Cooper had a reputation as a slow starter with a "stand-up old-lithograph style," as *Sports Illustrated* put it. But he defied expectations and came out aggressively, throwing his best punch — the left hook — over and over. Within thirty seconds he succeeded in bloodying Clay's nose. Clay blinked back tears and wiped his nose with the back of his glove.

"First blood to Cooper," said the British television announcer Harry Carpenter.

Cooper launched more lefts and then wrapped an arm around Clay's head. When Clay turned to the referee to complain, Cooper clobbered him again. Round one went to the Brit.

Cooper was more cautious in the second round, throwing jabs instead of hooks. Clay jabbed too and opened a small cut under Cooper's left eye. Still, Cooper was winning, landing far more big blows than Clay, and the crowd was growing more excited by the second at the prospect of an upset.

In the third round, Clay opened another cut, this time above Cooper's left eye. Cuts change everything in a fight. Cuts serve as overt reminders that punches are more than points scored in this sporting competition. Cuts are signs of damage and danger, and cuts above the eye are especially perilous because dripping blood blinds a fighter and forces him to do desperate things, to plunge headlong and headfirst, throwing wild punches to end the fight fast.

"This is what we always feared about Cooper," said Carpenter, the worried English TV announcer. "There's no telling how long he's got to go with that eye."

Clay grew more confident as Cooper began to look like a man who'd swan-dived into an empty pool. Hands low, Clay peered in at Cooper's red-streaked face, stalking his prey. He began teasing Cooper, opening his mouth, coaxing his opponent to throw a punch. But Clay wasn't throwing many punches of his own — he landed only eleven the entire round — perhaps because he had predicted a fifth-round knockout and this was only round three. By now Clay knew the press loved to talk about his knack for fulfilling predictions.

"Cut out the funny business," screamed Bill Faversham, head of the Louisville Sponsoring Group, from a ringside seat.

In the fourth, Cooper swung away with more lefts. Cooper's only chance was a knockout, and he needed one fast, before too much of his own blood spilled. With about five seconds left in the round, Cooper uncoiled a perfect left hook —'enry's 'ammer! — that caught Clay full on the jaw. Clay fell hard into the ropes, his gaze gone blank, his mouth agape. He sprang quickly to his feet, but he was dazed. He looked uncertain of where he was and what he had been doing five seconds earlier. The noise from the crowd obscured the clang of the bell signaling the round's end as Clay stumbled to his corner, sat on his stool, and then tried to get up again before his trainer, Angelo Dundee, shoved him back down.

In almost any other walk of life, the sight of a man bludgeoned senseless would have inspired concern for the man's health and immediate examination by a physician. Not in boxing. In Clay's corner, the panicked question was how to keep him in the fight. If their man didn't gather his senses in sixty seconds and come back to win, they were in deep trouble. Liston would fight another top contender, possibly Henry Cooper. Clay would likely have to wait years for a shot at the title. His earning power would fall. Jobs and fortunes could be lost.

"You OK?" Dundee asked as Clay slumped.

"Yeah," said Cassius, not skipping a beat, "but Cooper's getting tired."

Dundee, skeptical, mopped the fighter's brow and broke smelling salts under his nose. Then came a moment of inspiration for the trainer. Before the fight, Dundee had noticed a small split along the seam of one of Clay's gloves. He didn't think it was a problem. But now, with his fighter dumbstruck and on the verge of defeat, Dundee acted quickly. "I stuck my finger in the split, helping it along until it was a bigger split," Dundee wrote in his book, *My View from the Corner,* in 2009. "I then yelled at the ref . . . to come over and examine the glove."

While Dundee stalled, Chickie Ferrara, another of Clay's corner men, broke more vials of smelling salts under Clay's nose and dropped ice cubes down the front of his pants, a commonly used technique to jolt a fighter out of a stupor. In years to come, boxing lore would say that Dundee's glove trick provided Clay with three minutes to recover rather than the usual one-minute break between rounds. Film of the fight, however, suggests that Clay's extra recovery time amounted to no more than five seconds. "But even those few seconds," Dundee wrote, "were vital."

The extra five seconds benefited Cooper's corner too, where trainers worked to stanch the blood flow from their fighter's eye. Yet when the referee signaled for the fight to resume, Clay emerged the more energetic man. He moved toward his target like a tornado, wild, furious, punishing everything within reach. Pounding, pounding, Clay punched so hard and fast that Cooper could neither brace himself nor respond. Cooper tried to hold on to Clay, but Clay was too fast, too strong, and still punching. Soon the blood poured from Cooper's left eye like water from a broken main. Clay kept swinging. After about a minute and a quarter, the referee stopped the fight.

Rudy Clay jumped in the ring after the referee's signal, carrying his brother's crown. But Clay declined it. He was victorious, and he had won it in the fifth round, as predicted. But he had been humbled.

In the dressing room after the fight, a small, slender man in a carefully tailored suit approached Clay. He was Jack Nilon, manager for Sonny Liston.

"We want you bad in September, Cassius," he said. "I've come 3,500 miles to get your O.K."

The men discussed the possibility of having Clay fight Liston on September 30 at Philadelphia's 100,000-seat Municipal Stadium, assuming, of course, that Liston knocked off Floyd Patterson again in their upcoming bout.

Back in the United States, summer exploded. In June 1963, Medgar Evers, the field director for the NAACP in Mississippi, was assassinated outside his home. In Alabama, federal troops forced Governor George Wallace to admit black students at the University of Alabama. In the North, black men and women marched to protest police brutality, unfair wages, and discrimination in housing. Four years after closing its schools to avoid integration, officials in Prince Edward County, Virginia, finally gave in and agreed to allow black students to resume their educations. On August 10, Clay attended a rally in Harlem in which Malcolm X explained why he had no plans to join the upcoming March on Washington. Eighteen days later, Martin Luther King Jr. and a crowd of more than 200,000 people came together in Washington in what would prove to be one of the most powerful moments of the civil rights movement. "I have a dream," King chanted, "that one day on the red hills of Georgia the sons of former slaves and the sons of former slave owners will be able to sit down together at the table of brotherhood."

That was not the dream of Elijah Muhammad. Nor was it the dream of Malcolm X, who called King's march a "farce," an invention of black men with white hearts, subsidized by white liberals, and orchestrated by President Kennedy. Eighteen days after the great March on Washington, white supremacists used fifteen sticks of dynamite to blow apart a black church in Birmingham, Alabama, killing four black schoolgirls and injuring twenty others, a brutal reminder that not every American was ready for a seat at the table of brotherhood, not by a long shot.

In September, Cassius Clay attended a conference in Oakland on "The Mind of the Ghetto," organized by a black-nationalist group called the Afro-American Association. But even there, he preferred to play the clown rather than the rebel. "I don't stand for anything," he said. "I'm not a politician. I don't talk against anything. I'm a peaceful man. You know, Catholics, Protestants, KKKs, and NAACP members come to see me fight. I don't debate issues. I just fight." When a writer asked specifically about his interest in the Nation of Islam, he said, "I don't identify myself with anybody — anybody except Cassius Clay."

From Oakland, he traveled to Philadelphia to attend a lecture by Elijah Muhammad, leaping to his feet at times to cheer as the Messenger warned that black people would continue to die if they failed to separate themselves from white society.

"Separation is absolutely necessary," Muhammad told the audience. White people, he said, "are our enemies. The end of their time is at the door."

He went on to say black men and women had been fooled into worshiping a Christian God, "one that does not exist." But it was not too late to embrace Allah, said the man who considered himself Allah's divine messenger. "The old story of Jesus dying on the cross and going up to heaven is one of the worst falsehoods you could believe in," he continued. "I am here with the truth. I am asking for complete separation. There is no hope for a good future for the so-called Negro under the American flag."

Clay wore "an expensive silk mohair suit and a sullen expression on his face," the *Philadelphia Tribune* reported, and when reporters approached, he brushed them aside, telling them to talk to Malcolm X. "He's really got some-thing important to say," Clay said.

Although Clay continued to deny that he had joined the Nation of Islam, members of the Louisville Sponsoring Group grew more concerned by the day. These wealthy white businessmen expressed worry that Clay's associa-tion with a radical group that opposed integration and labeled white people devils would damage his career and their investment.

Was Clay lying about his connections to the Nation of Islam to avoid con-troversy? Was he buying himself more time to think? It's not clear. Clay was acting like a young man who thought he could have everything he wanted, do whatever he wanted, and say anything he wanted. So far, the facts of his life had supported that notion. How else to explain a man attending a Nation of Islam rally one day and playing the clown another day on a talk show hosted by the white comedian Jerry Lewis? How else to explain Clay's appearance on the *Jack Paar Show,* where he recited poems while Liberace in a beaded jacket plinked the piano beside a glittering candelabra? "For a change," Liberace joked with Clay as he prepared to recite a poem, "do the one about you."

If Clay believed black nationalism offered the only path out of oppression for his people, how else to explain his willingness in the summer of 1963 to record a comedy album?

The comedy album was hatched by the Louisville Sponsoring Group as part of their contingency plans in case Clay lost to Sonny Liston or otherwise found his boxing career abbreviated. Clay seemed like a born entertainer, one who gabbed and joked almost as well as he boxed. An album consisting of jokes and poems would send a message to television and film producers that Clay had another marketable talent.

Until then, the boxer's poetry had been juvenile stuff:

> *This guy's a bum.*
> *He'll fall in one.*

But for his album, *I Am the Greatest!,* Clay upgraded his material, employ-ing more sophisticated humor and subtler rhymes while still displaying the cockiness that fans and critics had come to expect. The album was recorded August 8 in front of a live audience at Columbia Records in New York. Clay recited this refrain:

Clay comes out to meet Liston
And Liston starts to retreat
But if he goes back an inch farther
He'll end up in a ringside seat.
Clay swings with his left,
Clay swings with his right,
Look at young Cassius
Carry the fight.
Liston keeps backing
But there's not enough room.
It's a matter of time.
There, Clay lowers the boom.
Now Clay lands a right,
What a beautiful swing,
The punch raises Liston
Clear out of the ring.
Liston is still rising
And the ref wears a frown,
For he can't start counting,
Till Sonny comes down.
Now Liston disappears from view.
The crowd is getting frantic,
But our radar stations have picked him up.
He's somewhere over the Atlantic.
Who would have thought
When they came to the fight
That they'd witness the launching
Of a human satellite?
Yes, the crowd did not dream
When they put down their money
That they would see
A total eclipse of the Sonny!

In addition to poems, the album contained an assortment of corny gags, including references to those inferior wordsmiths Keats and Shelley, fat jokes about Sonny Liston, and a riff on President Kennedy: "I don't ask what box-ing can do for me but what I can do for boxing."

Clay's material improved for one reason: he didn't write most of it. The man responsible was Gary Belkin, a comedy industry veteran who was listed as producer on the album's liner notes but received no writing credit. While Clay may not have written the verses, he was more than clever enough to memorize Belkin's poems. As he recited them on TV and in press confer-ences, his popularity grew. He was becoming boxing's first made-for-TV hero, tough but playful, rebellious but not frightening.

"Cassius," said the *New York Times,* "is a delightful young man."

Only a handful of writers — most of them black — sensed something deeper stirring beneath the playful personality.

"For when Cassius Clay declares, 'I am the greatest,' he is not just thinking about boxing," wrote Alex Poinsett in *Ebony.* "Lingering behind those words is the bitter sarcasm of Dick Gregory, the shrill defiance of Miles Davis, the utter contempt of Malcolm X. He smiles easily, but, behind it all . . . is a blast furnace of race pride."

12

The Ugly Bear

Look at that big, ugly bear. He can't even shoot craps."

More than half a century earlier, an argument over a craps game had led to murder and sent his grandfather to prison, but Cassius Clay probably didn't know that.

"Look at the big, ugly bear," he called out.

Clay had traveled to Las Vegas to see Sonny Liston fight Floyd Patterson, and now, Clay eyed Liston across the floor of a casino and jumped at the opportunity to provoke his rival.

Liston threw the dice. Craps. Down four hundred dollars, he glared as Clay chirped again: "What's the matter with you? You can't even shoot dice."

Clay wasn't done.

"Look at that big, ugly bear. He can't do nothin' right."

The other gamblers at the table were silent, possibly afraid. Liston dropped the dice and walked to Clay.

"Listen, you nigger faggot," Liston said. "If you don't get out of here in ten seconds I'm gonna pull that big tongue out of your mouth and stick it up your ass."

Clay would reenact the story of the casino confrontation countless times in the weeks ahead, acting it out for friends and journalists as if he were performing a scene from his favorite Western, describing how the crowd in the casino hushed and parted, how they whispered, "It's Cassius Clay, Cassius Clay . . ."

With each telling, his courage would grow in proportion to Liston's threat.

In truth, his response to Liston was not so brave: he got away as fast as he could.

Patterson versus Liston was a classic conflict between Good and Evil, with Evil winning in a first-round knockout. Patterson was so afraid of repeating his first disaster that he kept his hands low and charged straight at his man. He might as well have charged a wrecking ball. Liston knocked him down three times in the first round and ended the fight after two minutes and ten seconds.

"I felt good until I got hit," said Patterson, which is like saying the glass was half full before you dropped it.

When it was over, Clay climbed into the ring, slithered out of the grasp of three members of the Nevada sheriff's guard, and made a beeline not for Liston but for the nearest TV camera.

"The fight was a disgrace!" Clay shouted. "Liston is a tramp! I'm the champ!"

He flashed a fake newspaper — "Clay Has a Very Big Lip That Sonny Will Sure Zip," the headline read — and made a big show of tearing the paper to shreds.

"I want that big, ugly bear," Clay said. "I want that big, ugly bum as soon as I can get him."

Liston threw up his hands in mock terror, this time happy to go along with Clay's act.

Jack Nilon wanted Liston to fight Clay quickly. No one else in the heavyweight division had Clay's charisma. No one else had his name recognition. Clay was, as *Sports Illustrated* put it, "widely acclaimed as the savior of boxing," which was a veiled way of saying the sport needed saving from the monster currently in possession of the heavyweight crown. "Everything [Clay] does is exciting," reported a British journalist. "This unbelievably handsome youngster, a Harry Belafonte with muscles, has thrown the tradition of two-and-a-half centuries of boxing out of the window — without even bothering to open the window first."

But before Nilon could cut a deal with Clay and the Louisville Sponsoring Group, business troubles interfered. A few days after the second Liston-Patterson fight, Nilon announced the establishment of Inter-Continental Promotions, Inc., a new company to promote all of Liston's fights. Sonny was to be president, and Nilon and his two brothers were to be principal officers. Given that the Nilon brothers were long rumored to have connections to the mob, newspaper reporters greeted the formation of the new company skeptically, assuming some kind of skullduggery. On July 28, Estes Kefauver, chairman of a special U.S. Senate committee investigating organized crime, announced that he intended to scrutinize Inter-Continental Promotions. Three days later, Pennsylvania boxing officials refused to grant the new company a promoter's license, saying that it was illegal for Liston to own stock in the company promoting his fights.

That meant there would be no fight in Pennsylvania. But other states were eager to have the money and publicity that would come with hosting a championship bout. After a short period of negotiation, the Louisville Sponsoring Group and the Nilons reached agreement: the fight would be held February 25 in Miami Beach.

Although they were still new to the fight business and unaccustomed to dealing with unsavory characters like the Nilon brothers, and though they were uncomfortable with some of the agreement's terms, members of the Louisville Sponsoring Group secured a good deal for Clay, one that promised him 22.5 percent of ticket sales and concession revenues, as well as 22.5 percent of the lucrative closed-circuit TV receipts. Reporters covering the announcement said Clay would probably gross nearly $1 million.

Huston Horn, writing for *Sports Illustrated,* said Clay was wise to make the deal quickly. Horn questioned the young fighter's skill, saying that if not for Henry Cooper's tender facial tissue, Clay might have lost his last fight. What's more, the journalist said, Clay's jokes were getting old and his personality was beginning to grate. His character had come into question, too. "He has gained nothing, for example . . . by attending meetings of the Black Muslims — about whom he understands virtually nothing," wrote Horn. "Equally unbecoming has been his recent criticism of his long-suffering trainer, Angelo Dundee, whom he childishly calls a 'bum.'"

The Nilons and the Louisville Sponsoring Group scheduled a press conference for November 5 to announce their deal. Clay traveled to Denver for the announcement in a recently purchased secondhand bus. Little Red, he called the bus, for its red-and-white exterior. Cassius Clay Sr. painted signs that hung from the outside of the bus reading "THE GREATEST," "WORLD'S MOST COLORFUL FIGHTER," and "SONNY LISTON WILL GO IN EIGHT."

As the bus neared Denver, Clay stopped to phone reporters, telling them to get over to Sonny Liston's house if they wanted a good story. The reporters were already assembled at one in the morning when Clay's bus reached Liston's home, which was located in a mostly white neighborhood where thirty-two "FOR-SALE" signs had supposedly gone up when Liston moved in earlier that year. Clay honked the horn and flashed the headlights. Then he sent his friend Howard Bingham, who spoke with a persistent stutter, to knock on Liston's door.

Liston answered in a gold smoking jacket and brandishing a gold-crowned cane.

"What you want, you black motherfucker?" he asked.

"Come on out of there!" Clay shouted from the curb. "I'm going to whip you right now! Come on out of there and protect your home!"

Liston walked toward Clay as the men exchanged threats, but soon there were seven police cars surrounding Clay's bus and a police dog on a leash inches away from Clay's knees. When a police officer told Clay to "move on right away or be taken in," Clay climbed back on his bus and drove off.

The next afternoon at a luncheon for the press, Clay employed his usual material to charm reporters and irk Liston. He recited one of the poems that Gary Belkin had written for him that summer, the one that referred to Liston as a "human satellite."

Liston just laughed.

"I'm the champ of fightin'," he said, "but you the champ of talkin'."

The champ of fighting displayed a pair of fur boxing gloves, saying that he liked to use them against weaker opponents such as Clay.

As Liston's jokes scored and Clay's fell flat, Clay went silent and turned to eat the plate of chicken on his table.

"You eat like you headed to the electric chair!" Liston cracked. "The fight ain't tonight!"

With the bout set for February, after Clay's twenty-second birthday, he would not have the chance to become the youngest heavyweight champion in history. But that wasn't his biggest concern as 1963 neared its end; his biggest concern was an order to appear before the U.S. Army draft board in Louisville for a pre-induction physical exam.

There was no great international crisis at the time. The United States had fifteen thousand members of the military in South Vietnam, but the government was calling them advisors, not combatants, and there was no reason to expect an escalation of the confrontation in Asia. Clay was at a motel on the South Side of Chicago, driving back to New York from Denver, when a reporter caught up to ask him how he felt about serving in the military.

"I ain't worried about nothing 'till I get the official greetings from the draft board," he said, noting that the letter had been sent to Louisville and a copy had not yet reached him in his travels. Then he added a wisecrack: "Looks like Uncle Sam wants to miss out on the tax money from 15 million dollars, don't it?" The implication being that he would soon be earning enormous sums of money, great chunks of which would go to the federal government through income tax.

Two weeks later, President John F. Kennedy was assassinated as he rode in a motorcade through downtown Dallas. Bob Nilon, who was Jack Nilon's brother and a top executive with Inter-Continental, said plans for the fight would continue despite the national tragedy and despite concerns that Clay could face the draft. Clay would request a four-month deferment from the draft board, Nilon said, "so he can make the most of the greatest opportunity of his life — to fight for the world heavyweight crown and the wealth that goes with it."

Sonny Liston wasn't worried about Clay's military induction, either. The army, he said, would have no use for Clay "after I'm done with him."

13

"So What's Wrong with the Muslims?"

Clay was something new: a feisty black man who seemed to think he could say and do whatever he pleased, without fear of punishment. To some, he was an "uppity nigger" who needed to be put in his place. To others, he was an inspiration. For almost everyone, he was a curiosity and all but impossible to ignore.

"That audacity! That youth!" recalled Jesse Jackson, who was pursuing a college degree in sociology at the time and would soon become active in the civil rights movement. "Float like a butterfly! Sting like a bee! He talked that trash, too!"

By 1964, Ali had three Cadillacs, a tour bus, a new house in Louisville for his parents, and a rented home in Miami. He was also considering buying a house in Long Island, New York, so he could spend more time with Malcolm X. Win or lose, he had a massive payday coming after his fight with Liston, and he sounded at times as if he were more excited about the money than the championship.

"I've been boxing since I was twelve years old," Clay said, "and I'm getting mighty tired of training and always having somebody try to pop me in the mouth. But I probably won't ever get tired of money. I love money . . . The fame and pride of doing something real well — like being the world champion — is a pretty nice thing to think about sometimes, but the money I'm making is nice to think about all the time. I suppose it's the one thing that keeps me going."

If he came across as callow and self-absorbed, he was. Clay was preparing for the biggest fight of his life against a man so dangerous that *Sport* magazine called Clay's doom "almost inevitable," the writer noting that he included the word *almost* in case the fight was unexpectedly canceled. Yet the young fighter betrayed no signs of stress, no obvious worries beyond how to spend the great fortune he would soon accumulate.

"I have to go into the Army pretty soon, and after that I don't know," he said. "Maybe I'll buy a big housing project and get married and settle down and think about being rich."

Boxing's wise men believed that Clay would soon have plenty of time for military service, real-estate speculation, romance, and the consideration of a new career. Clay wasn't prepared for Liston, they said. He needed more experience in the ring. He needed more time. That was the nearly unanimous view among the press corps and former fighters.

"I don't see the kid going more than one, two rounds," said Mike DeJohn, a boxer who had lost to Liston in 1959 and had sparred with Clay. "Maybe in a year, two years . . . Liston is too strong."

Clay's mere existence offended some men who covered boxing, including columnist Arthur Daley of the *New York Times,* who wrote, "The loudmouth from Louisville is likely to have a lot of vainglorious boasts jammed down his throat by a hamlike fist belonging to Sonny Liston." Jimmy Cannon of the *New York Journal-American* was considered the most powerful sports columnist of the day, which made him the most powerful figure in all of sports journalism at a time when newspapers dominated, and he, too, believed that Clay had no business in the ring with Liston. "Look at that!" Cannon said one day to the young magazine writer George Plimpton as the men watched Clay spar at the Fifth Street Gym in Miami. Clay was skittering around the ring, flicking jabs and sliding around the ring on his toes, as if uninformed that heavyweights were not supposed to dance and throw pitty-pat punches. "I mean, that's terrible. He can't get away with that. Not possibly."

"Perhaps his speed will make up for it," Plimpton said.

"He's the fifth Beatle," Cannon said. "Except that's not right. The Beatles have no hokum to them."

"It's a good name," Plimpton said. "The fifth Beatle."

"Not accurate," Cannon said. "He's all pretense and gas, that fellow . . . No honesty."

To writers like Cannon, Clay was a child, naturally playful, incapable of understanding his own inferiority and making up for it with grandiose delusions, a child with the capacity to despise his elders in one moment and love them the next. It was a kind of intellectual constipation common among older white men. After grumbling to Plimpton, Cannon refined his statement in a column: "Clay is part of the Beatle movement. He fits in with the famous singers no one can hear . . . and the boys with their long dirty hair and the girls with the unwashed look and the college kids dancing naked at secret proms held in apartments and the revolt of students who get a check from Dad every first of the month and the painters who copy the labels off soup cans and the surf bums who refuse to work and the whole pampered style-making cult of the bored young."

The actual Beatles were in Miami to do *The Ed Sullivan Show* for a second time. A week earlier, they'd appeared on the show in New York, singing five songs before a screaming live audience and 73 million television viewers. For their second appearance on the show, Sonny Liston attended, along with Joe Louis and the dapper publicist Harold Conrad, who had been hired to promote the Clay-Liston fight. Conrad claimed it was his idea to bring the boys with the long dirty hair over to the Fifth Street Gym to see what would happen when they mixed with the pitty-pat puncher Clay. Conrad was a legend in the PR business, a veteran of dozens of prizefights, countless Broadway shows, and, according to legend, Bugsy Siegel's first choice to sell Americans on the neon splendor of Las Vegas. He was the jazz-talking, action-loving kind of guy Damon Runyon wrote stories about, a remnant of an age when people thought there was no end to how much faster, taller, louder, and brighter the world would get, and no limit to how much money a clever man could make along the way. Conrad figured that Clay and the Beatles had enough in common — they were young, they were new, they were smart-alecks — to justify getting them in the same room.

When the musicians arrived, walking up the worn wooden steps to the gym, the boxer wasn't there. The Beatles were not accustomed to being stood up.

"Where the fuck's Clay?" Ringo Starr asked.

Finally, as the young men from England prepared to leave, Clay appeared.

"Hello there, Beatles," he said, playing to the press gathered in the gym. "We oughta do some road shows together. We'll get rich."

The Beatles liked money too, so they had that in common.

"You're not as stupid as you look," Clay teased Lennon.

"No, but you are," Lennon teased back.

Life magazine photographer Harry Benson urged the Beatles into the ring, where they pretended to fight four against one. After that, Benson arranged the Beatles in a line so Clay could fake a punch that knocked them down like dominos.

The Beatles, unaccustomed to having someone else play the wise guy, weren't happy about it. "You made us look like monkeys," Lennon complained later to the photographer.

For some of the men in the press, this stunt offered further proof that Clay was a phony, all style and no substance. But those men were wrong, and Harold Conrad was right. He, along with a few of the younger reporters in the room, could see that a shift was taking place in American culture. Clay and the Beatles not only possessed real talent; they also represented something new. They were rebel-clowns, a compelling hybrid with the potential for danger and profit.

On the evening of January 14, 1964, Malcolm X, his wife, Betty, and their three daughters flew to Miami for a family vacation. Cassius Clay was paying for their trip, and he waited in his car to greet them at the airport.

Both men had cause for anxiety. Clay had the biggest fight of his life coming up in less than six weeks, and Malcolm had even more pressing concerns. He had recently given credence to the rumors swirling around Elijah Muhammad, and he had accused Muhammad of impregnating his secretaries. Muhammad in turn had suspended Malcolm indefinitely from the organization, supposedly because Malcolm had defied an order not to comment on the assassination of John Kennedy.

Despite the enormous strains of his life, the trip still qualified as a vacation for Malcolm. He sat by the pool at his motel. He strapped a camera around his neck and went for long walks.

Clay knew about Malcolm's suspension, but it wasn't in the boxer's nature to take sides in a squabble. He enjoyed Malcolm's company. The men had more in common than it might first appear. Both loved attention. Both enjoyed sparring with their enemies, manipulating the media, and stoking fears with outrageous language. Both rejected authority. Clay also may have felt that time spent with Malcolm X strengthened his connection to the Nation of Islam. To spend time and learn from Malcolm was only one small step removed from spending time and learning from the Messenger.

Malcolm had something to gain from time spent with Clay, too. If Clay somehow beat Liston, the young boxer might become a valuable asset to the Nation of Islam, and Malcolm might be more valuable to Elijah Muhammad as a result of his alliance with the boxer. Together, Clay and Malcolm would bring an image of youth and power to the movement, assuming that Elijah Muhammad did not find such a prospect threatening to his authority. There were rumors among reporters that if Clay beat Liston, Clay and Malcolm would travel the day after the fight to Chicago in time for a Nation of Islam convention. There, Clay would be welcomed by Elijah Muhammad, and Malcolm X would have his suspension lifted.

To Clay, Malcolm was like an older brother; "The Big M," he called his new mentor. To Malcolm, Clay was a promising protégé.

Malcolm told George Plimpton he had no interest in sport. In all of sporting history, Malcolm said, the Negro had never once come out ahead. Plimpton pointed out that Clay might be the exception. But Malcolm insisted he wasn't interested in Clay as a boxer. "I'm interested in him as a human being." Malcolm tapped his head as he spoke. "Not many people know the quality of the mind he's got in there. He fools them . . . He is sensitive, very humble, yet shrewd — with as much untapped mental energy as he has physical power. He should be a diplomat. He has that instinct of seeing a tricky situation shaping up — my own presence in Miami, for example — and resolving how to sidestep it . . . He gains strength from being around people. He can't stand being alone. The more people around, the better."

Malcolm understood that his presence in Miami made for a tricky situation, as he called it. Tricky because white reporters now saw plainly that Clay was connected to the Nation of Islam. Tricky because someone — possibly the FBI — was leaking information to the press about the widening rift between Elijah Muhammad and Malcolm X. Tricky because Malcolm's presence put Clay between the two men. Clay did his best during Malcolm's Miami vacation to avoid commenting on his connections to the Muslims. He was afraid that if the newspapermen labeled him a member of the Nation of Islam it would hurt ticket sales. Soon, though, he found the subject impossible to avoid.

On January 19, Malcolm's wife and children flew home to New York. Two days later, Malcolm and Clay also flew to New York, Clay telling Angelo Dundee that he was taking a few days off from training and not explaining why. The fight was less than five weeks away.

In New York, Clay ate dinner with Malcolm before attending a Nation of Islam rally at the Rockland Palace Ballroom. At the rally, Clay made a short speech, saying he was inspired every time he attended a Muslim meeting.

When the FBI got word from an informant that Clay had attended the rally, agents leaked the news to the white press. Two days later, the *Herald-Tribune* published a front-page story noting Clay's presence at the assembly. Although Clay had no comment for the *Herald-Tribune,* he began to speak openly to the white press of his support for the Black Muslims. "Sure I talked to the Muslims and I'm going back again," he said. "I like the Muslims. I'm not going to get killed trying to force myself on people who don't want me. I like my life. Integration is wrong. The white people don't want integration. I don't believe in forcing it, and the Muslims don't believe in it. So what's wrong with the Muslims?"

Meanwhile, Elijah Muhammad watched and waited. The Nation of Islam's newspaper, *Muhammad Speaks,* would not send a reporter to cover Clay's fight against Liston and made no mention of Clay's friendship with Malcolm X. The Messenger, like most Americans, probably thought Clay had little chance of winning. If Clay lost, it wouldn't matter if the boxer and Malcolm X were friends, and it wouldn't matter if Clay were a member of the Nation of Islam. He'd be quickly forgotten, tossed aside like yesterday's newspaper.

Clay and Malcolm returned to Miami. One morning over breakfast, Malcolm showed Clay pictures of Floyd Patterson and Sonny Liston accompanied by white Catholic priests who served as spiritual advisors to the boxers. Clay was already familiar with the Nation of Islam's view that Christianity had been forced on black Americans during slavery. Now Malcolm encouraged Clay to make the next logical leap: his fight against Liston was a fight pitting Islam against Christianity.

"This fight is the truth," Malcolm said. In private conservation his voice was gentle yet strong, and calmly reassuring. "It's the Cross and the Crescent fighting in a prize ring — for the first time. It's a modern Crusades — a Christian and a Muslim facing each other with television to beam it off

Telstar for the whole world to see what happens! Do you think Allah has brought about all this intending for you to leave the ring as anything but the champion?"

Clay never lacked for confidence, but now Malcolm offered him even more reason to believe in himself.

"Maybe I can be beat," he said. "I doubt it. But the man is going to have to knock me down and then I'll get up and he'll have to knock me down again and I'll get up and he'll have to knock me down and I'll still get up. I've worked too hard and too long to get this chance. I'm gonna have to be killed before I lose, and I ain't going to die easy."

As the fight drew closer, every reporter in Miami knew about Clay's association with the Nation of Islam.

Federal agents interviewed Angelo and Chris Dundee. The Dundees offered the agents a list of Muslims with whom Clay had been spending time. In an interview years later, Angelo Dundee said he knew nothing about the Nation of Islam at that time and thought the word *Muslim* meant "a piece of cloth." He would also say that he thought a man was entitled to follow whatever religion he liked. Even so, the Dundees were not happy about their fighter's new associates, and when FBI agents came around asking questions, the brothers agreed to help. They told the FBI they were worried that white fans would boycott the Liston fight if word spread about Clay's beliefs. According to an FBI memo dated February 13, 1964, twelve days before the fight: "The DUNDEES stated that they would keep the Miami Office fully informed of any further developments along this line."

In Miami, Clay lived at 4610 NW 15th Court, a small white house in an all-black neighborhood. There were louvered windows in front and a porch big enough for one chair. The screen door was always opening and closing, no need to knock, as children and young men and women from the neighborhood stopped by to see what their local celebrity was doing. At night, Clay showed movies on a big screen, outside in the yard, with moths fluttering in the projector light beam and traffic rumbling by. Most of the time, no one paid much attention to the movie, because there was too much laughter and noise. Clay had a habit of explaining the action on the screen for the children seated around him. Only the scary movies — *The Invasion of the Body*

Snatchers, for one — kept the racket down. When the movies were over, Clay's entourage remained, sleeping two or three to a room. In Clay's bedroom, a tiny oil painting of a New England harbor scene hung on one wall, along with taped-up newspaper articles about the upcoming fight. Every morning, Bundini Brown would wake Clay at 5 or 5:30 so the boxer could lace up a pair of heavy army boots, size 13EEE, and run three or four miles. After running, Clay would eat a big breakfast and head to the Fifth Street Gym, where he would hit the bags, spar a few rounds, and entertain the press corps. After that, he would go home and nap.

Everyone talked about Liston's incredible might, and it was true that the champ was one of the heaviest punchers the sport had ever seen. But sports-writers covering the fight were so bothered by Clay's unusual boxing style and so in awe of Liston's power that they failed to notice something that should have been obvious: Clay was growing. When he'd started his professional career against Tunney Hunsaker in 1960, the Olympic gold medalist weighed 192 pounds. Now, he was up to 210½ pounds, and it looked like he'd added most of the weight in his chest and shoulders. He was strong as new rope. If Clay and Liston had been strangers standing toe to toe in a saloon and getting ready to brawl, Clay might have been the barroom favorite. He was about a decade younger, two inches taller, only seven-and-a-half pounds lighter, and much, much faster. He was also training harder. While Clay was running the streets every morning and punishing his body in brutal sessions with brawny sparring partners at the Fifth Street Gym, Liston was coasting, and the Nilon brothers were letting him coast. Liston worked out in the air-conditioned Surfside Civic Auditorium in North Miami Beach, skipping rope, pounding the heavy bag, absorbing the blows from a medicine ball hurled at his gut, and running a mile or two outside when the mood struck him, which wasn't often. He sparred, but none of his sparring partners were as big or as fast as Clay. At night, Liston ate hot dogs, drank beer, played cards, and screwed around with prostitutes. He was training like a man who believed he could knock out his opponent with a hard stare.

"When has there ever been a heavyweight in history who could punch as hard as Sonny and still be able to take as good a punch as he does?" asked Liston's trainer, Willie Reddish. "Never! That's when."

Clay, on the other hand, was not only in top shape; he was a diligent student of his sport who had watched countless hours of fights on film, especially Jake LaMotta versus Sugar Ray Robinson, a big, bruising puncher going against a faster, smoother man. He watched the same Robinson-LaMotta fight "over and over," he said. When someone asked how he felt about being listed as a ten-to-one underdog, Clay explained calmly why the odds makers were wrong:

"Ten to one? Don't make this man look like a monster. He was nothing 'til he whipped a scared Patterson . . . I'm a natural fighter. I go to bed fightin', eat fightin', and even dream fightin'. This will be a mismatch and the easiest fight of my whole career . . . What makes you think I'm gonna get whipped? Ain't you convinced yet? Do you think I'm gonna stand there like a fool? How's he gonna body punch me? If he falls on me and wants to wrestle, I will tie him up and push him off and pop the left hand. Floyd Patterson didn't move, but I'll move. The secret of my success is speed . . . I'm the fastest heavy who ever lived. Do you suppose that two-hundred-thirty-pound bear is going to catch me? Liston has the whole world believing he is going to whip me. Well, there is nothing more to write about and nothing more to say. I'm ready to fight now. And when I become champ I'm really going to holler. I'll be in such demand all over the world I'll need four chauffeurs and two helicopters to get me around. I'll need twenty-five policemen to guard me. My autographs will cost one hundred dollars apiece. I'll get $20,000 each for my personal appearances.

"So remember that."

Ringside seats for the fight were $250 (about $1,900 in 2016 dollars), the highest price ever seen in boxing and a sign of the great optimism of William B. MacDonald, the former bus driver turned millionaire who had invested $800,000 to bring the bout to Miami. Clay was the greatest self-promoter the pugilistic world had ever seen. He was the brave, young hero out to destroy the ogre who terrorized the countryside. Even the Beatles were publicizing the event. What could go wrong?

But as the fight drew near, it was clear that something *had* gone wrong. Tickets weren't selling. The Miami Beach Convention Center held 15,744 people, but it looked to MacDonald as if he'd be lucky to fill half the seats. The high prices might have been a factor. The press wasn't helping either.

Reporters almost all agreed that Liston was going to crush Clay, and as much as spectators usually adored violence, 250 bucks was a lot to pay to see one man take three steps across a ring and cave in the side of another man's head with a single punch.

Bill MacDonald believed there was another reason for weak interest in the fight. Cassius Clay was supposed to be the plucky young underdog, the fresh-faced kid who might knock off the bully Liston. But news reports on Clay's relationship with Malcolm X and the Nation of Islam had changed the storyline. Now, it was the Black Muslim radical against the bully, and it was not at all clear to fight fans which one was less evil. Ambiguity was not the thing sports fans craved.

Three days before the fight, MacDonald, desperate, went to Clay and told him the fight would be canceled if he didn't retract his statements of support for the Nation of Islam. Given that MacDonald was probably going to lose hundreds of thousands of dollars on the fight, he might have been looking for an excuse to cancel. But his threat to Clay didn't work.

"I ain't denying it because it's true," Clay said, "and if you want to call the fight off that's your business. My religion's more important to me than the fight." It may have been the first time Clay had referred to Islam as his religion.

Harold Conrad urged MacDonald not to cancel the fight.

"Suppose Malcolm X got out of town right away?" Conrad asked. "Would that change your mind?"

When MacDonald said it might, Conrad visited Malcolm and explained the predicament. Malcolm agreed to disappear for a few days as long as he could return in time for the big event.

Clay had been disrespecting Liston for months, waking him from bed, waiting for him in casinos, surprising him at airports, and always with the same refrain: "You're a chump. Big, ugly bear! I'll whup you right now." It was all by design, as he said later. Angry fighters don't think clearly. They don't stick to their plans. They get frustrated, sloppy. Clay knew that Liston was sensitive about his image, that he yearned for respect, and so Clay worked to deny him that respect. By labeling Liston an ugly bear, Clay was tweaking his opponent's most sensitive nerve and perhaps using racism to do it, suggesting that Liston would never be more than a dumb animal. You can strap a shiny belt on a big, ugly bear and call him the heavyweight champion of the world, but he'll still be a big, ugly bear. Clay never relented. He said it so many times that everyone — possibly even Clay — got tired of hearing it. The campaign of psychological warfare built up to the day of the fight, when Clay put on his biggest and best show of all.

On the morning of February 25, a cold, wet, windy day, Clay arrived early for the pre-fight weigh-in at the Convention Center, dressed in a blue denim jacket with the words "Bear Huntin'" embroidered across the shoulders in red. Accompanying him were Sugar Ray Robinson, Bill Faversham, Angelo Dundee, and Bundini Brown. Malcolm X remained out of sight. In unison, Clay and Bundini shouted, "Float like a butterfly, sting like a bee." The men walked into a dressing room, where Clay changed into a white terrycloth robe. Dundee and a member of the Miami Beach Boxing Commission issued stern reminders, telling Clay to "act right," as Dundee put it, as if decorum were expected.

Clay didn't listen. "I'm the champ!" he shouted. "I'm ready to rumble." He and Bundini marched out to the area of the weigh-in, only to find it deserted. They were an hour early. So everyone went away and killed time. At 11:09, Clay and Bundini started screaming again. Liston arrived two minutes later, and the show began.

Now the weigh-in area room was packed with reporters, the air thick with cigarette smoke and the smell of aftershave. No public spectacle was required for the fighters to have their weights recorded prior to a fight, but, like the coin toss before a football game or the seventh-inning stretch in baseball, it was a ritual no one questioned. For reporters who would have to file their stories prior to that evening's fight, it gave them a shot at one last interview and one last scene to describe to their readers. But the press had never seen a weigh-in like this one.

"I am ready to rumble now!" Clay shouted. "I can beat you anytime, chump. Somebody gonna die at ringside tonight! You're scared, chump! You ain't no giant. I'm gonna eat you alive!"

Clay lunged. Bundini held him back. Clay lunged again, and Sugar Ray Robinson tried to pin him against a wall.

"Round eight to prove I'm great!" Clay shouted, holding up eight fingers.

Liston smirked and held up two fingers.

"Hey, sucker!" Clay yelled at Liston as Liston stepped on the scale. "You're a chump! You been tricked, chump!"

Clay continued: "You're too ugly! I'm going to whup you so bad. You're a chump, a chump, a chump . . ."

The reporters in the room thought Clay had lost his mind, that he was suffering a panic attack because he actually feared Liston.

Clay's wild performance was not well received. "Suddenly almost everyone in the room hated Cassius Clay," Murray Kempton wrote. "Sonny Liston just looked at him. Liston used to be a hoodlum; now he was our cop; he was the big Negro we pay to keep sassy Negroes in line and he was just waiting until his boss told him it was time to throw this kid out."

Clay kept it up, even after boxing officials announced he would be fined $2,500 for his behavior. He kept it up even after a boxing commission doctor asked him to sit still so they could measure his pulse rate. He kept it up even after the doctor said his pulse and blood pressure were soaring dangerously high and warned that the fight would be canceled if his condition didn't improve.

Later, he would call it "my finest piece of acting," adding that if he really set his mind to it he could probably become Hollywood's top movie star. As he changed back into his street clothes, Clay asked his entourage for reviews of his performance. How did he do? Great, right? Was Liston upset? He was really upset, right? He answered his own question: "I think he was shaken up."

Fight night finally arrived.

Forty-three of forty-six boxing writers surveyed picked Liston to win, most of them forecasting an early knockout. "It's even money Clay won't last the National Anthem," one writer quipped.

The Convention Center hall was half empty. The crowds stayed away because the tickets were too expensive, because Liston was too tough, and perhaps because a lot of white fight fans couldn't bring themselves to root for either man. But to make matters worse, a local radio station erroneously reported that Clay had been seen at the airport, buying a ticket to a foreign country, fleeing in fear. If anyone was thinking of buying a ticket to the fight at the last moment, that rumor didn't help.

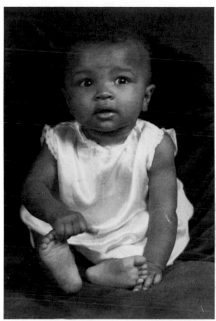

Even as a baby, Cassius Jr. was
not camera shy.
Courtesy of Victor and Brenda Bender

Rudy Clay (left) helps his brother Cassius prepare
for the 1960 Olympics. *Associated Press*

Ready to rumble at age twelve and
95 pounds. *Associated Press*

Cassius Clay Sr. and Odessa complained that the Nation of Islam brainwashed their son, but they remained involved in his life. *Associated Press*

In 1961, the young boxer's entourage included his ever-present brother, his mother, and a small but growing following of women. © *Art Shay*

After a poor start, Clay nailed Alex Miteff with a right to win his ninth professional fight in 1961. © *Art Shay*

Soon after turning pro, Clay left trainer
Joe Martin to work with Angelo Dundee.
Associated Press, Dan Grossi

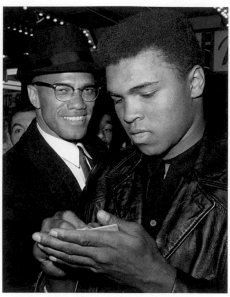

In June 1962, Clay met Malcolm X,
who would become a close friend and
spiritual mentor until their relationship's
abrupt end. *Associated Press*

Heavily favored, Sonny Liston was unprepared for the speed, power, and unrelenting jab of
the challenger Cassius Clay. *Associated Press*

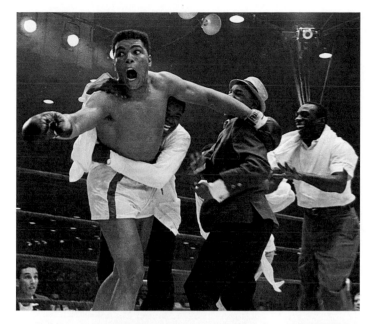

"I shook up the world": Clay becomes heavyweight champ at age twenty-two.
Associated Press

After winning the heavyweight title, Ali announced his loyalty to the Nation of Islam and Elijah Muhammad. Elijah honored the boxer with a new name, Muhammad Ali. Rudy Clay (left) also joined the Nation and became Rahaman Ali. © *Lowell K. Riley*

Sonji Roi, Ali's first wife, was a dancer, a barmaid, and a model. They eventually clashed over her refusal to follow the Nation of Islam's dress code.
Associated Press

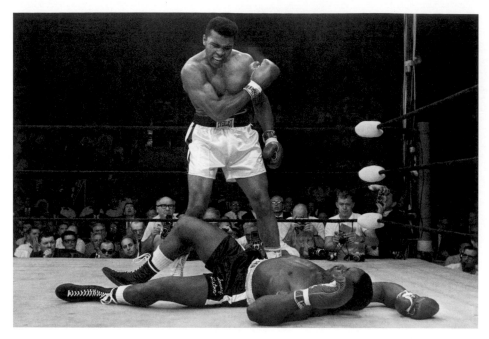

In the remationt, Ali knocked out Liston in the first round, although rumors swirled that Liston took a dive. *Associated Press, John Rooney*

Don King, Ali, Herbert Muhammad, and jazz trumpeter Dizzy Gillespie.
Courtesy of Safiyya Mohammed-Rahmah

Ali loved a crowd, and often found one on 79th Street in Chicago, near the offices of *Muhammad Speaks* and the popular Tiger Lounge.
© *Lowell K. Riley*

Ali cheers at a Nation of Islam rally, dressed in the uniform of the Fruit of Islam, a male-only paramilitary wing within the organization. © *Lowell K. Riley*

Howard Cosell (in hat) interviews Ali in 1967 as the fighter refused induction to the Army, saying he was a conscientious objector. Ali was convicted of draft evasion and banned from boxing. *Associated Press*

"I married a man with no job": Belinda Ali, a faithful member of the Nation of Islam, was seventeen years old and working two jobs when she became Ali's second wife. *Associated Press*

The Fight of the Century: Ali got up but lost a fifteen-round decision to Joe Frazier in one of the greatest and most brutal heavyweight bouts of all time. *Associated Press*

Drew "Bundini" Brown, Ali's friend and chief motivator, tapes the fighter's hands at their new training camp in Deer Lake, Pennsylvania. © *Kwame Brathwaite*

The crowd in the arena was overwhelmingly male, overwhelmingly white, inhaling cigarette and cigar smoke. Malcolm X was ringside in seat number seven, joined by the singer Sam Cooke and the football star Jim Brown. Other celebrities in the crowd included Norman Mailer, Truman Capote, Rocky Marciano, Joe DiMaggio, Yogi Berra, Arthur Godfrey, Ed Sullivan, Joe E. Lewis, George Jessel, Rocky Marciano, and fashion icon Gloria Guinness. Odessa and Cassius Clay Sr. were there too, of course, as were several members of the Louisville Sponsoring Group. Back in Kentucky, more than ten thousand people crowded Louisville's Freedom Hall to watch the broadcast on closed-circuit TV. Around the country, about 700,000 fans paid to watch the broadcast in movie theaters, the biggest closed-circuit audience ever assembled for a fight. Fans paid an average price of $6.42 per ticket, bringing the total revenue to $4.5 million. In 1964, by way of comparison, television rights for all twenty Major League Baseball teams cost $13.6 million. In other words, the broadcast of a single boxing match generated about a third as much revenue as a whole season of baseball, in part because closed-circuit viewing was new, but also because Clay had singlehandedly captured so much attention. The fight was shown in Europe, with an audience estimated at 165 million people, thanks to a deal struck with the National Aeronautics and Space Administration (NASA) that permitted a videotaped broadcast to be bounced by satellite from a NASA station in Maine to a receiving station in Europe, and then transmitted across the continent. So while the arena in Miami was half empty, Clay v. Liston would be seen and heard by one of the largest audiences ever gathered for a single event, a sign of a new era for television and sports and an unparalleled opportunity for a young man starved for fame.

Before his fight, when most observers thought Clay would have been in his dressing room, saying his prayers or writing his will, he was instead in the arena, dressed in a tight-fitting black suit with a black bowtie and white dress shirt, standing on tiptoes to watch his brother Rudy win his first professional fight, an unimpressive, four-round decision over a nobody named Chip Johnson. Siblings understand each other. They see personality traits that others miss, thanks in part to the countless thousands of hours spent together as children, before anyone is sophisticated enough to apply artifice. Rudy would always see his big brother as a hero, and the more famous Cassius became, the more convinced Rudy became that his worship was justified. When Rudy's fight was over, Cassius told him: "After tonight, Rudy," he said, "you won't have to fight no more."

Then, at about 10 p.m., it was big brother's turn. In his dressing room, Clay bowed in the direction of Mecca before walking to the ring. Clay arrived first, as is customary for the challenger. He wore white shorts with a vertical red stripe on each side and a short white robe. Liston entered the ring looking like a giant sweat sock, his neck and shoulders wrapped in white towels, with a white terrycloth robe over the towels and a white hood over his head. He looked solemn, even bored, as he shuffled his feet and stared at the mat. The referee, Barney Felix, instructed the men to join him in the center of the ring, and Clay and Liston stepped close enough to feel each other's breath. It was time for Liston to intimidate, as he had intimidated all his other opponents, but Clay wasn't going for it. Liston stared ahead blankly, motionless. Clay stood straight, possibly rising slightly on his tiptoes. When Felix told the men to shake hands, they didn't. They turned and walked to their corners.

The bell rang and Clay rushed across the ring. Now the crowd in the arena and everyone on TV could see, almost shockingly, that Clay was not only faster but also bigger than Liston. Liston threw a left jab that missed, then another left jab that missed, then a big knockout right that also missed. Clay circled left, away from Liston's left hand. Another Liston left . . . missed. Another . . . missed. And on it went. Liston threw the first eight punches and missed them all. Then, at last, he drove a strong right that struck Clay below the heart. A cry went up from the audience at the sound of leather on skin, and Clay's body thrust backward, but Clay spun away fast and poked Liston with a good jab. Whatever else happened, Clay had survived Liston's first charge and stung Sonny with a good punch of his own. He was not going to fall at the first solid shot as so many had predicted.

Liston attacked again. A wild left missed. Three more jabs missed. Clay stuck a jab in Liston's face, a punch designed to insult more than injure. The men circled. Clay ducked a jab. With a minute to go in the round, Clay's feet slowed. He set himself for a moment, looking for an opportunity to hit Liston hard. Liston looked for an opportunity of his own. Clay struck first, with his best jab of the round, the best punch either man had thrown. It smacked loud enough to be heard on TV. Clay circled halfway around Liston and threw a combination, left-right-left, and then another combination. Clay hit him again and again, with big, wide punches. Every punch Clay threw found a piece of Liston's head. The big, ugly bear, overwhelmed by his speedy attacker, backed up and ducked for cover, then swung wildly and missed with a left hook.

It had been more than two years since an opponent had lasted more than a round with Sonny Liston. Already, Clay had done better than most of the press corps had expected. Liston threw forty-five punches in the first round and landed only six. None seriously hurt Clay. The champ knew now that he wasn't going to win the fight with his usual combination of a scowl and a single punch; he was going to have to work. And he wasn't prepared to work.

Clay clowned for the cameras between rounds, opening his mouth in a big O and looking at the ringside reporters, as if to remind them that no one was going to shut him up. Liston sat patiently and listened to Willie Reddish.

In the second round, Clay slowed. He stood still and allowed Liston to land solid shots. Liston won the round, but Clay was never hurt, and the mere fact that he remained standing after two rounds surprised his critics and may have surprised and dismayed Liston.

In the opening moments of round three, Clay offered another surprise. Instead of running, he came hard after Liston, mixing jabs and hooks in wild flurries. With everyone screaming, Liston hit him back, but Clay responded with more flurries and pinpoint jabs. The punches landed — hard. Liston looked confused.

"He's getting hit with all the punches in the book!" the TV announcer, Steve Ellis, shouted.

Desperate, Liston launched his biggest blow of the night. Clay sidestepped. Liston missed so badly he almost flung himself into the ropes. Clay jabbed again, concentrating his punches on Liston's left eye, where a big red welt was rising, and then, at roughly the midpoint of the round, he began to circle. Clay was catching his breath and jabbing when Liston uncoiled a left hook that jolted Clay's head side to side. Liston, eager to end the fight fast, moved in for the kill as Clay backpedaled and jabbed. The round ended and the fighters returned to their corners.

The ringside press began to buzz. What was happening? How dare Clay put up a fight? The kid had taken Liston's best punch. The last thing anyone expected, least of all Liston, was a slugfest, but that's how this was shaping up. Through four rounds, Liston had landed fifty-eight punches, including at least three that looked potent enough to knock down telephone poles. Clay had landed sixty-nine punches. The vast majority of them were jabs, but they were jabs that cut, jabs that hurt, and jabs that even spectators in the cheap seats could hear snap like lashes on a snare drum when they met skin. Blood seeped from Liston's nose as well as his left eye. The reporters, talking among themselves, agreed that the fight was nearly even. That was shocking enough. But even more shocking was that if anyone had the edge, it was Clay, who had clearly won the opening round, who had proven he could take Liston's best punch, and who was in better condition as the battle wore on.

Then everything changed. Clay sat on his stool, and Dundee began mopping the fighter's forehead.

"There's something in my eyes!" Clay said, blinking.

Dundee wiped his fighter's eyes.

"I can't see. Cut my gloves off!"

Clay was blinded. It wasn't clear why. He wanted to quit.

Meanwhile, at ringside, Joe Louis was telling viewers: "Clay is surprising the whole world."

Clay stood up and put his hands in the air, as if to surrender.

In Dundee's version of the story, it was he, Dundee, who sent the fighter back into the ring, shouting, "Cut the bullshit! We're not quitting now."

Bundini Brown, however, said he was the one who compelled Clay to fight on, saying, "You can't quit. You're not fighting for yourself anymore, you're fighting for God!"

No one in Clay's corner was going to stop the fight. He would have to run until his vision cleared.

"Something's wrong with Clay," Louis told viewers. "Something's wrong with Clay's eyes."

The bell rang. Clay blinked and blinked and tried to keep his distance from Liston. Liston pounded him, first to the body, then to the head. Clay turtled, not even trying to throw punches, just covering up. He reached out feebly for Liston's face and then turtled again. Liston launched big left hooks while Clay hunched over and tried to absorb the blows with his arms. With less than a minute to go, Clay's vision cleared enough for him to tease Liston, sticking his left hand out and rubbing it all over Liston's nose. Liston was dominating the round but he couldn't land the big punch he needed, and the effort sapped him so much he didn't bother to swat away Clay's glove as it massaged his nose. Clay, for his part, had fought sightlessly against the so-called toughest man on the planet for the better part of a round. Billy Conn, the former light-heavyweight champion, had predicted that Liston would knock Clay out with his first punch. Now Clay had taken thirty-seven punches in one round and lived to tell about it. He hadn't quit. He hadn't gone down. For Sonny Liston, that might have hurt more than any punch Clay had thus far landed.

Later, all sorts of speculation would arise as to what had blinded Clay. Film of the fight suggests that Clay didn't start blinking or complaining about his eyes until Angelo Dundee wiped his face with a towel at the end of round four. Some of his Muslim friends had been warning Clay not to trust Dundee, saying the trainer had mafia ties. Now they wondered if Dundee had blinded his own fighter. After the fight, Dundee said he had checked his sponge and towel by wiping his own eyes but there had been nothing wrong with them. Had Liston's trainer put something on Sonny's gloves hoping that it would blind his opponent? Had some kind of liniment used on Liston's cut migrated accidentally to Clay's eyes? Had an ointment used on Liston's aching shoulder somehow blinded Clay? Barney Felix, the referee, said he checked Liston's gloves and found no trace of any foreign substance, but no one would ever know, and three minutes later no one would care.

Liston's face showed cuts and welts as he sat in his corner, waiting for the bell to signal the start of the sixth round. Over the past three and a half years, all his fights combined had lasted less than six rounds. Liston was a demolition man; he knocked things down and moved on. He was not accustomed to work that taxed his attention span or his stamina, and, now, Clay was coming out clear-eyed and as fast as ever, having proved he could take Liston's best shots. Clay threw eight jabs to open the round, finding Liston's face at the end of every punch.

"Easy target!" Steve Ellis told viewers. "EASY!"

Clay threw combinations that jolted Liston's head. Liston jabbed in return but never launched a sustained attack. Clay was hurting the champion, and the champion could do nothing about it. He was too old, too slow, and found his tank nearly empty. The round was more than a minute gone before Liston connected with a punch.

Clay could fight like this all night long, mixing jabs and combinations and waltzing circles around the ring, while Liston's fatigue and frustration would only grow. Clay could see it and feel it. With a minute left in the sixth round, he attacked with blurring speed. He hit Liston with two left hooks to the head. Liston wobbled. He was in danger. The bell rang, and Liston walked solemnly to his corner.

As Liston sat, his trainers put ice under his swollen eyes and rubbed his left shoulder. The champ was a mess.

"I think Clay's got all the confidence he needs now," Joe Louis said. "I think he's gonna win it now."

The bell rang to begin the seventh.

Clay, ready, rose from his stool.

Liston did not.

"You gotta fight!" one of the men in his corner shouted. "You gotta get up, Sonny! You're gonna be a bum all your life if you don't get up!"

Liston wouldn't budge

Suddenly Clay was dancing and leaping and raising his hands in the air. Liston had quit. The fight was over, and Clay was the new heavyweight champion.

In barrooms and movie theaters across the country, the cry rang out: Liston had thrown the fight, thrown the heavyweight championship of the world. How else to explain it? Liston said later that he had hurt his left shoulder in the first round of the fight on a wild punch that missed its mark. After the sixth round, he said, he had numbness running from the shoulder to the forearm. He would later get a note from his doctor to prove it. Still, it was hard to believe that a champion would give up so easily. Hard to believe that a man could throw 171 jabs with his left hand, including 21 in the final round, and then say his bum left shoulder made it impossible to go on. Hard to believe Liston would have thrown three times more lefts than rights in the final round if his left shoulder had been seriously impaired. Hard to believe a man as tough as Liston, a man who had gone the distance once with a broken jaw, couldn't fight through numbness. Hard to believe that a man with the most powerful right hand in boxing and a man supposedly impervious to punches wouldn't carry on one-handed given the stakes.

Later, there would be rumors that members of Liston's camp bet $300,000 on Clay at seven-to-one odds. Also later there would be news that the Nilon brothers paid fifty thousand dollars to the Louisville Sponsoring Group for the rights to Clay's first fight after Liston — a deal that made sense only if they believed Clay would win.

But those were mysteries to be unwrapped at another time, if ever. In the meantime, the arena erupted in pandemonium. Clay was up, running around the ring, Bundini wrapped around him like a human cloak, brother Rudy following behind.

"I am the king!" Clay shouted. "I am the king! King of the world! Eat your words! Eat! Eat your words!"

ABC radio reporter Howard Cosell reached Clay first, sticking a microphone in front of Clay's face as the fighter peered over a row of newspapermen. "I am the greatest! I am the greatest! I am the king of the world!" Clay shouted.

Cosell asked Clay what had happened in the fourth round.

"He had liniment on his hands, gloves," Clay said. "I couldn't see all that round. Almighty God was with me! Almighty God was with me!"

He moved over to a TV camera and continued, "I'm the greatest fighter who ever lived! I'm so great I don't have a mark on my face, and I upset Sonny Liston, and I just turned twenty-two years old. I must be the greatest! I showed the world! I talk to God every day! If God's with me, can't nobody be against me! I shook up the world! I know God! I know the real God!"

He raised his arms in the air.

"I'm the king of the world! I'm pretty! I'm a baaad man! I shook up the world! I shook up the world! I shook up the world!"

14

Becoming Muhammad Ali

It was not the wildest victory party in boxing history, but it may have been the oddest. While the Louisville Sponsoring Group hurried to organize a celebration at the Roney Plaza Hotel, Clay and Malcolm X slipped away to a soda fountain for big bowls of vanilla ice cream. From there, the men drove to the Hampton House motel, where Sam Cooke, Jim Brown, Howard Bingham, Rudy Clay, and a few others gathered in Malcolm's room for a night of sober conversation that lasted deep into the morning.

Cooke, nicknamed "The King of Soul," was the man behind the hit songs "Chain Gang" and "You Send Me," a man who had recently cofounded a record label to assert control of his business affairs, and a man, at age thirty-three, who had never cared for the Nation of Islam but admired much of Malcolm's message. Brown was one of America's greatest athletes, star fullback of the Cleveland Browns. While he was not a member of the Nation of Islam, the twenty-eight-year-old Brown respected Malcolm X and Elijah Muhammad for instilling pride in black people.

"Well, Brown," Malcolm said to the football player that night, "don't you think it's time for this young man to stop spouting off and get serious?"

Brown agreed. It was time for Clay to get serious. But Brown also sensed a crisis coming. Clay would soon be forced to choose between his two spiritual mentors, Elijah Muhammad and Malcolm X, and the choice would be difficult and potentially dangerous.

Clay stretched out and dozed on Malcolm's bed at one point. But he didn't sleep long. Sometime after two in the morning, he returned to his home, where neighbors were waiting on the lawn to congratulate him.

The next morning Clay did his best to get serious. He returned to the Miami Beach Convention Hall for a press conference and answered questions plainly and simply, without rhyming or shouting. He told reporters that he intended to retire as soon as he made enough money. Boxing was a means to an end. He didn't want to hurt anyone, and he didn't want to be hurt. If there had been any doubt that his histrionics before the fight had been part of a scheme to discombobulate Sonny Liston, Clay's mild post-fight demeanor proved it.

"I'm through talking," he said. "All I have to do is be a nice, clean gentleman."

But the press wasn't letting him off so easily. Wasn't it true, a reporter asked, that Clay was a "card-carrying member of the Black Muslims?"

With that, Clay's calm demeanor cracked.

"'Card-carrying?' What does that mean?" he asked. Members of the Nation of Islam didn't like being called Black Muslims, and "card-carrying" suggested shades of McCarthyism. He continued, "I believe in Allah and in peace. I don't try to move into white neighborhoods. I don't want to marry a white woman. I was baptized when I was twelve, but I didn't know what I was doing. I'm not a Christian anymore. I know where I'm going and I know the truth and I don't have to be what you want me to be. I'm free to be what I want."

Suddenly, this was no longer a press conference about a boxing match; it was a declaration of independence. Clay was casting aside the role black athletes were supposed to play in society and striking out on his own. He was taking stands on race, politics, and religion, refusing to be owned or manipulated by anyone.

Black and white people, he said, were better off apart. "In the jungle," he said, "lions are with lions, and tigers with tigers, and redbirds stay with redbirds, and bluebirds with bluebirds."

Although they were likely informed by discussions the night before with Malcolm X, Jim Brown, and Sam Cooke, Clay's remarks were his own. He could not have spoken more clearly in scorning integration or in renouncing Christianity in favor of Islam, but his heaviest punch was this: "I don't have to be what you want me to me to be." With that, he rejected the old promise that black people would get a fair chance if they played by the rules, worked hard, and showed proper respect for the white establishment. It wasn't just Sonny Liston who couldn't touch him, he suggested. Nobody could. Nobody could tell him how to behave or how to worship God. He didn't know exactly what he believed or what he wanted to be — he was only twenty-two years old, after all — but he had seen enough to understand the liberating power of self-determination.

The newsmen scrambled. What was this kid talking about? How could a black person oppose integration? What was the Nation of Islam exactly? A religion? A cult? A hate-mongering gang of thugs? And how were they supposed to write about such subtle matters within the confines of the sports pages?

The next day, Clay and Malcolm X continued to educate the white working press. Clay said he had been studying Islam for months and had not made his decision lightly.

"A rooster crows only when it sees the light," he said. "I have seen the light and I'm crowing."

He explained that he was not a part of a fringe group, that there were 750 million Muslims around the world. "You call it Black Muslims, I don't," he said. "The real name is Islam. That means peace. Yet people brand us a hate group. They say we want to take over the country. They say we're Communists. That is not true. Followers of Allah are the sweetest people in the world. They don't carry knives. They don't tote weapons. They pray five times a day. The women wear dresses that come all the way to the floor and they don't commit adultery. The men don't marry white women. All they want to do is live in peace with the world. They don't hate anybody. They don't want to stir up any kind of trouble."

Clay expressed a controversial view in asserting that integration would never work, but he was hardly being cynical. In America, black citizens were still excluded, officially or unofficially, from countless neighborhoods, churches, labor unions, social clubs, corporate offices, hospitals, hotels, retirement homes, and schools. There were no black governors, no black U.S. senators, no black Supreme Court justices in 1964. Of the 435 members of the House of Representatives, only 5 were black. It was certainly reasonable for

Clay, who had never attended an integrated school or lived in an integrated neighborhood, to believe that democratic principles did not apply to people of color, and, more to the point, that white people intended to keep it that way. Most of American history told him so.

"I get telephone calls every day," Clay said. "They want me to carry signs. They want me to picket. They tell me it would be a wonderful thing if I married a white woman because this would be good for brotherhood." But to do so would be to invite violent attack, he said. And to what end? "I don't want to be blown up. I don't want to be washed down sewers. I just want to be happy with my own kind. I'm a good boy. I never have done anything wrong. I have never been in jail . . . I like white people. I like my own people. They can live together without infringing on each other. You can't condemn a man for wanting peace. If you do, you condemn peace itself."

In his last refrain, he sounded more like Malcolm X than ever. And no wonder: the men had been nearly inseparable for weeks. Malcolm not only enjoyed Clay's company but also, increasingly, had come to believe that the boxer had an opportunity to shake up black-white relations and rally more young black men and women to join a popular uprising more aggressive than the one led by Martin Luther King Jr. "The power structure had successfully created the image of the American Negro as someone with no confidence, no militancy," Malcolm told one reporter shortly after Clay's victory. "And they had done this by giving him images of heroes that weren't truly militant or confident. And now here comes Cassius, the exact contrast of everything that was representative of the Negro image. He said he was the greatest, all of the odds were against him, he upset the odds makers, he won . . . They knew that if people began to identify with Cassius and the type of image he was creating they were going to have trouble out of these Negroes because they'd have Negroes walking around the streets saying 'I'm the greatest.'"

Malcolm understood how ordinary black men and women were responding to the young boxer. They were unbothered by his embrace of the Nation of Islam and unbothered by his rejection of integration, even if they didn't share his religion or his politics. The little that most white Americans knew about the Nation of Islam came from a 1959 Mike Wallace documentary called *The Hate That Hate Produced,* which made the Nation sound as bizarre as it was frightening. Black Americans, however, knew that the Nation, for all its oddities, was a powerful grassroots organization dedicated to self-empowerment. They knew that Clay, regardless of his religion, carried himself with pride.

"I remember the day I became aware of the Champ," the writer Walter Mosley said. "My mother was driving me to school after he won the heavyweight title from Sonny Liston. At a crosswalk a black man passing in front of our car suddenly turned and, raising his fists into the air, announced loudly, 'I am the greatest!' I was frightened by the man's violent outburst, but even then I heard the pride and hurt, the dashed ambition and the shard of hope that cut through him. Cassius Clay's declaration had become his own. The Black Pride movement was on, and one of its pillars were those four words."

On the same day Clay clarified his religious views, February 26, 1964, Elijah Muhammad spoke to thousands of Muslims at a Saviours' Day assembly at the Chicago Coliseum. Muhammad did not address his ongoing rift with Malcolm X, but he did use the occasion to welcome Cassius Clay to the Nation of Islam, and he offered Cassius's brother Rudy a seat on the dais. Until that moment, Muhammad had reserved judgment on the boxer, perhaps because he thought Clay would lose and also perhaps because the Messenger took a dim view of professional sports.

Elijah Muhammad opposed "sport and play," said John Ali, who served as national secretary under Muhammad at the time and functioned as the Nation of Islam's top business manager. But the Messenger overcame his bias in this instance, according to John Ali, because he thought he could protect Clay from the white businessmen who ran boxing and treated black boxers like slaves, casting them aside, penniless and brain damaged, when they could no longer perform.

That may indeed have been Elijah Muhammad's primary reason to welcome Cassius Clay, but the Messenger no doubt saw additional benefits. Clay had just become one of the most famous black men on the planet — possibly *the* most famous. He was clean-living, youthful, and handsome — a symbol of strength with a rebellious streak as wide as an interstate highway. Until then, Malcolm X had been the most visible representative of the Nation of Islam, but, in Muhammad's view, Malcolm was causing too much trouble. Cassius Clay did not have Malcolm's talent for leadership, but he would attract more attention than Malcolm ever had, and he would cause less trouble, too.

· · ·

After the Liston fight, Clay drove from Miami to New York, where he took a room at the Hotel Theresa in Harlem.

In an interview with *Jet,* a magazine with a mostly black readership, Clay announced that he was entering a new phase in life, one in which he would devote himself to religious observance and the pursuit of racial equality. "My mouth has made me the greatest, but nobody can be big in this country if they're black," he said. His drive from Florida proved that, he said, when he found himself unwelcome in restaurants along the way and forced to fill up on bologna. He said he was thinking about retiring from the boxing ring and devoting his life to traveling and "seeking a peaceful, workable solution to the race problem." Another possibility: "I just might run for mayor of New York or something."

His transition from boisterous boxer to calm spiritual leader proceeded gradually. One day, Clay went to a theater in Times Square to cheer for himself while watching a replay of the Liston fight. On another day, he and Sam Cooke visited the Columbia Records building to record a new song, a raucous version of "The Gang's All Here," with Clay interrupting the session at one point to instruct the engineer: "Play that over. I don't think you've got my voice loud enough in there yet. Remember, I'm the loudest."

On March 2, black newspapers around the country, following up on a report first published in the *New York Courier,* announced that Malcolm X might soon break with the Nation of Islam and form a new organization with the backing of Clay. Citing an unnamed "insider," the reporter for the *Courier* said Clay was "solidly in Malcolm's corner and would lend the influence of his nation-wide standing to any efforts of his friend to establish a cult of his own." Malcolm's ambition, according to the news reports, was "to participate more actively with other Negro groups in every phase of the current Negro revolution," while Elijah Muhammad had long insisted that his organization avoid political engagement. The same day, Clay told a reporter from the *Amsterdam News* he was changing his name to Cassius X. The press took this as another sign that Clay would stand in solidarity with brother Malcolm. Elijah Muhammad took notice, saying that Malcolm was "nursing" the young boxer "like a baby," according to an FBI informant.

On March 4, Malcolm and Cassius toured the United Nations, where Clay told African and Asian delegates he was eager to visit their countries and especially eager to see Mecca. Cassius and Malcolm talked about making the trip together. Perhaps it was Malcolm who first realized that the heavyweight champion could become an important international political figure, but his friend the boxer soon caught on.

"I'm the champion of the whole world," Cassius said, "and I want to meet the people I'm champion of."

Two days later, on March 6, Elijah Muhammad announced in a radio address that boxing's heavyweight champion, Cassius Clay, now a follower of the Nation of Islam, was to receive the honor of a full Muslim name.

"This Clay name has no divine meaning," Elijah Muhammad said. "Muhammad Ali is what I will give to him as long as he believes in Allah and follows me."

The last two words of that pronouncement would prove as important as the first two.

In a phone call, Elijah Muhammad told the boxer that his new name carried special meaning. Most members of the Nation of Islam merely replaced their so-called slave names with the letter X, as Malcolm Little had done and as Cassius Clay had intended to do. Only in unusual instances did Elijah Muhammad assign full Muslim names to his followers, and such honors were bestowed in most instances after many years of loyal service. Cassius Clay's new name was special for another reason as well, as the Messenger explained: the founder of the Nation of Islam, W. D. Fard, had once gone by the name Muhammad Ali, among others. "Muhammad," he explained, meant worthy of praise. "Ali" meant lofty.

Cassius Marcellus Clay Jr. had always adored his name. He had said it reminded him of a Roman gladiator, that it was the prettiest name he had ever heard, perfect for the prettiest and greatest heavyweight champion of all time. But now Elijah Muhammad called on him to abandon the name, and the boxer agreed without hesitation.

Malcolm X got the news when the voice of Elijah Muhammad came over his car radio in New York. To Malcolm, Elijah Muhammad's motive was obvious: the Messenger was in poor health and under attack for his sexual behavior. If he didn't fight, he might lose the organization he built. Malcolm X already posed a threat, but he would pose a far greater threat with the popular young boxer in his camp. That's why Elijah was trying to buy his impressionable young follower's loyalty with a designation of honor that suggested

Muhammad Ali would hold a privileged ranking within the Nation of Islam and a special relationship with the organization's leader. It was a political move. "He did it to prevent him from coming with me," Malcolm said.

Malcolm wasn't the only one angered by Elijah Muhammad's announcement. Cassius Clay Sr. couldn't understand why his son would abandon a name that was not only easy on the ear but also increasingly valuable. And to trade it for "Muhammad Ali," a name no one could spell? "They've been hammering at him and brainwashing him since he was eighteen," Cash Clay said. "He's so confused he doesn't even know where he's at." The Muslims were ruining both of his boys, Cash complained, noting that Rudy, too, had committed to this new faith. "They should run those Black Muslims out of the country before they ruin other fine young people."

Odessa Clay was angry as well. "They don't like me because I'm light," she said, referring to the shade of her skin. She also complained that the Nation of Islam never would have attracted her son if the Louisville Sponsoring Group hadn't sent him to Miami. Odessa conveniently overlooked the fact that her husband had raised their boys on stories of lynching and rape and the white man's endless deceit, laying the groundwork for the boys' rebellion.

Joe Louis joined Odessa in blaming the fighter's white management team for failing to protect their boxer, saying, "They stayed on one side of town and him on the other." Lyman T. Johnson, president of the Louisville chapter of the NAACP and one of the boxer's former history teachers, said he was "embarrassed for Clay, who is naïve." Louisville's black newspaper, the *Defender,* expressed concern that the young man's stance would hurt the integration movement. Martin Luther King, now at the height of his influence, voiced his disappointment, as well: "When he joined the Black Muslims and started calling himself Cassius X," King said, "he became a champion of racial segregation and that is what we are fighting against. I think perhaps Cassius should spend more time proving his boxing skill and do less talking."

What the newly named Muhammad Ali and others in the Nation of Islam failed to understand, said Jesse Jackson, who worked alongside Dr. King, is that civil rights activists were not merely fighting for integration; they were not merely fighting for black and white children to be mingled in society. The real fight was to kill segregation, to destroy the laws and customs that forced black Americans to accept second-class schools, second-class jobs, second-class neighborhoods, and second-class lives. "The idea that integration was our goal, that was the white people's definition of our struggle," Jackson said. "We were fighting for desegregation, fighting for the right to use public facilities, not just to sit beside white people. We were marching against the humiliation of the fact that your money can't buy a hot dog, can't rent a Holiday Inn. It was sense of the dollar dignity. We weren't fighting just to be with white people."

Ferdie Pacheco, the doctor who worked in the corner for many of Dundee's fighters, described Muhammad Ali as an overgrown child driven fundamentally by a desire to be contrarian. "He longs to figure out what the public expects him to do and then do something else, even if it's the wrong thing sometimes," Pacheco said. Angelo Dundee agreed: "I think he is involved with these Muslims just because people don't want him to be."

White sportswriters — old cigar butts of men, as Norman Mailer called them — were horrified and dismissive. Jimmy Cannon wrote, "The fight racket, since its rotten beginnings, has been the red-light district of sports. But this is the first time it has been turned into an instrument of mass hate. It has maimed the bodies of numerous men and ruined their minds but now, as one of Elijah Muhammad's missionaries, Clay is using it as a weapon of wickedness in an attack on the spirit. I pity Clay and abhor what he represents. In the years of hunger during the Depression, the Communists used famous people the way the Black Muslims are exploiting Clay. This is a sect that deforms the beautiful purpose of religion." Boxer Max Schmeling had been a dupe for Hitler and the Nazis, but, according to Cannon, this was worse.

It was not hard to see why a white man of Cannon's generation might think Ali's behavior worse than Schmeling's. Black men in 1964 seemed to be taking over everything, from basketball to boxing to the streets of America's cities. There had never been such an overtly political athlete in America, and certainly not a black one. "What white America demands in her black champions," the Black Panther Eldridge Cleaver said a few years later, "is a brilliant, powerful body, and a dull, bestial mind — a tiger in the ring and a pussycat outside the ring." With one mighty roar, Muhammad Ali announced the old rule no longer applied.

Throughout his boxing career, Cassius Clay had worked hard to generate controversy and rankle boxing fans, mostly with the goal of selling tickets and spreading his fame. Now, as Muhammad Ali, he didn't have to work at all. With his new name and his expressed allegiance to a radical religious group poorly understood by most Americans, he was genuinely distrusted and disliked — and more widely discussed than ever.

Until that point, the Louisville Sponsoring Group had not only taken care of his finances; they had bestowed on him an important endorsement. These white men with southern accents and seersucker suits had helped to moderate his public image, like a wealthy benefactor standing behind a long-haired, dope-smoking artist. They had sent the message to fans and potential business partners that this young man could be trusted no matter how much he mouthed off, that it was all in the name of sport and capitalism. But now, the relationship became complicated in ways the Louisville businessmen could have never imagined and scarcely knew how to discuss. Jules Alberti, the head of the nation's biggest celebrity endorsement agency, questioned whether the boxer would be a "good label for anybody's product."

If those challenges were not enough, the Louisville businessmen still faced legal and ethical questions stemming from the Liston fight. Had it been fixed? The evidence remained inconclusive and at times contradictory. The once indomitable Liston had surely looked old and slow. But if Liston had planned to lose, what about the conspiracy theory going around that suggested he had somehow blinded Cassius Clay prior to the fifth round? And what about that fifth round? The greatest knockout puncher of his time couldn't knock out a blind man? And what about the finish? The toughest man in the world forfeits his title because of a strained tendon in his arm? None of it added up, and the calculation grew more muddled when word leaked to the press that Liston's management company, Inter-Continental Promotions, had signed a deal to promote Clay's next fight and name his next opponent. That gave Liston's team a financial incentive to see Clay win, and it raised enough suspicion to spur an investigation by the Antitrust and Monopoly Subcommittee of the U.S. Senate's Judicial Committee.

After the fight, a memo circulated among members of the Louisville Sponsoring Group confessing that the Louisville businessmen had been given no choice about the rematch clause. "At all stages of the negotiation . . . the Nilons made it absolutely clear that there could be no fight without the guarantee to Liston and Inter-Continental of a return bout if Clay should win the championship," according to this document, found only recently in the personal archives of one of the members of the group. Since the Nilons and the Louisville Sponsoring Group knew that the World Boxing Association disliked rematch clauses, the two sides agreed to hide the second contract from the WBA. They also agreed that the Nilons would hold some of the money from the first fight in escrow to guarantee that the rematch clause would be honored. "In other words," the memo continued, "the question of a return bout was a non-negotiable item."

When the Senate subcommittee met, a lawyer for Inter-Continental admitted that Liston and the Nilons held the right to choose Clay's next opponent and to promote his next fight, but he insisted there was nothing shady about it. "We were just being smart businessmen," the lawyer, Garland Cherry, said. "We made the agreement . . . just in case Clay should become champion. It is a legitimate contract."

When the investigation concluded, the subcommittee found no evidence of a fix. Something stunk, but no one could be sure what it was, and there was always the possibility that it was nothing more than the usual foul odor that hung around boxing.

That still left the Louisville Sponsoring Group in a squeeze, with the Nation of Islam on one side looking to assert control over Muhammad Ali's career, and the Nilon brothers on the other maintaining the contractual right to decide where and whom Ali would fight next.

Every day brought more troubling news. First, the president of the WBA called for Ali to be stripped of his title — not because of suspicions that the Liston fight had been fixed but because of Ali's association with the Nation of Islam, conduct "setting a very poor example for America's youth." On April 26, 1964, another WBA official warned that a Clay-Liston rematch "would make suckers out of millions of American boxing followers." Then came a report from the army that Ali had twice failed his pre-induction mental exam, which caused many reporters and boxing fans to assume that the boxer had taken a dive on the test to avoid service. After all, how could so clever a man be deemed too stupid to carry a rifle? How could the world's greatest professional fighter be designated unfit to fight for his country? The army said there was no evidence the boxer had flunked intentionally, and his former teachers at Central High agreed, telling reporters they were not at all surprised at the results.

The test Ali flunked included questions like these:

A man works from 6 in the morning till 3 in the afternoon with 1 hour for lunch. How many hours did he work?
   a) 7 b) 8 c) 9 d) 10

A clerk divided a number by 3.5 when it should be multiplied by 4.5. His answer is 3. What is the correct answer?
   a) 5.25 b) 10.50 c) 15.75 d) 47.25

Test takers needed to get thirty correct out of one hundred to pass, but Ali didn't make the grade. He said he had spent fifteen or twenty minutes "scratching around" on a question about apples and then found that he had run out of time for a whole row of additional questions.

"I just said I'm the greatest; I never said I was the smartest," he told reporters.

A reporter asked what would happen if he passed the test next time; would he ask for exemption from service as a conscientious objector based on his religious beliefs?

"Not as a conscientious objector," he said. "I don't like that name. It sounds ugly."

15

Choice

Muhammad Ali faced a decision: Elijah Muhammad or Malcolm X?
It was a choice that would change the course of the boxer's life and many others'.

With his victory over Sonny Liston, Ali had become one of the most visible black men in the world. In 1964, Malcolm X appeared in 100 articles in the *New York Times*. Elijah Muhammad's name appeared in 31. Although he fought only once the entire year, Muhammad Ali appeared in 203 *Times* articles (although the paper was still calling him Cassius Clay). Among black Americans, only Martin Luther King Jr., who won the Nobel Peace Prize that year, would receive more attention from the nation's leading newspaper, with 230 articles containing his name. In addition to newspapers, TV news broadcasts carried reports from the frontlines of the civil rights struggle, with black-and-white images of fire hoses, tear gas, and pointed guns, along with brief snippets of commentary from segregationists and civil rights activists. But those reports were boiled down to a few minutes per night and edited by white men. Editing mattered, and editing helps explain why Muhammad Ali held such power. He defied the white media's filters better than any black man alive — perhaps even better than Dr. King.

Dick Gregory, the comedian and activist who spent time in 1964 with Ali, King, and Malcolm X, explained it this way: "When you saw King, you saw sound bites. Most folks never heard, 'I have a dream.' They heard little tidbits of it." Ali was different because he was a boxer, Gregory said, and boxing put him in a realm white men couldn't control. "This motherfucker would be in your fucking face for as many rounds as the fight last. King never got that kind of time. You watch him beat a white boy down to the ground and there ain't a goddamn thing you can do about it. Then he'd go and talk, *praising Allah!* This had never happened before. Never, ever happened before in the history of the planet . . . Ali was everything everybody wanted their child to be, except some ignorant-ass white folks, and they don't count." Gregory said that black men and women all over the world saw Ali doing these outrageous things, things black people were never supposed to do, saying things black people were never supposed to say, saying it all on live television — and getting away with it. And it made them ask, "C'mon, Ali, who you praying to?"

In the campaign to win Ali's loyalty, Malcolm X enjoyed greater intimacy, but Elijah Muhammad had the power. Malcolm himself had once told Ali: "Nobody leaves the Muslims without trouble." Ali knew that choosing the Nation of Islam would cost him his friendship with Malcolm. But he may have feared that choosing Malcolm would cost him his life. In the end, he chose the father figure over the brother. In fact, Cash Clay and Elijah Muhammad were not entirely dissimilar. They both bewailed the tyranny of white men. They both enjoyed the company of women other than their wives. But Cash Clay had been violent, physically threatening and attacking his wife and children, while Elijah Muhammad was Cash Clay's opposite in that respect, a man who seemed to never raise his voice, who was never seen drunk, a man whose power rested in quiet confidence and calm deliberation. In that way, Elijah Muhammad represented more than a father figure; he was also a powerful jab to the face of Cassius Sr. What better way for a son to punish the father than to replace him — and to drop his name, too?

All over the country, followers of the Nation of Islam were being forced to choose between the Messenger and his disciple. When Malcolm announced he was forming his own organization, Muslim Mosque, Inc., the Nation of Islam lost about 20 percent of its membership in a matter of weeks, according to Karl Evanzz's biography of Elijah Muhammad. Louis Farrakhan, then known as Louis X, recalled it as a trying time for many in the organization. "I, who was mentored by brother Malcolm, and Ali, who was mentored by brother Malcolm, had to make a decision," he recalled as he sat in a gazebo outside his home one recent day in southern Michigan. "A very painful decision. I didn't just love brother Malcolm. I adored him, and would have given my life to protect his life because of the great value that he was to the Honorable Elijah Muhammad and the Nation of Islam. I had to decide to break my relationship with brother Malcolm or break my relationship with my teacher, the Honorable Elijah Muhammad. And it was a no-brainer; I had to go with the man that taught brother Malcolm, that taught me. I didn't come to follow brother Malcolm. I came to follow Elijah Muhammad . . . So I stayed the course. And so did Ali."

Malcolm was already in danger. But when Muhammad Ali stopped taking his calls, Malcolm became more easily expendable. Elijah Muhammad ordered Malcolm to vacate his house and turn over his car, both of which had been paid for by the Nation of Islam. The Messenger predicted in his public statements that Malcolm was sure to return, begging forgiveness. Privately, however, he warned that the only way to stop Malcolm was "to get rid of him the way Moses and the others did their bad ones," according to an FBI report. That report, dated March 23, 1964, continued, "ELIJAH states that with these hypocrites, when you find them cut their heads off."

Although he knew there were rumors that he would be killed, Malcolm grew more rebellious once separated from the Nation of Islam. He positioned his new organization as an alternative to Martin Luther King Jr.'s nonviolent movement and urged black activists to stop worrying about their "personal prestige, and concentrate our united efforts toward solving the unending hurt that is being done daily to our people here in America." By 1964, groups such as the Student Nonviolent Coordinating Committee and the Congress of Racial Equality were adopting more militant stances. Race riots would soon erupt in several cities in the Northeast. In one of its early statements released to the press, the Muslim Mosque declared, "Concerning nonviolence: it is criminal to teach a man not to defend himself when he is the constant victim of brutal attacks. It is legal and lawful to own a shotgun or a rifle . . . When our people are being bitten by dogs, they are within their rights to kill those dogs."

The reinvented Malcolm X expressed support for desegregation and voter registration. He studied proper Muslim rituals and learned that Elijah Muhammad's version of Muslim theology and practice was far from orthodox. He also began telling reporters with no trace of doubt that the Nation of Islam was plotting to murder him.

In April, Malcolm flew to Egypt, traveling under his own new Muslim name, El-Hajj Malik el-Shabazz. From Cairo, Malcolm went to Jeddah, Saudi

Arabia. Soon after, he began the Hajj, the Muslim pilgrimage to Mecca that is often described as the most important event in the life of a Muslim. After seeing Muslims of every color, Malcolm expressed regret for past statements in which he condemned the entire white race. "I am not a racist, and I do not subscribe to any of the tenets of racism," he wrote in a letter to the *Egyptian Gazette.* He continued, "My religious pilgrimage to Mecca has given me a new insight into the true brotherhood of Islam, which encompasses all the races of mankind."

Malcolm also traveled to Lagos and Ibadan in Nigeria, and then on to Ghana, giving lectures and meeting with religious and political leaders at every stop. At the Hotel Ambassador in Accra, as he was preparing to go to the airport for a flight to Morocco, Malcolm spotted Ali, who was making his own month-long visit to Africa. It had been almost three months since Ali's fight with Sonny Liston. He had done little training in that time, and it showed. His gut was soft and his cheeks full. No date had been set for his next fight, and, as a result, the boxer was enjoying his first sustained rest in years. Even with a few extra pounds on his frame, Ali was instantly recognized everywhere he went, and he was thrilled to know that accounts of his latest boxing triumph and his conversion to Islam had made him an international celebrity. Thousands greeted him at the airport in Ghana, and more lined the street to watch him wave from his convertible on the way to the hotel.

"Brother Muhammad!" Malcolm called out upon spotting his friend in the lobby. "Brother Muhammad!"

Malcolm was in a white robe and carried a walking stick. He had let his beard grow out. Ali greeted his former mentor coldly.

"You left the Honorable Elijah Muhammad," he said. "That was the wrong thing to do."

Malcolm said nothing.

Once Malcolm was out of earshot, Ali turned on him. "Man, did you get a look at him?" the fighter asked his traveling companion, Herbert Muhammad, the son of Elijah. "Dressed in that funny white robe and wearing a beard and walking with that cane that looked like a prophet's stick? Man, he's gone. He's gone so far out he's out completely. Doesn't that just go to show, Herbert, that Elijah is the most powerful? Nobody listens to that Malcolm anymore."

It was no way to treat a friend, and it was a sign of Ali's complexity and contradictions. From the depths of the kind and loyal Ali, the jovial Ali, up rose the cruel Ali, the self-centered, insolent young man who flared in anger when he felt threatened.

This was Ali's first full day in Africa, and he was eager to begin his tour. He told a reporter from the *New York Times* he looked forward to visiting the United Arab Republic (the outcome of a political union between Egypt and Syria), where the law would allow him to take four wives. He planned to bring them home and put them up in a new, $100,000 house. "It'll be like a castle and I'll have a throne room for my heavyweight crown. One of my wives — Abigail — will sit beside me feeding me grapes. Another one — Susie — will be running olive oil over my beautiful muscles. Cecilia will be shining my shoes. And then there'll be Peaches. I don't know yet what she'll do. Sing or play music, maybe."

With that settled, he returned to another favorite topic: money.

"Hey, Herbert," he said, looking at his watch. "When's the man coming to take us diamond hunting?"

"What man?" Herbert Muhammad asked.

"That man we met last night who told us about the diamond mines here. I heard they got a lake somewhere so full of diamonds you just wade in and feel around." Perhaps he thought he would soon need four engagement rings. In any case, a Ghanaian overheard Ali and told him there were no such lakes.

"Well," he said, "I'm still going to go diamond hunting wherever they hunt them here."

After breakfast, Ali went looking for admirers. He ran from the dining room to the terrace, where he shouted to waiters, bellboys, hotel guests, and a group of small boys loitering in the driveway. He called for their attention.

"Who's the king?" he shouted.

"You are," came voices from the crowd. "You are."

"Louder!" Ali demanded. "Now, who's the greatest?"

"You are!" came the answer.

"Okay," he said, headed for his convertible. "Let's go to the beach."

Ali met with political leaders and made headlines everywhere he went, although some of his hosts were struck by his shaky command of Islamic customs. On May 18, he met Kwame Nkrumah, Ghana's president, who presented the boxer with a kente cloth and a copy of his books, *Africa Must Unite* and *Consciencism*. The books were more than symbolic gifts; they were meant to show that Nkrumah and Ali shared the desire to fight the white powers that had subjugated black people for so long, that the civil rights movement in America shared common goals with the postcolonial liberation movement in Africa.

In Accra, Ali and his brother performed a demonstration of how Ali had beaten Sonny Liston. Next he flew to Lagos, Nigeria, but he offended the people of the continent's most populous country by cutting short his visit, canceling a boxing exhibition, and declaring that Egypt was more important. In Cairo, he watched a film about the 1956 battle with Israel over the Suez Canal and said that if another such aggression against Egypt occurred, "I should be pleased to fight on your side and under your flag."

Not long after their encounter in Ghana, Ali received a telegram from Malcolm. Although he'd been spurned, Malcolm was not giving up on his protégé.

"Because a billion of our people in Africa, Arabia, and Asia love you blindly," Malcolm wrote, "you must now be aware of your tremendous responsibilities to them. You must never say or do anything that will permit your enemies to distort the beautiful image you have here among our people."

Malcolm was beginning to see how the American civil rights movement could become a black freedom movement and how it could connect to freedom movements around the world. Whether Ali had the same sense or not, his trip to Africa provided a signal moment. Until then, when he'd boasted and cried for attention, he'd done it with youthful innocence, with a glimmer in his eye that said he was only having fun or only wanted to make himself more rich and famous. He was a kid, just twenty-two years old, still scared of girls, incapable of balancing a checkbook, relying on benefactors to pay his taxes and make his business decisions, not sure of how to do anything but box and make noise. But here he was, nearly six thousand miles from home, visiting countries he had scarcely heard of before the trip, where Muslims came in all different shades of skin, where world leaders were bestowing gifts, where people in remote villages lined the dusty roads and chanted his new name, and where he could thrill the masses with a mere wave of the hand.

"You should've seen them pour out of the hills," he said, "the villages of Africa, and they all knew me. Everybody knows me in the whole world."

16

"Girl, Will You Marry Me?"

Muhammad Ali did find a wife in Africa, but it wasn't Abigail, Susie, Cecilia, Peaches, or any other members of his make-believe harem. Instead, it was a Chicago barmaid and part-time fashion model. Her name was Sonji Roi. Herbert Muhammad carried her picture in his briefcase on their African journey, showed it one day to Ali, and promised to make an introduction when they returned to the United States.

Why would Herbert Muhammad keep a Chicago girl's picture in his briefcase as he traveled to Africa? The simple answer: Herbert operated a photo studio on Chicago's South Side. He enjoyed taking pictures of scantily clad women and showing off his work. At the time, the FBI was closely following Herbert Muhammad and others in the Nation of Islam as part of a program to disrupt organizations that FBI director J. Edgar Hoover considered subversive. The bureau's reports were not always accurate, as they reflected the biases of mostly white agents eager to please their supervisors. FBI memos said Herbert plied women with expensive gifts to disrobe before his cameras, making not only portraits but also pornographic films, which he kept in the basement of his home and showed to friends. According to Muhammad Ali's brother, Herbert had already slept with Sonji, and so had other members of the Nation of Islam. Showing off the photo was Herbert's way of bragging and promoting the young woman's services. According to the FBI and one of Herbert's closest friends, Sonji Roi may have been a prostitute.

"She was a feisty little thing," said Lowell Riley, a photographer who shared the Star Studio with Herbert on 79th Street.

Ali and Sonji had their first date on July 3, 1964. Ali was staying in room 101 at the Roberts Motel on East 63rd Street in Chicago when Herbert knocked on the door of his room and ushered her in. She wore a straight, black wig; tight blue jeans; and a long-sleeved sweater-jacket with red stripes. As Sonji recalled the moment years later, Ali leapt from his bed and said, "I swear to God, Herbert, you know what I was doing? I was laying across the bed praying to Allah for a wife, and here she comes through the door. Here she comes with the Messenger's son, so she's gotta be the one." Then he turned to Sonji, with whom he had yet to exchange a word, and asked, "Girl, will you marry me?"

"Just that quick?" she shot back.

"Just that quick," he said.

They went across the street for ice cream, then to a Chinese restaurant for chop suey, and then back to Sonji's apartment at 71st and Crieger, where Sonji turned on music and slipped off her clothes.

The next morning, Ali took her back to the Roberts Motel, installed her in room 102, and told her they would never part. Later that day, he removed her wig and shampooed her hair.

"The way you touched my head," she recalled, "I never thought a prize-fighter could have such a tender touch."

Less than a week later, they drove to Louisville to meet Odessa and Cash.

"I still couldn't believe it," Sonji recalled. "All so sudden . . . so sudden."

Sonji was alone in the world, with no parents. And she sensed that Ali needed someone, too. He was a man who overflowed with love and lust, a man who was not afraid to talk about his feelings, to express his desire for marriage, and to talk among friends about his appetite for sex. "He was young," said Ali's cousin Charlotte Waddell. "He was green. He hadn't been exposed to any fast-track women." But all his life he had displayed a stronger than usual need to be wanted, admired, loved — so it follows as no surprise that he would strongly want sex, and lots of it, and that marriage would follow.

Sonji Maria Roi was twenty-seven years old and beautiful — short, slender, brown-eyed, with a stylish, long, straight wig. She dressed in high heels and short, tight, brightly colored skirts, as if she were a backup singer for one of Berry Gordy's Motown acts. Sonji's father had been killed in a card game when she was two. Her mother had earned her living singing and dancing in nightclubs and had died when Sonji was eight. By the time she was fourteen,

Sonji had given birth to a son and dropped out of school. Soon after she had entered a few beauty contests and gone to work in nightclubs as a barmaid. Her life changed when she met Herbert Muhammad, a short, fat man who made up for a lack of formal education with pluck and guile. With his father's backing, Herbert owned or operated three businesses on 79th Street — a Muslim bakery that specialized in bean pies from his mother's recipe; Star Studio, where glamorous portraits decorated the shop window; and the Nation of Islam's newspaper, *Muhammad Speaks*. After she posed for pictures in Herbert's studio, Sonji was hired to make telephone solicitations for *Muhammad Speaks*.

But a part-time sales job with *Muhammad Speaks* did not make Sonji a Muslim. According to the rules of the Nation of Islam, Muslim women weren't supposed to apply makeup, wear revealing clothing, or drink alcohol. Sonji did all those things and more. Herbert knew his father would not approve of Ali's choice in a bride. The Messenger would have wanted his most famous follower to marry a member of the flock.

"We were trying to get him *not* to marry her," Lowell Riley recalled one day as he flipped through a photo album containing pictures of Sonji in swimwear. "But she whipped that sex out on him, and he thought there was nobody else who could do what she was doing."

Ali's brother Rudy — also a newly registered member of the Nation of Islam and now going by the name Rahaman Ali, or Rock, as friends called him — had a more romantic explanation: it was true love, he said.

Less than six weeks after their first date, on August 14, 1964, Sonji Roi and Muhammad Ali were married by a justice of the peace in Gary, Indiana. The bride wore a black-and-white checkered sheath dress with an orange scarf. A justice of the peace performed the ceremony because the Nation of Islam had no official wedding ritual. The groom signed the marriage certificate as "Muhammad Ali," even though he had not legally changed his name. The name had been given to him by Elijah Muhammad, he said, and "anything he do is legal."

Asked about their plans, Ali said he and Sonji wanted their children to be born "in the hereafter," not in America. When a reporter asked where the "the hereafter" was located, Ali replied, "Somewhere near Arabia."

• • •

Many parents would be concerned, to say the least, to hear that their wealthy young son had married a woman he'd known for only six weeks, especially if the woman had Sonji Roi's resume: orphan, single mother, part-time model, dancer, rumored prostitute. But Odessa and Cash Clay adored Sonji. The first day they met, Sonji and Odessa worked together to fry a batch of chicken in Odessa's kitchen. Sonji was amused to learned that Odessa still called her grown son "tinky baby" or "woody baby," a play on "little baby." Soon Sonji was calling Ali her "woody baby."

Sonji was charming, frank, funny, and, perhaps best of all as far as Mr. and Mrs. Clay were concerned, not a member of the Nation of Islam. It suggested to Ali's parents that Elijah Muhammad's control over their son might have limits. It was even possible for the Clays to imagine that their son's love for Sonji might prove stronger than his love for Elijah Muhammad, and that marriage might open a path leading their boy out of the Nation of Islam.

Cash Clay continued to harp on the Nation every chance he got, which explained in part why his son was paying fewer visits to his parents' home in Louisville. "I tell him he's gonna be broke from all those leeches," Cash told a reporter, failing to mention that he had been leeching too, persuading his son to invest in a nightclub that Cash Clay owned and operated, a place called the Olympic Club, which opened and closed in the course of only a few months as Cash alienated one customer after another.

Ali's aunt, Mary Clay Turner, said the Clays still hoped that Muhammad Ali would realize the mistake he'd made and return to his family, reclaim his old name, and break free of the Nation. "Why, you have to be almost totally illiterate to be sold that Muslim bill of goods," Turner said in an interview with Jack Olsen of *Sports Illustrated*. "Cassius is about the cleanest thing in the whole confounded Muslim organization. All the rest of them have scars and smears on their names. If they haven't once been hustlers, well, they're hustling now! If they haven't been robbers, they're robbing now! This is it, you know I'm not lying! Practically every one of 'em's been in prison. Cassius falls for all that business about no drinking and no smoking, but he don't know they drink behind the doors, and cuss, and whip their mamas, and do everything. And they'd kill you just as quick as they'd kill me, and don't you forget it!"

Ali had options beyond the Nation of Islam. He had met and befriended other activists. On September 4, 1964, with FBI agents listening in, Ali and Martin Luther King Jr. spoke on the phone. According to the FBI's wiretap log, Ali assured King "he is keeping up with MLK and MLK is his brother and he's with him 100 percent but can't take any chances, and that MLK should take care of himself and should 'watch out for them whites.'" Although it's not clear what Ali meant when he said he couldn't take any chances, he was probably worried about angering Elijah Muhammad more than he was worried about angering the white establishment or the FBI. His respect for the Messenger's authority was overpowering. At one point, Ali told Jack Olsen: "I can't drive no more. He didn't want to read about me in no trouble, so he said you can just quit driving, and I had to quit. He's that powerful. Anything he says, we do. Even the white man — the whole country is scared of him."

Elijah Muhammad never commented publicly on Ali's decision to marry Sonji Roi. Nonetheless, the marriage placed Ali at a crossroads. As he began his own family, he had a chance to decide anew what his future might look like. But he elected to maintain the same course where his religion was concerned, telling reporters that his wife had written a letter to John Ali, national secretary of the Nation of Islam, declaring her intention to register as a Muslim. "That was the onliest reason I married her," he said, "because she agreed to do everything I wanted her to do . . . I told her to be my wife she must wear dresses at least three inches below her knees, she must take off lipstick, she must quit drinking and smoking."

Those were minor concerns for a man so deeply in love.

"My wife and I will be together forever," Ali told the press.

Not long after Ali's wedding, he and Sonny Liston reached an agreement for a rematch on November 16, 1964, at the Boston Garden. The Louisville Sponsoring Group negotiated the contract with Inter-Continental. After four years in the fight business, the Louisville businessmen understood more fully what they'd gotten into, and they were not entirely happy about it. Not only were they being hammered in the press for making an under-the-table deal with Liston and the Nilon brothers for a return bout, but the Nilon brothers still hadn't paid hundreds of thousands of dollars owed to Ali from the first fight. So, even as the two sides worked out the details of a new contract, the

Louisville Sponsoring Group filed suit against Liston and Inter-Continental to force payment from their prior contract. Only in boxing could such arrangements pass for normal.

Ali paid little attention to business matters. Eleven days after his wedding, he was back in Miami to begin training. Some accounts said his weight had ballooned to 240 pounds, while others put it at 225. Either way, he had work to do, so he wore a pair of five-pound work boots and carried pound-and-a-half weights in each hand when he ran. Almost every day after his run he watched film of his first fight with Liston, and after viewing it often enough, he pinpointed the key to victory: It had come down to his ability to dodge Liston's jabs. Once Liston realized his jabs weren't connecting, the bigger, slower fighter had tried leading with left hooks, but that hadn't worked either, because Ali was too fast to get caught by a lead hook. That had left Liston with no options. Unable to play the aggressor, he grew frustrated and fatigued, while Ali slammed away.

If it worked the first time, it would work again, Ali concluded. Liston was like a shark; stop him from moving forward and he would die.

A week before the fight, Ali weighed 216 pounds — 5½ pounds more than he'd weighed when he'd beaten Liston in Miami to claim the title. But even with the extra pounds, he was perfectly fit. If anything, he appeared to be in even better shape. According to *Sports Illustrated*, he had grown half an inch to 6 foot 3; his biceps measured 17 inches around, and his thighs were 27 inches, a 2-inch improvement in both places. His waistline was unchanged at 34 inches.

"I'm so beautiful I should be chiseled in gold," he said.

Liston was in shape for the rematch, too. He knew that he'd taken his opponent too lightly in their earlier match. For the first time in years, Liston had trained as if he might be in for a long fight, running stairs, jogging five miles a day, and working out with a martial arts instructor to improve his speed and agility. He began his workouts in Denver and, then, as the fight drew nearer, moved to White Cliffs, a country club near Plymouth, Massachusetts. He gave up beer and late-night card games. By late October, he weighed 208 pounds — 10 pounds fewer than he'd weighed for the first contest. But not everyone thought that a leaner Liston would necessarily be a meaner Liston.

"He seemed to shrink in size," wrote Arthur Daley of the *Times,* "and instead of looking his announced age of 30 he looked closer to 40."

On October 26, Liston badly battered one of his sparring partners, busting a gash between the man's eyes that required eight stitches to close. The damage buoyed Liston's mood. Although Ali was undefeated and had beaten Liston convincingly in Miami, bookmakers and boxing writers made Liston the favorite again, this time with nine-to-five odds for those laying bets. Apparently, the experts believed what Liston and his wife and trainers continued to insist: that a bum arm had crippled the fighter in the first go-round. Liston, they reasoned, was too strong and too mean to lose twice. Yes, he'd quit the previous fight, but this time he'd be battling to save his career and reputation. Even Ali acknowledged that Liston would probably put up a better fight this time around, predicting that it would take him nine rounds to win. "I give him three more rounds for being in better shape," he said.

As champion, Ali had expanded his retinue. He still had his brother, who was there to repeat everything Ali said and tell him how funny it was, and he still had Bundini Brown, who told jokes, wrote poems, and turned up the volume on the TV at Ali's command. But now, in addition, he had three Muslim cooks, an assistant to the assistant trainer, a chauffeur for his new $12,000 Cadillac limousine, and a mascot. The mascot was Stepin Fetchit, an aging vaudeville comic who was described to the press as Ali's "secret strategist," and who claimed to be teaching the young boxer how to throw Jack Johnson's secret "anchor punch." This may have been purely fictional but sounded good to writers and to Ali. Fetchit's real name was Lincoln Theodore Monroe Andrew Perry, his father naming him after four presidents. Fetchit was America's first black movie star, but he had risen to fame playing lazy, shuffling, ass-kissing characters that embodied negative racial stereotypes. He was an unlikely companion for Ali and his proud Muslim comrades.

Some said Ali's friendship with Fetchit was proof of the fighter's emotional complexity, while others were less kind.

"To me, he's just a thoroughly confused person," Ferdie Pacheco said.

Ali and Fetchit were both great actors, and Fetchit seemed to have a keen understanding of the boxer's gift for showmanship. Before the Liston rematch, Fetchit said, "People don't understand the champ, but one day he'll be one of the country's greatest heroes. He's like one of those plays where a man is the villain in the first act and then turns out to be the hero in the last act . . .

And that's the way he wants it, because it's better for the box office for people to misunderstand him."

On Sunday, November 8, Ali and his brother attended a Muslim service led by Louis X at a temple in Boston. On November 13, three days before the fight, Ali was unwinding in room 611 of the Sherry Biltmore Hotel. He'd run five miles that morning, but he'd stopped sparring, taking care not to get hurt. The Boston Garden anticipated a sellout, and closed-circuit ticket sales were expected to top $3 million. In the days leading up to the fight, when he wasn't running or skipping rope or getting a massage from Luis Sarria, Ali spent most of his time in his hotel room, watching movies, listening to music, and joking with his brother, Bundini, Captain Sam Saxon, and others. Reporters came and went. So did members of the Nation of Islam, including Louis X, Clarence X (formerly known as Clarence Gill, one of the leaders of the Nation of Islam's mosque in Boston and a part-time Ali bodyguard), and John Ali. For dinner that night, Ali ate a steak, spinach, baked potato, toast, and a salad with oil-and-vinegar dressing before turning on a 16-millimeter projector to watch *Little Caesar,* the 1931 gangster classic starring Edward G. Robinson.

Fifteen or twenty minutes after finishing his meal, at about 6:30 p.m., Ali ran to the bathroom and vomited. Suddenly, he was in terrible pain.

"Oh, something is awful wrong," he said as he came out of the bathroom.

Someone called an ambulance. Saxon, Rudy, and a few others carried Ali down the hall to a service elevator, through a laundry room, and outside to the ambulance.

Doctors at Boston City Hospital said Ali had an incarcerated inguinal hernia, a swelling the size of an egg in the right bowel, a life-threatening condition that required immediate surgery.

Sonji, who was staying at the home of Louis X, rushed to the hospital. So did Angelo Dundee. William Faversham and Gordon Davidson of the Louisville Sponsoring Group were at the Boston Garden, watching the Celtics play the Los Angeles Lakers, when a police officer found them and told them to get to the hospital right away. Another police officer was sent to the opera house to fetch a surgeon who would go on to perform the operation in white tie and tails.

When it was over and Ali's life was no longer in danger, the rumors and conspiracy theories started at once: Liston's trainers had poisoned Ali. The Nation of Islam had poisoned Ali. Malcolm X had poisoned Ali. The mafia had poisoned Ali. Ali was faking the illness because he was afraid to fight.

When Liston got the news that the fight was canceled, he poured himself a screwdriver. He had trained hard, worked himself into top shape, and now he would have to do it again. Score another round for Clay, his tormentor.

"That damned fool," Liston said. "That damned fool."

17

Assassination

As he slept one night, an explosion shook Malcolm X's house. Cold air whipped through a shattered window and flames spread across the living room floor. Malcolm rushed his wife and children through the smoke and out the back door. It was 2:45 in the morning on Valentine's Day, 1965. Fire trucks screamed down the block, and neighbors stepped outside to see what was happening. Malcolm stood on the street in his pajamas, his fingers wrapped around a .25 caliber pistol.

When the flames were out, police found traces of Molotov cocktails that had been thrown through the living-room window of the modest brick home in Queens. Malcolm was angry — but not surprised. He had been saying for weeks that Elijah Muhammad wanted him dead. In *Muhammad Speaks,* Louis X had written, "The die is set, and Malcolm shall not escape . . . such a man as Malcolm is worthy of death."

Muhammad Ali was just as threatening, telling one journalist: "Malcolm X and anybody else who attacks or talks about attacking Elijah Muhammad will die."

In a televised interview with Chicago journalist Irv Kupcinet, Ali had hurled insults at Malcolm. "I don't even think about him," he said. "He's nothing but a fellow who was an ex-dope addict, a prisoner, a jailbird who had no education, couldn't read or write, who heard about the Honorable Elijah Muhammad, who took him off the streets, cleaned him up, and educated him enough to go out and debate . . . He is no longer Malcolm X . . . He is just Malcolm Little. Little, nothing."

Malcolm's wife, Betty Shabazz, pleaded with Ali to help. "You see what they are doing to my husband, don't you?" she asked during a chance encounter at the Theresa Hotel. Ali put his hands up in the air. "I haven't done anything," he said. "I'm not doing anything to him."

But Ali's proclamation of innocence rang false. The Nation of Islam had done everything short of offering a reward for the murder of Malcolm X. As the most prominent member of the organization, Ali could have used his power to call for a halt to malicious attacks. He could have intervened on his former friend's behalf. He chose not to. Indeed, he helped stoke the anger.

On February 18, four days after the firebombing of his house, Malcolm phoned the FBI to tell them, as if they hadn't noticed, that someone was trying to kill him. In addition to the firebombing, there had been car chases in Los Angeles and Chicago. Now, leaders of the Nation of Islam were arriving in New York, raising suspicion that another attack might soon be launched. Louis X of Boston presided over a meeting of the Newark Mosque No. 25, while National Secretary John Ali checked into the Americana Hotel in New York on Friday, February 19. Two days later, members of the Newark temple made the drive to New York to attend a Malcolm X rally at the Audubon Ballroom in Harlem. When Malcolm took the stage, one of the men from Newark threw a smoke bomb and leaped to apprehend a pretend thief. "Get your hands out of my pockets!" he shouted by way of distraction as three gunmen crept to the stage.

"Hold it! Hold it! Hold it! Hold it!" Malcolm shouted. Suddenly, a shotgun blast ripped holes in Malcolm's chest. More shots flew. Malcolm toppled backward, the back of his head crashing to the floor. He died almost instantly.

A few hours later, a fire ripped through Muhammad Ali's apartment at 7036 South Cregier Avenue on the South Side of Chicago. Ali and his wife were at a restaurant having dinner when John Ali called with the news about the fire. How did John Ali know where they were eating unless the couple had been followed? Sonji became suspicious, wondering if the fire had been meant to warn her husband to stay in line.

"That was a strange fire. Real strange," Muhammad Ali said years later. "I believe to this day someone started it on purpose."

Two days after that, a bomb nearly leveled the Nation of Islam's mosque in New York. Soon after, one of Ali's former bodyguards, Leon 4X Ameer, who had left the Nation of Islam, died in a hotel room from trauma inflicted during an earlier beating. Prior to the beating, Ameer, formerly known as Leon Lionel Phillips Jr., had been talking to the FBI. In one interview with an agent, Ameer said Ali had suffered his hernia during sexual intercourse with Sonji and that Ali's managers had been embarrassed because they had not been able to "prevent nightly cohabitation" between Ali and his wife in the days leading up to the second Liston fight. Ameer also told FBI agents the boxer was growing tired of the "numerous donations" the Nation of Islam expected him to make. According to one FBI memo, Ameer told Ali "he was foolish to let the NOI [Nation of Islam] 'milk him.'"

None of this caused Ali to publicly question Elijah Muhammad's leadership. "Malcolm X was my friend," he said, "and he was a friend of everybody as long as he was a member of Islam. Now I don't want to talk about him. All of us were shocked at the way he was killed. Elijah Muhammad has denied that the Muslims were responsible. We are not a violent people."

Years later, interviewed over lunch at a restaurant in Chicago, John Ali said the Nation of Islam had nothing to do with the assassination. "I was never interrogated," he said. "I was never charged. People know if we wanted to do it, we could've done it." He paused. "We didn't do it."

Sam Saxon agreed. "I wanted to kill Malcolm," he said in an interview years later, after changing his name to Abdul Rahman. "But the Honorable Elijah Muhammad told us not to bother him, so we didn't bother him." Saxon said he thought the FBI arranged the assassination to stir dissension within the Nation of Islam and to eliminate a man who might have gone on to become a powerful rebel leader.

Decades later, Ali would say that turning his back on Malcolm was one of the biggest regrets of his life. But at the time, he showed no remorse. After his hernia, Ali enjoyed a long break from boxing. Most mornings, Sonji cooked breakfast while Ali lounged around their Chicago apartment. He would go for walks, often visiting Herbert Muhammad at the office of *Muhammad Speaks*, and then come home and watch television while Sonji cooked dinner. When they went out at night to the movies or a restaurant, fans would swarm Ali, but Sonji didn't mind. She would stand back a few feet and let her husband enjoy his admirers until he would remember her and make an introduction, saying, "This is my wife, y'all."

Those were the simplest, happiest times, but they were not perfect. Sonji was a skeptic, "the kind that can't believe in anything just on blind faith, not even God," as she said. So she asked questions about her husband's beliefs. Why can't women wear short dresses? Why do you call white people "devils" when you have so many white friends? Why couldn't they go out to night-clubs to see white entertainers? A decade later, after they had divorced, Sonji and Ali discussed these questions and others in front of the writer Richard Durham. "You would never answer me yourself," Sonji complained. "You thought the man should be the only one in the house who really knew what he was talking about, so you would go and ask the Muslim officials . . . You couldn't understand why little insignificant me would not just go along with the program like the others and ask no questions."

To which Ali replied, "You wouldn't give me what I expected from a Muslim woman."

Once, Ali got mad when he saw his wife putting on eyeshadow.

"You grabbed a wet towel and started scrubbing my face, hard," Sonji re-called.

"Did I do that?" he asked. "I'm sorry. If I had known what I know now, we'd still be married. You see, I was like a religious fanatic at first . . . I acted like every difference was a threat."

In early March, when he was still recuperating from his hernia operation, Ali traveled to Kingston, Jamaica, to watch Sugar Ray Robinson fight Jimmy Beecham at the National Stadium. Although he was almost forty-four years old, Robinson was still active, fighting fourteen times in 1965. At an elegant party before the fight, Ali got angry with Sonji about the orange knit dress she'd chosen to wear. In front of guests, he stepped in front of his wife and yanked the bottom of the dress, trying to make it cover her knees. At first, Sonji thought he was joking. After all, there were no Muslims around, and Ali had not only purchased this dress for her but had helped her put it on earlier that evening. But when he kept trying to yank down the front of the dress, Sonji saw he was serious and became embarrassed. She went to the balcony and cried. When Ali came out on the balcony, he saw a white man staring at his wife in her short dress and his anger bubbled over.

"I was vexed over that dress," he told her years later in front of Durham.

"But you bought that damn dress!" she said. "You picked it! Then you snatch me right off the balcony and drag me straight through the living room, past the guests, past the movie stars, past the bank president, the opera star, past Ray Robinson and everybody. And I'm crying and pulling away and you're jerking on me and yelling and you've forgotten everybody's looking. You're yelling and everything! You threw me in the bathroom, came in, and slammed the door. I'm screaming and crying and you're trying to stretch my dress. And in trying to make my dress long, pulling and snatching on it, you tore it. You tore it bad. So now I'm nearly naked. I'm trying to break away, and you're fighting me, pulling on my clothes, slapping me. Sugar Ray comes to the bathroom door and starts knocking on it. 'Let me in, man! Let me in . . .' He's yelling through the door like he thought you was killing me."

When they got back to Miami, Sonji wrote a goodbye note and left it on her husband's pillow. When he returned from the gym that day, she was gone.

Eventually, Ali tracked her down in Chicago, they talked on the phone "eighty-five dollars' worth," as Sonji put it, referring to the cost of the long-distance call, until she agreed to give him another chance. She flew back to Florida as Ali resumed training for Liston. But their arguments continued. Sonji's wardrobe would continue to be a catalyst for anger and bitter feuds.

On April 1, 1965, Ali and Sonji split again, but this time it was for professional reasons. Ali boarded his custom-painted bus, Little Red, for the drive from Miami to Chicopee Falls, Massachusetts, where he would train for his rematch with Liston, which had been rescheduled for May 25. He had invited Bundini Brown, Howard Bingham, a few sparring partners, his cooks, and four white journalists to join him for the trip. Rahaman Ali would follow in his brother's tomato-red Cadillac.

The bus was parked in front of Ali's house, everyone on board and ready to go, when Sonji shouted out the door: "Ali, you see about my dry cleaning?"

"All sent," the heavyweight champ told his wife.

"How about my shoes at the shop?"

"Done."

"Then take out the garbage."

Ali put one finger to his lips.

"Shh. Champs don't take out garbage."

Sonji's tone hardened. "I'm telling you, Ali . . . ," she said. Ali took out the garbage and got on the bus.

The bus was a 1955 Flexible. It smelled of cigarette smoke, white-bean pie, and fried chicken, the latter cooked by Sonji and packed in strong supply in the hope that Ali and his fellow travelers would not have to stop and test racial tolerance among restaurant owners in Florida and Georgia. Ali drove, one hand on the wheel, unconcerned with Miami traffic, as he looked over his shoulder to inform his fellow travelers about their great fortune: "Just think, the whole world would love to be on this bus with me, but they ain't and you are. We're going to breathe fresh air and look at pretty trees and eat that chicken and you can interview me while I'm driving my beautiful bus along at the cruising speed of eighty-five."

He paused to ask a question: Did anybody have gas money?

He pointed at a reporter in glasses.

"What's your name?"

"Pope," said Edwin Pope of the *Miami Herald*.

"Pope, loan me a hundred dollars."

Pope and others on the bus still didn't know what to call Ali. Muhammad sounded silly. Clay, the boxer insisted, wasn't his name anymore. If he was in a good mood he would answer to Cassius, but most of the men played it safe and addressed him simply as "Champ." For the white passengers, it was difficult to imagine that the leader of their brigade was the same man caught up in the violent world of Malcolm X and Elijah Muhammad. He was delightful, full of jokes, including quips about the nation's racial unrest.

"Next stop Boston," he said. "But first we stopping in Selma and Bogalusa." He was joking about bringing an integrated bus through the Deep South and the trouble that might ensue. "Don't worry, when we shout at girls it's gonna be colored girls so nobody get hung."

He was the finest source of copy some of these reporters had ever met, a man whose every utterance and action begged to be recorded. Pope was typing his stories on a portable Smith Corona typewriter while the bus bounced along. When Ali wasn't driving, he would squeeze in next to Pope to see what he was typing and to make suggestions or offer additional comments. When the bus stopped, the journalist would find a pay phone, call his editor, and dictate a column. Fortunately for Pope and his readers, the bus stopped often, as Ali couldn't stand to pass a town without letting its citizens express their appreciation for his visit.

By suppertime on the journey's first day, the crew hadn't left Florida, and the supply of Sonji's fried chicken had already been exhausted. In Yulee, just south of the Georgia line, the bus slowed and pulled into a truck stop. Big gas pumps stood like gravestones under overhead lights and truck trailers filled the macadam lot. Bundini Brown and some of the white reporters got off the bus and walked into a diner.

"They don't want you," Ali warned Bundini. "Don't try."

Bundini, wearing a denim "Bear Huntin'" jacket, just like the one Ali owned, went in anyway. The champ and some of his sparring partners stood by the gas pumps, watching him go. Bundini was one of the few men in the entourage who argued race with Ali. He told Ali the Nation of Islam was steering him wrong, that black and white people were no different, that it was only a matter of time before people stopped fighting one another over racial prejudice. At one point, Elijah Muhammad offered Bundini fifty thousand dollars a year to become a Muslim, mostly so he would stop planting dangerous ideas in Ali's mind. Bundini scoffed at the offer, according to his son, saying, "What kind of religion do you have if you gotta pay someone to become a member?"

Ali would fire and rehire Bundini many times over the years, but, in truth, he seemed to like sparring with his motivator-in-chief. Most people in the entourage said whatever they thought the champ wanted to hear, but not Bundini; Bundini challenged him.

"Okay, Jackie Robinson," Ali said. "You my integrator. If you come back on your head I know they don't want us."

Bundini went through the screen door, walked past six or seven white couples, and took a seat at the counter. The reporters joined him.

"I'm sorry," the manager said, coming out from behind the counter. "We have a place out back. Separate facilities."

From the kitchen, two black cooks peeked out the door. Bundini and the reporters tried to argue, but the manager — talking to the reporters, not to Bundini — said there was nothing he could do.

The screen door opened and Ali walked in — not to save the day but to humiliate Bundini.

"You fool — what's the matter with you? You damn *fool.*" Ali's nostrils flared and his voice raged almost out of control, according to George Plimpton, one of the writers at the counter. "You clear out of this place, nigger, you ain't wanted here," Ali said. "Can't you see, they don't want you, you nigger?" Ali grabbed Bundini by the jacket and hauled him out the door. Bundini flew across the macadam "as if he had been launched from a sling," Plimpton wrote. The champ rushed after him, still yelling. "I'm glad, Bundini! I'm glad you got showed, Bundini, you got showed!"

Bundini looked at his feet. "Leave me alone," he said. "I'm good enough to eat here! I'm a free man. God made me."

He broke away from Ali and hid on the bus. But Ali kept after him, calling him Uncle Tom and telling him to bow his head.

Bundini argued. He had served his country in the military, he said. He should be able to eat anywhere he wanted. The truck-stop manager would regret his actions someday.

"Tom! Tom! Tom!" Ali shouted.

"Leave me alone," Bundini said, barely audibly, as he hung his head and cried.

Fifty miles up the road, in Brunswick, Georgia, the bus stopped at another roadside restaurant. This time, without explanation, Ali marched his crew inside, asked for a table, and sat down to eat. He was ruthless, like a dictator or tribal chief who might rally his followers to great heights one day and then order them to undertake a suicide mission the next, his judgment as mysterious as it was uncontested.

He picked up a pitcher and poured cream in his cup.

"Bundini," he called out. "I'm going to integrate the coffee."

Bundini laughed. "One of these days," he said, "we're going to find out which one of us is crazy. I think it's you."

18

Phantom Punch

In Fayetteville, North Carolina, Little Red burst into flames and had to be retired.

"My poor little red bus," Ali said softly, offering a roadside eulogy. "You was the most famousest bus ever in the history of the world. Leastwise you the onliest one ever to come on a trip like this."

Still reluctant to fly, Ali and his band made the rest of the trip on a Trailways bus, arriving fifty hours later in Chicopee Falls. To some skeptics in the press, the disastrous trip was an omen. Ali hadn't really beaten Sonny Liston last time; Liston had quit. There was a sense that the young boxer had gotten lucky, that David had slung a lucky stone and would be wise to leave Goliath alone. The odds makers in Las Vegas once more made Liston the favorite, same as before Ali's hernia.

In early May, with the fight weeks away, boxing officials in Massachusetts canceled the contest over concerns that Liston's promoters had ties to the mob. A cynic might say everyone in boxing had ties to the mob, but fight promoters had no interest in philosophical dialogue; they needed to find a new venue, and they needed to find it fast. When a promoter and pawnshop owner from Lewiston, Maine, offered the five-thousand-seat St. Dominic's Arena for the fight, improbably, a deal was struck. Lewiston, a textile town with a population of 41,000, would be the smallest town to host a heavyweight championship in forty-two years.

Everything about the fight was a mess. Although the arena was small, half the tickets went unsold. The prices, ranging from twenty-five to one hundred dollars, were too high for most Lewistonians. The official paid attendance of 2,434 was the lowest for a heavyweight title fight in modern history. One rumor circulating said followers of Malcolm X would try to kill Ali the night of the fight. Another rumor said a Nation of Islam hit squad would kill Sonny Liston if he didn't take a dive. Muslims had been almost invisible at the fight in Miami, but they were out in force in Maine. Men in dark suits and bow-ties surrounded Ali wherever he went, scanning the crowds and frightening white reporters who were accustomed to a more jovial atmosphere.

Then there was Liston, who not only seemed anxious but in far from peak condition. Drinking Scotch and working out half-heartedly, the former champ, age thirty-two at a minimum but more likely thirty-four, appeared worn and weary.

"Liston is burnt out," Ali said.

"You can see it in his eyes," one of Liston's sparring partners said. "They don't look so scary anymore."

His wife, Geraldine, noticed the same thing. "He just didn't seem like Sonny," she said. Before his first contest with Clay, Liston had been confident and calm. This time, on the day of the fight, he was nervous — and wracked with diarrhea.

Ali, on the other hand, trained like a man who thought he had become the King of the World, or at least the King of the Black World, and who would do everything possible to avoid disappointing his legions. He alternated between speedy sparring partners and sluggers. Jimmy Ellis would test his reflexes, and Joe "Shotgun" Shelton would bang away at Ali's gut while Ali leaned against the ropes, conditioning himself for late rounds against Liston, as if pain were no consideration.

On the night of the fight, hundreds of police officers from the surround-ing area were called for duty. They combed the arena for bombs and patted down spectators for guns. Security was so tight that many ticketholders were still standing outside when the fight began. The only consolation for those stranded ticketholders was that they didn't have to listen to Robert Goulet butcher the national anthem.

Ali left his hotel at nine, dressed in jeans and a sweatshirt. Riding along, Mort Sharnik of *Sports Illustrated* asked the champ for a prediction. Ali answered without a rhyme. "It may start out with me not even throwing a punch," he said calmly. "I'm just gonna go backwards and Liston will pursue and then, finally, *bam!* — I'll hit him with the right hand and it's gonna be over." A week earlier, he had told a reporter that he never liked to go into a fight with a plan. "Angelo, he got a fight plan," Ali said, "and I do it when I can. But it would be the worst thing I could do to go in there with my mind all made up what to do. I been fighting since I was a child, and I do everything on instinct. Sometimes I wonder at myself when I see a big fist coming at my head, and my head move without me thinking and the big fist go by. I wonder how I did it."

That was the plan.

The fight began at 10:40 p.m. Sonji — who had decided to take the last name Clay, even though her husband had dropped it — sat with her in-laws, Cash and Odessa. Not far from the Clays, Frank Sinatra, Jackie Gleason, and Elizabeth Taylor sat ringside — the first and last time Lewiston saw such an array of stars. The crowd booed Ali as he arrived and cheered for Liston, lending truth to the maxim that says my enemy's enemy is my friend. Ali may have been the most widely disliked man in America in 1965.

The referee, Jersey Joe Walcott, himself a former heavyweight champ, met the fighters in the center of the ring and reminded them of the rules. Before the bell, Ali bowed his head and offered a prayer in the direction of Mecca, while Liston shuffled heavily in the opposite corner.

The fight began. Ali, in white trunks, looked bigger and stronger than ever, his chest and shoulders easily as imposing as Liston's, his stomach lean, coiled with muscle. He didn't backpedal, as he told Sharnik he would. Instead, he rushed to the center of the ring and threw two quick punches. With that message sent, he did what everyone expected of him, backpedaling and circling while Liston chased and threw punches that mostly failed to connect. Every time Liston tried to corner his opponent, Ali slid away, usually to his left, and danced another circle around the ring. In most of his fights, Ali would jab, jab, jab while he moved, but this time he hardly bothered, content to dance and let his opponent give chase. Through the first ninety seconds of the fight, Ali threw only two jabs, and both missed. Perhaps he was measuring Liston, perhaps maintaining distance for his own safety.

Against the older, slower Archie Moore, Ali had thrown eighty-six punches in the first round. In his first fight with Liston, he'd thrown forty-seven in the first round. Now, in the first two minutes of his rematch with Liston, Ali had tried a mere eight punches, connecting with three. It was shaping up

as the most inoffensive and inconsequential round of his professional boxing career, accomplishing nothing, it seemed, except to test Liston's stamina.
Around and around went Ali, circling Liston, slipping away from punches.

With a minute left, Liston backed Ali toward the ropes and marched forward, applying pressure. Ali stayed on his toes, waggling his shoulders left
and right and left again, shifting his weight from side to side, making himself
a moving target. Liston lunged and threw a left. Ali's eyes went wide and his
mouth opened. He pulled back his chin and let the blow hit softly below the
right shoulder. Sonny cocked his right arm to throw another punch, but he
was too slow. Ali fired a short right hand. It caught Liston on the temple. Liston's head turned down, like a man who'd dropped his wallet. His right knee
buckled, and his body folded at the waist.

Ali followed with a left uppercut, but the punch missed because Liston
was flat on his back, hands above his head, legs wide, like a tossed rag doll.
Liston was down, and it had happened so fast that many spectators missed
it. Ali stood over the fallen fighter and roared, as photographers snapped
and rewound their cameras frantically. Liston rolled to his right, rose to one
knee, then toppled over again like a drunk who's decided to stay down and
sleep it off.

Ali jumped around the ring in joy.

After about eighteen seconds, Liston finally rose. The fight should have
been over, but Walcott had never begun counting because he'd been too busy
trying to control Ali, who had failed to go to a neutral corner as rules required. When Walcott realized his mistake, he hustled to the side of the ring
to confer with Nat Fleischer, the publisher of *The Ring* magazine and the
unofficial commissioner of boxing, who declared that Liston had been down
for ten seconds. While Walcott was gone, Ali and Liston began fighting again.
Ali threw four hooks — left, right, left, right — before Walcott returned and
separated the fighters, signaling that it was all over: Ali was the winner by
knockout.

Liston wandered back to his corner. Meanwhile, Bundini got to Ali first
and hoisted him in the air. Then came Rahaman, who reached in his brother's mouth and pulled out his mouth guard.

"He laid down," Ali told Rahaman.

"No, you hit him," Rahaman said.

"I think he . . ."

"No, man, you hit him."

The punch was so fast, and the results so shocking, that even Ali, it seemed, was unsure what had happened. To many, it certainly looked as though Liston had been in no rush to get up from the mat. Cries of "fix" rose immediately from the crowd and persisted long after the fight. Geraldine Liston couldn't believe such a glancing blow would crumple her husband. In his entire career, Sonny had never been knocked out, and he had been knocked down only once prior to this. Joe Louis doubted the authenticity of the knockout too, saying Ali's short right hand to Liston's cranium had as much effect as "throwing cornflakes at a battleship." And because that short right hand had been so quick, so well hidden by Liston's forward-moving body, some observers went further, insisting there had been no punch at all, that Liston had simply taken a dive. They called it "The Phantom Punch."

There was a punch, and it did land. Slow-motion replays leave little doubt that Ali's right hand landed hard enough to send Liston's head moving down and to his right.

"It was a perfect right hand," said Floyd Patterson, seated ringside.

George Chuvalo, also ringside, had doubts: "I saw Liston's eyes," he said. "They were the eyes of a man faking. Stunned eyes roll. Liston's eyes were darting from side to side."

"I didn't think he could hit that hard," Liston said.

After he had watched a replay on television, Ali started referring to the blow as "my karate punch" or the "famous anchor punch," passed down from Jack Johnson to Stepin Fetchit to Ali. He heard the cries of fix, and he had an answer to them. "Sonny is too dull and too slow to be a fixer in a fight," he said. "I hit him flush with all my two hundred and six pounds and they hated to give me credit."

If the punch was real, the only question is whether Liston faked the fall or, once down, decided to stay down — because the mob had told him to, because the Nation of Islam had threatened him, because he was ill, or because he knew he couldn't win and no longer wished to try. The FBI had suspicions but found no evidence to suggest a fix.

Still, even Liston's wife had doubts.

"I think Sonny gave that second fight away," Geraldine told a TV journalist thirty-five years later. "I don't know whether he was paid, I didn't see the money if he was paid to lose. I don't know, I don't know what went on. But I really do. That's my belief. And I told him."

Geraldine told her husband she thought he had thrown the fight. But Sonny denied it.

"He said, no, he said, 'You win and you lose,' you know? I say, 'In the first round?'"

19

True Love

The day after the fight, Ali should have been overjoyed. So many things in his life were going exactly as he'd dreamed — and his dreams had hardly been modest. He'd just beaten Sonny Liston again, in front of his mother, father, brother, hundreds of reporters, and millions of spectators around the world. He possessed wealth. He possessed fame. And, as he never stopped reminding everyone, he still possessed the prettiest face the boxing world had ever seen. But one thing was not working out exactly as he'd hoped, and he was growing increasingly frustrated about it.

Ali still loved Sonji. He still wanted to have children with her, even though he was surprised that she had not yet become pregnant, given the quality and quantity of their sexual activity. The problem was her behavior in the company of Ali's Muslim friends, and, in particular, her refusal to wear the long gowns and headscarves proscribed for female members of the Nation of Islam. Ali had explained that Muslim women were supposed to be deferential and treat their men with respect, but Sonji, who was brassy and outspoken by nature, refused to defer to Ali or any other man. She never stopped telling her husband when she felt like he was being used or cheated by some of his friends and hangers-on, including members of the Nation. She questioned everything, from the honesty of Elijah Muhammad to the very meaning of religion.

"How could I stand by seeing you act like a tiger in the ring and out of it your knees trembling before some religious superstition, like a man who believes in ghosts?" she asked her husband. She wanted a hero who would carry her away from it all, from her hard, sad life, and yet she wound up with a man who wasn't even his own master. "I asked you to question it," she said. "Just ask yourself the questions, and in the quiet dead of night, answer. Don't even whisper your answer out loud. Just to yourself. You world heavyweight champion muthafucker."

But he never did question it, or at least not to her satisfaction, and religion continued to cause friction between them, with Sonji seething every time she saw her husband cowering to the leaders of the Nation of Islam, and Ali erupting in anger whenever Sonji showed disdain or disrespect for his faith. He had made great sacrifices to join the Nation of Islam, confusing his fans, distancing his parents, losing valuable endorsements, and abandoning at least one of his closest friends in Malcolm X. Having made his choice and committed to Elijah Muhammad, he expected his wife to do the same. Some of his frustration had to do with religion, to be sure, and some of it was tied to ideas of masculinity and marriage.

In Maine, before the Liston fight, they had been at a Holiday Inn in Auburn, when Sonji leaned over a balcony and told her husband to come inside.

"I'll be right there," said Ali, who had been outside talking to the journalist Jerry Izenberg and Sam Saxon, the Muslim man Ali had befriended in Miami. Ali started up the stairs, but Captain Sam blocked his path.

"You're the man," Saxon said. "You don't go when the woman says go."

Ali stayed.

The morning after the Liston fight, the couple drove from Lewiston to Chicopee, back to the hotel where Ali had been staying while in training. In Chicopee, Ali recalled, "She put on a short short short tight dress with no sleeves or nothing . . . and she walked into the lobby in this dress, and went into the dining room in it, and I pulled her to the room and I asked her, 'Why would you walk into the lobby . . . embarrassing me in these type sexual designed clothes showing all parts or many parts of your body?' And she says, 'You have won your fight. I no longer have to pretend . . . I never will be a Muslim.'"

The couple argued. Once again, Sonji left in anger, returning to Chicago.

Ali and Sonji didn't see each other for two weeks. When they reunited in Chicago on June 11, Ali insisted on taking his wife to a dressmaker so she could acquire "plain and simple" floor-length dresses. One day, he pulled one of the full-length dresses he'd bought her out of the closet and laid it on the bed, but Sonji refused to wear it. It was the same old argument, the one that had caused Ali to slap Sonji at the party in Jamaica.

"That was the breaking point" for Ali, said Safiyya Mohammed-Rahmah, the daughter of Herbert Muhammad.

Captain Sam attempted to intervene. He believed the two were truly in love. Given more time, he said, Sonji might come around to the Nation of Islam. He appealed to her pragmatic side. "That man's gonna be on top for ten years," Saxon told Sonji. "All you gotta do is pull your dress down over your knees."

Just as Elijah Muhammad's son Herbert had previously drawn the couple together, he now shoved them apart. An FBI informant said that Herbert treated Ali "in a manner such as a 'pimp' would treat a prostitute . . . attempting to downgrade [him] as much as he can in order to keep him completely under his control." According to Rahaman, Muhammad Ali's brother, Herbert had tried to sleep with Sonji even after she and Ali had married. He was not the only member of the Nation of Islam making overtures toward Sonji, according to Rahaman. When Sonji refused, Herbert began maneuvering to get rid of her, whispering poisonous words and pronouncing her unfit to be a Muslim.

Rose Jennings, who worked with Herbert Muhammad and Sonji at *Muhammad Speaks,* said she didn't know if sex played a role in Herbert's frustration with Sonji, but Jennings said she was certain that Herbert felt threatened by Ali's new wife and orchestrated her exit. "Herbert couldn't control her," Jennings said. "She started telling Ali what was really going on. She became influential in his business affairs. Herbert couldn't have that. So he told Ali that Sonji was screwing a white guy. It wasn't true, but he was trying to break them up."

It worked. On June 23, Ali filed a complaint in the Dade County, Florida, circuit court asking a judge to annul his marriage. By seeking an annulment, rather than a divorce, he hoped to avoid paying alimony. But Sonji told reporters she still hoped to save her marriage.

"I just love my husband and I want to be with him," she said. "It's just this religion. I have tried to accept it, and I have explained this to him, but I just don't understand it. It's very hard to change to the way they want me to be."

A week later, she told reporters she had been traveling around the country,

trying to find her husband so that she could speak to him and attempt to re-
pair their marriage. "He won't see me," she said. "I hear where he is and I go
there. He'll leave and I'll follow."

At a pretrial hearing, a judge asked Ali if he had ever loved Sonji. He answered, "I would like to say that I loved her only if she would follow me in
my way of life and if she would take my name and everything else that I could
give her and be what I wanted her to be. That's the onliest reason I would love
her." The judge, perhaps unimpressed with that answer, ruled that Ali had no
grounds to annul the marriage. Ali and his lawyers worked out a deal, and
Sonji agreed to a divorce that paid her $22,500 for legal costs and $15,000 a
year for ten years.

When it was over, Sonji pronounced her own verdict: "They've stolen my
man's mind."

Ali, for his part, said he intended to marry again: "I have no one in mind,
but I'll tell you this: the next time I marry it'll be a girl of seventeen or eighteen — one that I can raise to my way of thinking."

It's not clear if Ali really wanted a woman he could raise to his own way of
thinking or merely one who adhered to the Nation of Islam's way. In either
case, his first marriage raised uncomfortable questions. For many a young
man, marriage provides a wake-up call, a jolt that forces him to become less
selfish, to put his wife's needs ahead of his own, and then, soon after, his children's needs, too. But that was not the case for Ali. When the Nation of Islam
and Herbert Muhammad pushed him, he dropped his wife, just as he had
dropped his friend Malcolm X.

Many years later, when Rahaman Ali was in his seventies, his short-term
memory faded but his long-term memory sharp, when he was living out of
his brother's shadow and in poverty in a tiny, government-subsidized Louisville apartment, he was asked to name the greatest ordeal of his brother's life.
Was it one of Ali's fights? An illness? Injury? The death of a parent? Rahaman
answered without hesitation: it was losing Sonji.

"He went through hell," his brother Rahaman said. "Not to be able to hold
her, make love to her. It hurt him real bad. She's the only one he ever really
loved. His true love, his only one."

Herbert Muhammad knew almost nothing about boxing. He was thirty-six
years old, with a soft, round body that one writer said bore witness "to long

and determined dining." Odessa Clay called him "fat and piggy looking." Cash Clay was even harsher, pronouncing, "He dirty. Muhammad dirty."

Before his association with boxing's heavyweight champion, Herbert Muhammad had made headlines once before, in 1962, when a woman pressed charges against him for breaking her jaw in four places. The former mistress said she had broken up with him when she learned he was married and had children. But Herbert broke into her apartment, beat her, and threatened to kill her if she left him. Soon after, the FBI began keeping tabs on Herbert. Reports from FBI agents were not always accurate, and they were often biased against minorities and others deemed by J. Edgar Hoover to be potential threats. Still, Herbert kept the agency's operatives busy. Agents reported that Herbert received kickbacks from his father's attorneys as well as from the publishing company that printed *Muhammad Speaks,* took nude photos of girls, made pornographic films, and fathered at least one child out of wedlock. "He is 'money crazy,'" the bureau noted in one report," and will do anything for money even if it is against the principles of the NOI."

Herbert wore baggy, nondescript suits with ties that seldom matched, looking every bit like a man who wished to be overlooked. Although he may have sinned in other ways, he didn't smoke or drink. He followed the teachings of his father so long as they didn't interfere with his appetite for extramarital sex, large meals, and expensive home decor. "The part of being a Muslim he embraced was having a lot of wives," said Bob Arum, a boxing promoter who worked closely with Herbert.

The Honorable Elijah Muhammad wouldn't let his children or grandchildren attend secular schools, so they were taught at home, primarily by their mother, Clara Muhammad. "Herbert Muhammad could not read," said Rose Jennings, but that didn't stop him from pursuing an education or from serving as one of the top editors of a newspaper. As a young man, Herbert enrolled in hypnotism classes and a Dale Carnegie correspondence course. He also studied to become a certified television repairman. It was photography he loved most, though, in part because it suited a man who lacked physical confidence, struggled to read anything more than numbers, and preferred not to be the subject of attention. With a camera strapped around his neck, he could approach beautiful girls on the beach and ask them to pose, and then invite them to visit his studio to see the resulting prints, purchase copies, and perhaps join him for a steak dinner at the Tiger Lounge.

When Ali informed members of the Louisville Sponsoring Group that Herbert Muhammad was coming on board as his new business manager, no one knew exactly what Herbert would do. Soon, though, Herbert became "the ultimate decider of everything," Arum said, "because he had the connection to the boss." The boss, of course, was the Honorable Elijah Muhammad, Herbert's father. But Ali did not embrace the son only because he admired the father. He and Herbert developed a tight and complicated bond. It was based in part on their mutual affection for mischief and easy money, but that wasn't all. Ali loved Herbert's easy laugh, his optimism, and his warmth. Herbert became Ali's manager and also one of his dearest and most trusted friends.

Yet even as his friendship with Herbert grew and his immersion in the Nation of Islam deepened, Ali remained loyal to and dependent on the Louisville Sponsoring Group, which had him under contract for one more year and which continued to handle most of his business affairs — including paying the rent on his houses; covering his medical bills; providing salaries for his trainers, chefs, sparring partners, and drivers; and setting aside money to pay his taxes. In addition, Ali had been borrowing money against future earnings — up to $5,000 at a time, with his debt climbing to $43,000 before his second fight with Liston. He gave away cash the way real-estate agents give away business cards. He would leave a hotel with five hundred dollars in his pocket, headed for lunch, and disburse it all before he sat down to eat. At even the hint of a hard-luck story, Ali would reach for the roll of cash in his pocket. Offered a chance to invest in a sure thing — any sure thing — he seldom declined. He didn't spend much on clothes, but he installed telephones and record players in his cars, and his phone bills alone sometimes approached eight hundred dollars a month, as he tended to let reporters and anyone else in his room call long distance and stay on the line as long as they liked. He paid medical expenses for members of his entourage. He bought film and camera equipment for Howard Bingham. He ate prodigiously. But his biggest expenses may have been his vehicles — the three cars that were registered in his own name, the two in his father's name, and the bus in his brother's name. Ali paid the insurance on all of them — and his premiums were sky high because of his age and poor driving record.

Ali appreciated that the Louisville Sponsoring Group paid his bills and kept track of his income. He told one boxing promoter after the second Liston fight that he intended to renew his contract with the group. He liked the men in the consortium so much that when one of them said he wanted to sell his stake, Ali took it as a personal affront. He couldn't stand the idea of anyone losing confidence in him. In December 1964, Bill Faversham, the leader of the Louisville group and the closest thing Ali had to a manager, suffered a major heart attack. When he heard the news, Ali got in his car immediately and drove all night from Chicago to Louisville to be with Faversham in the hospital.

Despite his warm feelings toward Faversham and the rest of the Louisville Sponsoring Group, tension arose between them and Ali as Herbert Muhammad got involved. In the days after the Liston fight, Ali told the Louisville businessmen he was eager to pay off his debts and start fighting again, at least three or four times a year, beginning with a bout against Floyd Patterson or George Chuvalo. But Herbert wanted the Louisville businessmen to guarantee the fighter $150,000 after taxes for his next bout. Ali's take from the Liston fight had been $160,000 before taxes and about $95,000 after. There was no way he was going to get $150,000 *after* taxes given that Patterson and Chuvalo were less compelling opponents than Liston. But when the businessmen told him that, Ali said he intended to hold off on paying his debt to the group — a debt that had climbed to $60,000 by August 1965 — until he got what he wanted.

Arthur Grafton, an attorney, wrote in a memo to the Louisville Group: "When we pointed out that this was contrary to our established precedent and that it would leave him with practically nothing net out of the next fight, he seemed to think that this attitude was unfair to him and indicated an unwillingness on our part to do him a little favor. In this he was both egged on and abetted by the language of Herbert Muhammid [sic]." Grafton went on to say he hoped that Ali — who owed money to Sonji now, as well as to his financial supporters — would come to his senses and realize he would quickly go broke if he didn't fight.

There was a degree of racism, or at least paternalism, in the way the Louisville Sponsoring Group treated Ali. There were references in their correspondence to "our boy" and "his unsophisticated mind." But there were also well-intentioned efforts to help. In one letter, a group member commended

Ali's desire to give money to his church — although he also pointed out that Herbert Muhammad had informed the business executives that the Nation of Islam did not qualify as a tax-exempt organization.

A meeting was organized to work out the differences between Ali and his Louisville backers. Archibald Foster, dressed in a dark blue custom-made suit with whalebone buttons and a candy-stripe shirt, hosted the assembly in his New York office. Worth Bingham, Bill Cutchins, and Foster represented the Louisville Sponsoring Group. Ali was joined by Herbert, Howard Bingham, and Angelo Dundee. When they began talking about a fight with Patterson or Chuvalo, Ali grew excited. He wanted to fight again. Then he asked about the money, saying he wanted to donate all or part of his income from the next bout to the Nation of Islam to support construction of a $3.5 million mosque in Chicago. When members of the group reminded him that he made only $95,000 from his last fight and still owed $65,000 to his financial backers, Ali cursed. "I don't see why I should fight any more if I can't make no money," he said.

The white men in the room told Ali that if he kept fighting and investing his money wisely, his wealth would grow, and before long he would have more than enough savings to make generous donations to the Nation of Islam. But Ali was impatient. Three or four times Herbert pulled him out of the office for private conversations while Howard Bingham stayed in the room to monitor the Louisville businessmen.

"The longer we talked, the more violent Cassius and Herbert became," Worth Bingham wrote. After another conference outside the office, Ali came back with a final and even more unrealistic proposition: he would agree to fight if the men would guarantee him $200,000 after taxes. When the businessmen said it was impossible, he dropped his demand to $150,000. Still impossible, they said. He would need to earn $500,000 to clear $150,000 after taxes. Ali also suggested that the Louisville Sponsoring Group pay him $150,000 to renew his contract. When that offer was greeted coolly, he asked if the men would consider forgiving his $65,000 debt. The businessmen offered him a compromise: if he paid off the $65,000 now, they would lend him another $30,000 immediately.

That hurt Ali's feelings. "You were right," he told Herbert. "I can't hardly believe it. I thought they believed in me more than that."

Worth Bingham said he thought it was a mistake to let Ali get in deeper debt because he would "always be behind the eight ball."

Then it was Herbert's turn to take offense. "What he say?" Herbert asked, apparently upset at the use of the term *eight ball,* which is sometimes used to refer to dark-skinned black people. "You hear what he say? Why a man want to talk like that? I don't think you ought to say things like that unless you mean them."

With that, Ali and his group got up and left.

Later the same day, Worth Bingham and the other members of the Louisville Group went to meet the Nilons, who still controlled the rights to promote Ali's next fight. Bingham was horrified to learn that the Nilons had been bribing newspaper reporters with miniature Sony TV sets — and that every reporter except Red Smith, Arthur Daley, and Shirley Povich had accepted the gifts. "It was a bruising day," Bingham wrote in a letter to his fellow members of the group, "full of shocking revelations. We are deep in with pretty undesirable characters who have us where they want us, at least for the timebeing. Through it all came the questioned [sic], repeated by almost everyone: 'What are men like you doing in this business?' A good question, I feel."

20

A Holy War

The crowd booed as he bounced down the aisle, booed louder as he climbed into the ring, and booed loudest when the ring announcer introduced the heavyweight champion as Muhammad Ali, not Cassius Clay. Ali ignored the noise. He walked to his corner, turned up his palms, and recited a brief, silent prayer before turning to meet his opponent, Floyd Patterson.

It was November 22, 1965, two years to the day after the assassination of John F. Kennedy and more than five years since Ali — then an Olympic hopeful named Cassius Clay — had first met Patterson in Rome.

Ali's body glistened under the lights of the Las Vegas Convention Center. The fight began.

By now he was accustomed to being booed. He knew it was good for business, but he was also fueled by a sense of righteousness. Elijah Muhammad's group, he said in the days leading up to the fight, was the only religion teaching "truth, fact, and reality." He continued, "I found within it a device by which the so-called Negroes could unite and do something for themselves instead of begging and forcing themselves on other people. United, we could accomplish things for ourselves the way other nations do . . . I never felt free until I gained the knowledge of myself and the history of our people. This taught me pride and gave me self-dignity . . . To sum it all up, I wish to make it understood that I am not an authority on religion, and not even thirty percent qualified to explain the complex world of religion. I am no leader and not a preacher. I am merely the heavyweight champion of the world who believes in his religion and who is misunderstood." The remarks sounded as if they'd been polished by the interviewer, the boxing publicist Hank Kaplan, and a note attached to Kaplan's original copy of the interview said that the document had been approved by Herbert Muhammad.

Still, these were some of the most succinct and thoughtful comments Ali had made on his conversion, and they aligned him with other young black men who were moving away from the mainstream civil rights movement and fighting for Black Power as opposed to the more pacifist goal of "equal rights." But Ali was different, too. His faith in a nonwestern religion confused many Americans, and his belief that a global union of nonwhites would eventually defeat the Caucasian minority infuriated many of those same people. What made Ali so controversial was that he was an athlete, not a radical political activist. He was more difficult for white Americans to ignore as a result of his boxing career and the media that followed him. In Ali v. Patterson, Ali stood for the black radicals while Patterson represented the integrators, at least in a general sense. Ali carried real animosity for Patterson, anger that had been brewing for at least a year, ever since Patterson had said he felt a sense of moral duty to win the heavyweight championship back from the Muslims. "It's going to be the first time I ever trained to develop in myself a brutal killer instinct," Ali told Alex Haley. "I've never felt that way about nobody else. Fighting is just a sport, a game, to me. But Patterson I would want to beat to the floor." Ali called Patterson the white man's champ. He mocked the former champion for buying a house in a white neighborhood only to move out when he discovered that the white neighbors didn't want him. Patterson, Ali said, was nothing but an "Uncle Tom Negro."

Patterson didn't back down. In an article in *Sports Illustrated* co-authored by Milton Gross, the former champ wrote: "I am a Negro and proud to be one, but I'm also an American. I'm not so stupid that I don't know that Negroes don't have all the rights and privileges that all Americans should have. I know that someday we will get them. God made us all, and whatever He made is good. All people — white, black, and yellow — are brothers and sisters. That will be acknowledged. It will just take time, but it will never come if we think the way the Black Muslims think. . . . Clay is so young and has been so misled by the wrong people that he doesn't appreciate how far we have come and how much harm he has done by joining the Black Muslims. He might just as well have joined the Ku Klux Klan."

Patterson didn't sound like an Uncle Tom any more than Martin Luther King did. He sounded like a man who believed that nonviolent resistance was the most practical and effective approach for black people seeking justice. Radical groups like the Nation of Islam made a lot of noise, but, in Patterson's view, they had accomplished nothing and probably never would. Patterson's mistake was not in arguing politics. His mistake, if it can be called one, was in attempting to make a boxing match stand for something more than a fist-fight. He declared his contest against Ali a holy war. Patterson said Ali had a right to believe in any religion he wanted. But, he added, "I have rights, too. I have the right to call the Black Muslims a menace to the United States and a menace to the Negro race. I have a right to say the Black Muslims stink. . . . So in addition to winning the world's heavyweight title for the third time, I have one other responsibility. The Black Muslim influence must be removed from boxing."

Ali's response was unambiguous: Patterson was going to get hurt.

Sportswriters, of course, love to depict athletic contests in the most gran-diose terms. When Jesse Owens won the gold medal at the 1936 Olympics, writers described it as a victory over Hitler's notions of Aryan supremacy. But first it was a simple footrace. In this case, too, Ali v. Patterson would be a punching contest before all else, and Ali, as the bigger, stronger, younger, faster man, held every advantage.

The fight began and no one in the crowd could understand what Ali was doing. He seemed to be throwing punches with no intention of hitting Patter-son. He was throwing them far above Patterson's head and far from his body, pulling back to make sure he never came close to making contact. When Patterson bulled in and tried to pummel Ali's body, Ali grabbed Patterson's head, hugged him, then pushed him away and began throwing more of those strange, fake punches. At one point, Ali threw both hands in the air, as if per-forming a jumping jack, and then danced away, bobbing, circling, and wag-ging his shoulders. At another moment, he drew circles with his right hand, as if winding up for a Popeye punch, only to drop his fist and retreat again.

"Come on, American! Come on, white American!" Ali taunted his oppo-nent.

Patterson must have felt as if he were fighting a ghost. He couldn't hit Ali, and Ali wasn't hitting him. It may have been the only time in the history of heavyweight boxing that the defending champion seemed entirely uninterested in punching. When the bell rang to end the round, Ali returned to his corner and raised his hands in triumph as the crowd once again booed.

What had happened to his intent to drive Patterson to the floor, to make the man suffer? Or was this strange opening round part of his plan? It seems unlikely that Ali felt the need to fatigue Patterson, as he had Liston. Ali always said he fought on instinct, and in the opening round against Patterson it looked as if he had so much energy and so much anger that he found himself pushing the bounds of his own creative forces, like Miles Davis waiting and waiting to play the first note of a trumpet solo until the audience couldn't stand it, letting the silence speak until it resounded more forcefully than any blown note ever could. Ali's punchless performance was pure electricity, possibly madness, possibly genius.

In round two, real blows were exchanged. The first five Ali jabs were quick as a cobra's tongue, each one grazing Patterson's left ear. Then Ali made the necessary calibrations and his punches began thumping Patterson's nose, chin, and forehead. They stung, but they served another purpose. Ali's arm span was seven inches longer than Patterson's, a massive advantage for a man trying to hit without being hit. Ali knew he didn't have to hurt Patterson with the jab. The jab would keep Patterson at a distance, off balance, and unable to attack. Ali didn't know it, but he had another advantage. Earlier in the week, Patterson had injured his back. He didn't want to call off the fight, but he was clearly impeded by the injury. In round two, Ali threw sixty five punches and connected on fourteen, and while that was not a great percentage, Patterson attempted only nineteen punches and connected four times. It was a one-sided fight, and it would continue that way, as Ali circled and jabbed, seemingly content to go on all night, popping Patterson in the face, calling him an Uncle Tom, and then popping him in the face again. Finally, in the twelfth round of a scheduled fifteen-round bout, Ali attacked with genuine fury, the kind he had promised to unleash against his opponent. He abandoned the jab and threw uppercuts and hooks with the full force of his body, all of them aimed at Patterson's face.

"A happiness feeling came over me," Patterson would tell writer Gay Talese later, referring to the twelfth round. "I knew the end was near ... I was feeling groggy and happy ... I wanted be hit by a really good one. I wanted to go out with a great punch, to go down that way."

But he didn't. The referee stopped the fight.

Ali had obliterated Patterson. Of course, the crowd booed him for it. The white press criticized Ali too, accusing him of torturing his opponent the way a psychopath might torture a defenseless animal, which seems an odd complaint given that the objective of boxing is to hurt, torture, and render a man unconscious. What had Ali done wrong? Was jabbing a man relentlessly for twelve rounds somehow crueler than jolting his skull and short-circuiting his brain with one whopping punch? Ali knew there was but one way he would please his critics, and that was to lose.

After the fight, there was a victory party at the Sands Hotel. Sonji, apparently uninvited, showed up in a slinky red dress. She chatted with Bundini and sat in the lap of Cassius Clay Sr.

Ali watched her from across the room but did not approach.

"I got a feeling I was born for a purpose," Ali had said before the Patterson fight. "I don't know what I'm here for. I just feel abnormal, a different kind of man. I don't know why I was born. I'm just here. A young man rumbling. I've always had that feeling since I was a little boy. Perhaps I was born to fulfill Biblical prophecies. I just feel I may be part of something — divine things. Everything seems strange to me."

In countless ways, Ali behaved as if he were special, different, a young man rumbling.

Ali liked to be paid in cash after a fight. Once, around the time of the Patterson fight, Arthur Grafton, one of the lawyers for the Louisville Sponsoring Group, accompanied Ali to the bank. "He had something like twenty-seven thousand dollars coming to him, I think it was," Grafton told writer Jack Olsen. "That was what was left after he paid his divorce lawyers and a thousand dollars extra to a sparring partner and another five thousand somewhere else and whatever it was he owed us. We walked to the bank and he asked for twenty-seven thousand-dollar bills. The bank didn't have it, and Cassius said, 'Well, how long would it take you to get it?' and the bank said about twenty minutes, from the Federal Reserve. Cassius said no, that'd take too long, and the tellers started making up his twenty-seven thousand in smaller denominations. We finally wound up with a great big pouch full of money, and on the side of it was written in big letters 'First National Bank,' and we had to carry that thing through the streets of Louisville to his hotel. Before we left, Cassius said to the lady teller: 'You know I'm gonna count this money back in my hotel room and you'll know it'll be an honest count because my lawyer will watch me.' On the way back he was kidding me — I was nervous about this whole idea — and he said, 'Do you think I'm gonna be held up? You do, don't you?' He said, 'Maybe we should hire a cop. How much would it cost to hire a cop to walk back with us?' We got to the hotel and he spilled all the money out on the bed and started counting, and would you believe it? It was a thousand dollars short! We counted it five times and then carried the whole bag right back to the bank. They had already realized it was short and were expecting us. Then Cassius, twenty-seven thousand dollars in cash and all, flew off to Chicago."

Ali liked to run his fingers through his money and show the piles of cash to friends. He needed to see it and feel it in part because so much of his income seemed to vanish before he could spend it. Before Ali could ever see his money, big chunks of it went to the IRS, Sonji, the Louisville Sponsoring Group, his lawyers, members of his entourage, and various car dealerships. He often asked members of the Louisville Group to give him photostats of his income-tax receipts. It wasn't that he wanted proof that the taxes were being paid; it was that he couldn't believe how much Uncle Sam was taking, and he liked to show off the receipts to friends. Of course, keeping all that cash on hand sometimes added to his loss. Once, in 1965, his limousine driver took off, never to return, with three thousand dollars that Ali had been keeping in the trunk of his Cadillac. But Ali grew accustomed to such losses.

As his contract with the Louisville Sponsoring Group neared its end, the boxer told his backers he intended to renew the deal. But members of the group encountered a complication, and they were not happy about it. In January 1966, Muhammad Ali summoned the press to announce a new business venture called Main Bout, Inc., that would manage the ancillary promotional rights to all his fights, including the live and tape-delayed broadcasts. "I am vitally interested in the company," he said, "and in seeing that it will be one in which Negroes are not used as fronts, but as stockholders, officers, and production and promotion agents."

Ali was making good money on his fights. The Patterson bout two months earlier had grossed about $3.5 million, with about $750,000 of that going to Ali and the Louisville Sponsorship Group. He was by far the biggest and most well-paid draw in all of sports. Now, in pronouncing the creation of his own promotional company, Ali was asserting unprecedented autonomy for a black athlete. He was also diverting the biggest stream of income so that it would no longer flow to the Louisville Sponsoring Group. It was a sign of how much the world had changed in six years. When he had come home from the Olympics, the young boxer had considered himself fortunate to have a group of white benefactors. Now, he was talking about black independence and economic empowerment in terms that would have been unimaginable in 1960.

Members of the Louisville Group, not surprisingly, were shaken. In an interview with the FBI, attorney Arthur Grafton of the Louisville Sponsoring Group said he did his best to warn Ali that Main Bout was not offering him a good deal. Ali told Grafton he didn't understand Grafton's concerns. The organizers of Main Bout were his friends, Ali said, and Herbert Muhammad was the son of Elijah Muhammad, "who gives me strength — if I can help the Muslims, it gives me strength — it doesn't hurt if I don't make as much money as I would." Grafton knew he couldn't change the fighter's mind. In a memo to the members of the Louisville Group, he wrote that Ali was "obviously now being completely dominated by the Muslims." In response, at least one member of the group said he wanted to sever his connection with the boxer.

The businessmen were not alone in their anger. "The fight racket has been turned into a crusade by the Muslims," complained the sports writer Jimmy Cannon. "Their great trophy is Clay." Doug Gilbert, writing in *Chicago's American,* said, "If the Muslims own Clay, and also own the television rights to all his fights, they have what amounts to a hammerlock on all that's lucrative in boxing."

But there was also irony in the racist fears surrounding Ali's move toward independence. To begin with, the so-called Muslim crusade to control the fight business was the brainchild of a white Jew, the New York lawyer Bob Arum. Arum presented the idea to Herbert Muhammad, who invited Arum to Chicago to seek the approval of Elijah Muhammad. Arum was summoned to a meeting at Elijah Muhammad's home, where a large entourage of Muslims stood and listened respectfully. After twenty or thirty minutes of cordial discussion about their shared business interests, Elijah Muhammad, seemingly for no reason, launched into a sermon about "blue-eyed devils" and the sins perpetrated upon the black man. Arum had the impression Elijah Muhammad was giving a performance for his entourage, and he took it as a sign of Muhammad's cunning intelligence. When the meeting was over, Elijah Muhammad gave the deal his blessings, but with one condition: he wanted John Ali, the national secretary of the Nation of Islam, to be included in the new business because John Ali had a more sophisticated knowledge of business than Herbert.

Did Elijah Muhammad approve the deal because it was good for the Nation of Islam? That wasn't Arum's sense of it. "It was a way for his son to make some decent bucks," Arum recalled. Herbert Muhammad was already getting about a third of Ali's boxing income — by some accounts it was 40 percent. Now, he would also receive $45,000 a year in salary plus a percentage of revenues from Main Bout. He was making so much money that members of his own family were growing jealous, according to an FBI memo. And Herbert's family didn't know that Herbert was also taking money "under the table," according to the FBI, cutting partners in on some of the Main Bout profits in exchange for cash up front.

Why was John Ali included in the Main Bout deal? Arum said he learned years later from a source in law enforcement that John Ali may have been one of the forces behind the murder of Malcolm X, "and this was his reward . . . the boxing money." John Ali denied it, saying neither he nor anyone else in the Nation of Islam had anything to do with Malcolm's murder.

Arum put together a group of five officers and stockholders that included himself; another white man named Mike Malitz, who controlled most of the nation's closed-circuit TV business; football star Jim Brown; Herbert Muhammad; and John Ali. Muhammad Ali had no ownership stake in the company and no seat on the board of directors. In an interview years later, John Ali said he and Herbert profited personally from Main Bout. Muhammad Ali was paid a percentage of revenues from each fight, and the Louisville Sponsorship Group was compensated until its contract with Ali expired. But none of the money flowed to the Nation of Islam, according to John Ali. "The Nation was not dependent on charity," he said.

"The more I think about the situation," Louisville Sponsoring Group member Archibald Foster wrote, "the more I want to be quit of my association with the champion. All our long-term purposes have been frustrated. We had hoped to be completely free of underworld connections, but we seem to have new ones in Chicago. Certainly we don't very much like the anti-American philosophy which attaches to us by association. Finally, the money rewards are so little that I can't believe any of us are interested in those. What I'd like to do is to give Cassius back his contract."

On February 16, 1966, Arthur Grafton circulated a memo saying they would begin making sure all their bills were paid and their obligations met so that they could "relinquish our contract to Clay" when the right time came. Meanwhile, Grafton said, he had reserved seventy-five ringside seats for Ali's fight against Ernie Terrell in Chicago if any members of the group wished to attend. It looked as if this would probably be their last chance to enjoy the perks of their association with boxing's heavyweight champion.

Many members of the group said they intended to attend the fight. For all the complications they had encountered, for all the frustrations, most of the men still adored and wished well for the young man whose career they had helped launch.

21

No Quarrel

Muhammad Ali stretched his long legs and sank back into his lawn chair as he sang a refrain from Bob Dylan: "The answer is blowin' in the wind." It was February 17, 1966, and the question on Ali's mind was this: why had a draft board in Louisville reversed its previous position and classified his status as 1-A, suddenly making him eligible for military service?

"Why me?" he asked as he reclined in front of his gray cement house in Miami, jawing with reporters, neighbors, and friends. "I can't understand it. How did they do this to me — the heavyweight champion of the world?"

Two years earlier, when he was calling himself Cassius Clay, he had failed his pre-induction mental exam. But since then, the war in Vietnam had escalated. From 1964 to 1965, the number of American soldiers dying in Vietnam increased ninefold, from about 200 to 1,900. In 1966, the death toll would triple to more than 6,000. More American soldiers were being called to duty, and many of those who had been deferred faced reevaluation. As the death count rose, so did the divide among American people. Many believed that if South Vietnam fell to a communist power, the rest of Southeast Asia would follow, while others argued that America had no reason to fight in a nation that even the new president, Lyndon B. Johnson, referred to privately as "a raggedy-ass, fourth-rate country."

Ali repeated his complaint to one TV reporter after another. Everyone knew the draft was rigged to protect wealthy white men from service, while the poor and dark-skinned served in disproportionately high numbers, he said. Around the house, members of the Nation of Islam warned Ali that he would be sent to the frontlines right away, that white cracker sergeants were going to torture him.

"How can they reclassify me 1-A?" Ali asked.

"How can they do this without another test to see if I'm any wiser or worser than last time?"

Reporter Bob Halloran of the CBS Evening News showed up with a cameraman. Halloran went inside, unplugged Ali's phone without Ali's knowing so they wouldn't be interrupted, and then began his interview, asking the boxer to react to the draft board's decision. Ali gave Halloran his reaction in a burst:

"Yes, sir, that was a great surprise to me," he said. "It was not me who said that I was classified 1-Y the last time. It was the government who tested me. It was the government who said that I'm not able. Now, in order to be 1-A I do not remember being called nowhere to be reclassified as 1-A. Two fellas got together and made the statement that I'm 1-A without knowing if I'm as good as I was last time or better. Now, they had 30 men to pick from in Louisville, Kentucky . . . To pick out the heavyweight champion of the whole world . . . You have a lot of men in baseball you could've called. You have a lot of young men in football they could've called. You have a lot of young men that they could've called . . . that have taken the test and are 1-A. Now, I was not 1-A last time they checked me. All of a sudden they seem to be anxious to put me in the army and throw me in the 1-A category out of thirty or forty men that they could've picked from, and two men made the decision. And another thing I don't understand, I really don't understand, is why me, a man who pays the salary of *at least* 50,000 men in Vietnam, a man who the government takes $6 million from a year off of two fights, a man who can pay in two fights for three bomber planes."

That evening, Ali and his friends gathered in front of the TV to watch Walter Cronkite deliver the evening news on CBS. After a report about riots at a penal institution for girls in Indianapolis ("End of times!" someone in the room shouted at the TV), Cronkite introduced the story Ali had been waiting to see.

"In Louisville today . . . ," Cronkite began.

"Shhh-shh," said Ali.

Cronkite continued: ". . . heavyweight champion Cassius Clay's draft board reclassified him 1-A, making him immediately eligible for military service."

Ali was on the screen next, reciting his fiery pronouncements, complaining about being classified as 1-A. When it was done, Cronkite appeared again on the black-and-white TV to say there was no indication when Clay might be inducted or if his March 29 fight against Ernie Terrell would be canceled.

"That was a good one, wasn't it?" Ali asked the room.

Affirmation, along with a commercial for Chiffon margarine, came promptly.

"Did Lyndon Johnson hear what I just said?" Ali asked. "Was he watching that?"

"He was watching it!" someone shouted.

"Lyndon Johnson watches that? Two of my fights I pay for three bomber planes!"

Whether LBJ heard Ali's comments or not, millions of others did. The war in Vietnam provoked heated debate, but the majority of Americans in 1966 still supported the effort to fight communism in Southeast Asia. When TV viewers and newspaper readers learned that Ali did not want to serve in the military, it sounded like further proof of his selfishness and disdain for his own country. Ali never said he opposed the war on political, philosophical, or religious grounds; all he said was that he didn't want to go, that the draft board ought to be able to find someone to take his place, and that he didn't mind if the nation used his tax money to buy bomber jets to kill the enemy in Vietnam.

Two days later, he refined his argument, telling a reporter for the *Chicago Daily News* in a telephone interview, "I am a member of the Muslims and we don't go to wars unless they are declared by Allah Himself. I don't have no personal quarrel with those Viet Congs." He added, "All I know is they are considered as Asiatic black people and I don't have no fight with black people. I have never been over there and I have nothing against them." He had probably heard that the Student Nonviolent Coordinating Committee had taken a stand against the war, saying it was wrong to send black Americans to fight for democracy in Vietnam when they were denied freedom in their own country. Ali said he'd seen white men burning their draft cards on TV, and he'd heard that some congressmen opposed the war in Vietnam. "If they're against the war . . . why should we Muslims be for it?" he asked.

Ali was making a moral and religious argument now, one likely inspired by his teacher, Elijah Muhammad, who had served four years in prison during World War II for refusing to fight. Sam Saxon, now going by the name Abdul Rahman, claimed he was the one who fed Ali the memorable line, "I don't have no personal quarrel with those Viet Congs." Later, a variation of the quote would be widely attributed to Ali: "I ain't got no quarrel with the Viet Cong." It would be coupled with another quote, one that would appear on T-shirts and posters bearing Ali's image, becoming one of the most powerful quotations ever attributed to an American athlete: "No Viet Cong ever called me nigger." There's little question that Ali uttered the first remark, or something close to it. But there's no evidence that he spoke the second sentence until years later on a movie set. As Stefan Fatsis noted in a 2016 essay, antiwar protesters had used the phrase "No Viet Cong ever called me nigger" before Ali spoke out on the war.

Nevertheless, in his refusal to accept the Viet Cong as his enemy, Ali showed how his views were coalescing. His enemy was not to be found in Southeast Asia, he said; his enemy was American racism.

When he recognized its resonance, Ali began repeating the line: "I have no quarrel with the Viet Cong," or the double-negative version, "I ain't got no quarrel with them Viet Cong." It would become his most memorable quote in a lifetime of them. It was witty. It was rebellious. Whether it was calculated or not didn't matter because, essentially, it was true. Alone, with almost no support from the nation's intellectuals or religious leaders, he had taken a position that was, ironically, very much American. Like Henry David Thoreau, who refused to pay taxes that helped fund slavery and the Mexican-American War, and like the black men and women who refused to leave all-white lunch counters in the South, Ali was making a stand for civil disobedience, for freedom.

On February 28, 1966, eleven days after being notified of his new draft status, Ali submitted paperwork to the Selective Service claiming to be a conscientious objector. He claimed exemption to both combat and noncombat service, based on religious belief. He named Elijah Muhammad as the person he relied on most for religious guidance, said he believed in the use of force "only in sports and self defense," and cited as proof of his consistent religious conviction that he had divorced his wife, "whom I loved because she wouldn't conform to my Muslim faith."

Much of the form was completed by a New York attorney, Edward W. Jackson, who said Ali had asked him to record his answers. But on the first page, where a signature was required, Ali wrote:

Slave Name Cassius M Clay Jr RIGHT NAME Muhammad Ali.

Not surprisingly, Ali's refusal to fight for his country inspired more hatred.

Jim Murray of the *Los Angeles Times* snidely called Ali "the greatest American patriot since Benedict Arnold, the No. 1 candidate for the Congressional Medal of Prudence." Murray had a suggestion for Ali, whom he still referred to as Cassius Clay: "Go to some mother in Iowa — or Harlem for that matter. She will be sure to understand. Tell her you got this chance to make a big-money shot. Tell her you got two Cadillacs, an ex-wife, a whole religion to support . . . Suggest she send her son instead. You got no quarrel with the Viet Cong, you said. Well, I think you're on solid ground there, Cash. Why go to war for a lousy principle? I mean, look at it this way: half-a-million guys get killed in the Civil War fighting slavery. I bet half of them didn't even know what it was . . . The dumb clucks should've burned their draft cards. Or hired a lawyer, like you're doing. Well, there's a good side of it, Cash. If they hadn't died to free your folks, think of all the lawyers who would be out of work. Lordy. Elijah Muhammad himself might be broke. You're supporting the whole fez industry." Others writers questioned Ali's intelligence, saying that he didn't understand the issues or principles involved. A few speculated that Ali opposed the draft simply to drum up interest in his fight with Ernie Terrell. Several others claimed Ali was nothing but a puppet for Elijah Muhammad, that Ali would serve if Elijah told him to.

In Chicago, where Ali was supposed to fight Ernie Terrell, local newspapers urged cancellation of the bout. For the editorial writers at *Chicago's American,* the issue was Ali's unconvincing series of excuses for refusing the draft. The *Tribune,* meanwhile, didn't want to see money from the fight going to the Nation of Islam by way of Main Bout, Inc. Soon, veterans groups and local politicians joined the call for cancellation of the fight. At one point, Ali offered a half-hearted apology. "If I knew everything I had said on politics would have been taken that seriously . . . I never would have opened my mouth," he told United Press International.

Ali's team requested a formal hearing before the Illinois State Athletic

Commission. Bob Arum, who flew with Ali from Miami, thought the fight could be saved if Ali presented his political views tactfully. But before the hearing, Ali visited Elijah Muhammad, who was furious to hear that the boxer was considering another apology. That got Ali's attention, apparently. When he addressed the committee, Ali expressed regret for anyone who would be hurt financially by cancellation of the fight and for politicians who'd been put in an uncomfortable spot. But when a commission member asked if he was sorry for his unpatriotic comments, Ali said no, "I'm not apologizing for anything like that because I don't have to." About half an hour after the hearing, Illinois Attorney General William Clark, citing technicalities in licensing procedures, declared the match illegal. As Arum put it, "That's when they threw us out of Chicago."

Whether Ali was inspired by religion, politics, or devotion to Elijah Muhammad, many Americans had underestimated his commitment. His decision stoked the anger of white people, who said that the heavyweight champion was supposed to stand as a role model for American youth and a symbol of American strength. Perhaps less obvious was his effect on the black community, and in particular on young black men, for whom Ali was emerging as a powerful icon. For many young and rebellious black people, Ali's religion didn't matter; the important thing was that he stood up to white authority and spoke out forcefully against racism. He proved it before the Athletic Commission in Illinois and in the ring against Patterson. As Eldridge Cleaver wrote in his 1968 autobiography *Soul on Ice:* "If the Bay of Pigs can be seen as a straight right hand to the psychological jaw of white America then [Ali/Patterson] was the perfect left hook to the gut." One sign of Ali's growing impact: in 1965, the Student Nonviolent Coordinating Committee in Lowndes, Alabama, chose the symbol of a black panther for its logo and attached to it a slogan inspired by the champ, "WE Are the Greatest." Suddenly, a blast of ego became a call to arms. Huey Newton, the cofounder of the Black Panthers, said that while he had no interest in God or Allah, the speeches of Malcolm X and Muhammad Ali were crucial in the process of his politicization.

Ali described his growing cultural influence in a 1970 interview in the *Black Scholar:* "I was determined to be the one nigger the white man didn't get. Go on and join something. If it isn't the Muslims, at least join the Black Panthers. Join something bad."

• • •

The Terrell fight fell apart. Ali had to choose a new opponent in a hurry. In the two years since he'd become champ, he'd only fought twice. It was time to make money, to cash in as quickly and as often as possible, especially given that the U.S. Army wanted to put him in uniform and out of work. But now Ali's team had to scrounge for a deal. After being rejected by Illinois and warned by several other locales that he was unwelcome, Ali and his managers turned to Canada, announcing a fight against George Chuvalo on March 29 at the Maple Leaf Gardens in Toronto.

Being forced to leave his own country filled Ali, once again, with a sense of his own importance. "It doesn't look right to the free world, the way I'm being treated," he said. "This all makes me bigger. I always knew I was meant for something. It's taking shape, a destiny. To be great you must suffer, you must pay the price."

Members of the Louisville Sponsoring Group tried to persuade Ali to compromise on his military service. They called in favors and received assurances from powerful men in government that if Ali agreed to serve his country, he would be assigned a role that kept him far from combat. In all likelihood, he would perform a series of boxing exhibitions for soldiers just as Joe Louis had done during World War II. Gordon Davidson, representing the group, flew to New York to make the pitch to Ali. Davidson believed that Ali was a fine young man but very impressionable. "Elijah Muhammad pumped a lot of poison into him," Davidson said. "Ali didn't believe all that." The lawyer hoped to impress upon the boxer how much he would lose by refusing the draft. He found Ali in a suite at the Sheraton Hotel in Manhattan, surrounded by about a dozen Muslims, all of them dressed in black suits. "I had on my desk contracts worth more than $1 million from various companies, including Coca-Cola," Davidson said. "I told him, 'You know, they're all going to go *whoosh,* out the window.'"

But Ali would not be moved.

"The conversation lasted two hours," Davidson recounted. "And at the end he said, 'I want to thank you because I know you had my best interests at heart.' He was very gracious and appreciative."

Chuvalo was one of those fighters, like Rocky Marciano, fueled by pride and guts, a tough guy who didn't mind taking a punch for every one he gave. For Arum, who was promoting the fight and using his personal credit card to cover his expenses, it was not an easy event to sell. Chuvalo's size and battered face would give even the toughest man pause in a bar fight, but the Canadian was considered no match for Ali. In an attempt to raise interest in the lack-luster matchup, Ali called it an international battle pitting Canada's champ against America's and did his best to make it sound as if he were worried about losing. As a "warrior on the battleground of freedom," Ali said, he had been too busy in recent months to train properly. When one of Ali's sparring partners, Jimmy Ellis, knocked him down during a practice session, sports-writers concluded the champ was telling the truth.

Chuvalo was twenty-eight years old, with a record of thirty-four wins, eleven losses, and two draws, but he was big and strong, and he'd never been knocked out. In the pre-fight media flurry, Chuvalo promised he would not go down easily, as Liston had. "Hell, my kid could've taken a better punch than that," he said, referring to the so-called phantom punch thrown in Lew-iston, Maine. A journalist asked if Chuvalo meant his eldest son, who was six years old. "No, no," Chuvalo corrected. "I mean Jesse, the youngest. He's two. It would be an insult to the oldest to say he can't take a harder shot than Liston did."

The bell rang. Ali jabbed. Chuvalo let him. Every time Ali stopped jab-bing, Chuvalo moved inside and pounded Ali's ribcage. At one point in the opening round, Chuvalo banged fourteen consecutive right hooks to the same spot on Ali's left side before Ali moved away and hit back.

"Harder! Harder!" Ali said.

In the second round, Ali raised his hands and stood still, inviting Chuvalo to hit him in the stomach again. Chuvalo obliged.

"It's the chance of a lifetime for Chuvalo," the ringside announcer said. Chuvalo outpunched Ali in the first four rounds, 120 to 92. That was star-tling enough. But even more important was Chuvalo's advantage in power punches. Ali landed only 30 of them in the first four rounds; Chuvalo landed 107.

Chuvalo exposed the weaknesses that legendary trainer Eddie Futch had spotted in Ali. The champ didn't have a great knockout punch, and he never worked the opponent's body, Futch said. And Ali's defense, the trainer said, was "monolithic," relying almost entirely on his ability to back away from punches rather than ducking or deflecting them. Ali made up for it, Futch said, with "his speed and his good reflexes and his big heart." Big heart, in boxing language, meant the ability to remain conscious while getting batted about the head. Ali and Chuvalo both had plenty of heart.

More than any man Ali had ever faced, Chuvalo forced the champ to fight all out, to abandon gimmicks and draw on the full extent of his talent, mixing jabs and hooks, punching until his arms grew weary and his hands sore.

In his first fight against Liston, Ali had landed 95 punches. In the rematch, he had needed only 4 punches. Against Patterson, he had landed 210 blows over twelve rounds. Now, against Chuvalo, Ali would land 474 punches while absorbing 335 — including more than 300 power punches. It was the heaviest beating Ali had ever taken. "In my own mind," Chuvalo once said, "I was, like, special . . . I always said to myself that I couldn't be hurt. I felt, a crazy part of me felt, indestructible." After the fourth round, Ali may have begun to sense that Chuvalo was indeed indestructible, or that he at least believed in his own indestructibility. Ali said after the fight that Chuvalo's head was "the hardest thing I've ever punched."

Pacing himself, Ali circled the ring. He fought like a man who expected a long night and recognized that the judges — not a cut to the head and not a knockout blow — would likely decide the outcome. Chuvalo more than any other fighter to that point had revealed how Ali might be beaten: plan for a long night of work, stay inside, work the body, and keep pounding. He gave Ali a vicious beating, forcing him to go fifteen rounds for the first time. But the judges, in a unanimous decision, named Ali the winner.

Chuvalo finished the night with a lumpy face yet an unbroken spirit. He noted years later that Ali had to go to the hospital after the fight because he was "pissing blood" from so many kidney shots.

"Me?" Chuvalo said. "I got to go dancing with my wife."

22

"What's My Name?"

At the moment when Ali should have been the king of boxing and the undisputed champion of sports commerce, he was so unpopular that he couldn't get a fight in the United States. One after another, politicians proved their patriotism by banning Ali from their provinces. Even Louisville refused him.

The Chuvalo fight, while entertaining enough, did not provide a windfall. The arena had sold out, but closed-circuit ticket sales were scant, in part because the fight had been arranged on short notice and in part because fans had not expected much from Chuvalo. Ali understood that his career might be halted at any moment if the army forced him to enlist. Meanwhile, he was broke. He had fifty thousand dollars socked away in the trust fund that the Louisville Sponsoring Group had all but forced upon him, and that was all.

So Ali did what Ali did best. He fought. Over the next twelve months, he would defend his heavyweight title six times. Not since the heyday of Joe Louis in 1941 had a champion fought so often.

"I am a fighter, and a fighter's years in business are not very long," he said. "So I stay in action, stay alert, stay on target. And because I can go into the ring and come out again without being hurt, I can afford to keep going, doing twice the amount of work other champions have done, because it takes less out of me." Or, as Herbert Muhammad put it: "Standard Oil doesn't try to sell a small amount of oil each year."

In those six fights, though his opponents were not uniformly top-rate, Ali lived up to his braggadocio. No one knew, of course, that they were seeing the boxer in his prime for the last time.

On May 21, 1966, before 46,000 people at the Arsenal Football Stadium in England, Ali fought Henry Cooper again. Starting slowly, Ali waltzed around the ring, throwing insignificant punches here and there, like a man bothered by a fly in the room. At last, in the fourth, he attacked, and from that point on he hit Cooper wherever and whenever he wanted. In the sixth, an Ali right ruptured the skin over Cooper's left eye — a cut that would require sixteen stitches to close — and the referee stepped in to stop a contest that was never much of one.

Less than three months later, once again in England, Ali needed only three rounds to knock out Brian London. In this fight, anyway, he proved that he really could go into the ring and come out unhurt. London landed only seven punches.

For his next fight, in Frankfurt, Germany, against Karl Mildenberger, Ali did not have the company of his brother, who had recently gotten married. Ali's parents tagged along instead. Three hours after taking off from Chicago, the champ was asleep when Odessa, the only woman in the traveling group, awakened her son with kisses on the forehead.

"Is my baby okay?" she cooed.

"Yes, Mama, I'm fine," he softly replied. "I'll bet you're nervous, huh, Mom — 35,000 feet up?"

"No, baby," she said. "As long as I'm with you, Mama's fine."

Mildenberger was a tough, experienced fighter, with a record of forty-nine wins, two losses, and three draws. He was also a lefty, a species that had given Ali trouble since his earliest days as an amateur.

Sure enough, Ali struggled. He couldn't jab as often as he liked. When he threw hooks, Mildenberger ducked them with ease. Only a quarter of Ali's punches were landing. Usually, he landed better than one in three. With each passing round, the crowd of more than fifty thousand at Frankfurt's Waldstadion cheered more loudly for the ten to one underdog Mildenberger. It was the first heavyweight championship fight ever held in Germany. Still, Mildenberger was more nuisance than hazard, like a developing nation trying to make the threats of a superpower. In the eighth round, Ali seemed to decide enough was enough and took control. An Ali right buckled the German's knees. As Mildenberger teetered, Ali shoved him to the mat. Mildenberger got up, but Ali dropped him again in the tenth. By now the challenger was a bleeding mess. Finally, in the twelfth, another straight right by Ali left Mildenberger dazed and helpless, and the referee stopped the fight.

The Mildenberger bout was Ali's last under the Louisville Sponsoring Group. On October 22, as the business relationship ended, members of the group received a summary of their investment in the boxer. It showed total income of $2.37 million, with $1.36 million of that, or about 58 percent, having gone to Ali. After expenses, the group's net profit amounted to about $200,000, to be divided thirteen ways. Ali had paid back his loans to the group, he had paid his taxes, and he had about $75,000 in a trust fund. Though the boxer had not taken good care of his money, and though the members of the Louisville Group had not seen much of a return on their investment, the businessmen felt satisfied. They'd helped guide the young boxer's career as he rose to become champion and helped him earn a great fortune. From 1964 to 1966, Ali had earned more than $1.2 million. Baseball's highest paid player during those same years was Willie Mays, who had earned only about $100,000 a year. Even adjusting for inflation, Ali was almost certainly the best-paid athlete in American history up to that point, and by a wide margin. Unfortunately, he had burned through his money quickly. He still had his trust fund, but that was about the extent of his savings. At one point in 1966, his personal bank account showed a balance of $109.

Gordon Davidson said the Louisville Sponsoring Group's primary goal had been to help Ali become champion. They had not only managed his career and his money well; they had also stuck with him when he joined the Nation of Islam. Ali appreciated it. At a boxing exhibition in Louisville near the end of his contract, he asked the members of the group to step into the ring so that he could thank them publicly. All things considered, Davidson said, the members of the group would look back on their time with Ali with enormous pride. They helped launch one of the greatest careers in American athletic history, he said, and "we also showed young men they can reach the top in the fight game without selling their souls."

Before his next fight at age twenty-four, Ali spoke of retirement. His back ached. His hands hurt. Cleveland "Big Cat" Williams would be his next opponent, he said, and probably one of his last. This time, Ali found a venue in the United States willing to let him fight. The bout would be held in America's newest temple of sport, Houston's Astrodome, the nation's first indoor stadium, then called the "Eighth Wonder of the World." Money would pour in not only from ticket sales but also, once again, from closed-circuit TV broadcasts in nearly fifty countries. The match would air on live TV in Mexico and Canada. Ali said he wanted to fight Williams, then Ernie Terrell, and then retire "with money in the bank."

Ali called Williams his "most dangerous opponent," and there was a time when that might have been true, but two years earlier Williams had been shot in the stomach by a .357 magnum bullet from a police officer's gun, and it had taken four operations to save his life. He hadn't been the same since.

More than 35,000 spectators filled the Astrodome for the fight, which turned out to be entirely one-sided. In the first round, Ali scored almost at will, moving fast around the ring, throwing jabs, hooks, and four-punch combinations. In the second round, Ali found an even easier target in the plodding big man. Ali's fists circled and sliced, furling lines in countless new ways, each line ending abruptly on Williams's chin. A spectator who had never boxed might think Ali was feeling good in the ring, like an artist in the moment of soulful expression, but for an athlete, unfortunately, that's not how it works. Boxing tortures the nerves. It requires complete attention, complete exertion. Ali said it many times: boxing was his job, not a means of expression. If he took the time to think about how he felt, if he allowed his concentration to flag for a moment, he might have found himself flat on the floor, staring up at the lights, felled by a single punch. Ali would appreciate his brilliance later, watching his fights on film, but never in the ring. In the ring, he was all energy and improvisation and fury, a warrior, not an artist.

With a left-right combination, Ali sent Williams to the canvas. Then he did it again. When Williams got up the second time, blood streamed from his nose and mouth. Ali moved in relentlessly and knocked him to the floor once more. This time Williams was saved by the bell. In most fights, the referee will declare a knockout if a fighter falls three times in a round, but this was a championship bout, so the rule had been waived. As Williams rose unsteadily from his stool to begin another round, Ali raked his opponent's face with more punches. More blood drizzled to the floor. Down went Williams.

One last time the wounded fighter struggled to his feet, "manfully and use-lessly," as *Sports Illustrated* noted, but Ali piled punches upon punches until the referee stopped the fight.

Boxing writers and former boxers continued to criticize Ali's unorthodox boxing style and to question his toughness. "Trouble with Clay, he thinks he knows it all," Joe Louis wrote in *The Ring* magazine. "He won't listen . . . With room to move, Clay's a champion, real dangerous. But he doesn't know a thing about fighting on the ropes, which is where he would be if he were in there with me." Still, Ali was winning, and winning impressively. Even grizzled boxing veterans admitted that the champion's performance against Williams had been extraordinary; seldom had one fighter inflicted so much damage while suffering so little. No one knew if Ali had been serious about retirement, but had he truly intended to quit boxing, this would have been a fine moment for it. He was one of the most handsome and handsomely paid men on the planet. He was largely undamaged by a sport that crippled and stupefied even its best practitioners. And he had just given a brilliant per-formance in front of one of the largest audiences to ever witness a sporting event. Had he quit then, it might have been enough to go down in history as one of the greatest boxers of all time.

But three months later, he fought again. Once more, it was in the won-drous Astrodome, this time against Ernie Terrell. No animosity brewed be-tween Ali and Terrell before the fight. In fact, Ali seemed to like Ernie, who had grown up in Mississippi. Like Ali, Terrell entertained notions of having a career as a singer and made recordings with a group he called Ernie Ter-rell and the Heavyweights. Both men had fought as light-heavyweights in the Golden Gloves and both lived on Chicago's South Side, although Ali had been spending so much time in Houston of late that he had begun calling Texas his home.

On December 28, 1966, the boxers were in New York promoting their match. Terrell, a tall, lean, soft-spoken man, was telling reporters that he'd been waiting years to face Ali, who he continued to refer to as Cassius Clay. Terrell said they'd fought and defeated many of the same men, including Cleveland Williams, George Chuvalo, and Doug Jones. While many state boxing commissions continued to recognize Ali as the heavyweight champ, and while most sports fans did the same, the World Boxing Association had vacated Ali's title to register its unhappiness with his political views. At least according to the WBA, the title belonged to Terrell. But Terrell knew that he needed to defeat Ali to stake a legitimate claim to the championship.

The boxers were in a small room talking to Howard Cosell of WABC-TV, jawing at each other in the way fighters often did while trying to hype a bout, inflating their chests and their egos, when Ali complained, "Why you want to say 'Cassius Clay' when Howard Cosell and everybody is calling me Muhammad Ali?" He continued, "My name is Muhammad Ali and you will announce it right there in the center of the ring after the fight if you don't do it now . . . You just acting like a old Uncle Tom, another Floyd Patterson. I'm gonna punish you!"

At the mention of "old Uncle Tom," Terrell turned to Ali, leaned in, and said, "Don't call me no Uncle Tom."

"That's what you are," Ali said. "Just back off of me, Uncle Tom!"

The men shoved at one another. Ali slapped Terrell in the face.

"Keep shooting," Cosell told his cameraman.

No doubt Ali was looking to irritate Terrell and to promote their fight, but he also had a legitimate and sincere gripe. People changed their names all the time — sometimes to hide their religion, sometimes to accentuate it. Few were the people who insisted on referring to Tony Curtis as Bernard Schwartz or Marilyn Monroe as Norma Jean Baker or Mother Teresa as Anjezë Gonxhe Bojaxhiu. Yet every major American newspaper continued referring to Muhammad Ali as Cassius Clay. So did Sonny Liston and Floyd Patterson. So did most of the fans approaching him for autographs. In the *New York Times* article reporting on the tiff between the two boxers, the headline referred to Muhammad Ali while the body of the story continued to call him Cassius Clay. Cosell was one of the few journalists consistently calling him Ali in December 1966.

Terrell was no Uncle Tom, and he had expressed no objection to Ali's faith. He had never said, as Floyd Patterson had, that Ali's religion was inferior to Christianity. In fact, Terrell told another reporter: "I got nothing against him or his religion." He went on to say he knew that Ali was only trying to rattle him, and maybe he was trying to rattle Ali in return. "He wants me to worry about what people think about me, wants to confuse the issue," Terrell said. "But it's dangerous to be distracted. I'll just concentrate more."

Leading up to the fight, Ali vowed to punish Terrell for disrespecting his faith and his new name. "I want to torture him," he said. "I want to give him the Patterson humiliation and punish him. A clean knockout is too good for him."

Ali did punish him, but not right away. The fighters exchanged punches evenly in the first two rounds, before Ali began to land his jabs effectively. Just as they had after the Patterson fight, reporters accused Ali of carrying Terrell, of making him suffer through a long night when he could have finished him off sooner. But there's little evidence to suggest that was true. In the seventh round, Ali spun Terrell around with a punch, shoved him into the ropes, and then unleashed a furious series of blows, lifting both feet off the mat to put all his body weight into the punches, clearly going for the knockout. Terrell's legs wobbled and both eyes bled, but the challenger gathered himself and fought back, hammering hard on Ali's head in the final minute of the round. It happened again and again. Every time Ali took control of the fight, Terrell fought back, even as his left eye puffed and closed.

"What's my name?" Ali taunted in the eighth, followed by a whistling left-right combination that make the question rhetorical. "What's my name?" he spat again through his mouthpiece. Terrell closed his eyes as the next combination flew.

When the bell clanged to end the round, Ali did not go to his corner. Instead, he stepped in close to Terrell. His eyes went wide. The tendons in his neck tightened. His arms fell to his sides and he leaned in. He barked it this time so it didn't sound like a question: "What's my name!"

The fight went on for seven more rounds, but not because Ali wanted it to; he tried and couldn't end it. In round twelve, Ali stood flat-footed and threw his biggest punches. Terrell took the blows and fought back. Ali threw 737 punches in the fight, almost all of them to Terrell's head. But Terrell's long jab kept Ali at a distance much of the time, and Ali, looking weary, couldn't land a big enough punch to put Terrell away. He stopped taunting.

When it was over and the judges unanimously named Ali the winner, announcer Howard Cosell got in the ring and asked Ali if he could have knocked out Terrell if he had wanted to.

"No, I don't believe I could've," Ali said. "After the eighth round I laid on him, but I found myself tiring."

It didn't matter to the white men covering the bout, who by now looked for any and every reason to criticize Ali. They said he lacked dignity. They called it "a disgusting exhibition of calculated cruelty," as if boxing were supposed to be anything else. Milton Gross said he almost yearned for a return to the days when the mafia controlled the sport. Arthur Daley called Ali "a mean and malicious man," and Jimmy Cannon, of all people, called Ali's treatment of Terrell "a kind of a lynching."

Ali had boxed beautifully, changing speed and direction like a kite, cracking jabs, digging hooks to the ribs, sliding away with a shuffle to survey the damage, and then cracking more jabs, moving in and out with no steady rhythm, no pattern. He was a revolutionary, like Charlie Parker, with an innate style and virtuosity no one would ever reproduce. He turned violence into craft like no heavyweight before or since.

But that doesn't mean boxing's inherent violence passed him over. Even in a relatively easy win, Ali took about eighty punches to the head and sixty to the body from a man who stood six-feet-six-inches tall and weighed 212½ pounds and never quit. If that made Ali a torturer or a thug, it made him a bad one.

23

"Against the Furies"

In 1967, Muhammad Ali was twenty-five years old, the world's heavyweight champion, the most widely recognized athlete on earth, the most prominent Muslim in America, and the most visible opponent of the war in Vietnam. He remained obsessed with cars and houses and money, and he was eager to find a new wife, but the thing he talked about most of all was race. Race was the live wire that ran through him.

"A house is on fire, pretend," he told Jack Olsen, a white reporter for *Sports Illustrated*. "You're sleeping next to your partner." Ali made the sound of snoring. "You open one eye and you see the house is on fire. Your partner's still sleeping." He added whistles to the snoring sounds. "And you see this hot lava and this burning two-by-four is getting ready to fall on your partner, and you get out of the bed. You run out of the house without waking him up! When you get outside, you say [he clasped his hands and looked to the sky], 'Oh, Lord, what have I done wrong? I was so selfish and greedy, worrying about myself until I left my partner inside. Oh, [wringing hands], he's probably dead, the house caved in."

He paused dramatically.

"*And then he comes out just in time and he looks in your face!* Right then you feel he's supposed to kill you. You know what *you'd* do if somebody left *you* in a burning house . . . And he says, 'Man, why didn't you wake me up? Why did you let me stay in that house? [Shouting] *The house was on fire! Man, you were gonna let me burn . . . !*'

"Well, that's what white Americans are like. The house's been on fire for

310 years, and the whites have let the blacks sleep. The Negro's been lynched, killed, raped, burned, dragged around all through the city hanging on the chains of cars, alcohol and turpentine poured into his wounds. That's why Negroes are so full of fear today. Been put into him from the time he's a baby. Imagine! Twenty-two million Negroes in America, suffering, fought in the wars, got more worse treatment than any human being can even imagine, walking the streets of America . . . hungry with no food to eat, walk the streets with no shoes on, existing on relief, living in charity and poorhouses, 22 million people who faithfully served America and who have worked and who still loves his enemy are still dogged and kicked around."

The words were powerful and prescient. But, at the same time, Ali's views could be slippery, even incongruous. That didn't make him unusual. What made him unusual is that so many people were listening. Reporters wrote down his remarks. Elijah Muhammad's followers heard him lecture several times a month at mosques around the country. FBI informants made notes and sent memos to the home office in Washington, DC.

"If total integration would make them happy, the whites as well as the blacks, I would totally integrate," he told one journalist. "If total separation, every man with his own, would make them happy, I'll do that. Whatever it takes to make people happy, where they won't be shooting and hiding in the bushes and blowing each other up and killing each other, rioting. But I don't think total integration can work."

Boxers are professional rebels. They are permitted to engage in violence that others are not. They are permitted to be uncivil. Ali merely extended it beyond the ring. He wanted to make everything he said and everything he did a protest. He declared every chance he got that he was not going to be tamed. He would fight, stand up, say it, do it, right away, every time. He would be the world's heavyweight rebel champion. He was living a life of superficiality, as most of us do, making a career as an entertainer, blowing his money on more cars than he could possibly drive, and yet an overriding spirit of rebellion guided him and perhaps redeemed him. That's why his refusal to accept the draft captured so much attention and stirred such anger, because everything about Ali's existence offended the majority of white Americans: his skin color, his loud mouth, his religion, and, now, his lack of patriotism. For the first time in almost forty years, The Ring magazine, the fight game's bible, declined to name a "Fighter of the Year," insisting that Ali (still referred to as Cassius Clay by the magazine) was "not to be held up as an example to the youngsters of the United States."

The criticism never bothered Ali, perhaps because he had little confidence in America to do right by him. The problem went back to slavery, he said: "Well, we weren't brought here to be citizens in white America. The intention was for us to work for them — and like it. They mated us up, the more the merrier. The big black slave was called the buck. 'This nigger slave can breed fifteen babies a month!' And as soon as the baby was born, it was separated from the mother. And that was the making of your 'negro.' He was a mental slave. And that's the people we still have in America today." Given all that, he asked, how could the black man in America ever expect to be treated fairly? "When you put your whole trust and your whole future in another people, then you're putting yourself in a position to be disappointed and deceived. You cannot disappoint me. You cannot deceive me if I'm not looking for anything from you."

Ali voiced plainly and simply what so many black Americans felt: that they would never get a fair deal because a fair deal wasn't possible under the long-standing conditions imposed on them. Even black Americans who cared little for boxing and knew nothing of the law had the overriding sense that Ali had been the victim of prejudice. But it was his response, not his victimhood, that made him a hero. It was his refusal to back down as the government and boxing officials threatened to punish him. "Six-foot-two and a half and 220 pounds, as pretty as a man could be, Muhammad Ali was a black hero in an American landscape that nourished few black heroes," journalist Jill Nelson wrote. "Articulate, funny, incredibly male, Ali took no shit from the white man and lived to tell the tale, the man of black women's collective dreams."

Ali's stand against Vietnam made him a symbol of protest against a war in which black men were dying at a wildly disproportionate rate. Black men accounted for 22 percent of all battlefield deaths when the black population in America was only 10 percent. Why was America spending money and tossing away lives in the name of freedom in a distant land while resisting the cause of freedom at home? Why, yet again, did the interests of black Americans seem to diverge from the interests of the nation as a whole? Ali raised these troubling questions as opposition to the war rapidly spread.

Martin Luther King Jr. had begun speaking out against America's involvement in Vietnam, although board members at the Southern Christian Leadership Conference (SCLC) were concerned that King would only serve to enrage President Johnson and set back the civil rights movement. King was contemplating a dramatic change in direction for the SCLC. After his failed campaign against segregated housing in Chicago in 1966 and after horrific riots in Detroit and Newark in the summer of 1967, the civil rights leader said American society could only be saved with "radical moral surgery." If something wasn't done quickly — to stop the war, combat discrimination, and end the government's oppression of the poor — King feared an all-out race war that would end with a right-wing, fascist police state in America. King intended to lead a more radical movement, and his opposition to the war in Vietnam would be one of its pillars.

Andrew Young Jr., executive director of the SCLC, said Ali's stance may have played a part in King's decision to publicly oppose the war. "It was about the same time that Muhammad declared he was a conscientious objector that Martin began to say, 'I can't segregate my conscience,'" Young recalled. "There's no question in my mind there was a subtle influence that connected the two of them in terms of conscience and the war in Vietnam."

In an editorial, the New York Times said the boxer "may become a new symbol and rallying point for opposition to the draft and the Vietnam war. In Harlem, the nation's largest Negro ghetto, there were indications . . . that Clay's refusal to be drafted was creating considerable emotional impact, particularly on the young."

Tom Wicker of the Times wondered what would happen if thousands of Americans followed Ali's lead and refused to fight. "The fact is," Wicker wrote, "that he is taking the ultimate position of civil disobedience; he is refusing to obey the law of the majority on the grounds of his personal beliefs, with full knowledge of the consequence . . . What would happen if all young men of draft age took the same position!" An answer to the question came from L. Mendel Rivers, chairman of the House Armed Services Committee, who said that if Ali, "that great theologian of Black Muslim power," won a deferment, the president's power to deploy the military would be undercut by a flood of double-talking conscientious objectors. U.S. Congressman Robert H. Michel of Illinois also condemned Ali, saying, "While thousands of our finest young men are fighting and dying in the jungles of Vietnam, this healthy specimen is profiteering from a series of shabby bouts. Apparently Cassius will fight anyone but the Viet Cong." Michel went on to say that while

Ali considered himself "the greatest, . . . I am sure history will look upon him as the least of all the men who have held the once-honorable title of Heavyweight Champion of the World."

Draft board officials worried too, saying Ali was making it difficult for them to do their jobs. One of them, Allen J. Rhorer, chairman of the draft board in Calcasieu Parish, Louisiana, wrote to the U.S. attorney general, Ramsey Clark, saying the members of his board would "seriously consider submitting their resignations" unless "prompt and vigorous action" were taken against Ali.

Ali claimed he was a Muslim minister, saying he spent 90 percent of his time preaching and 10 percent boxing. But Ali never held the formal title of minister or any other title within the Nation of Islam. In fact, Elijah Muhammad stated clearly that Ali was not a minister, according to an FBI memo dated March 17, 1966, and made public half a century later. According to the memo, Elijah told another member of the Nation of Islam that Ali was welcome to attend an upcoming Nation of Islam event, but he should not receive any special treatment or honors. "He can come," Elijah said. "That's up to him. Nobody barring him from the meeting. He won't be up on the speakers stand. He's no minister . . . He won't speak unless I ask him to say something and I will tell him what to say."

Nevertheless, Ali continued to call himself a minister, and officials in the Nation of Islam never publicly contradicted him. The FBI, in its memo, speculated that Elijah Muhammad allowed Ali to describe himself as a minister "because of his publicity value." The Nation also helped Ali find a lawyer, Hayden C. Covington of New York, who had successfully defended members of the Jehovah's Witnesses against draft-evasion charges. Covington and the Nation secured signed statements from nearly four thousand people — most of them members of the Nation of Islam — affirming that Ali was a full-time minister. The lawyer also asked Angelo Dundee to sign a statement confirming that boxing was merely Ali's "side line or avocation" and that preaching was his "main job or vocation." In a letter to Ali, Covington wrote, "I told the Honorable Elijah Muhammad that we will fight them until hell freezes over and in the end skate on the ice of victory."

The first judge who heard Ali's case sustained his claim as a conscientious objector. But the Justice Department's appeals board, perhaps fearing the kind of chain reaction the *New York Times*'s Tom Wicker had warned about, rejected the judge's recommendation, saying Ali's objections to military service were based on issues of politics and race, not on a moral objection to all war. Ali would have to serve or go to jail, the board ruled. In March, he received an order to report the following month for induction at a draft board office in Houston.

While his lawyers scrambled, Ali prepared for the kind of fight he knew how to win. On March 22, 1967, after minimal training, he took on Zora Folley in Madison Square Garden. Folley was almost thirty-six years old, with a record of seventy-four wins, seven losses, and four draws, a father of eight, a combat veteran of the Korean War, and one of the kindest, gentlest men in boxing. Even Ali couldn't find reason to get angry with Folley. Moments before the fight, Ali was asked what he would do if he lost. He answered without hesitation: "Retire. Tonight."

When the fight began, Ali seemed uninterested, like a man too bored by his dinner guest to bother making conversation. He landed only two punches in the first round, three in the second, and six in the third. He bounced around the ring as if his only goal were to burn calories. Folley landed a few good shots but hardly enough to bother Ali.

In the fourth, Ali delivered a jolt of excitement with a knockdown. But Folley rose from the canvas before the referee counted ten and hit back, landing his best punches of the fight. In the fifth, Ali poked steady, painful jabs. In the sixth, he did more of the same. The seventh was different, though. Ali was no longer bored. He advanced on Folley. He threw big right hands and left hooks, not jabs. That left him vulnerable, and Folley retaliated with his best punches of the night. Ali accepted the punishment as the cost of doing business and stepped in again. Midway through the round, Ali rotated his torso and wound up for a big right hand that caught Folley flush on the left cheek. Ali wound up again, threw the same punch, connected with the same spot on Folley's cheek, and watched as the veteran fighter fell flat on his face, settling to the mat with his arms by his sides like a sidewalk drunk.

When the television announcer found Ali, the champ had his brother on one side, Herbert Muhammad on the other, and his father behind him. Ali smiled: "First of all I would like to say *As-Salaam-Alaikum* to our dear beloved leader and teacher the Honorable Elijah Muhammad, and I'm feeling real fine tonight. I thank him for his blessings and prayers."

"Now, let's talk about the fight," said the announcer.

They did. Ali, as was custom, said he had never been hurt. He described the knockout punch and then he invited his father to get in front of the camera. "I would say he's the greatest of all time," a beaming, slick-haired Cash Clay said. "I'm not saying that because he's my son."

After he pried himself off the mat and regained his senses, Zora Folley, a more impartial judge, came to the same conclusion as Cash Clay. "He's smart," Folley said. "The trickiest fighter I've seen. He's had twenty-nine fights and acts like he's had a hundred. He could write the book on boxing, and anyone that fights him should be made to read it first." He continued, "There's just no way to train yourself for what he does. The moves, the speed, the punches, and the way he changes style every time you think you got him figured . . . This guy has a style all of his own. It's far ahead of any fighter's around today, so how could those old-time fighters, you know, Dempsey, Tunney or any of them keep up? Louis wouldn't have a chance — he was too slow. Marciano couldn't get to him, and would never get away from Ali's jab."

Finally, Ali was getting the respect he'd been saying he deserved since he was twelve years old. What's more, there were few opponents likely to challenge him. There was talk of a Chuvalo or Patterson rematch. And there was a young fighter named Joe Frazier, winner of the 1964 Olympic gold medal and undefeated through his first fourteen fights, looming on the horizon. But at that moment it was difficult to imagine anyone beating Ali.

His biggest threat was jail.

"I've left the sports pages," he said. "I've gone onto the front pages. I want to know what is right, what'll look good in history. I'm being tested by Allah. I'm giving up my title, my wealth, maybe my future. Many great men have been tested for their religious belief. If I pass this test, I'll come out stronger than ever . . . All I want is justice. Will I have to get that from history?"

PART II

24

Exile

Martin Luther King Jr. arrived in Louisville on March 28, 1967, just as Ali returned to his hometown after defeating Zora Folley. According to an FBI memo marked "secret," Ali and King met privately at King's hotel for about thirty minutes, and their time together "mainly consisted of joking and 'horse play.'"

When they finished, the men met with reporters.

"We're all black brothers," said Ali, who stood almost a full head taller than King. Both men wore suits and ties. "We use different approaches to our everyday problems, but the same dog that bit him bit me. When we go out, they don't ask if you are a Christian, a Catholic, a Baptist, or a Muslim. They just start whupping black heads."

"Yes, oh, yes," King chorused. "We discussed our common problems and our common concerns. We are victims of the same system of oppression. Although our religious beliefs differ, we are still brothers."

The FBI may have been right that the meeting between Ali and King consisted largely of jokes. Both men were great comics. Both knew how to establish emotional connections quickly, even with their critics. Both possessed a manic energy at times. But despite the joking, the meeting mattered. For one thing, it revealed King's continued willingness to stand publicly as an opponent of the war in Vietnam. It also served as a reminder of Ali's flexible ideology and his seemingly contradictory urges to rebel and make friends.

Finally, the meeting reflected the manner in which the civil rights movement and the antiwar movement were colliding.

On the same day he met King, Ali, dressed in an iridescent blue-green suit, appeared at a protest against segregated housing in Louisville. His remarks were not entirely in favor of integration, but he nonetheless spoke and lent his support. He wanted to be heard. He wanted to stand with black people. He wanted everyone to know he fought on the side of change.

"Check me out on this," he told the housing protesters, as he launched into a variation on some of the speeches he'd heard at Nation of Islam rallies. "The richest soil is the black soil. You want a strong cup of coffee, you say, 'I want it black.' The blacker the berry, the sweeter the juice." He went on to say black was not only beautiful, it was better off without white. That brought shouts of "No!" from audience members who, after all, had gathered for the purpose of integrating Louisville's housing supply. But Ali continued, "Let's quit worrying white people and forcing ourselves into their neighborhoods," he said. "Let's start cleaning up and do for ourselves. I am what they call a Muslim. I am a follower of another freedom fighter — his name is Elijah Muhammad." Again, the crowd expressed some disdain. Ali said black Christians had been deceived all their lives. "When we went to church we looked in the Bible . . . We saw Jesus. He's white. We see angels. They're white. You see pictures of the Last Supper. Everybody there is white. The president lives in the White House." On the other hand, he said, "Devil food cake is dark. Black cats are bad luck." He continued to insult his audience. "I realize this here's a small town and you're not too wise to these teachings . . . I say the solutions to our problems is getting together, cleaning ourselves up, and respecting our women. Then the whole world will respect us as a nation."

He went on to talk about his opposition to the war, making his most plainly political statement on the subject to date: "Why should they ask me, another so-called Negro, to put on a uniform and go ten thousand miles from home and drop bombs and bullets on brown people in Vietnam while so-called Negro people in Louisville are treated like dogs and denied simple human rights?" He went on to say that his real enemies were in the United States, and that he would not help the United States enslave others.

The audience members did not boo when he was done, but neither did they wildly applaud. Clearly, this was not what they had come to hear.

When Ali finished, a reporter asked him how he thought the audience felt about his sermon.

"Oh, they liked it," he said.

A few days later, Dr. King, speaking at New York's Riverside Church, made his most powerful statement to date about Vietnam, calling the United States "the greatest purveyor of violence in the world today" and saying he felt compelled to speak out as a "brother to the suffering poor of Vietnam" and on behalf of "the poor in America who are paying the double price of smashed hopes of home, and dealt death and corruption in Vietnam." The reverend was attacked from almost all sides for his remarks — branded unpatriotic, a communist sympathizer, and, in the words of FBI director J. Edgar Hoover, "an instrument in the hands of subversive forces seeking to undermine our nation." Meanwhile, antiwar demonstrations around the nation grew larger and louder.

On April 17, the U.S. Supreme Court rejected a request by Ali's lawyers for an injunction that would have blocked the boxer's military induction. The lawyers had argued that the Kentucky Selective Service had discriminated against the boxer because of his race. Faced with the disappointing news, Ali promised that he would appear at his scheduled induction ceremony on April 28, but he insisted he would not accept induction. He vowed to "stand up for my religious beliefs even if it means I am put in jail for fifty years or am stood up in front of a machine gun."

In Chicago, Ali conferred with Elijah Muhammad and Herbert Muhammad. Elijah told reporters he offered no advice to his disciple. Perhaps tellingly, though, he added, "I gave him no more advice than I gave the faithful ones who followed me to the penitentiary in 1942."

It was a cool, gray morning in Houston, a curtain of mist in the air. On the morning of his scheduled military induction, Muhammad Ali gazed at himself in the reflection of a coffee-shop mirror as he jabbed with his fork at four soft-boiled eggs on his plate. Perhaps he saw a historical figure looking back at him in the mirror. That was the take of a *Sports Illustrated* reporter seated by the boxer's side. In opposing the draft, Ali considered himself a fighter whose battle transcended sports. He was Davey Crockett now. He was John

Henry. Nat Turner. He was a leader of his people. A true believer. Or, as he might have been tempted to say, the greatest crusader of allll tiiiimes!!

If the government of the United States jailed him or took away his right to fight, "it could cost me $10 million in earnings," he said to the reporter and to his own reflection. "Does that sound like I'm serious about my religion?"

When they finished their breakfast, Ali and his group of friends, lawyers, and journalists crammed into two taxis for the ride to the Armed Forces Examining and Entrance Station on the third floor of the federal office building at 701 San Jacinto Street. As Ali stepped out of his cab, lights from the TV cameras popped on, brightening the boxer's blue suit. The boxer paused and smiled before entering the building but gave no comment to the press.

Ali was one of twenty-six pre-induction examinees reporting at 8 a.m. to Houston's Board No. 61. He was the only one with a lawyer. Most of the men brought duffel bags or suitcases, knowing that they would likely be leaving on a bus later that day for a military base, but Ali was empty-handed.

"You all look very dejected," he said to some of the other men awaiting induction. He told them jokes. He talked about the Floyd Patterson fight. He said that if he stayed home, the Viet Cong wouldn't get him, but some redneck from Georgia probably would. He signed an autograph for a pre-enlistee from Escondido, California. Another one of the young men awaiting the draft said he wished Ali would go with him to Vietnam because the boxer made for pleasant company and "it would lighten our trip."

Ali's lawyers told him that they planned to take his case to civil court, but they could only do so after they'd exhausted all administrative remedies and after he had formally disobeyed an order to serve. When the moment came, Ali refused to step forward and accept his induction. A Navy lieutenant summoned him to an office and warned that he was committing a felony punishable by five years in prison and a ten-thousand-dollar fine. Ali refused again and signed a paper confirming his stance. With that, he became the most prominent American to make a legal plea for exemption from the war.

When it was over, Ali, for once, had little to say. He read a prepared statement, went back to his room at the Hotel America, and phoned his mother, who had been urging him to accept his induction. By the end of the day, the World Boxing Association and the New York State Athletic Commission had suspended Ali's boxing license and stripped him of his championship title. Soon after, with a unity of spirit, all the other boxing commissions in the country fell into line. Never mind that they had long tolerated the mafia and professional gamblers in their sport. Never mind that Ali had not yet been convicted of a crime. Never mind that boxing's rules contained no requirement that its champion be a Christian or an American or a supporter of American wars. None of that mattered. Guided by anger, prejudice, or patriotism, boxing's rulers decided that Muhammad Ali was unfit to wear the sport's crown because he was a Muslim who refused to fight for his country.

"The action of the sports authorities could effectively end Clay's career," his hometown newspaper, the *Louisville Courier-Journal* reported.

"Mama, I'm all right," Ali said. "I did what I had to do. I sure am looking forward to coming home to eat some of your cooking."

25

Faith

His enemy was solitude. His enemy had always been solitude, but now, with no one to box, no reason even to train, with his lawyers handling his fight with the government, and with no crowds clamoring for him, Ali grew bored.

On May 18, 1967, he was pulled over by police in Miami and arrested for driving without a license and failing to appear in court on an earlier traffic violation. He spent about ten minutes in jail before posting bond.

Soon he was back in Chicago, where he visited the Shabazz Restaurant on 71st Street, which sold bean soup and bean pies baked according to the special recipe of Clara Muhammad, the wife of Elijah Muhammad. Ali spotted a familiar face behind the restaurant counter, a seventeen-year-old girl named Belinda Boyd, whom he had met at least once before while visiting the Muhammad University of Islam and whom he had also seen working at one of the Nation of Islam's bakeries. A scarf covered her head and a long dress draped her body. Herbert Muhammad had suggested Ali visit Belinda at the restaurant, suggesting she might make a good wife.

Muhammad Ali was the Nation of Islam's handsome prince. Every girl at Belinda's school loved him. But she loved him more than most. Her love was "exponential," recalled Safiyya Mohammed-Rahmah, Belinda's classmate and the daughter of Herbert Muhammad. She had been proclaiming that love for years. "She just knew she was going to marry him," Safiyya said.

Yet Belinda's knees did not wobble when the prince walked into the restaurant.

"Do you know who I am?" Ali asked.

Belinda did not smile or bat her eyelashes. She was tall and slender but no waif. She practiced karate. She stood squarely and confidently. Belinda watched out of the corner of her eye as Ali smiled and eased his way past the waiting customers to order a bowl of soup. When he got to the counter, Belinda addressed him sharply: "You gonna butt the line?"

Ali froze. He went back and waited his turn.

Belinda was the daughter of Raymond and Aminah Boyd of Blue Island, Illinois, a working-class suburb on Chicago's South Side. Having completed her studies at Elijah Muhammad's school for Muslim boys and girls, she was working two jobs, at the bakery and the restaurant. She loved work, loved engaging with customers, loved making money and saving for college. It was true that she'd long had a crush on Ali, and also true that she'd been jealous when she'd heard the boxer had married Sonji Roi. Sonji was the most beautiful woman Belinda had ever seen — a black Elizabeth Taylor, and Ali was her Richard Burton.

Had Sonji and Ali remained married, Belinda said, she would have been content to work hard, help her parents around the house, and live a quiet life of religious observation, following her prince's moves in the pages of *Muhammad Speaks* and on TV. "I wasn't interested in having no boyfriend," she said years later. "I wasn't interested in getting married at all." But after Ali's divorce and after she turned seventeen in the spring of 1967, Belinda's thoughts returned to the man of her dreams. It wasn't his fame or his good looks that appealed to her, she said, so much as his potential as a Muslim. For weeks, Ali visited her at her jobs and called her on the phone. Once, after work, when she was waiting in the rain for a bus to go home, Ali offered to drive her home in his long, silver Eldorado. She refused, saying it wasn't proper for a single girl to be alone with a man in a car. Ali, in his Eldorado, followed Belinda's bus all the way to 150th Street in Blue Island. When Belinda got off the bus, Ali once again offered her a ride. She said she preferred to walk. Ali turned on his car's emergency flashers and drove alongside her, his head out the window, chattering with her, as she completed the last three miles of her journey home.

Later, when Ali visited the house in Blue Island where Belinda lived with her parents, it was as if Sidney Poitier had pulled into the driveway. Neighbors stepped out of their houses to see him. Here was a girl of seventeen, a girl who had never traveled, a girl with little education beyond that offered by the Nation of Islam, and she found herself suddenly courted by one of the most handsome and famous men in the world, a real-life hero, an older man who had already traveled the planet, already been married, already met important people. He was so big and so good-lucking, too. She felt giddy in his presence, she said. But she made up her mind not to show it. She had the feeling that Ali, beneath the bluster, was an insecure little boy who wanted to be told what to do. She sensed that she needed to show him strength.

Belinda was a virgin. While they were courting, Ali never pressured her about sex, even as they began to discuss marriage. But one day when Ali was visiting her at home, he asked if he could see her legs. "I wanna see what I'm getting," he said. There was humor, not menace, in the way he asked, but Belinda wasn't laughing.

"You ain't seeing nothing," she said. "You ain't touching nothing. You ain't tasting nothing. You ain't smelling nothing."

Getting involved with a man like Ali, with his mighty ego and matching libido, wasn't easy, especially for a girl so young. But Belinda was no pushover. In her view, Ali had only begun to appreciate the power and beauty of Islam. He had only begun to behave the way a proper Muslim man should. "I wanted to mold him," she said, "so he could be like my father."

Her friend Safiyya had a different perspective, saying Belinda, too, wanted to be molded. Belinda knew everything about Ali. She quoted Ali. She imitated Ali. Although she didn't box, she did practice karate, which may have been her way of trying yet again to be like the champ. "She loved Ali so much," Safiyya said, "she wanted to *be* Ali."

They were married on August 18, 1967, by a Baptist minister, Dr. Morris H. Tynes, in a ceremony at Ali's home at 8500 South Jeffery Boulevard in Chicago. Ali's parents flew to Chicago for the service but arrived too late, making it in time only for the reception. Herbert Muhammad stood beside Ali as his best man. The wedding, oddly, was a Christian one, as the *Chicago Defender* noted, because "Muslims have no marriage ceremony of their own," although Tynes did include references to Islam in his remarks.

For their honeymoon, the couple traveled to New York City. The trip was a wedding present from Minister Louis X of the Nation of Islam, whose name had recently been changed to Louis Farrakhan.

Belinda was overjoyed, but she was also beginning to see that she and her new husband would not be living like royalty.

It dawned her only gradually, she said: "I married a man with no job."

While Ali awaited trial on charges of draft evasion, boxing officials began planning for a tournament of televised bouts to decide the next heavyweight champion. Even white sportswriters who had consistently maligned Ali admitted that none of the contenders — Oscar Bonavena, Jimmy Ellis, Leotis Martin, Karl Mildenberger, Floyd Patterson, Jerry Quarry, Thad Spencer, and Ernie Terrell — were superior or even equal to Ali. The winner of the tournament would probably fight Sonny Liston, the fading star, or Joe Frazier, the rising star.

The mediocre talent pool left some boxing executives wondering if they could somehow persuade Ali to accept a symbolic role in the U.S. military. If he would agree to perform boxing exhibitions for soldiers as Joe Louis had during World War II, Ali would avoid prison and he might be cleared to return to boxing in a year or two. If he continued to resist the draft, on the other hand, he might never fight again.

The Louisville Sponsoring Group had already tried to change Ali's mind by explaining how much money he stood to lose. Now, in the spring of 1967, Bob Arum, the lawyer who led Main Bout, planned to try again. That year, Main Bout was still a side project for Arum, who practiced law in New York. One of the senior partners at his firm, Arthur Krim, was a powerful entertainment lawyer and a top advisor to President Lyndon Johnson. "Krim went to see Lyndon Johnson," said Arum, "and that's when Lyndon Johnson proposed a deal . . . that he [Ali] doesn't have to go in, he doesn't have to wear a uniform, he just does exhibitions at the Army bases." If Ali took the deal, he might have been allowed to continue fighting professionally even while he served his country, Arum said.

Arum asked football's Jim Brown, one of his partners in Main Bout, to help sell the deal to his friend Ali. Brown organized a meeting of many of the nation's leading black athletes, including Bill Russell, Lew Alcindor (later known as Kareem Abdul-Jabbar), Curtis McClinton (of the Kansas City Chiefs), Bobby Mitchell (Washington Redskins), Sid Williams (Cleveland Browns), Jim Shorter (Redskins), Walter Beach (Browns), Willie Davis (Green Bay Packers), as well as Carl Stokes, a prominent black attorney in Cleveland who would go on to become the first black mayor of a major American city. The meeting was held in Cleveland, in the offices of Brown's Negro Industrial Economic Union. Years later, the gathering would be described by Brown and journalists as a test of Ali's sincerity, an opportunity for his black peers to declare their support for the boxer's principled stand. After listening to Ali's passionate speech and challenging him with hard questions, this impressive lineup of men agreed to address the media and lend their support, or so the story went years later.

In truth, the meeting was about money first, principle second.

Arum, Brown, Herbert Muhammad, and the other partners in Main Bout would lose a great source of income if Ali never boxed again. Main Bout depended on closed-circuit TV revenues to thrive, and it seemed unlikely that millions of customers were going to line up outside movie theaters to watch Jerry Quarry versus Thad Spencer. Nor was there any guarantee that other fighters would sign contracts with Main Bout. Ali was committed to the company because of his loyalty to Herbert Muhammad. Ali was the company's greatest asset, but he was worthless to them if he wasn't fighting. Arum hoped that Brown and the other leading black athletes would persuade Ali to make a deal with the military and continue boxing, and Arum was prepared to reward the athletes by cutting them in on Main Bout's business. He promised a kind of affirmative action plan — promising that black athletes would receive closed-circuit franchises in some of the nation's top markets. If Ali could be convinced to return to boxing, those athletes — including several of the men meeting in Cleveland — stood to make money from Ali's fights.

That was the main purpose of the gathering, according to Arum: "to convince Ali to take the deal because it opened up tremendous opportunities for black athletes." The average salary for a professional football player in 1967 was about $25,000. Professional basketball players made an average of about $20,000 a year. With closed-circuit deals, some of the athletes would double or triple their annual income, and they would continue to make money from their franchises long after their athletic careers ended.

"But I wasn't setting it up for the athletes to rally around Ali," Arum said of the meeting in Cleveland. "Who the fuck cared at that point?"

When Brown met with Ali the night before the summit, Ali made it clear he would not be swayed. Still, Ali would not be facing an easy crowd. The men assembling in Cleveland were strong-willed. Several of them were military veterans. Others believed that Elijah Muhammad's ideology was racist and, if followed through, would lead to an American apartheid. They arrived intent on lecturing Ali, if not changing his mind.

"My first reaction was that it was unpatriotic," recalled Willie Davis, who played defensive end for the Packers. Davis said he intended to tell Ali that he owed it to his country to serve in the military.

But when Ali walked in the room, everything changed. Usually, Ali could count on his size and physical grace to make an impression when he entered, using his presence alone the way he used his jab, to set up the big right hand, which, in this case, was his gregarious personality. This time, almost everyone in the room was big, strong, and confident. Still, Ali managed to stand out, overpowering the men with his energy and steady stream of lightning-fast speech. He never stayed in his seat long. He interrupted others to crack jokes, and when his turn came to speak at length, he walked quickly and purposefully, like a preacher working the aisles of his church, establishing eye contact, calling the men by their first names, making each person in the room feel as if he were addressing them individually. When the others aimed hard questions at him, Ali never got defensive. He spoke passionately and confidently and with good humor, clearly enjoying the debate.

"Well, I know what I must do," he told the group. "My fate is in the hands of Allah, and Allah will take care of me. If I walk out of this room today and get killed today, it will be Allah's doing and I will accept it. I'm not worried. In my first teachings I was told we would all be tested by Allah. This may be my test."

John Wooten confirmed that the point of the meeting was business, not morality. But, at the same time, he said, the men wanted to hear Ali explain why he was refusing the draft.

Curtis McClinton, a halfback with the Kansas City Chiefs, was a member of the U.S. Army's active reserves at the time. He told Ali that while he respected the boxer's religion, it was important to remember his nationality, too. McClinton said he told Ali: "Hey, man, all you'd do is get a uniform and you'd be boxing at all the bases around the country . . . Your presence on military bases gives that motivation to military men . . . that we recognize them and give them respect." Ali seemed to think about it, as if he could see the value in his service. "It was a very dynamic conflict within him," said McClinton, who compared Ali to a child on the verge of adulthood, realizing that he faced a life-changing decision and the options were not black and white. "The whole issue of his transition to Islam, all of that had to be laid out and baked like a good cake. He knew all the ingredients. But what was he really?" If Ali laughed a lot during the meeting, McClinton said, it probably reflected his uncertainty. "If you knew Muhammad Ali," he commented, the laughter "was really a way of dealing with it to move forward."

Bill Russell was fascinated by Ali's position. It would have been easy for the boxer to compromise, Russell said. Ali could have kept his faith but played it down in public. He could have convinced himself and others that he would be no good to the Nation of Islam and no good to the movement for Black Power if he had to spend time in jail. Russell said the men gathered in Cleveland were prepared to help Ali if he changed his mind and sought a compromise. The men were ready to say they had persuaded the boxer to cut a deal with the government so that he could continue to fight — in the ring and for his people. They were prepared to accept their share of criticism from the black community if Ali was attacked for waffling. But it was clear throughout the meeting, Russell said, that Ali would not compromise.

"Three, four, five hours — I don't know how long we stayed in that back room," Jim Brown recalled. "Everybody had a chance to ask him all the questions they wanted to. Eventually, everybody was satisfied that his stand was genuine based on his religion and that we would back him."

Brown led the group to a press conference. Ali, Brown, Russell, and Lew Alcindor sat at a long table, the rest of the men standing behind them.

"There's nothing new to say," Ali announced, perhaps recognizing that reporters expected him to make big news by backing down from his antiwar stand.

"We heard his views and know he is completely sincere in his beliefs," Brown told the media.

In an article for *Sports Illustrated* written shortly after the meeting, Russell wrote that he envied Ali: "He has something I have never been able to attain and something very few people I know possess. He has an absolute and sincere faith . . . I'm not worried about Muhammad Ali. He is better equipped than anyone I know to withstand the trials in store for him. What I'm worried about is the rest of us."

Two weeks later, an all-white jury needed only twenty minutes to find Ali guilty of draft evasion. Judge Joe Ingraham handed down the maximum sentence: five years in prison and a ten-thousand-dollar fine. Ali was permitted to remain free while his lawyers appealed the ruling, but his passport was taken as a condition of his bail. The severe punishment was no doubt intended to send a message to others contemplating draft evasion, and there were a growing number. The day of the conviction, Congress voted overwhelmingly to extend the draft four more years. Another vote, inspired by antiwar protesters, made desecration of the American flag a federal crime.

Boxing officials had already stripped Ali of his title. Now, as he faced more serious punishment, white newspaper reporters attacked again, calling him a coward and a traitor, wondering why he wasn't more thankful for all that America had done for him, allowing him (as if he had needed permission) to rise from modest circumstances to become one of the most famous men of his time, with the opportunity to be a hero to his people and example to youth.

Black journalists were sometimes more even-handed. While some complained that the boxer was letting down his country, others said he was clearly a victim of discrimination, that the government had targeted him for his race and religion. "Clay should serve his time in the Army just like any other young, healthy all-American boy," wrote James Hicks in the *Louisville Defender.* "But what better vehicle to use to put an uppity Negro back in his place than the United States Army." Before, Ali had been seen as a great athlete and a rebel with peculiar taste in religion; now, at least in some eyes, he was a martyr, a victim of racism, a battler of excessive American power, and a fighter for something bigger than money or championship belts.

Three days after his conviction, Ali stood atop a garbage can and addressed antiwar protesters in Los Angeles. "I'm with you," he said. "Anything designed for peace and to stop the killing I'm for one hundred percent. I'm not a leader. I'm not here to advise you. But I encourage you to express yourself and stop this war." Soon after Ali left the scene, police attacked the protesters. When Ali saw the ensuing riot on television that night, he vowed not to participate in further demonstrations.

The growing number of antiwar protests infuriated J. Edgar Hoover, the FBI director. Hoover used the Counter Intelligence Program (COINTEL-PRO) in an attempt to neutralize the growing movement of black activists who, like Ali and Martin Luther King, seemed to be expanding the scope of their protests. FBI agents watched Ali's house in Chicago, according to Ali's cousin, Charlotte Waddell, who lived for a little while in the basement and said FBI agents approached her and asked for her help in gathering information about the Nation of Islam and Ali. Waddell said she refused.

Hoover may have been paranoid. He may have been racist. He may have been behaving like an authoritarian. But he also may have had reason to worry: When people like Ali and King challenged the merits of the war in Vietnam, more Americans questioned the necessity of the military campaign; more people asked why they should send their sons to fight and die in a conflict they didn't fully understand. When Ali refused to fight, the civil rights activist Julian Bond said, the action reverberated. "You could hear people talking about it on street corners," Bond told writer Dave Zirin. "It was on everyone's lips. People who had never thought about the war — black and white — began to think it through because of Ali. The ripples were enormous." Ali's stance wasn't the only reason people began to think more critically about the war. Reporters in Vietnam sent back TV and newspaper stories about the horrors and seeming futility of the combat. At the same time, more young men were being called to service. The ripples, as Julian Bond called them, formed questions: Why was America willing to sacrifice so many lives for Vietnam? Why were black Americans suffering disproportionate numbers of casualties? Why were so many wealthy young white men avoiding service by enrolling in college or by hiring lawyers to exploit technicalities in draft laws while poorer men got swept up in the draft? And, as a leaflet distributed by the Students for a Democratic Society asked, "What kind of America is it whose response to the poverty and oppression in Vietnam is napalm and defoliation? Whose response to poverty and oppression in Mississippi is silence?"

In Newark, delegates at the First National Conference on Black Power voted to recommend that black athletes boycott the Olympics and all boxing matches until Muhammad Ali's status as champion was restored. "We've got to boycott all boxing, all fights, every sponsor on a national level," Dick Gregory told the assembly. "Wherever they are fighting. And only this will make them give him [Ali] back his title." The delegates, many of them in African clothing, also voted to boycott Negro publications that accepted advertisements for hair straighteners and bleaching creams.

Freedomways, a magazine aimed at black readers, was one of the few publications to recognize immediately the larger point of Ali's latest fight, writing in an editorial: "Mr. Ali's case raises questions of great import for the entire country, and most especially for the 22,000,000 Americans of African descent. This is quite aside from any consideration of the blatant immorality of the particular war against the Vietnamese people which Muhammad Ali is protesting together with millions of other Americans. It is also aside from considering his constitutionally guaranteed right to practice his religious beliefs as a matter of conscience.

"While we are not claiming any special privilege for Negro Americans, what we are challenging is the moral right of this nation, *based upon its record,* to insist that any Black man must put on the military uniform, at any time, and go thousands of miles away from these shores to risk his life for a society which has historically been his oppressor."

In one of the final poems before his death, Langston Hughes reflected on the white racist reaction to the civil rights movement and to the growing criticism among blacks of the war in Vietnam. In "Backlash Blues," Hughes wrote that America gave blacks second-class homes and second-class schools. He asked,

> *Do you think that colored folks*
> *Are just second-class fools?*

26

Martyr

Ali was broke. He was behind on alimony and facing criminal charges for failing to pay his ex-wife. He was squabbling with his parents. His own lawyer was suing him, claiming that Ali owed $284,615 in legal fees for the work that had gone into keeping him out of jail on draft-dodging charges.

Still, the stress didn't seem to get to him. With no fights to promote, no training schedule to follow, and no entourage accompanying him, he was free to lavish attention on his new wife. Belinda supported Ali's decision to buck the draft, even if it meant jail time for him and poverty for them both. They were still getting to know each other. They were adjusting to sharing space in the same house. Belinda had been trained at the Muhammad University of Islam to be a housewife, and now she put those skills to use, cooking every night for her husband and washing and ironing his clothes. "She was like a giddy little schoolgirl," said Charlotte Waddell, Ali's cousin, who lived in the basement of the newlyweds' home. "They were always joking and laughing, watching TV all the time, eating popcorn."

Muhammad and Belinda adored Westerns, and they pretended to be cowboys sometimes. "You better get out of town, Belinda," Ali would say, "and your horse better be fast." Belinda would give her husband a hard stare, put her hands on her hips, where her imaginary pistol was holstered, and answer, "Naw, cuz I'm about to draw!" One night, Belinda was asleep on the sofa when she heard the door open and a man's voice say, "Hey, you better get out of town before sunrise." The voice was familiar but it wasn't Ali's. Belinda sprang from the sofa and flicked on the light to see Hugh O'Brien, who played Wyatt Earp on TV, standing in her living room. Ali had met O'Brien and persuaded the actor to come home and play a gag on his wife.

"I think that's the time he was the best man in the whole world to me," Belinda said years later of her husband. "I was happy when he wasn't making money. I was most happy."

Ali had an extraordinary appetite for sex, and Belinda learned to enjoy it, too. Ali was gorgeous, with a body that might have been carved by Michelangelo, and exceptionally well equipped as a lover. He had only one flaw in the bedroom, although it was not evident to Belinda until years later, when she had been with other men: Ali was a selfish lover, paying scant attention to her pleasure, she said. Still, the seventeen-year-old was not complaining, and after only a month or so of marriage, she became pregnant.

The Alis, in some respects, were like a lot of newlyweds. Money was tight, the future uncertain, dreams big. Belinda worried that her in-laws were not crazy about her — perhaps because she was a Muslim and perhaps because Odessa and Cash were still fond of Sonji. But it didn't take Belinda long to establish a connection with Odessa. Odessa got along with everyone. Odessa was the only one who could put Muhammad Ali in his place and get away with it. "Oh, you're pretty, but Rock's handsome," Odessa would say, referring to her other son, Rahaman. "Rock's stronger, too!" It drove Ali crazy, but everything Odessa said came out sugarcoated. Cash was different. Cash was not like any man Belinda had ever met. She was stunned to hear Cash refer to himself as a "whore-runner." What sort of man brags about such things? Cash told Belinda he liked women with big legs and big chests — "them stallions," he called them. "But I ain't leaving my wife for that crap," he said, as if such fealty would impress his daughter-in-law. "My wife knows what I'm doing."

Odessa surely did know. Back in May, Cash's womanizing had made headlines in Louisville. He had been out with two friends at Billy Limp's Chicken Shack when a woman had come to the restaurant's door. "I'm in trouble now," Clay had told his friends upon spotting the woman. Cash had stepped outside, according to the *Louisville Courier-Journal*, whereupon the woman had stabbed him in the chest.

Belinda and Muhammad Ali spent most of the first year of marriage on the South Side of Chicago, in their 1,300-square-foot brick house at the corner of 85th Street and Jeffery Boulevard. Rahaman, still shadowing his big brother, rented a place a few blocks away. Belinda and Muhammad's house had been owned or rented by Herbert Muhammad, but Elijah Muhammad had ordered Herbert to give it to the Alis. It had two bedrooms and one bath, wall-to-wall carpeting, a blue velvet couch, and a color TV that nestled inside a marble fireplace opposite the couch.

One morning, a reporter from *Esquire* magazine visited. Ali was shirtless, stretched out on the couch and running his hands over his flabby belly. A game show flashed on the TV, depriving the reporter of Ali's full attention. The boxer showed off his newest gadget — a small remote control that allowed him to adjust the sound on the TV without getting up and crossing the room, perfect for when his brother and Bundini Brown weren't around. Ali's eyes drifted to the screen as he tried to convince his visitor he was a busy man, even in exile. "And tonight," Ali said, "they're having this big musical and they want me to say a few words about whatever I want to talk about. Then I got a call from this college in Hartford — I forget the name of it — and they want me up there . . . There's always something. Everybody wants me." One had the impression that Ali, if formally invited, would appear, no questions asked, for the opening of an envelope.

Behind the fireplace was a mirrored wall, and Ali checked it at times to see how his performance was getting across. "It's impossible for me to dry up and have nothing to do. I mean I just don't represent boxing. I'm taking a stand for what I believe in and being one thousand percent for the freedom of the black people. Naturally those who have the same fight, but on a smaller scale, they come to me," and then he whispered, quoting the average black man: "'You speak for me, too, brother, you speak for me, too. I make my money from Charley but I'm with you.'" He lifted his voice again. "So I got hundreds of places to go and talk and I'll always have them as long as I'm talking for freedom."

At about 12:30 in the afternoon, he put on a striped shirt and a black leather jacket and invited the reporter to get in the car, saying he needed to go downtown to pick up Belinda, who was attending secretarial school in the Loop so that she could learn to type Ali's letters. Ali drove her to school every morning and picked her up every afternoon. His Eldorado sat by the curb. As he drove north on Lake Shore Drive, careful to stay below the forty-five-mile-per-hour speed limit, he adjusted the small record player under the dashboard and talked more about how busy he was, how he scarcely found time for religious study. "You see, I'm a minister and I have to know these things because of the questions they ask me," he said.

When Ali reached the Loop, Belinda, now three months pregnant, climbed into the backseat of the car. Ali dropped her off at the house, asked her to cook steak and vegetables for dinner, and drove away, saying, "We got something important to do." Then he went to get a carwash for his already sparkling-clean Eldorado. When the carwash turned out to be closed, he went home to watch more TV. The reporter, Leonard Shecter, had a hard time making sense of Ali at times. On the one hand, Ali complained that Uncle Sam was trying to starve and humiliate him. On the other hand, he said he was grateful the government had decided to release him on bond and allow him to travel the country, and that he had to be careful not to say or do anything that might make the feds change their minds.

Belinda served the men dinner. Ali shook pepper on his boiled okra and cabbage.

"Belinda, bring me some diet cola," he said.

"Belinda, bring the steak."

"Belinda, bring me some brown sugar."

He declared the steak too tough.

"Bring me some chicken."

"It's cold," Belinda said.

"Bring it anyway."

He ate quickly, left the table, and went to his bedroom to change his clothes, singing *Ain't Too Proud to Beg* while he dressed. When Belinda joined him in the bedroom, Shecter could hear the couple cooing. Ali emerged wearing a shiny black suit, white shirt, and dark tie, and saying he was going to show the reporter what he did now that he wasn't boxing. They drove to LaTees Beauty Parlor and Barber Shop on South Drexel Avenue, then to 79th Street, where they dropped in on the reporters and editors at *Muhammad Speaks*. Ali paid no attention to no-parking signs as he moved from one destination to another. In later years, he would tell friends that when he saw a curb painted yellow or red, he took it to mean that the city had reserved a parking space for him; his friends were never sure if Ali meant it as a joke. At the newspaper office, he opened a cabinet drawer containing thousands of pictures from his boxing career. He pulled out a bunch, reminisced a while, and put them back.

Then they were on the move again, headed to the Shabazz restaurant on 71st Street for a big piece of chocolate cake, which Ali ate in five bites. On his way out, he bought a piece of bean pie and ate it in two bites. Whenever they got to the car, Ali did a search for his keys. They were always in a different pocket. Occasionally, he locked them in the car.

He arrived at a theater where he had been asked to speak, but he was two hours early and the doors were locked. To pass the time, he wandered along the sidewalk, trying to attract attention. "I'm looking for a fight!" he barked to anyone in earshot. "Who's the baddest man around here?"

The whole thing saddened Shecter. Ali seemed at a loss. A national magazine writer was accompanying him, recording his every word and every action, and it was not enough to sate his ego. With two hours to kill before his next audience could be assembled, he was incapable of enjoying a quiet moment of isolation or introspection, incapable of trying to get to know the man who'd been accompanying him around town all day. Before their time together ended, the reporter asked Ali how he felt about going to jail. Ali managed to turn his answer into a boast.

"Who wants to go to jail?" he said. "I'm used to running around free like a little bird. In jail, you got no wife, no freedom. You can't eat what you want . . . being in prison every day, looking out of the cell, not seeing nobody . . . A man's got to be serious in his beliefs to do that."

Esquire decided to put Shecter's story on its April cover, and the magazine's art director, George Lois, was assigned to come up with a design. When Ali arrived at a New York studio to be photographed, Lois showed the boxer a reproduction of Botticini's painting of St. Sebastian, an early Christian martyr, tied to a tree, his body pierced with arrows. Lois asked Ali to pose the same way.

Ali considered it for a moment.

"Hey, George!" he finally answered. "This cat's a *Christian!*"

Lois, a nonpracticing Greek Orthodox, explained that Sebastian had been executed for converting to Christianity, just as Ali had been excoriated for converting to Islam, and he asked Ali for permission to call Elijah Muhammad to explain. Ali agreed, and Lois spent the next ten minutes on the phone discussing imagery and religious symbolism with the Nation of Islam's leader. Elijah Muhammad, who understood the power of the media better than most, gave his blessings.

The arrows were too heavy to stick to Ali's body with glue, so the Esquire crew tied fishing line to the arrows and hung them from a bar high above Ali's head. Ali, wearing nothing but white Everlast boxing shorts, white boxing shoes, and white socks, had to hold still until photographer Carl Fischer and his assistants could line up the arrows with the fake blood painted on the boxer's body — two in the chest, one below the heart, two in the stomach, one in the thigh. Lois was struck by Ali's patience and good humor. At one point, the fighter pointed to the arrows and gave them each a name, "Lyndon Johnson, General William Westmoreland, Robert McNamara . . ."

The *Esquire* cover may have been the best publicity Ali ever received. The headline would read, "The Passion of Muhammad Ali," but it was the photo that made the greatest impact. The image of the mighty boxer as a martyr, his hands tied behind his back, blood dripping from his torso, his head tilted, mouth agape in anguish, brought together three of the most searing issues in American culture: race, religion, and the Vietnam War. And it made people think: Maybe there was more to the noisome boxer than they believed. Had Ali been a Christian, like St. Sebastian, would he have been treated differently? Would he have been admired for abandoning his personal and professional desires to follow the word of God? Would he have been deemed a hero for converting his religious ideals into action?

Of course, when Ali posed for George Lois, neither man could have imagined how the timing of that magazine cover would magnify its power. On April 4, 1968, just as the magazine was appearing on newsstands and in mailboxes, Martin Luther King Jr. was in Memphis to speak at a rally for striking sanitation workers and to promote his campaign against poverty. At 6:05 p.m., as King stood on the balcony of the Lorraine Motel, he was struck in the chest with one round from a rifle and killed.

Ali told reporters, "Dr. King was my great Black Brother, and he'll be remembered for thousands of years to come." Later, he would speak less kindly, calling King "the best friend White America ever had."

Robert F. Kennedy, who had recently announced plans to run for the presidency, learned of the murder moments before he was to give a speech in Indianapolis. He abandoned his prepared remarks and delivered an extemporaneous eulogy, saying, "Martin Luther King dedicated his life to love and to justice between fellow human beings. He died in the cause of that effort. In this difficult day, in this difficult time for the United States, it's perhaps well to ask what kind of a nation we are and what direction we want to move in. For those of you who are black . . . you can be filled with bitterness, and with hatred, and a desire for revenge. We can move in that direction as a country, in greater polarization — black people amongst blacks, and white amongst whites, filled with hatred toward one another. Or we can make an effort, as Martin Luther King did, to understand, and to comprehend, and replace that violence, that stain of bloodshed that has spread across our land, with an effort to understand, compassion, and love."

Two months later, Robert Kennedy was assassinated in a hotel kitchen after a speech in Los Angeles.

It would stand as one of the most tumultuous years in American history. Riots erupted at the Democratic National Convention in Chicago. Daniel and Philip Berrigan led a group of Catholic activists in seizing hundreds of draft cards and setting them aflame with homemade napalm, an act that inspired an escalation of antiwar protests around the country. Women fighting for equal rights tossed their bras, mops, frying pans, and girdles into garbage cans in protest at the Miss America beauty contest in Atlantic City. Richard M. Nixon won the presidential election, but the segregationist Alabama governor George Wallace, running as an independent, received almost 10 million votes. Black athletes Tommie Smith and John Carlos raised their fists in a black-power salute when "The Star Spangled Banner" was played at their medal ceremony during the Olympic Games in Mexico City, a gesture that would have been unthinkable before Ali.

It was in this context that Ali as St. Sebastian greeted Americans — as a man who divided and inspired and suffered for his beliefs, a man shot through with enemy arrows. If Ali's religion struck some black Americans as a con man's game, and if white Americans could only scratch their heads trying to understand why Ali would praise the segregationist views of George Wallace, the nuances mattered less with every passing day, every passing riot, every passing protest march. All around was chaos, bloodshed, and disorder. Ali wasn't the only one bleeding.

On May 6, 1968, the 5th U.S. Circuit Court of Appeals affirmed Ali's conviction for draft dodging, ruling that the boxer had no legitimate claim as a Muslim minister or conscientious objector to avoid military service. Nor had he been the victim of discrimination, the court declared. If he didn't join the army, he would go to jail.

Ali remained free as his lawyers prepared an appeal to the U.S. Supreme Court. The Nation of Islam had already lent him $27,000 to help him cover some of his legal and living expenses. He paid that back and soon after borrowed another $100,000. But even with the loans, he struggled to keep up with his bills. To make money, beginning in the fall of 1967, he began presenting lectures on college campuses, earning between five hundred and three thousand dollars per appearance.

The lectures produced anxiety in Ali, who was insecure about his reading and writing abilities and uncertain what kind of questions he might face from college students. He listened to recordings of Elijah Muhammad's sermons and read Muhammad's book *Message to the Blackman in America*, slowly copying lines and ideas from those sources onto index cards that he could keep in the pocket of his suit jacket. It was painstaking work. For Ali, it was the beginning of a battle to overcome the dyslexia and poor reading skills that had hampered him since childhood. In years to come, he would fill hundreds if not thousands of yellow legal pads with transcriptions from Elijah Muhammad's writings and from the Koran. He would read the Christian Bible too, trying to identify contradictions in the text, and he would write those down. He would invite reporters to his home or to his hotel rooms, pull out those legal pads, and read from them, sometimes for hours.

He hired an agent to arrange lectures, and the agent ran an ad in *Variety*. A picture showed Ali in boxing gloves with the following copy: "Muhammad Ali, world's heavyweight champion (Cassius Clay) — Available for Lectures — Nationwide Training Tour — Personal Appearances — Theaters — Country Fairs — Arenas — Colleges — Universities — One-nighters."

In addressing college students in 1967 and 1968, Ali typically kept his remarks brief. He swore allegiance to Elijah Muhammad. He reminded listeners that he had proved his religious commitment by divorcing his first wife and forfeiting millions of dollars in income. He bragged that he was still the true heavyweight champion and would remain champion until someone defeated him in the boxing ring. He mocked other fighters, and for those who looked at his rounder-than-usual face and wondered if he was getting out of shape, he demonstrated his speed and agility with a flurry of air punches and a display of his speedy footwork, always to great applause. Of course, he also spoke about his opposition to the war.

"DOWN WITH EVERYTHING": that was the message on a popular T-shirt. At the time, it seemed everything was up for grabs, under attack. Everybody had something to protest. Some young men and women protested in the broadest way. They attacked conformity. They dropped out — of school, of marriage, of life. They did drugs. They grew their hair long. They took to the road and lived out of their cars, beholden, they said, to no one but themselves. Others went to Mississippi and Alabama, into territory at the heart of the civil rights struggle, to register voters and organize protests. But as the fight for Black Power grew more radical and riots erupted in big cities, many white activists turned their energies to the antiwar movement. As that movement grew, protesters sensed, increasingly, that their voices might be heard, that if they were bold enough and numerous enough and determined enough, they might just force the U.S. government to leave Vietnam.

"I'm expected to go overseas to help free people in South Vietnam," Ali said in one lecture, "and at the same time my people here are being brutalized; hell no! I would like to say to those of you who think I have lost too much: I have gained everything. I have peace of heart; I have a clear, free conscience. And I am proud." He said he would face a firing squad before renouncing Elijah Muhammad and Islam.

He adapted his remarks depending on the makeup of his audience. For an all-black crowd at the University of Pennsylvania, he said integration would never work. "There's no sense in Negroes wanting to integrate with whites," he said. "White folks don't want any black babies walking around in their neighborhood and we don't need any white babies walking around in ours." No white man wanted a kinky-haired, light-brown son, he said, just as no black man wanted a cream-colored child.

At Appalachian State University in North Carolina, he once again expressed admiration for the white segregationist George Wallace and repeated his refrain about all the animals and people of the world preferring to be among their own. "Chinese like to be with Chinese," he said, "because they eat with chopsticks and they like that pling, ting, tong, ting music. They don't dig Johnny Cash." In the same lecture, he said, "The black man was robbed of his language, the slaves were mated like animals . . . he was robbed of his religion, he was robbed of his god, he was robbed of his culture. So we have a nation of people called Negroes who are suffering a mental death. And this death is going on 500 long years."

In Los Angeles, he mocked the Black Power movement as nothing but a fad, saying the modern Negro radical "has an African haircut and African clothes and a white girl on his arm." Haircuts mattered. Black activists made "Black Is Beautiful" a rallying cry, fighting back against longstanding prejudices. For many young men and women in the 1960s, being black and beautiful meant letting their hair grow high and wide. Ali's own hair was something of a compromise. He wore it longer than most members of the Nation of Islam, but not nearly as long as other young radicals.

"We're not Negroes," he said at a stop in Richmond, Virginia. "All people on this planet are named after a country. People from Mexico are called Mexicans. People from Russia are called Russians. People from Egypt are called Egyptians . . . Now what country is named 'Negroes'?" That one always got a great laugh, although many of the people who laughed scratched their heads later when they realized it didn't entirely make sense. Race and nationality were two different things.

In Springfield, Massachusetts, Ali compared the black American who rioted in protest to a bull who charged a train. "He's a brave, brave bull," Ali said. "But his tracks are his only monument."

In Phoenix, he said he was through with boxing, declaring that he intended to do nothing else but "fight for my people."

Hecklers occasionally interrupted, calling him a draft-dodger. Critics occasionally called out some of the flaws in his logic, pointing out, for example, that redbirds and bluebirds belong to different species, which makes mating extremely unlikely. But most of Ali's audience members — liberal white college students, in all likelihood — were charmed by his sincerity and good humor. Ali challenged them to reconsider their prejudices, but he did not issue threats of violence as Black Panther leaders did. He closed his remarks, usually, by rallying the crowds to shout his name as he asked, over and over again until the answer grew loud enough to satisfy him, "Whooooo's the greatest? Whooooo's the champ? Whooooo's the champ? Whooooo's the greatest of *alllll tiiiiimes?*"

On June 18, 1968, Belinda gave birth to her first child. Elijah Muhammad visited the hospital and suggested the baby's name: Maryum.

Ali loved Maryum, but he considered it Belinda's job to raise the child, and he grew impatient when Maryum fussed. "Allah," he said, "made men to look down on women and women to look up to men; it don't matter if the two are standin' up or layin' down. It's just natural." He told a reporter for *Ebony* that he had no special career ambitions for his daughter. "All I want her to become is a clean, righteous person, a good Muslim woman, a good sister, maybe a teacher of black children."

While Belinda stayed home in Chicago with the baby, Ali continued touring campuses. He also agreed to become a partner in a new, Miami-based fast-food restaurant chain called Champburger. Three white men — a stockbroker, an accountant, and a lawyer — founded the corporation and brought aboard Ali for his ability to market the brand and attract investors. When asked how he felt about going into business with white partners, Ali said, "We Muslims do business with the white man every day. But we don't depend on him and we don't Uncle Tom . . . They know that I believe that they are devils and I don't deny it when they ask me."

Champburger went public on the New York Stock Exchange at five dollars a share before the first of its restaurants opened its door. The goal was quick expansion, with restaurants located exclusively in black neighborhoods and with franchises owned predominantly by black franchisees, although the stock prospectus warned that growth might be inhibited if Ali were imprisoned for draft evasion. Ali owned 6 percent of the stock, and in exchange for those shares he was expected to promote the restaurants and allow his image to be used in advertisements. He told one reporter he expected the company to open five hundred restaurants within its first year of operations. The first Champburger was scheduled to open in December at 62nd Street and Northwest 17th Avenue in Miami. The restaurant's specialty would be the quarter-pound "Champburger with Soul Sauce," selling for forty-nine cents. The menu would also offer hot dogs, fried chicken, and fried fish.

"This is something to help black people go into business and get into the economical system," Ali said. "Everybody that you see working in these places will be black."

On December 16, with the opening of the first Champburger less than two weeks away, Ali was locked up in Dade County Jail for outstanding traffic charges.

"Maybe this will be good for me," he said, referring to his ten-day jail term.

"I've never suffered." He added that his short jail sentence might be good practice if he wound up serving five years for draft evasion. As it happened, Ali was released early for Christmas and in time for the grand opening of Champburger.

Ali earned another paycheck — this time for about ten thousand dollars — by filming a fake fight with former heavyweight champion Rocky Marciano. A computer was supposed to determine the winner, but producers filmed two endings — one with Ali stopping Rocky on cuts, the other with Marciano scoring an unconvincing knockout against the much bigger, much faster Ali. Marciano had dropped forty pounds to get in shape for the production, but the whole thing was a joke, and the sight of Ali in boxing trunks again proved only one thing: that the champ had been eating too many Champburgers.

Ali didn't seem to miss boxing, not as long as he could continue to attract crowds and capture the attention of reporters. One day he drove his pink Cadillac from New York City to Monmouth College near the Jersey Shore for a lecture, with a *New York Times* reporter in the passenger seat. Ali, the reporter observed, "is not a conversationalist, but a monologist. When he begins a subject that he has obviously been asked about repeatedly before, it is as though he simply activates a tape in his head, and out pour the words." When he reached the most quotable passages in his soliloquy, Ali would reach up and turn on the overhead light, signaling to the reporter that this was the good stuff and he should take notes.

In Chicago one day, the sports journalist Dick Schaap invited Ali to join him for dinner. Tom Seaver, the star pitcher for the New York Mets came along, too. Seaver had just finished a spectacular season in which he'd won twenty-five games and led the Mets to a World Series triumph. The conversation was loud, with Ali doing most of the talking. About halfway through the meal, Ali paused in the middle of one his monologues, turned to Seaver, and said: "Hey, you a nice fella. You a sportswriter?"

That was how it went, day after day. Every street and sidewalk was a red carpet, unfurled just for Ali. By traveling mostly in big cities and lecturing mostly on college campuses, where antiwar protests were common, Ali insulated himself from the Americans who deemed him unpatriotic. He likely didn't read the critical letters that appeared in newspapers, and he certainly didn't see the hundreds if not thousands of letters received by the White

House and U.S. Justice Department from ordinary Americans who couldn't understand why a man convicted of draft evasion had not been jailed for his crime. One such letter, sent to the Justice Department from a husband and wife in Tampa, Florida, encapsulated the sentiment of many. It read,

> Dear Sirs:
>
> Respectfully asking why that "super-patriot" Cassius Clay or whatever he calls himself now is still running around loose while other American boys are being killed, maimed, and shot at in Viet Nam. We have one son in Viet Nam and another about to go there.
>
> Could it be that our great Justice Dept. is afraid of jerk Clay and the Negro populace in general? We think so.

Army Specialist Bill Barwick, a black man, wrote to President Johnson from Vietnam, saying that "Cassius Clay, pardon me, Muhammad Ali," was a topic of much discussion among the troops. "There are very few people who speak of anything else over here," he wrote in a letter dated June 24, 1967. "If Cassius Clay can get away with something like this than my brother, or the kid downtown, or any darn fool wise-guy will want to try the same thing." To Barwick, Ali's case proved that the law worked differently for those, like Ali, who were "more powerful and financially successful than the people who are now serving in the Armed Forces."

Ali carried on in spite of the controversy. In New York one day, he exited a hotel lobby and, instead of moving swiftly to his waiting car, looked around, waiting for people to recognize him. They did. Most celebrities preferred to avoid autograph seekers and back-slappers. Not Ali. All his life, whenever people offered to sneak him out a back door or take him down a service elevator to avoid attention, he would refuse. When a limousine driver waited for him, he instructed the driver to park on the busiest stretch of the most congested street he could find. When there people around to admire him, he was never in a hurry.

"Yes, ma'am," he said, "that's right. You are lookin' at Muhammad Ali, the heavyweight champion of the *whole* world."

The crowd in front of the hotel thickened and spread.

"See my new limousine?" he asked. "Just bought it last week for $10,000 —

I mean cash, baby. They think they can bring me to my knees by takin' away my title and by not lettin' me fight . . . Shoot! I ain't worked for two years and I ain't been Tommin' to nobody and here I'm buyin' limousines — the President of the United States ain't got no better one. Just look at it! Ain't it purty? Y'all go and tell everybody that Muhammad Ali ain't licked yet."

27

Song and Dance and Prayer

One day in March 1969, Muhammad and Belinda Ali were summoned to the home of Elijah Muhammad on Chicago's South Side. Although they had both been to the Messenger's home before, it was unusual to be called on short notice. They were anxious.

As usual, the Messenger's tastefully furnished home was crowded with people: grim men in suits, quiet women in white dresses. They sat at a long dining room table, where almost every seat was filled with a high-ranking official of the Nation of Islam. Clara Muhammad and some of the women in white served tea and small dishes of food. Normally, Belinda would light up in the presence of Elijah, whom she addressed as "grandfather." Normally, Ali would work the room, slapping backs and shaking hands. But not this time.

"It was terrifying," Belinda recalled years later.

Elijah Muhammad was small and thin — tiny, compared to Ali — with big, warm eyes and a disarming smile. It was a smile, James Baldwin wrote, that "promised to take the burden of my life off my shoulders." But Elijah Muhammad showed little of the smile in this meeting. Speaking softly and calmly, he explained why he had asked the Alis to come to his home. A few days earlier, Elijah Muhammad said, he had seen Ali on TV with Howard Cosell and heard Ali say to the television journalist that he hoped to fight again soon because he needed the money. Elijah Muhammad had always followed Ali closely. As the most recognizable public figure in his movement, the boxer's words and actions mattered. Elijah had not been upset when Ali went into business with men to sell Champburgers with Soul Sauce. He had not been upset when Ali had exchanged pleasantries with Martin Luther King. Nor had he been upset when Ali had begun his tour of mostly white college campuses. But the sight of Ali on TV saying he wanted to fight again because he needed money had enraged the Nation of Islam leader.

Ali listened quietly as the Messenger explained. The Nation of Islam, he said, had always disapproved of the sporting life. The sporting life was worse than frivolous. The sporting life corrupted men's souls. The sporting life promoted greed and violence. The sporting life distracted men from religious observance. Elijah Muhammad said he was disappointed to hear that Ali wished to return to the sporting life, and he was even more disappointed to hear that he wished do so merely for the money. Hadn't the Messenger told him that Allah would provide for him? Had he lost faith?

Ali's punishment, Elijah Muhammad said, would be a one-year banishment from the Nation of Islam. Neither Ali nor his wife would be permitted to attend services or to fraternize with members in good standing. The matter was not open to discussion, and Ali accepted the verdict without argument. The Messenger often used expulsion to discipline his followers. He had banished one of his own children, Wallace D. Muhammad, for questioning some of the Nation's teachings, and, most famously, he had suspended Malcolm X — a suspension from which Malcolm had never returned.

For Belinda, who had grown up in the Nation of Islam and whose parents both belonged, the penalty was almost unbearable. "It was like going to prison," she said. A few days later, when Elijah Muhammad publicly announced his decision, he hit Ali where he knew it would hurt most: he took away the boxer's name. "We shall call him Cassius Clay," Elijah declared. "We take away the name of Allah (God) from him, until he proves himself worthy of that name."

At first glance, Elijah Muhammad's logic seemed strange. Ali had been a boxer when he had joined the Nation of Islam. He had fought nine times since announcing his religious conversion. He had often bragged about his love of money and the cars and houses he would buy. He had abandoned the Louisville Sponsoring Group so that the Messenger's son could manage his boxing career and help him earn more money. John Ali, the national secretary of the Nation of Islam, and Herbert Muhammad were each personally earning great sums of money from Ali's boxing career. *Muhammad Speaks* had celebrated Ali's pugilistic success with dozens of laudatory articles. So what did Elijah Muhammad's vitriolic statement mean, and why did it come now?

One day shortly after the announcement of Ali's suspension, Louis Farrakhan visited Elijah Muhammad's home. The Messenger asked John Ali to read his pronouncement aloud so Farrakhan could hear it. "That was one of the hardest moments I had at the table of my teacher," Farrakhan recalled. "I didn't fully understand. And after John Ali read the article, Elijah Muhammad looked at me as I am looking at you and said, 'Brother, I did that for you.'"

Farrakhan wasn't sure what that meant, at least not at first. But Elijah Muhammad knew that Farrakhan, a gifted musician, had given up his career as an entertainer because the Nation of Islam considered music and entertainment frivolous. Years earlier, Malcolm X had delivered a letter to Farrakhan saying Farrakhan had thirty days to "get out of music or get out of the temple." Elijah Muhammad knew that other members of the Nation of Islam had given up singing, acting, dancing, and other activities, professional and recreational, because their activities were deemed distractions. Elijah Muhammad understood that others in the Nation resented the fact that Ali was permitted to box. "He was the type of leader," Farrakhan said, "who kept one eye on the scripture and one eye on the person to whom he was speaking, so that he would know where you fit."

In his book *Message to the Blackman in America*, Elijah Muhammad wrote that sport and play caused "delinquency, murder, theft and other forms of wicked and immoral crimes." He added, "The poor so-called Negroes are the worst victims in this world of sport and play because they are trying to learn the white man's games of civilization. Sport and play (games of chance) take away the remembrance of Allah (God) and the doing of good, says the Holy Qur-an."

Elijah Muhammad had made an exception for Ali — perhaps because he had thought the boxer would boost recruitment and drive more sales of his newspaper, perhaps because Ali had donated money to the Nation of Islam, perhaps because Elijah had feared that Ali would ally himself with Malcolm X, or perhaps because he had seen potential in the young man. There can be no doubt that the Nation of Islam profited by its association with Ali. The boxer once fought an exhibition with Cody Jones as a fundraiser for the Nation, with tickets selling at prices between $1.50 and $10 each. On another occasion, *Muhammad Speaks* sponsored a contest for its readers: whoever sold the most subscriptions in a month would get a free trip to one of Ali's fights. Beginning in 1965, the newspaper ran a regular column called "From the Camp of the Champ," detailing Ali's daily routines and philosophies. At the same time, when Ali bragged about his abilities and failed to credit Allah for his victory over George Chuvalo, the newspaper criticized Ali, and Ali apologized.

If Elijah Muhammad was torn between the Koran and his accounts receivable, Ali's interview with Cosell pushed the sect leader back to the Koran, moving him to recapture some of the high moral ground he had lost. At the same time, Elijah may have been sending a message to Herbert, who had never been as religiously observant as his father would have liked and who had the most to gain financially if Ali returned to boxing. If sport and play were corrupting anyone, it was Herbert.

"I Called My Manger Herbert Muhammad today," Ali wrote on a sheet of lined yellow paper, "and he told me that he Could No Longer be My Manger. Because his father T.H.E.M. [The Honorable Elijah Muhammad] and the Muslims through the Country, Could Not be with Me in Returning to the Ring."

Here was Ali, still only twenty-seven years old. His devotion to the Nation of Islam had insulated him from some of American culture's insanity. Ali would be nowhere near Woodstock in the summer of 1969, for example. He had kept his distance from the Black Panthers, who, at times, seemed to be engaged in an armed revolution against the U.S. government. But in other ways, Ali's new religion had done as much if not more than boxing to shape his life. He had given up his first wife for his religion. He had changed his name, risked prison, sacrificed millions of dollars, and turned his back on friends and relatives. He had even sent his friend Bundini Brown packing, albeit temporarily, because Bundini had upset Muslim leadership. And now the man who had inspired Ali's actions, the man he worshiped as a prophet of God, was casting him aside, telling him he was no longer welcome as a Muslim because he refused to abandon boxing. It must have been bewildering.

Back in 1964, the Nation of Islam had kept the boxer's membership secret, fearing the bad publicity that would come if Cassius Clay had lost to Sonny Liston. Now, it failed to back a disciple in his time of need. Even as Ali maintained a moral stand based on the teachings of Elijah Muhammad,

Elijah Muhammad himself backed away from the boxer. Perhaps the Nation of Islam didn't need Ali anymore, now that he wasn't making money. Radio stations all over the country broadcast speeches by Elijah Muhammad and Louis Farrakhan, and their message was spreading into the mainstream. The Nation of Islam's newspaper, *Muhammad Speaks,* boasted that its circulation was growing rapidly. The Temptations scored a hit record with "Message from a Black Man," a song that not only carried a title similar to that of Elijah Muhammad's book but also included lyrics that the Messenger would have endorsed: "Yes, my skin is black," the song begin, "but that's no reason to hold me back." But Ali, no cynic, praised the Messenger's decision. He said the punishment was fair. He said he understood his mistake and would do everything he could to atone for his sin and regain his teacher's trust. "All that funnin' and fightin', runnin' around, bein' on television, is over," he said. "Now I'll concentrate on prayin', studyin' hard and learnin' to be a better Muslim minister."

Although his words seemed sincere, his actions in the months ahead would prove inconsistent. In October 1969, Ali announced that he would act in a Broadway musical, something that certainly seemed to contradict the wishes of Elijah Muhammad. The musical, *Buck White,* was adapted from a play written by a white man, Joseph Dolan Tuotti, with songs by Oscar Brown Jr., who was black. The play purported to take place at the meeting hall of a Black Power group called B.A.D., whose initials stood for Beautiful Alleluja Days. Ali was guaranteed a weekly salary in addition to a percentage of the box-office gross. The play's producer, Zev Bufman, whose earlier stagings had included *Mame* and *Plaza Suite,* said he had never paid an actor as much as he paid Ali. The actor's name — "Cassius Clay a/k/a Muhammad Ali" — would appear above the title of the play on the marquee for the George Abbott Theatre.

In *Buck White,* Ali would don a beard and an Afro wig to play a decidedly non-Muslim black activist, Buck White, as he sang the Dylanesque lyric, "Yeah, that's all over now, Mighty Whitey. We can't bear no more. We don't care no more."

Ali didn't see any problem with the play because, as he said, "It is wrapped up with black people comin' together . . . unitin' to stand up and do for self, clean up self, respect self." He boasted that he had turned down an invitation to play the boxer Jack Johnson in another Broadway play, *The Great White Hope,* because he didn't want to act in romantic scenes with white women. At least in Ali's mind, the logic cohered. He wasn't a member in good standing of the Nation of Islam, so it didn't matter if Elijah Muhammad approved of his theatrical debut. And if he were permitted to rejoin the Nation and learned that Elijah objected to his Broadway work, he had an option in his contract that would allow him to quit the play.

When the production opened, critics treated Ali kindly, saying he sang and acted reasonably well, and that his great energy and enthusiasm made up for any lack of polish. But beyond Ali's performance, the play was not well received, and *Buck White* closed after only seven performances.

The newspaperman Robert Lipsyte witnessed another humiliation. One night he walked with Ali back to his hotel. When Ali couldn't open the door to his room, the hotel manager explained that it had been locked because Ali owed $53.09.

When you're the champ, Ali said, seemingly surprised, they never make you pay right away.

He was out of boxing and out of the Nation of Islam. He was a new father. As opposition to the Vietnam War grew, he became more of a political figure than he'd ever been, with an opportunity to reach new audiences and address new issues. This might have been a time of reflection for Muhammad Ali, a time of reassessment, had he been inclined to such things. But, if anything, this period of uncertainty in Ali's life seemed to inspire more selfish behavior.

Despite Elijah Muhammad's warning, Ali continued to pursue opportunities to box. In the fall of 1969, Herbert Muhammad, Angelo Dundee, and Howard Cosell worked together on a plan to have Ali fight Jimmy Ellis in a television studio. The fight would be broadcast live, but there would be no tickets sold. Cosell would get fifty thousand dollars for brokering the deal, according to an FBI memo dated December 8, 1969. The men believed that if the fight were held privately, with no paying audience, it would require no approval from a state agency or boxing commission. It's not clear why they abandoned the effort.

At the same time, Ali surrounded himself with a growing assortment of questionable characters, including members of the Nation of Islam's Mosque

No. 12, located in Philadelphia, which the FBI labeled "the gangster mosque," where members were involved in "narcotics, contract murders, bank robberies, fraudulent credit card and check schemes, armed robberies, widespread extortion and loan sharking activities." And, apparently for the first time, he began having sex with women other than his wife. According to one member of the Philadelphia mosque, Ali carried on an affair with his ex-wife, Sonji. He also maintained a long-running affair with his first love from Central High School, Areatha Swint, who changed her name to Jamillah Muhammad. "He was a man who did what he wanted to do," Swint recalled.

But Belinda had the impression there was no one special, that he slept only with an assortment of prostitutes and one-night stands. Belinda caught him kissing women in the nooks and crannies of the George Abbott Theatre and in the halls of the Hotel Wellington, where she and Ali were living while he rehearsed for the play.

"He knew it was wrong," Belinda said years later. "As long as he was having fun he didn't care. I was battling against the hypocrisy, the chauvinism . . . I thought growing up if I was good and loyal my husband would be good and loyal. I was totally wrong. Totally wrong."

Maybe it was her experience with the Nation of Islam, where everyone knew that Elijah Muhammad had cheated on his wife, or maybe it was her exposure to Herbert Muhammad, who had long had an active sex life beyond his marriage; maybe it was seeing the way her husband craved attention and the way women fawned over him, but for whatever reason, Belinda was neither surprised nor crushed by her husband's behavior.

"I knew things like this would happen," she recalled years later. "I was prepared to [accept] that, as long as he don't bring it in my home, I don't care what he does. I'm not his mother . . . I'm not going to tell him what to do. But I did tell him, it's not good for you to do that. You're trying to build up your reputation, and I'm trying to build a family reputation around you so you look good in the eyes of the people."

He didn't listen.

"I had no control over him then," she said years later.

Even when it happened more than once, she never considered leaving him. Where would she have gone? What would she have done? She was young and taking care of a child, and she loved him. "No, I didn't want to, I wasn't going to leave him," she said. "We had something to do, and I said I was going to help him. I knew we was going to go through some trials like this. I knew it was going to happen because of who he is and he's weak and I tried to make him strong. I tried to stand by him and stuff like that. He said, 'I'm just weak.' And he would tell me, 'I'm just weak, man. I'm just grateful you're not jumping off leaving me.' I said I'm not going to leave you. I said we got children. I'm not going to let no woman destroy my marriage. I'm not going to let that happen. And he would say, 'I don't love these people, it was just bam, bam, thank you ma'am. I ain't in love with nobody.' And he would tell me that. I said as long as you ain't in love with nobody, fine. But he took advantage of that. He took advantage. He just loved sex. He was a sex addict . . . He would bam, bam and he gone, he done."

Ali apologized when he was caught. He cried. He proclaimed his love for Belinda. The sight of this enormous man sitting on the edge of the bed, his shoulders slouched, tears streaming down his cheeks, never failed to move her. But then he would do it again. At times, Ali was so callous he would ask his wife to arrange his extramarital affairs, to book hotel rooms for his mistresses, to take care not to disturb him when he was with one of the other women. "And then he'd tell me, 'I'll use that against you,'" she recalled. She took that to mean that if she filed for divorce, Ali would tell the world his wife was complicit in his affairs, that she was practically his pimp. "I figured, let him sow his oats. Let him get it over with. You get tired of that shit after a while. I was a young girl. I didn't know what to do . . . And so he made me help him. He said, 'You supposed to do everything I tell you, you're my wife. Look at Herbert, he got women and stuff.' He said, 'If you help me, then you'll be doing something no wife would do.'" He made it sound like a compliment, a testament to her fidelity, proof of her love. Only the greatest and most loyal of wives would help her husband have sex as often as he wanted with all the women he wanted.

"Ali had a dark side, an evil side," Belinda said. "He manipulated me to do that. It was called manipulation. I didn't know what manipulation meant . . . I thought by my husband telling me everything, I thought he was being true and honest. I didn't like it, but he conned me to do certain things"

She tried telling her parents, but they didn't believe her. She saw no point in telling anyone else. "Everybody else knew," she said. "They watched him.

They knew Ali, what he was doing. I didn't have to tell nobody, but there was no way I could talk to people. I had to hold all that in . . . I had to do a lot of stuff all by myself. I had to deal with it all by myself."

Early in 1970, before her twentieth birthday, Belinda discovered she was pregnant again, this time with twins.

28

The Greatest Book of All Time

In the spring of 1970, Ali began work on his autobiography, promising, of course, that it would "outdo everything that's ever been written."

Random House paid an advance of more than $200,000 for the memoir, assigning one of its most talented editors, Toni Morrison, to shepherd the project. Richard Durham, the former editor of *Muhammad Speaks* and a writer with a longtime interest in Marxism, agreed to write the book based on a series of extensive interviews with Ali.

"The public doesn't know too much about me," Ali said at the press conference announcing his book deal. At first, the remark seemed funny, considering that Ali was perhaps the most widely publicized man on the planet and had been telling his own story virtually without pause since he first gained fame as an Olympian a decade earlier. But how well did the public really know Ali? How well did Ali know himself at age twenty-eight? Who was he? What did he hope to become? The questions no longer hung about him in the vague way they hang about most men and women. Now the questions demanded answers in writing.

Was he Muhammad Ali or Cassius Marcellus Clay Jr.? It was difficult to say. He had been born Clay and taken the name Ali, but he had never legally changed his name in the six years he had been calling himself Muhammad Ali. The paperwork had been too much trouble. And then Elijah Muhammad had taken away the name, saying that as far as the Nation of Islam was concerned, Cassius Clay was Cassius Clay again. Ali, meanwhile, continued to call himself Ali.

Was he the heavyweight champion of the world? He'd won the title by defeating Sonny Liston and defending it successfully, but boxing officials had stripped him of his crown, saying a Muslim draft dodger was not entitled to be the sport's titleholder. Yet the champ continued to call himself the champ.

Was he a boxer? A war protester? A leader of the Black Power movement? A humble follower of Elijah Muhammad? Who was he? What did he want? Like others, he wanted money, attention, sex, adventure, and power. He wanted to be special, and he wanted to be seen as special by people around the world, especially black people. "Who's the champ?" he asked audiences wherever he went. "Who's the champ?" He repeated the question until the answer came in the form of a chant: "Ali! Ali! Ali!"

Constantly craving attention wasn't easy. It forced him into endless contradictions. It turned him into a fighter who said he didn't care to fight, a writer who didn't write, a minister without a ministry, a radical who wanted to be a popular entertainer, an extravagant spender who said money meant nothing to him, a dietary ascetic who guzzled soft drinks and sold greasy hamburgers to his fans, an antiwar protester who avoided organized demonstrations even when President Nixon's decision to invade Cambodia provoked the largest student strike in the nation's history, and a religiously devout and demanding husband who openly cheated on his wife. As the 1970s began, Ali's desire to be all things to all people would send him on a wild ride as he sought to define himself in his own life, in the public's eye, and in the pages of his biography.

Fortunately for Ali, the political and social dynamic was changing, and forces beyond his own control also defined him. When he had won the heavyweight championship as Cassius Clay, he had been merely a promising boxer with manic energy and a loud mouth. When he had joined the Nation of Islam, he had become a prominent member of the most radical wing of the black movement in America. When he had refused the draft and been banned from boxing, his position in American society shifted again. Thousands of other draft-age young men followed his example and evaded military service, although most of them did so without risking imprisonment. Some fled to Canada. Others enrolled in graduate study. Those with clout called in favors. Of course, many young Americans lacked the clout and the money to avoid the draft. They didn't have a team of lawyers to file appeals in court, as Ali had. These young men faced the unpleasant choice of running away, going to jail, or accepting enlistment. Ali was no ordinary demonstrator. Still, as millions of Americans protested the war, the boxer's actions seemed less treasonous and more courageous, especially among young white protesters. After the demonstrations at the 1968 Olympics and countless other protests by black athletes, the sight of an outspoken black athlete no longer shocked. Mainstream black leaders such as Julian Bond and Ralph Abernathy, who had once disdained Ali, began to cheer him. As other black activists grew more radical, the Nation of Islam seemed less frightening. When boxing officials denied Ali the right to box and the government revoked his passport, even some of the white sportswriters who had criticized the fighter questioned whether he was being singled out unfairly because of his color and his religious and political beliefs. It wasn't that Ali moved toward the mainstream but that the mainstream moved toward Ali.

Years later, the writer Stanley Crouch would compare Ali to a bear. When he was a newly minted Muslim calling white people devils, Crouch said, Ali was a real bear, deadly dangerous and impossible to control. But as Ali found popularity, the boxer began to behave more like a circus bear, one that flashes its teeth and claws but only threatens harm.

In the spring of 1970, Belinda and Muhammad moved to Philadelphia, mostly so Ali could entertain business and entertainment opportunities in New York. In August, Belinda gave birth to twins, Jamillah and Rasheda.

His life in the early months of 1970 lacked structure. He no longer rose early each morning to exercise. His calendar contained few appointments. Ever since Elijah Muhammad had expelled him from the Nation of Islam, Ali had stopped attending Muslim rallies or prayer meetings, although he continued to pray at home several times a day.

Some of Ali's friends wondered if he would leave the Nation of Islam rather than wait for Elijah Muhammad to grant forgiveness. The Nation of Islam was growing weaker. Huey Newton and the Black Panther Party captivated young black men more than Elijah Muhammad, who turned seventy-three in 1970 and had begun to lose key members from his inner circle. Accusations of corruption dogged the organization. Karl Evanzz, in his biography of Elijah Muhammad, said that expelling Ali may have been the best thing the

Messenger ever did for the boxer. Just as the Nation of Islam was beginning to self-destruct, Ali gained distance from the organization, yet another example of the great luck and timing that had marked his life to date.

When the civil rights activist Jesse Jackson spent time with Ali in the early 1970s, he was struck by the casual nature of Ali's relationship to the Nation of Islam. Jackson remembered one day when he and Ali visited Jackson's mother. She had baked cracklin' bread, named for the fried pork skin that gives the bread its crunch, and Ali dove into it with vigor. Between bites, Ali asked what was in the bread, but Jackson wasn't fooled. "He knew what was in it!" And did he continue eating it after he was told that the bread contained an ingredient forbidden to Muslims? "He ate a pan full," Jackson said, laughing.

In hours of conversation during his years of exile, Jackson never heard Ali express misgivings about the Nation of Islam. At the same time, he never saw Ali with a prayer rug. Why did the boxer remain loyal to the Elijah Muhammad, even as the Messenger's power waned?

Jackson had a theory: "I think there was always anxiety about what happened to Malcolm."

Ali was not an active member of the Nation of Islam. He was not a boxer. He was a convicted draft dodger, but even that remained unresolved, as his lawyers continued working on his appeal. It was difficult if not impossible to say when anything would be decided. Yet, even in private discussions with friends, he never expressed doubt about his decision to refuse the draft.

Joc Frazier was heavyweight champion now. Although smaller than Ali, at five-foot-eleven, Frazier was a skull-shattering puncher. After beating Ali's former sparring partner Jimmy Ellis, Frazier possessed a record of twenty-five wins and no losses. To prove he was still the best, Ali would eventually have to beat Frazier. There was talk of an Ali-Frazier fight in Mexico, then Canada, but Ali couldn't get a passport. "I have officially retired from boxing," Ali said after the Canadian fight with Frazier was rejected. "I am busy with my autobiography and they want to make it into a movie. I don't have a title yet, but I am thinking of—'If I Had a Passport I'd Be a Billionaire.'"

He continued, "I am a freedom fighter now."

29

Stand by Me

One day in August 1970, Joe Frazier picked up Muhammad Ali in Frazier's gold-colored Cadillac. Frazier sat askew in the driver's seat, as if he were riding a horse sidesaddle, spinning the steering wheel with his left hand and gesturing to Ali with his right. Frazier wore a yellow shirt, yellow striped pants, brown boots, and a tan cowboy hat. They drove from Philadelphia to New York, Ali in the passenger seat and Ali's ghostwriter, Richard Durham, in back, his tape recorder rolling.

The trip had been Ali's idea, to get material for his book, which would be titled *The Greatest: My Own Story*.

After ten minutes of silence, Ali spoke first:

ALI: How long this take?

FRAZIER: We'll be there by five.

ALI: Hope so. I got an appointment at five.

FRAZIER: What you complaining about? I was supposed to be there at three. Fooled around waiting for you.

ALI (*long pause*): How's your leg? The one you broke in Vegas?

FRAZIER: I'll be all right. 'Nother two, three weeks from now, be able to get back in the ring. Got my weight down good, man. Look.

ALI: Yeah, you look good.

FRAZIER: Believe me, I ain't fat.

ALI: But you like me; you gain weight easy, don't you?

FRAZIER: Too easy. Well, that come from eating all that good food the wives
cook.

ALI: All that good cooking.

FRAZIER: You sit home when you laid up . . . in the house most of the time . . .

ALI: Yeah, getting that late trim, then going to sleep. That's what gets you.

FRAZIER: Yeah. Gets you fat right away.

ALI: So eat unsweetened grapefruits, man.

They spotted a police car and wondered why the officers were staring at
them. They talked about Frazier's upcoming fights.

ALI: But tell the truth, now, man. If you fought me, wouldn't you be scared?

FRAZIER: No, man. Honest to God.

ALI: You really wouldn't be scared?

FRAZIER: No kinda way!

ALI: I mean my fast left jab, the way I dance?

FRAZIER: Noooooo! I'd get close to you. They talk about how fast you is,
moving away. But you gonna find out how fast I am moving *in*.

Ali pressed him. Surely Frazier would admit he was scared. "It's impossible
for you to get away from my jab," he said. "Impossible!"

FRAZIER: See, them other cats out there let you have your way. They let you
jump around the ring and dance and all that —

ALI: You couldn't stop me from jumping around the ring and dancing. What
you gonna do?

FRAZIER: I'd get right dead on you! Every time you breathe, you be breathing
right down on my head.

ALI: You be tired after five, six rounds of scuffling.

FRAZIER: You be tired trying to get away, too. Running and jabbing and
ducking and dodging . . . you be tired, too.

The car stopped at a red light and Ali leaned out the window: "Hey, you
two foxes out there on the corner! Better watch it!" The girls recognized Ali
but not Frazier. Score that round for Ali.

The car moved and Frazier said he was eager to fight. "'Cause you ain't afraid of me, and I ain't afraid of you."

Ali paused. "But I really believe you afraid of me," he said.

Now Frazier paused: "No, I sure ain't."

The argument went on, pleasantly, until Ali said Frazier had no jab. When he heard that, Frazier hit the brakes.

FRAZIER: I don't have a jab?

ALI: Keep driving! Watch it! No, you don't have no jab.

FRAZIER: Man, I'd tear your head off with a jab. I'd hit you with a jab like a machine gun.

ALI: Naw, man. You don't have no footwork. You don't dance.

FRAZIER: Listen! Some guys get the wrong impression about what's happening out there. When I'm stepping into a man's jab, I'm not gonna step in with my head. I'm gonna step in with these hands. In front of me, see? And if your jab extend out to hit me, I got my hand here to catch it. Then mine can hit you. It's easy as that.

ALI (*disdainfully*): I throw 'em a little too quick for you to block.

FRAZIER (*shaking his head*): I'd like to get this thing together.

ALI: I sure would like to get it on, too. 'Cause I got something for you, Joe. And why you always talk about you gonna come out smokin'?

FRAZIER: That's what I do! Ain't nobody that could put that smoke out. They slow down the fire a bit, but when that fire's gone, that smoke still right there.

ALI: Naw, man. I wrote a poem on you. Went like this:

> *Joe's gonna come out smokin'*
> *And I ain't gonna be jokin'*
> *I'll be peckin' and pokin'*
> *Pourin' water on his smokin'*
> *This might shock and amaze ya,*
> *But I'll retire Joe Frazier!*

FRAZIER (*after pause*): Yeah? Smoke still smokin' It's still smokin'.

They laughed. They reminisced. They talked about the one man they both admired: Muhammad Ali. Frazier admitted that he pushed himself harder when he ran and sparred because he knew one day he would fight Ali. They went on for miles, as the New Jersey Turnpike passed from rolling farmland to the putrid oil tanks of Elizabeth, talking trash, comparing past performances, each man making a case for his superiority. Ali interrupted Frazier constantly, but Frazier accepted it in good humor.

FRAZIER: All the fellows I destroy, I don't have no hard feelings. After I whip your ass, I'll buy you some ice cream. (*Ali tries to interrupt.*) Let me talk! You finished now? Let me talk. I got no hard feelings with you here or no other place. But when we get in the ring, you on your own.

ALI: You be on your own, too.

FRAZIER: That's the only way I know how to be.

There followed a long Ali monologue, a round-by-round description, with sound effects, of how Ali v. Frazier would unfold, with Ali dancing through the first round without punching, then using nothing but left jabs in round two, then adding right crosses and left hooks in the third . . .

Frazier cursed and tried to interrupt but Ali wouldn't let him. Finally, Frazier got a turn to speak and predicted he would knock out Ali in the sixth round. That upset Ali. Predictions were *his* game.

After a bit more banter, Ali, seemingly serious, told Frazier he needed a job and asked if Frazier would consider hiring him as a sparring partner.

ALI: Suppose I'm never allowed to fight. But still I want to keep my body fit and sharp. Now, you needs a good fast man to keep you sharp because you go through so many sparring partners. Wouldn't you like to have the type sparring partner that could rumble with you four and five good rounds a day until you got enough? I mean, where you don't have to keep changing 'em because they can't stand up to you?

FRAZIER: That's good . . .

ALI: I mean, wouldn't you like to have a good sparring partner that could tag you? And you can tag him, and he ain't gonna quit on you? I need a job.

FRAZIER: You don't need no goddamn job.

ALI: Don't tell nobody; it's between us, but I do. How much you pay?

FRAZIER: How much you want?

ALI: Couple hundred a week. That means eight hundred by the end of the
     month.

FRAZIER: Shit! You want a whole lot.

Ali said he was serious. He would go to work as a sparring partner for
Frazier. While Frazier didn't say yes or no, he offered Ali a key to the gym
he owned so Ali could work out there anytime he wanted. Frazier said he
wanted Ali to be sharp if and when they did fight.

As they neared New York, they sounded like two good friends killing time
and enjoying each other's company. Ali offered Frazier financial advice, saying he had learned from his mistakes. Buy a house, he said. Resist the urge
to buy a lot of cars. One good Cadillac was enough. He urged Frazier to
give up his motorcycle, saying it was dangerous. They talked about which
fighters were Uncle Toms, agreeing on Jimmy Ellis, George Foreman, Floyd
Patterson, and Buster Mathis. They talked about their pregnant wives. They
compared singing voices, with Ali performing his Mighty Whitey song, and
the two of them singing "Stand by Me" in unison.

When Frazier boasted that he had earned thirty thousand dollars singing
in Las Vegas, Ali finally admitted he was impressed.

ALI: Awww, you ain't got that kind of money, man. Wow, you carry that much
     dough in your wallet?

FRAZIER: Four, five hundred. Need some?

ALI: How about a hundred? I may stay overnight.

FRAZIER: Yeah, okay.

Frazier handed Ali a hundred-dollar bill. Ali promised to pay him back
the following week. More singing followed, and as they arrived in New York,
Ali asked Frazier to open the Cadillac's sunroof.

ALI: Wow, damn! Look at that fox out there. HEY! I'M MUHAMMAD ALI.
     JOE FRAZIER AND MUHAMMAD ALI ... COME ON OVER HERE!
     I've always loved New York. This is our city, Joe; the world is right
     here.

• • •

Frazier pulled over on West 52nd Street to let Ali out.

ALI: We don't wanna be seen too much together, you know.
FRAZIER: Yeah. They'll think we're buddies. That'll be bad for the gate.
ALI: Yeah. Ain't nobody gonna pay nothing to see two buddies.

With that, they went their separate ways.

30

Comeback

When Ali moved to Philadelphia in 1970, he purchased the home of a hustler named Major Benjamin Coxson. Major was his Christian name, but Coxson wore it like a royal title. "The Maje," as people called him, owned carwashes and car dealerships, but the biggest chunk of his income came from flagrantly illegal activities. Coxson, a flamboyant dresser, bribed city officials, financed drug deals, and served as an intermediary between Italian and black gangsters in the so-called City of Brotherly Love. He also allegedly served as an informant to the FBI.

Ali met Coxson in 1968 when the boxer attended a fundraiser in Philadelphia for a neighborhood organization called the Black Coalition, which counted Coxson and Jeremiah Shabazz among its board members. In 1969, one newspaper identified Coxson as Ali's agent. When Ali decided to leave Chicago for the East Coast, he said, perhaps jokingly, "The Major made me move to Philadelphia." At that point, Coxson offered to sell his own home to the boxer. It was a split-level in the posh, mostly white Overbrook neighborhood, and it was already decorated, with a round bed in the master bedroom, color TVs in every room (including the bathrooms), twenty-two phones, and wall-to-wall carpeting in the garage. Ali agreed to pay $92,000 — more than double the home's assessed value.

When newspapers reported that Ali had moved to fancy digs in a white section of Philadelphia, college students at one of his lectures challenged him, asking why a black man who opposed integration didn't select a house in a black neighborhood. Ali answered with a question of his own: "Do you want me to buy a home in the ghetto? Why do I want to live in a rat bin and have a rat bite my child?"

Major Coxson wasn't the only new member of Ali's entourage in 1970. Without his usual retinue surrounding him and with no daily routine, Ali was more receptive — and vulnerable — to strangers than ever. "Ali would go in the bathroom and meet a guy, and the next thing you know it's his new best friend," said Gene Kilroy, a white man who became Ali's business manager — and one of the few who did not appear to be working an angle toward self-enrichment. Kilroy met Ali for the first time in Rome, at the Olympics. Later, he worked in New York for Metro-Goldwyn-Mayer. When Ali was out of boxing, Kilroy helped organize his speaking engagements, made sure Ali sent money home to his parents when he got paid, and enlisted an accounting firm to ensure the fighter's taxes were paid. It was part of Ali's charm that he remained so unguarded, that he saw everyone he met as someone worth knowing, even after ten years of intense celebrity, and even as many of those newcomers took advantage of him.

One day in 1970, a white Philadelphia schoolteacher named Marc Satalof asked his wife if she wanted to go for a drive and see if they could find Ali's new home. After all, they didn't have a lot of celebrities in the neighborhood. Finding Ali proved easy. Everyone in Overbrook knew which house belonged to Ali. When Satalof knocked on Ali's door, Belinda answered and invited him in. Ali was in the living room watching TV with friends. Satalof introduced himself and asked Ali if he would visit his school, Strawberry Mansion Junior High, in an all-black, gang-infested section of North Philly. Ali agreed without hesitation. He showed up on the day he said he would and spoke to several groups of students. When Ali complained that he was getting tired, Satalof thought the boxer was politely suggesting he was ready to leave. But Ali said no, he didn't want to quit; he hoped instead to take a short nap and then come back to the school and address the rest of the students. Ali proposed a trip to Satalof's house, which was near the school. While Ali was napping, one of Satalof's neighbors knocked on the door, checking to see if he was okay, because it was unusual to see Satalof's car in the driveway in the middle of a school day. Satalof asked the neighbor to be quiet because Muhammad Ali was sleeping in the next room. The neighbor laughed. If you're cheating on your wife, the neighbor said, don't worry, I won't tell anyone. No, really, Satalof said, it's Muhammad Ali. At that moment, Ali, having heard the conversation, stormed out of the bedroom, throwing air punches and pretending to be mad. After signing an autograph for Satalof's friend, Ali went back to school and stayed three hours, until every student had a chance to hear him speak and every request for an autograph had been fulfilled.

At about the same time, a fan named Reggie Barrett invited Ali to box in a fundraiser for an amateur boxing team in Charleston, South Carolina. Joe Frazier had been Barrett's first choice, but Frazier had turned down the request, so Barrett called Bob Arum, who said to get in touch with Chauncey Eskridge, who said that Ali might be willing to appear if the state of South Carolina permitted the event. Barrett's next step was to contact ABC to see if the television network would broadcast an Ali exhibition from South Carolina. When ABC executives said yes, Barrett signed a contract to rent the four-thousand-seat County Hall in Charleston.

Ali arrived two days before the scheduled exhibition, which had already sold out. "You're a *bad* brother to do all this in Charleston, South Carolina," the boxer said, putting an arm around Barrett's shoulder. "You out of your mind?"

Ali's draft-dodging case was still on appeal. He hadn't been seen in a boxing ring in two and a half years. He remained deeply unpopular among white Americans, and particularly so in the South. As news of his appearance in South Carolina spread, political pressure mounted to cancel the event. On the day Ali arrived in Charleston, county officials withdrew Barrett's permit for the hall. Barrett searched for another venue, without success. As Ali prepared to depart, Barrett offered to pay Ali for his time, but Ali refused the money. He gave Barrett his phone number and said to call if he could ever be of help. Ali extended such offers all the time. *Call me. Come visit me. Come work for me. I'm lecturing at a college next week; meet me there. Come see my next fight.* Not surprisingly, a good many people accepted his invitations, because Ali was great fun to be with, because he was famous, and because he seemed sincere when he extended the invitations and happy to see these virtual strangers when they reappeared seemingly by magic.

Barrett did call Ali, and he soon after went to work trying to get Ali another fight. He quickly became one of the boxer's business advisors, not replacing Herbert Muhammad or Gene Kilroy but supplementing them, because the Ali entourage always had room for one more man. Years later, when Barrett was convicted on cocaine trafficking charges, Ali testified as a character witness. "Right away, I got the feeling he was a good person to have for a friend," Ali told the judge on behalf of his friend, in a refrain he might have repeated about any number of people. "If I was the Lone Ranger, he'd be my Tonto."

Ali had other Tontos. Harold Conrad, the promoter who had worked to publicize the first Sonny Liston fight, contacted twenty-two states on Ali's behalf, checking to see if any governor or athletic commission chairman might be bold enough to give Ali the chance to fight. Kilroy wrote letters and made phone calls, too. In California, the athletic commission seemed open to the idea, but Governor Ronald Reagan said no. In Nevada, boxing officials agreed to let Ali fight, but the mobsters who ran the big hotels in Las Vegas killed the deal. Conrad hatched a plan for Ali to fight Frazier in a Tijuana bullring, promising the U.S. Department of Justice that Ali would spend no more than six hours beyond American borders. But that didn't work either. Other locations were considered: Detroit, Miami, even Boley, Oklahoma, an all-black town with a population of 720. Gene Kilroy and former pro football player Ed Khayat lobbied officials in Mississippi to license the fight. At one point, the prominent attorney Melvin Belli encouraged Ali to sue the states that were denying him the right to earn a living, but Ali declined.

When Ali went into exile, Bob Arum started a new boxing company, which he called Sports Action. Now that Ali was out of boxing, Arum had no reason to share closed-circuit-TV profits with Herbert Muhammad and John Ali. With Sports Action, he didn't have to. Arum asked one of his new business partners, Bob Kassel, to see if he could figure out a way to put together an Ali-Frazier fight. Kassel called his father-in-law, who lived in Atlanta, and Kassel's father-in-law put Kassel in touch with one of Georgia's most powerful black politicians, the state senator Leroy Johnson, who was not only beloved among his black constituents but also respected for his power-brokering skills by many of Georgia's white legislators.

Johnson researched the law and found the state of Georgia had no state boxing commission and no rules governing boxing. That meant Atlanta could license the fight if the mayor and Board of Aldermen approved, and since Johnson had helped the mayor and several members of the board get elected, Johnson was confident he could win their support. Kassel and Arum offered Johnson all the money from ticket sales; Sports Action would keep the more lucrative closed-circuit-TV income. Johnson pitched it to local political leaders as a chance for Atlanta to show the world it had become the most socially sophisticated and least racially divided of all major American cities, the city that was "too busy to hate," as one of the fight's sponsors said. Atlanta's mayor, Sam Massell, agreed to go along if Ali's team donated fifty thousand dollars to one of the city's crime-fighting programs. To make sure there would be no interference from the state, Johnson met with Lester Maddox, the Georgia governor who had risen to fame as a restaurant owner defiantly refusing to serve black customers after the passage of the Civil Rights Act in 1964. As governor, Maddox had surprised both supporters and opponents by hiring and promoting black officials and by initiating an early release program for the state prison system. Johnson, knowing that Maddox hated welfare programs for the poor, told the governor that Ali had no way to make a living without boxing and might end up on the public dole if he couldn't box.

"On with the fight!" Maddox pronounced.

To prove he could deliver Ali and pull off an event in the Deep South without prompting riots or Ku Klux Klan attacks, Johnson staged an exhibition at Morehouse College, where three thousand people crowded a gym on September 2, 1970, to watch Ali spar for eight rounds with three opponents. "The roof did not fall in," reported *Sports Illustrated*. "No one threw a bomb. Fire and brimstone did not rain down from heaven and no one was turned into a pillar of salt. There wasn't even a picket."

The old gang reunited for Ali. In his corner once more were Angelo Dundee and Bundini Brown, who'd been forgiven again after pawning Ali's bejeweled championship belt to a Harlem barber for five hundred dollars ("It wasn't as if I pawned it to a hock shop," Bundini said in his own defense. "I pawned it to a friend.").

A bit of fat wiggled at Ali's waist when he took off his robe and began to bounce around the ring. He drifted, flicking jabs, showing his footwork, which remained fine, and paused at times to allow his opponents to hit him on his arms and on the top of his head, as if this, too, were something he would have to get used to again. When it was over, Ali sat naked in his dressing room and spoke to reporters, telling them he wasn't ready yet for Frazier, but he would be soon.

Dundee agreed. "It was all there," said the trainer. "Everything. He can still fake with the hip, the hand, and the shoulder."

Not everyone was convinced. Cus D'Amato, the trainer, who considered himself one of the sport's salty oracles, said Ali's hand speed looked as good as ever, but his defense was sharply diminished. "Clay was saying he let his sparring partners get to him," D'Amato said, "let them hit him those heavy shots in the head and body. Well, I'm telling you, no fighter ever lets anybody hit him. It hurts. It rattles your brain. Clay simply couldn't stay away from those guys."

And those guys were sparring partners, not opponents fighting with their careers and lives in the balance. To D'Amato, it was a sign of trouble.

Frazier wouldn't agree yet to fight Ali. With no obvious second choice lined up, the PR man Harold Conrad knew what to do: get a white man to take on Ali, the black freedom fighter.

They settled on Jerry Quarry, who was twenty-five years old, a good-looking Irish kid and the son of a migrant farmer. In 1969, Quarry had gone punch for punch with Joe Frazier in a furious battle before a cut over Quarry's eye had forced him to stop. In a division dominated by black fighters, sportswriters of course referred to Quarry as "The Great White Hope." He might not have been great, but Quarry was certainly good, and he represented a bold choice for Ali. For his first fight back after a three-and-a-half-year hiatus, he might have been better off taking on a bum. But Ali was confident he could handle Quarry.

The bout was set for October 26, 1970, with a contract that gave Ali $200,000 guaranteed against a 42.5 percent share of the revenues. Quarry would get $150,000, against 22.5 percent of revenues. One month after Atlanta granted Ali a license to fight, a judge in the U.S. District Court for the Southern District of New York ruled that the state's athletic commission had violated Ali's rights by barring him from his profession. The NAACP Legal Defense Fund had filed the suit on behalf of Ali, noting that other convicted criminals had been licensed to fight in New York. Judge Walter R. Mansfield agreed, calling the commission's decision to ban Ali "intentional, arbitrary and unreasonable."

Prison remained a possibility, as Ali continued to appeal his draft-evasion conviction. But, in the meantime, he was permitted once again to box, at least in Atlanta and New York.

• • •

Ali understood the stakes. He understood that if he lost to Quarry every-thing would change. He understood that the safer move would have been to retire. He would have gone out on top, undefeated. He would have won the respect of Elijah Muhammad. He would have completed his martyrdom by sacrificing his career. He would have been remembered forever as a cham-pion. He would have had his good looks, his health, his celebrity. He would have remained frozen in time, in a sense, as the prince of boxing and one of America's most brilliant and influential sportsmen.

But he couldn't quit. He needed to fight. He needed the money. He needed the attention.

Ali took a room at a hotel in Miami Beach, leaving Belinda and their three children in Philadelphia, and began training again at the Fifth Street Gym. A new coat of paint had been added since the last time he'd trained, but the place was as beautifully foul as ever.

He went to work, doing what he did best, beginning at five or so each morning with a long run, trying to melt away his flab, preparing his body to do damage and endure damage. He taped a picture of himself to a mirror at the gym — a picture taken five years earlier, before the second Liston fight, when he was as taut and muscular as he had ever been. "That's when I was at my top condition," he said one day. "See how narrow and trim I was. Maybe I'll never look like that again." He asked the reporters to tell him how he looked. Was he trim? He said he was ready to be tested. He said he was run-ning hard, sacrificing more, that he was sure he would make no mistakes in preparing. "I'm crazy with loneliness, though. Durin' all the years I was away, I was never lonely. Oh, I had a ball, drivin' to the colleges and stayin' at the inns and meetin' students, the black power groups, the white hippies." Now he was alone, more or less, up at five, in bed by ten, hungry all the time, re-fusing the advances of women, and all because he was "thinkin' of that short walk to the ring, and all those faces there, lookin' at me and sayin': 'Why it's a miracle! He looks sooooo beautiful.'"

Everyone was counting on him, he said. "I get letters from black brothers beggin' me to be careful. . . . Nobody has to tell me this is serious business. I'm not just fightin' one man, I'm fightin' a lot of men, showin' a lot of 'em here is one man they couldn't defeat, couldn't conquer. . . . If I lose I'll be in jail for the rest of my life. If I lose I will not be free. I'll have to listen to all this about how I was a bum, I was fat, I joined the wrong movement, they misled me. So I'm fightin' for my freedom."

"Ali! Ali! Ali! Ali! Ali! Ali! Ali! Ali!"

This was new. He had never been cheered like this. Not as Ali and not as Clay. In almost every one of his prior fights, he had been the bad guy, the loud-mouth, the upstart, the traitor, the one everyone wanted to see leave the ring on a stretcher, preferably with droplets of blood trailing him. Yet now, here he was, still facing prison for draft evasion, still a Muslim, still one of the most loathed black men in America, moments away from fighting a white man in the great state of Georgia . . . and the mostly white crowd was on his side? It was like a scene from Lester Maddox's strangest nightmare, like watching Paul Robeson play Rhett in *Gone with the Wind* . . . except it was real.

Black fans arrived from all over the country, their ranks including celebri-ties, sports stars, and civic leaders: Sidney Poitier, Diana Ross, Hank Aaron, Coretta Scott King, Mary Wilson, Julian Bond, and Andrew Young. Curtis Mayfield strummed an acoustic guitar as he sang the national anthem, and comedian Bill Cosby sat ringside, working as one of the television analysts, providing commentary that was neither comedic nor particularly analytical. Rev. Jesse Jackson, his afro almost as big and wide as that of the pop mu-sic star Diana Ross, joined Ali in his dressing room before the fight and, at Ali's suggestion, led everyone in an ecumenical prayer. Boxing historian Bert Sugar called it the greatest collection of black power and money ever assem-bled. Some of the nation's most prominent black drug dealers, pimps, and street hustlers were also in attendance, thanks in part to the work of Richard "Pee Wee" Kirkland, the legendary playground basketball player from New York City and a soon-to-be-convicted drug trafficker, who said he bought five-hundred tickets to the fight, "because I thought it would be real good if a lot of people from Harlem that I grew up with was able to see Ali in ringside seats."

The Harlemites strolled up and down Peachtree Street and through the city's finest hotels with an ebullience that said they'd been waiting for this moment, waiting for the day when black men and women could strut arro-gantly across a southern city, dressed like royalty, the pimps and drug deal-ers dressed even more luxuriantly than the women by their sides, everyone laughing, showing no deference, taking Ali's swagger and making it their own. Only Ali could inspire such a show. Ali was a phenomenon, a spirit, an attitude, a challenge to democracy and decorum. He was the Great Equalizer. He was the fist to the white man's face.

It didn't matter if the man himself seemed to be guided more by effusive moods than a concrete philosophy. In fact, it may have helped. Ali was harder to pin down now that Elijah Muhammad had suspended him from the Nation of Islam. Ali at that moment, said the writer Budd Schulberg, "had managed to merge a score of ideological conflicts in his own transcendental black beauty. Somehow he had become Marcus Garvey and W. E. B. Du Bois and Paul Robeson, Adam Clayton Powell, Elijah Muhammad and Malcolm X, John Coltrane, Dizzy Gillespie, Bill Cosby, Jimmy Brown, and Dick Gregory all in one."

On the night of the fight there were limousines painted in psychedelic designs. There were men in purple tuxedoes with lapels wide as Cessna wings. There were silk shirts unbuttoned to the navel. There were men's platform shoes rising four inches high. There were ankle-length mink coats, mink fedoras, and silver mink bowties. Doing his best to keep up with the fashion show, Cash Clay wore a white, double-breasted suit and a wide-brimmed hat with a red band. Many of the ornately dressed men in the arena accessorized their wardrobes with concealed handguns, a fact that Mayor Sam Massell learned from his bodyguard only after the fight.

If Ali was anxious, he didn't show it. He walked among his fans with élan, boasting, shadowboxing, spinning, flashing his famous gap-toothed grin, enjoying every minute, reminding all that he had not grown fat or big-headed; that he was a man of the people and the King of the World, and King of the Black World in particular; that his time away from boxing had not diminished the strength of his ego. He was gorgeous and proud.

He spent the morning of the fight taking phone calls, then drove to the Municipal Auditorium, which looked, as one writer said, "as though it were constructed to hold a good sized PTA meeting." Ali's dressing room was small, barely wider than the length of the rubbing table at one end. On the opposite wall was a dressing table with mirrors outlined with light bulbs. Jesse Jackson, Angelo Dundee, and Bundini Brown crowded into the room. In one corner, George Plimpton crouched with a notebook and pen, jot-ting notes as Ali argued with Dundee about which protective cup to wear. Ali thought the standard-sized cup made him look fat. Dundee insisted Ali wear it.

Ali admired his image in his dressing-room mirror. He was strong and lean again, thicker in the chest and stomach than before his layoff. He combed his hair. He shadowboxed until his chest and shoulders shined with sweat. Then came a knock at the door and a voice: "It's time." Ali took one last look in the mirror and stepped outside.

It was the first time Ali would fight a younger man. Dundee, Bundini, and Jesse Jackson accompanied Ali as he walked through the arena and into the ring. Jackson told reporters over the noise: "If he loses tonight, it will mean, symbolically, that the forces of blind patriotism are right, that dissent is wrong; that protest means you don't love the country. This fight is love-it-or-leave-it versus love-it-and-change-it. They tried to railroad him. They refused to accept his testimony about his religious convictions. They took away his right to practice his profession. They tried to break him in body and mind. Martin Luther King used to say, 'Truth crushed to the earth will rise again.' That's the black ethos. And it's happening here in Georgia, of all places, and against a white man."

No pressure though.

For the old Ali, Quarry would have been no trouble. He was shorter than Ali. He was slower than Ali (every heavyweight was). He weighed less than Ali. He had shorter arms than Ali. He had lost not only to Joe Frazier but also to George Chuvalo, Jimmy Ellis, and Eddie Machen. Still, Quarry hit hard and took a good punch, and he claimed to have trained harder for this contest than he had ever trained, no doubt aware that if he suffered one more loss he might be labeled with the word no boxer wanted to hear: journeyman.

Ali came out fast, determined, throwing jabs and combinations, his gloves *whap-whap-whapping* Quarry's face. He wasn't teasing or playing around, as he had in some of the fights prior to his exile. Young Ali had jabbed and dance, jabbed and danced, but the twenty-eight-year-old Ali jabbed and threw, jabbed and threw, using his quick left hand to set up a quick left-right-left combination. From the opening minute, one thing was clear: Ali's jab was as good as ever, even if he wasn't using it quite as much. He was bigger now, at 213½ pounds, and that made the sight of those sizzling jabs even more astonishing, like flame flaring from a dragon's mouth.

It remained to be seen how his legs would hold up, which might explain why Ali worked so hard. In the first round, he threw sixty-one punches, landing twenty-five, including sixteen jabs and nine power shots. When the first round ended, Ali looked exhausted, slumped on his stool "like a beached whale," reporter Jerry Izenberg said.

In the second round, Ali was almost as active, throwing forty-nine and landing twenty punches. But in the third round, he slowed down, "bordering on exhaustion" according to Angelo Dundee, but still hitting, throwing thirty-nine punches, landing twelve. Fortunately for Ali, one of those twelve punches in the third round opened a cut over Quarry's left eye. When the round ended, the referee stopped the fight.

Bundini, Dundee, Jesse Jackson, and the painter LeRoy Neiman surrounded Ali in the ring, sharing his victory. Ali did not boast. He did not thank Allah or Elijah Muhammad. Instead, he praised Quarry and said "hello to the Supremes, the Temptations, Sidney Poitier, Bill Cosby, all of my friends here in the audience, and Gale Sayers also in Chicago."

Later, he admitted that he'd been disappointed by his performance, surprised that his body no longer performed as it had four years earlier.

Still, he'd won, and it felt good to be back.

After the fight, there was a party. The printed invitations, handed out at the fight to many of the best-dressed black men and women, said someone named "Fireball" was hosting a soiree at 2819 Handy Drive, a ranch house in the Collier Heights section of Atlanta, where many prominent black Atlantans lived. The house belonged to a well-known street hustler named Gordon "Chicken Man" Williams. The guests were mostly pushers, pimps, and mobsters. Upon arrival, masked men with shotguns met them. The would-be revelers were led to the basement, stripped to their underwear, ordered to place their handguns and valuables in a pile, and spread out on the floor. When space in the basement ran out, the men and women were ordered to lie on top of one another, stacked like cordwood. By three in the morning, there were at least eighty people in the basement, including Cash Clay. Two days later, the *Atlanta Journal* reported that $200,000 had been stolen, although only five victims filed reports with the police. Most, like Cash Clay, were too embarrassed to admit they'd been scammed. Six months after the holdup, two of the suspected robbers were gunned down outside a Bronx pool hall.

"If the robbers had known who they were robbing," an Atlanta police detective said after the murders, "they never would've robbed 'em."

31

"The World Is Watching You"

Ali-Frazier was the fight everyone wanted to see next. Ali-Frazier promised the biggest payday in the history of boxing. Ali-Frazier would determine which of the two undefeated heavyweight champions deserved to be called the true champion. But instead of Frazier, a mere forty-two days after the Quarry bout, Ali fought Oscar Bonavena at Madison Square Garden in New York.

Bonavena was twenty-eight years old, an Argentinian often referred to as Ringo for his long, Beatles-inspired haircut. He was a rough fighter with a record of forty-six wins against six losses and one draw. Although he had lost twice to Joe Frazier, Bonavena had gone the distance in both bouts and hurt Frazier badly, knocking him down twice in the second round of their first contest. He was an awkward boxer, throwing punches from all angles, seemingly with no plan or pattern. For Ali, Bonavena represented another risky choice, and if the Argentine beat the rusty former champ, there would be no Ali-Frazier, no meeting of two undefeated champs, no big payday.

For the first three rounds against Bonavena, Ali did little dancing. He stood in the middle of the ring, on his toes at times, on his heels at times, trading punches, letting Bonavena hunch his shoulders and bore in, pounding away, making Ali suffer. Gone was the dancer. Gone was the fighter who pulled back his head to let punches whistle by. In the fourth round, Ali tried something even more unusual: He stood still in the middle of the ring, hunched over, and covered his head with his arms — intentionally taking a beating or taking a rest, it was impossible to tell which one. Finally, in the fifth round, he showed flashes of the old footwork, circling the ring and throwing jabs, but not for the whole round, and then he went back to lumbering around and trading punches with Bonavena. As the rounds dragged on, Howard Cosell, broadcasting the fight, complained about the dullness of the action and the disappearance of Ali's panache.

At the end of the eighth round, Bonavena stung Ali with a big left. In the ninth, Bonavena sent a wild left hook crashing into Ali's jaw. Ali went reeling backward, his legs wobbling, eyes open in alarm. He collided with the ropes, bounced back, and grabbed for Bonavena like a drowning man thrusting at a life preserver. Later, Ali would say the punch made him feel "numb all over. . . . Shock and vibrations is all I felt, that's how I knew I was alive. I mean I was jarred. Even my toes felt the vibrations. Bong!" The only thing he could do, he said, was stall for time until he "could let the daze clear up."

One more punch and Bonavena might have ended it. But he didn't.

The fight went on, clumsily.

The crowd booed as Ali failed to deliver the kind of performance fans expected.

"The world is watching you!" Bundini yelled.

Even Herbert Muhammad was concerned enough to get out of his seat and climb up onto the ring apron to implore Ali.

In the fifteenth and final round, with both fighters exhausted, Ali ducked a left, threw a left of his own, and knocked Bonavena to the mat. Bonavena rose and Ali knocked him back down. Bonavena rose yet again and Ali knocked him down yet again, winning by a TKO.

After the fight, Ali had a cut on his mouth and a bruise on one eye. He was sore. But, again, he was the winner. Cosell climbed in the ring for an interview. He held a telephone with a long cord and handed it to Ali, saying Joe Frazier was on the line.

"How ya doing, Joe?" Ali said into the phone. "You're not frightened of me, are you?"

Ali continued, "Since we can't get along we're just gonna have to get it on!"

He made a few more remarks before Cosell interrupted. Television viewers couldn't hear Frazier, only Ali.

"What is Joe saying?" Cosell asked.

Ali looked down at Cosell and replied without missing a beat: "I haven't heard Joe."

32

A Different Fighter

He's much slower . . ."

José Torres, the former light-heavyweight champion, offered the diagnosis the way a doctor might: as a statement of fact and a prognosis of danger.

Angelo Dundee saw it, too. For about one minute of each three-minute round, Dundee said, Ali looked like the Ali of old. For the other two minutes, he was sluggish, easier to hit, vulnerable.

Years later, a statistical analysis of Ali's career compiled by CompuBox, Inc., would confirm what Torres and Dundee detected: beginning in 1970, Ali was a different fighter. CompuBox analyzed sixteen Ali fights from 1960 to 1967—the sixteen fights in which complete films have survived—and counted every punch. In those sixteen fights, Ali was at his best, landing 2,245 punches while getting hit by his opponents only 1,414 times. Put another way, he did 61.4 percent of the hitting.

Over the course of the rest of his career, however, Ali took as much punishment if not more than he gave. He hit opponents 5,706 times and got hit 5,596 times. In other words, the man often regarded as the greatest heavyweight of all time was being struck almost as often he was striking his opponents. Even the 50–50 ratio wasn't as good as it seemed, because the overwhelming majority of Ali's punches were jabs, while his opponents employed more hooks and uppercuts, which tend to do greater damage.

CompuBox assesses fighters based on the percentage of punches landed compared to the percentage of punches landed by their opponents. Boxing aficionados are generally wary of statistics, and it's fair to say numbers alone can never tell a fight's story or measure a fighter's skill. Still, this is the most telling of all boxing statistics. The welterweight Floyd Mayweather Jr. ranked best of all modern boxers in this category, having landed 44 percent of all his punches while his opponents hit him with an astonishingly low 18.8 percent of theirs. That gave Mayweather an overall plus/minus rating of plus-25.2 percent (44 minus 18.8). Ali's contemporary, Joe Frazier, a brutally efficient puncher, would finish his career with an excellent rating of plus-18.9 percent. Ali's ranking, on the other hand, was negative-1.7 percent over the course of his full career. Even when CompuBox added other factors to its statistical analysis, including total punches thrown, total punches landed, power punches landed, and jabs landed, Ali failed to rank among history's top heavyweights.

Numbers don't reveal a fighter's style, or his strengths and weaknesses, and they don't help describe the back and forth of hand-to-hand combat. But these statistics nevertheless raise questions about Ali. Did judges award him rounds that he didn't deserve because he possessed a flashy style and seemed never to be hurt by his opponents' punches? Was he winning rounds because he was the great Muhammad Ali?

Ali posted weak numbers in part because he used his jab as a defensive weapon, throwing it to keep his opponents away, which meant he didn't connect as often as other fighters. At the same time, beginning with his return to boxing in 1970, he began to pay a price for his relatively weak grasp of boxing fundamentals. He had never learned to properly block or duck punches because he hadn't needed to. As a result, as he slowed, he absorbed more punishment, curling up against the ropes and trying to absorb or deflect their blows instead of dodging them. Ali let some of the strongest men in the world punch, punch, punch, until their arms grew weary and their breath grew short — and *then* he would fight back. That strategy would come to be called the "rope-a-dope," a name that suggested Ali's opponents were falling into a clever trap. In the last stage of his career, as he relied increasingly on "rope-a-dope," Ali would compile a rating of minus-9.8 percent. In his final nine fights, Ali would end up absorbing 2,197 punches while landing only 1,349. More telling: Ali would be out-hit with power shots in those last nine fights by a count of 1,565 to 833. In his two final fights, opponents would land 371 power punches to Ali's 51.

By all these statistical measures, the man who called himself "The Greatest" was below average for much of his career.

Although the numbers would not become clear until many years later, Torres and Dundee were not the only ones who noticed dramatic changes upon Ali's return from his exile. Ferdie Pacheco, who called himself "The Fight Doctor," said that in 1970 Ali began complaining of soreness in his hands. That's when Pacheco began numbing the boxer's fists before fights with cortisone and an anesthetic called Xylazine, two shots in each hand. "Ali's hands were so shot he couldn't hit a pillow," Gene Kilroy said. The drugs gave Ali the confidence he needed to punch hard, but there was risk involved. If Ali couldn't feel the pain, he was exposing the structure of his hands to more damage. It was a risk he deemed worth taking, considering that his livelihood was on the line. Later, Kilroy introduced Ali to an orthopedic surgeon who recommended the boxer soak his hands in paraffin wax, which helped ease the pain. But nothing could be done about the fighter's legs.

"Ali came back and his legs weren't like they'd been before," Pacheco told writer Thomas Hauser. "And when he lost his legs, he lost his first line of defense. That was when he discovered something which was both very good and very bad . . . He discovered he could take a punch. Before the layoff, he wouldn't let anyone touch him in the gym. Workouts consisted of Ali running and saying, 'This guy can't hit me.' But afterward, when he couldn't run that way anymore, he found he could dog it. He could run for a round and rest for a round, and let himself get punched against the ropes . . . And when he started to get lazy in the gym, which came before his greatest glories, that was the beginning of the end."

When Pacheco was asked years later why he helped Ali continue fighting despite the boxer's diminished skills, he responded angrily, rising from his chair as he spoke: "You're in the corner to keep them fighting," he said, "not to tell them *not* to fight. If you didn't tell them to fight, you were fired immediately."

Ali and Oscar Bonavena had fought more or less to a draw statistically. Ali had landed 191 punches compared to Bonavena's 186, while Bonavena had landed more power punches, 152 to 97. In his locker room after the fight, Ali was modest and thoughtful. He said he hadn't trained as hard as he should have. He wondered aloud if his reflexes had slowed. But Ali was still the heavyweight champion of cockiness, and his swagger quickly returned. "Tonight I did what Frazier wasn't able to do in twenty-five rounds," he said. "People said I couldn't take a punch and I took everything he threw, and he hits hard . . . People said I had to cut a man to stop him, and I took him out with a left hook, a fighter who fought the best and was never knocked out in his life before."

After Bonavena, Ali might have been wise to schedule another fight or two against soft competition while working to get back shape, but that wasn't his plan. Instead, he intended to fight the man who had taken possession of his championship title, the man who would become his greatest rival. He explained his plan in verse:

> *Maybe this will shock and amaze ya*
> *But I'm gonna retire Joe Frazier.*

Ernest Hemingway once said, "If you fight a great left-hooker, sooner or later he will knock you on your deletion. He will get the left out where you can't see it, and in it comes like a brick. Life is the greatest left-hooker so far, although many say it was Charley White of Chicago."

Life is indeed a great left-hooker. Charley White was, too. But ask a boxing fan of the late twentieth century, and he'll likely tell you that Smokin' Joe Frazier was the greatest of all.

Joseph Frazier was born January 12, 1944, in Beaufort, South Carolina. He was the son of farmhands and the second youngest of ten children, a position that may have inclined him toward a career in fighting. If nothing else, it toughened him. At fifteen, Frazier quit school and moved to New York City to make money. When jobs proved difficult to find, he stole cars instead. He moved to Philadelphia, where he went to work in a slaughterhouse and where he pretended to be Joe Louis, hitting the heavy bag as he punched sides of beef in a refrigerated meat locker. In 1961, at the relatively late age of seventeen, he learned boxing under the trainer Yancey "Yank" Durham, a light-skinned black man with gray hair and a gray mustache, who knew as well as any trainer in the world how to take a tough kid off the street and make him a professional pugilist. Frazier's belief in Durham was total. When they traveled, Durham made his fighters double up in hotel rooms and he made them keep the bathroom doors open so no one could masturbate, his theory being that even the slightest bit of sexual activity would sap a fighter's vital energies. Three years after meeting Durham, Frazier won the Olympic gold medal. By 1968, he was heavyweight champion.

Frazier surprised. He looked too small at five-foot-eleven to be a heavyweight champion. Some said he was blind or nearly blind in his left eye. But he had a crooked left arm perfect for hooking, and he used that left hook to keep his wary opponents moving to his right, where he could see them better. He also had a good chin, rock-hard concentration, and a relentless style that made it all but impossible for opponents to mount a prolonged attack or a reliable defense. Frazier was a raging, bobbing, battering puncher who moved relentlessly in on his opponent's gut, crouching, slamming, pummeling, until he was ready to deliver that deadly hook. "Frazier was the human equivalent of a war machine," Norman Mailer wrote.

Frazier earned the nickname Smoke, or Smokin' Joe, because, like smoke, he seemed to be everywhere at one time, shapeless, immovable, rolling, smothering. Getting hit by Joe Frazier, one of his sparring partners said, was like getting run over by a bus — except a bus only hit you once.

Frazier was suited perfectly to serve as Ali's foil. While Ali danced, Frazier barreled. While Ali relied on the jab, Frazier's best punch was the left hook, the punch that had given Ali trouble ever since he first stepped into a boxing ring. While Ali had taken up boxing with dreams of becoming the greatest of all time, Frazier had done so hoping to lose weight. While Ali was the "black Adonis on parade," as *Time* called him, Frazier was "awkward and introspective, given to sullen moods he called 'the slouchies.'" While Ali rhymed and bragged, Frazier spoke in the plainest terms and made little effort to charm the public. "I like it, fighting," he once said. "There's a man out there trying to take what you got. You're supposed to destroy him. He's trying to do the same to you. Why should you have pity on him?"

In the summer before his comeback, Ali had challenged Frazier to fight in Frazier's gym, and later in a public park, in their street clothes, before a crowd that had gathered spontaneously. Frazier had refused to take the bait. After Frazier had decimated Jimmy Ellis, one of Ali's former sparring partners, Ali made this appraisal of the man who had taken his championship title: "Frazier ain't got no rhythm," he said. "He just keeps coming, punching from his knees up. Ducks and keeps coming, trying to get you on the ropes and hold you like some old robot. There wasn't no boxing in that fight with Ellis. When I was fighting, I boxed. You remember? Pop, pop, pop, pop — dance around — pip, pip, pip, real fast — dancing and faking — WHAARUP! — back off and circle — pop, pop, rat-a-ta-rata-ta-ta like a typewriter — POW! That's championship fighting. Frazier can't do things like that. He's an old plowhorse . . . But against Ellis he was pretty good for his kind of fighter. He wasn't afraid of nothing Ellis threw, he just kept on coming. And he had a tricky, fast left jab that surprised me."

Frazier liked Ali. He thought they'd established a real friendship. But one day in the autumn of 1969, when Frazier was in the gym with his friend Gypsy Joe Harris, he heard Ali's voice over the radio. Ali was doing an interview with WHAT-AM in Philadelphia, and he was calling Frazier a coward; a classless, clumsy fighter; an Uncle Tom. Frazier got so mad he crushed the radio with his foot, as Gypsy Joe Harris recalled in an interview with journalist Mark Kram. Over the radio, Ali challenged Frazier to meet him at a nearby gym to fight, immediately, for no money, to prove who was the better man. Frazier showed up at the gym but refused to fight, even as Ali once again called him names. After yet another similar incident, Frazier got so angry he drove to Ali's house to demand an apology.

Ali came to the door with some of his Muslim friends by his side. He told Frazier it was all in fun, that he was merely trying to promote their rivalry. Frazier said he didn't think it was fun, and he didn't like having his manhood or his blackness questioned. Ali had no right, he said. Ali had never plowed a field or worked ankle-deep in cow blood. Ali was the one with a white trainer in his corner, the one who'd been bankrolled by a bunch of wealthy white Kentuckians, the one with white lawyers keeping him out of jail, the one who clowned with Howard Cosell like they were vaudeville partners. Who was he to call Frazier a Tom?

"Coward? Uncle Tom?" Frazier said. "Only one I've been Tommin' for is you!" he said, according to Gypsy Joe, who was at Frazier's side. "Those sorry-ass Muslims leadin' you on me. It gonna stop right here."

"Don't talk about my religion," Ali said. "I can't let ya do that. Go home and cool down."

"Ain't ever gonna be coolin' down now," Frazier said. "Fuck your religion.

Ali loved entertaining crowds at his cabin in Deer Lake. © *Peter Angelo Simon*

Stokely Carmichael looks on as Ali works the speed bag.
© *Peter Angelo Simon*

Gene Kilroy (front left) adjusts the TV as Ali and a few friends gather in the champ's hotel suite to watch one of his fights. © *Michael Gaffney Photo*

To regain his championship, Ali would have to go to Zaire and defeat the seemingly invincible George Foreman. *Associated Press*

Promoter Don King brought heavyweight boxing to Africa, bragging that the ancestors of slaves were returning to conquer the continent.
Associated Press, Horst Faas

In Zaire, Ali met and fell in love with Veronica Porche, one of the young women hired to promote the fight (seated second from the right, next to Foreman).
Associated Press, Horst Faas

"I know what I'm doing," Ali shouted as he let one of the greatest punchers in heavyweight history bang away in a technique he would later dub "rope-a-dope."
Associated Press, REX, Shutterstock

After the Foreman fight, Ali relied increasingly on the rope-a-dope style, which endangered him against powerful punchers like Earnie Shavers, shown here in 1977.
© *Michael Gaffney Photo*

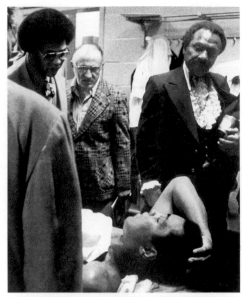

"Quit, son, before you get hurt," says Cassius Clay Sr. to his son in the locker room after the Shavers fight.
© *Michael Gaffney Photo*

In 1978, Ali trained lightly and suffered a shocking loss to Leon Spinks. "I lost fair and square," he said after the fight.
© *Michael Gaffney Photo*

After divorcing Belinda, Ali married Veronica Porche. With their daughter Hana, the couple is seen here on a bus headed to Washington, D.C., for a meeting with President Jimmy Carter. © *Michael Gaffney Photo*

Ferdie Pacheco (left) quit the Ali camp, saying it was unhealthy for the fighter to continue, but most others stuck with Ali. © *Michael Gaffney Photo*

Ali came out of retirement in 1981 and lost a hopelessly brutal fight to Larry Holmes, his former sparring partner. *Associated Press*

Ali stands before a Che Guevara mural on a 1998 visit to Havana.
© *David Turnley*

Hands shaking, feet shuffling, Ali lit the Olympic torch in 1996 in Atlanta, shocking the crowd and helping to remake his image as a man fighting illness. *Associated Press, Doug Mills*

In 2005, President George W. Bush presented Ali with the Presidential Medal of Freedom, calling him "a fierce fighter and a man of peace." *Associated Press, Evan Vucci*

We're talking about me. Who *I* am." Joe extended a hand. "This is black. You can't take who I am. You turn on a friend for what? So you impress those Muslim fools, so you be the big man?"

"We're finished talkin," Ali said, as he turned and went back in the house.

But Ali was only getting started.

33

The Five-Million-Dollar Match

Time magazine put Ali and Frazier on the cover. "The $5,000,000 Fighters" the headline read. Five million dollars for a boxing match. Who could comprehend the enormity of it?

Only in America could such wonders occur. Only in America — where men hit golf balls on the moon, where miraculous little pills permitted women to have sex without fear of pregnancy, where electronic calculators were small enough to hold in one hand, baseball teams played on plastic grass, new cars rolled off assembly lines with built-in pushbutton AM/FM stereo radios with integrated eight-track tape players — only here could the great-grandsons of slaves each earn $2.5 million for a single night of work. That was more than baseball superstar Hank Aaron would earn over his entire twenty-three-year career in the big leagues.

The money alone made the fight something bigger than a fight and sent writers searching for grandiose adjectives and cultural context. It made Ali-Frazier a declaration on the state of the union. Look how far America had come! How racist could a nation be, really, if it offered such opportunity to a couple of black men? Never mind that the astonishing riches were going to black men competing in the animalistic ritual of boxing. Never mind that the black men were, in fact, being wildly underpaid while the white men promoting the fight would capture the really big money.

Never mind all that.

Ali-Frazier became the Fight of the Century because it was the first time two undefeated heavyweight champions had ever met in the ring, and because it spoke somehow to the strength and resilience of America, and because, no matter how you cut it, $5 million qualified as heavy dough. After a decade of rioting and war, it felt good to get worked up about something as red-bloodedly pure and simple as a high-priced boxing match.

Ali and Frazier both said they might retire after the fight, regardless of the outcome. Frazier with dead calm predicted he would win. Ali, in a long, rambling press conference, said he was going to "have a ball," that there would be no need to dance or even put his hands up in defense against the slow, predictable Frazier. Boxing, he said to the assembled congregation of reporters, "looks frightful to you fellas, you sittin' with the typewriter, and you drinkin' every night, and you layin' up with your girlfriends, and boxing looks rough to you. But this easy when you're in shape and young and look good like I am. It ain't hard. It's easy. Boxin' is easy."

If fights were won with rhetoric instead of punches, Ali would have already scored the KO.

"It's impossible," he said, "for Frazier to outbox me, outclass me, whip me."

Ali may have had more on the line than Frazier did. Although Herbert Muhammad was back in his corner, Ali remained under suspension by the Nation of Islam. He continued to await the outcome of his draft case. In January, the U.S. Supreme Court announced it would hear the boxer's appeal. With jail still a strong possibility, there was no telling when or if Ali would get another chance to reclaim the championship. It was possible that his fight against Frazier would be his last.

He trained in Miami, saying he was trying to lose 10 pounds from his 228-pound frame, but even without his wife and children around, he was easily distracted, surrounded by a traveling circus that included Bundini Brown, Norman Mailer, the actor Burt Lancaster, Cassius Clay Sr., Major Coxson, and Ali's ever-present brother, Rahaman. There were newspaper and TV reporters too, of course — a seemingly endless stream of them. Although Ali no longer lectured on college campuses or performed work as a Muslim minister, he still jotted homilies on notecards and legal pads and recited them now for journalists as proof that he was more than a mere pugilist.

"Pleasure is the shadow of happiness," he preached.

"Yeah, man," answered Rahaman.

"People are unhappy because they are victims of propaganda," he said.

"Heavy, brother, heavy," answered Rahaman.

Angelo Dundee wanted Ali to fight two more "warm-ups" before taking on Frazier, but Herbert overruled the trainer. In negotiating the deal for the fight, Herbert told Frazier's manager, Yank Durham, that he wanted Ali to receive the same pay as Frazier, even though Frazier was champ. Durham agreed. Initially, the fight promoters offered each of the boxers $1.25 million against 35 percent of the gross income, but Durham and Herbert Muhammad held out for a flat $2.5 million each, or about $15 million in today's dollars. It was by far the largest sum ever guaranteed a boxer for one fight, and by taking a flat fee, the men didn't have to worry about whether the fight's promoters supplied an honest accounting of total revenues for the event. Even so, it was probably a miscalculation. Had they taken the first offer — $1.25 million per fighter against 35 percent of the gross — each fighter probably would have earned at least $3.5 million. Instead of becoming partners in the business enterprise, Ali and Frazier were entertainers hired for one night's work.

Tickets for the fight, to be held March 8, 1971, at Madison Square Garden, sold out immediately. Ringside seats were priced at $150 each, but they were soon being flipped on the secondary market for $700 and more. No one in the business could recall such buildup for a fight. The Hollywood talent agent who promoted the event, Jerry Perenchio, said he expected 300 million people in twenty-six countries to see the bout on closed-circuit TV. At the conclusion of the event, Perenchio said, in a comment that struck some as absurd at the time, he intended to take the fighters' shoes, trunks, robes, and gloves and auction them off to the highest bidders.

"This one transcends boxing — it's a show business spectacular," Perenchio said. "You've got to throw away the book on this fight. It's potentially the single greatest grosser in the history of the world."

Ali, of course, embraced the spectacle. He promised to go back to his old routine of predicting the outcomes of his fights, only this time with a twist. Five minutes before the bout, he said, on live TV he would remove a sheet of paper from a sealed envelope, the paper containing his prediction on when Frazier would fall. If he were to win, it would be a comeback for the ages, a divine destiny, at least in Ali's own eyes, and one of the greatest storylines the sporting world had ever seen: the martyr returns . . . with vengeance.

But strange things were happening to Ali in his heroic journey. The man who had aligned himself with radical black separatists, who had refused to go to war for a country he called racist, was suddenly and unexpectedly beginning to transcend categories of race and religion and attract a number of fans that had once despised him. Young people in America were seeking their own cultural voice. Like Bob Dylan's lyrics, Muhammad Ali didn't have to make perfect sense. All he had to do was stand up against the status quo.

He toned down the vitriol slightly. He seldom referred to whites as devils. He remained devoted to Elijah Muhammad, but he didn't talk about that devotion quite as much. The change was a subtle one, and it put Ali in a tricky position. He had taunted white America his entire career. But now, as he resumed his career, the white establishment expected him to be a sportsman again, to be thankful, to play the games that public figures are supposed to play. And, to a degree, Ali went along. It's not easy for a rebel to remain a rebel all his life. It's exhausting. The world changes and the rebel adapts or falls out of step. The rebel matures and his values change. When a rebel drives a Rolls-Royce, it doesn't guarantee that he will no longer be a rebel, but it factors into the equation.

"Muhammad Ali had become Lucky Lindy and the Brown Bomber, Bobby Kennedy and Joan Baez, all rolled up into one irrepressible folk hero hailed as our favorite defender of the truth and resister of authority," Budd Schulberg wrote. But that was a big job, one that made his life a tangle of contradictions. Ali still wanted to be seen as the champion of black America, but he was becoming more of a celebrity-rebel, a winking bomb thrower. *Time* magazine cited Ali as Exhibit A in an article entitled "The Athlete as Peacock," arguing that athletes "answer only to themselves these days." They dressed like Hollywood stars. They were as comfortable on TV as they were in the weight room. They organized boycotts and strikes. They criticized their coaches. "Nothing is deader than the old locker-room adage that there is no 'I' in T . . . E . . . A . . . M, or that coach equates with king," the magazine complained.

As his popularity grew, Ali found an unfortunate way to assert his claim as a warrior for his people: he did it by attacking Joe Frazier with malice, calling him dumb and ugly, labeling his opponent a spineless Uncle Tom. His statements bordered on the absurd. At one point, Ali said only Alabama sheriffs, rich white men in white suits, Ku Klux Klan members, and possibly Richard Nixon would root for Frazier. If any black man really believed Frazier could win, *that* black man was a Tom, too. No amount of bile was too much for Ali to heap on Frazier.

He explained why he did it. "When he gets to ringside, Frazier will feel like a traitor, though he's not," Ali said. "When he sees those women and those men aren't for him, he'll feel a little weakening. He'll have a funny feeling, an angry feeling. Fear is going to come over him. He will realize Muhammad Ali is the real champ. And he'll feel he's the underdog with the people. And he'll lose a little pride. The pressure will be so great that he'll feel it. Just gettin' in the ring alone with thousands and millions of eyes lookin' at you in those big arenas, and those hot lights . . . It's going to be real frightful when he goes to his corner. He doesn't have nothing. But me . . . I have a cause."

Ali didn't care if Frazier's feelings were hurt or if Frazier's son Marvis faced taunting at school from classmates who thought Joe Frazier was the white man's lackey because Ali had called Frazier an Uncle Tom.

Frazier's approach, in contrast, seemed far more humane: He said he intended to hammer Ali's gut until his kidneys popped out.

On the night of January 5, 1971, at about 8:30, Geraldine Liston returned home from a weeklong trip and found her husband lying down, stiff and bloated, on an upholstered bench at the end of their bed. His feet were on the floor, next to his socks and shoes. He had a holstered .38 revolver on his dresser, a quarter ounce of heroin in the kitchen, a bag of reefer in a pocket of the trousers draped over a bedroom chair, and a week of newspapers stacked outside his front door. The coroner said Liston died of natural causes. Later, some would speculate that a drug overdose had done him in. Others would say it was the mafia.

Liston was forty years old, give or take.

When Ali got the news, he expressed admiration for his former opponent, saying, "He was an awful nice fellow and I liked him a lot." Then, for old time's sake, he threw one more jab at Liston, and a nonsensical one at that, saying, "But just like any fighter who gets old, he had begun to show signs of age."

Less than two weeks later, Ali turned twenty-nine. He celebrated with a giant birthday cake with two chocolate boxing gloves made of icing on top. When he dove into his second big slice, he drew a warning from Jack Kent Cooke, the big investor behind Ali's upcoming fight.

"Will you stop eating that?" Cooke said, in mock horror.

Ali brushed it off, saying, "I don't have to train too hard for Frazier." Frazier's only chance, Ali said, was to score a knockout. But, he added, "I don't get knocked out or even hit a lot. To knock me out, he will have to come in to me and when he does, he'll get hit ten or fifteen times. It'll be easy to see that Frazier is an amateur compared to me."

The fight was seven weeks away. Ali said he would begin training in a few days. In the meantime, he offered a new poem:

> *Frazier will catch hell*
> *From the start of the bell,*
> *Then I'll jump out*
> *With Howard Cosell.*

Ali was becoming wiser with age, or so he claimed in interviews. "I don't like fighting," he told one reporter. "Nobody human could enjoy beating up somebody." After Frazier, he said, he would have enough money to last the rest of his life. He promised he would retire to a ranch somewhere in the Southwest with his wife and children.

Ali gave another interview while driving with a reporter in Los Angeles, saying that he had been getting instruction from Herbert Muhammad on how to control his emotions and moderate his public pronouncements, "because the results from a lot of my wild statements in the past, of not thinkin' and mixin' sport with religion and religion with sport, wasn't wise." But where Joe Frazier was concerned, Ali still found it impossible to modulate. "I'm going to WHUP Joe Frazier and OUTCLASS him and make him look like a AMATEUR," he said. "He don't stand a chance. It will be a mismatch. And people will be saying, 'How *could* we be so wrong?'"

Don Newcombe, the former Dodger pitcher, was in the car during the interview. After listening a while to Ali's bragging, Newcombe asked Ali if he had ever tried self-hypnosis "to make yourself believe something?"

"I guess that's what I do automatically and I don't know I'm doin'," Ali said.

It was true. Ali was the kind of person who could argue for the fun of it but with absolute conviction that his ice cube was colder than yours. Wasn't all that bragging a kind of self-hypnosis? But getting to the matter at hand,

Ali insisted that his mind wasn't playing tricks when it came to his upcoming fight: "I honestly believe I can whup Joe Frazier."

The newspaper reporter turned to a member of Ali's entourage: "Does this go on all day?"

"Yeah," he said. "And every day it gets better."

34

Ali v. Frazier

Imagine 10 million people, Ali said. Imagine if there were one stadium capable of holding 10 million people, a stadium so large that you could fly an airplane over the crowd and soar for an hour before you reached the end of all the people. That's how many people would be watching him fight Joe Frazier. And those who couldn't watch, those in remote towns and villages on every continent, would be waiting anxiously to hear if he won.

"It's the greatest event in the history of the world," he said.

At last, Ali was getting the kind of attention he had always craved. If anything, he had underestimated the magnitude of his fame. About 300 million people across the globe, not 10 million, would watch him fight Joe Frazier on March 8, 1971. If it wasn't the greatest event in history, it was certainly one of the most widely viewed.

Before the big bout, George Plimpton threw a party at Elaine's, where Norman Mailer, Pete Hamill, and Bruce Jay Friedman, among others, held court. The writers and intellectuals talked about boxing's deeper meanings. They talked about Ali and how, somewhat irrationally, he had become a superhero to Muslims, poor black people, white liberals, hippies, draft dodgers, and just about anyone who believed the cards were stacked in favor of the establishment. At Jack Kent Cooke's party, millionaires mingled with Hollywood stars including Elia Kazan, Lorne Green, and Peter Falk. Frank Sinatra and his Las Vegas pals had a boozy celebration of their own, of course. President Nixon had a special line installed at the White House so he could watch the bout everyone in America was talking about.

On the day of the fight, Ali, who feared isolation far more than he feared Joe Frazier, invited a small group of reporters to his room at the New Yorker Hotel. They watched TV.

Later the same day, Belinda dropped by the room, looking for her husband. He wasn't there, and no one seemed to know where he'd gone. She became suspicious, then angry. When she phoned the room of one of the members of Ali's entourage, a woman answered. When the woman spoke, Belinda heard a man's voice in the background.

"Who's on the phone?" she heard the man say.

"Is that my husband?" Belinda shouted into the receiver. "Is that Muhammad Ali?"

"Yeah," the woman said.

"Put him on the phone. That's who I'm looking for."

Ali got on the phone. "What you want?" he asked, as Belinda recalled years later in an interview.

She had been complaining to Ali for weeks that he hadn't trained hard enough. Now, her anger boiled over. "Why you in there?" she asked. "This is what I'm talking about, Ali! This is *just* what I'm talking about! I'm gonna come up there and knock the hell out you!"

She hung up and went to the room and tried to kick the door in, but it wouldn't give. She banged until Ali opened the door. He was naked. Belinda stepped inside and found a woman hiding in the shower, also naked.

"It's not what you think!" the woman yelled.

"You know what," Belinda shouted, "I don't even see what I'm seeing right now. This is not what I see. I'm gonna need to kill both y'all up in here." She picked up a steak knife.

"I was just on the street!" the girl screamed. "He gave me forty dollars! I didn't mean it!"

In that moment, Belinda couldn't sort out what made her angriest: her husband's infidelity, his casual approach to the fight hours away, the fact that Ali would sleep with a whore in the same hotel where his wife and children were staying, or the fact that the whore was ugly.

"And I cried," she said. "And then, when I said, 'Look. Ali . . . none of this happened. I'm just dreamin' this, alright? Because if you mention this to me, I'm gonna slap the hell outta you. I will swing and knock your head off. If you mention this to me again! Ever!' He said, 'Alright. Alright. Alright. Alright.'

So I left. And I was so upset. I might have been bold when I was in there, but when I got out, I cried like a baby. And I sat down in one of the hassocks in the hallway near the window of the hotel and just cried. And I got myself together, cleaned my face off, and went back down to the room with the babies. And then just shook my head. I said, 'Lord, have mercy. What have I gotten myself into?' I said, 'This is not gonna last. This is not gonna last.'"

She also made a wish: for Joe Frazier to defeat her husband.

The crowd was multicultural before anyone used the term, an explosion of pride, a funk fashion show, a drug-addled parade of ego and power. Everyone was there, and those who weren't lied and said they were. Among those verifiably in attendance and breathing the same stale Madison Square Garden air were Sinatra, Barbra Streisand, the Apollo 14 astronauts, Sammy Davis Jr., Colonel Harlan Sanders of Kentucky Fried Chicken fame, Hugh Hefner, Barbi Benton (who was Hefner's date, and wearing a see-through blouse under a monkey-fur coat), Hubert Humphrey, Woody Allen, Diane Keaton, Miles Davis, Dustin Hoffman, Diana Ross (in black velvet hot pants), Ethel Kennedy, Ted Kennedy, Mayor John Lindsay, Burt Bacharach, Sargent Shriver, William Saroyan, and Marcello Mastroianni. Bing Crosby settled for a seat at the sold-out Radio City Music Hall, where he would watch via closed circuit.

Earlier in the evening, Ali's brother, Rahaman, had his eighth fight as a professional. Rahaman had never been beaten, but he had never fought an opponent of any consequence either. In the Garden, before the biggest fight of his brother's career, Rahaman took his first loss, a bad beating from an English fighter named Danny McAlinden.

Then it was time. Time for *The Fight*. A thing so immense as to overload the senses of those in Madison Square Garden who watched the fighters march to the ring. Ali arrived first, wearing a red velvet robe, red trunks, and white shoes with red tassels. Frazier wore a green-and-gold brocade robe with matching trunks. Both men were in excellent physical shape. Television producers had gone over every detail, even helping the men select the colors of their trunks, with a darker color chosen to contrast Ali's lighter skin, and lighter-colored trunks for Frazier's darker-toned skin. Ali danced around the ring during the introductions, dipping in close to Frazier and calling out to him: "Chump!"

Frazier showed no interest.

As the referee gave instructions, Ali jawed at Frazier and Frazier jawed back.

The opening of a fight, Mailer wrote, "is equivalent to the first kiss in a love affair." But it's more like the first missile in a war. In either case, the opening punches in Ali v. Frazier missed their mark. Ali threw jabs and flurries. Frazier ducked, his head moving as fast as his fists, and steamed forward, trying to push through Ali's jabs. Ali backed up and threw more jabs, but Frazier's head was always moving and seldom where Ali expected to find it. Ali stung like a bee but didn't float like a butterfly. He didn't float at all. It was obvious right away that he wasn't trying to tire Frazier; he was trying to hurt him, to disconnect Frazier's synapses, the sooner the better. Ali stood flat-footed and threw jabs followed by flashing hooks, trying to capitalize on his big advantage in height and reach, and trying to end the fight quickly. Joe stayed low, something he had worked on for long hours under Eddie Futch's watch. In the gym, they'd stretched ropes across the ring and Frazier had practiced ducking them, bobbing, punching, bobbing, punching, hundreds, thousands of times. Now, he bobbed and punched and barreled forward, firing punches as he moved.

Ali won the first two rounds on points, landing more shots than Frazier. But when the third round opened, Frazier smiled, waving for Ali to come out and fight. Frazier threw hooks to the head and body, still shoving his way forward. Every time Frazier landed a thumping blow, Ali would shake his head vigorously, signaling to the crowd that the punch hadn't bothered him. At the end of the round, Ali returned to his corner and stood tall, declining a seat, showing Frazier he wasn't tired. Ali was acting like a kid on a playground sticking out his tongue and taunting his enemy, but the enemy in this case didn't seem to care.

Boxing fans were surprised to see Ali fighting Frazier's fight, standing toe-to-toe and exchanging punches instead of dancing and jabbing. Ali was fighting as if he believed his own hype — as if he believed that he was so much bigger and stronger now that he no longer needed to rely on speed. Frazier's eyes puffed. His mouth filled with blood. But he kept coming, kept snarling. Even Ali's punishing left jab didn't stop Frazier. He took his share, but every so often he managed to slip under one of the jabs and throw his money shot, the left hook.

Ali had predicted a sixth-round knockout, but by the sixth round Frazier was going strong, and Ali showed signs of fatigue. He wrapped his arms around Frazier's neck, leaned against the ropes, and brushed his hands lightly back and forth across Frazier's face like a man painting a fence. In the seventh and eighth, he did more of the same, resting and perhaps trying to sap Frazier's will by pretending he could go on this way all night, that the ropes were his hammock, a nice place to unwind for a while until he was ready to go back to work. Throughout the bout, Ali taunted Frazier, telling him he couldn't win.

"Don't you know I'm God!" he shouted.

"God, you're in the wrong place tonight," Frazier shot back. "Be somewhere else, not here. I'm kicking butt and taking names!"

The ninth round was shockingly violent, Ali's gloves caroming off Frazier's rocklike head, Frazier returning fire with uppercuts that made Ali's whole body rise and fall. Both men threw their strongest punches and landed them. Frazier's whole face grew lumpy, as if it had recently been inserted in a beehive. The crowd was on its feet. If the fight had ended there, Ali probably would have won on points. If Ali could have kept fighting this way, he would have knocked Frazier out or won a unanimous decision. But he couldn't keep it up. He had emptied his tank.

In the eleventh, instead of attacking, Ali backed off. He not only leaned on the ropes again but beckoned Frazier to move in close and hit him, the equivalent of a mobile home beckoning a tornado.

"What is he doing?" asked José Torres, the former light-heavyweight champ. "Is he punchy? He had the fight won in the final seconds of the tenth, and now he's spoiling it."

Frazier accepted Ali's invitation to punch, leaving his feet to throw a chin rattling left hook and following it with a mean left to the body. They were punches that Ali once would have avoided, but this time, if his mind was telling him to move, his body wasn't answering. Ali's knees buckled, and he tried to find his balance. He looked like he was going down, wounded like he had never been wounded in his professional career. But, somehow, he recovered and kept his feet on the ground. He had a phrase for this feeling of semiconsciousness. He called it the "half-dream room." He described it once: "A heavy blow takes you to the door of this room. It opens, and you see neon, orange and green lights blinking. You see bats blowing trumpets, alligators play trombones, and snakes are screaming. Weird masks and actors' clothes hang on the wall. The first time the blow sends you there, you panic and run, but when you wake up you say, 'Well, since it was only a dream, why didn't I play it cool . . . Only you have to fix it in your mind and plan to do it long before the half-dream comes . . . The blow makes your mind vibrate like a tuning fork. You can't let your opponent follow up. You got to stop the fork from vibrating."

Ali was in the half-dream room. At the bell, his corner men threw water in his face before he got to his stool, trying to snap him out of it. Bundini Brown pointed a finger and shouted, "You got God in your corner, Champ!" The referee, Arthur Mercante, came over to see if the fighter needed a doctor. He was persuaded to let the fight continue.

Ali came out moving in the twelfth as if to test his legs. Frazier pummeled him again. Ali fought back, but it was clear he had strength enough to fight only in flurries, not for an entire round. In the thirteenth, Ali started strongly again, moving with agility. He scored points by landing jabs, but he never hurt Frazier. After about a minute of playing the aggressor, Ali returned to the ropes, and Frazier, seeing an opportunity, exploded, connecting with an extraordinary forty-six punches. With bloody saliva dripping from his swollen lips and his face a mask of grotesque bruises, Frazier lashed out, throwing punches with the full force of his body and landing almost every one. If Ali's rope strategy had worked, if it had allowed him to regain energy while his opponent lost steam, he might have been hailed once more for his fistic genius. But it wasn't working at all. For Frazier, it was as if Ahab had discovered his great white whale lying on the beach and waiting to be carved up. Frazier punched, punched, punched, working the body, working the head, striking at will. He planted himself practically inside Ali's navel and stayed there, so that Ali couldn't see anything but the top of the shorter man's head. Frazier was so close that Ali couldn't extend his arms to strike back even if he'd wanted to. The more Frazier hurled punches, the more Ali assumed the stationary position of a punching bag. His jaw began to swell like a brown balloon, prompting concern in his corner that it had been broken.

Ali mustered one last reserve of strength and fought gamely in the fourteenth. But now both men were exhausted. It was a wonder either one of them could stand, much less punch and be punched. Ali, who liked to call himself the most scientific boxer in the history of the sport, may have been reconsidering, because this contest was anything but scientific. This was a bloody brawl. This was hell.

The men touched gloves to begin the fifteenth and final round. The bright overhead lights cast ugly shadows over both their swollen faces. The air reeked of sweat and smoke. Even the crowd was exhausted, but they were on their feet and screaming for more.

Ali came out dancing, as if to tell the world he was still strong, still fast, not yet done. He opened with a left that shot a spray of blood from Frazier's mouth. Frazier hammered a few blows to Ali's gut that made it clear he wasn't done either, and then grabbed Ali in a clinch. They broke and circled. Frazier moved forward, as he had the whole fight. Ali retreated. Frazier reached back with his left — reached all the way back, as he would say later, to the hot turnip fields of South Carolina, to his childhood days of poverty and hate — and let fly a left hook. Perspiration sprayed from Ali's head as the punch made impact. Ali's head jolted. His eyes closed, his mouth opened, and his legs folded. He landed on his back and elbows, head bouncing on the mat, legs flailing in the air.

Unbelievably, though, Ali got up.

He got up as soon as his body hit the mat.

He got up and resumed fighting.

Later, Angelo Dundee would say that Ali was out cold as he fell and regained consciousness when his ass hit the floor, which is exactly how it looked. When Frazier hit Ali with the left hook, it shook Ali's brain, causing brain cells to stretch and tear, and temporarily disrupting cell function and communication. Hooks do more damage to brain tissue than jabs because the neck helps absorb the impact of a punch that comes straight toward the face. When a punch comes from the side, the head rotates and rocks, the neck offers less help in blunting the force, and the whole brain shakes like Jell-O. That explains why Ali fell. What it doesn't explain is how he got up, and how he did it so quickly — before the referee could count four. A solid blow to the head can damage the brain's axons (the long, thin branches that transmit signals throughout the nervous system), and complete recovery might take weeks, months, or never come at all. But Ali rose and stayed on his feet and battled for the last two and a half minutes of the fight, as 20,000 people at Madison Square Garden and 300 million around the world screamed.

Was it courage that carried them? Was it neurology? Was it hubris overriding physiology? The men fought on until, finally, the bell rang and the referee stepped between them, signaling the end of one of the most intense and best-fought boxing matches in history. Fans swarmed the ring as Frazier was announced the winner by a unanimous decision.

Writers such as Norman Mailer attempted to describe the battle between these two men as something quasi-spiritual, something far beyond man-to-man combat. "There are languages other than words, languages of symbol and languages of nature," Mailer wrote. "There are languages of the body. And prizefighting is one of them. There is no attempting to comprehend a prizefighter unless we are willing to recognize that he speaks with a command of the body which is as detached, subtle and comprehensive in its intelligence as any exercise of mind by such social engineers as Herman Kahn or Henry Kissinger." After the fight, abstractions such as those gave way to the hard truths of pain and injury. Ali stretched out on a long table, motionless, eyes closed, naked but for a white towel. Angelo Dundee wandered around the room as if lost or bereft. Odessa Clay sat on a bench next to the table holding her son. "He'll be all right," she said over and over again.

Belinda was nowhere in sight, but Ali sat up when Diana Ross arrived in the dressing room. Ross took an ice bag from Bundini, pressed it to Ali's jaw, and whispered in the fallen fighter's ear. Ali managed a wink.

With his jaw the size of a small pumpkin, Ali went to Flower First Avenue Hospital for X-rays. Doctors said the jaw wasn't broken, but they suggested Ali stay overnight. He refused. He didn't want to let Frazier think he had been badly hurt. Ali was already talking about a rematch, and by refusing medical care he was launching the first attack in his psychological battle.

35

Freedom

In Harlem, they called it a fix. In the White House, President Nixon rejoiced, cheering the defeat of "that draft dodger asshole." Everyone had an opinion, but none of them mattered. Frazier had won, and Ali would have to fight his way back if he hoped to be champion again.

After the fight, *Sports Illustrated* sent George Plimpton to Ali's new home in Cherry Hill, New Jersey, to see how he was handling his first defeat. Plimpton found Ali in the driveway, entertaining neighbors, tussling with dogs, hugging small children, and signing autographs. He invited not only Plimpton but also the sightseers gathered on the street to come inside for a tour of his house, which was still only partly decorated. An oil painting of Elijah Muhammad sat on the floor in one room, propped against a wall next to bouquet of flowers with a card from the singer Aretha Franklin. In another room, Belinda sat on the floor watching television, ignoring Ali and his guests.

After the tour, Ali told Plimpton he was ready to talk—but Plimpton would have to share the interview with two other journalists, boys from a nearby high school who were producing an article for their school paper, one of them clutching a tape recorder, the other a Polaroid camera. When the boy with the Polaroid snapped a picture, Ali asked to see if the photo made his jaw look swollen. The other boy turned on his tape recorder and asked Ali to hold the microphone.

"When is this going to appear?" Ali asked. "What's the name of the paper?"

"The *Sentinel*," the reporter said. "It's mimeographed." The photos would be hung from the school's bulletin board because the mimeograph machine wouldn't reproduce pictures, he explained.

That sounded fine to Ali. He began by saying he and ten of his friends had gone to a theater in Cherry Hill the night before to watch a twenty-five-minute recapitulation of the Frazier fight. He got up from the sofa and reenacted his favorite part, in the eleventh round, when he backed around the ring and Frazier chased after him, strutting, with his hands down, before throwing the left that shook Ali like he had seldom been shaken. "That long long walk of Frazier's," he said. "Oh, my, we were laughing at that."

Throughout the fight, he said, that left hook had constantly surprised him. Why did he keep getting hit? He had thought the first couple had been lucky shots, but they had kept coming and coming.

The photographer asked: "How . . . I mean, what was wrong?"

Ali raised a hand to his head. "Here's how you're supposed to do it," he said. "I had my hands too low."

"Couldn't you bring them up?" the boy asked.

"That sounds simple, don't it?" Ali said.

The photographer asked if Ali was still dwelling on his loss.

"Not as much as I thought I would," Ali said. "For me now, fighting is more a business than the glory of who won. After all, when the praise is over" — and, according to Plimpton, Ali shifted here into the lower, hypnotic voice that he reserved for poetry and inspirational sermons — "when all the fanfare is done, all that counts is what you have to show for it. All the bleeding, the world still turns. I was so tired. I lost it. But I didn't shed one tear. I got to keep living. I'm not ashamed."

In the meantime, Ali had another fight to worry about — the legal battle over his draft status — and there was every reason to believe he was going to lose that one, too.

In 1969, the U.S. Supreme Court had voted not to hear Ali's case. Ali was saved from prison only by an acknowledgment from the Department of Justice that they had wiretapped some of the boxer's conversations, which led the Supreme Court to send the case back to the district court. Ali lost again in district court, and in January 1971 the justices of the Supreme Court appeared uninterested in hearing his case. That meant the district court's conviction would be affirmed and Ali would go to jail for five years.

But Ali got a big break. Supreme Court justice William Brennan urged the court to hear Ali's case, and he made an unusual argument. He didn't expect his colleagues to change their minds. He didn't expect Ali to prevail. But given the boxer's fame and given the outcry over Vietnam, Brennan worried that Americans would misunderstand the decision. He feared that Ali might appear to be the victim of a political prosecution if he didn't at least get a chance to argue his case before the court.

On April 19, 1971, the Supreme Court heard oral arguments in *Cassius Marsellus Clay Jr. v. United States*. The case referred to Ali by his old name because Ali still had not filed paperwork to make his name change official. It used the middle name "Marsellus" instead of "Marcellus" because Ali had misspelled his own name on his original Selective Service forms when he had registered for the draft in 1961.

Ali did not attend the oral arguments. Chauncey Eskridge represented him, but Eskridge's arguments, described later by one of the justices as "confused," were greeted coolly. Erwin Griswold, the U.S. solicitor general, argued on behalf of the government and questioned the basis of Ali's antiwar status. When Ali had said he had "no quarrel" with the Viet Cong, according to Griswold, he wasn't saying he opposed all war; he was really saying that he opposed this particular war. If the Viet Cong had been attacking Muslims, Griswold argued, Ali would have fought. Also, when Ali said he didn't want to fight for a country that treated him like a second-class citizen, he wasn't saying he was a pacifist; he was really making a political statement, saying he didn't want to fight for this particular government at this particular time.

Four days later, the justices voted five to three (with Thurgood Marshall abstaining) to affirm Ali's conviction. Justice John M. Harlan was assigned to write the majority opinion. Ordinarily, drafting the opinion is a mere formality. But this time it wasn't.

Harlan was a conservative justice who believed that social issues should be decided by legislators, not judges. His grandfather had been a close friend of the original Cassius Marcellus Clay, the white slave owner and abolitionist from Kentucky. In the summer of 1971, Harlan was seventy-two years old and suffering terrible pain, unaware he was dying of spinal cancer. As Harlan prepared to write his opinion, one of his clerks, Thomas Krattenmaker, volunteered to help with research. Clerks to the justices of the Supreme Court tended to be young, they tended to be among the best law-school students in the country, and they tended to be opposed to the war in Vietnam. Krattenmaker was a twenty-six-year-old white man who had marched in antiwar protests while studying law at Columbia University. Before going to work as a Supreme Court clerk, he had read *The Autobiography of Malcolm X*. The book gave him a sense of the passion and sincerity with which Malcolm and Muhammad Ali approached their religion. He had also been impressed by the clarity with which Ali had expressed his opposition to the war. "When he said, 'I ain't got no quarrel with the Vietcong,'" Krattenmaker recalled in an interview, "he spoke to every man in America who wasn't already enlisted. There was no threat to our nation, no threat to our culture. Why were we fighting?"

Krattenmaker understood why the justices would believe that Ali's opposition to the war was based on race and politics. Ali's opposition *was* based on those factors, in part. But the young court clerk was convinced that Ali's refusal to fight was also religious, and Ali was entitled to have more than one reason for refusing to fight as long as he was sincere about the reason that the court deemed valid: the opposition to all war based on his religion. The test for conscientious objector status required that an individual sincerely opposed participation in war in any form based on his religious training and beliefs. Quakers and other pacifists passed that test, but Catholics who viewed the Vietnam War as immoral did not pass it. True pacifists didn't get to choose their wars, as the court had decided earlier in the same term. Ali had conceded that he would fight in a so-called Holy War if Allah commanded him to. Did that mean he could not legitimately claim to be a conscientious objector?

Krattenmaker didn't think so. He urged Justice Harlan to read Elijah Muhammad's book *Message to the Blackman in America*. In that book, the Muslim Holy War was described as something entirely hypothetical and abstract — as unlikely as the Armageddon that Jehovah's Witnesses talked about. In other words, as a practical matter, followers of Elijah Muhammad were sincerely and religiously opposed to all earthly wars.

Justice Harlan's eyesight was failing, but he agreed to investigate *Message to the Blackman,* and, after doing so, he decided Krattenmaker was right. On June 9, in a memo to the court, Harlan said he was changing his vote. He included a long description of the teachings of the Nation of Islam and quoted from *Message to the Blackman:* "The very dominant idea in Islam is the making of peace and not war; our refusing to go armed is our proof that we want peace. We felt that we had no right to take part in a war with nonbelievers of Islam who have always denied us justice and equal rights; and if we were going to be examples of peace and righteousness (as Allah has chosen us to be) we felt we had no right to join hands with the murderers of people or to help murder those who have done us no wrong . . . We believe that we who declared ourselves to be righteous Muslims should not participate in any wars which take the lives of humans."

Justice William Douglas challenged that, saying the Koran allowed Muslims to fight in a *jihad* against nonbelievers. How could the same people willing to fight a *jihad* be deemed pacifists?

With Harlan switching sides, the court was tied four-four. That meant the boxer's conviction would still be affirmed. Ali would still go to jail. But Justice Potter Stewart was upset. He believed Ali had been convicted for political purposes, and now it would it appear that the Supreme Court was going to send him to jail because some of his fellow justices were afraid of the political backlash that might ensue if they ruled that supporters of the Nation of Islam were exempt from military service. Such a decision — accompanied by no written opinion — would have been a public-relations disaster for the Department of Defense, and it might have turned tens of thousands of black Americans into newly minted Muslims.

Justice Stewart suggested a compromise, based on a legal technicality, one that would allow the court to reverse Ali's conviction without setting any legal precedent and without deciding whether Ali and the rest of the Nation of Islam's followers sincerely opposed all war. The appeal board that had rejected Ali's first claim had not given any basis for its finding, Stewart pointed out. Was Ali rejected because the panel didn't believe he was opposed to all wars? Did the panel decide that Ali's views were not based on religion? Or did the panel question the sincerity of his religious beliefs? Without knowing why Ali's claim was rejected, there was no way to move forward and give him a fair hearing. The only choice was to reverse the conviction.

Harlan referred to the decision as a "pee-wee," Krattenmaker said, because it corrected an injustice while setting no legal precedent. It was a decision everyone on the court could live with. The ruling was unanimous.

It was 9:15 a.m. on June 28, 1971, on the South Side of Chicago when Ali got the news. He was out for a drive in his green-and-white Lincoln Continental Mark III and stopped at a small grocery to buy a cup of orange juice. He was holding his orange juice and walking back to his car when the store-owner came running out.

"I just heard on the radio," the man said excitedly, "the Supreme Court said you're free, an 8–0 vote." The news arrived fifty months after Ali's initial refusal to accept induction. In that time, Ali had spent about $250,000 in legal fees, a bill that would have been higher if he had paid in full and if the NAACP and American Civil Liberties Union had not donated their services. The grocer hugged Ali. Ali let out a whoop and went back inside, where he bought orange juice for the store's customers.

By the time he reached the 50th on the Lake TraveLodge, where he and his wife and children were staying, a gaggle of newspaper and TV reporters waited for him. Ali played it cool for the cameras. "I'm not going to cele-brate," he said. "I've already said a long prayer to Allah, that's my celebration." He continued, "All praises are due to Allah who came in the person of Master Faroud Muhammad, and I thank Allah for giving to me the Honorable Elijah Muhammad and I thank the Supreme Court for recognizing the sincerity of the religious teachings that I've accepted."

Ali was training for a July 26 fight against Jimmy Ellis, his former spar-ring partner and Louisville friend. He was also exploring the possibility of a fight with basketball superstar Wilt Chamberlain, who would have made an interesting opponent given that he stood seven-foot-one and weighed more than 275 pounds. The fight never came about, perhaps in part because Ali, upon posing for publicity shots with Chamberlain and pretending to throw a punch, couldn't resist shouting "Timber!"

Ali said he intended to retire after three or four more bouts. Once he beat Frazier and won back the championship, he would quit, return to the Nation of Islam as a minister, and pass his days in the company of his wife and chil-dren. He and Belinda, he said, wanted to have seven more kids, at least five of them boys. "I can't represent the Muslims again until I quit sports," he said. "I spoke with the Honorable Elijah Muhammad, and he told me, 'If boxing's in your blood, get it out.'"

Ali's body told him that boxing was not a good long-term option. He'd gained at least ten pounds since the Frazier fight. Ever since he'd taken that beating at Madison Square Garden, he'd found that he lacked the energy for training. Before his exile from boxing, he said, he would run five or six miles a day, then hit the gym for sparring, jumping rope, and heavy-bag work. Now he ran two miles and needed a nap. Was it age? Was it his three-and-a-half-year layoff? Was it cognitive damage from too many shots to the head? It was impossible to say. But Ali wasn't the same in the ring or out, and he knew it. "I used to dance every minute, to the left, to the right, always moving and sticking. You don't see that no more. I got another year and that's it. I could fight for eight more years but I'd be flatfooted. I'd start getting bruised up. I'd start getting knocked down more."

A reporter asked if Ali would sue to recover damages from those who had taken away his career for three and a half years. "No," he said. "They only did what they thought was right at the time. I did what I thought was right. That was all."

Ali had defeated America. To Donald Reeves, a black student who briefly met Ali when the boxer visited Cornell University, Ali was everything: The Black Prince, Br'er Rabbit, David-Who-Fought-Goliath, an Invisible Man who refused to be unseen, a battered fighter who showed black people what it took to remain undefeated. Ali was special to Reeves and others because he wasn't the leader of an organization — he was simply a man who seemed to be at the heart of so many of the central cultural issues of his time. Ali used skill rather than force to defeat his opponents; he refused to play by the rules of the establishment; he disdained materialism; he approached life with a sly smile and great sense of humor. Ali was a fantastic role model for Reeves, and he inspired the college student to compose an essay, which he submitted for publication to the New York Times. "Every time Ali wins," Reeves wrote, "I see it as a victory for black people. For a black man to exist, he must be the greatest. He must say it over and over again — I am the greatest, because white people might forget . . . Ali insists on being seen, heard, known, and knowing himself. He has transcended all those limitations the white system has imposed on the black man — of course they are trying to send him to jail."

Ali had more power than ever outside the ring. He had risked his career, taken on the federal government, and won. But when a reporter asked how he would use his enormous influence, Ali's answer was uncertain at best, jibberish at worst. "I wouldn't say that I have become a symbol or power," he said. "I stand . . . for what I believe. Some can say it's an American, some argue that it's against the country and it's bad. The individual must regard it to whatever . . . they want to. As far as what I think about the human rights of the black movement, then we are back to the same answer. You see, it depends on the individual. I try to live up to my own beliefs according to religious reasons. But I do hope that it may help encourage black people to do what they feel is right and to help their own people on the road to freedom and equality. But it is good to know that what ever I do will help someone else do good also." He continued, "I'd like to say to the black people: right on! Keep pushing. If you can just keep respecting one another and get the youngsters educated where they can go out and do for themselves. I'd like for all black people to read the *Muhammad Speaks* newspaper . . . You can't buy the understanding, wisdom and knowledge that's in that newspaper — get to the Muhammad's Mosque of Islam. This is what I see, this is what I believe, and if you love me, then you will like my teacher."

After the Supreme Court's decision, Ali did not speak out against the war on college campuses. Nor did he deliver speeches in the Nation of Islam's mosques, where he remained unwelcome according to Elijah Muhammad's edict. It was remarkable, really, how little he said about race and politics in the wake of the court's decision. He gave the impression of a man who, above all else, was glad to be a boxer again. With only four weeks to go before his fight with Ellis, he had a lot of work to do and a lot of weight to lose.

On June 25, Ali fought a seven-round exhibition in Dayton, including several rounds against a young fighter named Eddie Brooks of Milwaukee, who hit the former champion with sharp shots, "right on the button," according to Rolly Schwartz, an Olympic boxing referee who watched the sparring match. When it was over, Ali was exhausted, and it was reasonable to believe he meant it when he talked of retiring soon. "Another year and I'm through," he said. "I'm getting too old for this."

Ali wanted his sparring partners to hurt him. He believed that suffering was an important part of his preparation for a fight, that a man could build up tolerance for blows to the head and body in much the same way that one might build up tolerance for spicy food by eating jalapeno peppers. The effect of all those sparring session blows over the course of a career would never be quantified, but sometimes, even in the short term, it was clear that

Ali's strategy backfired. While sparring one day in July, Brooks hit Ali on the chin and Ali went down, flat on his back, as suddenly and stunningly as he'd gone down against Frazier. According to some accounts in the press, Brooks floored him two more times in the same sparring session, which suggests that Ali may have suffered a concussion from the first knockdown. In another sparring session, the European heavyweight champion Joe Bugner popped Ali consistently with quick left jabs, and Ali, flat-footed, seemed either incapable of or uninterested in getting out of the way. Avoiding Bugner's jab would have required the type of sharp reflexes and boxing technique Ali no longer possessed.

A week before the fight, Ali was still complaining about the roll of fat around his waist and still talking about giving up boxing. He said he was entertaining an offer from a large company in South Africa to give a series of speeches in that racially divided country, adding that he had no ethical qualms about touring South Africa for a white corporation: "I ain't going to start nothing," he said. "I'll talk to blacks and whites and integrated groups, all kinds. Maybe they like the way we (Muslims) talk separation."

Against Jimmy Ellis, Ali had to worry not about his poor condition but about fighting without Angelo Dundee in his corner. Dundee trained both boxers, but he felt a greater responsibility to Ellis because he also served as his manager.

Ellis had a record of 30–6, with fourteen knockouts, and he had beaten Floyd Patterson, Jerry Quarry, and Oscar Bonavena. Dundee thought Ellis had a chance against Ali so long as Ellis roughed up Ali's body and stayed away from his jab.

But it didn't work out the way Dundee had hoped. Ali was lazy against Ellis. He was overweight and sluggish, but he was thirty pounds heavier than his opponent and much stronger. Ali used his cracking jab to keep Ellis from working his way inside the way Joe Frazier had. Ali and Ellis had been friends since childhood. They'd sparred hundreds of rounds and fought each other as amateurs. Ali was comfortable and confident, thumbing his nose, lowering his hands, dancing around, and daring Ellis to try to hit him. Still, he let the fight go almost the full distance. In the opening moments of the twelfth and final round, Ali opened the kind of full-throttled attack that fans had been waiting to see. Only then did the referee stop the bout.

When it was over, Ali made no apologies for his lackluster performance. "I wasn't going to kill myself for this one," he said. "I'm training for Frazier."

If Ali was indeed training for Frazier, he went about it in a less than optimal way. Over the course of twenty-seven months, beginning with the Ellis bout, Ali fought an astonishing thirteen times, or roughly once every sixty days. In that same period, Frazier fought only four bouts. Even the unheralded Jerry Quarry fought less frequently than Ali during the same stretch.

Why would a man fight thirteen times in twenty-seven months when he didn't have to? Why would he endure 139 rounds of punishment against some of boxing's toughest heavyweights, plus thousands more rounds of sparring? Why would he absorb about 1,800 punches in those thirteen fights? What was he thinking? Was his schedule an acknowledgment that he disdained the rigors of training? That he felt compelled to prove himself? That the only way he could stay sharp was by scheduling a steady string of bouts? That he needed the money? That he needed to fight often to prove he deserved another shot at the championship? Or was it something even worse? Was Ali's judgment clouded by brain damage? Was his lost appetite for rigorous training connected somehow to a dulling of the mind from too many blows to the head?

Ferdie Pacheco, the doctor working in Ali's corner at the time, said he saw signs of lasting brain damage after the Frazier fight in 1971. Pacheco said he told Ali to quit after that fight.

Why didn't Ali listen?

"There is no fucking cure to quick money," Pacheco said. "There is none."

No one can say with certainty when brain damage begins to affect a person, although scientists have become much better in recent years at recognizing signs of trouble, particularly in athletes who suffer repeated blows to the head. When a person nears the age of thirty, his brain tissue becomes progressively less elastic, making him more susceptible to permanent damage with each passing year and each passing shock to the skull. Boxers are especially susceptible. After all, the point of boxing is to concuss the opponent, to knock him down and knock him out. If attempts were made to render boxing safe for boxers, it would likely mean the end of the sport. Boxers take far more hits to the head than other athletes, and they are less likely to receive proper evaluation after a damaging blow. In football, if a player is removed for a concussion or for concussion testing, another player takes his place. The game goes on. In boxing, if a fighter can't continue, the fight is over; the audience goes home. In boxing, the ability to shake off brain trauma and go on is considered testament to a fighter's strength and courage. When Ali bounced back up after he was floored by Frazier's left hook, boxing fans and writers admired him for his grit, for the steel in his spine. No one stepped in to offer a concussion test. The crowd cheered. The men in his corner urged him on. Even after the fight, no one checked him for a concussion.

Boxing's long-term hazards have been studied since 1928, when an American doctor first used the term *punch-drunk* to describe fighters suffering cognitive dysfunctions including memory loss, aggression, confusion, depression, slurred speech, and, eventually, dementia. Today, punch-drunkenness is referred to as chronic traumatic encephalopathy (CTE), a progressive, degenerative brain disease caused by repetitive trauma. Scientists now understand that even small jolts to the brain, when repeated, can cause lasting damage. Researchers have studied the effects of head injuries on football players, and the National Football League has taken steps to make the game safer. But boxers absorb many more blows to the head than football players, and boxers don't wear helmets to mitigate the damage. A boxer with a busy schedule probably takes more than a thousand shots to the head a year in his bouts and thousands more in sparring sessions. Over a ten-year career, a boxer will likely absorb tens of thousands of blows to the head. But boxing has no policy to determine when in the course of a career a fighter has had enough. State commissions govern the sport. A boxer who can't get a license in one state merely tries another. No national or international governing body sets the rules and offers accountability.

Did Ali suffer for all those blows to the head? In all likelihood, he did. Even as he entered what would later be described as the greatest phase of his career, there were signs of trouble, clues that have might might have raised a warning, and they were noticeable every time Ali opened his mouth beginning around 1971.

The act of speaking is not as simple as it seems. Speech and language circuits in the brain work together to form a message, translate that message into movement across more than one hundred muscles from the lungs to the throat to the tongue and lips, and execute those intricate muscle movements to produce sound waves. It's a lot harder than throwing a jab or ducking one. That's why slurred speech is often one of the first indicators of moderate to severe neurological damage or disease. That's why drunks and stroke victims and victims of neurological disorders such as Parkinson's disease or Lou Gehrig's disease often slur their words. The signals from the brain to the body are too impaired to get the job done smoothly. In 1967, Ali spoke at a rate of 4.07 syllables per second, which is close to average for healthy adults. By 1971, his rate of speech had fallen to 3.8 syllables per second, and it would continue sliding steadily, year by year, fight by fight, over the course of his career, according to a study published in 2017 by speech scientists at Arizona State University. The study examined Ali's speech by evaluating dozens of recordings of television interviews and analyzing Ali's voice over time. An ordinary adult would see little or no decline in his speaking rate between the ages of twenty-five and forty, but Ali experienced a drop of more than 26 percent in that period. His ability to clearly articulate words also declined significantly.

The brash boxer was slowly being hushed, and not by the government or by his critics; he was doing it to himself.

Ali had always said he would never wind up the way so many old fighters did — drooling, incoherent, memories fogged, displaying the effects of all those punches for the rest of their lives like shadows in a trophy case.

But those fighters never saw it coming, and neither did Ali.

One hundred fourteen days after his fight against Ellis, Ali fought Buster Mathis. Ticket sales for the Astrodome fight were moving sluggishly, and Ali couldn't think of anything nasty to say about Mathis to stoke interest in the competition. His act was getting old. His poems had grown familiar. His teasing of Howard Cosell had the feel of a well-polished routine. His bragging no longer startled. Ali still knew how to entertain, but he no longer rankled or surprised.

When the publicity man Bob Goodman complained to Ali that they needed something to attract attention, Ali lit up. "I got it!" he told Goodman. "You can have me kidnapped! Set me up in a cabin in the woods. I'll train up there. Nobody will know. A few days before the fight you can find me!" Goodman humored Ali and said it was a good idea — except that people probably weren't going to buy tickets to a fight when one of the combatants had gone missing. A crowd of only 21,000 showed up as Ali beat Mathis by a unanimous decision in twelve rounds.

Thirty-nine days later, Ali fought Juergen Blin, winning in a seven-round knockout. Ninety-seven days later, he fought Mac Foster, who lasted fifteen hopeless rounds. Thirty days later, Ali fought George Chuvalo for the second time and beat him for the second time. Fifty-seven days after that, he stopped Jerry Quarry on cuts in the seventh round. Twenty-two days later, he punished Alvin Blue Lewis before taking him out in the eleventh round. After another sixty-three days, he danced around with Floyd Patterson for a few rounds before landing a punch that opened a cut over Floyd's eye and caused the fight, Patterson's last, to be stopped. Sixty-two days later, Ali knocked out Bob Foster in the eighth round (Foster fired off a lot of sharp jabs and one of the best lines ever uttered about the difficulty in fighting Ali: "He was never in one place at the same time!").

Eighty-five days after that, on St. Valentine's Day 1973, Ali battered Joe Bugner but couldn't knock him out, winning it in a bloody unanimous decision.

Ali made it all look easy — nothing remotely like reality. That thudding jab, that smooth footwork, that surprising power. He delivered it all with confidence and grace: "Sorry, man," he seemed to say, "but I'm Ali."

He was on the road constantly, happy as could be. He trained in the morning and watched TV at night. He enjoyed a steady stream of women. He joked with Bundini. He played pranks on Dundee — the same sorts of pranks he'd played on his parents as a child, tying a cord to the blind in his hotel room and running it out the door, hiding in the closet and jumping out with a sheet over his head. Among his boxing friends, Ali could be the child again.

After the Bugner fight, Ali had padded his record to forty wins and one loss. Were all those fights necessary? Probably not. But they did help him recover some his finesse as a boxer, and it was clear that he was not ready to give up his athletic career.

He certainly had options. Warner Brothers had offered him $250,000 plus a percentage of revenues to star in *Heaven Can Wait*, the remake of a 1941 film called *Here Comes Mr. Jordan*, about a boxer who is removed from his body prematurely by an overanxious angel and who returns to life in the body of a recently murdered millionaire. When Ali turned down the part, director Warren Beatty cast himself in the lead role and changed the character from a boxer to a football player. The movie, released in 1978, performed extraordinarily well at the box office and earned glowing reviews. If Ali had taken the part, and if his performance had been well received, there's no telling whether his career path might have changed. For the time being, he remained a boxer. Hollywood was a possibility, but boxing was a certainty, and the money was simply too good to resist. Unfortunately, he also paid a price. Even in those ten relatively easy fights, Ali took more than 1,200 punches.

The problem, in part, was that Ali lacked the punching power to put a quick end to fights, even against middling competition. Bob Foster got knocked down seven times in his fight with Ali, but when it was over, he was dismissive of his opponent's power. When Joe Frazier hit him, Foster said, "I saw birds and all different colors, you know? They say I got up, but I don't remember." Not so with Ali. Even when Ali won easily, he seldom overwhelmed opponents. "He wasn't knocking them guys out," Foster said. "Shit, them guys was just getting tired. They were running out of gas and failing . . . He had me down six, seven times, but he never hurt me, you know . . . Ali know he didn't hurt me!"

36

Trickeration

I t's never about the money. It's always about the money."

It was one of Bob Arum's favorite lines, and the truth of it never failed the promoter. Boxers would say they loved to box. They would say they did it for the thrill of the competition, to settle scores, to prove their skills, to earn a place in the pantheon of greats. These boxers would say that when the time came to hang up their gloves, they would do so without hesitation — only to hesitate, time and time again, unable to resist the money. When his jaw was swollen after his clash with Frazier, Ali had announced he was ready to quit. Two or three more fights, culminating with the rematch with Frazier, and that would be it. He would be set for life, done.

Then he went on to fight ten times in twenty-four months, with Arum arranging most of the events. Ali still spoke eagerly of getting another shot at Frazier, but he no longer seemed to be in a hurry, not when he could make millions beating up men like Juergen Blin and Joe Bugner.

"Don't let nuthin' happen to Joe Frazier," Ali said, as he knocked off one tomato can after another.

He admitted the money mattered. "It ain't too late to start saving," he said. "I get $100,000 for a fight, I buy something costing $8,000, something else cost $24,000, and the one-hundred goes like hell. It costs me $10,000 a month to live. I can't keep that up."

His assets included two Rolls-Royces, a small collection of Cadillacs, a home in New Jersey, and a home for his parents in Louisville. Gene Kilroy, who served as Ali's all-purpose facilitator and handled many of his day-today business transactions, introduced Ali to accountants at Peat Marwick International, and the accountants told Ali that he could save a fortune in taxes by writing off more of his business expenses. With that in mind, Ali bought a six-acre property in Deer Lake, Pennsylvania, about twenty-five miles north of Reading. Ali had the land cleared and began building log cabins. This would be his new training center, where he could get away from the hustle and hustlers of New York and Miami, and where he could prepare in isolation for his upcoming fights. He planned to build enough cabins to house about twenty, he said, so that his sparring partners, his cooks, his wife, his children, his friends, and his entourage members would always have a place to sleep. With Ali, isolation was a relative term.

The training camp would help save money too, Ali said, because he would no longer have to pay for gym time and hotel rooms. Ali had other ideas for cutting back on spending. "I'm going to make my wife make her own clothes," he said in an interview with the *New York Times*. "She don't have to, but I'm going to make her do it." His goal, he said, was to put 75 percent of his income into savings until he had a million dollars socked away. He estimated that he had earned about $7 million before taxes so far in his boxing career. He and Belinda had four children now: Maryum, the twins Jamillah and Rasheda, and a four-month-old boy they called Muhammad Jr. The children spent most of their time with Belinda's parents, who lived in a working-class suburb of Chicago.

"It was very normal," Jamillah said, recalling the years spent primarily with her grandparents, "and that's why my grandmother took on the responsibility, because she wanted us to have a normal childhood." When their father visited, Jamillah said, it was like a holiday. The children put on their nicest clothes. Neighbors rang the doorbell to see Ali and get his autograph. Herbert Muhammad and others dropped by. When Ali left, their ordinary lives resumed.

Ali said he wanted to see the children more often. "I'm never home too much and they don't know me too well," he said. He told reporters that he and Belinda planned to sell their home in New Jersey and move to Chicago soon.

Ali liked to play with his children, but he had little interest in the day-to-day work of being a father, little interest in setting and enforcing rules. Certain parental responsibilities, he said, belonged solely to women. When the *Sports Illustrated* photographer Neil Leifer visited Ali one day and asked if he could take a picture of Ali changing his son's diaper, Ali plopped little Muhammad on a bed and wrapped a diaper around his middle, but he had no idea what to do with the safety pins. And this was his fourth child. "Belinda," he said, after the pictures had been taken, "come on over here and finish this job."

Ali said his role as a father was to make sure his children understood the importance of education and had enough money to live comfortably. "I don't want nobody whispering, 'See that waitress, that's Muhammad Ali's daughter.' That's pitiful when you think about it . . . But it ain't gonna happen. I'm going to be the first black fighter you can look at and say, 'There's a wise, wealthy man with property, camps, businesses, and $2 million in the bank.'"

Ali was still waiting to fight Frazier, but no date had been announced. In the meantime, he continued scheduling bouts against men who were less than top contenders. His next fight, he said, would be in South Africa, where he had been offered a tremendous payday. The plans for a bout in South Africa never came together, but Ali's announcement was enough to irk a black reporter, who asked why the boxer would support a government that imprisoned Nelson Mandela and forced black people to live under a brutal system of apartheid.

Ali responded, "Because my black brothers there haven't seen me."

Herbert Muhammad and Bob Arum made most of Ali's business decisions, consulting with Ali and Angelo Dundee in choosing opponents as they plotted Ali's path toward a rematch with Frazier. But in the summer of 1972, a new figure entered Ali's life and made a play to supplant Arum as promoter.

Don King was a hustler from Cleveland, a large man (at about six-foot-three, 240 pounds) given to large assertions. "I transcend earthly bounds," he once told a journalist. "I never cease to amaze myself; I haven't yet found my limits. I am ready to accept the limits of what I can do, but every time I feel that way, boom! — God touches me, and I do something even more stupendous." It was no wonder he and Ali hit it off. King carried himself like the black Al Capone, with a big afro, lots of sparkling jewelry, and pockets full of cash. The writer Jack Newfield called him "a street Machiavelli, a ghetto Einstein" who "dressed like a pimp, talked like an evangelical storefront preacher, and thought like a chess grand master." Mark Kram of *Sports Illustrated* called him "a 50-carat setting of sparkling vulgarity and raw energy, a man who wants to swallow mountains, walk on oceans, and sleep on clouds." Before his foray into boxing, King ran a gambling operation. To make it work as smoothly as possible, he ratted on competitors. In the late 1960s, he was said to be grossing fifteen thousand dollars a day, most of that money coming from poor, black Cleveland men and women who hoped to hit it big playing his rigged numbers games.

One day in April 1966, King had walked into the Manhattan Tap Room in Cleveland. Sam Garrett, a former employee of King's operation, sat at the bar. Garrett owed King six hundred dollars, and King wanted the money. An argument turned into a fight, and the fight turned into a beating, with Garrett on the sidewalk outside the bar and King kicking the smaller man in the head until blood flowed from Garrett's ears and King's footprints marked his victim's cheekbone. Garrett later died. A jury found King guilty of second-degree murder, punishable by life in prison. But, in a move that puzzled prosecutors and raised suspicions of bribery, the judge hearing the case reduced the conviction to manslaughter. King emerged from prison after serving three years and eleven months, and he was later pardoned. A few years after his release from prison, King arranged for Muhammad Ali to campaign for the judge and record a radio commercial endorsing his reelection.

In 1971, on his first day out of prison, King got a visit from his friend Lloyd Price, the legendary singer and songwriter who had gained fame with the songs "Lawdy Miss Clawdy," "Stagger Lee," and "Personality." The men talked about what King would do now that he was free. King said he was interested in the boxing business because it would give him a legitimate way to make money and asked if Price could arrange an introduction to Ali. Price knew Ali well. The men had met when Ali was a teenager hanging around music clubs in the West End of Louisville, and they had been friends ever since.

Price arranged first for King to speak to Herbert Muhammad. King told Herbert he wanted to bring Ali to Cleveland for a boxing exhibition that would raise money for a hospital in a black neighborhood that was on the verge of bankruptcy.

Even over the phone, Don King was a force of nature. He shouted with ear-splitting force, using laughter for exclamation points. He blustered and blew so fiercely and at such length that, eventually, more often than not, he got what he wanted, and when he didn't get what he wanted, he would get down on his knees and cry, pounding his fists on the floor like a three-year-old throwing a tantrum. In prison, he had borrowed heavily from the library and memorized passages from Shakespeare, which he quoted liberally. But his favorite expressions were curses, and his favorite curse, unequivocally, was "motherfucker," along with its adjectival form, "motherfucking." He once said, "We're blacks and we have nothing. We don't have expensive suits, or big houses, or luxury vacations. We're poor. All we got is the word. Our only invention that belongs to us is a word. And that word is *motherfucker!* Nobody can take that away from us. That's our word. That's a black word. It's our heritage . . . We should be standing on top of buildings, shouting our word — *motherfucker!*"

What King wanted from Herbert Muhammad was Ali. Ali, he said, *had* to come to Cleveland. Ali *had* to save this black hospital. Ali *had* to come to Cleveland or else poor black people would die and black doctors would lose their motherfucking jobs! Herbert Muhammad agreed. Ali went to Cleveland to box a ten-round exhibition for charity on August 28, 1972. Later, *Boxing Illustrated* reported that the hospital got only fifteen thousand dollars from the benefit. The hospital closed its doors a few years later. But from King's standpoint, the exhibition was a huge success because it allowed him to establish a working relationship with Ali and Herbert Muhammad.

King knew little about the business of boxing, but he was a huckster. He could sell anything — even freezers to Eskimos, as he liked to brag. Selling Muhammad Ali would be easy. Anybody could sell Muhammad Ali, but Don King was going to sell Muhammad Ali like no one had ever sold him before. It would be glorious. Stupendous. Exhilarating. It would make King a king of the ring.

When Ali and King first met, King showed up carrying a man's purse. Inside, he had $225,000 in cash according to Ali friend Reggie Barrett, who said in an interview years later that he had witnessed the encounter. Soon after, Ali visited King's home in Cleveland, where there was yet more cash on hand, much of it lying loose in dresser drawers.

"I had tons of cash," King said, recalling Ali's first visit to his home. "So I threw open the drawer."

As Ali's eyes bugged wide at the sight of so much green, King asked the boxer if he was familiar with the claw machines commonly found in bars and arcades, the ones that allow players one chance to drop a metal claw into a pile of toys and grab a prize. King told Ali he could reach in the drawer one time — only one time, with only one hand, and with his fingers pointed down, like the claw — and he could keep as much cash as he cleanly grasped and carried away.

Ali rolled up his sleeve and stretched his fingers wide.

"All he could pick up, he could keep," King said with a smile. "You know what I mean? You couldn't scoop like that, you had to pick it up, bring it out . . . But knowing the psychological elements of humanism . . . Greed! You know what I mean? You gonna get too much in your hand, it's gonna fall, plop, plop, plop, plop, plop." King laughed at the memory. If Ali had taken his time, he could have looked carefully in the drawer, seen where the big wads of bills in large denominations were sitting, and plucked them out cleanly. But King assumed, correctly, that the boxer would get excited, rush, and fumble. Ali played the game every time he visited King in those early years of their relationship, and every time the boxer tried it, he rushed and fumbled. "One time, he got thirty-five thousand, and a couple times twenty-five thousand," King said, laughing harder and harder as the story went on. "You know what I mean? But if he would've stopped, reconnoitered, looked around for the ten thousand (dollar bundles), he could've got much more. But the excitement of getting all that . . . That's what the thrill was for me. He would wind up trying to grab so much, and he would lose it all. That teaches you a lesson. Be patient, be objective, and go out there and get it all. Get as much as you can. So it was a thrill for me."

The thrill for King was that he had spotted vulnerability in Ali. Greed is a kind of fear, and fear is a kind of weakness, and King was a master at exploiting weakness.

"Ali, he wanted it all," King said. "You go meet five or six girls or something, or two girls. Okay, you get one, I get one. No! Ali wanted 'em both. He had an insatiable appetite. You couldn't take that away from him."

By flashing cash, King did more than use greed to his advantage. He also sent the message to the black men with whom he did business that he understood them, understood that black success looked different from white success in 1970s America, understood that the black man still suspected that if he struck it rich or got too much power the white man would take it all away. But cash! Cash was difficult to take away! Cash was something a man could hold in his hand, count, stash, hide, or spend, no permission required.

"Cash is king and King is cash," he said. "This is what it's always been. Dealing with human nature. And dealing with those who are the downtrodden, the underprivileged, people who have been denied, those who are not accustomed to being able to deal with me, you've got an opportunity, because white and black alike, that green is always there, it stands out. People that think you're gonna have some type of trickeration . . . you give 'em a check, you got to wait till they cash it . . . But if you give 'em cash, it's instant, they can't stop payment on that. You know what I mean? They can give you a check for two million, you know what I mean, before you get to the bank they stop payment on it. Then they got nothing to show for what they did. If they give you cash, they can't get that back."

King related to black boxers in ways white promoters could not. He reminded fighters that he shared their plight. Like them, he'd been cheated and mistreated by a white power structure designed to subjugate black men. Yet in spite of racism, in spite of prison, in spite of a system built to knock him down and hold him back, he'd clawed his way to wealth and fame, as he reminded them again and again, not only with his black-is-beautiful sermonettes but also with his ostentatious displays of wealth.

"They could not get another black to fight for them," King said, referring to the fighters who hired him as their promoter. "They came to me because I would become this savior, that I would be able to understand and tolerate the indiscretions and disloyalty, because I resonate from slavery . . . I come and deal with them as a human being. Black success was unacceptable . . . That's why they had to knock down Muhammad Ali, that's why they had to knock down me."

But for all his intelligence, for all his powers of persuasion, and for all his cash, Don King still needed the blessings of Elijah Muhammad to do business with Ali, so he made an appointment to see the Messenger in Chicago. Ali remained formally divorced from the Nation of Islam, but the boxer continued to practice Islam and continued to believe Elijah Muhammad to be Allah's true prophet. During their meeting, Elijah Muhammad tried to convince Don King to join the Nation of Islam. King, as he recalled years later in an interview, was open to the idea. He expressed enthusiasm for Elijah Muhammad's brand of Islam and said he would have considered joining if not for one big problem. "I would have become a Muslim," he said, "but I just couldn't give up pork." In fact, King said, he tried to convince Elijah Muhammad to drop the Nation of Islam's ban on pork.

Although Elijah rejected that suggestion, King was not discouraged. He went on to talk about the importance of putting black men in positions of power surrounding Muhammad Ali. Why continue to let Bob Arum promote the champ's fights, King asked, when a black man was ready to step in and do it better?

That was the right approach. The Messenger gave King his blessing.

After his fight with Ali, Joe Frazier spent three weeks in the hospital recovering from dangerously high blood pressure and a bruised kidney. After that, he took a ten-month break from boxing, scored an easy victory over Terry Daniels, and then took a four-month rest. He chose to fight infrequently in part because he didn't want to risk losing the championship but also because of the damage Ali had inflicted. His sparring partners and corner men could see that Frazier had been diminished, that he lacked some indescribable part of himself. Before facing Ali, hunger and fury had made Joe Frazier the meanest fighter on earth, not size or strength. But now some of that hunger and fury was gone — smashed, destroyed, or merely dissipated with the satisfaction of his victory — and it wasn't clear if or when he would get it back.

On January 22, 1973, in Kingston, Jamaica, Frazier fought George Foreman, winner of the gold medal in the heavyweight division at the 1968 Olympics. Foreman was the first high-ranking contender Frazier had battled since Ali. He was also perhaps the worst opponent Frazier could have selected. Foreman had no boxing style. He had no assortment of punches. He had no speed. He had nothing but power, and he had a ton of it. Foreman was a brooding, reclusive former street hooligan with a punch that could coldcock a rhinoceros. He was Sonny Liston without the personality. Foreman had fought thirty-seven men as a professional and beaten them all, thirty-four by knockout. Joe Frazier liked to work the body and stay close to his opponents, a prospect that excited Foreman. "He just comes on in," Foreman said, "and I'll know where to find him."

The press liked to make Foreman out to be a sociopath, mostly because he hit so hard. In truth, he was a pleasantly simple man. When he won gold at the 1968 Olympics, he became famous for waving a small American flag in the ring after his gold-medal-winning match, a gesture that some saw as a rebuttal of black militancy. But Foreman, who called himself "The Fighting Corpsman" for his time in President Lyndon Johnson's poverty-fighting Job Corps program, claimed he wasn't trying to be political. "I just pulled out the flag," he said. "People saw it and clapped, so I waved it. I didn't look at it as protest or anti-protest. It was just the way I felt at the moment. I'm not interested in politics or movements. I spend so much time trying to be a good fighter I can hardly be an intellectual." When asked how he felt about earning $375,000 for taking on Frazier, he said, "That's real nice. But money is the least of things. It comes and goes. Pride and responsibility and association with friends, those stay. There's more at stake in any sport than just money. Fighting just for money, you start getting all knocked down and bloodied up. I don't want to represent the sport like that."

George Foreman did not get knocked down and bloodied up against Frazier. It was Frazier who took the beating. Foreman humiliated the champion, knocking him down six times in little more than four and a half minutes.

"I got hit and hit and hit," Frazier said, summarizing more deftly than he had fought. Frazier's only accomplishment, really, was getting up as often as he did.

Don King attended the fight as a guest of Joe Frazier's, but when Foreman began to scatter Frazier around the ring, King eased his way toward Foreman's corner, and by the time the fight was over, there was King, in the ring, embracing the winner. When Foreman left the arena in a limousine, King was sitting next to him. Over the years, King would tell the story many times as a testament to his business skills if not his loyalty. "I came with the champion," he said, "and I left with the champion!"

While King gloated, Ali mourned. *Ali* was supposed to beat Frazier. *Ali* was supposed to be the next heavyweight champion. Now, his path to redemption had been complicated. He would need to beat both Frazier and Foreman to prove he was truly the greatest. Still, he managed to find something positive to say: if Frazier could be so easily defeated, it proved that Frazier's victory over Ali had been a fluke, possibly even an error by the judges. Beating Joe would be easy next time. And Foreman would be no match for him, either.

"I'm still greater than boxing," Ali said. "I am the best."

But before he could prove himself against Frazier or Foreman, Ali had another bout scheduled, on March 31, 1973, at the San Diego Sports Arena, with a man who seemed to pose little threat, a former Joe Frazier sparring partner with decent power and solid but unspectacular skills. His name was Ken Norton.

Bundini Brown compared boxing to sex. "You got to get the hard-on," Bundini said, "and then you got to keep it. You want to be careful not to lose the hard-on, and cautious not to come."

But Ali had no hard-on for Norton. He wanted Joe Frazier. He wanted George Foreman. But Norton? Norton's most recent fight had been in front of a crowd of seven hundred and had paid only three hundred dollars. Norton didn't belong in the same ring as Ali. That's what Howard Cosell said, that's what the bookmakers in Vegas said in making Ali a five-to-one favorite, and that's what Ali believed. Norton was a quickie, an easy paycheck. Promoters tried to pitch the fight as a battle between a draft dodger and an ex-Marine, but even that wasn't enough to generate excitement.

America had mellowed. The war in Vietnam slogged on, along with the protest movement. Bobby Seale, one of the founders of the Black Panthers, toned down his radicalism and announced he would run for mayor of Oakland. Richard Nixon won reelection in a landslide. Even Elijah Muhammad quit calling whites "blue-eyed devils" and began stressing the importance of self-improvement within the black community. Radical groups continued to protest. During one eighteen-month period in 1971 and 1972, the FBI reported more than 2,500 bombings in the United States, an average of nearly five a day. But the bombings seldom took lives, and their sheer number led to a lack of interest. As the writer Bryan Burrough put it, "bombs basically functioned as exploding press releases."

Ali, meanwhile, had little to say about race and politics, except to point out that he hadn't voted in the presidential election — and, in fact, that he had never voted in any election, local or national. Norton, meanwhile, refused to criticize Ali for his antiwar stance, saying he respected the man for standing up for his beliefs. The buildup to Norton v. Ali had all the drama of a church bingo contest. Interest was so soft that promoters decided to show the bout live on ABC rather than on closed circuit, marking the first time in six years than an Ali fight would be shown live on network television.

The week of the fight, Ali sprained an ankle while attempting to revolutionize the game of golf. Ali was not a golfer, but he made the contention that the game would be more amusing and the ball would go a lot farther if people hit the ball on the run rather than standing over the tee and wiggling their rear ends. In offering a demonstration of his technique, Ali badly twisted his ankle. He quit running for the rest of the week, and the ankle remained tender the day of the fight. Ali didn't think it would be a problem. He figured he could beat Norton on one leg.

The night before the fight, Ali attended a party. Two hours before the fight, he was in bed with two hookers. They took the mirror off the dresser and propped it next to the bed so they could watch themselves. Ali used Reggie Barrett's room at the LeBaron Hotel, hoping to escape Belinda's attention. After an hour had passed, Barrett knocked on the door, telling Ali the fight started soon.

"Oh, shit!" Ali said. "I gotta take a shower."

Norton was tall and broad, all muscle and bone, with shoulders spreading from his thick neck like redwood branches. He was in the finest shape of his life, exploding with confidence, a stunning specimen. He may not have been prettier than Ali, but he was certainly in better shape. "That night, I could have beaten Godzilla," he said. "I was that sure of myself. And in that kind of shape, I could have fought fifty rounds, easy."

Norton had another edge: He had the savvy trainer Eddie Futch in his corner. While most boxing experts considered Norton no match for Ali, Futch believed that Ali had fundamental flaws in his boxing style and that Norton's style would expose those defects. Trainers will tell you until your ears bleed that boxing isn't merely a clash of men; it's also a clash of styles, as Foreman versus Frazier had recently reminded people. Futch knew Ali wasn't as fast as he used to be. He knew that Ali relied almost exclusively on the jab, not bothering to grind down his opponents with body blows. He knew Ali didn't keep his hands up after he punched. He knew Ali backed away from blows instead of ducking or blocking them. Futch told Norton to match Ali jab for jab. When Norton jabbed, the trainer predicted, Ali would backpedal. When Ali backpedaled, Futch said, Norton would jab him into the ropes, batter his ribs until his kidneys hurt, and then, finally, when Ali got tired, take off his head.

On the night of the fight, Ali looked like a man entirely at ease as he walked through the arena to the ring. Bundini Brown and Angelo Dundee accompanied him, as did Don King, dressed like an astronaut pimp in a shiny silver tuxedo and matching bowtie. Ali stepped slowly and smoothly through the ropes, his body wrapped in a bejeweled robe with purple satin lining that had been a gift from Elvis Presley. The robe bore the words "PEOPLE'S CHOICE" in rhinestones across the back. When he took it off, a layer of flab jiggled from Ali's chest and belly. He weighed 221 pounds.

At the bell, Norton followed instructions. He jabbed and stepped forward as Ali shifted into reverse, just as Futch had predicted. Norton landed roughly two jabs for every one of Ali's in the opening rounds. In the third round, Ali showed flashes of his former self. He danced around the ring instead of backing up, kept his distance, flicked jabs, and skittered out of range, raising the hopes of fans who had come to see the dazzling fighter who had whupped Sonny Liston and outclassed Cleveland Williams. But it proved only a flash. In the fourth, Ali not only quit moving; he quit jabbing too, and he looked like he was already fatiguing.

From ringside, Howard Cosell, broadcasting the fight for ABC, carped about Ali's desultory performance. "Is he now but a relic of the fighter he was?" Cosell asked. TV viewers all over the country were asking the same. Had Ali lost his edge? Was this the best he could do? Or was he merely coasting, assuming he could flick the switch, turn on the Greatness, and finish off Norton anytime he liked? Not content to ask the question rhetorically, Cosell turned to Ali's corner and shouted at Angelo Dundee during his broadcast.

Cosell spoke in a Brooklyn accent, with vowels that got trapped in the back of his nose and consonants that exploded from his mouth with unexpected force and speed. It was a voice that reminded listeners of a trumpet in the hands of a non-trumpeter. Like Ali, Cosell was his own greatest admirer, and, like Ali, he could get on people's nerves. Including Angelo Dundee's — *right now!*

"Angie!" he said. "What's wrong with your fighter?"

Dundee yelled at Cosell, saying Ali was fine. Just watch, the trainer said, Norton would tire any minute now, and Ali would take charge.

But Norton didn't tire, and Ali didn't take charge. In the sixth round, Ali injured the second knuckle on his right hand. As the eighth round began, he was scarcely using his right hand and scarcely dancing. Most unusual of all, he wasn't talking. He wasn't taunting Norton. It was then Cosell noticed that Ali seemed to be moving his mouth in an odd way, as if something were wrong with his jaw. Cosell turned again to Ali's corner, this time addressing Dr. Ferdie Pacheco live on the air: Was something wrong with Ali's mouth?

"No," Pacheco said, loud enough for audiences watching on TV to hear. "I think he's loosened a tooth, but there's no fracture, there's no broken anything, there's nothing, you know . . . There's not much wrong with him right now, he's fighting pretty good, Howard."

Cosell hadn't asked if anything was broken. In his nervous lie, Pacheco had revealed the truth: Norton had broken Ali's jaw, perhaps as early as the first round.

Norton kept jabbing, forcing Ali into the ropes. At one point, when Ali grabbed Norton around the neck and tried to hold him, Norton bear-hugged Ali, hoisted him off the ground, and quickly dropped him again, a gesture that seemed to say: *I'm stronger than you! I'm younger than you! I'm beating you!*

In the eleventh round, Norton wobbled Ali. Chairs scraped the floor. The audience got up, stomped their feet, clapped, screamed. In the twelfth and final round, Norton knocked Ali around with no evident fear of reprisal. Blood poured from Ali's mouth.

When the bell rang to end the fight, Ali went to his corner. He rubbed his lopsided jaw solemnly, as if it were a math problem he couldn't solve. He combed his hair, same as he always did after a fight, because even after combat — and even after combat in which he had fared poorly — he wanted to look good for the cameras.

The ring announcer declared Norton the winner. Ali congratulated his opponent and departed in silence.

After the fight, Ali went to Clairemont General Hospital where he underwent surgery on his jaw. Belinda went to the hospital too, but not to visit her husband. She traveled by police ambulance because she had become hysterical after the fight. Belinda was so angry — angry about her husband's performance in the ring, about the prostitutes, about things buried deep in the intimate folds of marriage that she declined to discuss even decades later — that when San Diego police officers approached and tried to calm her down, she attacked them.

"I put three cops in the hospital," she recalled proudly. "Bundini said, 'We should've put *her* in the ring!'"

In the chaos after the fight, a reporter asked Dundee if he thought this loss would mark the end of Ali's career.

"I think you're a jerk," Dundee said.

It was not a stupid question. Ali was thirty-one, and longevity was neither the rule nor a blessing for boxers. Rocky Marciano had retired at thirty-two; Joe Louis, at least initially, at thirty-four. Ali had been fighting since age twelve with a style that depended on speed. He still possessed enough speed to remain competitive with the world's finest heavyweights, but it was not enough speed to avoid getting hit and getting hurt. Now, he had lost twice in twelve tries. More troublingly, some of the men in his corner believed that he had never fully recovered from the damage inflicted on him in his fifteen-round clash with Frazier in 1971.

Then there was the matter of the boxer's jaw. Pacheco said a broken jaw was as serious for a boxer as a broken hand for a pianist. The analogy wasn't exactly right. A pianist needs his hands to perform precision work; a boxer needs his jaw to do the blunt work of absorbing punishment, like a car needs a bumper. Still, Pacheco was right about the seriousness of the injury. Ali had suffered a badly swollen jaw against Frazier, and now the same jaw had been broken. It was not unreasonable to think that such an injury might compel a fighter to consider retirement.

Perhaps, as the newspaper columnist Lee Winfrey wrote, Ali was losing his relevance as well as his boxing skills. This was the Age of Nixon, not the Age of Aquarius, Winfrey wrote. The loudmouthed fighter had been entertaining when he had come along, a breath of vitality for a dull, thuggish sport. He really had shaken up the world. He had made people think, made them angry, made them reimagine what a young black athlete could say and do. But that was then. Now, in Winfrey's view, Ali was a boxer past his prime, a relic of the 1960s. "He's no different from Chubby Checker," the columnist wrote. "People don't want to dance to his music anymore."

PART III

37

A Fight to the Finish

Ali parked his gray Rolls-Royce a few feet from the entrance of the Roosevelt Hotel in New York and told one of his pals to keep an eye on the car so he didn't get a ticket. He stepped out of the car, into the warm sun, and then into the hotel, where he and Ken Norton were to hold a joint press conference announcing their intention to fight again September 10 at the Forum in Inglewood, California. But instead of marching to the front of the room where reporters and photographers had assembled for the press conference, Ali slipped into a seat in the back and waited for reporters to come to him. Of course, they did.

For Ali, it was an attempt to show humility. It was such a good acting job, in fact, that one reporter said Ali should have been given the Academy Award that Marlon Brando had recently turned down for *The Godfather*.

"Best thing ever happened to me," the new, supposedly unpretentious Ali said, referring to the beating Norton had given him.

He still had some of the wires in his mouth from surgery on the broken jaw. Doctors said he would be fine, but Ali claimed that losing to Norton and suffering a severe injury had forced him to reevaluate his life, to slow down, take his phone off the hook, and spend more time with his children.

"I needed that," Ali said, rubbing his jaw and looking at Norton. "Thank you very much."

Ali, wearing a short-sleeved dress shirt, vowed that he would be less arrogant from now on. He would work harder to prepare for the next fight. If he lost again to Norton, he said, no one would care if he fought Frazier or

Foreman. Norton would be next in line for a shot at the championship, and Ali would be an afterthought.

"Losing that fight was just what I needed," he said. "It made me humble. I'm going into the woods and train at my camp in Deer Lake, Pennsylvania, then I'm going to arrive in Los Angeles a few days before the fight and stay at a private home, no more hotels, no more of that stuff. That's all over. No more fooling around."

If anything good resulted from his broken jaw, it was this: Ali went four and a half months without getting punched in the head. Until mid-August, he worked himself into shape without sparring. Only then, with the fight three weeks out, did Ali let his sparring partners swing away. Afterward, he shared the good news with reporters: the jaw was fine. In another encouraging sign, he said, he had slimmed down to 211 pounds, 10 pounds fewer than he had weighed for the previous fight.

The older he got, the more difficult it became to focus like a champ. At Deer Lake, Ali woke every morning at 4:30 and rang an eight-hundred-pound church bell that he had purchased from a local antiques dealer, sending a signal to everyone in camp that he was up early and hard at work. Ali loaded the place with antiques. He wanted the camp to feel rugged. When Belinda visited, they would sit in an old wooden surrey and scan the skies for the mothership Elijah Muhammad talked about in his sermons.

Ali hired a man to haul boulders to the property, and Ali's father painted the names of great former fighters on the stones, the first two going to Joe Louis and Rocky Marciano.

There was nothing remotely fancy about the place. There were metal folding chairs, wooden rocking chairs, plywood tables, and plain wood floors. The gym's walls were decorated with photos and magazine covers depicting Ali. There were lots of mirrors, too. When Ali wasn't training, the log-cabin dining hall was the center of activity, the place where everyone gathered around long tables to eat, talk, and tell jokes. The kitchen had two stoves, a double sink, two refrigerators, a chopping table, and two coffee machines. On the wall opposite the door, Ali's father painted a big sign that read:

Rules of My KYTCHEN
   1. PLEASE TO KEEP OUTE except on express permission of cooke

2. COOKE shall designate pot scourers pan polishers peelers scrapers and COOKE has supreme AUTHORITY AT ALL TIMES.

3. NO REMARKS AT ALL WILL BE TOLORATED concerning the blackening of toast the weakness of soupe or the strength of the garlic stewe.

4. What goes in stews & soups is NOBODY'S dam business.

5. If you MUST sticke your finger in something stick it in the garbage disposal.

6. DON'T CRITICIZE the coffee you may be olde and weak yourself someday.

7. ANYONE bringinge guests in for dinner without PRIOR NOTICE will be awarded thwacks on skull with a sharpe object.

8. PLEASE WAITE Rome wasn't burnt in a day and it takes awhile to burne the ROASTE.

9. IF YOU MUST pinche somethinge in this KITCHYN PINCHIE the COOKE!

10. this is my kitchen if you don't belive it START SOMETHING.

The compound had no gate. Most of the doors had no locks. Visitors came and went as they pleased. Ali was entirely accessible. "The camp was like a revolving door of celebrities and entertainers, people who wanted to be boxers, people who wanted to be somebody," recalled Bob Goodman, the boxing publicist. That's how Ali liked it. When he made new friends, he would invite them to come work at the camp. When a fresh face arrived, the regulars would ask: "What's *he* do?" Ali didn't care. He assumed his new employees would make themselves useful or get bored and leave.

"Every guy that shakes hands with Muhammad, they're his manager, they're his agent . . . they're the ones that can do everything for you," an exasperated Angelo Dundee said.

At one point, Ali estimated that in the six-week buildup to a typical fight, he paid members of his entourage about $200,000, including $50,000 for Dundee, $5,000 for Rahaman, $10,000 for Gene Kilroy, and on and on. Kilroy was one of the few with a clear role. He arranged the travel. When the phone rang, Kilroy answered and decided which callers were worthy of Ali's time. When Marlon Brando or Ted Kennedy wanted to meet the champ, Kilroy made it happen. When Ali saw a TV news report saying that a Jewish old-folks' home was closing its doors because it couldn't make the rent, Kilroy made the phone calls, arranged for a quiet visit from Ali, and took care of getting the old folks the money they needed. Pat Patterson, a former Chicago police officer, handled security. Walter "Blood" Youngblood, who later changed his name to Wali Muhammad, also provided security. Lloyd Wells, a former journalist, arranged for women to visit the camp, for the pleasure of Ali and anyone else seeking casual sex. C. B. Atkins served as a driver and advisor. Lana Shabazz cooked, serving up lamb shanks, steaks, and bean pies with heaping bowls of ice cream for dessert. Bundini ate, drank, motivated, and entertained. Howard Bingham and Lowell Riley snapped pictures. Ralph Thornton parked cars and swept floors. Booker Johnson helped in the kitchen. Luis Sarria, the masseuse, doubled as Ali's exercise guru, putting the fighter through hours of sit-ups and squats.

Belinda and the children visited Deer Lake but usually did not stay long. Ali's parents came around often. Rahaman was a mainstay; he was also Ali's best sparring partner. Angelo Dundee arrived only when fights were approaching and training got serious.

Conflict was inevitable, fistfights not uncommon. The only thing that held this motley bunch together was Ali, whose happiness was contagious. "These people are like a little town for Ali," Herbert Muhammad once said. "He is the sheriff, the judge, the mayor, and the treasurer." When bored, Ali would suggest a visit to a children's hospital or a stroll through a crowded hotel lobby where he knew he'd be recognized. Sometimes he would open a phonebook and call numbers at random to see how strangers would react to receiving a phone call from Muhammad Ali. When Kilroy's mother suffered a heart attack, Ali called the hospital, spoke to the nurses, and said he wanted Mrs. Kilroy to receive the best care possible. "They treated her like the Queen of Sheba," Kilroy recalled. And when Mrs. Kilroy recovered, Ali visited the hospital in Bucks County, Pennsylvania, to thank those who had cared for her.

"We all loved Ali," said Lowell Riley, the photographer who'd been hired by Herbert to take pictures for *Muhammad Speaks*. "We didn't have no grudges. I think all of us just wanted to be with Ali because he was who he was . . . We didn't even know how much we were going to get paid. After the fight, Herbert and Ali would sit down and you'd get a check. We didn't have no contracts."

Ali lost one of the more colorful characters in his circle. In the summer of 1973, Major Coxson and his wife were murdered, execution-style, in their New Jersey home. Rumors circulated that the Black Mafia of Philadelphia did it. Even without Coxson, the camp was a carnival, with reporters coming and going so quickly Ali never bothered to learn most of their names. Some of the men who called themselves managers or agents had tricks to make side money. One of them told reporters that interviews with Ali cost fifty dollars — and pocketed the cash, of course. Once, a member of the entourage introduced Ali to a black man wearing a Dodgers cap and seated in a wheelchair. The man, whose legs had been amputated, identified himself as Roy Campanella, the former Dodger, and said he was in desperate need of money. Everyone in the camp, including Ali, knew the man was not really Campanella.

Nevertheless, Ali pulled out a wad of cash and gave it to the man.

Later, Angelo asked Ali why — why give money to an obvious con artist?

Ali replied, "Ang, we got legs."

Despite the distractions at Deer Lake, Ali worked hard to prepare for Norton. Dundee pronounced his fighter in the best shape of his life.

Ali, no longer feigning humility, agreed: "I'm a sight for the world," he said.

He continued, "Norton don't stand a chance, because I will be dancin' all night long! Oh, man, I'm gonna have no fat, no fat at all, I'm at my dancin' weight. Come one, come all to the Muhammad Ali Dance Ball."

"You the boss with the hot sauce," Bundini shouted as Ali crossed the ring to meet Norton in the first round.

Norton came forward, right hand by his chin, left hand wagging out in front. Ali assumed the same stance, but with his hands noticeably lower than Norton's. Their left feet were inches apart as the first punches flew, a short left by Norton followed by a short right by Ali.

All around, there were shouts and sharp breaths.

Ali danced, as promised, and that was enough to excite the crowd at first. This was the Ali they had paid to see, even if no great punches had yet to land and no blood had yet to pour.

Norton acted as if Ali's blows weren't hurting him, that he would gladly take the jabs so long as he had the opportunity to retaliate, which he did.

In the fifth round, Ali slowed down by the slightest bit. He was still on his toes, still moving, but Norton advanced more easily. At the end of the round, Norton got inside and stayed there, driving punch after punch deep into Ali's gut.

"I own you!" Norton shouted at the round's end.

In the sixth, both men landed hard shots, and the skin under Norton's right eye began to puff. Norton's confidence seesawed. In the seventh, Norton knocked Ali around the ring with thunderous punches. He continued his assault in round eight, landing an uppercut that made Ali's eyes go wide in pain or shock. In the ninth, the men traded their biggest punches, cannon fire at short range. Television announcers shouted with excitement. The crowd hollered for more.

Going into the twelfth and final round, it was difficult to say which man had the edge. They were both exhausted, both damaged. Barring a knockout, the decision would be in the hands of the ringside judges.

Ali came out dancing again, no doubt trying to show off for the judges that he was still fresh, still strong, even if he wasn't. He threw the first good punches of the round, and he kept throwing. He poured over Kenny Norton, flooding him with blows, making it impossible for Norton to think or fight back. The twelfth round was a test of wills, and Ali won it. When the bell rang, he was so stoked with adrenaline — or perhaps so angry that he had failed to take command of the fight earlier — that he marched to his corner and threw an errant punch at Bundini Brown. Then Ali leaned on the turn-buckles, quietly waiting for the judges to determine his fate.

The announcement came quickly: Ali had won it in a split decision.

He didn't gloat. He didn't jump around the ring and declare himself "the Greatest." He smiled grimly and offered a confession.

"I'm tireder than usual," he said as he stood center ring. He paused and added, "because of my age." He was four months away from his thirty-second birthday.

Four and a half months after beating Norton, Ali got his second crack at Joe Frazier. With no championship on the line, and with Frazier having been battered by George Foreman, the fight lacked the drama of their first encounter. Even so, the winner of this contest would get a chance to face Foreman and win back the crown. Also, there was no question that Frazier lit a spark and brought out some of Ali's basest traits.

Ali had always taunted opponents. Interestingly, he had usually harassed his black opponents more than the white ones. With white opponents, he tended to joke. Sometimes he even praised them for their intelligence and toughness. Perhaps with the white opponents he didn't feel he needed to work as hard to sell tickets. But with his black opponents, he flashed real anger. He tried to dehumanize many of the black men he fought, just as white supremacists had long tried to do. Ali had branded Sonny Liston an ugly bear, Floyd Patterson a rabbit, and Ernie Terrell an Uncle Tom. Some said he did it out of insecurity — because he came from a relatively stable family and a relatively comfortable neighborhood, unlike some of his opponents who had risen from more humble circumstances. Such behavior was especially perverse given Ali's longtime dedication to the uplift of his race. Now, in anticipation of his second go-round with Frazier, Ali was at his worst. His attacks were meaner, more personal, and more scornful, suggesting that Ali, for once, may have felt genuinely threatened.

Ali had convinced himself that he'd really won the first fight with Frazier and that the judges had erred in their decision. In the run-up to the rematch, Ali worked to convince the press and boxing fans of the same. He also resurrected his old complaints about Frazier, calling Joe too ignorant and too ugly to be champion. In one interview after another, Ali referred to Frazier as stupid and undeserving of respect from black fans. While other opponents had managed to brush off or laugh at Ali's condemnations, Frazier couldn't. He was hurt, and it showed. Frazier went on the defensive, citing his credentials as a man of the people and reminding reporters that he'd always been good to Ali, had always liked Ali, had even tried to help Ali during his exile from boxing.

Ali seemed to make no distinction between a rival and an enemy, and no one would tell Ali to shut up. No one told him he was behaving immaturely. On January 24, 1974, with the fight four days away, Ali and Frazier met at a TV studio in New York, where they had agreed to sit with Howard Cosell, watch a replay of their first fight, and provide commentary on the action. They had promised in advance not to talk about their respective hospital visits. Ali was still sensitive about the damage Frazier had done to his jaw, and Frazier was still angry that Ali had been bragging that his hospitalization after the fight had been briefer than Frazier's.

For a long time during the broadcast, the men played nice. But as the replay of the fight neared its end and the camera flashed on Ali's ballooning jaw, Frazier couldn't resist a potshot: "That's what he went to the hospital for," Joe said.

Ali looked at Frazier. "I went to the hospital for ten minutes," he said. "You went for a month, now be quiet."

"I was resting," Frazier said.

"I wasn't even gonna bring up the hospital . . . that shows how dumb you are," Ali shot back. "See how ignorant the man is?"

Frazier shot out of his seat, removed his earpiece, and glared down at Ali.

"Boy, how you figure I'm ignorant?" he said.

A mischievous look lit up Ali's face.

"Sit down, Joe," he said. "Sit down, Joe."

Ali's brother walked on to the set, ready to fight Frazier himself.

"You want to get in on this, too?" Frazier asked Rahaman.

Ali rose and wrapped an arm around Frazier's neck. Frazier ducked, trying to get away. "Sit down, quick Joe," Ali said. Frazier lowered his shoulder into Ali's gut, and then both men were rolling on the floor as members of their respective entourages poured in and tried to break it up. No real punches flew and no one was hurt.

Frazier got up and walked out. Ali straightened his suit and returned to his seat alongside Cosell.

Later, Ali and Frazier were fined five thousand dollars each for conduct that was deemed demeaning to the sport of boxing.

Four days after their televised spat, the real fight took place at Madison Square Garden. In boxing, as in movies, sequels tend to disappoint. In Ali-Frazier II, both men were a little older, a little slower, but their second clash was far from a disappointment.

Ali didn't clown this time. He danced. He shuffled. He threw jabs and flurries and overwhelmed Frazier in the first round. He dominated again in the second round and had Frazier in trouble, but Frazier caught a break. With ten seconds to go, referee Tony Perez mistakenly thought the round had ended and interrupted a strong Ali finish.

As the fight wore on, Ali avoided toe-to-toe exchanges. He stayed off the ropes. He moved laterally, bouncing, using the entire ring, and he did not rely too heavily on the jab, mixing in plenty of hooks and combinations. When

Frazier stepped forward and tried to shovel punches to the abdomen, Ali threw his left arm around Frazier's neck and his right around Frazier's left arm. Another referee might have warned Ali to quit grabbing and deducted points for the failure to obey, but Perez let Ali get away with it for the most part.

Although the fight lacked some of the speed and terror of the first encounter, it was more than violent enough. Hundreds of big punches found their marks. After five rounds, Ali slowed a bit and Frazier's right eye swelled. Frazier landed strong left hooks, especially in the seventh and eighth rounds, but Ali responded time after time by clinching, thwarting the attacks. At the start of round nine, Frazier came out grinning, urging Ali to come and get him, and Ali responded. Even as his nose began to bleed and his face grew puffy, Ali enjoyed his best round of the night, scoring with speedy combinations as the crowd chanted his name.

Over the final three rounds, the fighters maintained a furious pace, trading big punches one after another, holding nothing back. The noise of the crowd at Madison Square Garden rose with the violence of the battle. It was close. The men had landed almost the same number of punches. Frazier's punches probably hit with more force, but Ali moved more stylishly and appeared to be busier. Frazier wasn't fast enough or strong enough to keep Ali on the ropes as he had three years prior.

Ali's nose bled and his eyes puffed. Frazier's face looked like an old aluminum garbage can, only roughly retaining its original shape. In the twelfth round, Ali shuffled and threw lightning-quick combinations, but Frazier answered with several shots to Ali's head. "You gotta stop him to win!" Dundee yelled as Ali chased Frazier around the ring and the clock wound down. Dundee may have been inciting his fighter, or he may have genuinely believed the scoring favored Frazier.

When the final bell rang, Ali went to his corner. A strange mix of men gathered there: Ali rocking from one foot to another, Bundini frowning, Kilroy patrolling the perimeter, Rahaman and Angelo Dundee looking as helpless and anxious as soon-to-be fathers in the lobby of a maternity ward. The ring filled with photographers, reporters, and fans pretending to belong. Everyone waited.

Red Smith of the *New York Times,* always tough on Ali, believed Frazier had won, that Joe's aggressive, thudding punches had done more damage than Ali's flicking, backpedaling jabs. It may have been true. It also may have been true, as Smith suggested, that Ali won rounds because he was Muhammad Ali, the biggest star in boxing's firmament. That doesn't necessarily mean the judges leaned his way because they liked him or wanted to see him win for the financial benefit of all those involved in the sport. The bias may have stemmed from something simpler and subtler. Ali simply commanded more attention than other fighters. He fought with so much flair that it was difficult to take one's eyes off him.

Whether the judges were biased or not, they came to a unanimous decision: Ali was the winner.

Later, in his dressing room, Ali licked an ice cream pop through puffed lips. He gave Frazier credit, saying, "He had me out on my feet twice." But Ali had survived, he added, "because I'm skillful enough to get out of trouble."

Ali had beaten Frazier because he had trained hard, fought cleverly, gotten away with holding Frazier, and displayed a stunning capacity for remaining upright while being pummeled by punches that would have floored almost any other human being.

Later, someone asked Ali how it felt to get punched by Frazier: "Take a stiff tree branch in your hand and hit it against the floor and you'll feel your hand go *boingggggg*," he said. "Well, getting tagged is the same kind of jar on your whole body, and you need at least ten or twenty seconds to make that go away. You get hit again before that, you got another *boingggggg* . . . You're just numb and you don't know where you're at. There's no pain, just that jarring feeling. But I automatically know what to do when that happens to me, sort of like a sprinkler system going off when a fire starts up. When I get stunned, I'm not really conscious of exactly where I'm at or what's happening, but I always tell myself that I'm to dance, run, tie my man up, or hold my head way down. I tell myself all that when I'm conscious, and when I get tagged, I automatically do it."

In the weeks and months after the fight, reporters and boxing fans argued angrily over whether the judges had made the right call, but those were just the usual paroxysms that follow close-fought sporting contests. Ali had won, and two facts were beyond dispute: first, that Ali and Frazier were great warriors despite their diminished skills, and, second, that there was already an outcry for the men to fight again.

38

Heart of Darkness

It was Valentine's Day, 1974, and George Foreman was walking in circles around the parking lot of a motel in Dublin, California, thirty-five miles east of San Francisco. Don King matched him step for step.

Foreman was heavyweight champion of the world, yet he wasn't happy. His marriage had collapsed. He lacked faith in his business managers. He viewed warily the celebrities and financial schemers who acted as if they were all his new best friends. He missed his mother, too. To Ali, the heavyweight championship had been a magic carpet ride, all thrills and fast turns and journeys to exotic destinations. To Foreman, it was the cause of sadness. It had created in him a "terrible emptiness." He said he was growing "meaner by the day."

Big George was preparing to fight Ken Norton, and the financial schemers were already pressing him to look ahead and make a deal to face Ali, saying it would be the biggest and best payday in the history of all sport. Foreman didn't know whom to trust. Now it was Don King's turn to woo the champion. As Foreman circled the parking lot, King kept pace, talking nonstop and waving sheets of white paper.

From one of the rooms in the motel, King's business partner, Hank Schwartz, looked out the window, watching the two big men make their loops. This was exactly why Schwartz had hired King to work for his closed-circuit broadcast company, Video Techniques; he needed someone who could relate to the fighters and gain their trust. But now he wondered: What was King saying? Why was it taking so long? What were the papers in King's hand?

Later, King recalled his conversation with Foreman.

"George," he said, "I know people been screwin' you. But I tell you this. I'm going to give you a chance to make $5 million. Don't lose this chance."

Foreman didn't believe it. He didn't believe Ali would fight him.

"I can deliver him," King said. "I have his word."

In fact, King had already met with Ali and Herbert Muhammad, urging Ali to reject a deal from Bob Arum that would have had Ali fighting a re-match with Jerry Quarry. King argued that Arum failed to understand Ali's blackness, failed to appreciate how much it would mean to people of color all over the world for Ali to regain the championship that America's racist white government had stolen from him. "This isn't just another fight," King had told Ali. "Freedom. Justice. That's what you'll be gainin' for your people by gettin' back the title." Then he got down to business, saying he would agree to pay Ali and Foreman each $5 million — an almost ridiculous sum, double what Ali and Frazier had been paid for their record-setting bout in 1971. To prove he was serious, King said he would give Ali an advance of $100,000 for signing a contract on February 15, another $100,000 on February 25, a $2.3 million letter of credit on March 15, and a letter of credit for the re-maining $2.5 million ninety days before the fight. If King missed any of the payment deadlines, Ali could keep the money he had already been paid and walk away from the fight. If King failed to reach a similar agreement with Foreman, the deal would be voided and Ali would keep the initial $100,000 payment.

That's how King found himself in front of Foreman's motel, pleading his case. King was telling the truth when he said Ali had agreed to the fight. King didn't know how he was going to get the money to pay the fighters — he and Schwartz didn't even have enough to make the first payment of $100,000 to each fighter. But that was a concern for another day.

"This is my promotion," King told Foreman. He stopped walking and Foreman did, too. King pointed to the skin on his arm. "And I'm black. Here is a chance, a big chance to show all blacks that black men together can suc-ceed like no one has ever believed we could."

King thrust papers in front of Foreman. Finally, after two hours of circling the parking lot, Foreman signed.

Later that day, King found Schwartz at the motel bar and showed him the papers. The pages were entirely blank except for Foreman's signatures. One was signed a third of the way down the page, one was signed in the middle, and one was signed at the bottom. King had told Foreman that he would fill in the blank pages with all the necessary details and show them to Foreman's lawyer. They would decide which one of Foreman's signatures to use based on the length of the contract.

In the end, King promised, Foreman would wind up getting $200,000 more than Ali. He had told Ali the opposite, that Ali would get $200,000 more than Foreman.

Ali versus Foreman would not, despite Don King's ministrations, deliver freedom and justice to black Americans. But it still qualified as a big deal. After three and a half years out of boxing, Ali had fought his way back, beaten the only two professional fighters who had ever beaten him, and earned the chance to compete for the world's heavyweight championship, the highest individual honor in all of sports, the title he had taken from Sonny Liston and the title the U.S. government had taken from him, the one he had dreamed of holding ever since he was Cassius Clay Jr., a skinny little boy training with a white police officer in the basement of the Columbia Auditorium in the segregated city of Louisville, Kentucky.

Ali was thirty-two. For years he had been calling himself "The Greatest of All Times," stretching the last two syllables for dramatic purposes and adding an "s" to the end as if to suggest that one eternity wasn't enough. "The Greatest of Aaaaaaall Tiiiiiimes!"

Now he would have another chance to prove it.

It had been twenty years since he'd first laced on a pair of boxing gloves under the eye of Joe Martin and ten years since he'd beaten Liston and announced his membership in the Nation of Islam. In the span of that decade, he had gone from hero to villain and back to hero again. He'd fought the law, fought racism, fought white authority figures who'd said a black athlete should ply his trade and keep his mouth shut. He had always been fighting something, even if, to the casual observer, he had seemed to be making it up as he went along, settling on his religious and political views as capriciously as a bird might settle on a telephone wire. He had a straightforward manner and an enthusiasm that made people want to believe in him no matter what he said. The artist Andy Warhol, who knew better than most about imagery and popular icons, had this to say after meeting Ali in the early 1970s: "He just repeats the same simplicity over and over and then it drums on people's ears. But he can say the things that he can because he's so good-looking."

By 1973, American and Vietnamese leaders had agreed to end their war. The civil rights struggle had moved largely out of the streets and into the courts and state and federal legislatures. Time after time, on issue after issue, Ali looked like a winner, like a man who had been on the right side of every important social question.

Even in his relationship with the Nation of Islam, Ali's instincts and good fortune served him well. When the boxer had first announced his commitment to the religious group, it had cost him popularity and endorsements. It had forced him to make a painful choice between his friend Malcolm X and his mentor Elijah Muhammad. It had made him an outcast from the mainstream civil rights movement. But, at the same time, the Nation had given him discipline and focus, it had given him codes by which to live, it had granted him a sense of purpose and community. "If it wasn't for the Nation of Islam," Gene Kilroy said, "he could have been cleaning bus stations in Louisville."

Even Ali's suspension from the Nation of Islam had worked out advantageously. The Nation was losing sway in American culture and beginning to unravel in the early 1970s. An investigation by the *New York Times* found that the organization was running out of money and that some members had turned to burglary, extortion, and robbery. To refill the organization's coffers, Muhammad Ali had been dispatched to Libya, where he met with Libyan president Muammar el-Qaddafi and Ugandan dictator Idi Amin to ask for loans and donations. In Uganda, Idi Amin wanted to fight Ali and offered him $500,000 in cash for the privilege. When Ali hesitated, Amin pointed a gun: "Now what do you say, Muhammad Ali?" Ali said it was time to get out of Uganda. Qaddafi was friendlier and came through with $3 million. But the Nation still had problems. Elijah Muhammad was suffering from senility, according to the *Times,* and had lost control of the organization. Working in his place, John Ali, the organization's national secretary, was seeking more funding from Middle East leaders and promising that the Nation of Islam would relax its strict antiwhite doctrines and move toward traditional Islam. As Muhammad Ali fought his way back to a shot at the heavyweight championship and his popularity rose, it was no coincidence that he had also stopped talking about spaceships that would arrive to wipe out the white race, stopped demanding that white America turn over vast amounts of real estate to create an independent black nation, stopped referring to white people as blue-eyed devils, stopped praising segregationists like George Wallace, and stopped appearing in his bowtie and fez at Muslim rallies. If not for the prayer rug in the trunk of his car and the occasional cries of "draft-dodging nigger" shouted in his direction, he was not so different from a lot of other American sports heroes. In the 1970s, it was not unusual to walk into the bedroom of a twelve-year-old suburban white boy and see posters on the walls depicting Ali along with Mark Spitz, Walt Frazier, Pete Rose, or Franco Harris.

Not everyone loved the new, 1970s edition of Muhammad Ali. "When Ali came back from exile," Jim Brown said, "he became the darling of America, which was good for America because it brought black and white together. But the Ali that America ended up loving was not the Ali I loved most. I didn't feel the same way about him anymore, because the warrior I loved was gone. In a way, he became part of the establishment." Brown was also troubled by Ali's use of the Uncle Tom label to slander Joe Frazier and other black fighters, describing it as "hitting a little bit below the belt."

Brown was right. Ali had moved toward the American mainstream, and the American mainstream had moved toward Ali. Proof came in 1974, two nights after Ali and Frazier had battled in Madison Square Garden, when Bob Dylan performed in the same arena. Ali had been denounced in the 1960s as unpatriotic, Dylan as a hippie folksinger. They'd each held their ground, but, still, there was sadness for some in seeing them now, seemingly hanging on in a decade to which neither truly belonged. The 1960s were over, and for all the noise and strong points protesters had made during that extraordinary decade, the sense remained that an opportunity to forge fundamental change had been missed, that the American government was as unresponsive and autocratic as ever, that America remained divided as ever by inequalities of race and class. The great rebellion had fallen short. The hippies were moving on, taking jobs, and moving to the suburbs. They would pull out their dirty old T-shirts and bell-bottomed jeans to attend Dylan concerts, but the next morning they would dress again in suits and ties and head to their office jobs downtown. Their strident songs and stances hadn't quite done the job.

In his fight with Foreman, Ali would get one more shot at relevance. He would find himself at the center of one of the biggest entertainment events the world had ever seen, one that would do more than perhaps anything to set his legacy not only as a fighter but as a heroic black man.

Now that Foreman and Ali had signed contracts, or blank pieces of paper that would eventually become contracts, Don King and Hank Schwartz had to come up with a quick $10 million and a venue for the fight. Two or three days after obtaining Foreman's signatures, Schwartz flew to London to meet a prospective investor, while King appealed to Jerry Perenchio, the man who had arranged the first Ali-Frazier fight. They both struck out. They had only days to make the initial payment — $100,000 to each fighter — and only months to find the remaining $10 million.

Scrambling, Schwartz identified a British investor willing to give him $200,000. That bought him a little time. King and Schwartz also received $500,000 from an organized crime figure from King's hometown of Cleveland, according to an FBI memo. But they still needed more. Then one day, Schwartz received a phone call from an American working as a financial advisor in Germany and Belgium. One of the American's clients was Joseph Mobutu, the murderous despot who ruled Zaire and who possessed ill-gotten billions in Swiss banks after years of blurring the lines between Zaire's treasury and his personal accounts. Mobutu was once referred to as "a walking bank vault in a leopard-skin hat," a man who had stolen his country's wealth and bankrupted its morality. Mobutu's financial advisor said his client would cover all the expenses of the fight, with $10 million up front, if Schwartz would agree to stage the event in Zaire.

Antarctica? Siberia? A boat in the middle of the Indian Ocean? Was there any place on Earth less likely than Zaire to hold a major sporting event?

Zaire was one of the poorest, most corrupt, most politically unstable, most inaccessible, most incomprehensible places on earth; it was the inspiration for Joseph Conrad's *Heart of Darkness,* a place where well into the twentieth century the vast majority of people still lived as hunters and gatherers in rural villages without electricity or running water and still communicated not by telephone or television or radio but by a network of jungle-covered rivers; a place where people who opposed or disappointed the nation's leader were routinely executed.

About all this and more, Schwartz said, "I didn't give a shit."

Schwartz, a Jewish, Brooklyn-born World War II veteran, didn't give a shit that he was dealing with a financial advisor representing a homicidal dictator. Schwartz and Don King didn't care that Zaire's largest sports stadium contained only 35,000 seats and had no parking lot. They didn't care that the fight would have to go on at 4 a.m. in Kinshasa in order to reach viewers in the United States at 10 p.m. Eastern Daylight Time, or that the contest might be washed out if Zaire's seasonal rains arrived a little earlier than usual. They didn't care that almost every piece of electronic broadcasting equipment would have to be flown in from the United States or Europe. They didn't care that Kinshasa, a city of 1.5 million, had only about five hundred decent hotel rooms. They didn't care that reporters or fight fans traveling to Zaire for the fight would make the journey, as Norman Mailer wrote, only "after inoculations for cholera, smallpox, typhoid, tetanus, hepatitis . . . not to speak of shots for yellow fever and pills for malaria." They also didn't care that a heavyweight championship fight in Zaire would strengthen Mobutu's hold on power and cause more suffering for 22 million Zairians, who were already suffering plenty.

Muhammad Ali didn't care, either. If Ali was concerned about the political conditions in Zaire or about the moral consequences of doing business in that country, he didn't say. He was Ali; the normal standards of conduct did not apply. His race, his religion, his defiance of his own government, and his refusal to fight in the Vietnam War had made him one of the world's most visible symbols of rebellion. In that way, fighting in Africa made sense, and that was enough to trump all other concerns. Don King called it "a symbolic black happening," and that vague glorification resonated with Ali. So did the $5 million, of course. But Ali the showman and public-relations wizard recognized immediately the powerful imagery of two American black men fighting for the heavyweight championship of the world in the heart of Africa, the continent from which their ancestors had been sold into slavery, a place where black Africans still struggled to shake free from colonialism. The winner of this fight would be the greatest black warrior in the world, the man who dared to face his demons, the man who conquered white supremacy, the true champion of disenfranchised, downtrodden dark-skinned people all the world over.

The deal was made. Ali would fight Foreman on September 25, 1974, in Kinshasa, Zaire.

Ali had cause to be at least dimly aware of Zaire's recent history. In 1963, after the assassination of John F. Kennedy, Malcolm X had infuriated Elijah Muhammad by criticizing Kennedy and suggesting the president had deserved to die. Malcolm's comment about "chickens coming home to roost" received most of the attention at the time, but in the rest of his remarks, Malcolm listed the crimes for which Kennedy and his administration bore responsibility, and those crimes included the murder of Patrice Lumumba, the first black prime minister of Zaire (then known as the Republic of the Congo).

Zaire's troubles, of course, began long before Kennedy. For more than a century, the central African nation was at the heart of some of the darkest scandals, dirtiest swindles, and deadliest double-dealings the world had ever seen. The nation, roughly the size of Western Europe, had wondrous riches. It had gold. It had diamonds. It had cobalt and copper, tin and tantalum. In the nineteenth century, Belgium's King Leopold II built his personal fortune and strengthened Belgium's economy by exporting vast resources from the Congo. Leopold, without ever visiting the place, treated the Congo as if it were his personal colony. He used forced labor to remove the nation's minerals, and when the labor couldn't be forced, it was punished. Backs were carved open with whips, hands chopped off with machetes, bodies sliced through with bayonets and dumped in rivers. In *Heart of Darkness,* Conrad drew on figures from this era to create Mr. Kurtz, who placed on fence posts the severed heads of the Africans he'd disciplined while working to extract ivory, rubber, and more from the Congo. In 1908, the Congo became a formal colony of Belgium. It gained its independence in 1960, as the Republic of the Congo, and then became the Democratic Republic of the Congo. In 1965, at the age of thirty-five, Joseph-Désiré Mobutu assumed the presidency, with backing from the United States. In 1971, he changed his country's name to Zaire (pronounced to rhyme with High-ear) and then changed his own name to Mobutu Sese Seko Kuku Ngbendu Wa Za Banga, which meant "the all-powerful warrior who because of his endurance and inflexible will to win will go from conquest to conquest leaving fire in his wake." To show his humility, Mobutu banished all titles such as "Excellency" and "President." It was in that same spirit of modesty and egalitarianism that Mobutu banned neckties in Zaire, a move that would score him points with more than a few sportswriters in 1974.

Mobutu understood the power of money. Money allowed him to buy fighter jets for his nation's military, which gave him the power he needed to assure his position in office, which gave him the ability to make more money, which permitted him to send his children to school in Belgium and to own extravagant homes in Brussels and Paris. Money would compel the great Muhammad Ali to come to Zaire, and with Muhammad Ali would come cameras. Muhammad Ali was not going to solve all of Zaire's problems. He was not going to catapult the country into the twentieth century and end hundreds of years of suffering. But his presence would boost the reputation of Mobutu, and it would show the world that at least some degree of order had been delivered to what had long been one of the most chaotic and dangerous nations on Earth.

39

Fighter's Heaven

Ali vowed that his fight with George Foreman, win or lose, would be his last.

"One more and I'll be finished," he said.

Unless he lost. In which case, he said, he might fight one more time. Or a few more times . . . until he could get another crack at Foreman.

But he wasn't planning to lose. One more fight, a victory, and he would retire as champion.

In March 1974, Ali went on a tour of the Middle East, one organized by Herbert Muhammad to solicit funds from Arab leaders to prop up the Nation of Islam. Ali returned from the Middle East in time to travel to Caracas, Venezuela, where he watched George Foreman knock out Ken Norton in less than two rounds. With that, Foreman had won his last three championship fights in a total of eleven minutes and thirty-five seconds. He had taken two good fighters, Frazier and Norton, and made them look like kittens. It wasn't that Foreman outboxed his opponents. He merely flattened them the way a wrecking ball flattened an old house, with massive blows that made resistance futile. After decimating Norton, Foreman huffed and stomped around the ring. Looking up from ringside, Ali went to work taunting the champ and promoting their fight in Zaire. "If you behave like that," Ali shouted, "my African friends will put you in the pot."

When that quote appeared in the *New York Times,* it prompted a phone call from an aide to Mobutu Sese Seko. Mobutu's aide said his boss wished to remind Ali that Zaire was sponsoring the Ali-Foreman fight to present itself to the world as a modern and sophisticated nation. It would help, he said, if Ali would not talk about boiling George Foreman or anyone else in pots. Mobuto didn't resort to such crude methods of punishment.

Ali's managers promised it wouldn't happen again.

In July, Foreman held a press conference to announce that he would train in Pleasanton, California, for his fight against Ali. The taciturn champion announced that this press conference would be his last until the time of the fight. He had work to do, and he didn't need reporters getting in the way. Foreman was a man of few syllables. When asked to predict how he would fare against the "aging Ali," as one of the wire services called the challenger, Foreman refused to take the bait. He had won all forty of his professional fights, including thirty-seven by knockout. He saw no need for bluster. "I'll be trying to get him in every round," he said.

Asked about his strategy, Foreman said, "I'll just try to beat him."

Told that Ali planned to retire after the fight, Foreman said, "I think he should. He's been hit a lot."

Ali began training in July, same as Foreman, but with greater fanfare. He organized a picnic and invited reporters to his camp in Deer Lake, Pennsylvania, and told them they were welcome to come around as often as they liked. He was always happy to talk. In explaining why he was so confident of victory, Ali performed an imitation of Foreman, lumbering across the ring and punching in slow motion before falling on his back when struck. Referring to Zaire, Ali said, "There's gonna be a rumble in the jungle."

As the Rumble in the Jungle approached, the business-minded men around Ali discovered riches to be mined in Africa. John Ali, the national secretary of the Nation of Islam, traveled to Gabon and promised President Omar Bongo that, for a price, Ali would stop in Gabon and conduct a boxing exhibition on his way to Zaire. Something went wrong, though, and John Ali wound up in a Gabonese prison. Muhammad Ali and Herbert Muhammad called in favors to win his release.

Don King had a more sophisticated money-making plan. He and Hank Schwartz formed a company called Festival in Zaire, Inc., to function as a travel agency that would bring fans from America and Europe to Africa for the fight, providing up to seven thousand spectators with plane tickets, deluxe hotel accommodations, and tickets for the big event. For King, logistical problems would be solved at a later date. Or not. What mattered was that he had a hot item on his hands — one of the biggest international sporting events the world had ever seen — and there was only one way for Americans and Europeans to see it in person: through Festivals in Zaire, Inc., with prices starting at $2,100 — the equivalent of about $10,000 today. The government of Zaire had taken control of every available hotel room and dormitory in Kinshasa and assigned them to Don King and Hank Schwartz. If all the hotel rooms and dormitories sold out, some guests would be housed in ships docked hundreds of miles away, and then flown or driven to Kinshasa in time for the fight. That was the plan, at least for the time being.

In justifying the high price and the unusual lodging options, Schwartz told the *New York Times* that "this event is like no other, and rules don't apply."

He was certainly right about that. But some rules did apply, including this one: it's not easy to sell thousands of American sports fans on a trip that costs thousands of dollars, requires inoculation for multiple diseases, necessitates about fifty hours and ten thousand miles of travel, and ends, possibly, with lodging on a ship off the coast of Africa hundreds of miles from the sporting event said fans were paying to see. It was a lot to ask, especially for a fight that could end in a minute or less if George Foreman's recent performances offered any precedent.

To begin his marketing campaign, King hired four beautiful young black women to serve as his ambassadors. The women would wear bikinis and boxing gloves, and they would appear at promotional events. They would pose for pamphlets and brochures. If potential customers wanted more information on the travel packages, one or two of the girls might be dispatched to present a slideshow with pictures of Kinshasa's modern buildings and finest stores and restaurants. To find the women, King advertised on a soul-music station in Los Angeles, inviting women to attend open auditions at the Century Plaza Hotel. More than 250 applicants showed up, most of them clad in bikinis. "How did we pick the women?" asked Bill Caplan, who was Foreman's public-relations manager and served as one of the judges. He paused as if he weren't sure the question really required an answer. "Looks! They didn't have to tell us they wanted world peace and the end of hunger in America. All that mattered was looks!"

While King and Schwartz worked to sell the fight to Americans, Mobutu

prepared Zaire for what was expected to be the biggest spectacle in the nation's history. Workers began rebuilding Kinshasa's soccer stadium, qua-
drupling its capacity to 120,000, and adding a half-mile-wide parking lot.
Mobuto ordered a fleet of buses so that thousands of Zairians could travel
from around the country to see Ali v. Foreman. The government announced
that the fight would come at the end of a three-day festival featuring black
American entertainers such as James Brown and B. B. King.

Ali paid no attention to business matters, as usual. He never expressed
interest in seeing the books or understanding the finances involved in this or
any of his fights. He trusted those things to Herbert Muhammad. "Zaire's foreign minister said Herbert reminded him of an African potentate," recalled
Rose Jennings, who had been hired by Herbert to serve as a special liaison
between the American press and Mobutu's government. Jennings said she
was stunned by Ali's negligence. "Some of the things I saw would turn your
stomach," she said, "but Ali was oblivious to it all."

Ali did his part to sell tourists on his African adventure. He talked to reporters every day at Deer Lake, even allowing them to join him when he woke
each morning to run three or four miles along Pleasant Run Road. He took
to calling his camp "Fighter's Heaven," because he had everything he needed
there, and perhaps because the place had the feel of an ashram, a holy place,
with Ali as its leader, its prophet, its guru.

Ali's sparring partners now included a promising young Pennsylvania
fighter named Larry Holmes. Fans arrived every day at Deer Lake to do nothing more than watch the boxer jump rope or swat a punching bag. There
were drugs and prostitutes available for those who chose to indulge. The
place offered a nice view of the changes afoot in American culture in the
1970s, which the journalist Tom Wolfe labeled the "Me Decade." As the historian Thomas Borstelmann wrote, "A new emphasis on self-improvement,
self-expression, self-gratification, and self-indulgence moved to the center of
American culture, to the detriment of more community-oriented values." It
was as if all the hopeful longing of the 1960s counterculture had been washed
away by cynicism, leaving a lot of easy sex and drugs in its aftermath.

If more Americans were living in the moment and living for themselves,
Ali fit in nicely. Self-expression, self-gratification, and self-indulgences had

long been specialties of his. Even with boxing writers predicting almost unanimously that Ali would lose, perhaps badly, his public demeanor never changed, his confidence never dimmed.

He explained why in an interview with Dave Kindred, a reporter from Louisville. "Round One — bing! — I'm out on him — boom, boom! — I shake him up — I beat him to the draw — He was a kid when I beat Sonny Liston ten years ago — They're sayin', 'How much time will Ali last with George Foreman?' And I say, 'How long will *he* last' — See, they say I can't hit — And when have I ever been stopped — When have I ever given a record I go quick? — That ain't right, that don't even sound right. This is a kid. No skill, no speed — That's belittlin' to me, my greatness — He's not fightin' Joe Frazier, he's fightin' Muhammad Ali — I'm actually the greatest fighter of all time."

During the same interview, Kindred asked if Ali had any regrets. If he had his life to live over again, would he do it the same way?

Ali was not usually introspective, but he paused momentarily to think about the question before answering: "I wouldn't have said that thing about the Viet Cong. I would have handled the draft different. There wasn't any reason to make so many people mad." He went on to say he was proud of his decision not to enlist. His only regret was "the Viet Cong thing."

It was a puzzling comment, to say the least. Ali's statement about having no quarrel with the Viet Cong had been hugely influential. It had neatly and powerfully tied the civil rights movement to the antiwar movement. It had compelled countless Americans, black and white, young and old, to ask themselves what, if anything, *they* had against the Viet Cong. It had made Ali a champion to millions of people who cared not at all for boxing. Yet Ali went on to repeat this expression of regret several times through the years, leaving no doubt that he genuinely questioned the wisdom of his remark, that he felt truly sorry for upsetting so many people. It was a revealing comment. For one thing, it suggested that Ali didn't appreciate or else didn't care that his opposition to the war had made him an influential figure for his generation. But Ali's comment also offered a clue to some of his deepest feelings. He loved being loved more than he loved being admired.

Less than a year later, in another interview, Ali went a step further, suggesting he was not necessarily a conscientious objector. "The way I feel," he told *Playboy* magazine, "if America was attacked and some foreign force was prowling the streets and shooting, naturally I'd fight. I'm on the side of

America, not them, because I'm fighting for myself, my children, and my people . . . So, yeah, I'd fight if America was attacked."

If Ali betrayed signs of confusion or evolving values, he was nevertheless happy at this particular moment — happy to be a boxer again and not an antiwar crusader or a college lecturer, and happy to have the world watching him do the things he did best. His weight was down to 218 pounds, almost where he wanted it. When he caught himself in the mirror, he liked what he saw even more than he usually did. He said he was confident he would win, that Foreman wasn't as tough as everyone believed, that Ali would once again be the heavyweight champion of the world, which was all he had really ever wanted.

When Ali preened, others worried about his safety.

"Ali's had it," said Jerry Quarry, Ali's recent opponent. "He's at road's end."

"The time may have come to say good-bye to Muhammad Ali," Howard Cosell told television viewers, "because, very honestly, I don't think he can beat George Foreman."

Ali seemed unbothered. He loved Cosell, and Cosell loved Ali. Cosell had shown Ali respect when most journalists had mocked the fighter. Over time, they'd developed a good act, one that helped them each gain fame. Now, Ali responded to the broadcaster with one of their familiar toupee gags: "Cosell, you're a phony, and that thing on your head came from the tail of a pony!" When another reporter predicted a first-round knockout victory for Foreman, Ali pulled him aside and tried to educate him. "I'm going to tell you something," Ali said, "and I don't want you ever to forget it . . . Black men scare white men more than black men scare black men."

Even Ali's wife had doubts about her husband's chances. Belinda didn't believe Foreman was unbeatable, but she worried that Ali was doing too much talking and not enough training, and she couldn't understand it. Losing in Africa would be a tragedy, she told Ali. Not only would he blow his shot at the championship; he would blow the chance to be a hero to black people all over the world. She yelled at him sometimes, but the yelling only worked temporarily, as if she were blowing up a balloon with a pinprick in it. Ali would work hard for a few days, perhaps even for a week or two, and then he would slack off again.

One day, Belinda went to Hersheypark, the giant amusement park in Hershey, Pennsylvania, where she saw a gift shop that sold custom T-shirts. She decided to buy one. On the front, in block letters, she had the shop print: "I LOVE HIM BECAUSE HE'S THE GREATEST." On the back, she had them iron on the name: "GEORGE FOREMAN."

When Ali saw Belinda wearing the T-shirt at Deer Lake, he demanded she take it off.

"I ain't takin' it off until you start training seriously," she said. "You can't stop like that just because you worked two weeks."

Ali got angry, saying Belinda was embarrassing him.

"You embarrassing *me* by not trying!" she answered, as she recalled the encounter years later. She wore the shirt several days in a row until she felt Ali had resumed his good work habits.

But tension remained. One night in August, Belinda suggested they go see the new Mel Brooks movie *Blazing Saddles*. She knew Ali loved Western movies, and she'd heard this one had a lot of racial humor, so she thought her husband would like it. Ali and Belinda brought their eldest girl, six-year-old Maryum — or May May, as everyone called her. Rahaman, C. B. Atkins, and one of Belinda's cousins all tagged along. They all piled into Rahaman Ali's black-and-white Oldsmobile and drove to a theater in nearby Pottsville. *Blazing Saddles* was very much a movie of the times. Straightforward joke telling was giving way to irony in the 1970s, just as the spirit of rebelliousness was giving way to anger and dismay over the country's military failure in Southeast Asia and the revelations of corruption in the White House. Sincere passions that had been embraced in the 1960s seemed naive in the 1970s. In *Blazing Saddles,* a sly black sheriff and an alcoholic white gunslinger arrive to save a desert town's racist white citizens. In the end, when the heroes ride off into the sunset, the camera lingers until the cowboys dismount, slap hands, hand off their horses to assistants, and step into a waiting limousine, no doubt headed back to their movie-star homes in Hollywood.

Belinda loved the movie. She laughed and laughed, but Ali watched in silence. When they left the theater, it was raining. Belinda offered to drive back to Deer Lake. As they got going, she could tell her husband was angry. Irony was not a punch Ali knew how to throw — he was, after all, one of those earnest symbols of the 1960s — and, as a result, he had either missed or failed to enjoy the wit of *Blazing Saddles*. "He said it wasn't that funny, it was racist, it was this, it was that," Belinda recalled. That, in turn, made Belinda angry.

Where was his sense of humor? Why couldn't he simply enjoy the movie in-stead of complaining and starting an argument?

Ali changed the subject and began bragging about what he would do to George Foreman. Even cocooned in the Oldsmobile, surrounded by family and friends, he felt compelled to boast, to psych himself up and put Foreman down. That made Belinda even angrier — about her husband's silly reaction to the movie, about his half-hearted training, about everything. She muttered just loud enough for Ali to hear: "Yeah, you just tryin' to convince yourself you gonna win. You ain't gonna win . . . not the way you trainin.'"

Ali raised a fist like he was going to hit her and waved it in her direction. Belinda ducked.

"Man, are you tryin' to hit me?" she said, still holding the steering wheel and watching the road. "You *not* tryin' to hit me!"

Ali raised his fist again. "And I'm driving a car in the rain," she recalled, "and I took my hand and swung at him. I gave him a backhand to his face, because he was trying to hit me again, and I stopped him." A ring she was wearing may have caught Ali over his eye. "So he gets a little mouse over his eye and he starts bleeding a little bit, because I hit him harder than I thought I hit him. And he said, 'Man, she hit me!' Then he looked in the mirror and saw the blood, and he started cursing. 'Bitch! That bitch! Man, we'll kill you! Stop the car! Stop the car!'"

Belinda shouted at Ali: "Don't put your hands on me! You do not raise your hands at me again!"

The next morning, Ali apologized and bought her flowers. She hugged and kissed him and said she accepted the apology. But she reminded Ali that he had only about a month to prepare for the fight. He needed to get serious. She said she would take the kids to Chicago to stay with her parents, and when she returned, she intended to clean up the camp — getting rid of "the hang-erbangers, the niggers smoking reefer up there . . . all his damn girlfriends." She told Ali: "If you want the girlfriends, you go down to the hotel." She was referring to the Deer Lake Motel on Route 61, where the business cards read "Discreet Lodging" under the name of the establishment and where the rooms all smelled of Shell No-Pest Strips. "You don't bring 'em up in the camp no more," she said.

Ali agreed.

. . .

He continued to promise he would retire after fighting and beating Foreman. Even with Herbert Muhammad and the IRS taking their cuts, $5 million would provide a soft landing as Ali got out of boxing and explored new career options.

"It is befitting that I leave the game just like I came in," he said one day at a press conference in New York City, "beating a big, bad monster who knocks out everybody and no one can whup him. That's when that little Cassius Clay from Louisville, Kentucky, came up and stopped Sonny Liston, the man who annihilated Floyd Patterson twice. He was gonna kill me! He hit harder than George. His reach was longer than George. He was a better boxer than George, and I'm better now than I was when you saw that twenty-two-year-old undeveloped kid running from Sonny Liston. I'm experienced now . . . I'm *bad!* I done something new for this fight. I done wrestled with an alligator . . . I done tussled with a whale, I done handcuffed lightning, throwed thunder in jail! That's bad! Only last week I murdered a rock, injured a stone, hospitalized a brick! I'm so mean I make medicine sick!"

He looked to his left where Don King sat, smiling. It was difficult to say which man had more riding on the fight.

"It will be the greatest spectacle in the history of the world," King pronounced.

"Some people might pick the original Exodus," one of the reporters countered.

"Some people," King said, "have no imagination."

Before taking off for Zaire, Ali showed up for a boxing exhibition at the Salt Palace in Salt Lake City. Comedian Bob Hope told jokes. Joe Louis and Sugar Ray Robinson waved to the crowd. Ali, Frazier, and Foreman each sparred a few rounds against partners of their own choosing.

Organizers billed the event as a fundraiser for victims of a devastating drought in Africa, but three out of every four seats went unsold and precious little money was raised. Ali composed a new poem for the occasion, one that made reference to the recent resignation of President Nixon, who had stepped down rather than face impeachment hearings related to his involvement in the Watergate scandal. Ali admitted that he had not been paying attention to the details of Watergate, but he knew enough to rhyme: "If you think the world was shook when Nixon resigned / Wait till I whip this Fore-man's behind."

The entire trip to Salt Lake City might have been forgotten if not for one thing. Upon arrival at the airport in Utah, Ali's friend Gene Kilroy spotted someone he would later describe as "the most beautiful woman" he had ever seen. The next day, Kilroy saw the woman again, and he pointed her out to Ali. The boxer agreed that the woman was truly breathtaking — tall, slender, with caramel-colored skin and flowing waves of brown hair framing the deli-cate features of her face. Her name was Veronica Porche (pronounced *porsh*), and she was one of the four women selected by Don King and his panel of judges to help promote the fight in Zaire.

Not surprisingly, very few Americans were signing up for the travel pack-ages to Zaire. As he made his final sales push, King paid Porche and the other young women to fly to Salt Lake City, hoping they might cajole a few more boxing fans to come along with Ali and Foreman to Africa.

Porche was eighteen years old. Her father was a construction worker, her mother a registered nurse. She was one year removed from high school, still living at home with her parents, working at a department store and attending the University of Southern California in the hopes of becoming a doctor. She knew little about boxing. In her high-school chemistry class, she had once heard a classmate call Muhammad Ali a loudmouth, and that was more or less all she knew about the famous boxer. Veronica was the product of a sta-ble, middle-class family. She always knew when her parents would be home from work and always knew what time dinner would be on the table. She had attended Catholic schools and considered herself shy and well behaved. She was completely unaccustomed to the worlds of sport and celebrity, and she had no interest in meeting Ali. She assumed that if she did meet him, she probably wouldn't like him.

In fact, while she noticed Ali in Salt Lake City, and while Ali noticed her, they were not formally introduced. They never spoke. Ali looked at her, whispered his approval to Kilroy, and walked away.

"That was it," Porche said of their first encounter.

But that wasn't it.

40

"Ali Boma Ye!"

The following week, they were on their way, just Ali, his wife, his parents, his brother, his trainer, his manager, his three sparring partners, his two assistant trainers, his two photographers, his two training camp supervisors, his cook, his masseur, his biographer, and thirteen other friends and relations, all of them flying from New York to Boston to Paris to Kinshasa, Zaire, all of them, with the possible exception of Ali, contemplating that this might be their last journey together.

In Paris, they boarded one of Mobutu's private 747s for the final leg of the trip. Ali was gambling his entire career on this fight, but he betrayed no signs of stress. The sight of two black pilots in the cockpit and an all-black team of flight attendants thrilled him. Africa had black pilots! A black president with his own 747! What other wonders did the continent hold?

"This is strange to the American Negro," he said. "We never dreamed of this." But Ali had in fact dreamed of this, or at least spoken of it. So had Elijah Muhammad. So had Malcolm X. The Nation of Islam had been preaching for years that black Americans needed their own country so that they, too, could make their own laws, run their own schools, own their own businesses, and, presumably, fly their own 747s. Ali had been telling people for ten years that he was fighting in order to call attention to the struggles of his people and to help spread the word of Elijah Muhammad, the Messenger of Allah, who had predicted that the black man would one day throw off the shackles of his white oppressors and find true freedom. Now, here he was, a black man with a black manager and a black promoter traveling to a black nation to fight another black man in an event seen by the whole world. Who would have dared dream such a thing when Ali had first declared his loyalty to the Nation of Islam? And if something as unlikely as this could come to pass, why was it so difficult to believe that Elijah Muhammad's prophecies might come true? At the very least, one might ask, why was it so difficult to imagine that Ali might be capable of another miracle in the boxing ring? Why was it so difficult to imagine that he might beat George Foreman?

To Ali, Foreman was Sonny Liston all over again. Foreman was the bad guy, and Ali was the good guy. Why should the good guy fear the bad guy? The good guy always won.

During the flight, Ali rehearsed his verbal attacks, calling Foreman a robot, a mummy, a slow-moving goon. He'd been saying for months that Foreman would crack under pressure. He was going to distract and discombobulate Foreman, same as he had Liston. Even if no one believed him, Ali scored points for consistency. He'd been boasting that 2 billion people would watch this fight — the equivalent, he said, of "100,000 new faces every night for 170 *years!* Imagine that!" His math was off, but his point was good. It isn't easy performing in front of such a colossal crowd. It tries a man's nerves, he said: "Then you got the world's greatest fighter or one of the world's best, taking punches at your face, your body, and little hard gloves on, and everything at stake — your future, your life, your family's investments — everything's at stake. This worries you. And the pressure, the excitement, the drama."

Ali had been trying to cast Foreman as the fighter for the establishment, offering as evidence the fact that Foreman had waved an American flag when he'd won the gold medal at the 1968 Olympics. Sometimes it was hard to tell if he was saying these things to rile Foreman, to capture the attention of the press, or to convince himself that Foreman was truly the morally inferior man. "If he wins, we're slaves for three hundred more years," Ali told English journalist David Frost in a TV interview from Deer Lake. "If I win, we're free."

At a boxing writers' dinner in June at the Waldorf-Astoria Hotel in New York, for example, Ali began with his usual taunts, telling Foreman that Zaire was "my country," that thousands of Africans would be sticking pins in their George Foreman voodoo dolls. Seconds later, Ali's relatively benign racism grew more poisonous. "I'll beat your Christian ass, you white, flag-waving (expletive deleted) you!" Later, when Ali put an arm around Foreman's shoulder, Foreman slapped it away. Ali tried to grab Foreman's championship belt. Foreman ripped Ali's coat. Ali hurled drinking glasses at Foreman and against a drape-covered wall.

When Foreman walked away, Ali wasn't finished. He shouted as if he wanted to continue the tussle: "What hotel that nigger stay in?"

The behavior was so repulsive that it prompted Dave Anderson of the *Times* to offer this wish for Ali: "If he considers Zaire his country, maybe he'll stay there."

Later, Ali apologized, saying he should not have impugned another man's religion. But then, ten minutes after the apology, he did it again, saying, "I'm fightin' to represent Elijah Muhammad. This Foreman, he represents Christianity, America, the flag. I can't let him win. He represents the oppression of black people; he represents pork chops."

Until then, Foreman had admired Ali. He had even entertained notions of joining the Nation of Islam. But after the encounter in New York, he lost interest. "I figured if a religion couldn't make you into a better person," he said, "it had no purpose at all, and if his was the true face of Islam, I didn't want to see it in my mirror."

With his psychological tactics, Ali might have succeeded in firing up audiences and perhaps even prejudicing referees, but he was also undercutting what he claimed to be one of his primary goals: the uplift of black people. By slurring Joe Frazier as a Tom or George Foreman as a white, flag-waving Christian motherfucker (or whatever expletive the *New York Times* deleted from his quote), Ali was redefining race as a state of mind. He was also denigrating strong, honorable, hard-working black men with whom he should have stood shoulder to shoulder as symbols of pride, men worthy of admiration from black and white Americans. Ali's words not only stung Foreman and Frazier; they influenced millions of Ali's fans. Film director Spike Lee, who was seventeen years old in 1974 and living in Brooklyn, called Ali "our shining black prince; to black people, he was like God." Lee added, "I gotta admit, like a lot of young African-Americans, I got . . . hornswoggled by Ali, and we bought into thinking that Joe was not a black man."

On the flight to Zaire, it was pointed out to Ali that some of his attacks on Foreman might not work as well in Africa as they did in the United States.

The majority of Zairians were Christian (with no special aversion to pork chops), and few would understand the term *Uncle Tom.*

Ali thought about that for a little while and then asked, "Who do these people hate?"

"The Belgians," Gene Kilroy said.

That was all Ali needed to know.

Huge crowds greeted Ali and Belinda, both dressed in blue, as they stepped off the plane in Kinshasa. A bare-chested Zairian man wearing a beaded headdress and carrying a small wooden shield in one hand and a spear in the other led Ali through the airport.

Immediately, Ali began working the audience. Africa did not play a central part in the story of the Nation of Islam. The Nation of Islam talked about black Americans returning to their Asiatic roots, not their African roots. But Ali had always had a brilliant instinct for shaping his own biography. He had long ago discarded his American name and challenged the American government's right to tell him what to do. "I'm the king of the world!" he had shouted after beating Sonny Liston in 1964. He had not said king of America. *King of the World!* Most men and women invent their identities by the time they reach adulthood. In the story of Ali's invention — shaped by his Jim Crow childhood, his rambunctious father, Elijah Muhammad's religious vision, and Ali's own grandiose appetite for attention — he was the African American King, and he had come to Zaire to please his people and retake the crown that obviously belonged to him. Most men and women don't know they're making history until after they've made it, but Ali worked on the simple and liberating assumption that he was always making history.

He asked a reporter how many people lived in Zaire. When the reporter told him 22 million, Ali asked how many of the 22 million were pulling for Ali and how many for Foreman. The reporter said he didn't know. But Ali was taking no chances; he went to work from the moment he stepped foot in Africa campaigning for the support of the Zairian people.

"I am the greatest!" he shouted. Then he added, "George Foreman is a Belgian!"

First Ali had labeled Foreman white. Now he was calling him a colonialist oppressor of the Congolese. At one point, he went even further, calling Foreman "the oppressor of all black nations."

It might have been laughable, except that no one laughed. Foreman, unintentionally, made matters worse by bringing his German shepherd to Zaire. The Zairian people were not fond of dogs, and particularly not fond of German shepherds, a breed the Belgian colonials had used to control the Congolese.

Soon the crowds began to chant in Lingala: "Ali boma ye! Ali boma ye!"

Translation: Ali, kill him!

When Ali learned what they were saying, he led the cheers everywhere he went, waving his arms like the conductor of a marching band: "Ali boma ye! Ali boma ye!"

Ali and his entourage stayed at one of Mobutu's presidential compounds in N'Sele, about twenty-five miles from Kinshasa, on the banks of the Congo River. The compound included a handsomely furnished riverside house, a swimming pool, a grocery store, and a restaurant. Foreman was assigned to a military encampment. Unhappy with both the accommodations and food, Foreman soon moved to the presidential suite at the Inter-Continental Hotel in Kinshasa.

While Ali played the part of cheerleader everywhere he went, Foreman would not be bothered with unnecessary displays of charisma. His demeanor suggested he had no interest in Ali's games. He had traveled many miles to knock out Ali, and he wanted to get it done and go home.

"He did not look like a man so much as a lion standing just as erectly as a man," Norman Mailer wrote of Foreman.

When Mailer stuck out a hand and introduced himself, the champion merely nodded. "Excuse me for not shaking hands with you," Foreman said, "but you see I am keeping my hands in my pockets." Mailer found it difficult to argue with that logic. Every time Foreman refused to shake hands or refused to give an interview or refused to smile for a photograph, he gave the impression of a thundercloud holding back a great storm, storing every drop of energy until the time came to pound down upon the earth.

The sight of Foreman hitting the heavy bag at the compound in N'Sele provoked fear in Ali's camp. Foreman's manager, Dick Sadler, wrapped his arms around the bag, trying to hold it steady, but Foreman's blows were so powerful they lifted Sadler in the air. By the time Foreman finished, the bag had a dent the size of a man's head. The sportswriters worried: What would become of Ali's internal organs when they received that sort of beating? What would happen to his head? Even Ali's most trusted confidantes fretted. They knew Ali was a smart, resourceful fighter. They knew he always had a chance. But smarts and resourcefulness only got a fighter so far. Boxing is two human bodies in combat, "a stylized mimicry of a fight to the death," as Joyce Carol Oates put it, and Foreman in almost every way appeared to be the more destructive force of the two. Ali's talent for taking a punch offered little consolation.

Years later, Ali would admit he was worried, too. How hard did Foreman hit? Would he be able to take it? But, at least publicly, he showed no signs of concern. He acted as if the heavyweight championship were already his, that it had always been his. He acted as if Zaire were his, too. He went on long walks, marveling every time he met a black doctor or a black lawyer or a black politician, marveling that he was recognized even by people who had no televisions. He seemed just as excited in Kinshasa as he had been in 1960 at the Olympics in Rome — perhaps more, because he had the sense in Zaire that these were his people, and that they were expecting something from him.

"You could actually see and feel him drawing strength from the exuberant love of his people," said Stokely Carmichael, the head of the Student Nonviolent Coordinating Committee, who had traveled to Zaire at Ali's expense. "It was unbelievable. Wherever we went. I mean, even when he ran — no matter what time — it was as if the youth of the entire city ran with him. All around him, trailing behind, a joyous procession of ragged black youth, eyes shining with pride and excitement."

Don King and Hank Schwartz had hoped to find seven thousand European and American customers willing to pay thousands of dollars to travel to Zaire. In the end, they found about thirty-five. Not thirty-five thousand, just thirty-five. Thirty-five people. Thirty-five high-priced boxing tourists.

The American promoters had promised that Zaire's government would receive a share of the money made from sponsorships — things like Foreman-Ali bubble gum, Foreman-Ali candy bars, Foreman-Ali T-shirts, Foreman-Ali programs, Foreman-Ali postcards. None of those deals came to pass. In addition, Zaire was supposed to receive all the money from ticket sales for the live event in Kinshasa, but only Zairians were buying tickets, and they were paying such low prices that their contributions would not begin to offset the government's costs in putting on the fight. Zaire's leader advertised the bout as a "Gift from President Mobutu to the people of Zaire." Pale-green road signs with yellow lettering in French and English were posted around the country with messages reading:

A fight between two Blacks in Black nation, organized by Blacks and seen by the whole world; that is a victory of Mobutism.

The country of Zaire which has been bled because of pillage and systematic exploitation must become a fortress against imperialism and a spearhead for the liberation of the African continent.

The Foreman-Ali fight is not a war between two enemies, but a sport between two brothers.

Given the great public-relations value of the event, and given the way he had been pillaging billions of dollars from his own country, it's unlikely Mobutu was fretting about the fight's finances.

With plenty of plane tickets and hotel rooms unsold, not to mention thousands of servings of quiche Lorraine and chicken Kiev stored in Zairian freezers in anticipation of the American visitors, Don King decided to invite a few guests to join his African expedition free of charge, including the four beautiful women from Los Angeles who had been hired to help promote the travel packages. Veronica Porche initially declined the invitation, saying she didn't want to miss her classes at USC. But she changed her mind and agreed to go, mostly because she had never traveled outside the United States and didn't know when or if she would ever have such a chance again. One day in Kinshasa, she was approached by C. B. Atkins, a member of Ali's entourage, who asked Veronica if she wanted to visit Ali's training camp. She said yes, and asked if Trina, one of the other women selected by Don King for the trip, might come along, too.

Trina, who was four or five years older than Veronica, wore a white sleeveless T-shirt and no bra. Veronica dressed more conservatively, in a longsleeved pink blouse and matching pink slacks. When they met Ali, the boxer ignored Porche and flirted with Trina. But later, when the young women boarded a bus to go back to Kinshasa, Ali offered to ride with them, and he settled into the seat next to Veronica. The two chatted nonstop for the forty-minute ride, speaking mostly about their childhoods and their families.

When they reached Kinshasa, Ali said goodbye. There were no kisses, no invitations to extend the evening. But Porche had the feeling Ali liked her, and she was surprised at how much she liked him. It was a wonder, really, that someone so gloriously handsome and so famous could seem so simple and so charming—"like a country boy," she said.

Soon she was seeing Ali every day. They timed their get-togethers to avoid Belinda. "He just overwhelmed Veronica," recalled Rose Jennings. "He wouldn't leave her alone."

When reporters began to notice Ali's new companion and asked about her, he laughed it off. "My babysitter," he said. He didn't care, and neither did Veronica. She was young. They were in Africa. The most handsome man she had ever seen turned out to be sweet and kind and definitely, definitely attracted to her. It was overpoweringly romantic.

"I remember the moment I fell in love with him, the exact moment," she said years later. They were in his villa in N'Selc. Ali wore a black, short-sleeved shirt and slacks. "He had these lectures he had written out on cards, and they were really beautiful, on friendship, love. He was saying his lecture on love and . . . I fell in love with him. I felt there was sort of a palpable feeling . . . a certain energy that I felt hit me at a certain point in the lecture. And I knew."

Later, she learned the words were not Ali's. They were tracts he had copied from religious books. But it didn't matter. She was in love for the first time in her life.

On September 16, nine days before the scheduled fight, George Foreman suffered a cut over his right eye during a sparring session. The cut was bad enough that the bout had to be postponed—for how long, no one knew. Initial reports said it would be a week, at least. Soon, there were indications that it would be a month or more.

For everyone involved, this was a disaster. Mobutu feared that Ali, Foreman, and the reporters covering them would flee Zaire and never return. To prevent that from occurring, he ordered the fighters and their managers to turn over their passports.

Ali was despondent, describing the postponement as "the worst thing that could have happened." First he suggested that the fight should go on as scheduled, adding that if the cut over Foreman's eye opened up during the fight, he would agree to a rematch in six months. Then he suggested flying Joe Frazier to Kinshasa to take Foreman's place.

Foreman declined stitches, saying he didn't trust local doctors. With a butterfly bandage over his eye, Foreman had to avoid sparring, but he continued to train. Ali continued training, too. He also persuaded Veronica Porche to take time off from college and stay with him in Zaire. Belinda — apparently still unaware of her husband's new relationship — had returned to the United States.

Beginning September 22, a three-day music festival kicked off in Zaire, with performances by James Brown, B. B. King, Miriam Makeba, Celia Cruz, the Spinners, and Bill Withers. The music was electric, in no small part because the marijuana in Zaire — which the Americans called *binji* — was heavy-duty and sold by the handful at third-world prices. One night, Ali asked Veronica to join him at the stadium for the concert. She didn't want to go, but she waited in N'Sele for Ali to return, and that night they had their first kiss. Soon she was spending most of her days and nights with Ali at N'Sele.

When Belinda returned to Africa, she and Ali clashed violently — but not because Belinda caught Ali with Veronica. The fight started when Ali accused Belinda of sleeping with another man.

"Ali comes in the room," Belinda said, "he comes and hits me in my face like this, *Bam!* — and my face swells ... My whole face swole up. It was a black eye underneath ... He hit real hard."

Belinda lashed out, scratching Ali's face and leaving a gash running down the left side of his face from his hairline to his temple, one that would be visible in photos for days to come. Later, he cried and apologized.

"I could've had him arrested," she said, adding that she decided to hide her injury because she didn't want the fight stopped. She wore sunglasses and stayed out of sight until the swelling went down.

Veronica said she didn't know whether Ali hit Belinda, but she confirmed Belinda was hiding two black eyes beneath her sunglasses the day after the incident. Kilroy said he did not believe Ali struck his wife.

In the weeks leading up to the fight, Belinda could be seen wearing a George Foreman button. Ali and Porche continued their romance, with Porche falling more deeply in love by the day. She assumed Ali was going to lose to Foreman, as everyone predicted, but she didn't care. Although they had known each other only a matter of weeks, when Ali proposed marriage, Veronica answered yes without hesitation. She had the impression, she said, that Ali's marriage to Belinda was all but officially over. That's what Ali told her. A Zairian minister was summoned to N'Sele, and a wedding ceremony was performed in Ali's villa. "I can't say how legal it was," she said years later. "I know it's crazy, but we got married."

Ali promised that a proper American wedding would follow as soon as he divorced Belinda.

More than six hundred reporters had arrived in Zaire, and, with the possible exception of *Rolling Stone*'s Hunter S. Thompson, who spent much of his time shopping for elephant tusks, smoking marijuana, and getting drunk, most of the journalists were miserable. Hotel-room phones were mere ornaments. The government provided only a handful of telex machines for reporters to transmit stories, and when officials did finally deliver more of the point-to-point printing machines, they forgot to provide sockets for connecting them. Everywhere they went, visitors were expected to lay out a *matabiche,* a tip or bribe. Clothes had to be regularly laundered and ironed to kill the *michango,* a parasite that bored under the skin, settled in the soft pouches under the eyes, and required surgery to remove. Worst of all, perhaps: Zairian bartenders were inept. "They didn't understand 'screwdriver,'" Rose Jennings recalled. "You had to say vodka and orange juice. If you asked for iced tea, they'd bring you ice cream." When Jennings griped about one particularly incompetent bartender, the American seated next to her said, "Rose, you don't understand. A month ago this guy didn't know how to flush a toilet."

The most miserable American of all may have been George Foreman. When the boxer asked Dick Sadler to arrange a flight to Belgium or France so he could have a qualified doctor look at his wound, Mobutu wouldn't let him go. The Zairian dictator feared that Foreman would never return, and he was probably right. Mobutu made it clear that Foreman and Ali would stay in Zaire as long as necessary; nothing was going to stop this fight.

With Foreman moping, reporters turned for amusement and good copy to Don King, who had taken to wearing brightly colored dashikis and who seemed to have grown his afro to new and previously unexplored heights, inspiring Norman Mailer to write that King looked like a man falling down an elevator shaft, "*whoosh* went the hair up from his head." King paraphrased Shakespeare in commenting on the postponement of the fight, saying, "Adversity is ugly and venomous like a toad, yet wears a precious jewel in her head." The extra suspense surrounding the fight would turn the event, he said, from colossal to super-colossal.

Ali, meanwhile, did one of the things he liked best: he entertained. He continued getting to know Veronica. He practiced a set of rudimentary magic tricks. He learned to hammer out two or three boogie-woogie songs on the piano. He watched movies that the American embassy sent to his camp. He offered daily press conferences and informal interviews to journalists who were starving for copy and getting little from Foreman, enjoying the fact that some of the reporters from Africa and Europe had not heard his old poems before. He even came up with a new one, a long ode called "A Bad Morning Shave." He explored Zaire. And he continued to train. To make sure that neither he nor his sparring partners grew weak or got sick from the local food during the long wait, he ordered meat flown in from Europe.

One week before the contest, Ali repeated his oath to make this his final fight. "I plan to retire as soon as I win," he said at a news conference. "There won't be no lose."

The journalists who had been following Ali for years and had come to love him marveled at his demeanor. Even some of the men in his entourage were awestruck. How did he do it? How did he manage to stay so sunny and to convey such confidence? Ali was not naive. He knew Foreman was young and strong and undefeated. He knew that Foreman was one of the greatest knockout punchers the sport had ever seen. He knew that Las Vegas made Foreman a three-to-one favorite. Even if Ali genuinely believed he was the better and smarter boxer, he had to be concerned that Foreman might hurt him, that one good punch might end his comeback, end his career. Red Smith of the *New York Times* called Ali's chances of winning "as remote as Zaire." Smith added, "There is much loose talk in the fight mob about the fix being in for Ali, but on its merits this shapes up as a match between a rising young power hitter and a folk hero far past his peak." A British writer quipped that Foreman could be stopped only one way: "Shell him for three days and then send in the infantry."

But stress rolled off Ali like water off a marble statue. He spoke only of winning, of being champ again, of getting back in the good graces of Elijah Muhammad.

"I have a dream," Ali said, "in which I put on my suit and get my briefcase ready, and my suitcase packed, and I'm going to see what the Leader say my mission is going to be. The championship strengthens my reputation as a prophet. No more am I the onliest lil' voice crying in the wilderness. The stage is set."

41

Rumble in the Jungle

It was two in the morning on October 30, the day of the fight. Muhammad Ali stood by the side of the mighty Zaire River, formerly known as the Congo River. Fallen trees cascaded down the river like matchsticks. A pale moon shone. The air was warm and humid. Ali, dressed in black, stood surrounded by his most trusted men. They were quiet, like soldiers preparing to leave on a dangerous mission.

An hour later, in his dressing room at the stadium in Kinshasa, Ali tried to relieve the pressure.

"What's wrong around here?" he asked. "Everybody scared?"

The horror film he had watched earlier in evening, *Baron Blood,* now *that* had been scary, he said; fighting George Foreman wasn't. "This ain't nothing but another day in the dramatic life of Muhammad Ali!" He rolled his eyes in mock fear and switched his clothes for white boxing trunks with black stripes and a long white robe fringed with a black African pattern. Usually, Bundini designed Ali's robes, and he had one in his arms — it was trimmed in Zairian colors and had a map of the country over the heart. But Ali didn't want to wear Bundini's robe.

"Look how much better *this* one looks," Ali said, spinning in front of a mirror. "It's African. Look in the mirror."

Bundini refused to look.

Ali slapped him.

"You look when I tell you! Don't ever do a thing like that."

Bundini wouldn't look.

Ali slapped him again.

Still, Bundini would not acknowledge Ali's robe.

Ali shrugged and sat at the end of his training table under slowly spinning ceiling fans. In a low, singsong voice, he murmured to himself. He recited old rhymes and favorite catchphrases, as if in a review of his boxing career: "Float like a butterfly, sting like a bee . . . you can't hit what you can't see . . . I been broke . . . I been down . . . but not knocked out . . . it must be dark when you get knocked out . . . it's strange getting stopped." He concluded with "Now! Let's rumble in the jungle!"

He hopped off the table and tried to make Bundini feel better. "Bundini!" he shouted. "We gonna dance?"

No answer.

"Ain't we gonna dance, Bundini? You know I can't dance without you."

Bundini was still sad. Finally, he answered, "Aw, hell, Champ. All night long."

"Are we going to dance with him?"

"All night long!"

Someone called out: "Ten minutes."

Dundee taped Ali's hands. The trainer checked to make sure he had everything he needed for the fight: Q-tips in his shirt pocket, a vial of smelling salts tucked behind his ear, coagulant powders and gauze in his left hip pocket, liquid coagulants and surgical scissors in his right hip pocket, and a kit stuffed with an ice bag, more gauze pads, an extra pair of shoelaces, an extra mouthpiece, and extra smelling salts.

Herbert Muhammad led Ali into a toilet stall — the only place where they could have privacy — and, together, the men prayed.

Ali walked calmly through the stadium and into the ring, surrounded by his usual coterie — Rahaman, Dundee, Herbert, Bundini, Kilroy — all of them bearing expressions suitable for pallbearers, plus dozens of Zairian soldiers in white helmets. A giant portrait of Mobutu loomed over the stadium. Ali smiled as he passed Joe Frazier seated at ringside, and then he climbed through the ropes and began to shuffle and shadowbox. He removed his robe, brown body shining in the ring lights as a panoply of brown faces watched him move. As he danced and waved his arms, the crowd chanted his name as if they'd rehearsed for this moment for months. In a sense, they had.

It was approaching 4 a.m. Thousands of seats sat empty near the ring, those priced at $250 each and reserved for the Americans and Europeans that Don King had hoped to entice. But beyond the inner circle, more than forty thousand Zairians stood waiting in a wide, low oval that stretched far from the ring. For those in the cheap seats, Ali and Foreman would be small, dark specks, their swift, subtle moves impossible to discern. A corrugated tin roof had been built over the ring to protect against a tropical downpour, which only further obstructed views from the outlying seats. The spectators didn't seem to care that their views were partially blocked or that they'd all be drenched if it rained. They'd been up all night waiting. The time had finally come for action. "Ali boma ye!" they chanted. Ali waved his hand, leading them like an orchestra conductor.

All over the world, people sat down to watch. In many countries, the fight would appear live on free television in people's homes. In the United States, Britain, and Canada, people went to theaters and paid to see it on big screens. About two thousand people were expected to fill the Grand Ballroom of New York's Waldorf-Astoria — where eighty-five dollars bought a ticket to view the fight as well as dinner and unlimited whiskey, and where the fight would begin at about 10 p.m. At drive-in movie theaters in the New York region, the price was about eighty dollars per carload. At Madison Square Garden, where former champs Jack Dempsey, Jimmy Braddock, and Gene Tunney would be watching, ticket prices topped out at thirty dollars. Even outside New York, tickets were expensive, at twenty dollars in Milwaukee, for example, and seventeen in Salt Lake City. At one point, Ali had bragged that 2 billion people would be watching around the world. That wasn't going to happen. About 50 million would see the fight live, and another 300 to 500 million would watch a delayed tape. Still, 500 million qualified as an enormous number of spectators, and for many of those watching, Ali stood as more than an underdog boxer, more than an American black man, and more than a Muslim; he stood as a symbol of defiance.

In Kinshasa, the threat of rain weighed heavy in the air. There was the threat of violence, too. An entire nation had been waiting months for this moment. Hundreds of soldiers surrounded the ring and stood at strategic points throughout the stadium — enough to make a show of force but not enough to control forty thousand Zairians if the clouds opened and rain washed out the fight, or, worse, if Foreman finished Ali with one whopping punch.

Foreman arrived. The band played America's national anthem, followed by that of Zaire. While Dundee slipped eight-ounce boxing gloves on his fighter's hands, Ali shouted across the ring at Foreman, taunting the champion. He continued taunting as referee Zack Clayton called the men to the center of the ring for a review of the fight's rules. "Chump!" Ali snapped at Foreman. "You're gonna get yourself beat in front of all these Africans!"

The referee told Ali to shut up. Ali did not. "You been hearing about how bad I am since you were a little kid with mess in your pants," he barked. "Tonight, I'm gonna whip you till you cry like a baby!"

The bell rang. After saying endlessly for months that he would dance, that the way to beat the slow-footed Foreman was to dance, and after repeating just moments earlier in his dressing room that, finally, at long last, the time had come to dance, Ali did not dance. Instead, he walked flat-footed to the center of the ring, like a man with a death wish, to meet George Foreman.

The reporters perched at the hem of the ring stood.

"Oh, Christ, it's a fix," Plimpton shouted, hardly able to hear himself in the oceanic roar. Plimpton thought Ali was going to stand still, take one punch from Foreman, and fall down as Sonny Liston had in Lewiston, Maine.

But Ali had something else in mind. Weeks before the fight, he had sought advice from the legendary trainer Cus D'Amato. D'Amato had told Ali that Foreman was a bully. The best way to fight a bully, D'Amato had said, is to hit him first and hit him hard. Show him you're not scared.

That's what Ali did. He landed the first two punches, and for thirty seconds he continued to swing away, too busy to think about dancing. When Foreman asserted control, forcing Ali into the corner, Ali's corner men screamed wildly in warning, as if Ali were a swimmer who had accidentally drifted close to a shark. But, even then, instead of dancing away, Ali moved from the corner to the ropes, which, as Plimpton, writing for *Sports Illustrated,* put it, was "traditionally a sort of halfway house to the canvas for the exhausted fighter." It looked like pugilistic suicide, except that most of Foreman's punches were missing or catching Ali's arms. Soon, Ali was back in the center of the ring, where he popped Foreman with a solid right lead to the head. Foreman repaid it with a stiff left to Ali's face.

The round went on that way, two big men giving and taking tremendous punches, the crowd screaming, Ali surprising everyone by his willingness to stand up straight and fight, Foreman throwing big, round, inefficient punches, assuming he needed only one really good one. It was a furious, thrilling three minutes of action. When it was over, Foreman sat on his stool and smiled. This was his kind of fight. If Ali wanted to trade punches, Foreman would happily oblige. If Ali wanted to stand against the ropes and let Foreman take his best shots, Foreman would do that too, even more gladly.

Ali said later he wanted to see if Foreman knew how to fight his way out of the "half-dream room," the place where a man goes when his brain signals get fuzzy. Given that Foreman had won most of his fights with ease, Ali suspected that Foreman might lack the ability to escape the room. But Ali's surprising strategy caused panic in his corner at the end of the first round.

"What you doin'?"

"Why don't you dance?"

"You *got* to dance!"

"Stay off the ropes . . ."

To which Ali replied: "Don't talk. I know what I'm doing."

Rounds two and three looked the same, only slower. Foreman bulled forward, sending Ali to the ropes. Ali leaned back, eyes popped wide, alert for danger, as Foreman swung away. Instead of sliding off the ropes and dancing around the ring, using speed to his advantage, Ali stayed put, settling for short, quick counterpunches, landing one punch for every two or three thrown by Foreman. Soon, Ali was shaking his head and hollering at Foreman — "Is that all you got? Is that all you got?" — just as he had against Joe Frazier in their first fight. Was that his plan? To let Foreman hit him? To absorb the best punches his opponent could throw and hope the man ran out of gas? The thought of it horrified the contingent in Ali's corner. It was a strategy that had failed against Frazier and Norton, and it seemed even more likely to fail against the mighty Foreman.

"Dance! Dance!" came the shouts from Ali's men.

In the third round, Ali stuck with the same approach, fighting off the ropes, grabbing Foreman around the head to slow him down, and whispering words of discouragement in his ear. With a minute remaining in the round, Foreman hit Ali with his best punches of the night, three good rights, each landing solidly on Ali's head. Ali grabbed Foreman around the neck and talked to him again, no doubt belittling Foreman's punching power before responding with rat-a-tat-tat concussive shots of his own in the round's final ten seconds.

Ali's punches hurt Foreman, even staggered him at times. But Foreman remained dangerous as he continued to stomp forward. When Foreman charged, Ali backed up against the ropes, letting his body hang over the typewriters in press row at the angle, Plimpton wrote, "of someone looking out his window to see if there's a cat on his roof."

"Is that the best you can do?" he taunted through his mouthpiece in round four. "You can't punch . . . Show me something! . . . Give it *back* to me! It's mine! Now it's my turn!"

In the final thirty seconds of the round, it was indeed Ali's turn. He came off the ropes and attacked, throwing stinging punches too fast for Foreman to block.

Foreman's eyes puffed. He moved more and more slowly until he resembled a man in need of a nap.

Foreman had no backup plan. He knew but one way to fight. As Foreman's punches slowed, Ali stayed on the ropes, patiently waiting to counterattack. After the fifth round, Foreman's corner men, Dick Sadler and Archie Moore, began to complain that the ring ropes were too loose, that Ali was leaning so far back that their man couldn't land punches. The complaints were useless. To casual observers, it may have looked as if Ali were letting Foreman do all the work. But it wasn't so. In fact, Ali was landing almost as many punches as Foreman. The big difference was that Ali made his punches count while Foreman banged away wildly with shots that missed or merely struck Ali's arms. The other big difference: Foreman was fighting for three minutes of each round while Ali conserved his energy and waited for the final thirty seconds to go all out. He knew Foreman would be tired from throwing and missing so many big punches and would be even more tired in the final seconds of each round. He knew his punches would hurt more by then. He knew George would have little time to counterattack. He knew his late flurries would impress judges. At one point, after emerging from his prone position and popping Foreman with a particularly sharp burst, Ali looked over at Jim Brown, who was serving as one of the announcers for the fight, and winked, as if to say, *I've got this.*

In the sixth, Ali surprised Foreman by coming to the center of the ring right away and shooting three crisp lefts to Foreman's forehead. Each time he jabbed, the crowd screamed his name as if they were his personal chorus.

Jab.

"Ali!"

Jab.

"Ali!"

Jab.

"Ali!"

In the middle of the round, Ali went back to the ropes to rest. He set his rear end on the second strand from the top and waited for Foreman to come over and hit him. There's an adage in boxing that if a fighter tries to go fifteen rounds with a heavy bag, the bag will win. Ali was the bag. Later, he and others would call this passive defense "the rope-a-dope," suggesting that Ali had lured the dope Foreman into a trap. In truth, the rope-a-dope had not been planned and hardly qualified as a stroke of genius on Ali's part. In truth, it made for a dull fight. But it was borne of necessity. It was a feat of masochism. Ali lacked the speed to escape and lacked the power and stamina to fight back for more than a fraction of each round. The best he could hope to do was outlast Foreman. "In the entire history of boxing," Mike Silver wrote in *The Arc of Boxing,* "this non-strategy worked exactly once." This was the one time.

"Is that all you got?" Ali asked Foreman.

That was all Foreman had.

By the end of the round, the biggest and scariest heavyweight since Sonny Liston was throwing punches that could barely knock over a vase. Foreman looked like the mummy Ali had made him out to be, a half-dead creature too slow to hurt anyone.

When the bell rang to start round seven, Ali went back to the ropes, taking a seat and waiting for Foreman to come over and start hitting. Once again, he attacked with thirty seconds left in the round. As the clock ticked down, Ali hit Foreman with a right cross that spun Foreman's head almost 180 degrees. Perspiration flew in a halo from Foreman's hair. The wounded fighter staggered and righted himself.

Ali shouted, "You got eight — EIGHT — long rounds to go, sucker!"

"I got a feeling that George is not gonna make it," Joe Frazier told viewers around the world as the seventh round came to a close.

Foreman wobbled as he rose from his stool to start the eighth. In need of a knockout, he threw big, wild punches, most of which missed or landed with little effect.

Once again, Ali waited. With twenty-one seconds to go in the round, he let fly a left-right combination. Both shots landed. Ali covered up in anticipation of a counterpunch, stuck out the left, landed another right, and then threw another combination. A great burst of energy moved him now. He spun out of the corner and into the center of ring where he let loose a left, a right, and another left. Foreman fell off balance. His hands flew up in the air like a man facing an armed robber as Ali's fifth unanswered punch came.

"Oh my Lawdy!" Bundini shouted. "He on Queer Street!"

The next shot was a right to the head. Foreman stumbled a few paces and reached wildly into empty space as he tumbled to the ground. Ali cocked his arm and circled around his opponent, but there was no need to punch again. Foreman collapsed to the canvas.

Ali raised his arms, and a moment later he was mobbed in the ring.

Years later, Foreman would say he'd been drugged before the fight by his own trainer. The decades gone by served to harden his certainty. He explained it this way: Before his fights he usually avoided drinking water, trying to dry out so that his body would look lean and rippled with muscle. He would wait until the fight was moments away from beginning and only then would he take a drink of water. In Zaire, Sadler gave him water moments before the start of the fight. To Foreman, the water tasted like medicine. But when he complained about it, Sadler told him he was crazy, that it was the same water he'd been drinking every day in Zaire. Foreman swallowed the rest. When he got in the ring, the fighter said he felt groggy. It wasn't the heat or the humidity. This was a kind of sluggishness he'd never felt before. After the fight, he remembered the water and became convinced that he'd been drugged.

"I know it," he said in an interview almost forty years later. "I know what happened."

Why would Foreman's manager drug him? Foreman suspected that Sadler had cut a deal with Herbert Muhammad — let Ali win this one, and we'll both cash in on the rematch.

Foreman waffled on whether he'd lost because he'd been drugged or because Ali had been the superior fighter, sounding like a man still burning with resentment but wishing to be magnanimous. "It's not like the water beat me," he said. "Muhammad beat me. With a straight right hand. Fastest right hand I'd ever been hit with in my life. That's what beat me. But they put drugs in my water there."

Foreman also complained that the referee, Zack Clayton, had given him only eight seconds instead of ten to get up after the knockdown. Replays of the fight suggest Foreman may have been right. Clayton's count appeared to be quick and short. When the referee began his count, only eight seconds remained in the round. The bell should have ended the round before Clayton counted ten. But even without factoring for the bell, Foreman appeared to be on his feet before Clayton's count reached ten.

Nevertheless, as Foreman stood, Clayton waved his arms, declaring Ali the winner by knockout.

Before the fight, Foreman said Sadler asked him for $25,000 in cash. The money, Foreman said, was for Clayton, to make sure the referee didn't show any favoritism toward Ali. Foreman said he gave Sadler the cash and Sadler gave it to Clayton. Years later, though, Foreman said, he discovered that Herbert Muhammad had also made a cash payment to Clayton for the same ostensible purpose — to make sure the referee wasn't prejudiced. Herbert's payment, according to Foreman, was "a little bit more" than $25,000.

When asked if Foreman's story was true, Gene Kilroy shouted angrily: "That's bullshit! We only paid ten thousand!"

The conspiracy theories would live on for decades, but they would make no difference. It had been ten and a half years since Cassius Clay had used a felt-tipped pen to write the words "heavyweight champion of the world" next to his name on a mattress in his Miami home in the days before his first fight with Sonny Liston. Now, his name had changed, but the title was his again, making him only the second man in heavyweight boxing history to lose and regain the championship.

It was dawn when Ali left the arena. He and Belinda got into the back of a silver Citroën. The rest of Ali's camp boarded two buses. They formed a caravan, led by a police car with an orange beacon, that rolled through Kinshasa "like . . . a military column through a liberated territory," as Plimpton described it. Crowds filled the street in celebration, everyone chanting "Ali! Ali! Ali!" As the caravan moved out of the city and back toward Ali's training camp, crowds that had heard the news came out along the road. Low, heavy clouds hung over the hills. The morning sky turned green. A pounding rain began to fall, drumming the roofs of the buses and Ali's car. Plimpton recalled that it had rained in Miami too, after Ali's shocking defeat of Sonny Liston. Then the boxer had been a plucky upstart; now he was a king, gazing through rainstreaked windows at another piece of his kingdom.

"Bulldogs is falling out of the sky," Bundini said as the caravan slowed for storm.

The next day, Ali laughed and took credit for holding back the rain long enough to finish the fight.

With his victory over the mighty Foreman, the Ali myth grew again. He was John Henry hammering on the mountain but greater, because Ali had hammered over and over through the years — hammered on Liston, hammered on Patterson, hammered on white reporters who told him to shut up and box, hammered on LBJ, on Nixon, on the U.S. Supreme Court, on Norton, on Frazier, and now on big, bad George Foreman.

For a decade and a half now he had been telling the world: "I am the greatest!" How could anyone disagree?

Through it all, he remained an appealing figure, which may have been his most surprising accomplishment. For all his bragging, Ali knew how to laugh at himself. He recognized that he was the court jester who'd become king, not the obvious heir to the throne. One minute he was saying he might call on President Gerald Ford to see if he could be of service to his country as a diplomat, and the next minute he was performing a magic trick with three pieces of rope of three different lengths that, abracadabra, became all the same length. Despite his bluster and the fundamental brutality of his sport, Ali's happy-go-lucky manner endeared him to people, black and white. Racism still permeated American society. Wounds from Vietnam remained open and raw as veterans settled in back home with missing limbs, suicidal thoughts, and a noticeable dearth of victory parades. Ordinary Americans had lost trust in their leaders, lost all sense of what heroism and gallantry were supposed to look like in an age of growing cynicism and despair. And here was Ali — a man with every right to be angry — still exuberant, still hopeful, still pretty, still winning. He wasn't the ideal American hero, merely the ideal one for his time.

What would he do next?

Ali admitted he wasn't sure.

"But I know," he said, "that beating George Foreman and conquering the world with my fists does not bring freedom to my people. I am well aware that I must go beyond all this and prepare myself for more.

"I know," he said, "that I enter a new arena."

42

Moving on Up

Ali returned home to a hero's welcome. After landing in Chicago, the boxer traveled by motorcade to City Hall, where Mayor Richard J. Daley declared November 1, 1974, Muhammad Ali Day. Dressed like a dandy in a blue suit with a neck scarf and carrying an ornate walking stick that had been a gift from Zaire's ruler, Ali thanked the mayor. He posed for photographs. He told reporters he was eager to see his four children "and my great leader, Elijah Muhammad."

From City Hall, Ali traveled to the Nation of Islam's Salaam Restaurant on the South Side. The next day, when he went to the home of Elijah Muhammad, he saw a man much diminished in health, intellect, and power. For years, there had been rumors that the Messenger's mind had been slipping. Some of Elijah Muhammad's recent pronouncements differed from his core principles. When he spoke at his annual Saviours' Day assembly in 1974, for example, he had urged followers to stop condemning the white man and to stop blaming American society for their problems. "The fault is not on the slavemaster any more," he had said, "since he said you can go free and we see that he is not angry with us." He told Leon Forrest, one of the writers working on *Muhammad Speaks*: "Let's not talk no more about any blue-eyed devils." FBI reports suggested that Elijah Muhammad was seriously considering granting permission for his followers to vote.

Ali was still officially barred from the Nation of Islam, but, in the meantime, the fighter continued to describe himself as a firm believer. Also in the meantime, Elijah Muhammad and the Nation of Islam continued to benefit financially from their association with the boxer. With Ali's return from Africa, Elijah told Ali once again: he should retire from boxing and return to the Nation of Islam as a minister. Elijah Muhammad had shaped Ali's life as much as anyone. The Messenger had given Ali a new religion and a new name, had pushed him to divorce his first wife, to abandon his friend and mentor Malcolm X, and to reject the draft. "My whole life is Elijah Muhammad," Ali said in an interview a month after his return from Africa. "Everything."

Still, he could not bring himself to obey this order. After regaining the championship, he was not prepared to retire.

Had Ali's faith weakened? Had his greed grown? Was it a combination of these forces?

"I feel real guilty, makin' so much money so easy," he said during one press conference after the fight in Africa. "Fighting George Foreman was an easy $5 million . . . From here on out, in all my championship fights, I don't want nothing but what it costs to train. I want my share to go to needy groups." He mentioned, specifically, the Nation of Islam and the NAACP, even though the groups maintained conflicting missions. Asked if Ali might someday become the leader of the Nation of Islam, he said, "No, sir. I don't want to be a leader. I don't live clean enough to be a spiritual leader."

A week after Chicago celebrated Muhammad Ali Day, Louisville did the same. Cheerleaders and a marching band from Central High greeted Ali upon arrival in his hometown. Odessa Clay was there too, wearing a white mink stole that had been a recent gift from her son. The mayor announced that a downtown street, Armory Place, would be renamed Muhammad Ali Place, and Ali announced that after all his global travel he still considered Louisville the greatest city in the world — "because I'm from here, mainly." He told the students of Central High to do their homework so they wouldn't wind up needing as many lawyers as he did. After a ten-minute speech at the airport, Ali climbed into a white Cadillac limousine with two telephones, a television, and a refrigerator; stood up and stuck his head through the sliding roof; and waved goodbye to the crowd.

"You are the *greatest,* my man!" a fan shouted to Ali, who winked back.

Ali's victory over Foreman had generated powerful new feelings of admiration among his fans, according to *Ebony* magazine. The magazine asked, "Is it far-fetched to say there are elements of religion of some kind involved in the very special relationship that those people have with Muhammad Ali?" *Ebony* quoted a black dermatologist who had watched the Rumble in the Jungle at a Washington, DC, arena packed with seventeen thousand people. "Most were black," the dermatologist told the magazine, "and as we watched Ali fighting round after round to take back a title he lost because he was black man enough to stand on his own two feet and suffer the consequences, well, something just seemed to go through the crowd, something warm and good-feeling . . . When he won, it seemed as though everybody in the arena was suddenly cleansed of any negative thoughts we had about our black selves and about one another and we walked out filled with pride and broth-erliness and black self-love."

His effect on white Americans was powerful, too. Pat Harris was eighteen years old, the son of a longshoreman, and raised in Weehawken, New Jersey. He'd hated Ali in 1971, hated his refusal to fight for his country, hated his ar-rogance, hated the way he'd bad-mouthed Joe Frazier, and he'd been ecstatic when Frazier had won their first contest. He and his buddies paid twenty dollars each for seats in the last row of Madison Square Garden to watch the Ali-Foreman fight. Even though the fight was broadcast via closed-circuit TV, the energy in the arena was incredible. Everyone booed when Foreman's face appeared on the screen, and everyone cheered Ali. "All of a sudden I was an Ali fan," Harris recalled. Only later did he realize how Ali shaped his views on race. "As kids, I don't think race affected us that much," he said, because almost everyone around him was white. "Black people, they were ballplayers," he said. "They were boxers." Harris and his friends weren't per-mitted to use "the n-word," as Harris put it, "but Ali used it all the time. He called Joe Frazier a nigger. We got a kick out of that. Archie Bunker and Ali were the only ones who were allowed to say that." Harris didn't have much interaction with black people until years later when he moved to New York City and became a sportscaster. But as a teenager in 1974, it struck him that Ali wasn't angry anymore, at least not angry at white America, and that made him appealing. "If you followed his career and watched his progression, you couldn't help but love him . . . I think he liked making people laugh. I think he liked making people happy."

Ali knew he mattered to people like Harris, and especially to people like the black dermatologist in Washington. He also knew he would have to do something special to top his victory over Foreman. In Louisville, Ali told reporter Dave Kindred of the *Courier-Journal* that he wanted to fight George Foreman and Joe Frazier on the same night, as part of the same television broadcast, for a $10-million payday. He insisted he was serious. Perhaps Ali thought it was the only way he could top the Rumble in the Jungle. When two of his Nation of Islam bodyguards interrupted the interview to say Ali had to move on to another appointment, Ali told them to wait until he and Kindred finished. When the bodyguards left, Ali whispered, telling Kindred he would have left the Nation of Islam long ago if not for fear for his own safety. "But you saw what they did to Malcolm X," Ali said, in a comment Kindred reported years later in a book. "I can't leave the Muslims. They'd shoot me, too."

Three months later, on February 25, 1975, Elijah Muhammad died of heart failure at age seventy-seven. When he heard the news, Ali left his training camp in Deer Lake to attend the funeral service in Chicago. Publicly, he had little to say about his mentor's death. But Ali spoke at length in a private memorial service for Elijah Muhammad, in remarks that were never reported by the press or previous biographers.

"After hearing of the death of the Honorable Elijah Muhammad," said Ali, wearing a brown suit and glancing at notes, "immediately I took a jet to Chicago . . . to see Herbert because I knew Herbert would tell me just what's happening, how I should feel, what I should say, what I should do."

Ali explained that Elijah Muhammad had told him many years ago that he should accept Herbert Muhammad's orders and advice as if it had come directly from the Messenger. It was Elijah Muhammad who had inspired Ali's faith, but it was Herbert who Ali had seen or spoken to virtually every day for more than a decade. It was Herbert who had been his teacher. And it was Herbert who had been told by his father to take care of Ali, to "never leave his side," according to the journalist Mark Kram, because Ali was vulnerable, easily persuaded, and would always "follow the last person to have his ear." Now, Ali said, it was Herbert who told him what he should do in response to the Messenger's death: he would embrace another one of Elijah Muhammad's sons, Wallace D. Muhammad, as the new leader of the Nation of Islam. "If every Muslim was killed tomorrow," Ali told the mourners gathered in Chicago, "and I was the onliest one left, I would go out somewhere and set me up a little mosque and continue from there on what the Honorable Elijah Muhammad taught me." He concluded, "I make my pledge here today . . . that I will be faithful and loyal and honorable to the Honorable Wallace Muham-

mad, and I'm sure that everyone here today who feels the same will be happy
to stand up right now and let the world know that you're behind this man."

The crowd stood as Ali turned and hugged his new spiritual leader.

Back in Deer Lake, Ali continued to talk about fighting Foreman and Frazier
in one night. No one took him seriously. Don King and Herbert Muhammad
were selecting Ali's opponents now. "Herbert was not that fond of Don," said
Lloyd Price, who had introduced the men, "but they made money together."
King and Herbert Muhammad were in no rush to schedule a fight with anyone who posed a serious threat to their man. The better, safer strategy was to
line up a few small- to medium-sized events against so-so fighters. For start-
ers, Don King suggested Ali fight Joe Bugner, whom Ali had already beaten
once in 1973. King, who was eager to solidify his position as boxing's newest
big-time promoter, promised Ali $2 million for the fight.

"Joe Bugner?" Ali asked Gene Kilroy incredulously. "How do you turn
down Joe Bugner, two million dollars? I wouldn't hire him as a sparring partner."

Although Ali had said he intended to retire after facing Foreman, he now
gave it little thought. How do you quit when you're flying high, when you're
the best in the world at what you do? How do you go from being heavyweight
champ to . . . what? A chatty celebrity? A TV game-show host? What would
he do for the next forty or fifty years? It wasn't as if he could pick up where
he left off when he was twelve. He was not going to return to school. He was
not going to peddle life insurance. He could have joined Howard Cosell as
a television commentator, but was Ali really ready to let other athletes command the spotlight while he sat on the sidelines in a garish sport coat and
tie? He might have enjoyed diplomatic work, as he suggested in interviews
after the Foreman fight, but he was not the sort who would operate happily
and efficiently in a bureaucratic machine. He joked in a December visit to the
White House that he might run for president, but that seemed unlikely too,
especially given that he had never so much as voted.

The mere sight of Ali sharing a laugh with President Ford offered evidence
of Ali's strange place in American culture and the difficulties he might face
in trying to become something more than a celebrity prizefighter. Ali's fame
had long rested on his rejection of American values. Yet here he was, officially welcomed to the highest office in the land, and here he was, happy to be

welcomed, making no waves, raising no political or social issues, just smiling and joking with the president. Ali was now an American hero, a symbol of national identity. He had earned that position by pulling off the great upset of George Foreman but also by riding waves of good fortune beyond his control. America had changed. A comedy called *The Jeffersons* debuted on CBS in 1975. It was a show about a black family in New York that was "moving on up, to the east side, to a deluxe apartment in the sky," and it encouraged viewers to consider the payoff of the civil rights movement, to see one version of racial progress, even if it portrayed George Jefferson and his family as foreigners in upper-class society, as the historian Bruce J. Schulman has noted. "Separate but equal," the battle cry of Southern segregationists, was dead now. But it had been replaced by something more complicated than equality. A new ideal of diversity was taking shape, with racial and ethnic groups fighting to maintain their distinctions. George Jefferson was moving on up, but he wasn't looking to blend into white society, and neither was Muhammad Ali. But others were. O. J. Simpson, the star running back for the Buffalo Bills, avoided politics because he thought it might damage his brand and impair his income, and he was rewarded for it, becoming one of the first black pitchmen for corporate America.

Ali adapted to the changes in popular culture as well as anyone. Even the death of Elijah Muhammad and the ascendancy of his son played to the boxer's advantage. Wallace D. Muhammad moved quickly to disavow many of his father's teachings and reinvent the Nation of Islam. Wallace turned the organization toward orthodox Islam. He eliminated dress codes. At a reception held in honor of Muhammad Ali, Wallace allowed smoking and dancing for the first time. He dropped demands for a black-only state. He even invited white people to join the organization. Finally, about a year and a half after the death of Elijah, Wallace Muhammad announced that the Nation of Islam would no longer exist, and he launched a new organization called the World Community of al-Islam in the West, the first of many name changes.

Suddenly, Ali had a clean slate. He was the champion, he was immensely popular, and he was unfettered from Elijah Muhammad. But who would Ali be without the order and sense of obedience his spiritual advisor had long imposed?

Ali would be a celebrity all his life, just as Joe Louis and Rocky Marciano and Jack Dempsey had remained celebrities. Of that there could be little doubt. But his words and actions suggested that he believed his fame at this point in his career derived almost exclusively from boxing, which made it difficult to know how far that fame would carry when he retired. It was even less clear what mattered to Ali most beyond his sport. Almost every professional athlete faced a similar challenge toward career's end. For an athlete, achieving greatness is the second hardest thing to do. The hardest thing to do is to quit.

"Ali has entered folklore," Wilfrid Sheed wrote, "and has no place to go but down."

In January, a week after his thirty-third birthday, Ali began that downward trek when he joined Don King and Dick Sadler at Chicago's Hyatt Regency Hotel to announce his next fight. It wasn't a rematch with Foreman. It wasn't a third tilt with Joe Frazier or Ken Norton. It wasn't even a contest with the previously advertised Joe Bugner. No, Don King and Herbert Muhammad had gone even lower on the food chain and chosen as Ali's opponent the journeyman fighter and part-time liquor salesman Chuck Wepner of Bayonne, New Jersey, a man known as the Bayonne Bleeder for the ease with which his face sprung leaks. Wepner was thirty-six years old and possessed a record of thirty wins, nine losses, two draws, and more than two hundred stitches.

Was this Ali's plan to ease into retirement? Was he going to dabble in boxing? Was he going to perform on the TV talk-show circuit and dust off his boxing gloves every three or four months to beat up a human marshmallow like Chuck Wepner?

Desperate to hype the humdrum fight, Don King tried to exploit racism, saying Wepner had been chosen to "to give the white race a chance." When that failed to get a reaction, he said fifty cents from every ticket sold would go to Project Survival, the same unheard-of charity he'd mentioned a year earlier to generate interest in his Salt Lake City boxing exhibition. Even Ali couldn't manage to make Wepner sound threatening. He always did better razzing black opponents than white ones, perhaps because he perceived black boxers as his true rivals in the contest to be America's baddest black man. At one point, casting about wildly to hype his upcoming fight, Ali said boxing fans ought to buy tickets because Wepner was "a good family man who could use the money." Then he said he promised to make the fight more interesting by confining his punches to the region between Wepner's belly button and Adam's apple, avoiding the targets from which Wepner was most likely to bleed. In conclusion, he said, he didn't really have to explain why he had chosen Wepner. He was, he declared, "still the greatest fighter of all time," and boxing fans and "pretty foxes" would pay to see him perform no matter the opponent.

The press conference in Chicago raised another uncomfortable question: why was Dick Sadler, manager to George Foreman, standing by King's side? In the months ahead, Sadler and King would work together promoting Ali's fights, and Sadler would work at Deer Lake as an assistant trainer for Ali. Was this Sadler's reward for poisoning George Foreman? The answer may never be known. King was still new to the fight business. It's possible that he merely seized on the breakup of Sadler and Foreman, reaching out to Sadler at a low point in his career and gaining a valuable new ally.

To make sure he didn't lose Ali, King made monthly cash payments to the men who surrounded the champ and urged them to say good things about King to Ali. He took special care to pay the Muslims surrounding the fighter, including Abdul Rahman, formerly known as Captain Sam Saxon, who received five hundred dollars a week plus expenses to serve as the boxer's spiritual mentor. King also threw a party in Chicago for Herbert Muhammad, celebrating the "unsung genius" who had guided Muhammad Ali's career for so long. King invited Howard Cosell, Ken Norton, George Foreman, Redd Foxx, B. B. King, Lola Falana, Horace Silver, Paul Anka, Lou Rawls, and Nikki Giovanni, among others. But even as he did his best to ensure the continuing loyalty of Herbert Muhammad and Ali, King knew he would need additional fighters, and Sadler could help deliver them.

For the Wepner fight, Ali would receive $1.5 million, plus $200,000 in training expenses; Wepner got $100,000. The money didn't come out of Don King's pocket. He had investors — investors with alleged underworld ties. By overpaying Ali and spreading around cash to members of the fighter's coterie, King solidified his control over boxing's biggest star. No one believed that Wepner had a chance to beat Ali. In 1970, in the last fight before his death, Sonny Liston had used Wepner's face to paint the boxing ring red. Wepner had needed seventy stitches to close the cuts in his face after the fight, but the underdog had refused to quit. "The referee was Barney Felix," Wepner recalled. "He came up to me before the ninth round. I said, 'Barney, give me one more round.'" The referee asked Wepner how many fingers he was holding up. "How many guesses do I get?" Wepner joked. Wepner's manager tapped his back three times. "Three!" Wepner shouted. Felix allowed the fight to continue. "But in the ninth I threw a wild punch that hit the ref in the shoulder, and after that they stopped the fight," Wepner recalled.

Despite Wepner's winning personality and the clash of black versus white man, champion versus man-on-the-street, ticket sales were soft. So was Ali's gut. "I'm over-tired and under-trained," he admitted. "It's a grinding, grueling job. There's no pleasure in the ring for me . . . I'll be OK for that Wepner, though."

The fight, held March 24 at the Richfield Coliseum in Ohio, would be remembered primarily for four things:

1. Ali's inability to finish off his brave and bloodied opponent until only nineteen seconds remained in the fifteenth and final round.
2. The sight of Ali sneaking glances at TV monitors near the ring to see how he looked as he fought.
3. Wepner's ninth-round knockdown of Ali, which may have been the result of a trip or a slip as well as a good shot to Ali's chest.
4. Even in the loss, Wepner inspired a young man watching the fight to develop a screenplay about a blue-collar boxer who goes the distance against boxing's heavyweight champion. The young man's name was Sylvester Stallone, and his screenplay became the movie *Rocky,* which would win the Academy Award for best picture in 1977.

After beating Wepner, Ali fought again seven weeks later. In a bout televised live on ABC from Las Vegas, Ron Lyle gave Ali a surprisingly hard time. Lyle had learned to box while in prison on a murder charge. Now, after studying Ali's recent fights, Lyle refused to fall for the champ's rope-a-dope tactic. Instead, he waited patiently for Ali to meet him in the center of the ring. In the first round, Ali didn't land a single punch. Through the first six rounds, he landed only eighteen, looking very much like a fighter hoping to win by a popular vote. In the tenth round, Ali did more gabbing than jabbing, leaning to his right and talking to Lyle while Lyle threw punch after punch, aiming for the nasty purple welt rising under Ali's right eye. Finally, in the eleventh round, Ali rocked Lyle with a right. One punch changed everything. Lyle stumbled and rested on the ropes, trying to clear his head and find his legs. Ali attacked with his first real burst of energy of the night. Soon, the referee stepped in and put an end to it, declaring Ali the winner by a TKO.

Six weeks later, Ali fought yet again, this time against Bugner in Kuala Lumpur, Malaysia, where a crowd of twenty thousand greeted him at the airport. The temperature in the ring hit more than 100 degrees Fahrenheit, and the men went fifteen grueling rounds. Ali won by unanimous decision.

Once more, Ali had to work hard for a fight that his trainers and promoters had treated almost as if it were an exhibition, a supposedly easy paycheck with little risk involved. Ali did get paid handsomely for his fights against Wepner, Lyle, and Bugner, but the fights were not without cost. Against three heavy hitters, Ali fought forty-one rounds and took 483 punches. There were even more blows in the same period, from countless thousands thrown in sparring sessions and exhibitions. In fact, during one five-round exhibition at the Louisville Convention Center, a fundraiser for the new Ali School of Boxing in Louisville, Ali was knocked down four times by Jimmy Ellis. Later, he said the first knockdown was real, and he faked the others to convince the crowd that the first one had been phony, too. When he and Ellis finished, Ali welcomed to the ring a sixteen-year-old fighter named Greg Page, a future heavyweight champion. For three rounds, Ali and Page exchanged heavy blows. When they were done, Ali joked, "That boy hit me so hard, it jarred my kinfolk back in Africa."

Ali didn't mind getting hit between fights. In fact, he believed it helped him prepare for combat with men who were trying in earnest to knock him out. "I let my sparring partners beat up on me about eighty percent of the time," he said in a 1975 interview. "I go on the defense and take a couple of hits to the head and the body, which is good. You gotta condition your body and brain to take those shots, 'cause you're gonna get hit hard a couple of times in every fight."

Larry Holmes, one of his sparring partners at the time, said Ali made it clear to the men he hired that they were supposed to hit him hard — and not try to avoid the head. "If you didn't hit Ali, he'd probably fire you," Holmes recalled. Years later, Holmes would laugh at Ali's notion that taking punches during sparring sessions somehow hardened him for battle. He ridiculed Ali for acting as though he were proud of his ability to take a punch in sparring sessions and in fights. "The object of the game of boxing is hit and don't be hit," he said. "Don't be no fool! Don't prove shit to nobody. You wanna show people how strong you are, show 'em how strong you are by *not* taking those shots. But you know, he didn't do that. *Hit me! Show me something!* And they did."

Ali had entered a troubling career phase. After saying throughout most of 1973 that his retirement was imminent, he continued fighting through 1974 at a pace usually reserved for up-and-comers. These one-sided bouts were no good for boxing. They turned the sport into a mockery. They undercut the democratic idea that fighters could work their way to a shot at the title. The mismatches were no good for Ali, either. He was older, slower, and heavier now. He gulped down Coca-Cola like it was water. He could pour six packets of sugar into one cup of coffee. Ali liked to say he was so fast he could turn out the lights and get in bed before it got dark, but he also might have said he could finish a piece of pie and a scoop of ice cream before the plate hit his table. For Lyle and Bugner, he'd weighed in at 224½ pounds, which was 8 pounds more than he'd weighed against George Foreman and almost 19 pounds more than he'd weighed for his second Sonny Liston fight. He didn't take these fights as seriously as he'd taken his earlier contests. Now, his fellow boxers could see that he was risking his health.

"For Ali to come out there and fight George Foreman," Larry Holmes said, "George is a big ol' man, and getting hit by that! That motherfucker's a horse! You beat up a horse. You make him run and run and run and run out of gas like Ali did, but you don't stay on the ropes for five or six rounds and get punched! Thirty, forty times a round getting hit! You get hit upside the head thirty times a round and you got hit a lot . . . You can't do wrong all the time and think you're gonna come out of it whole."

Ali remained in denial. He did think he was going to come out of it whole. He continued to tell reporters that he was a scientific fighter who never got hurt, that he was special, that even though he didn't dodge punches as well as he once did, and even though he didn't dance away from punches as quickly as he once did, that he still *saw* punches better than anyone and still managed to shift the angle of his head and torso just enough, at the last possible moment, so that most of the blows failed to land with full impact. He continued at age thirty-three to believe he could avoid the damage that almost inevitably befell boxers.

But that would soon change, because Ali was getting ready once again to fight Joe Frazier. After Ali-Frazier III, the cruelty of boxing and its lasting impact on a fighter's mental and physical health would be clear to everyone, even Ali.

43

Impulses

Belinda learned about her husband's affair with Veronica Porche soon after everyone had returned from Zaire. It did not come as a shock. A few years earlier, Wilma Rudolph, Ali's Olympic teammate, had come to the Alis' house in New Jersey asking for money to support a child that Rudolph claimed belonged to Ali. Ali admitted the affair with Rudolph but told Belinda he didn't believe the child was his. After seeing the baby, Belinda decided her husband was probably telling the truth; the child didn't look like Ali.

There were other women and other children, some that Belinda knew about and some that she didn't. According to one of Ali's former bodyguards, the boxer continued to see Sonji Roi, his first wife, during the late 1960s and early 1970s. Areatha Swint, Ali's old girlfriend from Central High School in Louisville, said she carried on an affair with Ali during his marriage to Belinda and traveled with the boxer to some of his fights. A woman named Barbara Mensah said she began a long-running affair with Ali in 1967, when she was seventeen years old, and eventually had his daughter. In 1972, Ali and a woman named Patricia Harvell had a daughter named Miya, a child Ali acknowledged as his own. In 1973, Ali met a high-school senior named Wanda Bolton who was visiting the Deer Lake training camp with her parents. In 1974, Ali became the father of Bolton's daughter, and the year after the child's birth, Ali married Bolton in an Islamic ceremony that was never legally recognized. Ali and Belinda were still married at the time. Islamic law allowed a man to have up to four wives, although the vast majority of American Muslims did not practice polygamy because it violated

American law. Bolton, who joined Ali in Zaire for the Foreman fight, later sued and settled her case with Ali for child support. Another teenaged girl, Temica Williams, claimed she began an affair with Ali in 1975 and soon after had his son. In a lawsuit filed in Cook County, Illinois, Williams claimed that Ali provided only four years of financial support for her boy. Williams sued Ali for sexual assault, alleging that she had been only twelve years old at the start of the relationship and had still been a minor at the time Ali purportedly fathered her child. Her case was dismissed because the statute of limitations had expired. Years later, Veronica said she knew about Temica. Ali had admitted the affair, but he told Veronica he didn't believe Temica's child was his. "He would have claimed that baby," Veronica said, "but everybody in the camp was going with that girl." Also, when Muhammad and Veronica talked about it, they concluded that the child was likely conceived at a time when Ali had been traveling.

"Ali's weakness was coochie," said Leon Muhammad of the Philadelphia mosque. "Ali did a lot of things because he was Ali. People would say to him, 'Hey, be loyal to Belinda . . .' How can you tell a guy that when he's the boss, when he's paying you?"

Years later, others would wonder whether some of Ali's behavior was connected to brain injury from repeated blows to the head. Ali complained of difficulty sleeping and compensated with frequent naps. He described lacking the motivation to go for long runs. He engaged in risky behavior, letting opponents and sparring partners swing away at him, even though he had said years earlier that he knew his long-term health and success in boxing depended on his ability to avoid being hit. But Belinda said she never saw any signs of cognitive damage in her husband. "He was automatically stupid and crazy," she said years later. "He got that DNA-wise."

Ali knew his philandering was wrong. He knew it hurt his wife. He knew it undermined his public image. But as long as he was enjoying himself, Belinda said, those things didn't matter. He seemed entirely unable to control his impulses. Years later, Belinda listened to a Muslim sermon on a CD and heard the imam say that when a man made his primary goal the pursuit of fame, he inevitably failed as a man. "I said, yeah, that's true. Because Ali failed as a man. He was a successful fighter, but he failed as a man. He failed as a father. He failed as a leader, as a role model."

Belinda tolerated it, for the most part. When they argued, Ali would cry and say he was sorry and say he didn't love the other women. He would say it was just sex, that it didn't mean anything. He would say he couldn't help himself. Among friends, Ali would joke about it: "*My wife* is married," he'd say.

But Ali didn't accept all the blame. Sometimes he would point out that Belinda had no right to complain because she had helped arrange for him to see the other women. Sometimes he would threaten to go public with her complicity if she sought a divorce or told reporters her side of the story. She put up with all of it. "The problem I had was when he started bringing them home," she said. "One time he asked me to go to the grocery, and I came back because I forgot my wallet, and she's in my bed. I felt like my whole body was on fire . . . The children were down the hall. He didn't care. He's Muhammad Ali. He can do whatever he wants."

Black women, white women, young women, old women, Hollywood actresses, chamber maids: Ali didn't discriminate. Everyone close to the fighter knew his proclivities. His friends laughed about it. His entourage members and business associates supported it. Within Ali's closest circle, a special set of coded signals developed to be used in noisy crowds. The men would cluck their tongues loudly. One cluck meant *where are you?* Two clucks might mean *I'm here* or *okay, understood.* Multiple clucks meant *stop whatever you're doing, this is important,* or, more specifically, *Belinda has been spotted and Ali needs to ditch the woman he's with.*

Bob Arum told the story of traveling with Ali to Mexico, where their hosts presented them with a roomful of gorgeous women to choose from. In one interview, Arum said that Ali took six women back to his room, while Arum took one. In another interview, Arum said Ali took three women. In either case, Arum's story ends the same way every time. A few hours later, Ali sent a messenger to Arum's room saying Muhammad wanted Arum's girl, too.

Belinda thought she could handle it. Most of the time she did handle it. She booked hotel rooms for the mistresses and occasionally invited them to go shopping with her. But over time, as the affairs piled up, as flings with women like Wanda Bolton and Veronica Porche evolved into long-term relationships, as children were born to some of these women, as sexually transmitted diseases got passed around, Belinda said, "the love I had for him started dwindling, fading away, fading away."

She blamed Ali, of course. But she also blamed Ali's father, Cash Clay, for setting a bad example. She blamed Herbert Muhammad for his cavalier attitude toward women and for suggesting that the Nation of Islam sanctioned marital infidelity. She blamed the all-male domain of boxing. She blamed the men in Ali's entourage, particularly Lloyd Wells, a pimp in a white yachting cap, who supplied the boxer and others in his training camp with a steady stream of women, many of them prostitutes. She blamed the culture of celebrity too, which seemed to say that men of wealth and power were entitled to anything they wanted anytime they wanted, especially where sex was concerned. She blamed American society in the 1970s, when sex outside of marriage became something close to the norm, when women asserted their desires more boldly, when divorce rates and drug addiction surged, and when Donna Summer recorded the disco hit "Love to Love You Baby," a song that included sixteen minutes of passionate moaning and inspired rumors that Summer had been masturbating during the recording session, which is just what she appeared to be doing in the photo on her album cover. But most of all, Belinda blamed Ali.

Belinda and Veronica had crossed paths but never met in Zaire. Their first meeting came in Las Vegas, shortly before the Ron Lyle fight. The day after their introduction, the women were standing on a patio at the Tropicana Hotel, looking over a railing at the neon-lit Vegas Strip. Belinda said she'd had a dream about Veronica. In the dream, Veronica had fallen from a railing just like the one they were leaning on now, landed on her face, and died. Veronica took it as a warning.

Upon returning from Zaire, Veronica had moved to Chicago to be close to Ali. He had just purchased a twenty-eight-room Tudor mansion in Chicago's Hyde Park neighborhood, at 4944 South Woodlawn Avenue, across the street from the home where Elijah Muhammad had lived. The house was so big that, eventually, Herbert Muhammad would keep an office there. While it was under renovation, Ali and Belinda kept an apartment in the penthouse of a building Ali owned, but Veronica got the impression that Belinda had the place to herself. Ali seldom stayed with his wife, she said. The children lived with Belinda's parents. Ali purchased a condominium in Chicago for Veronica.

One day in June, Ali invited Belinda and Veronica to join him in Boston, where Ali was scheduled to deliver a speech to Harvard's graduating seniors. Before leaving on the trip, Belinda and Veronica stopped at a Muslim restaurant to get steak sandwiches and went to Belinda's apartment to eat. Belinda unwrapped the sandwiches in the kitchen while Veronica waited in the living room. Soon after, as they boarded their plane, Veronica became sick to her stomach. She spent the entire flight in the airplane's lavatory. "She didn't get sick, but I did," Veronica recalled.

Ali's friend Howard Bingham also made the trip to Boston, snapping pictures along the way. One of Bingham's photos, which seemed innocent enough at the time, captured the complexity of Ali's romantic life. In the picture, Ali stands near a nondescript glass door. He wears a pinstriped suit and striped tie. Three women stand to his left. They are, from right to left, Veronica Porche, wearing large hooped earrings, a white purse over her shoulder, one hand holding the other in front of her stomach; Belinda Ali, dressed all in white, clutching a manila folder, her right hand reaching for Ali's arm, her eyes turning to the camera as it flashes; and, next to Belinda, an eighteen-year-old Louisville woman named Lonnie Williams, wearing glasses and gazing in the direction of Veronica. Lonnie was fifteen years younger than the boxer, but she had recently had an epiphany: "I knew I was going to marry Muhammad," she said. "I was just a kid in school, and I had things I needed to do, but I knew . . . The thought was like an umbrella, always over my head."

Her epiphany would prove accurate, but at the time of the photo Belinda was still married to Ali and had no intention of divorcing him. Veronica considered herself already married to Ali, but she was waiting for him to get a divorce so she could make it official. Lonnie would have to wait.

In Bingham's photo, Ali betrays no hint of discomfort as he stands beside his second wife, his future third wife, and his future fourth wife. His shoulders are loose. His hands rest by his sides. His mouth is open slightly as if he's speaking. His eyes are wandering to his right, away from the three women. At what—or at whom—he's gazing, no one knows.

Ali told Veronica that he had a good reason for welcoming Lonnie. Belinda didn't want to grant Ali a divorce, and in her frustration, she often lashed out at Veronica. By introducing Lonnie to the mix, Ali hoped that Belinda would have a new target for her anger. "He said Lonnie would be a third wife and then all the pressure wouldn't be on me," Veronica recalled. In hindsight, she said, it sounds crazy.

She paused and laughed.

"However," she said, "it did work."

During his lecture at Harvard, an audience member asked Ali for a poem. He thought about it for a moment, leaned into the microphone, and recited what may have been the greatest rhyme of his life, his complete autobiography in two syllables:

"Me! Wheeeee!"

About two weeks later, Ali took Belinda and Veronica with him to Malaysia for his fight against Bugner. Ali made no attempt to hide the fact he traveled with both women. The three of them shared a suite with two bedrooms in Kuala Lumpur. Ali told Belinda: "Every two nights, I'll take you as my wife, you'll stay with me for two nights. Veronica stays in that room. And when those two nights is over, you'll go to that room and Veronica will stay with me two nights." When Ali didn't want to sleep with either of them, he said, Veronica and Belinda would share the suite's second bedroom, which contained twin beds.

Once again, Belinda accepted the conditions imposed by her husband. "I'm biting my teeth, going, 'Is this really happening to me?'" she recalled.

She took Veronica shopping, trying to help her dress more like a proper Muslim, she said. Belinda bought Veronica a silver perfume amulet for four hundred dollars. She tried to turn her rival into an ally. After about a week, though, when people in Malaysia began to mistake Veronica for Ali's wife, Belinda lost patience. She told Ali that Veronica had to go.

But Veronica stayed.

Veronica hated the way Belinda treated her, and she wished Ali would have defended her, wished he would have told Belinda to knock it off, or would have made a complete break with Belinda and initiated the divorce proceedings. But he wouldn't do any of those things. Still, she stayed. "It was totally unfair to me," Veronica recalled years later, "but I remember thinking,

'Well, it's too late. I'm in love. Love supersedes everything.' I was that ideal-istic."

Before his fight with Bugner, Ali had spoken again of retirement. But no one believed him at all. Everyone knew that Don King had already begun negoti-ating for Ali to fight Joe Frazier for a third time, perhaps in Madison Square Garden, perhaps in the Philippines, where authoritarian leader Ferdinand Marcos was as eager as Mobutu had been in Zaire to improve his public im-age by palling around with Muhammad Ali. No man in the world provided more powerful propaganda.

Filipinos adored Ali, but there wasn't all that much excitement about Ali-Frazier III, the feeling being that Frazier was washed up after having been bounced around by Foreman like a beach ball.

Still, Ali was the biggest attraction in the sport. He was not only on top of the boxing game; he was at the top of the list of celebrity athletes, a category he had virtually invented. He was a superstar, as big as they came. His auto-biography, written with Richard Durham, was in bookstores, selling well and getting strong reviews. Soon, there would be a movie based on the book and starring none other than Muhammad Ali as Muhammad Ali. "It's going to be big," Ali said of the film, "like 'Godfather.' 'The Magnificent Seven.' They could make ten films from my life."

Ali's autobiography was not only the work of his coauthor, Richard Durham, and his editor, Toni Morrison; it was also very much the creation of Herbert Muhammad, who wound up sharing the copyright. The book pre-sented Ali as a boxer, a rebel, and a proud Muslim, and Durham was granted creative license to get the job done.

One of his fictional anecdotes proved particularly compelling. At some point several years after his return to Louisville from the 1960 Rome Olym-pics, Ali had lost his gold medal. He didn't know how it had happened. One day he had it, and the next he didn't. It might have been stolen or mis-placed, according to his brother, Rahaman, who said he helped hunt for it. But Durham used the lost medal to fashion a fable. As Durham told it, Ali flung the gold medal into the Ohio River because he was upset at having been turned away at a whites-only restaurant and chased from the restaurant by a white motorcycle gang. Clay was, in fact, denied service at a Louisville restaurant, and he was indeed angry that such a thing could happen even to an Olympic hero. But no gang of bikers chased him, and there's no evidence to suggest he threw his medal in the river. He certainly didn't do so in 1960, as his autobiography suggests, given that photographs show him holding the medal as late as 1963.

After the book's publication, Ali admitted at a press conference that he had lost the medal, not thrown it in the river. He also admitted that he hadn't read Durham's work. Nevertheless, the myth of the medal tossed in protest would live on for decades to come.

Ali-Frazier III was set for October 1, 1975, in Manila. Ali was guaranteed $4 million; Frazier would collect $2 million.

Three weeks before the fight, *Newsweek* reporter Pete Bonventre received an assignment from his editor: go to Manila with Ali, get past the showmanship, get past the sports-page clichés, and dig for the truth about the man.

Most of the reporters covering Ali were sportswriters. Many had been covering him for years. They loved Ali, and they were familiar with his antics, as well as with his cast of supporting characters. By sending Bonventre, *Newsweek* hoped to get the outsider's perspective and, perhaps, to get past the hagiography already clinging to Ali.

Bonventre loved Ali, too. "Here's this guy," the reporter said, "this magnetic force, who's probably the most famous guy in the world, and he's telling reporters, 'Open your notebooks and I'll fill them up.' I mean, how could you not love a guy like that?"

Bonventre traveled to Manila ahead of the pack of sportswriters to get time with Ali and his merry band of men. Bonventre watched one day as a Filipino man presented Ali with a scroll that had been printed with beautiful calligraphy and decorated in silver and gold. Ali signed it, rolled it up, and bowed as he handed it back.

"Thank you," the Filipino man said. "You are now the godfather of my child."

Ali turned with a wide grin to Bonventre.

"How do you like that!" he said, proud as could be.

Still, it didn't take long for the reporter to see that Ali's world had changed, and not for the better. Ali arrived in Manila with thirty-eight "handlers," a number that did not include his girlfriends. In addition to Veronica, Ali's old high-school girlfriend Areatha Swint had made the trip to Manila. "You couldn't be around a man like that without the she-wolf pack," Swint recalled years later. "There's was no way you let that get under your skin."

Bonventre described the change in Ali's world this way: "Solemn Muslim guards have given way to street-wise hustlers. Liberals who cherished him as a symbol of pro-black, anti-war attitudes have been replaced by wry connoisseurs of his pure showmanship. Even Ali's women, invariably beautiful and black, have now been brought out of the back rooms of his life and openly flaunted." While this was not a hard-hitting investigative piece, it was very much in the spirit of Watergate, when journalists were challenging authority, knocking over idols, and, to use a catchphrase popular at the time, telling it like it is.

Bonventre reported what other reporters had long known, that Ali now seemed "unfettered by marital convention," and that Veronica Porche was known to everyone in the fighter's camp as "Ali's other wife." A photograph accompanying the article showed "Baby-sitter Veronica" walking hand in hand with three of Ali's four children — May May, Jamillah, and Rasheda. The reporter also wrote about the cruel, "almost Nixonian" way that Ali pitted the men in his entourage against one another, once even forcing two of his followers to climb into a boxing ring and duke it out for his amusement.

Bonventre wasn't the only reporter who'd decided that Ali's adultery should no longer be a private matter. After an encounter between Ali and Marcos at the presidential palace in Manila, Ali's affair with Veronica became impossible for reporters to ignore.

At the palace, Marcos had his wife, Imelda, by his side. Veronica accompanied Ali.

"You have a beautiful wife," Ali told Marcos, smiling at Imelda.

"From the looks of yours," said Marcos, "you're not far behind."

Joe Frazier snickered at the remark, and Veronica wasn't sure whether to take it as an insult.

Ali did not attempt to correct Marcos.

Journalists reported on the incident, saying that Ali had introduced Veronica to Marcos as his wife. It wasn't exactly true, but it was close enough to make things uncomfortable. Dave Anderson of the *New York Times* asked Ali if he had taken two wives.

"No, we ain't gonna go against the law of the land," Ali said, making a veiled reference to the fact that Islamic law permitted him to have more than one spouse. "But ain't she beautiful?"

Back in the United States, photos appeared in newspapers of Veronica and Ali at the Philippine presidential palace. Belinda surely knew that Veronica was in Manila. But it was one thing to know about his affair and another to see it making international news. Belinda got on a plane, flew to Manila, and interrupted her husband in the middle of an interview. The couple retreated to Ali's bedroom, where Belinda shouted, knocked over furniture, and threatened to break Veronica's neck the next time she saw her.

"I'm not wanted here," Belinda told reporters in Manila. "Muhammad Ali doesn't want me here. Nobody wants me here. I'm not going to force myself. I don't like an impostor coming in and taking over my family after eight years and destroying my life."

With that, Belinda went back to the airport and flew home.

"You really couldn't blame her," Areatha Swint said.

Ali told Bonventre he had no intention of letting mundane domestic matters interfere with his work. He was on a divine mission. "It ain't no accident that I'm the greatest man in the world at this time in history," he said. Allah had chosen him for a reason.

"It's time for me to face another test," he told Bonventre. "Things have been going too good lately. Allah must make me pay for all this fame and power . . . Allah's always testing you. He don't let you get great for nothing."

Later, in an interview with the *New York Times,* Ali defended his right to sleep with as many women as he liked and hinted that he was spending time with others in addition to Veronica and Areatha. "I got three or four lady friends here," he said. "I can see some controversy if she was white, but she's not. But the only person I answer to is Belinda Ali and I don't worry about her . . . This is going too far. They got on me for the draft. They got on me for my religion. They got on me for all sorts of things. But they shouldn't be able to get on me for having a girlfriend . . . The only person I worry about if I do something wrong is Wallace Muhammad. If my wife catches me with ten women at a party, kissing them, that don't bother me, just so I don't get in trouble with Wallace Muhammad."

44

Ali-Frazier III

Two days before the fight, Ali was stretched out on a couch in his dressing room, giving himself a pep talk. There were reporters in the room, but they weren't gathered around, and Ali didn't seem to care if any of them were listening. His words flowed in a stream of consciousness: "Who'd he ever beat for the title?" Ali asked, referring to Joe Frazier, of course. "Buster Mathis and Jimmy Ellis. He ain't no champion. All he's got is a left hook, got no right hand, no jab, no rhythm. I was the real champion all the time. He reigned because I escaped the draft and he luckily got by me, but he was only an imitation champion. He just luckily got through because his head could take a lot of punches."

If he wasn't conducting an interview and if he didn't care whether anyone was listening, why did Ali feel compelled to run through this evaluation of Frazier's evidently meager skills and qualifications? Was this how he entertained himself? Was this the way he soothed his own doubts?

Once again, in the buildup to the fight, Ali had been merciless in his treatment of Frazier, questioning his intelligence, his manliness, and his blackness. Ali had waved a small rubber ape and called Frazier a gorilla and pretended to box a man in a gorilla suit. He had rhymed endlessly and unimaginatively about the gorilla and the "Thrilla in Manila." "He not only looks bad! You can smell him in another country!" Ali held his nose. "What will the people in Manila think? We can't have a gorilla for champ. They're gonna think, lookin' at him, that all black brothers are animals. Ignorant. Stupid. Ugly. If he's champ again, other nations will laugh at us." He dropped low, let his knuckles hang by his knees, and jumped around, snorting like an ape. At one point, Ali aimed an unloaded pistol at Frazier and pulled the trigger four or five times. Frazier claimed it was a real gun — "I know enough about guns to know that," he said — but Ali said it was a toy.

Frazier hated Ali for treating him this way. The wounds ran deep, and he would carry them the rest of his life. "I'm gonna eat this half-breed's heart right off his chest," Joe told his trainer, Eddie Futch. "I mean it," Joe said. "This is the end of him or me."

Ali didn't seem to care. He approached conflict the way he had approached George Foreman in the biggest fight of his life, improvising, counting on his good instincts, good looks, and good luck to get him through. Would it matter if he made Frazier mad? Maybe. Maybe not. Who cares? Anyway, boxing was never intended to be polite. Ali and Frazier had something bigger than the heavyweight championship on the line. They were competing for their own championship, to see once and for all which one of them was the greater fighter.

The day of the fight, October 1, 1975, was another day of scorching sun, high humidity, and cantankerous heat. The Araneta Coliseum in Manila had air-conditioning, but not enough. Even at 10 a.m., as a crowd of 28,000 packed the arena tight, everyone felt the ferocious heat. In the United States and Canada, the fight was shown live on a closed-circuit telecast in 350 arenas and theaters. The vast majority of boxing fans listened to the action on the radio, as they did for most big fights. But for this fight, a new option became available, if only for the 100,000 or so American homeowners who subscribed to Home Box Office, the fledgling cable TV station. On the night of the fight, HBO became the first network to broadcast nationally via satellite. To make it work, a transmitter in the Philippines bounced a signal across the Pacific Ocean via satellite to a station in Jamesburg, California. The station in Jamesburg transmitted the signal by AT&T land lines to a telephone switching center in Manhattan, where it was rerouted to the HBO studios on 23rd Street, and then relayed by satellite to Valley Forge, Pennsylvania; beamed to a station in Fort Pierce, Florida; and delivered by microwave link to cable providers. As Ali and Frazier appeared live via satellite in HBO subscribers' homes, a new age of television began. Suddenly, it became much easier and much less expensive for cable TV operators to reach big audiences with live and original programming.

Ali wore white satin trunks, Frazier blue denim. Both men were in excellent condition. Even so, the heat was so oppressive that it was impossible to know how either boxer would hold up if the fight went more than a few rounds.

The bell rang, and they were going at it for the third time in four and a half years.

Ali moved to the center of the ring and kept his hands up in front of his face, displaying the perfect boxing form that had escaped him most of his career, although he maintained it only briefly. He threw five left jabs before launching his first right. After about thirty seconds, he stopped moving around the ring, dropped his hands, and began throwing powerful hooks aimed for Frazier's head, one after another. Frazier bobbed and barreled his way inside but Ali moved out of danger. He wasn't dancing out of the way. He wasn't dancing at all. But in the early rounds, he nonetheless set the pace for the fight. Ali stuck out his left hand, taking advantage of a big edge in reach, to keep Frazier at a distance, and then whipped the right cross when Joe tried to swat away the left. Ali threw far more punches than Frazier in the first two rounds, and he was landing many of them — big, solid, thudding shots, his face taut in a sneer, his feet solidly planted, body corkscrewing to bring maximum force. Ali wanted a knockout. He wanted to end it before Frazier or the heat could get to him.

Frazier wobbled at times. The sweat flew from his face. At the end of round two, he looked like he was going to fall. But he didn't. He grunted and burrowed in on Ali and flayed the bigger man's ribs with punches that sounded like big mallets on a bass drum.

The third round opened, and Ali resorted to his rope-a-dope technique, curling up in the corner and letting Frazier in so close Ali could feel the heat of his breath. After about forty seconds of pounding, Ali stood tall and went after Frazier. He threw right-hand leads that jerked Frazier's head back. The round ended with both men in all-out attack, arms flying, heads spinning, Ali shouting at Frazier, Frazier grunting at Ali. Ali won the round but not before Frazier caught him with a nasty left to the chin.

"Stay mean with him, Champ!" someone screamed from Ali's corner.

In the fourth and fifth rounds, Ali leaned back in the corner as Frazier fired shots at his arms and hips. In the sixth, Frazier wedged himself under Ali's chest and began banging like a man trying to get out of a locked trunk, the only difference being that the trunk hit back from time to time. Seemingly in defiance of possibility, the temperature in the arena was rising, the cigar and cigarette smoke forming a dense cloud that clung to the ceiling, the scent putrid. Ali was drenched in his own sweat and Frazier's. It was difficult to imagine either of these men, or any human, lasting fifteen rounds in these conditions and under this sort of attack. Two left hooks seemed to daze Ali, but he kept fighting. Another left hook rocked Ali's head. One veteran sportswriter said it was the hardest punch he'd ever seen, harder than the one that had knocked Ali to the mat in 1971.

"Old Joe Frazier," Ali said, as the men came off their stools to begin the seventh, "Why, I thought you were washed up."

"Somebody told you all wrong, pretty boy," Joe answered.

In the eighth, Ali tried again to end it. He abandoned defense, gritted his teeth, and reached back to throw the biggest punches he could. But Frazier didn't fall, and Ali couldn't keep it up for a full round. When Ali returned to the ropes to rest, Frazier squatted down and dug into his opponent's ribs again. He did what he did best. He ripped at Ali's midsection with eight or nine straight shots before trying the left hook that might end it all. Ali swayed but never went down.

The fight stayed even through the ninth and tenth. Frazier was the more aggressive of the two fighters. He accepted that he would have to take Ali's best punches to muscle his way inside. For part of each round, Ali let Frazier punish him. If boxing is ultimately a test of strength, Ali was betting that he would be the stronger man in the end, that he would endure to win. All his life, Ali had made his body answer his call. As a boy, fighting Corky Baker, he'd jitterbugged and flicked jabs and eluded the big, strong neighborhood bully until the bully quit in shame. Against Sonny Liston, when Ali had been expected to run and hide, he'd come out firing missiles no one knew he possessed. Against George Foreman, he'd turned himself into a sponge, absorbing his opponent's energy. He had always had a great talent for exploiting the weaknesses of his opponents, but now he relied heavily on a different talent: simple endurance. Against Frazier, he made up his mind he would triumph by suffering, by accepting more pain than Frazier could. Ali had always been willing to suffer — for his sport, for his religion, for his pleasure — but he had never suffered physical pain like this.

"It was like death," he would say when it was over. "Closest thing to dyin' that I know of."

Ali spoke often of death, as many religious men and women do. Although he had been blessed with one of the most handsome and graceful bodies anyone had ever seen, he had always accepted that body's limitations, always acknowledged that no one lived forever. As the Muslim prayer says, "Surely we belong to Allah, and to Him we return." For now, it was clear that Ali was willing to pay a phenomenal cost to keep fighting, willing to push himself beyond anyplace he had ever gone.

Between the tenth and eleventh rounds, Ali sagged on his stool. He looked beaten, finished.

"The world needs ya, champ!" Bundini shouted, tears streaming down his face.

Ali rose and gazed across the ring at Frazier. Both men's faces were swollen, empurpled around the eyes, and soaked in sweat and blood. All around them, agitated men shouted for more.

In the eleventh, Ali somehow found a new store of energy. He threw more punches, harder punches, faster punches, seventy-six punches in all, one punch for every 2.37 seconds. Most of the shots found their target — which was Frazier's head. Gobs of blood flew from Frazier's distorted face. Still, punch after punch, Frazier moved forward.

"Lawd have mercy!" Bundini screamed.

In the twelfth, Frazier finally slowed down. Ali stretched his arms long and wide and landed his best blow of the night. Bumps rose from the bumps already on Frazier's brow. He looked like someone had just scraped him off the highway. In the thirteenth, Ali knocked out Frazier's mouthpiece, and that accomplishment seemed to give Ali another surge of adrenaline. Standing in the center of the ring, he threw a right that nearly floored Frazier. Somehow, Frazier remained vertical. He found Ali through closing eyelids, shoved him in the corner, and slammed his fists again and again into Ali's gut. Ali's eyes rolled to the heavens, as if to ask, *How is this man still hitting me?*

In the fourteenth, Frazier could not see. With his left eye closed and his right eye damaged, he couldn't aim his hook unless he straightened up and turned his head to the left. But when he did that, he couldn't make out the right crosses flying at his head. Ali nailed him with nine straight.

Ali, emboldened, grew stronger. When he should have been exhausted . . . no, when he was beyond exhausted, he maintained a pace that defied not only the heat but also logic and perhaps physiology. And Frazier, practically blind, caught them flush. Plumes of sweat, mucus, and blood flew from his brow with every shot. Joe, hopelessly resisting, looked around with one eye for Ali. He stomped forward like an apparition, a haint, one that would haunt Ali the rest of his life no matter who won this fight. Frazier was hit and hit and hit, defenseless, but he would not fall. His feet slid forward, his arms churned. He tried to crash one more left hook, his only hope. But he couldn't do it.

When the bell rang, he walked shakily back to his corner. He slumped on his stool, where he heard his manager, Eddie Futch, say, "Joe, it's over."

"No, no," Frazier said, "ya can't do that to me."

But Futch had been a trainer at four fights in which a fighter had died. He said later he was thinking of Frazier's kids when he insisted on stopping the fight with only one round to go. Later, some people close to Ali's corner said they heard Ali tell Dundee he wanted to quit. Dundee never confirmed those accounts, but he did say he wasn't sure Ali would have lasted another round.

It didn't matter. Futch, mercifully, ended it.

Ali rose slowly from stool, the winner, or at least the survivor. He raised his right hand in the air. As Cash Clay, Rahaman Ali, Don King, and Herbert Muhammad climbed into the ring to celebrate, Ali fell to the mat.

That night, Imelda Marcos led Ali up a red-carpeted staircase to a party in his honor at Malacañang Palace. Ali sat quietly, gently sliding food past his scraped and swollen lips. Frazier was too badly beaten to appear at the same reception, but Ali insisted on carrying on in the image of the triumphant warrior, even if he felt more like a wounded one.

The next day, he was urinating blood (and would continue to do so for weeks). His eyes were red, his face misshapen, his right hand swollen and sore.

As he gazed out the window of his hotel room at a dark red sunset, he turned to a reporter and asked, "Why I do this?"

45

Getting Old

He was done. Finished. He meant it. He had beaten everyone worth beating. He had proven everything he could possibly prove. It was time to quit, he said.

But a few weeks passed.

"I've changed my mind," he told Howard Cosell, "and I feel I can go another few years. The fans want to see it." He said he had international business plans, "and being an active champion I can do more business and other things, and I just want to stay active so I can have more power doing things I'm doing on the side."

He sounded like a man fighting for money. He also sounded, more than ever, like a man who was sacrificing his health and reputation for the pursuit of the next paycheck. Perhaps he was contemplating the possibility of another expensive divorce. Perhaps he had read his wife's recent interview with *Ebony*, in which she had said, "I'm not going to break our marriage in any way. Nothing can come between us. I don't care how many Veronicas come on the scene; I'm not leaving . . . I've got four children and I've got to look out for them, right?"

Sitting beside Cosell, Ali spoke slowly and somnolently. When asked why he had not fulfilled his promise to knock out Frazier in the first round, Ali seemed to need a moment to prime the pump before the words would flow. "Well, yes," he said, "this is, uhh, psy . . . chological warfare on your opponent."

Nearly five months after the Thrilla in Manila, Ali took on Jean-Pierre

Coopman in a fight Ali couldn't muster enough energy to rhyme about. The Belgian heavyweight was known as the Lion of Flanders, but Ali described this fight as a kind of a vacation, saying he deserved an easy opponent or two after his war with Frazier. Ali was slow and overweight, but he could have beaten Coopman sitting down. He chatted with the audience during the fight, played for laughs by wiggling his ass as he moved around the ring, and may or may not have broken a sweat. In the fifth round, he finished an easy night of work, knocking out Coopman with an unremarkable combination of punches. If the bout proved anything, it proved a thirty-four-year-old, overweight Ali was still far superior to a middle-of-the-pack heavyweight.

Two months later, Ali fought again, this time against Jimmy Young at the Capital Centre in Landover, Maryland. Ali would make $1.6 million for the contest, while Young would get about $100,000. Ali said he planned to fight Young, Ken Norton, George Foreman, and then retire. He neglected to mention that he had already signed a contract to fight Richard Dunn in Germany on May 24, a mere twenty-four days after facing Young, meaning that he would be defending his title an astonishing three times in ninety-four days. Oh, and he also intended to challenge Japan's heavyweight wrestling champion, Antonio Inoki, on June 25 in Tokyo, in a bout that would be a hybrid between boxing and wrestling and for which no rules had yet been determined. But that was it: Young, Dunn, Norton, Foreman, Inoki, and then retirement. Count on it, he said.

"I'm so far in my own class that I have to look for other things," he said, explaining why he would fight a wrestler, someone who might kick him or throw him to the floor or twist his neck. "This is what I'm involved in — publicity, controversy, acting just to . . . draw crowds. Why am I me? Because I do things that are ridiculous."

For his fight with Young, Ali's face was moon-shaped, his chest and belly jiggling, his weight at an all-time high of 230 pounds, almost 40 pounds heavier than he'd been at the start of his career. Young was six-foot-two, quick but not too quick, strong but not too strong. He had been fighting professionally for nearly seven years and training at Joe Frazier's gym in Philadelphia.

At this point in his career, Ali no longer believed he needed to be in top shape to beat most opponents. He counted on savvy and on the fact that he was almost impossible to knock out. As long as he remained standing, he figured, he would find a way to beat most men.

His explanations for his poor condition made little sense. All in the same press conference, he said:

"I'm heavy because I need energy."

"I'll fight only as hard as I have to until his resistance is low."

"To me, it's just another day of havin' a little fun."

"The only thing that can beat me is me."

"If I got down to 215 for this one, I'd hate the gym."

"I've been eating too much pie, too much ice cream."

Ali was not only out of shape and overconfident; he had also failed to do his homework, had failed to watch film of Jimmy Young's fights. If he'd watched, if he'd cared, he would have known he was in for trouble. Young was far from the best fighter Ali had ever faced, but he was one of the cleverest. He was also hungry and superbly conditioned. From the opening moments of the fight, the challenger shocked the crowd and broadcaster Howard Cosell by turning the tables on Ali, by fighting more like Ali than Ali was capable of fighting at that point in his career. Young recognized that Ali liked to counterattack. But what would happen if Ali had no attack to counter? What would happen if Young waited and forced Ali to be the aggressor? What would happen if he forced Ali to fight fifteen full rounds, without resting on the ropes for long stretches? Young decided to find out.

Ali was flummoxed. In the opening round, he attempted only five punches, landing none. In the entire fight, he landed only about 110 punches, or about 7 per round. He found no rhythm. His punches flew soft and slow. When he circled the ring and waited for Young to come after him, Young circled too, waiting for Ali to attack. In round three, Ali, clearly frustrated, leaned back on the ropes and signaled for Young to come and get him. It was rope-a-dope time. Young calmly walked away, as if to say, no thanks, I've seen that trick before. Somewhere, George Foreman must have been weeping at the sight Over and over, Young out-Ali-ed Ali, ducking jabs with a mere bob of his head, grabbing his opponent by the arms and shoulders to slow the action, even taking a knee and sticking his head between the ropes at times to disrupt his opponent's rhythm. Ali had no answer.

"Go to work," Bundini shouted in the sixth.

"You're losing," Rahaman screamed in the eleventh.

"You can't be thirty-four and balloon up and not train . . . fighting only for the money," Howard Cosell complained on the air.

When it was over, the crowd booed Ali. Everyone but the judges thought Ali had lost. Young had outlanded the champion by a margin of almost two to one. But there's an old unwritten rule in boxing that a challenger has to *take* a title away from the champion, winning by a knockout or at least by overwhelming violence; the judges shouldn't do the job for him. But then why have judges at all? Ali did nothing to earn the decision against Young; he was awarded the victory because he was Muhammad Ali. It was a gift from his admirers.

When Cosell found him in the ring, Ali stated the obvious: he should have taken Young more seriously.

"I'm getting old, Howard," he said. "That's why I'm quittin' this year."

Ali's ring doctor, Ferdie Pacheco, said it wasn't just age and lazy work habits slowing Ali down, however. "He was more than just overweight," Pacheco said. "This repetitive fighting saps him of his desire to get into proper shape. This was the worst he's ever taken an opponent . . . He was getting tired a lot sooner than usual. His reflexes were only 25 to 30 percent of what they should be."

Angelo Dundee noticed a difference in Ali, too. For years, Dundee would tell Ali about watching old fighters come in to the gym, how he could tell even when they loosened up, even when they jumped rope, that they were losing their agility. "The bounce wasn't the same," he said, "the fluidness wasn't the same." He called it stuttering, referring not to the fighters' speech but to the way their bodies moved.

"Hey, man," Dundee told Ali one day. "You're starting to stutter."

But Ali didn't listen.

"You don't want to take the message," Dundee said, "I can't help it."

Dundee also noticed a worrisome change in Ali's voice. He became concerned, he said, "because I couldn't . . . hear him talk. I would sort of get on Muhammad . . . don't bend your throat, talk."

A reporter asked Ali if, given his poor performance against Young, he would consider taking a break before fighting Ken Norton, a match that was expected to take place in September at Yankee Stadium or Madison Square Garden. Would he at least consider canceling his bout against the Japanese wrestler in Tokyo?

No, Ali said. He wasn't going to cancel it.

The reporter asked, Why not?

"Six million dollars," he answered.

46

"They May Not Let Me Quit"

By 1976, Muhammad Ali was everywhere. A name that had once sounded so foreign as to be incomprehensible was now an instantly recognizable brand. There were Muhammad Ali books, Muhammad Ali movies, Muhammad Ali toys, Muhammad Ali posters, even another fledgling hamburger chain, this one called Ali's Trolley. And, of course, there were still Muhammad Ali boxing matches, too. But it was clear that Ali's boxing fame had outlasted his boxing skills.

To help fill the arena in Munich for his fight with Richard Dunn, Ali gave free tickets to American servicemen stationed in Germany. When reporter Mike Katz of the *New York Times* asked Ali if he saw irony in a conscientious objector inviting soldiers to see him fight, Ali replied with one of his favorite lines: "You're not as dumb as you look." Then, Ali added, "I was against the war. I wasn't against the soldiers."

Ali lost ten pounds in three weeks to prepare for Dunn. He beat Dunn soundly, but there was nothing impressive about the performance. In five rounds, only twelve Ali jabs found their mark. The jab had always provided offense and defense for Ali. He had jabbed so quickly and so well that opponents didn't have time to fight back. The jab had allowed Ali to control the fight, keeping his opponent at a safe distance but within striking range. But Dunn, as a left-handed fighter, was not as vulnerable to Ali's jab. Without his best punch and without his speedy footwork, Ali had little protection. When he threw big, looping punches, Dunn did the same. At least twice, Dunn staggered Ali. Finally, Ali took over, knocking down Dunn four times in the fourth before ending the fight with another knockdown in the fifth. But it was clear even to casual fans that Ali was an entirely different fighter now. Even against no-name boxers, he no longer escaped unharmed. Shots to the head were the price he would pay to continue his career.

In his televised interview from the ring after the fight, Ali thanked Allah; his spiritual leader, Wallace D. Muhammad; President Gerald Ford; Dick Gregory, who was running across America to call attention to hunger; and the karate masters who were getting the boxer ready for his fight against Antonio Inoki. He sent greetings to "all my family at home" without mentioning any names.

Ali's frenzied fight schedule in 1976 reflected the frenzied nature of his life. His nine-year marriage had become an echo of a marriage, a trace of what it had been, and was nearing its end.

Belinda had recently changed her name to Khalilah, saying the name had been given to her by the Nation of Islam's Supreme Minister Wallace D. Muhammad. In an interview with *People* magazine, Belinda said, "There isn't any marriage. It's past me now."

Khalilah, Veronica, and Muhammad now kept separate apartments in Chicago, and Veronica was pregnant with Ali's child.

Ali's parents were separated. Odessa stayed home in Louisville, ensconced in a new house paid for by her son, while Cash jetted around the world, lapping up the pleasures that came with being the father of the champ — pleasures that included a lot of free drinks and attention from women who did not ordinarily look twice at a man twice their age.

Ali's financial affairs were in chaos, too. Gene Kilroy paid the bills and tried to scare off vultures. Herbert Muhammad negotiated the deals. Bob Arum and Don King made the fights. But, often, Herbert, Arum, and King wound up competing to make deals. If Ali had served as chief executive officer, setting the strategy, defining the long-term goals, and making a plan to ensure his long-term financial health, he might have been well prepared for retirement. But he didn't. Instead, in the fall of 1976, he named Spiros Anthony, a lawyer from Fairfax, Virginia, as his trustee. Anthony opened an office and hired a small staff to cull through Ali's business offers. "He was literally the most sought-after celebrity in the world," Anthony said. "You can imagine what people were trying to throw at him, to get him to buy or

endorse. Watches, prayer rugs. It was an unbelievable deluge of proposals."
Anthony invested Ali's money in real estate — mostly office buildings and
condominiums. But Ali soon accused Anthony of siphoning off his money
and using it to cover gambling debts, a charge Anthony denied. Ali sued.
Although he continued to claim his innocence — and, in fact, claimed that
the real-estate investments he'd made had earned Ali millions of dollars —
Anthony agreed to settle the suit and paid Ali $390,000.

Anthony made several good investments for Ali, and he brought in a respected accountant in an attempt to reduce Ali's tax liability. But after examining Ali's limited business records, the accountant, Richard W. Skillman of
Caplin & Drysdale, found it all but impossible to distinguish Ali's legitimate
business expenses from his seemingly endless list of loans and investments
to Ali's friends. "I think he knew he was throwing the money away," Skillman
said.

The boxer's money troubles continued.

"I really want to quit," he said. "But if someone offers you ten million, it
ain't easy." He said he wanted to go out on top, with his health, but he also
wanted to go out with $10 million in U.S. Treasury bonds, "so I can have a
check that says $85,000, tax free, in my mailbox every month." If Ali's busi-
ness affairs had been properly managed from the beginning, if he'd employed
tax shelters and invested his income wisely, he could have received a monthly
check for much more than $85,000 a month in retirement. But, now, as he
neared the end of his career, that wasn't the case. Now, he needed to make
as much money as he could while he was still capable of fighting in an attempt to make up for lost time, poor decisions, expensive marriages, and
wasted opportunities. Many of the men around him — including Ali's father,
his brother, Bundini, and others — also counted on Ali to continue earning
for as long as possible.

"They may not let me quit until I can't fight no more," he said.

The Inoki fight — if it could even be called a fight — was Herbert's idea.
Promoters in Japan had promised Ali $6 million to see what would happen
when a boxing champion and a wrestling champion met in the ring. But
as the fight approached, no one seemed to know if the contest was to be
scripted, a gentle exhibition, or a true competition with a set of rules that
blended the sports of boxing and wrestling.

The fourteen-thousand-seat Budokan arena in Tokyo was sold out for the

June 26 bout. In the United States, nearly 33,000 paid $10 each to attend a closed-circuit telecast at Shea Stadium in New York. At Shea, fans would also see a live match between the boxer Chuck Wepner and professional wrestler André the Giant. Ali, always the master of self-promotion, told interviewers that this fight would draw more viewers than any of his others. He promised the action would be real and probably bloody.

As the fight neared, and as it became clear that Inoki wanted to fight and win legitimately, Ali's team came up with a set of rules that pretty much prevented the wrestler from doing anything that would physically harm his opponent. Ali would wear flimsy four-ounce gloves while Inoki would fight barehanded. No kneeing or hitting below the belt was allowed. No punching was permitted when the fighters were on the canvas. Kicking was allowed, but only if the fighter doing the kicking kept one knee on the ground. The rules were not announced to the public before the fight. If they had been, it's a fair bet that no one would have paid to see a competition that sounded more like a game of Twister than martial arts.

The Ali-Inoki fight began with Inoki running across the ring and throwing himself feet first in Ali's direction, trying to use his legs to make a tackle. He missed, tried again, and missed again. Instead of getting up, though, Inoki stayed on the mat, scooting like a crab, swinging out at Ali with his legs from time to time, trying to clip Ali behind the knees and bring him down. Inoki knew Ali had only one way to fight: with his fists. But Ali couldn't throw a punch so long as Inoki stayed on the ground. As Inoki scooted and kicked, Ali hopped around like a man trying to stomp a snake.

Round after round, Inoki stayed on his back, trying to kick Ali in the calves and thighs. In the fourth, Ali hopped onto the ropes to escape, shouting in horror. In the sixth, Ali tried to grab Inoki's leg, but Inoki got the better of it, wrapping his other leg around Ali's calf and flipping Ali on to the canvas for the first takedown of the night. Inoki climbed quickly atop Ali's chest and squatted on his face.

How much indignity will a man suffer for $6 million? Ali had provided his answer.

That would turn out to be the best action of the fight.

Ali mocked Inoki, telling him to get up and fight. "One punch! I want one punch!" he shouted. Inoki, preferring not to be punched, stayed down. Soon,

Ali's legs were swollen and bleeding. Angelo Dundee insisted that Inoki tape his shoes so they wouldn't cut Ali's legs any further.

A pillow fight would have offered more drama. When it was over, Ali had thrown six ineffectual punches. "One million dollars a punch," he later bragged. In fact, his payday was better than that. Only two of Ali's punches landed, which means he was paid $3 million a punch. Or would have made $3 million a punch, if the fight had generated as much income as expected.

Fans booed and threw garbage in the ring. Judges declared the bout a draw; paying customers used more profane language.

For Ali, the fight proved more than an embarrassment. After examining Ali's swollen leg, Ferdie Pacheco urged the fighter to stay in bed for a few days. Ali instead flew the next day to Seoul, South Korea, where he boxed in a four-round exhibition for U.S. servicemen. By the time he flew back the United States, Ali had developed blood clots in his legs and had to be hospitalized for several weeks.

If that were not bad enough, Inoki later sued Ali, claiming that last-minute rule changes left him unable to fight and resulted in lost ticket sales.

About a month after Ali's return from Japan, Veronica Porche gave birth to a girl named Hana. Three weeks after the baby's arrival, on September 2, 1976, Khalilah filed for divorce, citing adultery and "extreme and repeated mental cruelty." The case was settled quickly, with Ali agreeing to pay his wife $670,000 over five years. He also gave her a home in Chicago, an apartment building, and other property. And he promised to place $1 million in a trust fund for their four children.

Now Ali had a new child to support and a new ex-wife to compensate. That meant he had greater incentive to continue boxing. At the same time, however, his discipline was flagging. When he felt invigorated, he would wake up at 5:30 in the morning, drive his Stutz Blackhawk one mile from his home on Woodlawn Avenue to Washington Park, and then run around the perimeter for about an hour. But he was not feeling as invigorated as he used to, and on many mornings he skipped his workouts entirely. Since Veronica didn't cook often, Ali would eat fried chicken and French fries coated in spicy orange sauce from Harold's Chicken Shack.

As he prepared to fight Ken Norton at Yankee Stadium, Ali no longer spoke of retirement. He also began looking for more business opportunities. He signed a contract to promote "Ali African Feelings" bed sheets, with a photo of Ali in a tuxedo on every package. "We've got bedspreads and towels, comforters, too / Sheets made for blacks, for whites, and for you," Ali rhymed at a press conference announcing his deal.

> The fight game gets harder for an old man like me
> Selling sheets is easy as drinking iced tea
> The patterns are pretty, the idea's a honey
> And would you believe, they are paying me money?

A company called Mego International was making Muhammad Ali dolls (as well as dolls resembling Cher, Farrah Fawcett-Majors, and The Fonz from TV's hit show *Happy Days*). Ali had his own animated cartoon television show called *The Adventures of Muhammad Ali,* in which he wrestled alligators, fought off poachers in the African jungle, and battled space warriors. There was even a song about Ali called "Black Superman," with lyrics that rhymed the words "scar" and "king of the ring by far," which became a hit outside the United States. Soon there would be endorsements for Muhammad Ali Sportswear, Saudi Arabian Toyota dealerships, Muhammad Ali Champion brand shoe polish, Gino's fast-food restaurants, Bulova watches, Muhammad Ali rope-a-dope-soap-on-a-rope, the Muhammad Ali Peanut Butter Crisp Crunch Candy Bar, Birds Eye Quarterpounders (launched in England with Ali saying, "It takes a big mouth to eat a big burger"), Ore-Ida Hash Browns, Pizza Hut, and Brut cologne ("Float like a butterfly, sting like a bee, the smell of Brut, and the punch of Ali"). Ali partnered with a Saudi Arabian company that planned to sell "Mr. Champ's" soft drinks, paint, and other products to underdeveloped nations. He also approved a Superman versus Muhammad Ali comic book, and signed on to do television and magazine ads for d-CON brand cockroach traps and cockroach sprays. The d-CON products would come with Ali's picture on every box.

Was this a sign? A preview of how the next chapter in the boxer's life would unfold? Already, Ali had stopped picking fights over race, religion, and politics. Soon, he would stop punching people, too. When that happened, he would become the pitchman for products, not the product itself. But would that be all? Would that be enough? Ali wasn't saying, and he seemed to be in no hurry to find out.

In their first fight, Norton had broken Ali's jaw. In their second fight, Ali had escaped with a close and controversial decision. Norton didn't pummel opponents the way Frazier did, and he didn't clobber with the power of Foreman, but he was a strong, smart, defensive fighter, and Ali knew he had to be at his best to win. The question remained, however: was his best good enough?

Ali trained for the contest not in Deer Lake but at the Concord Resort Hotel in the Catskills region of New York. He sparred only about one hundred rounds — roughly half his usual workload for a fight — and generally left reporters unimpressed with his work ethic. One quipped that "the only thing he does with the same ferocity . . . as in the past is look in the mirrors." Between workouts one day, he drove Veronica around in a golf cart and tried — but mostly failed — to hit a few golf balls. On another day, he welcomed a group of army sergeants who asked Ali if he would pose for pictures to help promote recruiting for the military, which by now had done away with the draft. Ali, wearing a white robe over boxing trunks, happily agreed. If he commented on the irony of it all, reporters didn't mention it. On another day, he drove to Port Jervis to see a piece of property he claimed to have recently purchased, but he got lost on the trip and couldn't find it.

He slimmed down for the contest, but he still looked a little soft. His chest lacked definition and traces of fat hung around his waist. He had the physique of a man who had been working to lose weight, not a man trying to get strong. Still, he bragged that he was a more powerful fighter than ever, that his new fighting style required neither speed nor subtlety. "I'm almost twice as better as the first Norton fight," he said. "Frazier and Foreman do nothing to stop me. How Norton gonna do it?"

Ticket sales were sluggish. Demand for seats at the closed-circuit venues was far from overwhelming. Ali-Norton promised to be a good fight. It was the rubber match. But it lacked the excitement of Ali-Frazier or Ali-Foreman. Ali didn't even bother to taunt his opponent. "I wanna leave him be," he said. "He don't arouse me."

He tried to get aroused at the weigh-in, barking, "I want you, nigger!" and "Be at that fight, nigger!" But Norton seemed uninterested.

The fight took place on a cool, rainy night before a crowd of about twenty thousand at Yankee Stadium. A pun-loving headline writer for one of the city's tabloids called it "Yankee Afraidium," while *Sports Illustrated* went with "Junkie Stadium." New York City was in crisis, with crime rates soaring, the government flirting with bankruptcy. The rest of the country was only slightly better off. The world's greatest superpower had become heavily dependent on foreign oil, and now there was a desperate shortage of fuel. Gasoline and heating oil prices rose sharply. Many Americans traded their gas-guzzling Cadillacs and Oldsmobiles for fuel-efficient, Japanese-built cars, but they weren't necessarily happy about it. It felt like an admission of weakness. For the first time in decades, America looked like a country in decline. Inflation roared and the economy sputtered. Stories of fear and frustration filled the nightly news.

The Bronx could be dangerous any night of the week, but it was especially dangerous on the night of the fight as off-duty police officers, agitated by new work schedules and deferred pay raises, protested outside Yankee Stadium, blocking traffic, encouraging young men without tickets to crash the gates and sneak into the fight, and more or less advertising that no one was going to get arrested. Limousines were looted. People were mugged. Red Smith of the *New York Times* got his pocket picked. Still, Odessa Clay made it to the fight. She wore a long black evening gown and sat apart from her husband. The motorcycle stunt rider Evel Knievel was there, wearing diamond rings and cowboy boots made from the skins of boa constrictors. Also in attendance were the painter LeRoy Neiman, actor Telly Savalas, tennis star Jimmy Connors, Caroline Kennedy, and Joe Louis. The fight was delayed slightly because even the fighters had trouble reaching the stadium.

When the action finally began, Ali looked for an early knockout. He fought now as if he were Sonny Liston, a heavy hitter who liked to finish his work quickly. But Ali didn't have the knockout power of Liston, and when he stood flat-footed in the center of ring and swung away, Norton blocked most of the punches or evaded them. As the fight went on, Norton was never seriously hurt. Neither was Ali, for that matter, but Norton was doing most of the punching. He was the busier fighter, the more aggressive fighter, the more artful fighter. Ali employed many of his now-familiar tricks, shaking his ass, winding up his arms as if loading springs before punches, and fighting harder in the final seconds of many rounds to leave good lasting impressions in the minds of the judges. He did an especially good job in the final minute of the fight of loading up and throwing a lot of punches, while Norton fought the final round as if he were confident of victory and no longer needed to take chances.

Ali's jabs landed softly. He never shook Norton, never cut him, never slowed him. Through fifteen unexciting rounds, Norton landed 286 punches to Ali's 199, including 192 power punches to Ali's 128. Numbers don't measure pain. They don't measure damage. But in this case, the numbers told the story pretty well. Norton was the better fighter and the stronger fighter. He landed more punches, a higher percentage of punches, and harder punches.

When the final bell rang, Norton barked at Ali: "I beat you!"

Ali, having no answer, turned and walked to his corner, head down, shoulders slumped.

But Norton was wrong. He didn't beat Ali — at least not according to the judges scoring the fight. In one of the most controversial decisions in boxing history, Ali was declared the winner.

"I was robbed," Norton said, sobbing, as he left the ring.

Later, in his dressing room, Ali admitted that he probably won on style points. "The judges always like dancing," he said. "I switched 'cause the flat-footed fighting wasn't going like I thought it would." Far from declaring himself the Greatest, Ali said he had triumphed thanks to diminished expectations. "I tell you," he said, "for my age and all I been through . . . it was a perfect performance tonight."

If that was Ali's idea of a perfect performance, his standards were too low for his own good. After the fight, reporter Paul Zimmerman of the *New York Post* asked his fellow scribes who they thought had won. Seventeen out of twenty-one picked Norton. As did Joe Frazier: "You think they're going to give Ken the decision," Frazier asked, "as much money as Ali makes for people?"

A black reporter asked Ali, "How much longer can you fight with your mouth?"

"You're an Uncle Tom nigger to ask me something like that," Ali shot back.

"I'm asking you," the brave reporter repeated, "how much longer can you fight with your mouth?"

"Long enough to whup your black ass," Ali answered, not smiling.

Ali had fought four times in 1976 (not including his farcical exhibition with Inoki), and if not for the generosity of judges, he probably would have lost two of the four. Even his admirers in the press were beginning to describe him as washed up. "There is no question now," wrote Mark Kram in *Sports Illustrated*, "that Ali is through as a fighter. The hard work, the life and death of Manila, the endless parade of women provided by the fools close to him, have cut him down."

A few days after the fight, Ali flew to Turkey with Wallace Muhammad to meet with Muslim leaders. In an interview at the airport in Istanbul, he said he would probably retire after one more fight with George Foreman. Ali and Wallace, along with Turkey's deputy premier Necmettin Erbakan, attended a noon prayer service at Istanbul's celebrated Sultan Ahmet Mosque (also known as the Blue Mosque). When it was over, Ali made a big announcement: "At the urging of my leader, Wallace Muhammad, I declare that I am quitting fighting as of now and from now on I will join the struggle of the Islamic cause."

"It has been my lifetime dream to be champion and retire from the ring and then use my influence and fame in the work of Islam and Allah," he said. "I have many people advising me to retire and many people advising me to fight just a few more times. I do not want to lose a fight, and if I keep boxing I may lose. I may gain much money, but the love of the Muslims and the hearts of my people are more valuable than personal gain. So I am going to stop while everyone is happy and I am still winning. This is my leader," he said, gesturing to Wallace Muhammad, "this is my spiritual teacher in Islam, and I want to retire anyway. Now he has advised me it will be wise. I have no confusion in my mind."

Under the tutelage of Wallace, Ali was learning more about orthodox Islam. He bowed to say his prayers every day, and he often invited his non-Muslim friends to pray with him. He enjoyed explaining what the prayers meant and why they mattered. The word "Islam" means submission, or surrender, Ali said, and every Muslim knew that it was essential to submit humbly to God's will if one wished live in peace. The daily prayers were meant to help strengthen his bond with Allah, to remind him over and over that Allah was all knowing, merciful, and eternal. Ali had never been much good at submitting to the will of his fellow man, a characteristic that had helped make him great. But it was one thing to question the authority of a government and another to question the authority of God. He found comfort in the words of the Koran. The prayers, he told friends, gave him a sense that there was order to the universe.

But even so, Ali was not sure he was ready to give up boxing. As he and Wallace Muhammad flew home from Turkey, the boxer began to waffle. He told Wallace he had already spent most of his income from the Norton fight and knew he would face considerable pressure to continue boxing, especially when he started speaking to people like Bob Arum, Don King, and Herbert Muhammad.

Back in the United States, Wallace praised the boxer's decision to retire from boxing in a speech to his followers in Chicago. He said he understood that Ali might have trouble adjusting to life without boxing and might face financial pressures. "If he should lose his wealth because of his changing life," Wallace said, "I would give him all the wealth that I have." But Ali's religious instructor expressed confidence, saying he was proud that the boxer would henceforth fight for God instead of money.

"Muhammad Ali," he said, "congratulations for taking that stand whether you keep it or not."

47

"Do You Remember Muhammad Ali?"

Movie star!" Ali screamed. "I'm a mooooooo-veeeeeee starrrr!"

One month into his retirement, he was in Miami, filming the story of his own life and talking about his future as a Hollywood star.

"This face is worth billions," Ali said. "My roles have always got to be Number One. I can't be the boy in the kitchen. Some big football star plays the waiter in the movie while some homosexual gets the lead role. I got to be the hero. Like Charlton Heston, he's got a serious image. Moses. In 'Airport' he was the captain, a real man. Always distinguished, always high class." And there would be no sex scenes. "Kissinger wouldn't do that," he said, referring to the secretary of state, Henry Kissinger, "and I'm bigger than Kissinger."

Prettier, too, though that went without saying.

Two weeks later, while filming a scene in Houston, Ali told reporters he was ready to end his retirement from boxing.

"I want Foreman," he said. "I will destroy Foreman."

But he was in no hurry for Foreman, who was clearly the most dangerous opponent out there. First, Ali said, he would probably fight Duane Bobick or Earnie Shavers. Then he'd take on Foreman. Then, most likely, he'd retire.

Meanwhile, Ali continued to shell out money as if it were the equivalent of his own opinions and he would always have an endless supply. One winter day in Chicago, he told his friend Tim Shanahan he needed to buy a birthday present for Veronica. He had just been paid for the Norton fight, and he was thinking about getting Veronica a Mercedes. Ali and Shanahan drove in one of Ali's Cadillacs to go choose a Mercedes. On the way, Shanahan suggested that Ali buy something for himself, too.

Ali liked that idea, and said, "Let's a get a Rolls!"

Next stop: a Rolls-Royce dealership in suburban Lake Forest, where Ali picked out a two-tone kelly-green Corniche, which sold for about $88,000, as Shanahan recalled. In 1976, the average new house in America cost about half that much. Ali drove the car off the lot without paying for it, telling the salesman to call his lawyer to arrange the financial transaction. As they were leaving, though, Shanahan reminded Ali that they were supposed to be buying a gift for Veronica.

Ali turned around and went back into the dealership.

"Do you have any cute lady cars?" he asked.

The salesman showed him a silver convertible Alfa Romeo and offered a discount on the price. When Ali got home and presented his gift, Veronica climbed in, looked at Ali, and said, "I can't drive a stick shift."

Ali gave Shanahan the Alfa and went back out and bought a Mercedes for Veronica.

Ali had been promised $6 million for the Norton fight, but he received a fraction of that. Herbert Muhammad received between 30 and 40 percent of Ali's gross income — and not just his boxing income. Herbert joked that if someone approached the boxer on the street and offered him five bucks to urinate in a cup, he'd better remember to pay off his manager. Of the $6 million earned from the Norton fight, $2 million went directly to Herbert, and $2 million was put aside for the IRS. Ali also had to allocate funds for alimony, child support, property taxes, and the salaries for his drivers, security guards, and others.

It's never the money; it's always the money. And so, nearly eight months after fighting Norton and announcing his retirement, Ali was back in the ring, this time against the less-than-terrifying Alfredo Evangelista, "the Lynx of Montevideo," who had never fought before in the United States, who had had only sixteen professional fights, and who had recently been defeated by a no-name named Lorenzo Zanon. Even veteran boxing people knew little about Evangelista. "You know what the big story of this fight is?" Don King bragged. "It's that I got $2.7 million for Ali to fight a name in a book." Even Ali couldn't dream up a way to hype this contest. After watching film of Evangelista, he told reporters: "He doesn't look like he can hit too hard."

Evangelista didn't hit too hard. But neither did Ali. Evangelista lasted a long, dull fifteen rounds against Ali at the Capital Centre in Landover, Maryland. Ali won a unanimous decision, but he hardly won over the fans paying up to $150 each for tickets. He did a little dancing. He did a little shuffling. He did a little rope-a-dope. He did a little punching. But, for the most part, he looked like a man who knew exactly what was required to earn his paycheck and didn't wish to do more. Customers in the arena booed the action. After a few rounds, newspaper reporters stopped taking notes. For those watching at home, at least Howard Cosell's commentary offered a modicum of entertainment. "It's been a vaudeville act," Cosell said when it was still the first round.

"I suppose this entertains the crowd," he said later. "I can't say it's that amusing to me."

When the boxers moved around for long periods without punching, Cosell commented, drolly, "Well, I always thought the best pair of dancers I ever saw were the Nicholas Brothers a number of years back."

When Ali went to the corner, dropped his gloves, and beckoned for Evangelista to hit his chin, Cosell said, "I don't like this and, frankly, I'm sorry that it's on the air."

In the seventh, when Ali failed to land a punch, Cosell said, "You have to begin to wonder how much if anything Ali can do anymore, because, at this point in time, as a matter of self-respect, you would have expected him to do something. Look at this. It all speaks for itself."

"You don't like to beat an old horse," he said at the start of the eleventh, "but this has been dreadful."

"You have to suspect," he continued, "that there is little if anything left in the great fighter we once knew. Look at him miss. Look at him miss. Do you remember Muhammad Ali?"

Finally, he declared the entire fight "an exercise in torpor not to be believed."

When it was over, in an interview with Cosell from the center of the ring, Ali's words came out in a slurry of soft consonants and vowels as he plugged his upcoming movie, praised Wallace Muhammad, and tried to thank someone whose name he couldn't remember.

Once again, even in a lousy show, even in a fight about nothing but money, Ali had been forced to resort to the rope-a-dope, forced to fight fifteen rounds, and forced to take 141 punches from a big, strong, young man. He won in a unanimous decision, but he lost in so many other ways.

A month after defeating Evangelista, on June 19, 1977, Ali married Veronica Porche in a civil ceremony at the Beverly Wilshire Hotel in Los Angeles. The bride-to-be informed reporters that she had already become a Muslim. Ali wore white tails, white gloves, a white ruffled shirt, and white shoes. Veronica wore a white gown with a long white train. The couple stood under a metal canopy decorated with white carnations. There were two white birdcages, each one holding two white doves. They honeymooned in Hawaii. But Ali was not the sort to sit on the beach. He preferred to sign autographs and shadowbox with strangers he met on sidewalks and in hotel lobbies, so Ali brought Howard Bingham along on the honeymoon for company. The honeymoon lasted only a few days. Afterward, Ali returned to the gym to prepare for his next opponent: Earnie Shavers.

Shavers had been twenty-two years old and working on an automobile assembly line in Youngstown, Ohio, when he'd visited a boxing gym and tried on a pair of boxing gloves for the first time. He'd climbed in the ring with a young man who knew all the moves, who knew how to bob and weave, to keep his hands high, to poke fluid jabs, and fire rapid combinations. Shavers had thrown one punch and knocked him out cold.

Between 1969 and 1977, Shavers won fifty-four professional bouts, all but two of them by knockout. "Me and George Foreman," he said years later, "were maybe the greatest punchers ever." They were certainly among the greatest. Shavers was not a polished fighter. He did not throw sharp combinations. His jab inspired little fear. He moved with no special grace. But he didn't have to because he hit like a tire iron. He hit so hard, as one opponent said, "he can make July into June." He hit so hard that Joe Frazier and George Foreman wouldn't fight him.

Which raises the obvious question: why would Ali?

"God didn't make the chin to be punched," the trainer Ray Arcel once said. Ali knew his chin wasn't made to be punched, but he also knew his chin *could* be punched, and that he would very likely manage to keep his legs under him and his head relatively clear. That confidence carried him far. But Ali was taking a terrible risk in challenging Earnie Shavers. And Herbert Muhammad and the others who encouraged Ali to take the fight were doing him a grave disservice. Ferdie Pacheco called it "an act of criminal negligence."

They met on September 29, 1977, at Madison Square Garden, with about 70 million people watching the fight live on NBC-TV. An estimated 54.4 percent of all televisions in America were tuned to the fight. Normally, Shavers was the kind of boxer who expected to win quickly. But he knew, as everyone did, that Ali was not an easy man to knock out, so he conditioned himself in anticipation of a long fight. In the second round, it looked as if Shavers would not need endurance. Ali was standing toe to toe with this dangerous puncher, not dancing, not ducking. If he had trained seriously for this fight, Ali might have defeated Shavers the way he'd defeated George Foreman: by moving around the ring for a few rounds, letting his man tire, and then knocking him out. But Ali wasn't in top shape and wasn't moving well this time, and, as a result, he wound up trading punches with one of the most dangerous punchers of all time. Shavers uncoiled a right so strong it knocked Ali back three or four feet. Ali looked like a 225-pound beanbag as his body bounced off the ropes. His knees buckled, but, as his body flew forward, he regained his balance. He grabbed Shavers for support, and while he was leaning on his opponent, Ali clowned for the audience. He opened his mouth and eyes wide, as if to say, *Wow, that hurt!* Of course, by clowning, he was really trying to convey to the crowd that it hadn't hurt at all. After the fight, the *New York Times* compared him to an opera singer who fakes the high notes, a man getting by on fearlessness while bluffing to compensate for his diminished skills.

Shavers backed off a little to assess the man facing him. "Is this guy faking or is he really hurt?" he asked himself. With a minute left in the round, Shavers crowbarred Ali with another right. Again, Ali rocked backward, reached with one hand for the rope to balance, and then waved at Shavers to come on, to give him more of the same. Ali's eyes were glassy. There could be no mistake he was hurt. Shavers belted him. Ali waggled his rear end, clowning, pretending this was fun. Shavers landed another mighty blow. Ali backed up, shook his head, and waggled his ass once again.

Ali survived the round, but barely. Later, Shavers would say he regretted his decision not to fight more aggressively in the second. Still, he gave his opponent credit. "Ali took a great punch," he said.

Against Shavers, he took many great punches. Over and over, Ali shook his head to tell everyone he wasn't hurt, and yet he continued to let Shavers control the pace of the fight, continued to let Shavers thump him. In the thirteenth, Shavers buckled Ali's knees again, twice, with booming punches that landed right on the chin. Ali covered up and leaned on the ropes until his head cleared.

At the end of the fourteenth round, Ali was goggle-eyed, slack-jawed, and appeared to need help getting back to his corner. In the opening moments of the final round, he cringed as Shavers piled on more punches. But in the final seconds of the round, Ali rallied, exploding with one last burst of energy. Now it was Shavers wobbling. It was astonishing, really, watching these men throw punches with every ounce of strength they possessed, back and forth for three minutes. No one ducked. No one danced. For three minutes Ali and Shavers hurled bombs at each other. Heads spun. Legs trembled. Neither man fell. The bell rang.

Ali returned to his corner, appearing exhausted and perhaps defeated. Shavers had thrown more punches. He had landed more punches. He had landed more power punches. He had landed a higher percentage of punches. He had landed a higher percentage of power punches. He had hurt his opponent more than he'd been hurt. He had reason to hope for victory. But, once again, perhaps not surprisingly, the judges gave Ali the win.

In his dressing room after the fight, Ali collapsed on a table. Someone draped a towel over his chest. Cash Clay stood by his son's side as Ali closed his eyes and placed his right hand atop his head as if he were trying to keep it still or soothe a pain. Ali had once more escaped defeat, but he had not escaped damage. His hands hurt, as did his left knee. "Next to Joe Frazier in Manila, this was my toughest fight," he said. "The twilight zone, it's really coming up on me now. I can feel it in my bones."

Boxing was becoming more dangerous than ever for the thirty-five-year-old heavyweight champ, and some of the people around Ali could see it. He was speaking more slowly, enunciating less clearly, moving less smoothly. After the Shavers fight, Teddy Brenner, matchmaker for Madison Square Garden, told reporters at a press conference that if Ali insisted on continuing his career, he would have to do it elsewhere; the Garden would never offer him another fight. It was a boxing rarity: someone putting an athlete's health ahead of the desire to make money. And then it happened again: Ferdie Pacheco resigned as Ali's ring doctor, saying he would no longer be a part of the fighter's self-destruction. He obtained a lab report from the New York State

Athletic Commission that showed Ali's kidney function was failing and sent copies of the report to Ali, Veronica, and Herbert Muhammad. He got no response from any of them. Pacheco also wrote to the New York State Boxing Commission and urged them to pull Ali's boxing license.

Did he tell Ali that he was risking brain injury? "Yes, I told him," Pacheco said, his voice rising in anger, his body coming out of his seat as he spoke. "Every goddamn day I told him . . . He didn't see that. He didn't think he was brain damaged. He didn't remember things. He was stuttering and stammering . . . I couldn't stop him. I tried."

Cash Clay tried, too.

"Quit, son, before you get hurt," Cash said after the Shavers fight.

Ali couldn't do it. He told his father in a soft voice: "I'm on the tightrope."

48

Staggered

It was Ali's thirty-sixth birthday, and he celebrated with cake and a sparring session at the Fifth Street Gym in Miami, where his professional career had more or less begun.

At one point, Ali had vowed to take on the winner of the Ken Norton–Jimmy Young fight. But when Norton won, Ali changed his mind, even with Don King vowing to get Ali $8 million. Instead, Ali announced he would fight the 1976 Olympic gold medalist Leon Spinks. Sportswriters called it a farce, saying Spinks, with only seven professional fights to his name, was still more or less an amateur. Ali was insulting the sport, they said. The champ, of course, didn't see it that way. "I am the savior, the prophet, the resurrector," he said. "I am the onliest one keeping this thing [boxing] alive, and I'm still the greatest fighter of all time." Translation: I'll fight whomever I want.

As Ali jabbed at his birthday cake, Dundee discussed the fighter's weight.

"He's about 235, 236," the trainer said. "He'll come down about ten pounds. He'll soon have middle-age spread and never get rid of it."

The extra weight wasn't Ali's only problem. One day, the veteran boxing manager Moe Fleischer watched Ali spar and couldn't believe what he was seeing. "He lets his sparring partners bang him around," Fleischer told the sportswriter Red Smith. "I don't understand that. When I had a guy in training, my guy was always the boss." Sure enough, Ali was getting hit hard by his sparring partner, through one round, two rounds, three, four. "Pump 'em!" Ali grunted, his belly overflowing the waistband of his sweatpants as his sparring mate, Michael Dokes, blasted away.

The bell rang.

"One more!" Ali insisted. "You nineteen, I'm thirty-six. This is the last round. Show me!"

As they came out for the fifth, Dokes, determined to show him, pulled off his headgear and flung it aside. Ali did the same.

Dokes began fighting like the young Ali, showing his opponent his chin and then pulling it away every time a punch flew near.

"You moving today," Ali said.

Dokes cornered Ali and rapped him on the head.

"Keep pumpin'!" Ali said as Dokes threw punch after punch.

Ali landed a flurry of shots at the bell, but when he was done, he went straight to his dressing room. Jeremiah Shabazz announced that there would be no interviews, that Ali had adopted a new policy of silence to the press. That inspired the headline for Smith's column the next day: "Hell Has Now Frozen Over."

But Ali's silence was no joke. It continued in the weeks ahead. "I'm just tired of the press and I'm tired of people," he said.

"He's troubled about something," Bob Arum said, "and I think it may be because he's having a hell of a time training to get in shape at this stage of his career."

There were more money troubles, too.

The *New York Times,* in a front-page story, revealed that Ali had lost millions of dollars in a real-estate investment, had been having trouble raising enough money to pay his taxes, and had recently left behind a trail of unpaid bills. To come up with cash, according to the *Times,* Ali was trying to sell both his Deer Lake training camp and his home in Berrien Springs, Michigan. The newspaper said Ali had earned about $50 million over the course of his career — including $46.4 million over the past eight years — but still could not afford "to live in the style to which he and his friends have become accustomed."

Ali accepted some of the blame for the state of his finances. "I spent a lot of it foolishly," he said one day while bouncing one of his daughters on his knee. "When she grows up, she's gonna say, 'Daddy, where did all the money go?'"

Don King explained it this way: "Ali's got a costly personality. I don't think he's got any tax shelters at all. I don't think he's been handled properly."

Ali was getting about $3.5 million to fight Spinks, but it seemed not enough to cheer him up. He did his road work, taking a wake-up call every morning at five from Kilroy and hitting the road to run three or four miles around the Desert Inn golf course in Las Vegas, then wandering in, alone or with Kilroy, to the hotel coffee shop for breakfast. Reporters were mystified by his sullen disposition. He had two children now with Veronica — Hana, who was nineteen months old, and Laila, who was only six weeks. Veronica and the babies were with Ali before the fight in his penthouse suite at the Hilton in Vegas, so perhaps his sullenness was not sullenness at all but the ordinary fatigue of being a new father. But most reporters covering Ali interpreted his silence as a sign of fear — fear that he might lose to this younger, hungrier man; fear that he had broken the covenant with his own body; or fear that he had done the math and concluded that he would never fight enough to dig himself out of his financial hole.

Still, Ali was a huge favorite, with the odds running at about eight to one. Ali was a hero, and his devotees were not ready to let him fade away. His 1977 biopic, along with its popular theme song, "The Greatest Love of All," introduced a new generation of fans to his story. "It was the late 1970s, an eternity since Martin Luther King Jr. and the civil rights movement had died," wrote Kevin Powell, who was eleven years old at the time, "and . . . Ali was one of the last shining symbols of a historic era of immense black pride and achievement . . . one of the only black heroes I had." Spinks, on the other hand, was a raw, unknown talent, a mere boxer. The fight seemed so lopsided that at least one reporter wondered if it would score well enough in the ratings to top ABC's popular TV show *Charlie's Angels*, which would be on the air at the same time.

On February 15, 1978, at the Hilton Hotel in Las Vegas, as Ali climbed slowly into ring, Spinks joined with the audience in applauding the champ. The loudspeakers in the room blasted "Pomp and Circumstance." Ali smiled gently and walked around the ring before dancing a few steps and throwing a few punches at the air. The crowd was a small one at 5,300 people. Although the arena was sold out, and millions more watched on television, the scene nevertheless seemed beneath Ali's standards, like a low-budget movie propped up by a lone and fading star.

As the fight began, Ali went right to the ropes, letting Spinks hit him. And hit him. And hit him. There was not even the pretense of a fight from the defending champion. But the astonishing thing wasn't Ali's inaction; it was

Spinks's speed and energy. The twenty-four-year-old Spinks overwhelmed Ali. Spinks jabbed to keep Ali off balance and threw combinations that left Ali no time or space to respond. And it happened as soon as the fight began. Ali came off the ropes eventually and danced a little, but Spinks merely waited for him to finish his act, watched him to go back to the ropes for more rest, and whaled away again.

If you had never seen a boxing match and knew nothing about the sport and you dropped in to watch this one, and if someone told you that Spinks was getting paid about $300,000 while Ali was getting $3.5 million, you might reasonably conclude that the purpose of the competition was to measure which man could endure more violence. Only by that measure was Ali winning or justifying his enormous paycheck. In no way did Ali look like the more talented athlete or the man trying to prove he was the world's greatest fighter.

"I know what I'm doing!" he said as he went back to his corner after not fighting in the first round.

"Yeah, you look good," said the ever-encouraging Bundini Brown.

"I know what I'm doing," he said again after the second, perhaps trying to convince himself after another round in which he had done little punching.

Ali seemed to think the pressure or his insults would get to Spinks. "He was crazy, so I tried to hit him," Spinks said years later. "He talked shit all the time, so I tried to talk more shit than he did. I wanted to hit him more than he was hitting me. I wasn't having fun. I was scared as hell."

Ali came out dancing to start the third, but Spinks merely waited for the old man to stop. Ali soon did. Spinks was not a big heavyweight, at six-foot-one and a shade under two hundred pounds. But he was young and strong and fought like it. He wasn't smooth, but he kept the pressure on his opponents with a high-energy attack. Good boxers had no trouble hitting Spinks, but bad or lazy boxers were often overwhelmed by his onslaught. When the champ went to the ropes to rest again, Spinks moved in and threw thirty-eight unanswered punches. Ali absorbed many of them with his arms, but not all of them, and even when Ali did block the punches with his arms, he was still being hit. Ali's arms were being pummeled, and his gloved hands were crashing into his own head.

Through it all, Ali kept talking but not punching. His lips bled. A welt be-

gan to rise over his right eye. His punches were slow and often wide of their
mark.

"Things that you see you wanna do, you can't do it," he explained after the
fight.

Ali looked slow, dazed, like a man fighting through the fog of a bad head
cold. When he wasn't resting on the ropes, he was grabbing Spinks around
the neck, trying to stop the assault. Over the first seven rounds, Spinks
landed more than two hundred punches, while Ali landed roughly a third
of that. Ali applied more effort in the middle rounds, but he was still losing
badly, lacking the energy to fight back. In the ninth, Spinks staggered Ali
with a whopping right. Pain ripped through Ali's ribcage. The right side of
his head throbbed.

"That my round?" he asked Bundini as he came back to his corner after
the ninth.

Bundini lied and said it was.

Spinks was too young and strong. Every time Ali summoned the energy
to fight for thirty seconds or so, Spinks answered with an energy boost of his
own. In the tenth, Spinks tried the rope-a-dope, letting Ali punch away as he
covered up. It was one of only two rounds in which Ali landed more punches
than Spinks. By the eleventh, Spinks was the aggressor again, loading up
right hand after right hand, no longer worried about getting hit. The men
went head to head in the eleventh and twelfth, Ali aware now that he had to
make up for the rounds he'd given away early in the fight. Spinks would not
cooperate. Ali could see the big blows coming, but he couldn't get out of the
way. All he could do was cringe and take the shots.

Spinks grinned and patted Ali on the rump several times as the fighters
passed on the way to their corners. Ali's shoulders sagged.

The final round was brutal. It was like a playground brawl, wild punches
flying everywhere. Neither man bothered to duck, dodge, or block. These
were gunfighters closing their eyes and firing until their weapons were emptied. For Ali, it was pure desperation. He needed a knockout. For Spinks, it
was an adrenaline-fueled finish to the greatest night of his boxing life. In the
final seconds of the fight, Ali, his unprotected head hammered over and over
again, appeared ready to fall. The bell rang and saved him. When the judges
announced Spinks the winner, the new champion threw his arms in the air;

smiled an enormous, toothless smile; and floated in the air on the arms of his cornermen.

As Ali escaped quietly from the ring, an announcer for the BBC, describing the fight for television viewers in England, said, "we've obviously seen the last of him."

Ali walked out of the ring, his head held high, tears in his eyes.

Although he was tired and hurt, though his face had been bruised out of shape, he said almost immediately that he intended to fight again.

"I want to be the first man to win the heavyweight championship for the third time," he said.

49

Crown Prince

It was a warm Wednesday morning in August 1978. Ali had just dropped his daughter Hana at nursery school, and he was driving in his beige Stutz Blackhawk — "ALI78" on the Illinois license plates — to his training camp in Deer Lake. Ali had promised everyone that he would fight one more time and quit. He would beat Spinks in the rematch, reclaim the heavyweight championship, and retire. He guaranteed it. A reporter riding along asked how he felt knowing his career would be over soon and generations would grow up without seeing him fight.

"They never saw Jesus, either," Ali answered. "Or Einstein, or Franklin Delano Roosevelt. But they all read about them in history books. Everybody's going to die, everybody's going to get old. Even after you're dead and I'm dead, this hill is going to be here."

In any case, he said, he would still be famous when he finished boxing. "I'm going to be ten times bigger than the heavyweight champion," he said. "I found out fighting was just to introduce me to the world. I'm just now starting to be a man." It wasn't mere hyperbole, he said. He had a real plan: to launch an international organization called WORLD — the World Organization for Rights, Liberty, and Dignity — to "build boys' camps in this country, give people relief when they're hit by floods and other disasters, build hospitals wherever they're needed around the world, and work for better relationships between countries." He had recently traveled to Moscow and met Soviet leader Leonid Brezhnev, who had utterly charmed Ali and had promised to let him use an office in the Kremlin. "I'm going to be my own United Nations," he said.

Just one more fight, he said, and his career as a humanitarian and diplomat would begin.

At about the same time, another interviewer asked Ali if he worried that brain damage from boxing might inhibit his plans for the next phase of his life.

No, Ali said, the words coming slowly. "That happens to people who get hit too much."

But Ali was getting hit too much — more than 1,100 times in his past four fights alone. Accurate punch statistics don't exist for Ali's earliest fights, but this much is known: in twelve of his earliest fights (Johnson, Miteff, Banks, Moore, Jones, Cooper, Liston, Liston again, Patterson, Chuvalo, Cooper again, and London), he took fewer than 1,100 punches. In those days, young Cassius Clay really was fast and slippery enough to avoid the kind of damage inflicted routinely on other boxers. But those days were long gone. Now in sparring sessions as well as fights, Ali had come to resemble a punching bag with legs.

It should have been Ken Norton fighting Spinks. Norton was next in line for a shot at the championship. But when Ali lost, he insisted he was entitled to another shot at Spinks. It was a tradition, he said, that the fallen champ gets another go at the man who knocked him from the throne.

Boxing had two self-appointed sanctioning organizations: the World Boxing Association and the World Boxing Council, neither of which had any legal authority but both of which wielded power. It was a situation that led to confusion, corruption, and, sometimes, the exploitation of athletes. The World Boxing Council had stripped Spinks of the title and handed it to Norton, saying Norton should have been entitled to challenge Spinks before Ali got a rematch. But Spinks was still the WBA champ, and that was good enough for Ali.

At one point, Bob Arum announced that the Spinks-Ali rematch might be held in South Africa and sponsored by the South African–owned Southern Sun Hotel chain, but those plans collapsed when American civil rights leaders complained that Ali and Spinks would be "selling their souls" by endorsing South Africa's racist apartheid government. Instead, the fight was scheduled for September 15 at the Superdome in New Orleans.

Ali waited until August to begin training hard. Even then, though, Gene

Kilroy complained that the fighter was easily distracted. He answered his own phone and accepted invitations eagerly. He greeted guests and spent hours regaling them with stories and magic tricks. Ali had a folder full of business proposals in his cabin at Deer Lake, and he seemed to like every pitch he heard.

"He just can't say no," Kilroy told a reporter.

Ali did say no to one request.

One day, Louis Farrakhan stopped by Ali's house in Chicago's Hyde Park neighborhood, across the street from the home formerly owned by Elijah Muhammad.

The men stood in the kitchen. A football game flickered on TV.

Farrakhan told Ali he planned to rebuild the Nation of Islam and restore the importance of the teachings of the Honorable Elijah Muhammad, teachings that had been downplayed since Wallace Muhammad had taken over his father's leadership position and moved with Ali toward orthodox Islam. Now, Farrakhan was asking for Ali's support. He was asking the fighter to rededicate himself to the wisdom of their former mentor.

"I asked Ali, 'Would you help me rebuild the work of our teacher?'" Farrakhan recalled.

Ali gestured to the TV.

"'Farrakhan,' he said to me, 'Every one of the people in that stadium knows me.' He didn't finish the statement, but it was 'Hardly anybody in that stadium knows you.' So, in words unspoken, it was, 'Why would I follow you in rebuilding his work?' . . . So he turned me down, and he went on with his life and I went on with mine, to rebuild the work of our teacher."

Even the singer and songwriter Billy Joel expressed concern that the distractions in Ali's life were hurting his performance in the boxing ring, opening the song "Zanzibar" with the warning for Ali not to go downtown lest he give away "another round for free." But Ali said he was confident he would get in shape and win his next bout. "I know what I'm doing," he said. "I'm going to start turning it on today. This morning I weighed 226 pounds . . . I got six more weeks trying to come in at 217, 215. Six weeks is all I need . . . I'm already in better shape than I was for the last fight."

Once again, as he did in almost every interview, Ali vowed this would be his last fight. Joe Frazier had already announced his first retirement at age thirty-two. George Foreman, at age twenty-eight, had begun working as a minister at a church in Houston, his boxing career seemingly finished. Now, young fighters were coming up to take their places. Larry Holmes had recently won impressive decisions over Earnie Shavers and Ken Norton and said he was eager to fight Spinks for the title. Holmes must have assumed that Ali, his former boss, would soon be joining Frazier and Foreman in retirement. That's what Ali kept saying, after all.

"If I fought after this, I'd be pushing it," Ali said. "I got just enough mentally to train for this fight."

But Ali had been pushing it a long time.

"What can Ali do but further deteriorate his legend?" Ferdie Pacheco asked in a 1978 interview. "With each beating he takes, he gets less able to take a beating. I hope to hell I'm wrong, but if he could get lucky and beat Spinks it would be the unluckiest thing that ever happened to him. He would go on to so-called easy fights. But there are no easy fights for this guy. The body doesn't know whether you win or lose, and his body is getting beaten up on the way to the fight." Pacheco said Ali was making a big mistake by letting his sparring partners rough him up. "You don't toughen up the brains and kidney by letting them get hit a lot. It's not the same as putting calluses on hands. Cosmetically he looks the same, but his reflexes are not there. His legs used to get him out of trouble, nobody could hit him. Now everybody can hit him. And now he's slurring his words. Which is the *sine qua non* of brain damage."

Hunter S. Thompson, in a piece published that year for *Rolling Stone,* also suggested that Ali was taking a great risk by extending his career. "Muhammad Ali decided one day a long time ago not long after his twenty-first birthday that he was not only going to be King of the World *on his own turf,*" Thompson wrote, "but Crown Prince on *everybody else's* . . . Which is very, very *High* Thinking — even if you can't pull it off. Most people can't handle the action . . . and the few who can, usually have better sense than to push their luck any further.

"That was always the difference between Muhammad Ali and the rest of us. He came, he saw, and if he didn't entirely conquer — he came as close as anybody we are likely to see in the lifetime of this doomed generation."

• • •

Although he trained for only six weeks, Ali worked hard, confident he could beat Spinks if he got in shape. Spinks did not approach the fight with the same determination. Fame punished the new heavyweight champion, who had grown up in poverty in St. Louis, dropped out of school after tenth grade, and enlisted in the Marine Corps before launching his career in boxing. Now, old friends, distant relatives, newspapermen, television producers, and would-be agents surfaced, eager to ask favors of the newly wealthy young man. He ate and drank and spent too much. His training consisted at times of running a mile, smoking a joint, running another mile, and smoking another joint. He was arrested twice in his hometown of St. Louis, once for a traffic charge, once for possession of marijuana and cocaine, and had run-ins with police in other cities, as well. "Come on, man, I'm Leon," he said, greeting the arresting officer for his second St. Louis incarceration. In New Orleans, in the days leading up to the fight, Spinks got drunk every night in neighborhood bars where he knew his managers wouldn't find him.

Expectations were low for both fighters. Red Smith called it "a match between a novice who hasn't learned to fight and an overripe stager who has forgotten how." The FBI investigated a tip that officials at Top Rank—the boxing promotion company formed by Bob Arum and Herbert Muhammad—tried to bribe Spinks to throw the fight. Documents in the FBI's archives don't reveal the outcome of the investigation.

In his final press conference before the fight, Ali said goodbye the same way he had said hello fourteen and a half years ago before his fight with Sonny Liston. He rhapsodized and beat his breast and proclaimed himself the prettiest, the wittiest, the bravest, and most beautiful man ever to bloody another's nose. Instead of giving his farewell in his dressing room, he did it in the gym where he had been working out, so that 1,200 spectators could hear his words on what he called "my last day in a training gym."

He admitted that he hadn't looked very good in in recent weeks, admitted that he probably couldn't go on fighting much longer even if he wanted to. His weight still hovered around 220 pounds, higher than he would have liked it. But he wasn't worried. Ever since his victory over Foreman, he had become convinced that he was smarter than everyone else when it came to training and that he, uniquely, could prevail in fights by inuring himself to pain. "I wasn't training to beat my sparring partners," he admitted. "Some days I took punches just to toughen myself. I'm the best heavyweight in history to take a punch. I condition myself to take punishment."

Then he recited what he said would be the last pugilistic poem of his career, which was really just a rehash of one of his poems from the 1960s, with Leon Spinks's name replacing Sonny Liston's:

> *Ali comes out to meet Spinks*
> *But Spinks starts to retreat*
> *As Spinks goes back an inch farther*
> *He winds up in a ringside seat.*

And on it went. The audience ate it up, even if some of the reporters rolled their eyes at the familiar refrains.

The Superdome overflowed with more than 63,000 people. This was the biggest fight the city of New Orleans had witnessed since 1892, when John L. Sullivan and Jim Corbett squared off, and it was the largest crowd ever to see a fight indoors. Sylvester Stallone, Liza Minnelli, and John Travolta were there.

"The stars were for Ali," Ishmael Reed wrote, "but the busboys were for Spinks." The busboys, most of them black, could identify with a man who grew up in public housing and was put in handcuffs for a traffic offense. The busboys could identify with a man who drank too much and burned through his dough and got hassled by the cops.

The noise of the crowd was almost frightening. Ali came out dancing. He stayed in the center of the ring. When he needed to rest, instead of loafing on the ropes, he hooked his left hand around Spinks's neck and pulled his opponent into a hug. The referee let it go. In the first round, Ali landed only four punches. In the second round, he only landed nine. But Spinks wasn't doing better. Round after round, the pattern repeated. Ali jabbed and hugged, jabbed and hugged. Neither man was knocked down or badly hurt. But in staying on his toes for fifteen rounds, in fighting so much more energetically than he had in his recent bouts, by seeming to turn back the clock by at least a year or two, Ali impressed the crowd, the judges, and even the announcer, Howard Cosell. Cosell was moved enough by the fourteenth to break into song — or something like song, reciting lyrics to one of Bob Dylan's most sentimental numbers, "Forever Young."

Clay holds up five fingers to show how many rounds he predicted Henry Cooper would last in their fight in June 1963. His brash pronouncements offended many, but the crowds still flocked to get a sight of him. *PA Images*

Clay entered the ring in a red and white satin robe, made specially for the occasion at the cost of twenty pounds – here was the king! *Getty Images*

His prediction wasn't looking too good when Cooper knocked him down in the fourth round as 'enry's 'ammer found its target, but he ended the contest in the next round – just as predicted. *PA Images*

In 1966, and now known as Muhammad Ali, the world champion prepared himself for a rematch against Cooper, taking time out to visit a play group in Ladbroke Grove in London. *Getty Images*

Cooper required sixteen stitches to stem the bleeding after he was beaten in six rounds at Highbury Stadium on 21 May 1966. *PA Images*

Ali returned to England a few weeks later to take on Brian London when he was arguably at the peak of his career. *Getty Images*

London, who had fought Floyd Patterson for the world title in 1959, was no match for Ali, landing just seven punches before he was knocked out. *Getty Images*

In 1964, Ali visited Egypt to help develop his understanding of his new faith. *Getty Images*

During his goodwill visit to Pakistan in 1987, Ali is presented with a photograph of himself. He believed that such journeys helped draw him closer to Allah. *Getty Images*

In less than four months in the middle of 1972, Ali fought four bouts in four different countries, the last of them Ireland. He brought his mother Odessa with him for the journey. *Getty Images*

Alvin "Blue" Lewis out for the count in the eleventh round at Croke Park in Dublin. *Getty Images*

Richard Dunn may have hit the canvas on five occasions in his 1976 fight, but it was clear that Ali was no longer the boxer he had once been. *PA Images*

Ali arrived in Australia early in 1979 and went to visit Fitzroy, a deprived area of Melbourne, to see for himself the situation facing Aboriginal people there. *Getty Images*

Forty years after winning Olympic gold and twenty-five years since they last fought, Ali meets Joe Bugner at the Sydney Games in 2000. *Getty Images*

Ali and Veronica Porche visit a mosque in South Shields in the north-east of England in July 1977 to have their marriage blessed. *Mirrorpix*

David Beckham greets Ali at the BBC Sports Personality of the Year awards in 1999, at which the boxer was named Sports Personality of the Century. *Getty Images*

Ali visits Ricky Hatton's gym in Hyde, Manchester, in 2009. *PA Images*

Global icons: Nelson Mandela and Ali greet each other in June 2003 in Dublin. *Getty Images*

When the judges named Ali the winner by unanimous decision, Rahaman tried to lift his brother in the air. Ali, once again champion, raised one arm and blew kisses to the crowd.

Cosell asked the champion if he would announce his retirement.

"I don't know yet," Ali said softly. "I'm going to think about it."

50

Old

He was champion, the King of the World once again. To commemorate the occasion, he ordered gold rings for the men in his entourage. On the face of each ring sat a gold crown surrounded by the words "M. ALI WORLD CHAMPION THREE TIMES." He told reporters he was in no hurry to formalize his retirement. He preferred to hold on to the championship for six or seven months, relishing it, he said, basking in his own glory a little longer before letting go.

In November, the champ attended a black-tie fundraiser for Joe Louis, age sixty-four, who had to be rolled onto the dais in his wheelchair.

"I'm tired of people telling me it's a shame about Joe Louis," Ali said, perhaps referring to Joe's financial condition more than his physical condition, which was largely the result of a stroke. "I'm tired of people telling me, don't be like Joe Louis. Why is it a shame? Joe Louis is a true friend of everyone."

In December, Ali appeared on *This Is Your Life,* a British television show that reviewed his biography and surprised him by flying some of the most important people from his life to London, bringing them on the set one by one. Ali, wearing a black suit with a silver and gray tie, sat next to Veronica and watched his life roll before his eyes. Here they were: his parents; his brother; one of his schoolteachers; his first trainers, Joe Martin and Fred Stoner; friend and former sparring partner Jimmy Ellis; Howard Bingham; Angelo Dundee; Henry Cooper; Joe Frazier.

Through the years, even when he was joking with Howard Cosell or Johnny Carson, even when he was clowning for cameras with the Beatles or mugging with Bundini Brown, Ali seemed to be acting, always conscious of the image he wished to convey to television viewers. This was different. Ali seemed surprised and sincerely overcome with emotion — the main emotion being joy. He didn't preen. He didn't boast. It was one of the most genuine moments in Ali's television career (not including his fights, of course). He screamed and covered his face and laughed so hard he almost fell out of his chair. "He was still tickled to death when people made a big deal out of him," Veronica recalled years later. "He was like a little kid with surprises."

When the show ended and Hana and Laila came on the set, Ali smiled and laughed and bent over to pick up both girls at the same time. The cameras captured the image of one of life's great winners, a man who had accomplished everything he had set out to accomplish and had earned the right to celebrate.

But the image of satisfaction didn't last. Six months later, in July 1979, Ali sat for another interview with Cosell. The broadcaster was in New York, Ali in Los Angeles. Their faces appeared side by side on a split screen. There was no gleam in Ali's eye this time, no laughter in his voice. His face was rounder. His voice was a mere murmur, low in volume and full of air, as if he hadn't slept in days. He told Cosell he was making his retirement official now.

"Everybody gets old," he said.

Cosell asked if the reports were true that Bob Arum had paid Ali $300,000 to formally declare his retirement, so that Arum could schedule a fight to determine the new champ. "If that's true," Ali said, "I know nothing about it."

"Are you glad it's over?" Cosell asked.

"Yes, sir, Howard," Ali said. "So glad that it's all over. I'm glad that I'm still intelligent enough to speak. I'm glad that I'm three-time champion. I'm glad I got to know you."

"You are the greatest, aren't you?" Cosell asked.

Ali managed a small smile.

"I try to be," he said.

Ali had done no planning for retirement. Although he had spoken vaguely about a new, global charitable project, he had taken no steps to launch it. Nor had he saved enough to live comfortably without income. While Herbert Muhammad remained his close confidant and business manager, Ali complained at times to friends that Herbert had lined his pockets at Ali's expense, and that if his manager had done his job, Ali would have been set for life. One day, while complaining about the state of his finances to his friend Tim Shanahan, Ali said he was thinking about bringing in a new manager to straighten things out. "Get me a Jewish lawyer!" he said, half joking.

Ali did not find a Jewish lawyer, but he did get help after his second fight with Spinks. Robert Abboud, chairman of First National Bank of Chicago, read a story in the *New York Times* about the shaky state of Ali's finances and requested a meeting with the boxer. In the meeting, Abboud offered to put together an all-star squad of accountants, lawyers, and talent agents to manage Ali's post-boxing career — all at virtually no charge to Ali. Everyone would work for the privilege of helping the great Ali — and, of course, for the chance to hang framed photos on their walls and brag to friends and clients that they knew the champ. "I just thought he was a national treasure," Abboud recalled, sounding a lot like the members of the Louisville Sponsoring Group, who had set out in 1960 with the intention of boosting the career of a promising young athlete and perhaps making a little money along the way. It became clear to Abboud that Ali had paid attention to his money primarily when it had come time to spend it.

Abboud assigned a young bank officer named Robert Richley to audit Ali's finances and develop a plan. Richley summarized the state of Ali's problems: Herbert Muhammad was getting far too much of Ali's income, the boxer's expenses were too high, and he had been and remained the victim of far too many foolish business deals. The good news: he was still young and famous, which meant he still had time to "monetize his position and securitize his future," Richley said.

Abboud and Richley tried to "build a fence" around Ali, as Abboud put it. They told Ali he was no longer permitted to sign any contract or agree to any deal without the cosignature of one of his new financial advisors. The bank executives established a team to handle every aspect of Ali's business life. Marge Thomas would take care of bookkeeping and day-to-day financial needs. Barry Frank of International Management Group would develop endorsement and licensing deals. Michael Phenner of Hopkins & Sutter would serve as Ali's lawyer. Until then, Ali had been relying on Charles Lomax for most of his legal work. Given that Lomax also represented Herbert Muhammad and Don King, there were obvious conflicts of interest. When Phenner got involved, he arranged a meeting with Herbert and Lomax, reviewing all the contracts Ali had signed, making sure Ali got paid what he was promised, and insisting that he be informed of all future deals before they were completed. Phenner also insisted that Herbert reduce his cut of Ali's earnings. "Herbert was taking 30 to 40 percent," Phenner said, "and that was just a part of what they were able to take from him, because he was so generous." Years later, Phenner said he didn't recall the precise numbers, but after long and difficult negotiations, he said, Herbert agreed to accept a big pay cut.

"Michael Phenner saved us," Veronica Porche said. "I was so happy to have someone who wasn't a crook handling things."

Trust funds were established. Health insurance was purchased. Until then, Ali had been paying medical bills out of pocket for himself, his wife, his children, and his employees.

Barry Frank put together good deals for Ali. Idaho potato farmers agreed to pay the boxer $250,000 for his endorsement. Ali got $1 million to play the lead role in the television movie *Freedom Road,* which costarred Kris Kristofferson. Frank also arranged a televised *Farewell to Muhammad Ali* TV show that paid the boxer $800,000, as well as a ten-city European farewell tour that promised to pay additional millions. Meanwhile, Ali and Veronica moved to Los Angeles, purchasing a home on Fremont Place in the Hancock Park neighborhood, near Ali's friend Lou Rawls. Ali piled up a lot of new expenses in furnishing the house.

Robert Abboud said he watched with disappointment as his fence broke down — largely because Ali let friends and acquaintances trample it. One example: rather than selling his Chicago mansion, where he'd spent a fortune in remodeling costs, Ali was persuaded by Herbert Muhammad to donate the home. Phenner said the donation was arranged in such a way that Ali was unable to deduct the gift on his taxes. The boxer simply couldn't say no to people. A friend would call and say he knew a guy who would pay Ali three thousand dollars cash to show up for an hour at his car dealership or appliance store. Would Ali do it? Yes, he would — and he would stay for three hours, not one, because the line for autographs was invariably longer than organizers had expected. At one point, Barry Frank negotiated a lucrative deal for Ali to endorse Orangina, the carbonated soft drink. But the deal fell apart when a lawyer discovered that Ali had already taken ten thousand dollars cash to endorse Champ Cola and had signed a contract saying he would never endorse another soft drink.

"He was extremely naive," Frank said. "Beyond belief." When a business-man came to Ali and suggested they form a partnership to manufacture their own automobiles, Ali loved the idea. Think about how many people bought cars, he marveled. Millions! Surely there would be hundreds of thousands of people if not more who wanted to own cars made by Muhammad Ali. But Ali didn't understand or didn't realize the contract required him to invest $1 million of his own money toward the development of the product, nor did he understand how complicated the business of designing, manufacturing, and selling cars would be. "He was strangely unaware of what was going on in the world," Frank said. "He never understood. He thought Don King was just another black man trying to eke out a living like he was. He was overly impressed with a suitcase full of hundred-dollar bills and not sufficiently im-pressed with a check. He knew what you could do with hundred-dollar bills. He didn't fully understand checks. He did understand it, but emotionally, gut-wise, it didn't have the meaning that a suitcase full of dollar bills did."

Veronica grew frustrated at times, too. Chauffeurs would enter the house to fetch the couple's luggage and steal jewelry from her dresser or nightstand, but Ali wouldn't fire them. He possessed "the kindest, most pure heart of any-one I know," she said. He didn't care how much money he had in the bank. He didn't care if he stayed at a Ritz-Carlton Hotel or a Holiday Inn. Didn't care if his watch was a Rolex or a Timex. He did have one quirk when it came to shopping — he judged objects like furniture and appliances by their weight, the heavier the better, and would walk through his own house urging guests to pick up objects and measure their impressive heft. But other than that, Veronica said, he showed few signs of materialism.

Once, the boxer phoned Michael Phenner from a car dealership in Beverly Hills and asked for money to buy another Rolls-Royce. Phenner advised Ali to leave the showroom. The lawyer said he was confident he could negotiate a better price for the car once Ali had departed.

"Mike, how much do you think I'm going to save?" Ali asked.

Phenner said he could probably save ten thousand dollars, maybe more.

"Mike, do I have the money?" Ali asked.

Phenner said yes. Ali got in the car and drove it away.

At one point, Phenner and Abboud talked about hiring a twenty-four-hour financial security guard for Ali, someone who would be by his side to

intervene when he was approached with business offers. It proved imprac-
tical.

In 1979, a man calling himself Harold Smith (real name: Eugene Ross
Fields) set out to become the new Don King, the biggest promoter in boxing,
and he tossed around enough cash to make it happen. Smith persuaded Ali to
lend his name to an operation called Muhammad Ali Amateur Sports, which
sponsored track meets and boxing tournaments, as well as Muhammad Ali
Professional Sports, which promoted professional boxing matches. With Ali's
endorsement, and with a seemingly limitless supply of cash, Smith quickly
signed some of boxing's top talent, including Thomas Hearns, Ken Norton,
Gerry Cooney, Michael Spinks, Matthew Saad Muhammad, and Eddie Mus-
tafa Muhammad. The FBI eventually discovered that Smith had embezzled
more than $21 million, with the help of insiders, from Wells Fargo Bank in
California, making it one of the largest cases of bank fraud in American history at that time. While Ali was never accused of conspiring with Smith, the
boxer did receive at least $500,000 of Wells Fargo's money. When news of
the scam hit the press, Ali held a press conference to explain that he knew
nothing about the crime. He joked about it, saying, "A guy used my name to
embezzle $21 million. Ain't many names that can steal that much."

In addition to the bad business deals, there were also paternity suits and
threats of paternity suits, enough of them that Phenner and his colleagues
joked that they might wind up defending Ali in a class-action case for all his
extramarital affairs. Phenner adored Ali. It was impossible not to, he said. But
no matter how he tried, he could not protect the fighter because Ali would
not or could not protect himself. A reporter for the *New York Times* witnessed one all-too-typical scene. Ali was stretched out on a bed in his suite at
the Meadowlands Hilton in New Jersey — he often conducted interviews and
business meetings while lying in bed, clothed or unclothed — as a woman
showed him a brown bottle full of Muhammad Ali vitamins. "And they'll
be in the stores as soon you sign as this contract," the woman said. Without
getting up, Ali signed the contract. The woman put the document in her
briefcase and left. Soon after, a man handed Ali a pamphlet. He explained to
Ali that it was an advertisement for a proposed new school, the Muhammad
Ali Institute of Technology and Theatrics. "Yeah, man," Ali said. "Thanks,
man." He still didn't get out of bed.

"It got to the point where we felt we were at risk as a law firm," Phenner said, "because someone would say why didn't Sutter & Hopkins stop this?"

Phenner and Frank told Ali he would probably make about $8 million from his farewell tour, but before it began they found reason to worry. Ali was inviting everyone he knew to come along and offering to pay their expenses. Phenner and Frank insisted Ali pare down his list of travelers, which he agreed to do, settling on Veronica, Howard Bingham, and a few others. But when the boxer went to the airport to begin his journey, he encountered an uninvited guest: Bundini Brown, who was dragging an oversized trunk full of Muhammad Ali T-shirts, Muhammad Ali cigars, and other Muhammad Ali products he hoped to sell on the tour. Bundini did not have a plane ticket, but he begged, and Ali agreed to buy him one — at a cost of about $1,500 in each direction.

The tour was a success. Ali sparred with Jimmy Ellis. He went for long walks through new cities. He signed countless thousands of autographs. He ate countless slices of pie and cake (and proudly showed off his ballooning belly, joking that people were starting to ask if he was pregnant with twins). He sat with television interviewers and gave long interviews, recalling his earliest fights and favorite poems. His hair had begun to gray. His voice was slower and softer — a fact that became more obvious as television interviewers showed footage from earlier Ali television appearances and then cut back to Ali live in their studios — but his memory remained as sharp as ever. He recalled in vivid detail not just particular bouts but even particular rounds and particular punches. He said he was getting $75,000 to box exhibitions and thought he could get $1 million for going a few rounds with Teofilo Stevenson, the Cuban heavyweight who had won the past two Olympic gold medals for boxing. In July, Ali fought an exhibition against Lyle Alzado, a defensive end for the Denver Broncos football team and a former Golden Gloves boxer. Ali got $250,000 for the fight, which was supposed to be an eight-round affair. But when it became clear that Alzado was taking the fight seriously and hurting Ali at times, the fighters agreed to skip the seventh round. Ali weighed 234 pounds for the Alzado exhibition and admitted that he hadn't run one mile or spent one day in the gym in the six months since he had beaten Spinks.

It was easy to imagine going on this way for years, touring the world, picking up paychecks for giving speeches or endorsing products, offering interviews, putting on the trunks and pretending to box a few rounds, telling jokes. (One of his favorites at the time: "What did Abraham Lincoln say when he woke up after a three-day drunk? He said, 'I freed the *who?*'") As long as he was making people happy, Ali seemed happy. During an interview in New Zealand, one of the announcers had to apologize to his audience that the rest of the regularly scheduled news would have be postponed because Ali had gone on longer than expected, reviewing his whole life, his whole career, for more than eighty minutes.

"I'm through boxing," he vowed. "You'll never see me in the ring again." But he said he would continue to conduct exhibitions for ten more years to make sure that young people would always know his name and know, as he told one interviewer on the tour, that he was "the greatest fighter of all times, the most talked-about fighter of all times, the most controversial, and the fastest and the prettiest, dancing master, the greatest fist-fighter in the history of the whole world." He paused to admire himself in the television monitor, laughed, and asked the cameraman to move in for a close-up. He said he looked forward to getting on with his life: "Look how good I feel on your show. How I can brag, and how I can talk. All my life I have it made, 'cause I go out a winner. If you go out a loser, it worries you . . . I want to go out as champion, I want to retire as three-time champion . . . I'm just glad to be able to get out on top."

When he returned from his so-called farewell tour, Ali announced once again, in case there was any uncertainty, that he was formally and officially retired. The heavyweight title belonged to Ali's former sparring mate Larry Holmes, who'd been tearing apart every man he faced, showing flashes of Ali's fine footwork and a jab that was perhaps even superior to that of his mentor.

Some reporters greeted Ali's latest retirement with skepticism, but Red Smith, who had always been one of Ali's toughest critics, gave the fighter a fond farewell. "The fact is," Smith wrote, "Ali was a remarkable athlete, almost surely faster on his feet than any other heavyweight of any era. He was an imaginative and inventive showman, a tireless entertainer. He postured and clowned and faked it, and his speed compensated for his sins as a pure boxer. He was a fair puncher and could take more punishment than anyone of his era could inflict. An excellent fighter, he was great only against Joe Frazier, who brought out the champion in him . . . He defended the title more often than any other heavyweight and against more bums, starting with Liston. Whatever happened in their first meeting, Liston went in the water when they met again in Lewiston, Me. Of that there is no manner of doubt, no possible, probable shadow of doubt, no possible doubt whatever. Ali hasn't made a really good fight since Manila, though he was called the winner after eight of them. It is time to say goodbye. It is past time, but that's all right. He was an ornament on the sports scene. If he stayed too long, that was partly because we hated to see him go."

51

Humpty Dumpty

One day in the fall of 1979, Ali squeezed into a blue plastic chair and ad-dressed a roomful of students at the New School for Social Research in New York City. The students were enrolled in a class designed to explore Muhammad Ali's favorite subject: Muhammad Ali.

On this day, the final meeting of the seven-week course, students would hear from the man himself.

"My knowledge," he said, smiling as he set up the rhyme. "You can learn more from me than from any college."

Ali offered the students more poems. He told jokes. He also spoke at length about the crisis occurring in Iran. A month earlier, Jimmy Carter had allowed the Shah of Iran, Reza Pahlavi, to enter the United States for cancer treatments. In response, some of the Shah's political opponents had overrun the U.S. embassy in Tehran and seized fifty-two American hostages. Iran's leader, Ayatollah Ruhollah Khomeini, had labeled America "the Great Satan" and refused to negotiate the hostages' release. The attack on the embassy hit Americans hard. Just years after the country's demoralizing retreat from Vietnam, and with the economy increasingly damaged by oil shortages, here, it seemed, was another example of American weakness. Ali expressed ea-gerness to help. He offered to go to Iran and trade himself for the hostages. At one point, he struck a patriotic chord, saying, "No country is as great as America. Even our smallest city is greater than any country in the world." At another point, he argued that America deserved many of its problems. "This is a country based on lies," he said.

Despite the contradictions in his remarks, Ali was convinced he could be an effective diplomat — the "black Henry Kissinger," as he put it. In fact, soon after the hostages were taken in Iran, President Carter had considered using Ali as an intermediary, perhaps because he was America's best-known Muslim, and perhaps because he was so extraordinarily well liked. It never happened. But Carter did send Ali on a different diplomatic mission. When the Soviet Union invaded Afghanistan in December 1979, the United States, in protest, announced a boycott of the 1980 summer Olympics in Moscow. Ali was in India on a charity mission at the time. Carter called and asked the boxer if he would travel to Africa with a team from the State Department and explain to Africans why the United States would not participate in the Olympics and to see if he could persuade other nations to join the boycott.

There was irony in it, of course. The same government that had once prosecuted Ali for refusing to fight in an American invasion of Vietnam was enlisting his help now in trying to pressure the Soviet Union to withdraw from Afghanistan. Still, the job seemed simple enough. State Department officials briefed Ali: all he had to do was remind Africans that America was the land of the free, and that America would not stand by silently and let the Soviet Union overrun Afghanistan. Ali was widely admired in Africa, not only for his triumph over George Foreman in Zaire but also for his visit to the continent in 1964 after he had beaten Sonny Liston. If he had shown up and not a uttered a word, if he had merely waved to crowds, thrown punches at the air, and let State Department officials do most of the talking, his mission might have been a success. But Ali was highly impressionable, and this character trait undermined his diplomacy. He arrived by State Department plane in Dar es Salaam, Tanzania, the first stop on a five-nation tour, and quickly embarrassed himself. When a Tanzanian reporter asked Ali why Africans should support a ban on the Moscow games given that Moscow provided aid to a number of popular liberation movements in black African countries, Ali reacted with surprise, saying he hadn't been told of the Soviet Union's support for black African freedom fighters. "Maybe I'm being used to do something that ain't right," he said. "If I find out I'm wrong, I'm going back to America and cancel the whole trip." At the same time, Tanzanian president Julius Nyerere refused to meet with Ali, saying he was insulted that President Carter had sent a boxer.

Next stop: Kenya, where Ali went a step further in undermining President

Carter's cause, arguing that African athletes should feel free to decide for themselves whether or not to compete in the Moscow games. "I'm not here to push nothing on nobody," he said. Later, Ali was asked why the United States had failed to back an African boycott of the 1976 Montreal Olympics — a protest set off by the presence of New Zealand, which had sent a rugby team to South Africa. Ali said no one had told him about the 1976 boycott and if he'd know about it, he never would have undertaken his African campaign. *Time* magazine labeled it "the most bizarre diplomatic mission in U.S. history."

Less than a month after his return from Africa, Ali said he wanted to box again. He told promoter Bob Arum that he wanted to fight John Tate, who held the World Boxing Association heavyweight crown. Larry Holmes, Ali's former sparring partner, was the champion in the eyes of the World Boxing Council, the title having been divided as boxing's two governing bodies vied for supremacy.

The news of Ali's possible return thrilled some members of his entourage and dismayed others. It certainly upset the businessmen who had recently sold an Ali farewell tribute to network television and a series of Ali farewell performances to cities in the United States and Europe. The notion of a return to boxing for Ali also upset those who were concerned about the fighter's health. Ali had gained twenty pounds in retirement. Angelo Dundee warned that losing the weight and getting in condition to fight would be more taxing than ever. "I still don't think he'll come back, I hope not," the trainer said, "but if he wants me, I'll work with him again."

Ali was thirty-eight years old. His weight exceeded 240 pounds. He hadn't fought in eighteen months. The year before that, he'd only fought twice. It had been nearly four years since he'd knocked out an opponent and four and a half years since his last truly impressive win, that coming in the punishing battle with Frazier in Manila. Since his defeat of Leon Spinks, it was not clear that Ali had worked up a good sweat, much less labored to stay in shape. There was no reason beyond nostalgia to believe Ali belonged in the ring with John Tate or Larry Holmes. "Ali can't fight no more," said Freddie Brown, a seventy-three-year-old trainer who'd worked with Rocky Marciano, Rocky Graziano, and a lot of other Rockys nobody had heard of. "He can't go two good rounds in a row good . . . It's too bad he hung on too long like he did. If he'd have quit after Manila, then I'd say he was the best heavyweight we ever had."

And yet Don King, Bob Arum, Herbert Muhammad, and others promised to help if Ali decided to fight again. Arum said he tried to dissuade Ali but failed. But what if Arum and the others had refused to help? What if they had told Ali that no amount of money would change their minds? What if they had said his health was their top concern? Would he have changed his mind?

Veronica Ali said she opposed her husband's return to boxing.

"The last three fights or so," she said, "he fought because he had to fight, because he would've been broke if he didn't fight." Veronica blamed Herbert Muhammad and others who had made great fortunes and had never cared enough to help the boxer properly invest and protect his income. "People like Herbert were happy to keep him where he needed to keep working," she said.

Veronica had noticed for several years that Ali had been slurring his words, but she didn't give it much thought. She had also noticed Ali's left thumb "twitched a little," although in an interview years later she could not precisely recall when it had started. Her husband, she said, almost never complained about physical challenges. Ali's biggest physical problem in those days was difficulty sleeping. It got bad enough that he consented to see a doctor. Many patients with head injuries suffer from sleep disorders, but the doctor who saw Ali apparently didn't make that connection. He told the boxer that his difficulty sleeping was probably connected to his frequent traveling.

Odessa and Cash Clay expressed concern for their son and urged him not to fight again. "I thought he wasn't walking good," Cash said. "I thought maybe his hip was bothering him. I wasn't sure about his speech, either, but the way I look at it, that boy has been fighting since he was twelve years old. A man can only take so many licks to the head. With the brain, you know, one lick can be too many. The way he talks, I noticed that at times, it's not too clear. I told him to retire, not to keep going back constantly. Any more hits to the head, you don't need that. But he told me he wants to keep fighting."

Rahaman, too, urged his brother to quit. "He's only flesh and blood," he said. "I told him. He didn't care."

Rodrigo Sanchez, president of the WBA, warned that boxing authorities would not permit Ali to fight for the championship unless he proved himself fit with a warm-up bout. But that warning proved empty. As Ali and men like Arum and King surely knew, the lure of big money would overwhelm the reticence of Sanchez. It would also overwhelm the warnings of Ferdie Pacheco, who told one journalist: "Ali should not try to come back, absolutely not. At his age, with the wear and tear he's had as a fighter, even when he's trying to get back into shape, all the organs that have been abused will have to work harder — his heart, lungs, kidneys, liver. I've always had a great deal of trepidation about any boxer who stayed beyond his time . . . but for someone who has been in with such brutal punchers as Joe Frazier and George Foreman, there's no way for him to escape the attrition that his body has undergone."

When it became clear that Ali's opponent in a comeback would likely be Larry Holmes, Holmes, too, cautioned Ali to reconsider: "It'll be a sad day for boxing," he said, "because he's gonna get hurt."

On March 8, 1980, Ali went back to work at the Fifth Street Gym in Miami. Rather than working the bags and skipping rope to get in shape for the enervating business of punching and taking punches, Ali began sparring right away. In three rounds with a young and unexceptional Argentine fighter named Luis Acosta, Ali looked terrible. Still, immediately after finishing work with Acosta, Ali went eight rounds with a better fighter, an undefeated heavyweight named Jeff Sims, who battered the former champion with lefts and rights to the head until blood began gushing from Ali's mouth. Ali needed ten stitches. The injury was bad enough to keep Ali out of the ring for a time, and some thought it might crush his comeback plans. But it didn't.

Soon after the injury, in an interview with fourteen-year-old Michael Morris, a journalist at Booker T. Washington Junior High School in New York, Ali admitted that he had "lost a little of my speed, a little of my determination, a little of my stamina." And while he confessed that his reflexes had slowed, he said he was nonetheless confident that he was faster and more skilled than "the average younger man." Morris might have asked if Larry Holmes qualified as an average younger man, but instead he asked an even more challenging question, one that adults out of deference almost never posed to Ali: "How do you feel about physicians saying that you have brain damage?"

"Brain damage," Ali said, "I think somebody in England said that, or some physician in London heard me talk and saw my movements and the way I walk and he said I have brain damage. Sitting here, do I sound like I have brain damage?"

"No," Morris said.

"I think I sound more intelligent than anybody who would answer your questions, and I don't care who you talk to, your boxer, politician, president, mayor, governor; I don't think nobody on earth could answer questions more better or more precise than me."

The young journalist asked Ali how he would feel if he lost, if he wound up like all the other champions who "hung around too long and lost the title?"

"I'll feel terrible," he said, "oh, man, I'll feel terrible. For me to go out and lose it after I had won, and for them to say he's like all the other black fighters, stayed too long and went out losing, that would haunt me for the rest of my life."

But Ali insisted there was no possibility of his losing. If he thought there was even the slightest chance, he said, he wouldn't fight.

As he told another reporter: "You think I'd come back now and go out a loser? You think I'd be that stupid?"

Larry Holmes was one of twelve children of a Georgia sharecropper who relocated the family to Easton, Pennsylvania, in search of work. Soon after the move, Holmes's father abandoned his family, leaving Larry's mother to raise the children in government-subsidized, low-income housing. At thirteen, Holmes quit school and went to work in a carwash and later in a paint factory. He was still holding down the factory job when he became a sparring partner for Ali in Deer Lake. He was young and ebullient and excited to be in Ali's camp, where he often reminded the older men that if they needed paint he could get it for them at a discount. Everyone liked him.

When he became heavyweight champion, Holmes did not go in for flashy clothes or expensive cars. Even his nickname, "The Easton Assassin," was hardly a glamorous one. He remained married to the same woman all his adult life and still lived in Easton, where he used his boxing riches to build a $500,000 house. He bragged that he had $3 million in his savings account, more than enough to afford a fancy place in New York or Los Angeles. But he preferred Easton, he said, because he knew his friends would keep him humble and the police would cut him slack if he drove too fast or drank too much. His goal when he retired from boxing, he said, was to have enough money to open a restaurant in Easton and donate generously to the NAACP and the Easton Boys Club.

Holmes spent parts of four years in Muhammad Ali's employment, working for five hundred dollars a week as a sparring partner. He learned boxing.

But that wasn't all. He also learned that heavyweight champions attract too many "fucking freeloaders," as he put it. He learned that women could be a terrible distraction to a man who can't control his sexual urges. But, perhaps more than anything else, he learned that boxers shouldn't take too many punches, not in sparring sessions and not in bouts. There's nothing heroic about getting hit in the head, Holmes said, even in victory.

Holmes did his best to avoid punches. He mimicked only Ali's best habits in the ring. He moved well, and while he didn't have a devastating knockout punch, he wore fighters out with his jab until they were ready to fall or completely unable to fight back. Holmes had a jab like a defibrillator. It was quick, it was accurate, and it landed harder than a lot of fighter's hooks. Most fighters used the jab to set up combinations, but Holmes didn't have to. His jab alone won fights. Ali had a great jab — one of the greatest of all time — and Holmes had an even better one.

Holmes didn't want to fight Ali, but Don King talked him into it. King, who, as one writer put it, "would pick Joe Louis out of his wheelchair and feed him to Roberto Duran if the money were right," persuaded Holmes that he would never escape Ali's shadow if he didn't fight him.

Soon enough, Holmes sounded like a man who believed it.

"I don't care if he gets hurt," he said in reference to Ali. "He been denyin' me my just dues all this time . . . There'll be no mercy in there for him. He either gets knocked out or he gets hurt."

The fight was set for October 2. Don King had talked about staging it in Cairo, Egypt, Taiwan, or Rio de Janeiro. Instead, he settled on a temporary arena constructed in the parking lot of the Caesars Palace in Las Vegas. Ali would earn $8 million, while Holmes, the champion, would get roughly half that.

To ensure that they felt safe putting a thirty-eight-year-old man into the ring with a younger, fitter opponent, the Nevada State Athletic Commission announced that Ali would be required to undergo a strenuous physical examination, including a brain scan, before the bout.

As Ali prepared to fight Holmes, concern for the older boxer's health grew. A British doctor had recently told reporters of his fear that Ali had already suffered brain damage from too many blows to the head. Ali dismissed such concerns. "Only Allah knows about my brain," he said, "so I don't pay attention to all that."

Others, however, took the report seriously. Ferdie Pacheco said Ali "used to be an electrifying speaker. Now he has troubles. He says he's tired. He is tired. He suffers from tiredness of the brain."

Bob Arum agreed. "Just about everyone who is close to Ali has remarked on the way he has been slurring his words and talking slower," Arum said in June 1980. "I just talked to Ali Monday by phone, and my impression is that he isn't as articulate as he used to be. And he doesn't pronounce his words as well. It may very well be that he's become a product of being in the ring too long. After all, the guy has been fighting for twenty-six years, and has taken some real good shots from Norton, Shavers, and Spinks in his most recent bouts. He should undergo a thorough examination prior to his next fight."

In July, Ali did undergo a thorough examination. It took place over the course of three days at the Mayo Clinic. Two reports emerged from the Mayo Clinic, one from Dr. John Mitchell in the department of nephrology and internal medicine, which read, "Preliminary examinations would indicate that the patient is in excellent general medical health with no evidence of renal impairment or chronic or acute medical illness." The other came from Dr. Frank Howard of the Department of Neurology, who wrote that he had asked Ali about his slurred speech. The fighter responded, according to Dr. Howard's memo, that his slow speech was the result of fatigue, "and that he has always had some mild slurring of his speech for the past ten to twelve years." The report continued, "He stated that he was tired on the day of the examination here and that he had gotten little sleep. He denied any problems in coordination as far as running, sparring, or skipping rope. He also says that his memory is excellent and that he can deliver five forty-five minute lectures without notes . . . Other than occasional tingling of the hands in the morning when he awakens which clears promptly with movement of the hands, he denied any other neurological symptoms. On neurological examination, he seems to have a mild ataxic dysarthia (difficulty speaking). The remainder of his exam is normal except that he does not quite hop with the agility one might anticipate and on finger to nose testing there is a slight degree of missing the target. Both of these tests could be significantly influenced by fatigue.

"A CT scan of the head was performed and showed only a congenital variation in the form of a small cavum septum pellucidum. The remainder of the examination was normal, and the above mentioned structure is a congenital abnormality and not related in any way to any head trauma. On extensive psychometric testing, he showed a minimal decrease in memory that was more pronounced when he was fatigued, but all other intellectual functions appeared to be intact.

"In summary, there is no specific finding that would prohibit him from engaging in further prize fights. There is minimal evidence of some difficulty with his speech and memory and perhaps to a very slight degree with his coordination. All of these are more noticeable when he is fatigued."

The Mayo report raised questions. How much speech and memory loss did a boxer have to suffer before his condition prohibited him from engaging in more fights? How much loss of coordination was too much? And how did the doctors know that Ali's cavum septum pellucidum — a fluid-filled space in the brain   wasn't caused by brain trauma? This last question was the most perplexing, given that scientists had been saying for decades that cavum septum pellucidim frequently occurred among punch-drunk boxers.

Despite the questions, the Nevada State Athletic Commission granted Ali a license to fight.

With a month to go before the fight, Ali told reporters his weight was down to "about 226," from a peak of about 250. Even at 226, he looked flabby. He had grown a bushy mustache — perhaps to disguise a cut suffered in a sparring session — and had begun dyeing the gray out of his hair. He continued sparring, often with large crowds of fans watching him. But for Ali, sparring consisted mostly of leaning back and absorbing the blows of his sparring partners. He worked with younger, smaller, faster fighters. He worked with bigger, stronger punchers. But his approach seldom varied. He let them fire away.

Tim Witherspoon was twenty-two years old, a solid puncher with good boxing technique, when Ali hired him as a sparring partner in advance of the Holmes bout. Witherspoon was excited to step in the ring with his idol. The first time the men sparred, however, Witherspoon was shocked. "I noticed he wasn't that strong," he said. "His movement wasn't like I used to see on television." Ali's longtime associates reassured Witherspoon: Give it another week or two, you'll see. They don't call him the Greatest for nothing. Watch! Witherspoon watched, but he didn't see improvement.

To Witherspoon, it was as if a shabby impostor had taken his hero's place. But it was worse than that. It was frightening. "When we were in the ring sparring, he was constantly telling me to give him head shots. I was giving him head shots, but it was too easy and I noticed he wasn't getting any better, so I wouldn't really hit him with a full fist. I would hit him with like a slap. But he would get pissed at me if I didn't hit in the head. It went on and on. It was easier and easier to hit him. And he wasn't getting any stronger . . . I felt something was wrong with him."

Witherspoon wasn't the only one who saw it.

Newspapers in the summer of 1980 carried headlines like this one, from the *Capital Times* of Madison, Wisconsin: "Ali Showing Some Signs of Brain Damage."

"He's just a shell," said Billy Prezant, a veteran trainer, after watching Ali work out.

"You can't put Humpty Dumpty together again," said Teddy Brenner of Madison Square Garden.

"He's getting hit too much," said Bundini Brown.

"You shouldn't get hit that much by anybody," said Dundee.

"He was lonely," said Veronica. "He needed a challenge."

One sparring partner opened a cut on the bridge of Ali's nose. After rounds in which he did nothing but stand still and take punches, Ali gasped for breath. He wasn't moving his head. He wasn't throwing combinations. He wasn't dancing. He was just standing there and taking shots. It got so bad that Dundee began to cheat, shouting "time!" before the sparring-session rounds were over.

Ali was losing weight but perhaps not enough. About three weeks before the fight, while training in Las Vegas, he was visited by Dr. Charles Williams, who had been the personal physician to Elijah Muhammad and remained the physician of Herbert Muhammad. Williams had examined Ali once before — when Ali was preparing for his second fight against Leon Spinks — and had concluded that Ali was feeling sluggish as a result of hypothyroidism, according to an interview Williams gave to the writer Thomas Hauser. "I corrected it," Williams told Hauser. "I won't say how. I only had a day or two to correct it. Let's just say I corrected it and Ali whupped Leon Spinks." This time, as Ali prepared to fight Holmes, Dr. Williams gave Ali a thyroid drug and a weight-loss drug. The weight-loss drug, Didrex, was similar to an amphetamine and was often prescribed for obesity. Regardless of medical advice, Ali began popping them like they were mints, happy that the pills seemed to melt away fat and boost his energy.

On the morning of September 15, journalist Pete Dexter was in Ali's Las Vegas hotel room. Ali took a break from watching a Holmes fight on Betamax tape to get up and go to his closet, where he kept a scale and a tray filled with thirty different kinds of pills.

Ali picked out eight or ten pills to take with his breakfast, then peeked out the window, where a crowd stood waiting to see a young man named Gary Wells attempt to jump the water fountain at Caesars on a motorcycle, the same jump that had almost killed stunt rider Evel Knievel. Ali turned away.

"I don't want to see nobody get his head ripped off," he said. "They encourage him, but I know what people want to see when they watch something like that."

Ali gazed at himself in the mirror. He lay down on his bed and his rubdown man, Luis Sarria, closed the curtains.

"As sure as you hear my voice," he said, to whom it was not clear, "you and I will both die."

An hour later, the young man on the motorcycle missed his landing ramp and nearly killed himself crashing into a brick wall at eighty-five miles an hour.

By the week of the fight, Ali had shed his gut. But he had also shed much of the muscle mass in his thighs, shoulders, and arms. Still, with his hair dyed black and his mustache shaved, he gave the appearance of a more youthful man. He looked good enough, in fact, that some of the skeptics on press row wondered if they'd been wrong to dismiss him as over the hill. "He's 29 again," crowed Pat Putnam in *Sports Illustrated*, as if Ali in his sixtieth professional fight and after a layoff of two years might really have one more trick for his fans, one last way to shock the world.

"Now that I got my weight down and I'm in shape, I know I can do it," Ali said. "Man, I got confidence."

But anyone watching Ali train knew the weight loss was an illusion. He struggled even hitting the heavy bag. Sparring partners barreled across the ring like there was no one there to stop them.

"He couldn't run," said Gene Dibble, a longtime Ali friend. "Hell, he could hardly stay awake."

A month or so before the fight, Veronica Ali had felt confident her husband would beat Holmes. She was impressed with his conditioning, with his physique, with his attitude. But after Dr. Williams gave him drugs, Veronica said, Ali lost too much weight and lost it too fast. "Bingham and I both thought it was done purposely," Veronica said years later. "Maybe someone bet against him and wanted to make sure he lost . . . We think that somebody sabotaged that fight."

Two days before the bout, Ali went out for his usual early morning run. Temperatures at dawn that week in Las Vegas were about seventy degrees —not ideal running weather, but not dreadful either. Still, Ali conked out quickly, unable to run a mile. After one of those morning runs the week of the fight, Ali collapsed on the side of the road. He was taken to a hospital and treated for dehydration, according to Larry Kolb, who was Ali's friend and advisor.

When Kolb asked Hebert Muhammad what had happened, Herbert told him: "The dumb nigger tripled his doses." Still, Herbert insisted Ali had to fight Holmes; too much money was on the line to cancel the bout.

On the day of the fight, Tim Witherspoon said he overheard Ali's boxing and business managers discussing whether it was safe to let Ali step in the ring. He heard them using the words "dehydration" and "thyroid." Witherspoon had his own strong opinion. He had sparred with Ali for months. He had seen Ali's condition go from bad to slightly better to worse than ever. He was certain Ali would lose. But he wasn't worried about Ali losing; he was worried about Ali getting killed.

Moments before the fight, when his boxing trunks were on, his shoes laced, and his hands taped, as members of the entourage stood by nervously, Ali stretched out on a red chaise lounge chair and napped. Soon, he was up and headed toward the ring. The makeshift arena was hot, crowded, and fogged with cigarette smoke. Ali dragged his feet as he walked, shoulders slumped. His was not the body language usually associated with a challenger for boxing's heavyweight crown. It was certainly not the body language of a man primed to engage in violent, hand-to-hand conflict. Once he was in the ring, under the bright lights, Ali perked up slightly, urging fans to boo his opponent, pretending he wanted to begin the battle right away, before the bell. But the act was hardly convincing. If anything, he looked inebriated.

"I'm your master!" Ali yelled at Holmes.

Holmes stood stiff as a statue, glaring.

For the first minute or two of the fight, Holmes approached cautiously, as if waiting to see Ali's game plan. But when Ali didn't reveal one and didn't attempt to inflict damage, Holmes attacked with that resolute jab. Holmes jabbed and jabbed, and Ali gave no response. It appeared that Ali could not get out of the way, could not fight back. If his brain was telling his body to do either of these things, his body was failing to respond.

After the first round, he slumped on his stool, already exhausted.

"Oh, God," he thought to himself, as he would say later, "I still have fourteen rounds to go."

In round two, Ali landed one punch. One feeble punch. Still, he was a legend, so the crowd offered encouragement. "Ali! Ali!" they chanted. Ali responded by blocking more jabs with his face. Unable to fight back, he attempted to display bravado, pointing to his chin and telling Holmes to hit him again. Holmes did. Over and over.

The arena was so steamy even the reporters and fans were perspiring through their shirts. While Holmes's body glistened, no sweat glistened on Ali's body. His eyes glazed like a man in a stupor. He blinked as if trying to clear his head.

After three rounds of championship boxing, Ali appeared to be losing by default. He had landed only five punches. Meanwhile, Holmes continued popping that nasty jab. Every time he was hit, Ali appeared surprised, as if wondering where the fist had come from and why he hadn't tried to get out of its way.

Still, Ali's fans as well as the assembled journalists waited. They'd seen Ali start slowly before. They'd seen him play tricks with his opponents. They hung on to hope.

In the fifth, finally, Ali came out dancing, moving in circles around the ring. But he threw no punches as he danced, and when the dancing stopped, there was nothing for him to do but absorb more punches. His eyes grew red and puffy as more jabs found his face. In the final seconds of the round, Holmes threw a series of left leads that hurt Ali badly. The punch tally after five rounds was shocking: 141 shots landed for Holmes, 12 for Ali.

"You start punching or I'm going to stop it," Dundee yelled at his fighter.

"No, no, no, no, no, no, no," Ali said.

The crowd began to boo. Ali had been heckled many times before — taunted for his abrasive personality, for his politics, his religion, his clowning — but never before in more than a quarter century of competitive boxing had he been scorned for sheer lack of ability. Ali had no answer — not for the crowd and not for Holmes. He just leaned against a turnbuckle and barked at Holmes, his mouth the only thing working: "Hit! Hit! Hit!" he said.

In the seventh, Ali tried again. He danced a little. He attempted the jab, once his most effective punch, but found it no longer traveled quickly enough to reach its intended target. After a minute and fifteen seconds of dancing and punching at air, he wore himself out. It was as close as he would come all night to looking like a boxer, and it wasn't close enough. It was if he were putting on for audiences around the world a demonstration of the effects of aging — or, worse, boxing-related brain damage.

After the eighth round, Ali sat on his stool, his face swollen, both eyes blackened with bruises. Bundini Brown leaned in, tapping Ali's shoulder, trying to do the thing he'd always done best, getting Ali's attention, riling him, sparking him, finding words that would inspire. Ali stared ahead in silence, breathing hard through his open mouth. He gave no response. In the opposite corner, Holmes asked his trainer for advice, but not the kind fighters usually seek in the chaos of battle. He was hitting Ali at will. It was too easy. He was afraid he might seriously hurt his opponent. Now he asked his corner men if he should back off.

His trainer told him to fight harder, to fight so hard the referee would have no choice but to end it.

As the ninth round began, Ali appeared to be completely defenseless. Holmes threw a big right that dented Ali's jaw, followed by an uppercut. The uppercut was followed by something almost unheard of in the sport of boxing, something that shocked even the grizzled sportswriters who had watched countless hundreds of men struck by countless thousands of punches. But there it was: a scream. The great Muhammad Ali screamed — whether in pain or fear or shock, who knows? But he screamed. He screamed, and he tried to curl his body like a knuckle, shrinking to hide himself from Holmes, looking like a mugging victim who had no defense except to cover up and hope that his attacker would take whatever he wanted and leave him alone.

Long after the fight, it was the scream that the men in his corner and the men in the press box would remember.

Meanwhile, Holmes kept punching.

After the ninth, Angelo Dundee threatened once again to stop the fight. Ali offered no protest, but he rose at the bell and went out to meet Holmes. Holmes came at him fast and hard: jab, jab, jab, jab, right, right, jab, jab, a hook to the kidneys, a combination, and then a flurry of punches that seemed to blur, with no beginning and no end, leaving Ali helpless but still standing.

Throughout most of the fight, Herbert Muhammad had sat at ringside with his head down, unable to watch and yet unwilling to stop it, as Holmes landed 340 punches to Ali's 42. After the tenth round, finally, Herbert looked up, made eye contact with Dundee, and nodded. Dundee told the referee he was calling it.

No more.

Ali sat on his stool, eyes closed, mouth open, shoulders slumped. He neither spoke nor moved.

Holmes was crying when he reached Ali's corner. "I love you," he told the defeated fighter. "I really respect you. I hope we'll always be friends."

Ali went back to his hotel room, where Gene Kilroy asked him if he wanted to undress and take a shower.

"No," Ali said. "I think I just want to lie down and rest for a little while."

Half an hour later, Holmes and his brother Jake knocked on Ali's door.

"Are you OK, champ?" Holmes asked. "I didn't want to hurt you."

"Then why did you?" Ali asked, with a soft laugh.

"Now I want you to promise me one thing," Holmes said, "that you will never fight again."

Ali began to chant: "I want Holmes. I want Holmes. I want Holmes."

"Oh, Lord," said Holmes, laughing.

A few hours later, Ali returned to the empty arena where he had fought the night prior and sat for a live television interview.

His face was a lumpy mask. He had two black eyes but wore sunglasses to hide them. He lowered his head and gently rubbed his brow.

He was asked, of course, if he intended to fight again.

"I may return," he said. "I want to think about it, but we might go back and try again . . . Wait about a month, go back in the gym, see how I feel."

52

The Last Hurrah

Two weeks after the fight, the Nevada Athletic Commission reported that Ali had failed his post-fight drug test. A urine sample revealed codeine and phenothiazines — painkillers and antidepressants — in Ali's body.

The boxer claimed that he had taken the drugs immediately after his loss to Larry Holmes, to speed his recovery. Even if that were true, however, it would have been a violation of the commission's rules, as Ali and his team no doubt knew.

On December 29, 1980, the Nevada commission began a hearing on whether to strip Ali's boxing license. Ali appeared at the hearing, but before it began, he voluntarily gave up his license. By doing so, his lawyers argued, Ali was no longer subject to Nevada's rules and could not be punished. Ali promised he would never again apply for a license in Nevada, and the commission, in return, promised to close its hearing and drop additional questions about Ali's admitted use of thyroid drugs before the fight.

If Ali had been forced by Nevada to retire, other state commissions might have followed in withdrawing his license. "It would have been an awful precedent," attorney Michael Phenner told reporters.

In hindsight, Ali never should have been allowed to fight Holmes, said Sig Rogich, who was chairman of the Nevada Athletic Commission at the time. "We rushed it," Rogich said years later in an interview. "It was such a big event . . . It was such a huge sellout. I always tried to be objective. I thought part of our job was to promote our town, and we wanted to show we were the perfect town for these events."

Television networks didn't cover the news of Ali's failed drug test. Newspapers, for the most part, printed small stories deep inside their sports sections. Still, it was humiliating for Ali. And the humiliations kept coming. Like the punches of Larry Holmes, Ali could see them, but he couldn't stop them.

Ali's contract said he was entitled to $8 million dollars for fighting Holmes, but Don King paid him only $6.83 million, insisting that Ali had agreed in a conversation prior to the fight to amend the deal. In truth, King had asked Ali to formally amend the contract, but Michael Phenner had refused. King insisted, however, that Ali had given his word.

Phenner filed a lawsuit against King, demanding that he pay Ali the additional $1.2 million. King had already earned millions from a fight that never should have happened, a fight in which Ali had risked his life. Although King must have known he would lose if Phenner's case went to court, he wasn't prepared to give up. "Cash is king, and King is cash," the promoter always said. With that in mind, the promoter put fifty thousand dollars in a briefcase and instructed Jeremiah Shabazz to deliver it to Ali. King told Shabazz to turn over the cash only after Ali signed a letter releasing King "from any and all monies due to me, or for which I may have been entitled under the said Bout Agreement."

Shabazz brought a notary public with him when he went to see Ali in Los Angeles. The notary read Ali the letter from King and asked Ali if he understood what he was signing. Ali said yes. He took the cash and signed the letter, which not only allowed King to keep almost $1.2 million to which the promoter was not entitled but also gave King the right to promote Ali's next fight, should he decide to box again.

When Ali phoned Phenner to tell him what had happened, Phenner cried.

Was this how it ended for Muhammad Ali?

Writers compared his plight to that of Joe Louis, a great champion who'd fought too long, who'd wound up broke and looking a decade or two older than his age, but Ali's performance against Holmes had been far feebler than anything Louis had done in the ring. After the fight, newspapers and magazines around the world printed pictures of Ali seated woozily on his stool, his eyes blackened and half closed, his face swollen, his arms draped on the ropes. But even as he approached his thirty-ninth birthday, he couldn't bring himself to say it was over. He made excuses. All those pills had sapped his strength, he said. His old friend the mirror had let him down. The mirror had said he was in good shape. The mirror had told him he was young and strong again. Next time, he said, he wouldn't be fooled. Next time he would worry more about his strength and stamina than his weight. Next time . . .

"In two or three years," Ferdie Pacheco warned, "we'll see what the Holmes fight did to his brain and kidneys. That's when all the scar tissue in his brain will further erode his speech and balance . . . He was a damaged fighter before the fight, and now he's going to be damaged even more . . . For him to get up at a press conference the day after the fight and say he might fight Weaver is crazy. It's not publicity, it's part of the illness. He just can't think straight. The people around him need to make him think straight. That's where the responsibility lies."

But most of the people around Ali waffled. Herbert Muhammad said he hoped Ali would never fight again, but he promised to stand by his friend if he did. Don King said much the same. As long as there was money to be made, these men and others would not shun it.

On January 19, 1981, Ali was at home in Los Angeles when Howard Bingham called and said there was a man standing on the window ledge of a ninth-floor Miracle Mile office building, threatening to jump. Minutes later, Ali arrived in his two-tone brown Rolls-Royce, driving up the wrong side of the street. He hustled into the building, leaned out a window, and shouted to the man: "You're my brother! I love you, and I couldn't lie to you!" In a photograph taken at that moment, it appears that the suicidal man might fall as he tried to get a better look at Ali, but, after about thirty minutes, Ali talked him off the ledge. The next day, Ali visited the man in the hospital, where he promised to buy him clothes and help him find a job.

Three months later, on April 12, Joe Louis died of a heart attack at his home in Las Vegas. He was sixty-six years old. In its obituary, the *New York Times* said Louis had "held the heavyweight boxing championship of the world for almost twelve years and the affection of the American public for most of his adult life."

But Louis had been more than a boxer and more than a beloved man. He'd been one of the most influential black men in American history. The same could be said for Jack Johnson and Muhammad Ali. These were three men who took chances and absorbed pain, three men unafraid to strip bare to the waist and let the public see their limitations and their powers, showing the world that in a sphere of violence and suffering there is also the possibility of style and beauty.

Back in 1967, Joe Louis and a ghostwriter had published an article in *The Ring* magazine describing how Louis would have fought Muhammad Ali, or Cassius Clay as Louis called him at the time. Louis said he would have forced Ali to the ropes and pounded away. The older champion was confident of his superiority. Still, Louis expressed admiration for the man who had inherited his crown, and he told a sweet story about the young boxer:

"Once I happened to walk along when Clay was hollering 'I am the Greatest!' to some fellows outside the Theresa Hotel in Harlem. When he saw me, Clay came over and shouted to the crowd: 'This is Joe Louis. *WE* is the Greatest!'

"That was nice. Cassius Clay is a nice boy and a smart fighter. But I'm sure Joe Louis could have licked him."

In the fall of 1981, Ali announced he would fight Trevor Berbick in December. "The Drama in Bahama," he called it, for the fight was to be held in Nassau in the Bahamas. In truth, though, there was little drama in the competition between Ali and the relatively unknown and unaccomplished Berbick. Audiences were tiring of Ali's act. He'd been thrilling in his prime. He'd been entertaining in the twilight of his career. But now, it was clear even to his most loyal fans that he didn't belong in the ring, and it was becoming increasingly painful to watch Ali taking so many blows to the head. To be sure, those fans would have liked to see one last flash of brilliance from Ali. But was it worth it? Was it even possible? What would it prove?

Questions swirled around Ali's health and his failed drug test. At first, it wasn't clear if he would receive a license to fight. Promoters called it "The Last Hurrah." Even after contracts were signed, television networks in the United States balked at broadcasting the event. Three weeks before the day of the fight, tickets had not gone on sale.

Ali, who arrived in the Bahamas weighing 249 pounds, insisted he wasn't competing for the money or the attention. But even if that were true, his stated motivation hardly inspired admiration. The goal, he said, was to be the first man to win the heavyweight championship four times. "Nobody will ever do it five times because you know as well as I do that people get old too fast. I used to run six miles a day but now I got to make an effort for three . . . Not even Muhammad Ali could win the title five times . . . People tell me not to fight, but they are at the foot of the wall of knowledge and I am at the top. My horizon is greater than theirs. Why do people go to the moon? Why did Martin Luther King say he had a dream? People need challenges."

Aware of concerns about his health, Ali frequently asked reporters if they thought he had brain damage or if it sounded as if he were slurring his words. He also made the unusual move of releasing a medical report from an examination made shortly after his fight against Larry Holmes. The report from an endocrinologist at UCLA Medical Center said Ali had first come to the hospital on October 6, 1980, four days after his loss to Holmes, complaining of "lethargy, weakness and shortness of breath." The report covered four visits to the hospital and said, "The patient tended to talk softly and to almost mumble his speech at times; but when questioned about this, he was able to speak appropriately without any evidence of a speech disorder. He was evaluated by both a neurosurgeon and neurologist who felt that his speech pattern was not pathologic." The doctors at UCLA said they detected only one other problem in Ali's condition: he had lost his sense of smell, a problem that may have stemmed from boxing-related damage to his olfactory bulbs, which lie below the frontal lobes of the brain and transmit information from the nose to the brain.

In Nassau early one morning, Ali went for a run. It was five in the morning. Roosters crowed. The sun only hinted at its arrival over the Caribbean. Ali ran for about a mile and a half, stopped to walk for a while, and then climbed into a limousine for a ride back to the hotel. His sparring sessions were equally uninspiring, according to reporters on hand. In the days before the fight, Ali refused to step on a scale; he didn't want anyone to know how much he weighed.

Although he was clearly not in great condition, Ali remained confident he would beat Berbick, who was twenty-seven years old with a record of nineteen wins, two losses, and two draws, including a fifteen-round loss to Larry Holmes. Ali felt certain that his own loss to Holmes had been an anomaly, the result of a bad mix of drugs. This time, he promised to "sizzle and dance" all night, to stay out of Berbick's range, to build points round by round and win by an easy margin. He was so confident, in fact, that he was already discussing his next opponent.

"Berbick," he told Red Smith two weeks before the fight, "I'll handle him so easy. I'll outbox him and outclass him and talk to him. They say I have brain damage, cain't talk no more. How do I sound now?" Smith conceded that he sounded like Muhammad Ali. "My next opponent will be Mike Weaver. He's challenged the winner." And after Weaver, he said, he would fight Larry Holmes again. After Holmes, he told another reporter, "I'll defend my title a few times, then I'll retire, go preach all over the world. What's wrong with me trying it? You ever see so many people worried about one black guy in your life?"

He winked and asked the writer again: "Do I sound like I got brain damage to you?"

Four days before the fight, Don King was assaulted in his hotel room, suffering a broken nose, broken teeth, and a split lip. King alleged that the beating had been the work of the mysterious man promoting the fight, Cornelius Jace, who also went by the names James Cornelius, Cornelius James, and Jace Cornelius. No one knew where Jace had come from, although with Ali it was not surprising for business associates to appear and disappear without explanation. Only after the fight would the media learn that Jace was a convicted felon who had pleaded guilty in 1975 to five counts of theft in connection with a used-car dealership.

"He's a promoter," Herbert Muhammad said, when asked about Jace's background. "He promotes something, I don't know what."

Jace was issuing notes of credit instead of checks to people he had promised to pay. Tempers were running hot. No one had made arrangements to get Trevor Berbick to the Bahamas for the fight. Ticket sales were scant, despite steep price cuts. The makeshift arena — rickety chairs and a jumble of bleachers set in a converted baseball stadium — was still under construction. Some of the fighters on the undercard were threatening to leave because they hadn't been paid. Even Ali seemed unsure if his money had come through. Two days before the fight, when Ali learned that one of Jace's checks had bounced, the fighter packed his bags and said he was leaving. He agreed to stay, according to Larry Kolb, only after a group of Bahamian businessmen and government officials presented Ali with a suitcase filled with $1 million cash.

The fight started late because organizers couldn't find the keys to unlock the gates surrounding the baseball field where the arena had been built. Ali entered the ring slowly and somberly. He raised his arms halfway to acknowledge the cheers from the small crowd as he awaited Berbick's arrival.

Jace had forgotten to purchase boxing gloves for the event, which meant all the fighters on the card that night had to share the same two pairs. By the time of the main event, the gloves were heavy with sweat. Cornelius had also failed to arrange for a proper bell at ringside, so the timekeeper struck a cowbell with a hammer to signal the start of Muhammad Ali's final fight.

Ali walked to the center of the ring. He weighed 236 pounds, almost 20 pounds more than he had weighed against Holmes. He had promised to dance for ten rounds, but he abandoned that notion immediately and showed no flashes of the fighter who had once electrified his sport — no fancy footwork, no snake-tongue jabs, not even any mocking of his opponent. Ali simply stood in the center of the ring and tried to trade punches with Berbick.

Berbick was no great fighter, but he was stronger, faster, and younger than Ali, and it showed. Ali's jabs had no pop. His combinations were too slow to be effective. He would fight hard for a few seconds and then retreat to the ropes, where Berbick hit him without fear of retaliation, like a military unit shelling an abandoned outpost.

At the end of the third round, a round in which he had been hit but not hit terribly hard, Ali appeared to lose his footing while looking for his stool. In the fourth round, Berbick rocked Ali with hard punches to the jaw. Ali wobbled but didn't fall. He recovered and landed a good combination, but Berbick made him pay for it with another solid right to Ali's jaw. Round after round, Ali rose slowly from his stool. Round after round, he winced at Berbick's body blows. By the seventh, Ali looked thoroughly fatigued, unable to fight back for more than a few seconds at a time. To start the eighth, he came out on his toes for the first time, exciting the crowd, sparking chants of "Ali! Ali!" But the chorus ended when Ali stopped dancing and Berbick moved in again to attack. At the end of the ninth round, Ali paused before going to his corner. Through glazed eyes, he squinted at Berbick as if measuring the size and strength of his opponent, comparing the man's young, hard body to his own, and not liking the comparison.

In the final round of the final fight of his career, Ali tried to summon the magic of his youth. He came out dancing. It was a plodding dance, but it was the best he could do, and it was enough to bring one last cheer from the crowd. "Ali! Ali!" they shouted, their cries meant as encouragement, or wishful thinking, or reminiscence, or farewell, or all those things. Ali danced and jabbed for about ten seconds. After that, the crowd ceased its chanting and Berbick resumed his punching.

Now Berbick was all over him, smothering him, battering him, knocking him around the ring from rope to rope. With about forty-five seconds to go in the fight, Ali attempted a left hook that looked as if it was moving through water, so slowly and harmlessly did it travel. Berbick blocked it easily and followed with a jolting shot to Ali's head.

Thirty seconds to go and Ali tried to steal the round with one final flurry, as he had done so many times against his greatest rivals: Joe Frazier, Ken Norton, and George Foreman. But this time he was on the brink of losing to an inferior opponent, a man who was supposed to be an easy mark, and he needed one last bit of magic or one last knockout punch to avoid defeat. Ali summoned his arms to action and reared back. He tried. But the punches never flew. He couldn't fight at all. Berbick stepped in and threw a big left to the chin that spun Ali's head. Before Ali could recover, a right smashed the other side of his face. Ali retreated to the ropes, wrapped his arms around Berbick's neck, and slipped away. Berbick chased him, landing more big punches to the head. Ali was helpless now. He leaned once more against the ropes, and that's where his boxing career ended, with fists flying at his face until a cowbell clanged to say it was finally all done.

The decision was unanimous. Ali lost.

In the ring after the fight, Ali spoke to a television announcer in short sentences, as if it were too much effort to utter more than a few words a time. His voice was so soft and so slow he was difficult to understand.

"It was close, it was close," he said. "I have to submit to the judges. He was strong. He was good. I think he won . . . I saw the shots but couldn't take them. Father Time just got me."

He was asked if his career was finally over? Was this really his last fight?

"As of now," he said, "I'm retired. I don't think I'll change my mind."

In his dressing room, he slouched on a chair. Except for a small bruise over his left eye, he was unmarked.

"You can't beat Father Time," he said, his voice a whisper.

"Was this your last fight?" a reporter asked again.

"Yes," he said, "my last fight. I know it is. I'll never fight again."

He added, "At least I didn't go down ... No pictures of me on the floor, no pictures of me falling through the ropes, no broken teeth, no blood. The people of the world will love me more now, see that I'm like them. We all lose sometimes. We all grow old. We all die."

When it became clear that Ali really was quitting this time, members of his entourage wanted to memorialize their time together. They decided to pitch in money for a plaque that would go outside the log-cabin gym at Deer Lake, where they had shared so many good times, where they had come together to form their own strange and beautiful family, with Ali as their glorious, glowing leader. They would list their names alphabetically: Howard Bingham, Bundini Brown, Angelo Dundee, Jimmy Ellis, Gene Kilroy ...

The job of purchasing the plaque fell to Bundini.

He ordered a tombstone.

53

Too Many Punches

One day in November 1982, an elderly African man and a young boy rang the doorbell of Ali's big white house in Hancock Park.

Ali's friend Larry Kolb answered.

"We are here," the elderly man said, "because — before I die — I wish to introduce my grandson to the great Muhammad Ali."

Ali told Kolb to let them in. The boy carried a Big Mac in a paper bag: a food offering for Ali. Muhammad hugged the little boy and performed a magic trick for him. He ate the Big Mac.

The elderly man said they had traveled all the way from Tanzania, going first to Chicago in search of Ali. They had been in Los Angeles three days.

"Today we found you," he said, according to Kolb. "Tomorrow we can go home." Ali fed them and then drove them in his Rolls-Royce to their low-budget airport hotel. He hugged them and kissed them and told them to go with God.

On the drive home, Ali told Kolb he believed that every person on Earth had an angel watching him all the time. He called it a Tallying Angel, because the angel made a mark in a book every time someone did something good or bad. "When we die," Ali said, "if we've got more good marks than bad, we go to Paradise. If we've got more bad marks, we go to Hell." Hell, he said, was like mashing your hand down in a frying pan and holding it there, flesh sizzling, for eternity.

"I've done a lot of bad things," he told Kolb. "Gotta keep doing good now. I wanna go to Paradise."

Later the same month, Ali sat in the locker room of the Allen Park Youth Center in North Miami, a short drive from the spot where he had defeated Sonny Liston in 1964. He squeezed into a pair of boxing trunks and laced up his shoes, preparing for a workout, trying to get fit for a series of paid boxing exhibitions planned for the United Arab Emirates. The money raised during the trip would go to build a mosque in Chicago, he said.

A reporter asked when he would be back. He mumbled, words "clinging together as cobwebs of dust do," as the journalist put it. "I'll be gone six weeks," he said, counting with his fingers. "I'll be back November tenth," he said.

"You mean December tenth, don't you?" the reporter asked.

"Yeah," he said, lifting his eyes. "December tenth."

"Then you'll be away about three weeks, not six weeks."

"Yeah," he said, slowly. "I'll be away three weeks."

It had been one year since Ali's loss to Trevor Berbick. Since then, he had only joked about a comeback. "I will return . . . ," he liked to say, pausing before adding: "To my home in Los Angeles."

Now, he said, he was content to travel and raise money to promote his religion. He had come to the gym in North Miami to get in shape, to drop a few pounds, not with any interest in competing again, just so that he would look reasonably good when he boxed in exhibitions.

"My life just started at forty," he said. "All the boxing I did was in training for this. I'm not here training for boxing. I'm going over to those countries for donations. When I get there, I'll stop the whole city. You don't hear nothin' about Frazier, or Foreman, or Norton, or Holmes, or Cooney. But when I get to these cities, they'll be three million people at the airport. They'll be on the sides of the road going into the city."

With that he went downstairs to the gym, climbed slowly up the small wooden steps and into the ring. The bell rang. Ali moved toward his sparring partner and punches pounded his headgear.

Two days before Ali's interview at the gym in North Miami, a South Korean boxer named Duk Koo Kim had been knocked out and rendered comatose after a long, brutal fight with Ray "Boom Boom" Mancini. Soon after, Kim died of cerebral edema — swelling of the brain. The death prompted legislative committees in the United States to examine the safety of boxing. But, in the end, little changed. "What does the boxing profession think of the controversy?" asked U.S. representative James J. Florio of New Jersey. "Well, the answer is: There is no boxing profession. It's not a system, it's a nonsystem, and it's getting worse."

In 1983, a pair of editorials in the *Journal of the American Medical Association* called for the abolition of boxing. In other sports, one editorial said, injury was an undesired byproduct. But "the principal purpose of a boxing match is for one opponent to render the other injured, defenseless, incapacitated, unconscious." Muhammad Ali, interviewed on national TV, was asked for a response to the editorial. He appeared tired and unfocused as he sat in front of the fireplace in his Los Angeles home. His voice came through soft and muddy. Asked if it was possible that he suffered brain damage from boxing, he replied faintly: "It's possible."

On April 11, 1983, *Sports Illustrated* published a special report on brain injuries in boxing, pointing out that deaths in the ring had long prompted calls for reform, but scant attention had been paid to the chronic brain injuries caused by thousands of blows taken over the course of a career. The magazine pointed to Ali as a prime example, saying that the former champ was not only slurring his words but also "acting depressed of late."

To some observers, Ali seemed bored and emotionally detached. To amuse himself, he would take out his personal phone book and dial famous friends. But sometimes he would pause in the middle of the conversation, having forgotten to whom he was speaking. *Sports Illustrated* reported that "many observers" believed Ali was already punch-drunk.

The magazine asked Ali if he would agree to undergo a series of neurological tests, including a CAT (computerized axial tomography) scan, which was a relatively new tool for doctors at the time, one that was capable of revealing cerebral atrophy. Ali declined to undergo the test. But the magazine obtained scans of Ali's brain taken at an exam at New York University Medical Center in July 1981 and showed them to medical experts. The radiologist's report in 1981 had found Ali's brain to be normal, but the doctors reviewing the scans at the behest of the magazine were more familiar with boxing-related brain injuries than most radiologists, and they disagreed with the earlier conclusion. They saw signs of significant brain atrophy — specifically, enlarged ventricles and a cavum septum pellucidum, a cave in the septum that shouldn't be there.

"They read this as normal?" asked Dr. Ira Casson, a neurologist at the Long Island Jewish Medical Center. "I wouldn't have read this as normal. I don't see how you can say in a thirty-nine-year-old man that these ventricles aren't too big. His third ventricle's big. His lateral ventricles are big. He has a cavum septum pellucidum."

The Mayo Clinic had spotted some of the same things but had deemed them unrelated to boxing. In an interview decades later, Dr. Casson strongly disagreed with that conclusion: "It was all consistent with brain damage from boxing," he said.

Although he was finished as a fighter, Ali continued traveling extensively. He never tired of meeting new people and seeing new places. One night in Japan, as he was returning to his hotel room after dinner with his friend Larry Kolb, Ali stopped in front of his door and gazed down the long hallway. It was the custom at this hotel for guests to trade their shoes for slippers upon entering their rooms and to leave their shoes in the hall. Now, with most everyone asleep, there were shoes in front of every door. A mischievous look crossed Ali's face. He nodded at Kolb. Without a word, the two men moved up and down the hall, rearranging the shoes. When they were done, they giggled and retreated to their rooms.

In May 1983, Ali was in Las Vegas, where Don King was paying him $1,200 "hang-around money" to schmooze with fans before a Larry Holmes fight at the Dunes. King knew Ali would engage with fans all day, even for a mere $1,200. He did it without compensation every time he stepped out of his home. And so the former champ signed autographs and performed magic tricks and ran into Dave Kindred, one of the reporters who'd been covering him since his earliest days as a professional fighter. "He was an old man at forty-one," Kindred wrote.

Ali admitted he was worried about his condition. His friends and family were worried, too. He was drowsy all the time. He shuffled when he walked and murmured when he talked. His left thumb trembled. He drooled at times. He felt suddenly like an old man, and he wanted to know what was happening.

In October 1983, Ali returned to UCLA for more tests. This time, the signs of damage were impossible to ignore. A brain scan revealed an enlarged third ventricle in the brain, atrophy of the brain stem, and a pronounced cavum septum pellucidum. Neuropsychological testing indicated that he had trouble learning new material. When he was treated with Sinemet, a drug for patients with Parkinson's disease, he showed immediate improvement.

In interviews, Ali insisted there was nothing seriously wrong. "I've taken about 175,000 hard punches," he said. "I think that would affect anybody some. But that don't make me have brain damage." Even so, he said he wanted to find out why his body seemed to be betraying him. Ever since his fight against Joe Frazier in Manila, he said, he had felt damaged, and it was steadily getting worse.

In September 1984, Ali checked in to New York's Columbia-Presbyterian Medical Center, where he underwent several days of testing. He was seen by one of America's leading neurologists, Dr. Stanley Fahn, who said Ali displayed a range of symptoms, including slow speech, stiffness in the neck, and slow facial movements. "He was a little slow in his response to questions," Dr. Fahn told the writer Thomas Hauser, "but there was no hard data to suggest that he was declining in intelligence."

Ali was discharged after five days because he needed to travel to Germany. When he returned and was readmitted, news of his hospitalization spread around the world. Floyd Patterson paid a visit, and Rev. Jesse Jackson, who had recently given up a campaign for president, visited twice. Ali had given Jackson his endorsement in the Democratic primaries, but in the general election the former boxer threw his support to Republican candidate Ronald Reagan. In 1970, as governor of California, Reagan had shot down Ali's attempt to obtain a boxing license, saying, "Forget it. That draft-dodger will never fight in my state." When Larry Kolb reminded Ali of Reagan's statement, Ali shot back: "At least he didn't call me a *nigger* draft-dodger." Ali may have thought it was funny, but Jesse Jackson and others did not. "He's not thinking very fast these days," Jackson said after Ali's endorsement of Reagan. "He's a little punch drunk." Atlanta mayor Andrew Young was so upset he arranged a meeting with Ali, attempting in vain to change the former boxer's mind on the endorsement.

Kolb, Ali's friend and manager, stayed in a hospital room adjacent to Ali's to keep him company and handle his phone calls. Veronica arrived soon after. Every day, Ali looked out the window of his seventh-floor hospital room and saw reporters and fans gathered on the sidewalk.

One day, Ali ventured outside to greet the crowd. "I saw so many people waiting and thinking I'm dying," he told reporters, "so I got dressed and looking pretty to show you I'm not dying." He raised his chin and shouted, "I'm still the greatest . . . of . . . allllll . . . tiiiiimmmmme!"

While conducting his examination, Dr. Fahn spoke to reporters at a press conference, saying tests virtually ruled out Parkinson's disease as the cause of Ali's symptoms. Instead, he said, Ali was likely suffering from Parkinson's syndrome — an array of symptoms similar to those found in people with Parkinson's disease. Dr. Fahn said Ali would be treated with the drugs usually prescribed for Parkinson's patients, Sinemet and Symmetrel. Ali's condition, he added, was "very possibly" the result of blows to the head taken during his boxing career.

Only an autopsy could say for certain whether boxing had damaged Ali's brain, according to Dr. Fahn. A British survey of more than two hundred boxers published prior to Ali's diagnosis found that about 10 percent of all former boxers suffered symptoms similar to Ali's. In neurology textbooks, Parkinson's is listed as a degenerative disease of the brain. Nerve cells in the brain stem begin to die. As they die, the brain can't produce enough dopamine, and the loss of dopamine leads to the shortened, unsteady stride; the slurred speech; the lost facial expression; and the trembling hands. These were the same symptoms that led to the description of the term *punch drunk* half a century prior and the same symptoms described by *Sports Illustrated* a year earlier in its special report on boxing and brain injury.

In an interview years later, Dr. Fahn said it was possible that Ali had been afflicted with these symptoms as far back as 1975, when he fought Joe Frazier in Manila, although the damage was certainly not caused by one fight. Ferdie Pacheco, having watched Ali fight through the years, expressed much the same opinion. Ali's boxing record also offered evidence to support Fahn's theory. In the early years of his career, before his three-year ban from the sport, Ali had absorbed an average of 11.9 punches per round, according to an analysis by CompuBox. In his final ten fights, he had been hit an average of 18.6 times per round. The numbers don't prove that Ali suffered brain damage, but they strongly indicate that he was losing his speed and his reflexes, and that the cause may have been more than age.

"My assumption," Fahn said, "is that his physical condition resulted from repeated blows to the head over time. One might argue that his Parkinsonism could and should have been recognized earlier from the changes in his speech. That's speculative. But had that been the case, it would have kept him out of his last few fights and saved him from later damage. It was bad enough to have some damage, but getting hit in the head those last few years might have made his injuries worse. Also, since Parkinsonism causes, among other things, slowness of movement, one can question whether the beating Muhammad took in his last few fights was because he was suffering from Parkinsonism and couldn't move as quickly as before in the ring, and thus was more susceptible to being hit."

The good news, Fahn said, was that Ali seemed as clever and intelligent as ever. His life was not threatened. And medication would ameliorate some of his symptoms.

Ali's medicine kept his symptoms in check, but Ali didn't always take his daily doses.

"I'm lazy and I forget," he said. In truth, the pills made Ali so nauseated that he often preferred to endure his symptoms.

He continued traveling, continued boxing in exhibitions around the world, sometimes not sure where he was going one day to the next but trusting Herbert Muhammad to guide him. His ego, at least, was undiminished. "I'm more celebrated, have more fans, and I believe am more loved than all the superstars this nation has produced," he said. "We have a saying, 'Him whom Allah raises none can lower.' I believe I have been raised by God."

Even with his extensive travels, Ali spent more time at home now than ever, but he did not adjust easily to domesticity. The manly entourage had been his family most of his adult life. Now, he seemed unprepared for and perhaps uninterested in the life and work of parenthood. Rather than settling down with Veronica and their two girls — Hana, age eight, and Laila, age six — Ali entertained an endless stream of guests at his home and took every invitation to travel as an opportunity to escape boredom. Laila said she hated entering her father's study because there were always so many people — "advisers, friends, fans, hangers-on." After years of watching him on TV, she longed for her father's company, and she did not wish to share him with the strangers surrounding him. Ali was like a big kid, and his girls loved that. He took them to Bob's Big Boy and let them order "a whole dinner of desserts." He hid behind doors when they entered rooms and chased them around the house wearing scary masks. He swallowed all the kids' vitamins so they wouldn't have to. He tape-recorded conversations with his children, telling them they would be happy one day to have a record of their time together. He was enormous fun, but, as Laila told it, he did not provide the kind of warm, safe, and loving environment she craved.

"I never heard my parents fight," Laila wrote in her memoir, "but their separate bedrooms said it all."

In the memoir, she refers to her childhood home in Los Angeles as "the mansion" and "my father's mansion." With the exception of Thanksgiving, there were no family dinners. Maids and cooks kept the children clothed and fed. Laila was not impressed when celebrities such as Michael Jackson and John Travolta appeared in the living room. "I was drawn instead to another black family who lived down the street," she wrote. "They ate together every night . . . The parents gave the kids rules and made sure they were obeyed. All this made me envious. I longed for such a family."

Ali's children from his first marriage saw their father two or three times a year. Jamillah, in a recent interview, said that she and her sisters, Rasheda and May May, got along nicely with their stepsisters, Hana and Laila. Ali did a good job of making sure Khalilah's children got to know Veronica's children. When Veronica and Muhammad were married, the children often spent summers together at the house in Los Angeles. Sharing her father with her stepsisters was not difficult, Jamillah said. "We had to share him, anyway," she said. "We had to share him with the world."

Ali's illegitimate children enjoyed even less time with their father. Miya, Ali's daughter with Patricia Harvell, said her father phoned her regularly and invited her to Los Angeles from time to time. Once, Miya said, when children at school were teasing her because they didn't believe Ali was her father, Ali flew in, took her to school, and addressed an assembly of students, introducing himself as Miya's father and speaking individually with some of those who had doubted his daughter's claim. "That meant more to me than words can explain," Miya said.

Veronica had to share Ali, too. Often, she remained in her room, feeling like a prisoner in her own home. She was never comfortable coming into the kitchen or living room unless she was fully dressed because she never knew who might be there. Veronica possessed a shyness that people mistook for frostiness.

"I became numb," she said in an interview years later. "Yes, it was so much hurt. Too much hurt."

Ali cheated on Veronica throughout their marriage. "He'd bring a woman right in front of you," she recalled, "and later you'd find out he was fooling around with her." Even when she learned that Ali maintained a steady relationship with Lonnie Williams, Veronica said she accepted it because she didn't think her husband was really in love with the other woman.

Ali's second wife, Khalilah (formerly known as Belinda), had also moved to Los Angeles in the late 1970s, which further complicated matters. In 1979, Khalilah had landed a part in *The China Syndrome,* which starred Jane Fonda and Jack Lemmon. But after that, her acting career foundered, and she burned through most of the money she had received in the divorce. By the 1980s, she was working as a housecleaner in the same Los Angeles neighborhood in which her ex-husband and his new family resided. She had also been reduced to selling her plasma for ninety dollars a week.

Lonnie arrived in Los Angeles in the mid-1980s. She was fifteen years younger than Ali. She had first met the boxer in 1963, when her family had moved to a house on Verona Way in Louisville, across the street from the home Ali had purchased for his parents. Lonnie was a pigtailed first grader at the time. Her mother, Marguerite Williams, became one of Odessa Clay's dearest friends. Through the years, Ali brought each of his wives to Louisville, and Sonji, Khalilah, and Veronica each dined at the Williams's table. Lonnie watched them come and go. In 1982, on a visit to Louisville, Ali had invited Lonnie to lunch. During the lunch, Lonnie became disturbed by Ali's emotional and physical condition. "He was despondent," she told Thomas Hauser. "It wasn't the Muhammad I knew." Soon, a plan was made and agreed upon by Veronica: Lonnie would move to Los Angeles to help care for Ali. In return, Ali would pay all her expenses, including her tuition for graduate school at UCLA.

Ali made no effort to hide his new relationship from his wife and children. In fact, Laila wrote, "He'd sometimes bring us along when he visited . . . her Westwood apartment . . . At the time, I didn't know anything was wrong. It took me years to realize the inappropriateness of a married man introducing his kids to a special friend like Lonnie."

In the summer of 1985, Veronica and Muhammad decided to divorce. Ali told his lawyers to ignore the prenuptial agreement, saying he didn't want to be stingy. Some of Ali's friends believed that Veronica was divorcing Ali because he was ill, but Veronica strongly denied it, saying she believed her husband's condition was stable and he would enjoy a long and active life. She said she still loved Ali but left him because she'd been hurt too many times by his affairs with other women. "You cannot do that and then expect someone's love," she said.

On November 19, 1986, Ali married Lonnie before a small gathering of friends and family in Louisville. Lonnie's parents were there, as were Cash, Odessa, and Rahaman.

Lonnie was twenty-nine. Ali was forty-four. He was starting over, not only in marriage but also in his body. All his life, his body had done everything he'd asked of it. He had been beautiful and strong almost beyond measure. As a young fighter, he had danced and dodged out of danger, stinging his opponents so quickly and sharply that he seemed never in peril. After his three-year layoff from the sport, he had lost some of his speed but made up for it with cunning and power, making George Foreman his fool. In the final phase of his fighting career, he had lost his legs, lost his reflexes, lost his quick hands, lost everything but his guile and his willingness to suffer and endure.

Now, with his body abandoning him, with his voice a whisper, his feet shuffling, he would have to reinvent himself one more time.

54

"He's Human, Like Us"

Ali's hands shook. His face masked his emotions. His voice shushed and blurred. He nodded off at inconvenient moments. He was not an old man, but he gave the appearance of one at times. As he had in the ring in the latter stages of his career, Ali adapted; he turned weaknesses to advantage.

When he grew bored with an interview or a meeting, he pretended to fall asleep. When the person who had been boring him left the room, he sprang from his chair and sang a line from the old Platters tune: "Yes, I'm the great pretender!"

He also feigned sleep during interviews. With cameras rolling, he would act as if he were dreaming about one of his fights, and he would begin throwing punches, slowly at first, and then faster and with more force. Lonnie or Howard Bingham would play along, urging the stranger in the room not to wake Ali from his dream. That's when Ali would throw a punch that stopped mere inches from the face of his interviewer, open his eyes, and make it clear that it had been a show. It was a clever way to entertain without speaking and to disguise his genuine fatigue, giving the impression that he was in control —a rope-a-dope for the weary and middle-aged.

Despite his physical challenges, Ali loved to travel. The entourage was gone, but he still had Lonnie, Bingham, Larry Kolb, Herbert Muhammad, an assistant manager named Abuwi Mahdi, and others to accompany him. He did the rubber-chicken dinner circuit and never complained when he couldn't eat two consecutive bites without stopping to sign an autograph or pose for a photo. He told old jokes and stories as if they were new. He promoted products. He raised money for charity. He let reporters into his home and sat with them for hours, watching replays of his old fights, insisting he felt fine and had no regrets. He received standing ovations just for entering or exiting a restaurant. No matter where he went, he was the most famous person in the room, and even in his diminished condition, he made pulses quicken and left lasting impressions.

Kolb recalled a favorite moment. Ali was at a black-tie charity dinner in New York, seated next to Jersey Joe Walcott, the former heavyweight champion. Walcott was in his seventies at the time, wizened, tiny compared to Ali, and unnoticed. A long line snaked from Ali's seat right past Walcott, as dozens of men and women waited for Ali's autograph. Ali signaled for Kolb and whispered in his ear: "Larry, get up and go to that line and tell every one of those people that the man seated next to me was a great boxer, too. His name is Jersey Joe Walcott, and he was the heavyweight champion of the world. Tell them if they want my autograph they gotta ask Jersey Joe for his first."

In 1985, Ali went to Beirut along with Kolb, Herbert Muhammad, and others, including Robert Sensi, a CIA agent introduced to them by Vice President George H. W. Bush, according to Kolb. They were trying to win the release of more than forty hostages, including four Americans, held in Lebanon by Muslim extremists. News reports at the time described the mission as a fiasco, but the journey was more complicated than journalists covering the story were aware. Led by Sensi, Ali and his group flew first to London, where Ali met with Iranians said to be close to Iran's supreme leader Ayatollah Khomeini—believed by the White House to be the hidden hand controlling the hostage-takers in Lebanon. From London, Kolb said, Ali spoke by phone with Khomeini—or someone who said he was Khomeini. Soon after, one American hostage was released. But when Ali told a reporter that his conversation with Khomeini had won the hostage's release, the American mission bogged down. Khomeini aides told Ali that Iran had nothing to do with the hostages taken in Lebanon; they suggested Ali go to Lebanon if he really wanted to free more captives.

In Beirut, the Americans were taken in the middle of the night to a Hezbollah safe house, where they met with shadowy figures who presented conditions for releasing more hostages. No additional captives were freed. From his suite at the beachfront Summerland Hotel, and from the mosques and schools he visited, Ali heard the daily rocket fire, the whizzing bullets and explosions. On Middle East Airlines stationery, he wrote a letter to his old friend Gene Kilroy, who had moved on from his job as Ali's facilitator to one as a Las Vegas casino host, taking care of VIP guests with the same care he had long given Ali. The letter was dated February 20, 1985. It read,

Dear Gene

I'm just leaving Lebanon for Zurich, and I wanted to drop you a note. When you hear bombs go off around you it makes you think how much you like to be with the people you care about.

I hope to see you soon, but in the meantime, I Want you to know that I appreciate your loyalty over the years.

Love
Muhammad Ali
Your "Boy"

He drew a smiley face next to the word "Boy."

Even as Ali continued to travel, his condition worsened. His hands grew shakier, his voice weaker, his gait more awkward. Before, he had always been too quick, too clever; now, scandal and sadness touched him.

In the early 1980s, he began working with a lawyer named Richard M. Hirschfeld. Ali wasn't sure where or when he had first met the man, or what kind of law he practiced, but it didn't matter, because Hirschfeld always seemed to have a lot of cash and a lot of money-making ideas. In partnership with Herbert Muhammad and Ali, Hirschfeld launched Champion Sports Management, with plans to train and manage boxers at Ali's Deer Lake camp as well as another location in Virginia. But that wasn't all. Through other business entities, the men planned to invest in a luxury hotel, a Brazilian car company, a Sudanese oil refinery, and a West German herpes vaccine. Hirschfeld promised he would make them all rich.

If Ali or Herbert Muhammad had checked Hirschfeld's background, they might have kept their distance. Hirschfeld had already been charged once with stock fraud. In 1984, soon after entering into his partnership with Ali, Hirschfeld once again became the target of the Securities and Exchange Commission, which forced him to shut down Champion Sports Management. Gene Kilroy warned that Hirschfeld was "a bad guy," one of the worst to ever come around, but Ali continued to do business with him.

The former boxer rented an office on Wilshire Boulevard. The place contained nothing but a phone. No desk. No chairs. No pictures. Nothing. Ali drove his Rolls-Royce to the office, stood at the window, lay on the floor, and sometimes fell asleep. He told one of his friends that he wondered if the world knew where he was.

Ali paid for the crummy downtown Los Angeles motel room where Drew Bundini Brown had gone to drink himself to death. In the fall of 1987, at the age of fifty-seven, Bundini took a fall and suffered serious head and neck injuries. Ali visited him one day in the hospital.

"I'm . . . so . . . sorry . . . champ," Bundini said, looking up from his bed.

"Quiet, Drew," Ali told him.

The men held hands.

Ali picked up a towel.

"My turn to wipe your sweat off," he said.

Ali told Bundini he would soon be in heaven with God, or Shorty, as Bundini called the almighty. "And someday me too," he said.

Bundini gave no answer.

"Hey, Bundini," Ali tried again. "Float like a butterfly, sting like a bee! Rumble, young man, rumble!"

He said it softly, not like they used to do it when they were young and defiant, but with a sense of nostalgia, with love. Ali concluded with an open-mouthed "Aaaahhhh," softly.

Bundini smiled.

Ali kissed him on the forehead.

Within a week, Bundini was gone.

In the fall of 1987, after Bundini's death, Ali made a goodwill visit to Pakistan, where he visited mosques, shrines, schools, hospitals, orphanages, and government offices. Ali believed that such visits were an important part of his religious observance, that acts of charity were a means of purifying one's soul and drawing nearer to Allah. Throughout the late 1980s and early 1990s, he traveled hundreds of thousands of miles each year. Ali distributed countless autographed religious pamphlets on his journeys. He carried them in oversized briefcases, one in each arm, sometimes for hours a day. It kept him strong, he said. But the exercise was only a bonus. Ali said he felt a duty to explain Islam to Americans and to explain America to Muslims.

He'd conquered his fear of flying, enough so that he sometimes didn't bother to wear a seatbelt. Once, when a flight attendant instructed him to buckle up, Ali replied, "Superman don't need no seatbelt." To which the flight attendant answered, "Superman don't need no *plane!*" Ali loved being sassed and often repeated the exchange when he flew with friends.

Ali said he enjoyed retirement more than he had enjoyed life as a boxer. No longer did he have to wake up at five in the morning to exercise. No longer did he have to absorb punches from big, strong men. Now, all he had to do was bask in the love of his fans. Everywhere he went, people chanted his name — "Muhammad Ali Clay," they called him in the Middle East, to differentiate him from the many Muhammad Alis who lived in Muslim countries. People tossed flowers at his passing car and laced garlands around his neck. Dignitaries presented him with expensive gifts, which Ali would often leave behind for the hotel cleaning crews. Late at night, when he couldn't sleep, he would knock on the door of one of his traveling companions and spend hours talking about his favorite subjects: religion, power, money, and sex. "If I had one dollar from everybody that loves me," he sometimes said, "I'd be a billionaire." He seldom talked about boxing and engaged in surprisingly little bragging. "He was relentlessly sunny," Kolb said. "He made you feel safe . . . Deep down, he was one of the humblest guys I ever met."

In Pakistan, as his chauffeur-driven Mercedes rolled through village after village, Ali couldn't stay in his seat, same as he hadn't been able to stay seated in his stroller as a baby, and same as he hadn't been able to tolerate riding the bus to school with the other children at Central High in Louisville. Even though he had his window rolled down and was waving, most of the people in passing trucks and buses couldn't see him, so he wedged his big body through the window, sat on the sill, and hung far enough outside the car for almost everyone to catch a glimpse as he passed.

One day, a military band dressed all in white serenaded Ali with an instrumental version of "Black Superman." He heard the song everywhere he went in the Arab world. At the Khyber Pass, on the border between Pakistan and Afghanistan, Ali congratulated Afghans for fighting Soviet intervention in their country and promised the Afghani people his support. That night, an hour's drive down the mountain road from the Afghan border, he spoke again, this time in a rickety old auditorium in Peshawar. His voice was slurred but easily understood. "Many people in America know nothing about Muslims," Ali said. "Many people in America know nothing about Prophet Muhammad. America is a big country. America is a beautiful country. All peoples, all races, religions are in America, but the power structure and the news media present a bad picture of Muslims. Whenever Muslims are mentioned, people think about Palestini guerrillas — whenever Muslims are mentioned they think about Khomeini, they think about Colonel Qaddafi, and whatever he may do that they consider rebellious. My fight in the boxing ring was only to make me popular. I never enjoyed boxing. I never enjoyed hurting people, knocking people down. But this world only recognizes power, wealth, and fame — according to their procedures. And after hearing the powerful message of Islam, and seeing the beautiful unity in Muslims, after seeing how the children are raised, after seeing the procedures of prayer, after seeing the way we eat, the way we dress, just the whole attitude of Islam, it was so beautiful — I said this is something more people have to know about, this is something more people would accept and join if they really understood. Whether they be black or white, red, yellow, or brown, Christian, Jew, Hindu, Buddhist or atheist, if he hears Islam, reads the Koran, hears the plain truth about Muhammad, he'll have to be affected in one way or the other."

Larry Kolb had commissioned a video covering Ali's weeklong tour of Pakistan. On the video, during Ali's speech in Peshawar, seated in a sea of men wearing traditional Afghani and Pakistani clothing, a thin man with a long beard stands out. He's wearing an Arab thobe with a white ghutra on his head. He sits two rows from the back of the auditorium, listening to Ali speak. It appears to be Osama bin Laden, who lived in Peshawar at the time of the speech. After bin Laden became the prime suspect in the September 11, 2001, terrorist attacks on the United States, Kolb said he provided the videotape to experts in the U.S. intelligence community and that they told him the man was most likely bin Laden.

By the late 1980s, Lonnie and Muhammad had moved from Los Angeles to Ali's farm in Berrien Springs, Michigan, a place that had once been owned by Al Capone, according to local legend. Ali celebrated his forty-sixth birthday with a party in New York attended by dozens of celebrities, including Don King and Donald Trump. Ali still loved seeing old friends, loved talking about old times. It wasn't the fights he liked to recollect; it was the memories peripheral to the fights, the friendships he'd forged. His eyes would brighten and he would giggle like a little boy talking to his brother or Jimmy Ellis about their all-night drives from Louisville to Miami, recalling the way they had fiddled with the radio to find their favorite Atlanta radio station and sung along to the Motown hits of the early 1960s. He didn't brag like he used to, but his happiness was never in doubt.

"I've got Parkinson's syndrome," he told the writer Peter Tauber. "I'm in no pain. A slight slurring of my speech, a little tremor. Nothing critical. If I was in perfect health — if I had won my last two fights — if I had no problem, people would be afraid of me. Now they feel sorry for me. They thought I was Superman. Now they can go, 'He's human, like us. He has problems.'" If he had the choice, he said, he would do it all over again.

He continued making news, but it was not always good news; it was the kind of news made by humans. In 1988, Dave Kindred, now reporting for the *Atlanta Journal-Constitution*, broke a story that would have seemed preposterous had it involved anyone but Ali. Someone who sounded an awful lot like the former champ had been phoning politicians, journalists, and Capitol Hill staffers, talking about politics and lobbying for legislation. When Kindred received one such call, he knew immediately something was wrong. The voice sounded like Ali's, but Kindred strongly suspected a mimic. After twenty-one years of reporting on the boxer, Kindred knew that Ali usually did all the talking; he seldom listened to what reporters had to say. But the Ali who called him in 1988 engaged in a "pleasant back-and-forth conversation" and used words such as "fallacious" and "dispossessed," which were not normally a part of Ali's vocabulary. Not only that, his slurred speech was gone. He sounded sharp as ever.

It didn't take long for Kindred to solve the mystery. Ali began visiting U.S. senators at their offices in Washington, DC, five of them in all. Each time, the former boxer stood in silence while his attorney, Richard Hirschfeld, did the talking. Back in 1971, when the Supreme Court had overturned his draft-evasion conviction, Ali had been asked if he intended to sue the government for damages. He'd said no, that the prosecutors had only been doing what they had thought was right. But on Ali's behalf, Hirschfeld filed suit against the federal government in 1984, seeking $50 million in damages resulting from his lost wages. When the suit was dismissed because the statute of limitations had expired, Hirschfeld began lobbying in Congress for legislation that would give Ali a second chance.

Kindred suspected that it was Hirschfeld imitating Ali on the phone. The reporter asked Ali if he'd made the calls to the senators.

"I didn't call 'em," Ali said. "Why would a Black Muslim fuck with politicians? I don't care."

"Who made the calls?" Kindred asked.

Ali said he didn't know.

Was it Hirschfeld? The men had been virtually inseparable. They'd been involved in a long list of business deals. And Hirschfeld had been entertaining friends for years with his impersonation of Ali.

"I can't see Richie doing it."

"Why did you go to Capitol Hill with him?"

"The senators, Richie said they wanted to see me."

At one point, when Kindred persisted in asking questions, Ali warned him: "You're gonna get your ass sued."

"I just want to get the story right," Kindred said.

"That little Jewish lawyer's gonna sue your ass," Ali said.

Kindred's stories in the *Journal-Constitution* described a bold hoax perpetrated by Hirschfeld in an attempt to squeeze money from the U.S. government. But Hirschfeld denied impersonating Ali in phone calls, insisting he merely coached Ali on what to say. Ali was not accused of any crime, but it was hard to believe from reading Kindred's articles and other coverage of the scandal that Ali was entirely innocent. Larry Kolb, who was one of Ali's managers at the time, said Ali and Herbert Muhammad both knew exactly what Hirschfeld was doing. "I know for a fact that Muhammad was in on it," Kolb said. "I also know Muhammad didn't think he was doing anything wrong." Kolb said that Ali believed it was appropriate to let his attorney speak on his behalf. Ali was never accused of wrongdoing, and his public image suffered only a glancing blow. Hirschfeld was eventually convicted of income tax evasion and securities fraud. He spent eight years as a fugitive from the federal government. After his capture, he died in prison, apparently by suicide.

A few years later, in 1989, Lonnie and Muhammad went on a Hajj pilgrimage to Mecca. It moved him in much the way the Hajj had moved Malcolm X in 1964 and in much the way it had moved countless Muslims throughout history. "It was a spiritual journey for both of us," Lonnie recalled. "He was happy because it is one of the pillars of Islam that every Muslim who can afford it must do. He was awed by the thousands of Muslims who were gathered from all over the world to make Hajj . . . He delighted in the fact that Muslims of all colors from all over the world were coming together. He met and knew many men, Sheiks and others, of immense wealth who were dressed the same and enduring the same physical challenges of the Hajj as everyone else. Wealth had no influence. He was also struck by the number of young children who were making Hajj with their parents, some being carried on the shoulders of their fathers. Muhammad used this time to learn more about the meaning of Hajj, the life of the Prophet Muhammad and Islam. There would be long discussions in the evenings with those who were making Hajj with us or who Muhammad had befriended that day. People were very happy to see Muhammad but remained focused on why they were there. In other words, they didn't allow their fondness or physical proximity to Muhammad to distract them from their religious duty. Muhammad continued to speak about Hajj many weeks after returning home. He was so happy and relieved he was able to fulfill that obligation before he died."

Religion filled much of the space in Ali's life that had once been occupied by boxing. "When Muhammad started to get sick and realized he was no longer invulnerable," the writer Thomas Hauser said in an interview years later, "he started to get scared. That was one factor that led to his taking his religion more seriously."

One day, Ali was hired to sit at a table and sign autographs to promote a new television enterprise — Classic Sports Network — at a cable TV convention in New Orleans. His pay was five thousand dollars for four hours. Ali did more than sign autographs. He posed for photos and performed magic tricks, and, because he spent so long with each of his fans, the line to meet him stretched far out of sight. At 3:50 p.m., when Ali's time was almost up, the man who had hired him, Brian Bedol, began apologizing to the people standing in line and telling them that the champ would have to leave in ten minutes. Bedol heard a loud whisper from behind. "Hey boss man, what are you doing?" It was Ali. "These people are here to see *me!*"

Ali stayed two more hours, until everyone had an autograph or a picture. When he was done, he joined Bedol and his team for dinner — and insisted on picking up the two-thousand-dollar tab. When the meal ended, Ali in-

vited Bedol and the others to his hotel suite, where he passed around a Bible
and discussed the contradictions contained in the texts. There were thirty
thousand contradictions in the Bible, he said, and he went on to offer examples. As the night stretched on, Bedol had the feeling Ali was going to
mention every one, but he didn't. He was trying to make the point that Judaism, Christianity, and Islam sprang from the same set of beliefs. Muslims,
Ali explained, believed that Jewish and Christian holy books were divinely
revealed, but those books had lost their integrity through countless revisions
over the years, and only the Koran offered a perfect and complete account
of God's words as revealed to the prophet Muhammad. After midnight, Ali
stopped talking, pushed back his chair, rose, and walked to his bedroom.
After ten minutes, when Ali didn't return, Bedol and his colleagues looked at
one another and quietly exited the suite.

In an interview after his retirement, Ali was once asked who had helped
him most in his career. "In my career, everything . . ." He paused and smiled.
"Allah. All my success, all my protection, all my fearlessness, all my victories,
all my courage: Everything came from Allah."

On February 8, 1990, Cassius Marcellus Clay Sr. suffered a heart attack in the
parking lot of a Louisville department store and died. He was seventy-seven.
Ali's relationship with his father had always been a complicated one. For
years, Cash had drunk too much and mistreated his wife and children. But,
at the same time, he'd been a steady fixture in his son's life — never far from
home, always in attendance at his son's fights or hanging around his training
camp, and traveling the world as part of his son's adventures. He had not been
an ideal father, and in later years the father-son roles sometimes had seemed
reversed, with Ali relishing opportunities to show his father who was really
in charge. Upon news of the death, Ali told reporters: "He was a father, a
friend, my trainer, and my best buddy."

In November 1990, Ali traveled to Iraq to meet its president, Saddam Hussein, in an attempt to win the release of hundreds of American hostages. Ali
was mostly silent during the meeting, but when it was over, Hussein released
fifteen Americans and allowed them to travel home with the boxer.

The following year, Ali toured in support of his new biography, written by
Thomas Hauser with Ali's cooperation. The book put Ali back in the spot-

light and began the work of placing his achievements in historical context. By including interviews with Ali's doctors, who had been granted permission by Ali to speak openly, Hauser also called attention to the damage boxing had done to his story's hero. But even as he promoted it, Ali expressed ambivalence about his authorized biography.

"Book makes me look like a fool," he told Robert Lipsyte of the *New York Times.*

When Lipsyte asked if he'd read it, Ali whispered in Lipsyte's ear: "Shouldn't say this. Never read a book in my life."

What about the Koran? Lipsyte asked.

"Not cover to cover. Some pages forty times."

Ali cradled a baby while he spoke to Lipsyte. He and Lonnie had recently adopted a boy, Asaad.

As he spoke to Lipsyte and held Asaad, Ali watched a tape of his recent appearance on the *Today Show,* which he had done to help sell the book.

"Shouldn't have done it," he said, looking at his own shaking hands and rigid face on the replay. "If I was a fan, I'd be shocked."

Lonnie was saddened at times by Ali's reluctance to appear on camera and his frustration with his appearance. She knew how much he had once loved such attention. Now, she reassured him: "You know I tell the truth. That man is shaking, but he can be understood."

"That man look like he's dying," Ali said. The man who had always called himself pretty no longer liked what he saw.

"You were fine," Lipsyte said. "You give other people with problems inspiration."

In New York that same week, Ali met Chuck Wepner at a charity event. Wepner, who had fought hard against Ali in 1975, still swore he had scored a legitimate knockdown in their bout, while Ali insisted he'd gone down only because Wepner had stepped on his foot. It remained a sore point for Ali. When the men met again, sixteen years later, Lipsyte and others watched anxiously to see how Ali would react. Would he recognize Wepner? Would he say something?

Lipsyte's concerns quickly dissolved. The reporter watched as Ali and Wepner came together. Ali moved in close to his old rival, leaned forward, and stepped on his former opponent's foot.

55

A Torch

At about 10:15 one Saturday morning in the spring of 1994, Muhammad Ali and his brother Rahaman were eating breakfast at their mother's house in Louisville when the doorbell rang. Odessa Clay, wearing a flowery housedress with lace trim, answered.

Standing on the porch was a tall, sturdily built white man named Frank Sadlo. Odessa hadn't seen Frank in years, but she recognized him. He was the son of Henry Sadlo, who had been the Clay family's first lawyer. Back in the 1960s, Henry Sadlo had been the man Odessa called when her husband had had too many drinks and gotten tossed in jail. Henry Sadlo had been the man who had helped Cassius Jr. reclaim his driver's license after too many teenaged speeding tickets. He'd been the lawyer who had reviewed Cassius Jr.'s first professional boxing contract after the young boxer had returned from the Rome Olympics with a gold medal. Soon after, the Clay family replaced Henry Sadlo with attorneys of a higher pedigree. But the Clays, nevertheless, had always admired and respected Henry Sadlo; he had been one of the few white men who had shown kindness and respect before the family had been brushed with fame.

When he was five years old, Frank Sadlo would sometimes accompany his father on visits to the Clay home. Cassius and Rudy would put up their fists and pretend to box with the feisty youngster, but instead of saying "I'll fight you!" little Frank would shout, "I'll fish you!"

Now, Odessa looked up at Frank Sadlo, a grown man, as big as her two boys, and the memory floated back.

"I'll fish you!" she said with a laugh.

Frank bent down to hug Mrs. Clay.

Rahaman came to the door. He hugged Frank, too. Odessa invited him in.

Frank followed Rahaman and Odessa into the kitchen, where Muhammad sat at the table eating a bowl of cereal, his right hand shaking as he gripped a spoon. By 1994, Ali's life had slowed, same as his body. He didn't care for the way he looked and sounded. Some friends thought he was depressed.

Odessa reminded Muhammad that Frank was Henry Sadlo's son. Frank explained Henry Sadlo was at Norton Hospital in downtown Louisville, preparing to undergo heart surgery — a triple bypass and valve replacement. The likelihood of survival was 50 percent.

Before Frank could even ask the question — would Muhammad be willing to visit? — Ali put down his spoon, pressed both his fists into the tabletop, and pushed himself up out of his chair.

"Let's go," he said.

At the hospital, Ali and Henry Sadlo talked for forty-five minutes. When doctors told Ali that the patient needed to rest, Ali left Henry Sadlo's bedside but stuck around the hospital. Doctors and people visiting loved ones came in search of Ali, as if he were a physician or a priest, asking if he would attend to more people. Ali was told of a comatose man who was fading fast. Ali went to the patient's bed in the intensive-care unit and whispered in his ear, and Frank Sadlo swore that he saw the comatose man open his eyes. For the next hour, Ali made the rounds, holding hands with patients, sparring with orderlies in the hallways, flirting with nurses, performing magic tricks for kids.

When it was over, when Henry Sadlo recovered from his heart surgery and Ali left Louisville, Frank got to thinking: "I wanted to do something nice for Muhammad," he said. "What he did, getting up from his breakfast to rush to the hospital to see somebody . . . not a lot of people would do that. So I started thinking: what can I do for Muhammad?"

Shortly after Sadlo's visit to the Clay family home, Odessa suffered a stroke. Ali visited her in the hospital every day for weeks. Many nights he slept by her side. When Odessa was in the intensive-care unit and too sick to speak or open her eyes, Ali gently rubbed her nose and spoke to her in a murmuring monologue. "I love you, Bird," he said. "Are you in pain, Bird? You gonna get up?"

She died August 20, 1994. Not long after the funeral, Frank Sadlo helped Muhammad clean out his mother's house. In the basement, they found boxes full of mementos from Ali's career. Sadlo and Ali sat together on the floor and sorted through it all. Ali laughed as he told stories and decided which mementos to keep and which to toss. Sadlo listened and heard the arc of Ali's life: Odessa and Cash's little boy had lost his bicycle, he'd taken up boxing, won an Olympic gold medal, and gone on to charm the whole world with his athletic gifts, with the flair he'd inherited from his father and the kindness that had come from his mother. As Sadlo thought about it, one part of Ali's biography stood out: his victory in the 1960 Olympics. Winning the gold medal in Rome had been a turning point for Ali. That's when he had first tasted fame on a large level and first seen the potential of a life lived large.

For Sadlo, an idea began to form.

The Olympic games were coming to Atlanta in 1996. Sadlo wondered if Muhammad could be celebrated somehow. Would Olympic officials present Ali with a replacement for the medal he'd lost? Would they let him light the torch that signaled the start of the games? The more Sadlo thought about it, the more excited he became. Ali was an Olympic gold-medalist, an international hero, the twentieth century's greatest athlete. He was a Muslim grandson of slaves, the embodiment of diversity. He was America — big, beautiful, fast, loud, romantic, crazy, impulsive. Who better to represent his country to the world?

With nothing but postage stamps, a telephone, and a nine-year-old Oldsmobile Cutlass Supreme, Sadlo went to work. He was holding down two jobs: as a social worker and a waiter at Applebee's. But he had no wife and no children, which meant he had plenty of time for this project. Sadlo wrote letters to Olympic officials and telephoned the office of the mayor of Atlanta, Andrew Young. When a bureaucrat at the Atlanta Committee on the Olympic Games agreed to a meeting, Sadlo drove to Georgia. He was afraid that the officials in Atlanta would think he was a kook, "someone who didn't have all his oars in the water," so he brought along photos he'd taken with Muhammad to prove his connection with the legendary athlete. He knew it was a long shot, but he tried anyway. He made dozens of phone calls, possibly hundreds, and mailed dozens of letters. One January evening in 1995, he took Ali out for dinner and told him about his campaign. Ali smiled and thanked him.

That felt good. If nothing else, Ali would know that he had tried.

A week before the start of the Olympics, Sadlo put it out of mind. His work was done. He had never gotten a direct answer to any of his letters or calls. In the days before the start of the games, TV commentators and newspaper journalists speculated about who might receive the honor of lighting the torch. Most bets were on a pair of Atlantans: baseball legend Hank Aaron and boxer Evander Holyfield. The choice was meant to be a tightly held secret. Sadlo assumed nothing had come of his efforts.

Then, at 2:30 in the morning on July 16, three days before the opening ceremony, Sadlo received a strange phone call. It was Howard Bingham calling from Los Angeles to say that Muhammad and Lonnie wanted to thank Sadlo for what he had done. That was it. Bingham didn't say *what* Sadlo had done, only that Lonnie and Muhammad appreciated it.

On Friday night, June 19, Sadlo was waiting tables at Applebee's in Clarksville, Indiana, and keeping an eye on the televisions in the restaurant as the opening ceremony of the Olympics filled the screens. Eighty thousand people crammed a stadium in Atlanta. Around the world, hundreds of millions watched on television. Evander Holyfield carried the torch into the stadium and handed it to Janet Evans, the gold-medal-winning swimmer, who carried it up a long ramp. Evans was supposed to hand the torch to its final carrier, who would light the Olympic cauldron and signal the official start of the games.

There was no one in sight.

Then, from the shadows, came a large, slow-moving figure, an apparition dressed all in white.

A roar shot through the stadium. It began with a "Whoooaaaa!" and turned into a thrilled, throaty, rattling cheer. They chanted, "Ali! Ali!"

His right hand clutched an unlit torch. His left hand shook uncontrollably and shockingly to those who had not seen him in recent years. His face betrayed no emotion. When Evans touched her torch to Ali's, Ali's torch caught the flame. He stood tall and held it high. Cameras flashed. The crowd continued to roar. Ali's left arm continued to shake but he held tight to the torch with his right.

When he clutched the torch with both hands, his shaking stopped. His face tightened in concentration as he bent over to light the wick that would travel by pulley to the top of the stadium. But the wick wouldn't catch and the flame from the torch licked at Ali's hands. For a moment, it appeared Ali would need help, that he might drop the torch, or worse, set himself on fire. The arena fell silent, as if eighty thousand breaths were held. Then, finally, the wick caught. The cauldron was lit. The crowd roared again.

They cheered because they saw Ali as a rebel again. They saw a man who wasn't afraid to show his weakness, a man whose shaking hands reminded everyone of what he'd said countless times when he was young and vital and seemingly immortal: that he had no fear of death.

For Frank Sadlo, the scene was pure joy. He knew how much Ali loved the spotlight and how much he'd been missing it since his retirement from boxing. He didn't care whether he'd had anything to do with the Olympic Committee's selection. He knew it was entirely possible that his calls and letters had had nothing to do with it, that some Olympic official or television executive had come up with the idea entirely on his own. That didn't matter. Sadlo's wish had come true. And, as he stood on the floor of Applebee's, gazing up at the TV, fighting back tears, he wished again — wished for Ali to enjoy this moment and all the attention that would follow.

Two months after the Olympic ceremony, Muhammad and Lonnie sat for an interview with a reporter from *USA Today* at the couple's home in Michigan.

"Ali's lighting of the Olympic flame," the resulting story said, "has triggered a renaissance for The Greatest, one of the planet's most magical, beloved athletic heroes, and a man whose humanitarian efforts are being pushed by some for a Nobel Peace Prize.

"Since the Olympics, the 54-year-old former three-time heavyweight champion is viewed less as a victim of boxing and Parkinson's disease than an inspiration to millions of the disabled.

"After years of ducking the media because his neurological disorder made him self-conscious, Ali has re-emerged.

"He didn't just light a flame, he lit the way for others — and, perhaps, himself."

• • •

Suddenly, Ali was more than an aging sports legend.

"He's half real, half folktale," said Seth Abraham, the president of Time Warner Sports at the time. "I know Paul Bunyan and the blue ox don't exist, but it's such a part of Americana. He's almost Paul Bunyan . . . Muhammad Ali: was there really such a character?"

56

The Long, Black Cadillac

Ali had no one left to fight.

For most of his adult life, he had been at war — with his opponents in the ring, with reporters who tried to tell him how to behave, with American political and economic systems that relegated black Americans to the lowest social and economic stratum. Among boxers, Jack Johnson had taken the first good shot at American notions of white superiority; Joe Louis had followed, striking blows for integration and acceptance; and Muhammad Ali, during a period of national turmoil, had jabbed and danced and lashed out, unworried about angering the white man, insisting America's glory had been built by the thrashing of black backs, the destruction of black families, and the smothering of black voices, and that black Americans would never truly be free until they whupped the whole rotten system.

Now, with his voice but a whisper and no one left to antagonize, Ali grew quiet. He continued to travel, continued to accept awards, continued to perform certain polished routines, as Lonnie and Howard Bingham played along. Ali would scowl as Bingham introduced him as Joe Frazier. Ali would make a handkerchief disappear. He would appear to levitate. He would sit at a piano with Bingham and play "Heart and Soul."

The routines were mostly wordless. But the less Ali spoke, the sweeter and more saintly he became — at least in the eyes of white America. He had reputable businessmen and -women surrounding him now. He lived with Lonnie on a farm in Berrien Springs, Michigan, away from the media, away from the struggles of his people, away from the entourage, the sycophants, the con men, the women, away from everything. When reporters came calling, they were impressed that he wasn't ashamed to let the world see his trembling hands and clumsy gait. They described him as a man at peace. With his hushed voice and simple magic tricks, Ali seemed charming, especially compared to some of the churlish professional athletes who populated the world of the sports in the 1990s.

Lonnie, who had a master's degree in business, got rid of some of the shady businessmen who had attached themselves to her husband. She brought in lawyers and marketing executives with new ideas and negotiated better deals. In 1999, a picture of the young Ali appeared on the front of the Wheaties cereal box, where athletes of high achievement and good character had been honored for generations.

Ali, with Thomas Hauser's help, produced an inspirational book called *Healing: A Journal of Tolerance and Understanding.* The book contained quotes from famous figures as well as blank spaces for readers to pen their own inspirational messages reflecting on "tolerance, brotherhood and understanding." Lonnie and her team worked to stabilize Ali's finances and polish his image. Along the way, the hard-punching revolutionary became a shuffling, sweet-faced mystic, benevolent and wise.

At times, the veneration had a spiritual tone.

"More and more he is like a soul walking," wrote Frank Deford.

Ali's daughter Hana wrote a book in which she called her father "a prophet, a messenger of God, an angel."

Writing for *GQ,* Peter Richmond watched Ali shove a frosted raspberry coffee cake in his mouth and proffered, "As I watch him eat, I have never been more sure of a man's inner contentment. Except maybe when he eats the second piece."

The same writer composed a parable about Ali:

"For decades," it read, "Allah had Muhammad Ali doing Allah's work. Ali was the most remarkable young black man the nation had ever seen, unafraid to take on the mightiest of the white man's institutions, speaking out, yes, for the black man, but even more for Allah, in a fashion that Malcolm X and Elijah Muhammad never could have.

"But the older the disciple grew, the more he began to lose fights to people like Trevor Berbick. And the more he began to lose fights, the more he threatened to fall into the black hole wherein reside all the great athletes who tried to hang on too long. Allah knew that the closer Muhammad Ali got to the ultimate indignity of punch-drunkdom, the less use he was for Allah as an emissary on earth . . . So Allah hit upon a plan. Where Ali's voice once moved mountains, Allah struck him mute. Where Ali's swift fists once rained upon opponents with the precision of a surgeon, Allah struck them with terrible tremors so that they struggled to hold a piece of cake . . .

"And this is how Allah made sure that Muhammad Ali would be doing his work again. Tenfold. For in infirmity, Ali came to mean much more than he had ever been before."

It was a questionable notion — that the silent, suffering Ali meant more to the world than the angry young man who had challenged our country's racist hierarchies and fired imaginations — but it sounded nice.

Ali continued to give interviews in the years after lighting the Olympic torch, but he seldom discussed race or politics. In 1991, when four Los Angeles police officers were videotaped viciously beating a black man named Rodney King, an act that ignited riots, Ali said nothing. Three years later, when O. J. Simpson was arrested for murdering two white people, one of them his ex-wife, and when the trial turned into a referendum on racism among police, Ali made no public comment.

He still preferred to talk about himself.

In 2001, in an interview with the *New York Times,* he apologized for calling Joe Frazier an Uncle Tom and saying Frazier was too dumb and ugly to be champ. "I said a lot of things in the heat of the moment that I shouldn't have said," Ali noted. "Called him names that I shouldn't have called him. I apologize for that. I'm sorry. It was all meant to promote the fight."

The apology seemed genuine, as if Ali were thinking about the Tallying Angel. Along with apologizing to Frazier, he aided countless charitable and humanitarian organizations, including the United Nations, the National Parkinson Foundation, and the Make-a-Wish Foundation. He and Lonnie helped launch the Muhammad Ali Parkinson Center and Movement Disorder Clinic at Barrow Neurological Institute in Phoenix. "God will be the judge of the deeds we do, how we treat people, how we help charities," he said. "I can't cure nobody, so all I can do is help people raise money."

On September 11, 2001, Arab terrorists hijacked four commercial planes and crashed them into the World Trade Center in New York; the Pentagon in Washington, DC; and a field in Pennsylvania, killing about three thousand people and injuring thousands more. After the attack, anti-Muslim backlash flared in America. Innocent Muslims were detained. Graffiti was sprayed on mosques and the doors of Arab-owned businesses. A statement from Ali was released: "I am a Muslim," it said. "I am an American . . . Whoever performed, or is behind, the terrorist attacks in the United States of America does not represent Islam. God is not behind assassins."

On September 20, Ali traveled to New York.

"Tell me what happened again?" he asked during the flight.

When it was explained to him again about the terrorist assault, he turned to his wife and said, "They're not mad at me, are they?"

The day was gray and misty. Ali greeted firefighters who had been at the scene of the attack. He curled his hands into fists and pretended to launch punches as he posed for pictures with them. For the most part, the firefighters wanted to tell Ali where they had been when he'd fought Joe Frazier the first time, or what they remembered best about the Rumble in the Jungle. But Ali, wearing a Fire Department of New York baseball cap, used the occasion to discuss religion. "Islam is not a killing religion," he said. "Islam means peace. I couldn't just sit at home and watch people label Muslims as being the reason for this problem."

After the September 11 attacks, President George W. Bush sent American troops into battle in Afghanistan and Iraq, with the goal of routing Islamic terrorists and overthrowing Iraqi president Saddam Hussein. Newspapers at the time reported that Ali had agreed to appear in a Hollywood-produced ad campaign that would explain to audiences in the Middle East that America respected Muslims and intended to treat them with respect, even as American troops targeted terrorists. The *Final Call*, the newspaper published by the Nation of Islam under the leadership of Louis Farrakhan, urged Ali to reject the government's propaganda campaign. Instead, the *Final Call* said, Ali ought use his power to call attention to problems affecting black Americans in the twenty-first century, such as the AIDS epidemic and the rapidly growing black prison population.

Ali didn't address those issues anymore, leaving observers to wonder: Did he have any quarrel with Afghanis or Iraqis? Did he have any quarrel with President Bush in his rush to war?

"I dodge those questions," he told the English television interviewer David Frost. "I have people who love me. I've opened up businesses across the country, selling products, and I don't want to say nothing and be wrong, not knowing what I'm doing, not qualified, say the wrong thing and hurt my businesses and things I'm doing, hurt my image."

When Frost asked specifically about the American invasion of Iraq, Ali answered, "That's one of those questions that can get me in trouble. I'll dodge that." He put his hand over his mouth for emphasis.

The rough edges that had made Ali controversial and important were slowly being rubbed down. In 2001, Will Smith starred in *Ali*, a big-budget movie that covered ten years of the boxer's life, from 1964 to 1974, from Liston to Foreman, and from Sonji to Veronica, from Malcolm X to the last years of Elijah Muhammad.

In 2005, Ali received the Presidential Medal of Freedom, the nation's highest civilian honor. In presenting the award, President Bush called Ali "a fierce fighter and a man of peace" but made no mention of the former champion's decision in 1967 to refuse to serve in the U.S. Army. Ali, in turn, made no mention of Bush's decision to send troops to Afghanistan and Iraq. But Ali still had a little bit of the troublemaker in him. When the president turned and raised his fists, as if he were preparing to fight, Ali declined to play along. Instead of raising his fists, Ali lifted a finger to his head and twirled it in a gesture suggesting Bush was crazy. The room filled with laughter.

In the same year, a museum dedicated to the champ opened on the banks of the Ohio River in downtown Louisville. Lonnie and Muhammad led the drive to create the $80-million, 93,000-square-foot Muhammad Ali Center, with backing from General Electric, Ford Motor Company, and Yum! Brands. The city also renamed Walnut Street, one of its main thoroughfares, Muhammad Ali Boulevard.

With the help of Lonnie and lawyer Ron DiNicola, Ali finally severed his ties with Herbert Muhammad. In 2006, Lonnie and Muhammad struck a deal with the entertainment marketing company CKX, selling 80 percent of the marketing rights to the boxer's name and image for $50 million. Lonnie agreed to work with the firm in setting the strategy to build her husband's brand.

As the years passed under the CKX deal, Ali became a commodity. He endorsed companies and products that once would have had nothing to do with him — IBM, Porsche, Gillette, and Louis Vuitton, to name but a few. Some of his old fans and some of the journalists who had covered him in the 1960s complained that the new Ali stood for everything — for peace, love, unity, equality, justice, and high-end leather goods — and in standing for everything risked standing for nothing. At one point, he earned $750 per autograph and signed more than seven thousand items a year. He made many appearances for charities at no charge, but for other public events he earned six-figure fees. When he wasn't traveling or signing autographs, he spent hours a day on the phone, talking to his children and grandchildren and joking with old friends. When his son Asaad played on the baseball team at the University of Louisville, Muhammad and Lonnie often attended his games. "He was a man that never complained," Asaad said. "You never could tell what days were bad with Parkinson's, what days were good. Because he's that kind of person. He's tough, he's strong."

In 2009, he attended the inauguration of America's first black president, Barack Obama. In 2016, when presidential candidate Donald J. Trump proposed a ban on Muslim immigration to the United States, a statement issued on behalf of Ali reminded fans of the boxer's combative style but fell short of the vigor of earlier days. It read, in part: "Speaking as someone who has never been accused of political correctness, I believe that our political leaders should use their position to bring understanding about the religion of Islam."

Year by year, he grew weaker, quieter.

His children married and had children. His friends and loved ones died: Howard Cosell in 1995, Archie Moore in 1998, Sonji Roi in 2005, Floyd Patterson in 2006, Herbert Muhammad in 2008, Joe Frazier in 2011, Angelo Dundee in 2012, Ken Norton in 2013. Ali's visitors in those years found that his condition varied depending on the time of day they saw him and how well he'd been sleeping. Sometimes he smiled and laughed and reminisced in a clear voice, and sometimes the effort was too great and he sat quietly.

Muhammad and Lonnie spent less time in Michigan and more time in Paradise Valley, Arizona, in a single-story house in a gated community. Lonnie's sister Marilyn shared the home and helped with Ali's care. Numerous portraits of Ali, including a large series of Andy Warhol paintings, decorated the living room. Ali liked to sit near the kitchen, in a leather reclining chair that had a built-in vibrator to massage his back and legs. From there he could watch TV or look at videos on the Internet. He still watched Westerns and horror movies, but what he loved to watch most of all was himself — old fights, old interviews, old TV news clips. Sometimes guests would sit by his side as Ali gazed at his younger self in action, watching the most beautiful heavyweight of all time as he floated around the ring, dodging punches, sticking jabs, laughing, shouting, rejoicing, taunting. That was the real Ali. That was how he was supposed to be. That was the natural order of things. He was so elegant, so defiant, so strong, so completely in control, so free. Who wouldn't want to watch that?

In an interview with *AARP Bulletin,* the magazine published by the group formerly known as the American Association of Retired Persons, Lonnie talked about the challenges faced by a spouse who becomes a caregiver. "The relationship changes over time with the illness," she said. "Physically, [patients] are not as mobile; they are not able to do things with you like they used to. The medications might affect their cognitive ability. They may not speak as well." But Lonnie said she was fortunate because her husband maintained a winning attitude, never complaining, never getting depressed. Muhammad and Lonnie appeared on the cover of the magazine, he with his eyes closed and head tilted down, she with lips pressed to her husband's temple and a hand cradling his chin. "Everything now is about protecting him and making sure he is healthy," she said.

Lonnie became gatekeeper as well as caregiver, which led to complaints from some of Ali's children and friends, who said they didn't get to see Ali as often as they would have liked and couldn't reach him on the phone. Newspapers reported that Muhammad Jr. — Ali's son from his marriage to Belinda — lived in poverty on the South Side of Chicago and relied on charity to feed and clothe his family. Khalilah, Ali's second wife, lived in government-subsidized, low-income housing in Deerfield Beach, Florida. In her dimly lit, one-bedroom apartment, there remained only one visible reminder of her former life: a Muhammad Ali refrigerator magnet.

On October 1, 2015 — the fortieth anniversary of Ali's brutal fight against Frazier in Manila — Lonnie and Muhammad appeared at the Ali Center in Louisville for a private event sponsored by *Sports Illustrated* and Under Armour, the sports apparel company. George Foreman and Larry Holmes were there, talking to reporters, extolling the greatness of Ali, explaining that they had no hard feelings — even though they couldn't resist taking a few pokes at their former rival, shots that served as a useful reminder that these men were warriors who had constructed their identities from strength and pride.

All his life, Ali had fought to prove his superiority. He'd battled his father, he'd battled the boxing press, battled the government, battled Sonny Liston, Joe Frazier, Ken Norton, George Foreman, and Larry Holmes. He'd kept it up long after he should have—just as Foreman and Holmes were keeping it up even now, still looking to unload a few jabs. Foreman, at least in private, continued to insist that he'd been drugged before stepping into the ring with Ali in Zaire. Holmes, in an interview before the banquet, admitted he got tired of people behaving as if Ali were the Dalai Lama, tired of people carrying on as if Ali were a superhero and all other heavyweight champions were mere mortals. Ali was a good man and a great fighter, Holmes said, but he'd been a fool to take so many punches. "He wasn't no hero," Holmes said.

Ali's brother, Rahaman, was there, too. Ali had once promised Rahaman that he didn't have to box, that his older brother would always see to it that he lived comfortably. But now Rahaman and his wife struggled to pay bills. They lived in public housing, in an apartment decorated to look like their own low-budget Muhammad Ali Museum. Newspaper clippings were taped to the wall. A portrait of Odessa Clay that had been painted by her husband Cash hung over the sofa. Rahaman, who inherited some of his father's artistic talent, had painted a few portraits of his brother. Those paintings sat on the floor, leaning against a wall. Years earlier, Rahaman had had a falling out with Lonnie. As a result, he hadn't seen his brother in months. And while certain VIPs were invited to pose for pictures with the champ prior to the start of the ceremony at the Ali Center, Rahaman did not make the cut.

When the doors to the ballroom opened and guests were invited to find their seats, all eyes turned to Ali. He was seated at the head table, wearing a black suit, a white shirt, and a red tie, with Lonnie on his right and Lonnie's sister Marilyn on his left.

The ballroom filled quickly with invited guests, many of them making a beeline for Ali's table. Vic Bender got there first. He and Ali had been classmates at Central High. Earlier that afternoon, Bender had taken a writer on a tour of Ali's Louisville, starting with the Clay family home on Grand Avenue and proceeding along the route that Cassius and Rudy had run on their way to school, keeping pace with the city bus, stopping every time the bus stopped, just as interested in entertaining their friends as they had been in exercise. Now it was Bender running—running as best he could for a big man in his seventies—to get to Ali's side before anyone else. He said hello to Lonnie and then leaned over to hug Ali.

Ali didn't move. He didn't speak. He didn't look up. His body appeared small and frail, but his face was smooth and unlined. His hair was thinning but without a trace of gray. Still pretty.

As the ceremony began, videos flashed on big screens and long speeches were made. The highlights of his career were recounted, but Ali, wearing dark sunglasses, never reacted. When a *Sports Illustrated* executive presented the former boxer with a silver plate as his award, cameras flashed and guests stood to applaud, but Ali still didn't move, didn't smile, didn't reach out to accept the prize. He might as well have been sleeping. When the ceremony ended, he was sped from the room in a wheelchair.

As the ballroom emptied and busboys cleared the dishes, Rahaman and his wife, Caroline, stayed behind. They walked from table to table, taking the small photographs of Ali that had been used as decorations and stuffing them in a shopping bag.

"Wasn't it a beautiful night?" Rahaman asked.

Less than eight months later, Ali was hospitalized in Phoenix for a respiratory infection. He had been hospitalized before with infections, and he had always bounced back. But this time, after a few days of treatment, his condition worsened. Lonnie phoned the children and told them to come right away. They did. At 8:30 p.m. on June 3, with his family surrounding him in Room 263 of the Scottsdale Osborn Medical Center, Ali was disconnected from the ventilator keeping him alive. He fought to breathe.

An imam named Zaid Shakir stood by Ali's bed and watched as the pulse in Ali's neck began to slowly fade. Shakir leaned over until his mouth was next to Ali's right ear and began to sing the call to prayer, a song usually sung to newborns as they are ushered into the world. "There is no God but Allah, and Muhammad is his messenger," he sang in a loud, beautiful voice. One of Ali's grandsons offered a string of prayer beads. Shakir pressed the beads into Ali's hand. Shakir spoke to Ali: "Muhammad Ali, this is what it means. God is one; say it, repeat it, you've inspired so many, paradise is waiting."

When the imam finished the prayer, Ali was gone.

At 9:10 p.m., Muhammad Ali, seventy-four years old, was pronounced dead of septic shock.

• • •

Ali's body was flown to Louisville for the funeral. For years, Muhammad and Lonnie had talked about what the ceremony would look like, who would serve as pallbearers, and who would deliver eulogies. They had filled a black binder with elaborate plans. Ali had envisioned a magnificent sendoff.

He was remembered in print, on television, and on the Internet as a man of courage and principle. He was hailed as one of the great figures of the twentieth century. In the *New York Times,* his obituary ran for more than two full pages, followed less than a week later with a sixteen-page special section. From the White House, President Obama issued a statement that read, in part: "'I am America,' he once declared. 'I am the part you won't recognize. But get used to me — black, confident, cocky; my name, not yours; my religion, not yours; my goals, my own. Get used to me.' That's the Ali I came to know as I came of age — not just as skilled a poet on the mic as he was a fighter in the ring, but a man who fought for what was right. A man who fought for us. He stood with King and Mandela; stood up when it was hard; spoke out when others wouldn't. His fight outside the ring would cost him his title and his public standing. It would earn him enemies on the left and the right, make him reviled, and nearly send him to jail. But Ali stood his ground. And his victory helped us get used to the America we recognize today . . . Muhammad Ali shook up the world. And the world is better for it. We are all better for it."

Some writers said that Ali had "transcended" race. It was an attempt to whitewash his legacy, and it was dead wrong. Race was the theme of Ali's life. He insisted that America come to grips with a black man who wasn't afraid to speak out, who refused to be what others expected him to be. He didn't *overcome* race. He didn't *overcome* racism. He called it out. He faced it down. He refuted it. He insisted that racism shaped our notions of race, that it was never the other way around.

Born in the age of Jim Crow, Ali lived to see a black man elected president. Just as remarkable was the arc of his own life: the son of a poorly educated sign painter became the most famous man in the world; the greatest professional fighter of his time became his country's most important draft resister. Although he had always been ambitious and always yearned for wealth, he had somehow remained warm and genuine, a man of sincere feeling and wit. Bitterness and cynicism never touched him — perhaps because he recognized this lesson of his own life: that American society, for all its flaws, produced remarkable men from unremarkable origins. He himself, indubitably, was one.

Ali's funeral procession began on a hot Friday morning, June 10. Thousands upon thousands of people lined the streets of Louisville. People who had never met Ali took time off work and traveled hundreds of miles to be there. Standing beneath a scorching sun, they craned to catch a glimpse of Ali's hearse. People wore T-shirts reading "I AM ALI" and "I AM THE GREATEST" and held signs that said "THANK YOU" and "WE LOVE YOU." Little boys and grown men threw punches at the air, shadowboxing, when they saw Ali's car. Women tossed flowers. "Ali! Ali!" the crowds chanted, as they always had.

Ali's hearse was a Cadillac, of course, part of a seventeen-Cadillac procession.

As the procession moved from his childhood home on Grand Avenue toward downtown, it did not precisely follow the route young Ali had run on his way to school back in the 1950s, but it came close. The hearse moved along Broadway, where Ali had once dreamed of flying, passing Fourth Street, where his bicycle had been stolen and where he'd met his first boxing coach. At Sixth Street, spectators began to chant, "Ali boma ye" — "Ali, kill him" in Lingala — same as the people of Zaire had chanted forty-two years earlier, when Ali fought Foreman. The procession passed the Beecher Terrace apartments, where the teenaged Ali had kissed a pretty girl, fainted, and fallen down the stairs. It passed Central High, where Ali had been granted a diploma despite poor grades because the principal had detected something extraordinary about his student. It passed the former site of the Broadway Roller Rink, where Ali had picked up his first copy of *Muhammad Speaks* and begun to learn about Elijah Muhammad and the Nation of Islam. It passed the downtown Muhammad Ali Center, where the boxer's accomplishments were memorialized in a manner usually reserved for American presidents; and on, finally, to Cave Hill Cemetery, where Ali's body would be laid to rest.

The burial was a private ceremony, attended only by Ali's close family. This was followed by a public service at the city's largest downtown arena, where more than twenty thousand people gathered to hear speeches by religious leaders as well as eulogies from former President Bill Clinton, television broadcaster Bryant Gumbel, actor Billy Crystal, Lonnie Ali, and two of Ali's children, Maryum and Rasheda. Ali's former wives, Khalilah and Veronica, were there, as were Louis Farrakhan, Jesse Jackson, Gene Kilroy, Will Smith, Don King, Bob Arum, Mike Tyson, George Foreman, and Larry Holmes. The service, broadcast live on network television and seen around the world, lasted more than three hours.

"Muhammad fell in love with the masses," Lonnie Ali said in eulogizing her husband, "and the masses fell in love with him. In the diversity of men and their faiths, Muhammad saw the presence of God." Even though he was born in a society that treated black people as inferior, she continued, Ali had "two parents that nurtured and encouraged him. He was placed on the path of his dreams by a white cop, and he had teachers who understood his dreams and wanted him to succeed. The Olympic gold medal came, and the world started to take notice. A group of successful businessmen in Louisville, called the Louisville Sponsoring Group, saw his potential and helped him build a runway to launch his career. His timing was impeccable as he burst into the national stage just as television was hungry for a star to change the face of sports. You know, if Muhammad didn't like the rules, he rewrote them. His religion, his name, his beliefs were his to fashion no matter what the cost."

Ali's voice was noticeably absent from the memorial service, but Imam Zaid Shakir did his best to channel him.

He stepped to the lectern and offered a poem:

> He floated like a butterfly and stung like a bee
> The greatest fighter this world has yet to see . . .
> On the heart of every life he touched he left an indelible stamp,
> And he will always be known as the People's Champ.

Long before, Ali had spoken about the meaning of his life.

"God is watching me," he once said. "God don't praise me because I beat Joe Frazier . . . He wants to know how do we treat each other, how do we help each other."

In one of his final interviews, he assessed his own accomplishments: "I had to prove you could be a new kind of black man," he said. "I had to show that to the world."

POSTSCRIPT

Five months after Muhammad Ali's death, a political activist from the 1960s sat in a coffee shop on Chicago's South Side and told this story:

In the summer of 1966, Martin Luther King Jr. had come to Chicago, planning to put the city at the center of his ongoing, nonviolent revolution. He called it the Chicago Freedom Movement, and the main focus was an attack on discriminatory housing. King led marches into all-white neighborhoods, where he faced vicious attacks by mobs. He also organized a rent strike, urging tenants in derelict buildings to put their monthly rents into a special trust fund instead of paying it to their landlords, and vowing that the money would be used for badly needed home repairs.

One day, one of the volunteers in the movement got word that a family participating in the rent strike was being evicted from a home in the Garfield Park neighborhood. The volunteer, a young woman enrolled in law school at the University of Chicago, hurried to the scene. As she arrived, officials from the Cook County Sheriff's Office were emptying the family's apartment, cluttering the sidewalk with furniture, clothing, books, and family photos. The day was hot and humid. Hundreds of people lined the street, watching the eviction in progress.

As the young woman stood and stared, helpless, she felt a hand on her shoulder. She turned around and looked up. It was Ali. Until then, she had seen him only on television. He was wearing a beautiful blue seersucker coat, and he was gorgeous. He removed his coat and asked the young woman to hold it.

Ali was facing draft-dodging charges at the time, but he had not yet been barred from boxing. In fact, he was at his athletic peak: twenty-four years old, too fast to be hit, too strong to be resisted, as perfect a boxer as the world had ever seen.

Although he had spent much of the summer in Chicago, he had not marched with King during the Chicago Freedom Movement nor commented publicly on the protest. How had Ali heard about the eviction? Why was he there? Had he stumbled across it by accident? Had someone called him?

There were no reporters on hand to ask him, and no cameras to capture what happened next.

Without saying a word, Ali walked to where the family's belongings had been dumped on the sidewalk, picked up a kitchen chair, and carried it back into the apartment. The sheriff's deputies made no move to stop him. Within seconds, dozens of people followed Ali's lead. Soon, the apartment was full again.

Ali took back his jacket, got in his car, and drove away.

ACKNOWLEDGMENTS

You've got a big responsibility here," Gene Kilroy told me. "Don't screw it up." He repeated it at least a hundred times over four years, in case I forgot. I never did. I certainly could not have written this book without the help and trust of Kilroy and many others who loved Ali. I'd like to begin by thanking Lonnie Ali, Veronica Porche, Khalilah Camacho-Ali, Rahaman Ali, Caroline Sue Ali, Kilroy, Frank Sadlo, Vic and Brenda Bender, Larry Kolb, Bernie Yuman, Ron DiNicola, Howard Bingham, Michael Phenner, Mike Joyce, Elijah Muhammad III, Lowell K. Riley, Abdul Rahman, Louis Farrakhan, David Jones, Tim Shanahan, Keith Winstead, Seth Abraham, and Hank Schwartz.

I'd also like to thank the friends and writers who helped me in so many ways: Ron Jackson, Charlie Newton, Heidi Trilling, Richard Babcock, Robert Kurson, Joseph Epstein, Bryan Gruley, Kevin Helliker, Robert Kazel, Bob Spitz, David Garrow, Steve Hannah, Jamie Hannah, Dan Cattau, Tony Petrucci, Patrick Harris, Don Terry, Myron and Karen Uhlberg, T. J. Stiles, Richard Milstein, Rabbi Michael Siegel, Linda Ginzel, Boaz Keysar, Jeremy Gershfeld, Elizabeth Miller-Gershfeld, Stephen Fried, Joel Berg, Marshall Kaplan, Jeff Pearlman, Jeff Ruby, Tim Anderson, Ken Burns, Sarah Burns, David McMahon, Stephanie Jenkins, Jeremy Schaap, Willie Weinbaum, Douglas Alden, Ashley Logan, Steve Reiss, Caspar Gonzalez, Craig Sieben, Dan Shine, Tony Fitzpatrick, Solomon Lieberman, Jim Sigmon, Richard Cahan, Ethan Michaeli, Dan Cattau, Jay Lazar, Andy Kalish, Mike Williams, Louis Sahadi, Joe Favorito, Stefan Fatsis, Baron Wolman, A. J. Baime, Robin Monsky, Dan Kay, Audrey Wells, Stacey Rubin Silver, Ted Fishman, Kevin Merida, Lisa Pollak, Kwame Brathwaite, Richard Sandomir, Pat Byrnes, Mark

Caro, James Finn Garner, Jim Powers, Lou Carlozo, Michael Hassan, Rich Kaletsky, Marci Bailey, Amy Merrick, and Tom Tsatas.

Research help came from Lori Azim (who also did a knockout job as a fact-checker), Shirley Harmon, Tom Owen, Howard Breckenridge, Mark Plotkin, Britt Vogel, Maranda Bodas, Jack Cassidy, Shane Zimmer, Jake Milner, Eric Houghton, Madeline Lee, J. R. Reed, Bethel Habte, Meredith Wilson, Mary Hinds, Alison Martin, Liz Peterson, Jeff Noble, Steven Porter, Olivia Angeloff, Gabriella Moran, Jennifer-Leigh Oprihory, Michelle Martinelli, and Ally Pruitt.

For their expert fact-checking, thanks to Mike Silver, Bob Canobbio, and Lee Groves. Thanks to Robert Becker and Congressman Mike Quigley for helping to expedite some of my Freedom of Information Act requests. Thanks to Canobbio and CompuBox, Inc., for developing amazing new statistics on Ali's career. Thanks to Visar Berisha and Julie Liss for working with me to study the effect of boxing on Ali's speech rate. Thanks to Jimmy Walker and everyone at Celebrity Fight Night. Thanks to David Zindel and Graymalkin Media for permission to quote the Joe Frazier–Muhammad Ali dialogue from *The Greatest: My Own Story*. Thanks to Dr. Stanley Fahn for helping me understand Ali's health. Thanks to Ikenna Ezeh and everyone at ABG. Thanks to Abdur-Rahman Muhammad, Leon Muhammad, and Harlan Werner. Thanks to the many writers and photographers who shared their knowledge of Ali and in some cases shared their research materials, including David Remnick, George Sullivan, Karl Evanzz, Andy Quinn, Tom Junod, J. Michael Lennon, Michael Long, Stephen Brunt, Davis Miller, David Maraniss, Gordon Marino, Art Shay, David Turnley, Peter Angelo Simon, Michael Gaffney, Maureen Smith, Thomas Hauser, Mark Kram Jr., Michael Ezra, Dave Kindred, Robert Lipsyte, Neil Leifer, Edwin Pope, John Schulian, Richard Hoffer, Stan Hochman, Jerry Izenberg, Richard Feldstein, Ed Feldstein, Randy Roberts, and Johnny Smith.

Thanks to my friend and agent, David Black, and to everyone at Black, Inc., and especially Sarah Smith, Susan Raihofer, and Jennifer Herrera. Thanks to Lucy Stille, my agent at APA. At Houghton Mifflin Harcourt, thanks to my brilliant editor Susan Canavan and her team, including Jenny Xu, Megan Wilson, and Hannah Harlow. For her wonderful copyediting work, thanks to Margaret Hogan.

Thanks to my family for being in my corner: Phyllis Eig, David Eig, Matt Eig, Lewis Eig, Judy Eig, Penny Eig, Jake Eig, Ben Eig, Hayden Eig, Martin Karns, Don Tescher, SuAnn Tescher, Gail Tescher, Jonathan Tescher, and Leslie Silverman. Thanks and love to my kids: Jeffery Schams, Lillian Eig, and Lola Eig. This book is dedicated to Lola, who was five years old when she wrote a letter to Muhammad Ali. It read, "Dear Muhammad, Jonathan really loves you. Do you love him?" That letter earned us a phone call from Lonnie Ali. It earned Lola a birthday greeting from Lonnie and Muhammad. And it earned us both an invitation to visit Lonnie and Muhammad at their home in Phoenix.

Finally, and most of all, thanks to my amazing wife, Jennifer Tescher — the greatest of allllll tiiiiiimes!

NOTES

This book is the product of more than six hundred interviews with more than two hundred individuals. I conducted all the interviews myself, either on the phone or in person.

The notes that follow provide a detailed list of sources, including thousands of pages of FBI documents, hundreds of books, and thousands of newspaper and magazine stories. A few sources may require additional explanation.

In describing fight scenes, I relied heavily on YouTube videos. I have opted not to list the complete URLs for each of those videos. Most boxing statistics and dates for fights come from www.boxrec.com.

I was very fortunate to come along after so many brilliant writers had already covered Ali. Their names appear scattered through the book and in the following notes. Some of them met with me or took my calls and answered my questions. Those include Jerry Izenberg, Thomas Hauser, David Remnick, Edwin Pope, Stan Hochman, Robert Lipsyte, J. Michael Lennon, Stephen Brunt, Dave Kindred, Johnny Smith, Karl Evanzz, and David Garrow. Others — including Richard Durham, Tom Wolfe, Manning Marable, and Nick Thimmesch — left archives for me to explore. One archive worthy of particular mention is that of *Sports Illustrated* writer Jack Olsen, who spent weeks with Ali and had his tape recorder running for long and glorious hours. Those recordings, held now by the University of Oregon, were like time-travel machines, getting me as close as I could ever hope to being in the same room with young Cassius Clay, his mother, his father, and many others. Some of them had never been heard since Olsen listened to them.

Years from now, when another Ali biographer comes along and listens to the recordings of my interviews with Ferdie Pacheco, Gene Kilroy, Rahaman Ali, Khalilah Camacho-Ali, Don King, Veronica Porche, George Foreman, and many others, I hope they feel some of the same thrill that I did in listening to Jack Olsen's tapes.

I was also fortunate to gain access to FBI and Justice Department files on Ali, many of which had never previously been seen. For this I am thankful to the archivists and Freedom of Information officials who handled my requests, and especially to Robert Becker in U.S. Congressman Mike Quigley's office for helping to expedite my FOIA requests.

In describing Ali's relationship with the Louisville Sponsoring Group, I relied heavily on interviews with the group's lawyer, Gordon Davidson, as well as memos, letters, and business records stored at the Filson Historical Society in Louisville. Details on the murder conviction of Ali's grandfather — never previously reported and almost certainly unknown to Ali — come from newspaper clippings and trial transcripts held at the Kentucky Department for Libraries and Archives. Lonnie Ali helped me track down the marriage certificate for Cassius and Odessa Clay, which strongly suggests that Odessa was already pregnant at the time of her marriage — another fact that has never been previously reported and was likely unknown to Ali.

Finally, this book contains two completely new bodies of research. At my request, CompuBox, Inc., researchers watched every one of Ali's recorded fights and counted the punches. As a result, now, for the first time, we can describe with a high degree of accuracy how many times Ali was hit and how many times he hit opponents, round by round, fight by fight, and over the long arc of his career. I also asked speech scientists at Arizona State University to review Ali's television appearances and evaluate changes in his speech rate. The study, led by Visar Berisha and Julie Liss, sheds important new light on how Ali's boxing affected his cognitive skills.

PREFACE: MIAMI 1964

page

ix   *A long, black Cadillac:* "Clay's Act Plays Liston's Camp and Sonny Is a Kindly Critic," *New York Times,* February 20, 1964.
      custom-made denim jacket: BBC News footage, n.d., www.youtube.com.
      "I'm the biggest thing in history!": Ibid.
      Men in shorts and girls in tight pants: "Clay's Act Plays Liston's Camp."
      "Float like a butterfly": Ibid.
      "I'm pretty and move as fast as lightning": John Cottrell, *Muhammad Ali, Who Once Was Cassius Clay* (New York: Funk and Wagnalls, 1967), 127.

x   *"There's got to be good guys":* Nick Tosches, *The Devil and Sonny Liston* (New York: Little, Brown, 2000), 201.
      He swats away the outstretched hands: BBC News footage, n.d., www.youtube.com.
      "is just a little kid": "Clay's Act Plays Liston's Camp."
      In a cramped hotel room: "Malcolm Little (Malcolm X) HQ File," FBI memo, February 5, 1964, *Federal Bureau of Investigation,* https://vault.fbi.gov/malcolm-little-malcolm-x (hereafter FBI Vault), section 10.

xi   *"Being an old farm boy myself":* "Malcolm X Scores U.S. and Kennedy," *New York Times,* December 2, 1963.
      It's 2 in the morning: Malcolm X FBI file, February 5, 1964, section 10.
      According to an FBI informant: Malcolm X FBI file, January 21, 1964, section 9.

xii   *"You ain't got a chance":* BBC film footage, n.d., www.youtube.com.
      "I am the GREATEST!": Murray Kempton, "The Champ and the Chump: The Meaning of Liston-Clay I," *New Republic,* March 7, 1964, http://thestacks.deadspin.com/the-champ-and-the-chump-the-meaning-of-clay-liston-i-1440585986.
      "See, the different parts of the brain": William Nack, *My Turf: Horses, Boxers, Blood Money and the Sporting Life* (Cambridge, MA: Da Capo Press, 2003), 123.

xiii *"He fools them":* George Plimpton, "Author Notebook: Cassius Clay and Malcolm X," in George Kimball and John Schulian, eds., *At the Fights: American Writers on Boxing* (New York: Library of America, 2012), 190.

xiv *"That's the only time"*: David Remnick, *King of the World* (New York: Random House, 1998), xii.

"the very spirit of the 20th Century": Norman Mailer, *King of the Hill: Norman Mailer on the Fight of the Century* (New York: Signet, 1971), 11.

200,000 blows: At the request of the author, CompuBox, Inc., compiled punch-by-punch statistics from Muhammad Ali's fights. Complete footage was available for 47 of Ali's 61 professional bouts. The CompuBox review of those 47 fights showed that Ali absorbed 14.8 punches per round (slightly below the heavyweight average of 15.2 per round) over the course of his professional career. The estimate of 200,000 lifetime blows is based not only on the CompuBox data but also on author's interviews with managers, trainers, sparring partners, and opponents. Ali boxed 548 rounds as a professional, about 260 rounds as an amateur, an estimated 12,000 rounds of sparring as part of his training regimen, and at least 500 rounds of exhibitions. Ali probably took fewer than 14.8 shots per round as an amateur and in exhibitions, but he probably absorbed more than 14.8 shots per round during sparring sessions. Given those assumptions, the following calculation is likely a conservative one: 13,308 rounds multiplied by 14.8 punches per round equals 196,958 punches.

1. CASSIUS MARCELLUS CLAY

3 *convicted murderer*: "Shot through the Heart," *Louisville Courier-Journal*, November 5, 1900; trial transcript, November 12, 1900, *Commonwealth v. Herman Clay*, Kentucky Department for Libraries and Archives, Frankfort.

a drinker, a bar fighter: Rahaman Ali, Khalilah Camacho-Ali (formerly Belinda Ali), Gordon Davidson, and Coretta Bather, interviews by author, November 10, 2014; March 28, 2016; March 18, 2014; March 28, 2014.

slashed his eldest son: Jack Olsen, *Black Is Best: The Riddle of Cassius Clay* (New York: Dell, 1967), 49.

tall, strong, and handsome: John Henry Clay photo, courtesy of Keith Winstead, cousin of Muhammad Ali.

"a great evil": "The Day Henry Clay Refused to Compromise," Smithsonian.com, December 6, 2012, http://www.smithsonianmag.com/history/the-day-henry-clay-refused-to-compromise-153589853/.

continued to own scores: U.S. Census.

4 *that slave was John Henry Clay*: Keith Winstead, interview by author, June 16, 2016.

"For it is through our names": Ralph Ellison, *The Collected Essays of Ralph Ellison*, ed. John F. Callahan (New York: Modern Library, 1995), 192.

"John asks me to give his Xmas compliments": Henry Clay Jr. to Henry Clay, January 1, 1847, Henry Clay Memorial Foundation Papers, University of Kentucky Special Collections, Lexington.

Herman Heaton Clay quit school: 1940 U.S. Census, www.ancestry.com.

handsome man, strong and tall: Coretta Bather, interview by author, March 28, 2014.

had a baby boy: "Slave Inhabitants in District No. 2," Fayett County, Kentucky, 1850, U.S. Census, www.ancestry.com.

while playing craps in an alley: Trial transcript, November 12, 1900, *Commonwealth v. Herman Clay.*

"was going to get hurt": Ibid.

an illiterate day laborer: 1900 U.S. Census, www.ancestry.com.

5   *"I had this knife":* Trial transcript, November 12, 1900, *Commonwealth v. Herman Clay.*

"Death was instantaneous": "Shot through the Heart."

he and Priscilla divorced: "NINE DIVORCES GRANTED," *Louisville Courier-Journal,* November 10, 1901.

After six years in the state penitentiary: "Penitentiary Labor," *Louisville Courier-Journal,* May 2, 1906.

December 30, 1909: Kentucky Marriage Records, www.ancestry.com.

killing his wife with a razor: Death certificate, Kentucky Death Records, www.ancestry.com.

"For those who have respect": Remnick, *King of the World,* 83.

2. THE LOUDEST CHILD

7   *"Dark Gable":* Keith Winstead, interview by author, June 17, 2016.

luxurious vibrato of his singing voice: "Black Is Best: Mr. and Mrs. Cassius Clay, Sr., Interview," by Jack Olsen, n.d., sound recording, Jack Olsen Papers, Special Collections and University Archives, University of Oregon Libraries, Eugene.

KING KARL'S THREE ROOMS: Ibid.

twenty-five dollars and a free chicken dinner: Dave Kindred, *Sound and Fury: Two Powerful Lives, One Fateful Friendship* (New York: Free Press, 2007), 30.

A black man was better off: Rahaman Ali, interview by author, November 10, 2014.

8   *"When Cassius is working on a sign":* "Muhammad Ali's Father, Cassius M. Clay Sr., Dies," *Louisville Courier-Journal,* February 10, 1990.

gin was his usual: Olsen, *Black Is Best,* 49.

"He couldn't fight a lick": Ibid.

"You're a beautiful lady!": Rahaman Ali, interview by author, November 10, 2014.

9   *June 25 in St. Louis:* Marriage certificate, Cassius Clay to Odessa Grady, June 25, 1941, St. Louis, Missouri, City Recorder of Deeds, St. Louis.

six-pound, seven-ounce baby: Muhammad Ali and Richard Durham, *The Greatest: My Own Story* (New York: Random House, 1975), 33.

small rectangular mark: Kindred, *Sound and Fury,* 30.

"most beautiful name": Olsen, *Black Is Best,* 42.

West Oak Street: Birth certificate for Cassius Marcellus Clay Jr., January 17, 1942, Kentucky Cabinet for Health and Family Services, Department for Public Health, Office of Vital Statistics, Frankfort.

six or seven dollars a month: Population Schedule, *1940 U.S. Census,* www.ancestry.com.

10   *"He cried so much":* Ali and Durham, *The Greatest,* 33.

wallpaper white with red roses: Rahaman Ali, interview by author, November 10, 2014.

Cassius had the bed by the window: Rahaman Ali, interview by author, October 19, 2016.

seventy-two inches away: measured by author, October 19, 2016.

their clothes came from Goodwill: Ali and Durham, *The Greatest,* 39.

smelled of paint: Coretta Bather, interview by author, March 28, 2014.

the aroma of Odessa's fine cooking: Rahaman Ali, interview by author, November 10, 2014.

11 *"Of course, we knew everyone":* Georgia Powers, interview by author, August 6, 2014.

"Our childhood was not difficult": Alice Kean Houston, interview by author, April 18, 2014.

"Cassius Jr's life to me": Odessa Clay, untitled Cassius Clay biography, n.d., Jack Olsen Papers.

12 *"Woody Baby":* Rahaman Ali, interview by author, November 10, 2014.

13 *ate that on the way to school:* Olsen, *Black Is Best,* 43.

"We were like twins": Rahaman Ali, interview by author, October 19, 2016.

never letting his younger brother win: Rahaman Ali, interview by author, November 10, 2014.

"those kids had some large heads": Mary Turner, interview by Jack Olsen, transcript, n.d., Jack Olsen Papers.

couldn't swim at all: Larry Kolb, interview by author, January 2, 2017.

14 *"That Gee would run around":* Owen Sitgraves, interview by author, April 23, 2015.

his father's plum tree: "Black Is Best: Mr. and Mrs. Cassius Clay, Sr., Interview."

the police car: Owen Sitgraves, interview by author, April 23, 2015.

"I would make 'em take naps": Olsen, *Black Is Best,* 45.

"Cassius Jr. would always go in first": Ibid.

15 *"a more polite racism":* Tom Owen, interview by author, November 11, 2014.

granted the right to vote: Tracy E. K'Myer, *Civil Rights in the Gateway to the South: Louisville, Kentucky, 1945–1980* (Lexington: University Press of Kentucky, 2009), 10.

16 *"where do the colored people work?":* Ali and Durham, *The Greatest,* 34.

annual median income: U.S. Bureau of the Census, *United States Census of Population, 1950, vol. 2, Table 87* (Washington, DC: Government Printing Office, 1952), www.census.gov.

17 *he was permitted to play:* George C. Wright, *Life behind a Veil: Blacks in Louisville, Kentucky, 1865–1930* (Baton Rouge: Louisiana State University Press, 1985), 276.

"We'd stand by the fence": Rahaman Ali, interview by author, November 10, 2014.

colored people had to suffer so: Ali and Durham, *The Greatest,* 34.

Herman boasted: Ibid., 37.

18 *"If we hadn't stopped to drink":* W. Ralph Eubanks, "A Martyr for Civil Rights," *Wall Street Journal,* November 6, 2015.

19 *"Why can't I be rich?":* Nick Thimmesch, "The Dream," *Time,* March 22, 1963, 78.

3. THE BICYCLE

20 *twelve-year-old Cassius pedaled:* Rahaman Ali, interview by author, August 8, 2014.

Visitors registered to win: Advertisement, *Louisville Defender,* October 7, 1954.

popcorn and candy: Ali and Durham, *The Greatest*, 45.

"what my father would do": Ibid.

21 *Cassius and Rudy were supposed to share:* Rahaman Ali, interview by author, August 30, 2014.

"I almost forgot about the bike": Ali and Durham, *The Greatest,* 45.

"hotter'n a firecracker": Joe Martin, interview by Jack Olsen, Jack Olsen typed notes, n.d., Jack Olsen Papers.

emptying coins from parking meters: Ibid.

"Do you know how to fight?": Ibid.

"Why don't you come down here": Ibid.

22 *parents bought him a motorized scooter:* "Black Is Best: Mr. and Mrs. Cassius Clay, Sr., Interview."

It was all the prompting: Olsen, *Black Is Best*, 46.

"those boys really went at it": Ibid., 52.

"He was just ordinary": "'Who Made Me — Is Me!'" *Sports Illustrated,* September 25, 1961, 19.

23 *good at shooting marbles:* Rahaman Ali, interview by author, August 8, 2014.

"I wanted to be a big celebrity": Muhammad Ali television interview, *Good Morning America,* ABC, January 13, 1977.

24 *"One needed a handle":* James Baldwin, *The Fire Next Time* (New York: Vintage International, 1993), 21.

"racing the bus": Ali and Durham, *The Greatest,* 38–39.

When the bus stopped: Owen Sitgraves, interview by author, March 30, 2016.

25 *"Sometimes he'd hop on":* Ibid.

who drank almost every day: Vic Bender, interview by author, October 1, 2015.

looking in the mirror at his muscles: Rahaman Ali, interview by author, August 8, 2014.

"It was almost impossible": Thomas Hauser, with Muhammad Ali, *Muhammad Ali: His Life and Times* (New York: Simon and Schuster, 1991), 19.

"It's safe to say": Claude Lewis, *Cassius Clay: A No-Holds-Barred Biography of Boxing's Most Controversial Champion* (New York: Macfadden-Bartell, 1965), 23.

27 *"Any fighter who'd get":* Geoffrey C. Ward, *Unforgivable Blackness* (New York: Knopf, 2004), 17.

"We are in the midst": Ibid., 14.

28 *"I grew to love the Jack Johnson":* Remnick, *King of the World*, 224.

4. "EVERY DAY WAS HEAVEN"

29 *cut him with a knife:* Charles Kalbfleisch, interview by Jack Olsen, n.d., Jack Olsen Papers.

"They'll kill each other": Ibid.

30 *"He used to go with my aunt":* Howard Breckenridge, interview by author, November 20, 2014.

For three days after suffering: Kindred, *Sound and Fury*, 36.

"strapped": Story notes, March 13, 1963, *Time* magazine article, Nick Thimmesch Papers, University of Iowa Libraries, Iowa City.

two children out of wedlock: Rahaman Ali, interview by author, August 8, 2014.

"Every day was heaven": Ibid.

"I just know I had a nice time as a kid": Cottrell, *Muhammad Ali, Who Once Was Cassius Clay*, 11.

school's best athlete in 1959: *Centralian*, 1959, Jefferson County Public School Archives, Louisville.

31 *"About the onliest other sport"*: "Playboy Interview: Muhammad Ali," *Playboy*, November 1975.

shadowboxed in the halls: Victor Bender, interview by author, October 19, 2016.

"National Golden Gloves Champion": Olsen, *Black Is Best*, 64.

"are you listening": Lewis, *Cassius Clay*, 19.

27% of whom were black: Omer Carmichael and Weldon James, *The Louisville Story* (New York: Simon and Schuster, 1957), 14.

32 *"White and Negro children"*: "Louisville Quiet as Its Schools End Segregation." *New York Times*, September 11, 1956.

district agreed to choose: Ibid.

170 school boards: C. Vann Woodward, *The Strange Career of Jim Crow* (New York: Oxford University Press, 1966), 154.

33 *The building Cassius attended*: Thelma Cayne Tilford-Weathers, *A History of Louisville Central High School, 1882–1982* (Louisville: N.p., 1982), 18.

classes in dry-cleaning: Ibid., 19.

"dumb as a box of rocks": Marjorie Mimmes, interview by author, August 8, 2014.

"Not the sharpest tack": Owen Sitgraves, interview by author, April 23, 2015.

"I sat next to the skinny kid": "Ali Delights Pupils Here at a Tribute to Dr. King," *New York Times*, January 13, 1973.

he earned a sixty-five: Hauser, with Ali, *Muhammad Ali*, 22.

34 *"very dyslexic"*: Lonnie Ali, interview by author, January 31, 2016.

"made me feel like something different": Olsen, *Black Is Best*, 64.

pretended he was a girl: Marjorie Mimmes, interview by author, August 30, 2014.

money in a change purse: Nack, *My Turf*, 178.

"I don't know anybody": Vic Bender, interview by author, October 19, 2016.

35 *Scientists believe dyslexia*: "The Advantage of Dyslexia," *Scientific American*, August 19, 2014, www.scientificamerican.com.

Baker was a legend: Howard Breckinridge, interview by author, November 20, 2014.

"He was inhuman": Ibid.

outweighed Cassius: "The Legend That Became Muhammad Ali," *Louisville Courier-Journal*, January 28, 2011.

"You're crazy if you get in the ring with him": Ibid.

36 *"This ain't fair!"*: Ali and Durham, *The Greatest*, 43.

"baddest dude I know": Ibid.

167 amateur bouts: Ibid., 51.

82–8, with twenty-five knockouts: Bob Yalen, interview by author, August 6, 2016.

four-month respite imposed: Cottrell, *Muhammad Ali, Who Once Was Cassius Clay*, 19.

"Rudy had more potential": Vic Bender, interview by author, June 9, 2014.

eat meatloaf: Rahaman Ali, interview by author, August 30, 2014.

37 *"I know how far I can go":* Ali and Durham, *The Greatest*, 51.

38 *two trays to carry:* Remnick, *King of the World*, 93.

    "I started boxing because": José Torres, *Sting Like a Bee* (New York: Abelard-Schuman, 1971), 83.

    once found him sleeping: Cottrell, *Muhammad Ali, Who Once Was Cassius Clay*, 21.

    "the black boys couldn't go": Remnick, *King of the World*, 96.

    "I'm taller than you": Nack, *My Turf*, 181.

39 *Cassius told Dundee:* Angelo Dundee and Mike Winters, *I Only Talk Winning* (Worthing, UK: Littlehampton, 1985), 17.

40 *Turley was short:* "Legendary Cowpoke," *St. Petersburg Times*, October 1, 1980.

    Turley had bloodied: "T. J. Jones of Chinook Reaches Quarterfinals in Golden Gloves," *Billings Gazette*, February 26, 1958.

    Turley and Cassius traded punches: "Rocky Erickson: Boxer Francis Turley," *Rocky Erickson: Montana Sports Stories, vol. 1*, www.youtube.com.

    stepped out of the St. Clair Hotel: Ali and Durham, *The Greatest*, 90.

    "Well, that's some of everything": Ibid., 93.

41 *"getting shellacked pretty good":* Olsen, *Black Is Best*, 53.

42 *number of professional boxers:* Jeffrey T. Sammons, *Beyond the Ring* (Urbana: University of Illinois Press, 1990), 149.

    rivaled I Love Lucy *in the ratings:* Ibid., 149.

43 *"New York won an unprecedented":* "Louisville Youth Steal Spotlight in Golden Gloves," *Lawton Constitution*, March 26, 1959.

5. THE PROPHET

44 *on his feet, shadowboxing:* Lewis, *Cassius Clay*, 25.

    frightened before every one of his fights: Larry Kolb, interview by author, December 7, 2016.

    "We trained together": Hauser, with Ali, *Muhammad Ali*, 25.

45 *"almost everybody is against discrimination":* Gunnar Myrdal, *An American Dilemma* (New Brunswick, NJ: Transaction Publishers, 2009), 2:1010.

47 *Before he changed his name:* C. Eric Lincoln, *The Black Muslims in America* (Trenton, NJ: Africa World Press, 1994), 12.

    Fard began holding meetings: Ibid., 11.

    This philosophy, though unusual: Ibid., 47–48.

    He built a base: Ibid., 16.

48 *"an especially anti-American and violent cult":* FBI report, June 28, 1955, FBI Vault.

49 *"Without the failings of Western society":* Louis Lomax, *When the Word Is Given* (Chicago: Signet, 1963), 10–11.

    "Why are we called Negroes": Recorded by Louis X, www.youtube.com.

50 *"brainwashed, hypnotized":* Olsen, *Black Is Best*, 134.

"Cassius really knew how to fight": Ibid., 53.

51 *boxing almost constantly*: Cottrell, *Muhammad Ali, Who Once Was Cassius Clay*, 20.

"My mind was not as quick as his": Rahaman Ali, interview by author, August 30, 2014.

Cassius never wore a watch: "A Split Image of Cassius Clay," *Louisville Courier-Journal*, November 25, 1962.

made his brother a promise: Rahaman Ali, interview by author, August 30, 2014.

he competed as a heavyweight: "Jones, Clay Top Gloves Final Night," *Chicago Defender*, March 9, 1960.

52 *"WATCH CLAY in the future"*: Memo, n.d., Hank Kaplan Boxing Archive, Archives and Special Collections, Brooklyn College Library, Brooklyn, New York.

"Let's forget the Olympics": Cottrell, *Muhammad Ali, Who Once Was Cassius Clay*, 22.

6. "I'M JUST YOUNG AND DON'T GIVE A DAMN"

53 *"I'm just young"*: "Clay Making Great Mileage in Publicity and Contacts," *Louisville Times*, February 28, 1961.

54 *Some boys weren't interested*: Jamillah Muhammad (formerly Areatha Swint), interview by author, December 9, 2014.

55 *the same phobia*: Olsen, *Black Is Best*, 54.

"flips and things": Ibid., 54–55.

56 *"The decision by Clay"*: "Should an Athlete Be Forced to Fly? Clay May Miss Olympics," *Louisville Times*, May 2, 1960.

"But then he went to an army supply": "The Legend That Became Muhammad Ali."

flight to San Francisco hit turbulence: Cottrell, *Muhammad Ali, Who Once Was Cassius Clay*, 25.

His previous opponent had: "10 Finals in Olympic Ring Show Tonight," *Daily Independent Sun* (San Rafael, CA), May 20, 1960.

"He was the most obnoxious guy": Tommy Gallagher, interview by author, July 17, 2015.

57 *"I hate to say it"*: Ibid.

Hudson and Clay barked: "Black History Month: The Army Boxer Who Knocked Down Muhammad Ali (1960)," The CBZ Newswire, http://www.cyberboxingzone.com/blog/?p=19447.

58 *to lend him money for a train*: Joe Martin, interview by Jack Olsen, Jack Olsen typed notes, n.d., Jack Olsen Papers.

"He was not a good student": "The Legend That Became Muhammad Ali."

7. AMERICA'S HERO

60 *"Ain't he gonna get in trouble"*: Remnick, *King of the World*, 101.

61 *What struck newcomers*: Baldwin, *The Fire Next Time*, 48.

"I could've converted him to Judaism": Dick Schaap, interview, *ESPN Classic,* transcript of broadcast interview, August 25, 2000.

"with a pride and serenity": Baldwin, *The Fire Next Time,* 51.

no bragging for once: Dick Schaap, interview, *ESPN Classic.*

"His usual haughty, disdainful self": Ibid.

"I was so hurt": "Playboy Interview: Muhammad Ali," *Playboy,* November 1975.

62   *Cassius Marcellus Clay VII*: "Clay, McClure Most Colorful Pugilists," *Laredo Times,* September 4, 1960.

    Clay noticed: "Patterson Clay's Goal," *Louisville Times,* September 6, 1960.

    "Be seeing you in about": Cottrell, *Muhammad Ali, Who Once Was Cassius Clay,* 27.

63   *"Wouldn't it be wonderful"*: "The Press Box: Have to Make Good," *Louisville Times,* August 24, 1960.

    Twelve percent of the men: "U.S. Negroes Play Big Role at Olympics," *Winnipeg Free Press,* August 30, 1960.

64   *"Is there a crisis for Negroes"*: Ibid.

    "If there is a Rome winner": "U.S. Boxers Unimpressive," *El Paso Herald Post,* August 18, 1960.

65   *wearing a white tank top*: "Cassius Clay vs. Yvon Becot (Rome, 1960 Olympics)," www.youtube.com.

    "He's very tall and has a very fast left hand": Tony Madigan interview, n.d., www.youtube.com.

66   *"Do southpaws bother other fellows?"*: "Cassius II," *Warren* (PA) *Observer,* August 26, 1960.

    His coaches begged him: "Fleischer Talked Harmonica Boy Clay out of Jeopardy at Olympic Games in Rome," *Ring,* August 1967.

    He wasn't dancing much: "Muhammad Ali (Cassius Clay) vs. Zigzy Pietrzykowski HQ," www.youtube.com.

67   *For every punch Pietrzykowski landed*: Punch counts tabulated for the author by CompuBox, Inc.

    a three-tiered podium: "Muhammad Ali (Cassius Clay) vs. Zigzy Pietrzykowski HQ."

8. DREAMER

68   *"it's gonna be great to be great"*: "The Happiest Heavyweight," *Saturday Evening Post,* March 25, 1961.

    "Look at me!": Budd Schulberg, *Loser and Still Champion: Muhammad Ali* (Garden City, NY: Doubleday, 1972), 33.

    He wore his medal: Cottrell, *Muhammad Ali, Who Once Was Cassius Clay,* 30.

    Waldorf Towers Hotel: Ibid., 31.

69   *two steaks at $7.95 each*: Thimmesch, "The Dream," 79.

    He vowed that within three years: "Cass Clay to Turn Pro," *Phoenix Arizona Republic,* September 12, 1960.

    "Cassius Signs for Patterson Fight": Cottrell, *Muhammad Ali, Who Once Was Cassius Clay,* 32.

"Back home they'll think it's real": Remnick, *King of the World*, 104.

$2.50 check: Ibid.

"I dream I'm running down Broadway": "The Happiest Heavyweight."

"You really know who I am?": Ibid.

70   *"You mean your wife know who I am, too?"*: Ibid.

71   *"To make America the greatest is my goal"*: Remnick, *King of the World*, 106.

"Uncle Sam's defenses are down": Lyman Johnson, statement to FBI, June 6, 1966, Archives and Special Collections, University of Louisville, Louisville, Kentucky.

72   *boxing royalty lined up with offers*: Cottrell, *Muhammad Ali, Who Once Was Cassius Clay*, 32.

"I did some research": Gordon B. Davidson, interview by author, April 18, 2014.

Cassius Clay Sr. didn't want Joe Martin: Ibid.

Arab sheik: Typed notes, n.d., Jack Olsen Papers.

73   *"Oh, my, he was so proud"*: Dora Jean Malachi, interview by author, July 26, 2015.

"The old man, he don't care": Joe Martin, interview by Jack Olsen, typed notes, n.d. (c. 1963), Jack Olsen Papers.

a big, gravelly voiced: "The Eleven Men behind Cassius Clay," *Sports Illustrated*, March 11, 1963.

contract was for six years: Gordon B. Davidson, interview by author, April 18, 2014.

Seven were millionaires: Cottrell, *Muhammad Ali, Who Once Was Cassius Clay*, 33.

74   *"Ah wonder if you realize"*: Ibid.

"to do something nice": Ibid.

expected expenses of $9,015.86: Memorandum to the Louisville Sponsoring Group, December 19, 1960, George Barry Bingham Papers, Filson Historical Society, Louisville, Kentucky.

75   *revealing a balance of $6,217.12*: "'I Don't Want to Be a Joe Louis,' Says Louisville's Cassius Clay, '— Not with Income Tax Problems,'" *Louisville Courier-Journal*, November 2, 1960.

which had come to $2,500: Ibid.

get a driver's license: Ibid.

"me and the Pied Piper": "The Passion of Muhammad Ali," *Esquire*, April 1968.

On October 29, 1960: Muhammad Ali boxing record, www.boxrec.com.

76   *"He's six-three for one thing"*: "Young Cassius Clay Can Be the Champ," *Charleston Daily Mail*, November 5, 1960.

"attractive but not probative": A. J. Liebling, "Poet and Pedagogue," *The New Yorker*, March 3, 1962.

77   *base salary of $363.63*: Budget, Louisville Sponsoring Group, December 19, 1960, George Barry Bingham Papers.

"Archie," he said: Remnick, *King of the World*, 112.

paying two hundred dollars a week: Budget, Louisville Sponsoring Group, December 19, 1960, George Barry Bingham Papers.

"I think the boy needs": Cottrell, *Muhammad Ali, Who Once Was Cassius Clay*, 49.

Dundee would stand calmly: Ibid., 50.

Dundee was the son: Angelo Dundee, *My View from the Corner* (New York: McGraw Hill, 2009), 17–20.

78   *"the most engaging person"*: Ferdie Pacheco, *Tales from the Fifth Street Gym* (Gaines-
     ville: University Press of Florida, 2010), 13.
79   *Dundee kept a record*: Ibid., 14.
     December 19, 1960: Hank Kaplan, notes, n.d., biographical file, box 1, folder 1, Hank
     Kaplan Boxing Archive.
     "Training him was like jet propulsion": Ibid.
80   *"a pork and beaner"*: "Clay Making Great Mileage in Publicity and Contacts."
     "one way to handle a kid": "Champ 23: A Man-Child Taken in by the Muslims," *Life*,
     March 6, 1964.
81   *split of the gate*: "Clay Making Great Mileage in Publicity and Contacts."
     "The old man teed off": Typed notes, n.d., Jack Olsen Papers.
     form signed March 1, 1961: "Classification Questionnaire," Selective Service System,
     March 1, 1961, National Archives and Records Administration, College Park, Mary-
     land.
82   *"The world of the squared circle"*: "'Man, It's Great to Be Great,'" *New York Times*,
     December 9, 1962.
     "Six-foot-twenty": Angelo Dundee, interview, *ESPN Classic*, transcript of broadcast
     interview, January 3, 2003.
     "I'm not afraid of the fight": Hank Kaplan, Note, n.d., Hank Kaplan Boxing Archive.
     "He punches like a middleweight": Ibid.
     he made $100,000: "Perfumed, Coiffed and Grappling with Demons," *New York
     Times*, September 18, 2008.
83   *"I saw fifteen thousand people"*: Torres, *Sting Like a Bee*, 104.
     "He knocked me down": Alonzo Johnson, interview by author, June 3, 2015.
     gained fifteen pounds: "'Who Made Me — Is Me!'"
     "I just sit here": Ibid.
84   *Dundee told him after*: Cottrell, *Muhammad Ali, Who Once Was Cassius Clay*, 58.
85   *"I'm tired of being fed"*: Cottrell, *Muhammad Ali, Who Once Was Cassius Clay*, 60.

9. "TWENTIETH-CENTURY EXUBERANCE"

86   *left the rink at about 6*: Muhammad Ali to Khalilah Camacho-Ali, n.d., personal
     collection of author.
     "My brother": Ibid.
87   *"The Cartoon was about the first slaves"*: Ibid.
88   *"It gave him confidence"*: Rahaman Ali, interview by author, August 30, 2014.
     The front page of the issue: "What Is Un-American?" *Muhammad Speaks*, Decem-
     ber 1961, 1.
89   *"You are the man that is asleep"*: Taylor Branch, *Pillar of Fire: America in the King
     Years, 1963–65* (New York: Simon and Schuster, 1998), 3–4.
     "The mind is its own place": John Milton, *Paradise Lost* (Indianapolis: Hackett Pub-
     lishing, 1997), book 1, page 13, lines 254–55.
90   *Islam was a "facade"*: Bennett Johnson, interview by author, January 22, 2014.
     in a seersucker suit: Abdul Rahman (formerly Sam Saxon), interview by author,
     March 21, 2014.

"Why are we called Negroes?": Abdul Rahman, interview by author, August 19, 2016.
"third best pool shooter": Ibid.
91 *"I pulled him in"*: Ibid.
"This minister started teaching": Alex Haley, "Playboy Interview: Cassius Clay," *Playboy*, October 1964.
92 *his recent immersion into the Nation*: Remnick, *King of the World*, 135.
"Boxing is not as colorful": "Clay Expects to Enliven Boxing as Well as Win World Crown," *New York Times*, February 7, 1962.
"Whatever the other man": A. J. Liebling, "Ahab and Nemesis," *The New Yorker*, October 8, 1955.
It was no clash of titans: Ibid.
94 *"I view this man with mixed emotions"*: Cottrell, *Muhammad Ali, Who Once Was Cassius Clay*, 83.
"The money comes with the glory": Einar Thulin, "Coffee with Cassius," December 30, 1962, Hank Kaplan Boxing Archive.
Clay was booed so lustily: Cottrell, *Muhammad Ali, Who Once Was Cassius Clay*, 82.
"Cassius' love affair": Jim Murray, "Cassius on Clay," *Los Angeles Times*, April 20, 1962.
95 *"I'll take Sonny Liston right now"*: Cottrell, *Muhammad Ali, Who Once Was Cassius Clay*, 87.

10. "IT'S SHOW BUSINESS"

96 *"knocking out some bums"*: "Clay Didn't 'Eat Crow' but Will Devour Powell," *Chicago Defender*, January 21, 1963.
97 *"I don't care if this kid can fight a lick"*. Thimmesch, "The Dream," 80.
"I got a headline for you": "Headline Writing Pays Off," *Winnipeg Free Press*, January 30, 1963.
98 *with revenue of about $56,000*: Cottrell, *Muhammad Ali, Who Once Was Cassius Clay*, 92.
"When he first hit me": "Liston's Edge: A Lethal Left," *Sports Illustrated*, February 24, 1964.
99 *"Now take those Associated Press reporters"*: Story notes, March 13, 1963, *Time* magazine article, Nick Thimmesch Papers.
"I was marked": Ibid.
"Seventy-five percent": "A Split Image of Cassius Clay."
"Before going out to greet the pretty girls: William Faversham, interview by Jack Olsen, n.d., Jack Olsen Papers.
100 *fifty cents' worth of gas*: Ibid.
At the end of 1962, the financial ledger: Memo, James Ross Todd, treasurer, to the Louisville Sponsoring Group, January 30, 1963, George Barry Bingham Papers.
In a private meeting: "Minutes of the Meeting of the Louisville Sponsoring Group," December 21, 1962, George Barry Bingham Papers.
101 *"Cassius Clay is Hercules"*: Thimmesch, "The Dream."

In Esquire *soon after:* Tom Wolfe, "The Marvelous Mouth," in *The Muhammad Ali Reader,* ed. Gerald Early (New York: Ecco, 1998), 20.

102 *he felt like he "never got through": Conversations with Tom Wolfe,* ed. Dorothy Scura (Oxford: University of Mississippi Press, 1990), 11.

"*Here you are, boy*": Wolfe, "The Marvelous Mouth," 20.

"*The Negroes of the country*": James Baldwin, "Letter from a Region in My Mind," *The New Yorker,* November 17, 1962.

103 *for taking away his driver's license:* "Cassius the Quiet Wins License Bout with State," *Louisville Courier-Journal,* March 30, 1963.

Clay objected: "Clay Wary of Pictures with White Girl," *Chicago Defender,* March 18, 1963.

and eventually helping to kill four: Scott Sherman, "The Long Good-Bye," *Vanity Fair,* November 30, 2012, http://www.vanityfair.com/unchanged/2012/11/1963-newspaper-strike-bertram-powers.

"*How tall are you?*": "A Comeuppance for the Cocksure Cassius," *Sports Illustrated,* March 25, 1963.

"*The Garden is too small for me*": Cottrell, *Muhammad Ali, Who Once Was Cassius Clay,* 96–97.

104 *scalpers outside the Garden:* Lewis, *Cassius Clay,* 62.

"*I can't believe it*": Cottrell, *Muhammad Ali, Who Once Was Cassius Clay,* 96.

"*People come to see me*": Ibid.

When it was 9:47 p.m.: Lewis, *Cassius Clay,* 63.

105 "*Get that loudmouth!*": Ibid.

landing 21 punches: Punch counts tabulated for the author by CompuBox, Inc.

106 *Clay raised his arms:* "1963-3-13 Cassius Clay vs Doug Jones (FOTY)," www.youtube.com.

Then he picked up a peanut: Cottrell, *Muhammad Ali, Who Once Was Cassius Clay,* 100.

old friends from Louisville: Story notes, March 14, 1963, *Time* magazine article, Nick Thimmesch Papers.

"*I ain't Superman*": Cottrell, *Muhammad Ali, Who Once Was Cassius Clay,* 101.

columnist Al Monroe tried: Al Monroe, "Reporters Missed Boat in Not Quoting Liston," *Chicago Defender,* October 2, 1962.

In another column: Al Monroe, "What about 'The Lip' as Heavyweight King?" *Chicago Defender,* July 30, 1963.

107 "*an insurrectionary assault*": Woodward, *The Strange Career of Jim Crow,* 175.

108 "*Sonny Liston is the standard*": Cecil Brathwaite, "Ode to Cassius," *Chicago Defender,* April 1, 1963.

109 *Clay attended a victory party:* Story notes, March 14, 1963, *Time* magazine article, Nick Thimmesch Papers.

"*I got a little headache*": Story notes, March 15, 1963, *Time* magazine article, Nick Thimmesch Papers.

"*You mean it's a 50–50 split with us?*": Ibid.

110 *He paid $10,956:* Deed of Sale, May 9, 1963, Louisville, Kentucky, Jefferson County Clerk's Office, Louisville.

They hired a cook: Story notes, March 15, 1963, *Time* magazine article, Nick Thimmesch Papers.

"Tomato-red Cadillac convertible": Ibid.

111 *"I won so many amateur fights":* Ibid.

11. FLOAT LIKE A BUTTERFLY, STING LIKE A BEE

113 *Archie Robinson, a portly man:* Hank Kaplan, "Boxing — From the South" (unpublished, n.d.), Hank Kaplan Boxing Archive.

114 *"the clap doctor":* Bob Arum, interview by author, November 17, 2015; Gene Kilroy, interview by author, November 17, 2015.

"I got to go to the fights for nothing": Ferdie Pacheco, interview by author, December 30, 2013.

"Blue eyes and brown eyes": Drew Brown, interview by author, March 7, 2016.

"He was not an admirable character": Gordon B. Davidson, interview by author, April 18, 2014.

115 *A. J. Liebling had written of the "butterfly Cassius":* Liebling, "Poet and Pedagogue."

"If he hated": Ta-Nehisi Coates, *Between the World and Me* (New York: Spiegel and Grau, 2015), 36.

116 *"Cassius came up and pumped my hand":* Malcolm X as told to Alex Haley, *The Autobiography of Malcolm X* (New York: Ballantine, 1965), 350.

playful uncle to the kids: Attallah Shabazz, interview by author, October 1, 2015.

"a public figure's success": Malcolm X as told to Haley, *The Autobiography of Malcolm X,* 350.

117 *seven women who had been:* Claude Andrew Clegg III, *An Original Man: The Life and Times of Elijah Muhammad* (New York: St. Martin's Press, 1997), 185.

"I felt like something": Ibid.

118 *he and his brother attended a Nation of Islam rally:* Untitled photograph, *Muhammad Speaks,* December 20, 1963.

spotted Clay's red Cadillac: "Muslims Great, Says Cassius Clay, in Interview on Right of Way," *Chicago Sun-Times,* July 3, 1963.

119 *"I don't really know much about them":* Ibid.

Clay might thrive as an entertainer: Gordon Davidson to William Faversham, July 23, 1963, George Barry Bingham Papers.

Producers of the TV show: Ibid.

And Frank Sinatra inquired: William Faversham to Louisville Sponsoring Group, April 26, 1963, George Barry Bingham Papers.

Malcolm was "a charming sumbitch": Gordon B. Davidson, interview by author, April 18, 2014.

120 *it took a hiccup:* Randy Roberts and Johnny Smith, *Blood Brothers* (New York: Basic Books, 2016), 121.

"There has never been anything": Ibid., 119.

referring to Buckingham Palace: Dundee, *My View from the Corner,* 80.

121 *The king weighed in at 207 pounds:* "'E Said 'E Would and 'E Did," *Sports Illustrated,* July 1, 1963.
Had specially made for the occasion: Ibid.
in a conservative suit and tie: Jack Wood, "Henry Cooper v. Cassius Clay," *Daily Mail,* May 3, 2011, http://www.dailymail.co.uk/sport/othersports/article-1382819/ Henry-Cooper-v-Cassius-Clay-The-punch-changed-world.html.
"stand-up old-lithograph style": "'E Said 'E Would and 'E Did."
"First blood to Cooper": "Cassius Clay vs Henry Cooper 18.6.1963," www.youtube.com.
"This is what we always feared": Ibid.

122 *he landed only eleven:* Punch counts tabulated for the author by CompuBox, Inc.
"Cut out the funny business": "Cassius Clay vs Henry Cooper 18.6.1963," www.youtube.com.
"but Cooper's getting tired": "'E Said 'E Would and 'E Did."
"I stuck my finger in the split": Dundee, *My View from the Corner,* 83.

123 *"We want you bad in September, Cassius":* "'E Said 'E Would and 'E Did."
Four years after closing its schools: "Prince Edward Negroes to Get Schools after 4 Years without Them," *New York Times,* August 15, 1963.

124 *who called King's march a "farce":* "Minister Malcolm Exposes 'Farce' of D.C. 'March,'" *Muhammad Speaks,* October 25, 1963.
"I don't stand for anything": "Clay Here — 'Ugly Bear to Fall,'" *Oakland Tribune,* September 28, 1963.
the Messenger warned that black people: Roberts and Smith, *Blood Brothers,* 134.
"Separation is absolutely necessary": "Muhammad on Self-Defense — Defend Truth at All Costs," *Muhammad Speaks,* October 25, 1963.

125 *"He's really got something important":* "Angry Cassius Clay Snubs Newsmen at Black Muslim Rally," *Philadelphia Tribune,* October 1, 1963.
wealthy white businessmen expressed worry: "Far-from-Wealthy Clay Stays Solvent Because Louisvillians Twist His Arm," *Louisville Courier-Journal,* February 9, 1964.
"For a change": Jack Paar Show, www.youtube.com.
The album was recorded August 8: Ticket stub, Worth Bingham, August 8, 1963, George Barry Bingham Papers.

126 *"Clay comes out to meet Liston":* Cassius Clay, "I Am the Greatest!" *The Knockout* (Columbia Records, 1963), side 2, track 4.

127 *"is a delightful young man":* "Final Backward Look," *New York Times,* July 25, 1963.
"Lingering behind those words": Alex Poinsett, "A Look at Cassius Clay: The Biggest Mouth in Boxing," *Ebony,* March 1963.

12. THE UGLY BEAR

128 *"Look at that big, ugly bear":* Cottrell, *Muhammad Ali, Who Once Was Cassius Clay,* 113.
"Listen, you nigger faggot": Hauser, with Ali, *Muhammad Ali,* 59.

how they whispered, "It's Cassius Clay, Cassius Clay": Tom Wolfe, *The Kandy-Kolored Tangerine-Flake Streamline Baby* (New York: Picador, 2009), 108.

129 *"I felt good until I got hit"*: Remnick, *King of the World*, 75.

"Clay Has a Very Big Lip": Cottrell, *Muhammad Ali, Who Once Was Cassius Clay*, 116.

"widely acclaimed as the savior of boxing": Houston Horn, "A Rueful Dream Come True," *Sports Illustrated*, November 18, 1963.

"Everything [Clay] does is exciting": "Clay — It's the Mouth That Does It," March 12, 1963, Hank Kaplan Boxing Archive.

130 *After a short period of negotiation*: "Draft, Not Liston Worries Clay," *Chicago Defender*, December 30, 1963.

Clay was wise to make the deal quickly: Horn, "A Rueful Dream Come True."

131 *Liston answered in a gold smoking jacket*: "Once More, Sonny, with Feeling," *Pacific Stars and Stripes*, November 7, 1963.

as the men exchanged threats: "Police Dogs Route Clay from Home of Liston," *Greeley* (CO) *Daily Tribune*, November 5, 1963.

"I'm the champ of fightin'": Horn, "A Rueful Dream Come True."

"You eat like you headed to the electric chair!": Ibid.

132 *"I ain't worried about nothing"*: "Draft Board Could KO Clay," *Middlesboro* (KY) *Daily News*, November 9, 1963.

"so he can make the most": Ibid.

13. "SO WHAT'S WRONG WITH THE MUSLIMS?"

133 *"That audacity! That youth!"*: Jesse Jackson, interview by author, July 6, 2016.

"I've been boxing since I was twelve": "I'm a Little Special," *Sports Illustrated*, February 24, 1964.

called Clay's doom "almost inevitable": "Cassius Clay: The Man and the Challenge," *Sport*, March 1964.

"I have to go into the Army pretty soon": "I'm a Little Special," *Sports Illustrated*, February 24, 1964.

"I don't see the kid going more than one": "Liston's Edge: A Lethal Left."

"The loudmouth from Louisville": Arthur Daley, "An Unhappy Choice," *New York Times*, January 14, 1966.

"Look at that!": Remnick, *King of the World*, 151.

135 *"Clay is part of the Beatle movement"*: David Remnick, "American Hunger," *New Yorker*, October 12, 1998.

"Where the fuck's Clay?": Ibid.

136 *"You made us look like monkeys"*: Harry Benson, interview by author, September 12, 2016.

137 *There were rumors*: James Booker, story notes, March 14, 1963, *Time magazine* article, Nick Thimmesch Papers.

To Clay, Malcolm was like an older brother: Alex Haley, interview by Blackside, Inc., October 24, 1988, for *Eyes on the Prize II: America at the Racial Crossroads*

1965 to 1985, Henry Hampton Collection, Film and Media Archive, Washington University Libraries, St. Louis, http://digital.wustl.edu/cgi/t/text/text-idx?c=eop; cc=eop;q1=malcolm%20x;rgn=div2;view=text;idno=hal5427.0088 .062;node=hal5427.0088.062%3A1.7.

"The Big M": James Booker, story notes, March 14, 1963, *Time* magazine article, Nick Thimmesch Papers.

Malcolm told George Plimpton: George Plimpton, *Shadow Box* (New York: G. P. Putnam's Sons, 1977), 97.

138 *"Sure I talked to the Muslims":* Roberts and Smith, *Blood Brothers,* 164.

"This fight is the truth": Malcolm X as told to Haley, *The Autobiography of Malcolm X,* 354.

139 *"Maybe I can be beat":* "Liston's Edge: A Lethal Edge."

"The DUNDEES stated": FBI memo, Muhammad Ali files, February 13, 1964, FBI Archives, National Archives and Records Administration, Washington, DC.

Clay lived at 4610 NW 15th Court: George Plimpton, "Miami Notebook: Cassius Clay and Malcolm X," in Kimball and Schulian, eds., *At The Fights,* 195; Wolfe, "The Marvelous Mouth," 20.

Clay showed movies: Plimpton, *Shadow Box,* 107.

140 *size 13EEE:* Larry Kolb, interview by author, May 28, 2016.

"When has there ever been": Hank Kaplan, "Liston vs. Clay, from This Vantage Point" (unpublished, n.d.), Hank Kaplan Boxing Archive.

141 *watched countless hours of fights:* Hank Kaplan, "Clay-Liston, in Retrospect" (unpublished, n.d.), Hank Kaplan Boxing Archive.

Robinson-LaMotta fight "over and over": "Cassius Is Elated over Victory, but Is Angry Being Long-Odds Underdog," *New York Times,* February 26, 1964.

"Ten to one?": Hank Kaplan, "Nothing Left to Say—Nothing Left to Write About" (unpublished column, December, 1, 1963), Hank Kaplan Boxing Archive.

Ringside seats for the fight were $250: Seating chart, Hank Kaplan Boxing Archive.

142 *"I ain't denying it because it's true":* Harold Conrad, *Dear Muffo* (New York: Stein and Day, 1982), 169.

143 *telling Clay to "act right":* Remnick, *King of the World,* 178.

144 *"my finest piece of acting":* Cottrell, *Muhammad Ali, Who Once Was Cassius Clay,* 151.

"I think he was shaken up": Remnick, *King of the World,* 181.

Forty-three of forty-six boxing writers: "Boxing 'Experts' Get Ears Boxed," *New York Times,* February 26, 1964.

145 *Arthur Godfrey, Ed Sullivan, Joe E. Lewis:* Hank Kaplan, "Countdown to the Fight" (handwritten note, n.d.), Hank Kaplan Boxing Archive.

and fashion icon Gloria Guinness: Hank Kaplan "Brief Recall of the Day Cassius Clay Shook up the World" (unpublished, n.d.), Hank Kaplan Boxing Archive.

more than ten thousand people: "Louisville Glovers Dance for Cassius," *New York Times,* February 26, 1964.

Around the country, about 700,000 fans: "Record $3,200,000 Likely to Be Topped for Bout TV," *New York Times,* February 26, 1964.

Major League Baseball teams cost $13.6 million: Michael Ezra, *Muhammad Ali: The Making of an Icon* (Philadelphia: Temple University Press, 2009), 82.

The fight was shown in Europe: Ibid., 83.

dressed in a tight-fitting black suit: "Clay Is Exultant," *New York Times,* February 26, 1964.

146 *"After tonight, Rudy":* Remnick, *King of the World,* 186.

147 *"He's getting hit with all the punches":* Clay v. Liston, www.youtube.com.

148 *"You can't quit. You're not fighting":* Drew Brown, interview by author, March 7, 2016.

149 *he had checked his sponge and towel:* "Cassius Is Elated over Victory."

Barney Felix, the referee: "Felix Discloses 5th-Round Drama," *New York Times,* February 26, 1964.

150 *"I think Clay's got all the confidence":* Clay v. Liston, www.youtube.com.

"You gotta fight!": Harry Benson, interview by author, September 12, 2016.

151 *"I am the greatest!":* "Clay Liston Round 7 with Radio Broadcast," February 25, 1964, www.youtube.com.

"I'm the greatest fighter who ever lived!": "Sonny Liston vs Cassius Clay — February 25, 1964 — Round 6 & Interviews," www.youtube.com.

14. BECOMING MUHAMMAD ALI

152 *Clay and Malcolm X slipped away:* "Champ 23."

Cooke, nicknamed "The King of Soul": Peter Guralnick, *Dream Boogie: The Triumph of Sam Cooke* (New York: Little, Brown, 2005), 532.

Brown respected Malcolm X and Elijah Muhammad: Jim Brown, interview by author, June 25, 2014.

"don't you think it's time": Hauser, with Ali, *Muhammad Ali,* 106.

153 *"I'm through talking":* "Clay Discusses His Future, Liston and Black Muslims," *New York Times,* February 27, 1964.

"In the jungle": Ibid.

154 *"A rooster crows only when it sees the light":* "Clay Says He Has Adopted Islam Religion and Regards It as Way to Peace," *New York Times,* February 28, 1964.

155 *"I get telephone calls every day":* Ibid.

"The power structure": *Muhammad Ali: The Whole Story,* directed by Joseph Consentino and Sandra Consentino (1996, TV movie; Burbank, CA: Warner Home Video, 2001).

156 *"I remember the day I became aware":* "Muhammad Ali Shaped My Life," *New York Times,* June 5, 2016.

Elijah Muhammad opposed "sport and play": John Ali, interview by author, April 4, 2015.

157 *In an interview with* Jet: "Champ Offers $20,000 to Anyone Changing His Muslim Beliefs," *Jet,* March 26, 1964, 50–58.

"Play that over": Cottrell, *Muhammad Ali, Who Once Was Cassius Clay,* 175.

announced that Malcolm X: "Report Clay, Malcolm X Plan New Organization," *Chicago Defender,* March 2, 1964.

"nursing" the young boxer "like a baby": Memo, March 12, 1964, Malcolm X FBI file, section 10.

158 *"I'm the champion of the whole world"*: "Clay, on 2-Hour Tour of U.N., Tells of Plans to Visit Mecca," *New York Times*, March 5, 1964.

"This Clay name has no divine meaning": Clay Puts Black Muslim X in His Name," *New York Times*, March 7, 1964.

159 *"He did it to prevent him from coming with me"*: Manning Marable, *Malcolm X: A Life of Reinvention* (New York: Penguin Books, 2011), 292.

"They've been hammering": Olsen, *Black Is Best*, 133.

"They don't like me because I'm light": Audio tape, Ax 322, tapes 1–34, Jack Olsen Papers.

"They stayed on one side of town": Olsen, *Black Is Best*, 139.

"embarrassed for Clay": "Negro Leaders Criticize Clay for Supporting Black Muslims," *New York Times*, February 29, 1964.

"When he joined the Black Muslims": "Clay Criticized," *Louisville Courier-Journal*, March 20, 1964.

160 *"The idea that integration was our goal"*: Jesse Jackson, interview by author, July 6, 2016.

"He longs to figure out": Olsen, *Black Is Best*, 103.

"I think he is involved with these Muslims": "Champ 23."

"The fight racket": Remnick, *King of the World*, 209–10.

"What white America demands": Eldridge Cleaver, *Soul on Ice* (New York: Dell, 1992), 117.

161 *"good label for anybody's product"*: "Advertising: 'Greatest' — but Can He Sell?" *New York Times*, February 27, 1964.

"At all stages of the negotiation": Minutes of meeting, March 8, 1964, Louisville Sponsoring Group Papers, Filson Historical Society.

162 *"We were just being smart businessmen"*: "Fight Agreement to Be Scrutinized," *New York Times*, February 28, 1964.

"setting a very poor example for America's youth": Cottrell, *Muhammad Ali, Who Once Was Cassius Clay*, 154.

"would make suckers": "Greene Opposes 2d Bout between Clay and Liston," *New York Times*, April 27, 1964.

The test Ali flunked: Lewis, *Cassius Clay*, 101.

163 *"I just said I'm the greatest"*: "Clay Calmly Accepts Decision That Will Keep Him from Military Service," *New York Times*, March 21, 1964.

"Not as a conscientious objector": "Clay Admits Army's Test Baffled Him," *New York Times*, March 6, 1964.

15. CHOICE

164 *"When you saw King, you saw sound bites"*: Dick Gregory, interview by author, June 17, 2015.

165 *the Nation of Islam lost about 20 percent*: Karl Evanzz, *The Messenger: The Rise and Fall of Elijah Muhammad* (New York: Pantheon, 1999), 291.

"I, who was mentored": Louis Farrakhan, interview by author, August 8, 2015.

166   *vacate his house and turn over his car*: Memo, March 12, 1964, Malcolm X FBI file, section 10.

"to get rid of him the way Moses": Memo, March 23, 1964, Malcolm X FBI file, section 10.

urged black activists to stop worrying: Memo, March 13, 1964, Malcolm X FBI file, section 10.

"Concerning nonviolence": Marable, *Malcolm X*, 298.

167   *"I am not a racist"*: Ibid., 365.

"Man, did you get a look at him?": "Clay Makes Malcolm Ex-Friend," *New York Times,* May 18, 1964.

168   *"It'll be like a castle"*: Ibid.

some of his hosts were struck: "Clay Is an Enigma to Egyptians," *New York Times,* June 15, 1964.

kente cloth and a copy of his books: "Short Cuts," *London Review of Books,* May 19, 2016.

169   *he offended the people*: "Nigerian Tour Wins Cheers, but Leaves a Bad Taste," *New York Times,* June 4, 1964.

"I should be pleased to fight": "Clay Says He Would Answer an Egyptian Call to Arms," *New York Times,* June 11, 1964.

"Because a billion of our people": "Clay Makes Malcolm Ex-Friend," *New York Times,* May 18, 1964.

Malcolm was beginning to see: Marable, *Malcolm X*, 365.

"You should've seen them": "Day with Clay: TV, Song, Muslims," *New York Times,* June 27, 1964.

16. "GIRL, WILL YOU MARRY ME?"

170   *Herbert plied women*: Memo to FBI director, October 6, 1965, Herbert Muhammad File, Malcolm X Manning Marable Collection, Columbia University Libraries, New York.

Sonji Roi may have been a prostitute: Lowell Riley, interview by author, July 8, 2014.

171   *"I swear to God, Herbert"*: Ali and Durham, *The Greatest*, 184.

"The way you touched my head": Ibid., 187.

Sonji was alone: Hauser, with Ali, *Muhammad Ali*, 115.

"He was young": Charlotte Waddell, interview by author, October 2, 2015.

172   *work in nightclubs as a barmaid*: Safiyya Mohammed-Rahmah, interview by author, August 6, 2015.

"We were trying to get him not *to marry her"*: Lowell Riley, interview by author, July 8, 2014.

checkered sheath dress: "Clay Honeymoon May Be in Egypt," *Louisville Courier-Journal,* August 15, 1964.

"anything he do is legal": Ibid.

"in the hereafter": Olsen, *Black Is Best*, 151.

173   *Sonji and Odessa worked together*: Ali and Durham, *The Greatest*, 188.

"woodie baby": Rahaman Ali, interview by author, August 30, 2014.

"he's gonna be broke": Olsen, *Black Is Best*, 161.

"Why, you have to be almost totally illiterate": Ibid., 166–67.

174 *"I can't drive no more"*: Audio tape, Ax 322, tapes 1–34, Jack Olsen Papers.

"That was the onliest reason I married her": Olsen, *Black Is Best*, 153.

"My wife and I will be together forever": "Work, Play, Talk and All-Star Cast Fill Clay's Camp," *Louisville Times*, November 12, 1964.

175 *five-pound work boots*: "Clay Undergoes Successful Surgery for Hernia," *New York Times*, November 14, 1964.

carried pound-and-a-half weights: "Still Hurt and Lost," *Sports Illustrated*, November 16, 1964.

he had grown half an inch: Ibid.

176 *"He seemed to shrink in size"*: Arthur Daley, "Sports of the Times," *New York Times*, November 15, 1964.

"I give him three more rounds": "Still Hurt and Lost," *Sports Illustrated*, November 16, 1964.

told jokes, wrote poems: "Clay Shows No Worry over Folley or Draft," *Louisville Times*, March 21, 1967.

chauffeur for his new $12,000 Cadillac limousine: "Work, Play, Talk and All-Star Cast Fill Clay's Camp."

"To me, he's just a thoroughly confused person": Ferdie Pacheco, interview by Jack Olsen, typed notes, n.d., Jack Olsen Papers.

"People don't understand the champ": Remnick, *King of the World*, 246.

177 *a Muslim service led by Louis X*: Ferdie Pacheco, interview by Jack Olsen, typed notes, n.d., Jack Olsen Papers.

ticket sales were expected to top $3 million: "Clay Undergoes Successful Surgery for Hernia."

Ali ate a steak, spinach, baked potato: "Clay Undergoes Surgery; Fight Off," *Louisville Courier-Journal*, November 14, 1964.

Sonji, who was staying at the home of Louis X: Louis Farrakhan, interview by author, August 8, 2015.

William Faversham and Gordon Davidson of the Louisville Sponsoring Group: Gordon Davidson, interview by author, April 18, 2014.

178 *"That damned fool"*: Remnick, *King of the World*, 239.

17. ASSASSINATION

179 *"The die is set"*: Marable, *Malcolm X*, 398.

"Malcolm X and anybody else": *Muhammad Ali: Made In Miami*, produced by Gaspar Gonzalez and Alan Tomlinson (PBS, 2008).

"I don't even think about him": Muhammad Ali, interview by Irv Kupcinet, WRKB-TV, March 15, 1965; Malcolm X FBI file, FBI Vault, part 27.

180 *"You see what they are doing"*: Hauser, with Ali, *Muhammad Ali*, 110.

"Get your hands out of my pockets!": Marable, *Malcolm X*, 436.

Sonji became suspicious: Ali and Durham, *The Greatest*, 192.

"That was a strange fire": Ibid., 191.

181 *suffered his hernia during sexual intercourse:* Untitled memo, January 19, 1965, FBI Archives.

"he was foolish to let the NOI": Untitled confidential memo, dictated February 16, 1965, FBI Archives.

"Malcolm X was my friend": "Cassius Clay Says He's Unafraid; Walks Streets Daily — No Guards," *Montreal Gazette*, February 25, 1965.

"I was never interrogated": John Ali, interview by author, April 4, 2015.

"I wanted to kill Malcolm": Abdul Rahman, interview by author, August 19, 2016.

"This is my wife y'all": Ali and Durham, *The Greatest*, 191.

182 *"the kind that can't believe in anything"*: Ibid., 192.

"Did I do that?": Ibid., 193.

"I was vexed over that dress": Ibid., 194.

183 *goodbye note:* Ibid., 195.

Rahaman Ali would follow: "Earmuffs Help on Clay's Bus," *Boston Globe*, May 1, 1965.

"Ali, you see about my dry cleaning?": "Should a King Tote His Own Water?" *Miami Herald*, April 1, 1965.

Sonji's tone hardened: Kindred, *Sound and Fury*, 88.

The bus was a 1955 Flexible: Edwin Pope, interview by author, March 20, 2014.

184 *the latter cooked by Sonji:* "Should a King Tote His Own Water?"

Pope was typing his stories: Edwin Pope, interview by author, March 20, 2014.

185 *offered Bundini fifty thousand dollars:* Drew Brown, interview by author, March 7, 2016.

"Okay, Jackie Robinson": "Champ, Press Marooned in N.C. as Axle Burns," *Boston Globe*, May 2, 1965.

"You fool": Plimpton, *Shadow Box*, 118.

186 *"One of these days"*: "Ugliness in Yulee," *Miami Herald*, April 2, 1965.

18. PHANTOM PUNCH

187 *"My poor little red bus"*: "So Hard to Be Righteous," *Miami Herald*, April 4, 1965.

188 *"Drinking Scotch and working out"*: "A Birthday for Sonny Liston," ThisWeekScience .com, http://www.thesweetscience.com/news/articles-frontpage/15175-a-birth day-for-sonny-liston.

"Liston is burnt out": "Still Hurt and Lost."

"He just didn't seem": Geraldine Liston, interview, *ESPN Classic*, transcript of broadcast interview, May 2, 2001.

jeans and a sweatshirt: Remnick, *King of the World*, 254.

189 *"It may start out"*: Ibid.

"Angelo, he got a fight plan": "Cassius to Win a Thriller," *Sports Illustrated*, May 24, 1965.

190 *"He laid down"*: Remnick, *King of the World*, 261.

"It was a perfect": "A Quick, Hard Right and a Needless Storm of Protest," *Sports Illustrated*, June 7, 1965.

"*I saw Liston's eyes*": "Eyes Have It, Says Doctor," *Louisville Courier-Journal,* May 28, 1965.

"*I didn't think he could*": "A Quick, Hard Right and a Needless Storm of Protest," *Sports Illustrated,* June 7, 1965.

"*Sonny is too dull and too slow*": "No Fix," *Louisville Courier-Journal,* May 28, 1965.

The FBI had suspicions: FBI memo, July 30, 1965, FBI Vault.

"*I think Sonny gave that*": Geraldine Liston, interview, *ESPN Classic.*

19. TRUE LOVE

194   "*How could I stand by seeing you*": Ali and Durham, *The Greatest,* 200.

"*I'll be right there*": Jerry Izenberg, interview by author, January 20, 2015.

"*She put on a short short*": Olsen, *Black Is Best,* 155.

"*plain and simple*" *floor-length dresses:* "Muslim Dispute with Wife May Lead to Clay Divorce," *Fort Pierce (FL) News Tribune,* June 24, 1965.

195   "*That was the breaking point*": Safiyya Mohammed-Rahmah, interview by author, August 6, 2015.

"*That man's gonna be on top*": Abdul Rahman, interview by author, August 19, 2016.

"*in a manner such*": FBI report, February 6, 1968, Herbert Muhammad File, Malcolm X Manning Marable Collection.

Herbert had tried to sleep with Sonji: Rahaman Ali, interview by author, August 29, 2014.

"*Herbert couldn't control her*": Rose Jennings, interview by author March 10, 2014.

"*I just love my husband*": "Muslim Dispute with Wife May Lead to Clay Divorce."

196   "*He won't see me*": "Clay's Wife Gets $350 Partial Aid," *Fort Pierce (FL) News Tribune,* July 1, 1965.

"*I would like to say that I loved her*": Olsen, *Black Is Best,* 155.

"*They've stolen my man's mind*": Ibid., 149.

"*I have no one in mind*": Ibid., 156.

"*He went through hell*": Rahaman Ali, interview by author, August 29, 2014.

197   "*to long and determined dining*": Mark Kram, *Great Men Die Twice* (New York: St. Martin Griffin's, 2015), 76.

"*fat and piggy looking*": Odessa Clay, interview by Jack Olsen, n.d., Jack Olsen Papers.

"*He dirty. Muhammad dirty*": Ibid.

Herbert Muhammad had made: "Woman Beaten, Nab Son of Muhammad," *Chicago Defender,* October 13, 1962.

Agents reported that Herbert received: FBI report, January 14, 1966, Herbert Muhammad File, Malcolm X Manning Marable Collection.

"*He is 'money crazy'*": FBI report, January 16, 1967, Herbert Muhammad File, Malcolm X Manning Marable Collection.

"*The part of being*": Bob Arum, interview by author, November 17, 2015.

"*Herbert Muhammad could not read*": Rose Jennings, interview by author, March 10, 2014.

He also studied to: Safiyya Mohammed-Rahmah, interview by author, August 6, 2015.

198 *"the ultimate decider of everything"*: Bob Arum, interview by author, November 17, 2015.
Ali had been borrowing: Gordon Davidson to Muhammad Ali, January 6, 1965, Louisville Sponsoring Group Papers.
He didn't spend much: Memo: "Detail of Advances to Clay during 1964," March 17, 1965, Louisville Sponsoring Group Papers.
Ali paid the insurance: Gordon Davidson to Chauncey Eskridge, March 9, 1965, Louisville Sponsoring Group Papers.

199 *He told one boxing promoter*: Hank Kaplan, interview with Muhammad Ali, n.d., Hank Kaplan Boxing Archive.
took it as a personal affront: Gordon Davidson to Joseph Thomas, February 8, 1965, Louisville Sponsoring Group Papers.
Ali got in his car immediately: Gordon Davidson to Archibald Foster, December 9, 1964, Louisville Sponsoring Group Papers.
Ali's take from the Liston fight: Worth Bingham memo, n.d. (1965), Louisville Sponsoring Group Papers.
"When we pointed out": Arthur Grafton, memo to Louisville Sponsoring Group, August 5, 1965, Louisville Sponsoring Group Papers.
"our boy" and "his unsophisticated mind": Archibald Foster to Arthur Grafton, August 9, 1965, Louisville Sponsoring Group Papers.

200 *$3.5 million mosque*: Ibid.
"The longer we talked": Ibid.

201 *"It was a bruising day"*: Ibid.

20. A HOLY WAR

202 *"truth, fact, and reality"*: Muhammad Ali, interview with Hank Kaplan, n.d., Hank Kaplan Boxing Archive.
approved by Herbert Muhammad: Ibid.
"It's going to be the first time": "Playboy Interview: Cassius Clay," *Playboy*, October 1964.
"Uncle Tom Negro": Cottrell, *Muhammad Ali, Who Once Was Cassius Clay*, 240.
"I am a Negro and proud to be one: "'I Want to Destroy Clay,'" *Sports Illustrated*, October 19, 1964.

204 *"I have rights, too"*: Floyd Patterson, "Cassius Clay Must Be Beaten," *Sports Illustrated*, October 11, 1965.
"Come on, American!": Cottrell, *Muhammad Ali, Who Once Was Cassius Clay*, 243.

205 *"A happiness feeling came over me"*: Floyd Patterson and Gay Talese, "In Defense of Cassius Clay," *Esquire*, August 1966.

206 *"I got a feeling I was born"*: "Rabbit Hunt in Las Vegas," *Sports Illustrated*, November 22, 1965.
"He had something like": Olsen, *Black Is Best*, 166.

207 *"It wasn't that he wanted proof"*: Ibid., 167.
in the trunk of his Cadillac: Ali and Durham, *The Greatest*, 188.
As his contract with: "Memo to the Executive Committee of the Louisville Spon-

soring Group," January 11, 1966, Gordon B. Davidson Papers, Filson Historical Society.

"I am vitally interested": Ezra, *Muhammad Ali*, 93.

208 *"who gives me strength"*: FBI memo, June 14, 1967, FBI Vault.

"obviously now being completely": Arthur Grafton, "Memo to the Members of the Louisville Sponsoring Group," Louisville Sponsoring Group Papers.

at least one member of the group: Memo to the Executive Committee of the Louisville Sponsoring Group, January 11, 1966, Gordon B. Davidson Papers.

"The fight racket has been turned": Ezra, *Muhammad Ali*, 93.

Arum presented the idea: Bob Arum, interview by author, November, 17, 2015.

Arum was summoned to a meeting: Bob Arum, interview by author, June 22, 2016.

209 *When the meeting was over*: John Ali, interview by author, April 4, 2015.

getting about a third: FBI report, February 6, 1968, Herbert Muhammad File, Malcolm X Manning Marable Collection.

He was making so much: FBI report, January 16, 1967, Herbert Muhammad File, Malcolm X Manning Marable Collection.

"and this was his reward": Bob Arum, interview by author, November 17, 2015.

neither he nor anyone else in the Nation: John Ali, interview by author, April 4, 2015.

"The Nation was not dependent": Ibid.

"The more I think": Archibald Foster to Louisville Sponsoring Group, February 8, 1966, Louisville Sponsoring Group Papers.

210 *"relinquish our contract"*: Arthur Grafton, "Memo to the Members of the Louisville Sponsoring Group," Louisville Sponsoring Group Papers.

21. NO QUARREL

211 *"The answer is blowin'"*: "Fighter Charges Board with Bias," *New York Times*, February 18, 1966.

the death toll would triple: "Statistical Information about Casualties of the Vietnam War," April 29, 2008, National Archives, http://www.archives.gov/research/military/vietnam-war/casualty-statistics.html#date.

212 *white cracker sergeants*: Robert Lipsyte, *An Accidental Sportswriter* (New York: Ecco, 2012), 73.

"How can they reclassify me 1-A?": "Fighter Charges Board with Bias."

"Halloran went inside": Bob Halloran and Bob Arum, interview by author, November 17, 2015.

"Yes, sir, that was a great surprise": Muhammad Ali interview, n.d., sound recording, Jack Olsen Papers.

Ali and his friends gathered: Ibid.

213 *"I am a member of the Muslims"*: "Clay Wants KO in 'Flight of Century," *Tucson Daily Citizen*, March 28, 1966.

214 *antiwar protesters had used the phrase*: Stefan Fatsis, "No Viet Cong Ever Called Me Nigger," *Slate*, June 8, 2016, http://www.slate.com/articles/sports/sports_nut/2016/06/did_muhammad_ali_ever_say_no_viet_cong_ever_called_me_nigger.html.

He named Elijah Muhammad: "Selective Service System, Special Form for Conscientious Objector," February 28, 1966, National Archives and Records Administration.

215 *"Slave Name Cassius M Clay Jr":* Ibid.

"the greatest American patriot": "Jim Murray," *New Journal* (Mansfield, OH), February 23, 1966.

"If I knew everything I had said": "Clay Not on March Draft List," *Kokomo* (IN) *Morning Times,* February 22, 1966.

216 *But before the hearing:* FBI report, January 16, 1967, Herbert Muhammad File, Malcolm X Manning Marable Collection.

"That's when they threw us out of Chicago": Bob Arum, interview by author, November 17, 2015.

"If the Bay of Pigs": Cleaver, *Soul on Ice,* 118.

"I was determined to be the one nigger": "The *Black Scholar* Interviews: Muhammad Ali," in Early, ed., *The Muhammad Ali Reader,* 89.

217 *"It doesn't look right":* "Clay Says He Is a Jet Plane and All the Rest Are Prop Jobs," *New York Times,* March 25, 1966.

"Elijah Muhammad pumped a lot of poison": Gordon B. Davidson, interview by author, April 18, 2014.

218 *using his personal credit card:* Bob Arum, interview by author, November 17, 2015.

"warrior on the battleground of freedom": "Showdown with a Punching Bag," *Sports Illustrated,* March 28, 1966.

When one of Ali's sparring: "Clay Knocked Down by Sparring Partner," *New York Times,* March 20, 1966.

"I mean Jesse, the youngest": "Historicist: The Heavyweight Showdown," *Torontoist,* March 23, 2013, http://torontoist.com/2013/03/historicist-the-heavyweight-showdown/.

"Harder! Harder!": "The Battle of Toronto," *New York Times,* March 30, 1966.

Chuvalo outpunched Ali: Punch counts tabulated for the author by CompuBox, Inc.

"monolithic": Eddie Futch, interview by Ron Fried, n.d., courtesy of Ron Fried.

219 *"the hardest thing I've":* "Champion Hails His Rugged Rival," *New York Times,* March 30, 1966.

"I got to go dancing with my wife": George Chuvalo, *Chuvalo* (Toronto: HarperCollins, 2013), 176.

22. "WHAT'S MY NAME?"

220 *"Standard Oil doesn't try":* "Champ in the Jug?" *Sports Illustrated,* April 10, 1967.

"Is my baby okay?": "Intimate Look at the Champ," *Ebony,* November 1966.

Usually, he landed better: Punch counts tabulated for the author by CompuBox, Inc.

222 *"It showed total income":* Capital Accounts memo, Worth Bingham Papers, Louisville Sponsoring Group, October 20, 1966, Filson Historical Society.

a balance of $109: Bank Statement, Citizens Fidelity Bank and Trust Company, Worth Bingham Papers, May 15, 1966, Filson Historical Society.

"we also showed young men": "Cassius and His Angels Are Parting Friends," *Louisville Courier-Journal,* October 16, 1966.
223 *The match would air:* Ezra, *Muhammad Ali,* 115.
 Ali said he wanted: "The Massacre," *Sports Illustrated,* November 21, 1966.
224 *"manfully and uselessly"*: Ibid.
 "Trouble with Clay": Joe Louis, "How I Would Have Clobbered Cassius Clay," *The Ring,* February 1967.
225 *"Why you want to say 'Cassius Clay'"*: Howard Cosell interview with Muhammad Ali and Ernie Terrell, December 28, 1966, *ESPN Classic,* www.youtube.com.
 "I got nothing against": "The Left That Was," *Sports Illustrated,* February 6, 1967.
226 *"I want to torture"*: "Cruel Ali with All the Skills," *Sports Illustrated,* February, 13, 1967.
 "No, I don't believe": "Muhammad Ali vs Ernie Terrell [Full Fight]," www.youtube. com.
227 *"a kind of a lynching"*: Hauser, with Ali, *Muhammad Ali,* 165.

23. "AGAINST THE FURIES"

228 *"A house is on fire, pretend"*: "Learning Elijah's Advanced Lesson in Hate," *Sports Illustrated,* May 2, 1966.
229 *"If total integration would"*: "My Friend Cassius," *Louisville Courier-Journal Magazine,* July 31, 1966.
230 *"not to be held up as an example"*: Hauser, *Muhammad Ali,* 280.
 "Well, we weren't brought here": "The Black Scholar Interviews: Muhammad Ali," *Black Scholar,* June 1970.
 "Six-foot-two and a half": "The Sex Symbol," *Inside Sports,* November 30, 1980.
231 *Martin Luther King Jr. had begun speaking:* Andrew Young Jr., interview by author, August 11, 2014.
 "It was about the same time": Ibid.
 "may become a new symbol": "Cassius vs. Army," *New York Times,* April 30, 1967.
 "he is taking the ultimate position": Tom Wicker, "In The Nation: Muhammad Ali and Dissent," *New York Times,* May 2, 1967.
 "that great theologian": "Clay May Cause Draft Law Change," *San Antonio Express,* August 26, 1966.
 "While thousands of our finest": "Congressman Takes Swing at Clay's Draft Status," *San Antonio Express,* Feb. 22, 1967.
232 *"I am sure history will look"*: FBI memo, February 23, 1967, FBI Vault.
 "seriously consider submitting": Allen J. Rhorer to Ramsey Clark, May 9, 1967, Muhammad Ali Collection, National Archives and Records Administration.
 "He can come": FBI memo, Chicago bureau to director, March 17, 1966, FBI Vault.
 "because of his publicity value": Ibid.
 secured signed statements: Hayden C. Covington to Muhammad Ali, September 2, 1966, personal collection of author.

"I told the Honorable Elijah Muhammad": Ibid.

233 *"Retire. Tonight."*: "Muhammad Ali vs Zora Folley — March 22, 1967 — Entire fight — Rounds 1 — 7 & Interviews," www.youtube.com.

234 *"The trickiest fighter"*: "Zora Folley Ranks Muhammad Ali as No. 1," *Sports Illustrated*, April 10, 1967.
"I've left the sports": "Taps for the Champ," *Sports Illustrated*, May 8, 1967.

24. EXILE

237 *"mainly consisted of joking"*: FBI memo, February 6, 1968, Herbert Muhammad File, Malcolm X Manning Marable Collection.
"We're all black brothers": "Clay, Dr. King Call Talk 'Renewal of Fellowship,'" *Louisville Courier-Journal*, March 30, 1967.

238 *"Check me out on this"*: "As Preacher, Cassius Is Forced to Settle for a Split Decision," *Louisville Times*, March 30, 1967.
"Why should they ask": "Clay, Dr. King Call Talk 'Renewal of Fellowship.'"

239 *"Oh, they liked it"*: "As Preacher, Cassius Is Forced to Settle for a Split Decision."
"greatest purveyor of violence": "Beyond Vietnam," April 4, 1967, Martin Luther King Jr. Research and Education Institute, Stanford University, http://kingencyclopedia.stanford.edu/encyclopedia/documentsentry/doc_beyond_vietnam/.
"an instrument in the hands": David Garrow, *The FBI and Martin Luther King, Jr.* (New York: Penguin Books, 1981), 182.
"stand up for my religious": "High Court Delivers Blow to Clay," *Abiline Reporter News*, April 18, 1967.
"I gave him no more advice": Howard L. Bingham and Max Wallace, *Muhammad Ali's Greatest Fight* (Lanham, MD: Rowman and Littlefield, 2000), 145.
On the morning of his: "Taps for the Champ."

240 *"it would lighten our trip"*: "Cassius Joked, Danced Right up to Refusal," *Louisville Courier-Journal*, April 29, 1967.

241 *"The action of the sports"*: "Clay Refuses Induction, to Lose Boxing Crown," *Louisville Courier-Journal*, April 29, 1967.
"Mama, I'm all right": "Taps for the Champ."

25. FAITH

242 *about ten minutes in jail*: FBI memo, June 14, 1967, FBI Vault.
Herbert Muhammad had suggested: Khalilah Camacho-Ali, unpublished memoir, n.d., courtesy of Khalilah Camacho-Ali.
"exponential": Safiyya Mohammed-Rahmah, interview by author, August 6, 2015.

243 *"Do you know who I am?"*: Ibid.
she was working two jobs: Khalilah Camacho-Ali, interview by author, March 28, 2016.
silver Eldorado: Khalilah Camacho-Ali, unpublished memoir.

alone with a man in a car: Khalilah Camacho-Ali, interview by author, November 21, 2014.

completed the last three miles: Khalilah Camacho-Ali, unpublished memoir.

244 *"I wanna see what":* Khalilah Camacho-Ali, interview by author, March 1, 2016.

"She loved Ali so much": Safiyya Mohammed-Rahmah, author interview, August 6, 2015.

They were married: "Muhammad and Belinda's Wedding Cloaked in Secret Maneuvering," *Chicago Defender,* August 23, 1967.

Ali's parents flew to: "Cassius Takes Bride in Chicago Ceremony," *Atlanta Constitution,* August 19, 1967.

Herbert Muhammad stood: "Nuptials for Muhammad Ali," *Chicago Defender,* August 21, 1967.

For their honeymoon: Khalilah Camacho-Ali, interview by author, March 27, 2016.

245 *"I married a man with no job":* Ibid.

"Krim went to see Lyndon": Bob Arum, interview by author, June 22, 2016.

246 *"to convince Ali to take the deal":* Bob Arum, interview by author, November 17, 2015.

"But I wasn't setting it up": Ibid.

When Brown met with: Jim Brown, interview by author, June 25, 2014.

247 *"My first reaction was":* Willie Davis, interview by author, November 19, 2015.

"Well, I know what": "I'm Not Worried about Ali," *Sports Illustrated,* June 19, 1967.

John Wooten confirmed: John Wooten, interview by author, November 19, 2015.

"Hey, man, all you'd do": Curtis McClinton, interview by author, November 19, 2015.

248 *Bill Russell was fascinated:* "I'm Not Worried about Ali."

"Three, four, five hours": Jim Brown, interview by author, June 25, 2014.

"There's nothing new": "Clay Won't Reconsider," *Kokomo (IN) Morning Times,* June 5, 1967.

"We heard his views": Ibid.

"He has something": "I'm Not Worried about Ali."

Two weeks later, an all-white jury: "Clay Guilty in Draft Case; Gets Five Years in Prison," *New York Times,* June 21, 1967.

249 *"Clay should serve his time":* Bingham and Wallace, *Muhammad Ali's Greatest Fight,* 162.

"I'm with you": Ibid., 179.

FBI agents watched Ali's house: Charlotte Waddell, interview by author, October 2, 2015.

250 *"You could hear people talking about it":* Dave Zirin, *What's My Name, Fool? Sports and Resistance in the United States* (Chicago: Haymarket Books, 2005), 67.

"What kind of America is it": Mike Marqusee, *Redemption Song* (London: Verso, 1999), 165

In Newark, delegates: "Boycott of Sports by Negroes Asked," *New York Times,* July 24, 1967.

251 *"Mr. Ali's case raises":* "Muhammad Ali — The Measure of a Man," *Freedomways,* Spring 1967.

"Backlash Blues": "Backlash Blues," performed by Nina Simone, www.youtube.com.

26. MARTYR

252 *behind on alimony:* "Judge Orders Back Alimony Paid to Clay's Former Wife," *New York Times,* October 21, 1967.

His own lawyer was suing: "Lawyer Sues Cassius Clay for $284,615 Legal Fees," *New York Times,* October 17, 1967.

"She was like a giddy little schoolgirl": Charlotte Waddell, interview by author, October 2, 2015.

"You better get out of town": Khalilah Camacho-Ali, interview by author, November 21, 2014.

253 *"I think that's the time":* Khalilah Camacho-Ali, transcript of undated interview, personal collection of Khalilah Camacho-Ali.

"Oh, you're pretty": Rahaman Ali, interview by author, November 10, 2014.

"My wife knows what I'm doing": Khalilah Camacho-Ali, interview by author, November 21, 2014.

Cash had stepped outside: "Clay's Father Suffers Stab Wound in Chest; Woman Is Charged," *Louisville Courier-Journal,* May 9, 1967.

254 *owned or rented by Herbert Muhammad:* FBI report, February 6, 1968, Herbert Muhammad Files, Malcolm X Manning Marable Collection; Khalilah Camacho-Ali, unpublished memoir.

It had two bedrooms: "The Passion of Muhammad Ali."

"And tonight": Ibid.

255 *the city had reserved a parking space:* Tim Shanahan, interview by author, July 15, 2014.

256 *"Hey, George!":* George Lois, interview by author, June 30, 2015.

Elijah Muhammad, who understood: Ibid.

257 *"Lyndon Johnson":* Ibid.

"Dr. King was my great": "Ali Mourns King's Death in Solitude," *Chicago Defender,* April 11, 1968.

"best friend White America ever had": "'Cassius Le Grand' Is Too Big to 'Float,' but Still Has Sting," *Louisville Times,* February 15, 1969.

"Martin Luther King dedicated his life": "Robert F. Kennedy's Martin Luther King Jr. Assassination Speech," April 4, 1968, www.youtube.com

258 *If Ali's religion struck some:* "The Separate World of Muhammad Ali," *Boston Globe,* April 22, 1968.

259 *Nor had he been the victim:* "Clay Loses Appeal of Conviction," *Chicago Tribune,* May 7, 1968.

The Nation of Islam had already lent him: "Champ in the Jug?"

recordings of Elijah Muhammad's sermons: "Ali Faces His Precarious Future Unafraid," *Chicago Defender,* February 22, 1968.

ran an ad in Variety: "Return of Muhammad Ali, a/k/a Cassius Marcellus Clay Jr.," *New York Times,* November 30, 1969.

260 *"I'm expected to go overseas":* "Ali at 70: The Greatest's Greatness," *Los Angeles Times,* January 18, 2012.

"There's no sense in Negroes": "No Integration, Cassius Clay Says," *Bucks County Courier Times,* November 1, 1967.

"Chinese like to be with Chinese": Untitled article, *Watauga (NC) Democrat,* Sep-

tember 25, 1969, http://www.wataugademocrat.com/community/remembering-ali-s-visit-to-app-state/article_27044be6-90b8-58ef-bbe0-c3fa660e6d9e.html.

261 *"has an African haircut"*: "Muhammad Ali Urges Black 'Separatism,'" *Los Angeles Sentinel,* February 8, 1968.

"We're not Negroes": "The Old Cass-Mu," *Chicago Defender,* April 24, 1968.

"He's a brave, brave bull": "Clay in 'Holy War,'" *Lowell (MA) Sun,* September 6, 1967.

"fight for my people": "'Finished With Ring' — Cassius," *Atlanta Constitution,* February 9, 1968.

Elijah Muhammad visited the hospital: Khalilah Camacho-Ali, transcript of undated interview, personal collection of Khalilah Camacho-Ali.

262 *"Allah . . . made men"*: "Muhammad Ali," *Ebony,* April 1969.

"We Muslims do business": Ibid.

five hundred restaurants: "Going to Jail for Beliefs Appeals to Cassius, Deposed Champ," *Louisville Courier-Journal,* August 24, 1969.

"Champburger with Soul Sauce": Advertisement, *Miami Times,* September 12, 1969.

"This is something to help": "Ali Enters Miami Jail," *Fort Pierce (FL) News Tribune,* December 17, 1968.

"Maybe this will be good": "Clay Begins His 10-Day Term," *Register* (Danville, VA), December 17, 1968.

263 *about ten thousand dollars*: Hauser, with Ali, *Muhammad Ali,* 197.

"is not a conversationalist": "Return of Muhammad Ali, a/k/a Cassius Marcellus Clay Jr."

"Hey, you a nice fella": Dick Schaap, "Muhammad Ali Then and Now," in Kimball and Schulian, eds., *At the Fights,* 216.

264 *"Respectfully asking why"*: Letter to Department of Justice, Muhammad Ali Collection, February 13, 1969, National Archives and Records Administration.

"Cassius Clay, pardon me": Bill Barwick to President Lyndon B. Johnson, Muhammad Ali Collection, June 24, 1967, National Archives and Records Administration.

"Yes, ma'am": "Muhammad Ali," *Ebony,* April 1969.

27. SONG AND DANCE AND PRAYER

266 *They were anxious*: Khalilah Camacho-Ali, interview by author, April 29, 2016.

every seat was filled: Ibid.

"It was terrifying": Ibid.

"promised to take the burden": Baldwin, *The Fire Next Time,* 64.

267 *Elijah Muhammad said he was disappointed*: Khalilah Camacho-Ali, interview by author, April 29, 2016.

"We shall call him": "Muhammad Ali Loses His Title to the Muslims," *New York Times,* April 20, 1969.

268 *"That was one of the hardest moments"*: Louis Farrakhan interview by author, August 8, 2015.

"get out of music": Ibid.

"delinquency, murder, theft": Elijah Muhammad, *Message to the Blackman in Amer-*

ica (Phoenix: Secretarius MEMPS Publications, 1973), 246, http://www.finalcall. com/columns/hem/sport_play.html.

exhibition with Cody Jones: Maureen Smith, "*Muhammad Speaks* and Muhammad Ali: Intersection of the Nation of Islam and Sport in the 1960s," in *With God on Their Side: Sport in the Service of Religion,* ed. Timothy Chandler and Tara Magdalinski (London: Routledge, 2002), 177–96.

269   *newspaper ran a regular column:* Ibid.

"*I Called My Manger*": Muhammad Ali, handwritten note, n.d., courtesy of Khalilah Camacho-Ali.

sent his friend Bundini Brown packing: "The Art of Ali," *Sports Illustrated,* May 5, 1969.

270   "*All that funnin*'": Ibid.

"*It's wrapped up with black people*": "'I See No Prestige in Show Business,'" *New York Times,* November 23, 1969.

271   Buck White *closed after:* "Cassius Clay Musical Stopping the Count at 7," *New York Times,* December 5, 1969.

When you're the champ: Robert Lipsyte, *Free to Be Muhammad Ali* (New York: HarperCollins, 1977), 90.

Cosell would get fifty thousand dollars: "Cassius Marcellus Clay Jr.," FBI memo, December 8, 1969, Muhammad Ali Collection, National Archives and Records Administration.

272   "*gangster mosque*": "Black Mafia," FBI memo, November 30, 1973, FBI Vault.

carried on an affair with his ex-wife: Leon Muhammad, interview by author, June 13, 2016.

maintained a long-running affair: Jamillah Muhammad, interview by author, December 9, 2014.

"*He knew it was wrong*": Khalilah Camacho-Ali, interview by author, November 21, 2014.

"*I knew things like this would happen*": Ibid.

273   *ask his wife to arrange his extramarital affairs:* Khalilah Camacho-Ali, Veronica Porche, Jamillah Muhammad, multiple interviews by author, multiple dates, 2014–17.

"'*I'll use that against you*'": Khalilah Camacho-Ali, interview by author, November 21, 2014.

"*Ali had a dark side, an evil side*": Ibid.

28. THE GREATEST BOOK OF ALL TIME

275   "*outdo everything that's ever been written*": "Book Buzz," *Washington Post,* March 29, 1970.

"*The public doesn't know too much about me*": Ibid.

paperwork had been too much trouble: Khalilah Camacho-Ali, interview by author, November 21, 2014.

277   *Crouch would compare Ali to a bear:* Ishmael Reed, *The Complete Muhammad Ali* (Montreal: Baraka Books, 2015), 151.

278 *"He knew what was in it!":* Jesse Jackson, interview by author, July 6, 2016.
"I think there was always anxiety": Ibid.
even in private discussions: Ibid.; Gene Kilroy, interview by author, July 1, 2016.
"I have officially retired": "Clay 'Grants' World Title, *Washington Post,* May 27, 1970.

29. STAND BY ME

279 *"How long this take?":* All quotations, gestures, and details contained in this chapter come from Ali and Durham, *The Greatest.* Durham's original manuscript is held at the Carter G. Woodson Regional Library in Chicago, but the audiotapes are not. Durham's wife, Clarice, in an interview by the author, said she believed her husband quoted accurately from audiotaped conversations. Durham's biographer, Sonja D. Williams, wrote in her account of Durham's life that Durham and Ali, overcoming the objections of Herbert Muhammad, insisted that the book's dialogue should be authentic and uncensored. Some of Durham's parenthetical phrases have been edited in this account and some of his dialogue has been abridged, but no words or gestures have been added or altered.

30. COMEBACK

285 *"The Major made me move":* "Cherry Hill Played a Big Role in Muhammad Ali's Life," *Courier-Post* (Cherry Hill, NJ), September 13, 2012.
286 *"Do you want me to buy a home":* "Clay KO'd by Black Militants," *Indiana Evening Gazette,* January 30, 1970.
"Ali would go in the bathroom": Gene Kilroy, interview by author, May 4, 2016.
Satalof asked his wife: Marc Satalof, interview by author, April 15, 2015.
287 *"You're a bad brother":* Reggie Barrett, interview by author, March 22, 2016.
288 *"Right away, I got the feeling":* "A Strange Case of Friendship," *Inside Sports,* July 31, 1981.
Melvin Belli encouraged Ali to sue: Gene Kilroy, interview by author, August 22, 2016.
offered Johnson all the money: Leroy Johnson, interview by author, June 1, 2016.
289 *"too busy to hate":* "Welcome Back, Ali!" *Sports Illustrated,* September 14, 1970.
Atlanta's mayor, Sam Massell: Sam Massell, interview by author, May 10, 2016.
Johnson . . . told the governor: Leroy Johnson, interview by author, June 1, 2016.
"On with the fight!": Ibid.
"The roof did not fall in": "Welcome Back, Ali!," *Sports Illustrated,* September 14, 1970.
"It wasn't as if I pawned it": "Ali Despite Millions Won, Faces Toughest Fight, Balancing Budget," *New York Times,* March 25, 1978.
Ali sat naked: "Welcome Back, Ali!," *Sports Illustrated,* September 14, 1970.
"It was all there": Ibid.
290 *"Clay was saying he let":* "Clay Doesn't Feel D'Amato's Definition of Pressure," *Louisville Times,* October 26, 1970.

son of a migrant farmer: "Jerry Quarry, 53, Boxer Battered by Years in the Ring, Dies," *New York Times,* January 5, 1999.

"intentional, arbitrary": "3-Year Ring Ban Declared Unfair," *New York Times,* September 15, 1970.

291 *"That's when I was at my top condition":* "He Moves Like Silk, Hits Like a Ton," *Sports Illustrated,* October 26, 1970.

292 *ecumenical prayer:* Jesse Jackson, interview by author, July 6, 2016.

Boxing historian Bert Sugar called it: "Knockout," *Atlanta,* October 2005.

"I thought it would be real good": Ibid.

293 *"had managed to merge":* Schulberg, *Loser and Still Champion,* 78.

limousines painted in psychedelic designs: "Ringside Crowd Forms Dazzling Backdrop," *New York Times,* October 27, 1970.

silver mink bowties: "Sport and Sociology at the Auditorium," *Atlanta Constitution,* October 28, 1970.

white, double-breasted suit: "Ringside Crowd Forms Dazzling Backdrop."

concealed handguns: Sam Massell, interview by author, May 10, 2016.

"as though it were constructed": "Ali on Peachtree," *Harper's Magazine,* January 1971.

294 *made him look fat:* Plimpton, *Shadow Box,* 157.

chest and shoulders shined: Ibid., 163.

"If he loses tonight": Schulberg, *Loser and Still Champion,* 74.

295 *"like a beached whale":* Jerry Izenberg, interview by author, June 22, 2016.

"bordering on exhaustion": Dundee, *My View from the Corner,* 139.

"hello to the Supremes": "Muhammad Ali — Jerry Quarry. 1970 10 26. 1," www.youtube.com.

Later, he admitted that: Ali and Durham, *The Greatest,* 326.

including Cash Clay: Gene Kilroy, interview by author, May 4, 2016.

296 *"If the robbers had known":* "$200,000 Robbery — 'Bare Minimum,'" *Atlanta Constitution,* November 1, 1970.

31. "THE WORLD IS WATCHING YOU"

298 *"numb all over":* "It's Gonna Be the Champ and the Tramp," *Sports Illustrated,* February 1, 1971.

"let the daze clear up": Kindred, *Sound and Fury,* 137.

"How ya doing, Joe?": "Ali v. Bonavena," ESPN broadcast, www.youtube.com.

32. A DIFFERENT FIGHTER

299 *"He's much slower":* "Diana Ross Sums It Up: Clay Looked Great," *Louisville Times,* October 27, 1970.

one minute of each three-minute round: Dundee, *My View from the Corner,* 143.

2,245 punches: Punch counts tabulated for the author by CompuBox, Inc.

CompuBox assesses fighters: Statistics compiled for the author by CompuBox, Inc.

301 *"Ali's hands were so shot"*: Gene Kilroy, interview by author, September 16, 2016.
"Ali came back": Hauser, with Ali, *Muhammad Ali*, 213.
"You're in the corner to keep them fighting": Ferdie Pacheco, interview by author, December 30, 2013.

302 *"Tonight I did what Frazier"*: Schulberg, *Loser and Still Champion*, 96.
"Maybe this will shock and amaze ya": Ibid.
"If you fight a good left-hooker": "Talk with Mr. Hemingway," *New York Times*, September 17, 1950.
second youngest of ten: Mark Kram Jr., interview by author, August 13, 2016.

303 *no one could masturbate*: Joe Hand Sr., interview by author, March 21, 2014.
"Frazier was the human equivalent": Mailer, *King of the Hill*, 67.
a bus only hit you once: "Bull v. Butterfly: A Clash of Champions," *Time*, March 8, 1971.
hoping to lose weight: "In This Corner . . . The Official Heavyweight Champ," *New York Times*, November 15, 1970.
"black Adonis on parade": "Bull v. Butterfly: A Clash of Champions."
"I like it, fighting": "In This Corner . . . The Official Heavyweight Champ."
"Frazier ain't got no rhythm": Ibid.

304 *crushed the radio with his foot*: Mark Kram, *Ghosts of Manila* (New York: Harper Perennial, 2002), 28.
"Coward? Uncle Tom?": Ibid., 29.

33. THE FIVE-MILLION-DOLLAR MATCH

306 *"The $500,000,000 Fighters"*: *Time*, March 8, 1971.

307 *"have a ball"*: "Muhammad Ali vs Joe Frazier (I) 1971-03-08," www.youtube.com.
228-pound frame: "It's Gonna Be the Champ and the Tramp."
"Pleasure is the shadow of happiness": Ibid.

308 *two more "warm-ups"*: Jim Dundee, interview by author, June 11, 2015.
earned at least $3.5 million: "Frazier-Ali Bout Income Near $20-Million Mark," *New York Times*, May 9, 1971.
"This one transcends": "Sport's $5 Million Payday," *Sports Illustrated*, January 25, 1971.

309 *"Muhammad Ali had become Lucky Lindy"*: Schulberg, *Loser and Still Champion*, 128.
"Nothing is deader": "The Athlete as Peacock," *Time*, January 4, 1971.
Alabama sheriffs: Kindred, *Sound and Fury*, 165.

310 *"When he gets to ringside"*: "At the Bell . . . ," *Sports Illustrated*, March 8, 1971.
Marvis faced taunting: Marvis Frazier, interview by author, March 8, 2014.
he intended to hammer: "I Got a Surprise for Clay," *Sports Illustrated*, February 22, 1971.
"He was an awful nice fellow": "Patterson, Ali Mourn Liston," *Chicago Defender*, January 7, 1971.
giant birthday cake: "'Mellow' Ali Predicts Win," *Los Angeles Times*, January 16, 1971.

311 *"Will you stop eating that?"*: Ibid.
"Frazier will catch hell": Ibid.
"I don't like fighting": "Explains Boasting," *Oakland Post,* February 4, 1971.
"because the results from a lot": "'Mellow' Ali Predicts Win," *Los Angeles Times,* January 16, 1971.
"I guess that's what I do": Ibid.

34. ALI V. FRAZIER

313 *Imagine 10 million people:* Mailer, *King of the Hill,* 62.
President Nixon had a special line: Connie Bruck, *When Hollywood Had a King* (New York, Random House, 2004), 309.
314 *Belinda heard a man's voice:* Khalilah Camacho-Ali, interview by author, December 23, 2014.
"And I cried": Ibid.
315 *Bing Crosby settled:* "Where Were You on March 8, 1971," ESPN.com, http://espn.go.com/classic/s/silver_ali_frazier.html.
Television producers had gone over: "The Telecast of the Century," *New York Times,* August 21, 1972.
316 *"is equivalent to the first kiss"*. Mailer, *King of the Hill,* 76.
317 *"Don't you know I'm God!"*: Kram, *Ghosts of Manila,* 144.
"God, you're in the wrong place": Joe Frazier, interview, *ESPN Classic,* transcript of broadcast interview, January 17, 2001, courtesy of ESPN.
"What is he doing?": Torres, *Sting Like a Bee,* 208.
"half-dream room": Ali and Durham, *The Greatest,* 405.
318 *"You got God in your corner"*: "'Everyone Will Remember What Happened,'" *Sports Illustrated,* March 15, 1971.
320 *"There are languages other than words"*: Mailer, *King of the Hill,* 17.
motionless, eyes closed, naked: "'I Ain't No Champ,' Says Muhammad Ali," *Charleston Daily Mail,* March 9, 1971.
Flower First Avenue Hospital: "Frazier Earns the Crown," *New York Times,* March 8, 1971.

35. FREEDOM

321 *"that draft dodger asshole"*: "Muhammad Ali's Philadelphia Story," *Philadelphia Citizen,* June 6, 2016.
Plimpton found Ali in the driveway: Plimpton, *Shadow Box,* 200.
An oil painting of Elijah Muhammad: Ibid., 201.
"When is this going to appear?": Ibid., 203.
322 *"That long long walk"*: Ibid., 204.
"Not as much as I thought I would": Ibid., 206.
323 *Ali had misspelled his own name:* "Classification Questionnaire," Selective Service System, March 13, 1961, National Archives and Records Administration.

described later by one of the justices as "confused": Marty Lederman, "The Story of *Cassius Clay v. United States*," ScotusBlog.com, June 8, 2016, http://www.scotusblog.com/2016/06/muhammad-ali-conscientious-objection-and-the-supreme-courts-struggle-to-understand-jihad-and-holy-war-the-story-of-cassius-clay-v-united-states/.

324 *read* The Autobiography of Malcolm X: Ibid.
"*The very dominant idea in Islam*": Muhammad, *Message to the Blackman in America*, 322.

325 "*pee-wee*": Thomas Krattenmaker, interview by author, June 29, 2016.
It was 9:15 a.m.: "A Day for Victory Outside Ring," *New York Times*, June 29, 1971.

326 "*I just heard on the radio*": Ibid.
$250,000 in legal fees: "Judges' Decision Today: 5-3-1, Favor Ali?" *New York Times*, June 28, 1971.
"*I'm not going to celebrate*": "A Day for Victory Outside Ring."
"*Timber!*": "Ali's Remark Ended Wilt's Ring Career," *Los Angeles Times*, January 15, 1989.
"*I can't represent the Muslims again*": "Ali Will Quit after Fighting Joe," *Lompoc (CA) Record*, June 23, 1971.
lacked the energy for training: "A Day for Victory Outside Ring."

327 "*They only did what they thought*": Ibid.
"*Every time Ali wins*": Donald Reeves, "The Black Prince," *New York Times*, May 17, 1971.
"*I wouldn't say that I have become a symbol*": "Muhammad Ali: World's Greatest Fighter," *Sacramento Observer*, February 25, 1971.

328 "*right on the button*": "Tired Ali Unimpressive in Dayton Exhibition, Hints at Retirement," *Xenia (OH) Daily Gazette*, June 26, 1971.
"*Another year and I'm through*": Ibid.

329 *Bugner popped Ali consistently*: "Ali Gets Down to Serious Work," *New York Times*, July 24, 1971.
"*I ain't going to start nothing*": "The Lip Hits Deck," *Pacific Stars and Stripes*, July 24, 1971.
Dundee thought Ellis had a chance: Ibid.

330 "*I wasn't going to kill myself*": "Ali Stops Ellis in Closing Minute of 12th Round," *New York Times*, July 27, 1971.
saw signs of lasting brain damage: Ferdie Pacheco, interview by author, December 30, 2013.
"*There is no fucking cure*": Ibid.

332 "*You can have me kidnapped!*": Bob Goodman, interview by author, December 4, 2014.

333 "*He was never in one place*": Bob Foster, interview by author, June 12, 2014.
played pranks on Dundee: Angelo Dundee, interview, *ESPN Classic*.

334 "*I saw birds and all different colors*": Bob Foster, interview by author, June 12, 2014.

36. TRICKERATION

335 *"It's never about the money"*: Bob Arum, interview by author, November 17, 2015.
"Don't let nuthin' happen to Joe Frazier": "An Abrupt End to the Frazier Reign," *New York Times,* January 23, 1973.
"It ain't too late": "At 30 a Man Learns, Even Muhammad Ali," *New York Times,* September 14, 1972.

336 *accounts at Peat Marwick:* Gene Kilroy, interview by author, December 13, 2014.
"I'm going to make my wife": "At 30 a Man Learns, Even Muhammad Ali."
"It was very normal": Jamillah Ali, interview by author, July 25, 2015.
"I'm never home too much": Muhammad Ali, interview by Nikki Giovanni, 1971, www.youtube.com.

337 *"Belinda . . . come on over here"*: Thomas Hauser, *Muhammad Ali Memories* (New York: Rizzoli, 1992), unnumbered page.
"I don't want nobody whispering": "At 30 a Man Learns, Even Muhammad Ali," *New York Times,* September 14, 1972.
"Because my black brothers": "Ali Deflects Quick Jab after Fight," *New York Times,* September 21, 1972.
"I transcend earthly bounds": "Playboy Interview: Don King," *Playboy,* May 1988.
"a street Machiavelli": Jack Newfield, *Only in America* (New York: William Morrow, 1995), 3–4.

338 *"a 50-carat setting"*: "The Fight's Lone Arranger," *Sports Illustrated,* September 2, 1974.
grossing fifteen thousand dollars a day: Newfield, *Only in America,* 3.
Garrett owed King six hundred dollars: Ibid.
it would give him a legitimate: Lloyd Price, interview by author, July 30, 2015.
Price arranged first for King: Ibid.

339 *"We're blacks and we have nothing"*: Newfield, *Only in America,* 37.
King made thirty thousand dollars: Ibid., 30.
freezers to Eskimos: "Playboy Interview: Don King," *Playboy,* May 1988.
$225,000 in cash: Reggie Barrett, interview by author, March 4, 2016.
"I had tons of cash": Don King, interview by author, December 13, 2015.

340 *"Ali, he wanted it all"*: Don King, video interview by independent journalist Andy Quinn, December 14, 2014, courtesy of Andy Quinn.

341 *"Cash is king"*: Don King, interview by author, December 13, 2015.
"They could not get another black": Don King, video interview by Andy Quinn, December 14, 2014.
During their meeting, Elijah Muhammad: Don King, interview by author, December 13, 2015.

342 *three weeks in the hospital:* Kram, *Ghosts of Manila,* 149.
He just comes on in: "Set for a Wood Chopper's Brawl," *Sports Illustrated,* January 15, 1973.

343 *"I just pulled out the flag"*: Ibid.
"I got hit and hit and hit": "People in Sports: Same Old Ali," *New York Times,* February 13, 1973.

King eased his way toward Foreman's corner: "Playboy Interview: Don King," *Playboy,* May 1988.

"I came with the champion": Newfield, *Only in America,* 47.

"I'm still greater than boxing": "People in Sports: Same Old Ali."

344 *"You got to get the hard-on":* Joyce Carol Oates, *On Boxing* (New York: Harper Perennial, 2006), 30.

paid only three hundred dollars: "The Bugle Call Champion," *Sports Illustrated,* June 12, 1978.

five-to-one favorite: "Ali-Frazier Match Goes Way of Devalued Dollar," *New York Times,* April 2, 1973.

more than 2,500 bombings: Bryan Burrough, *Days of Rage* (New York: Penguin, 2016), 5.

"bombs basically functioned": Ibid.

sprained an ankle: Gene Kilroy, interview by author, July 19, 2016.

345 *in bed with two hookers:* Reggie Barrett, interview by author, March 4, 2016; Khalilah Camacho-Ali, interview by author, March 4, 2016.

mirror off the dresser: Reggie Barrett, interview by author, March 4, 2016.

"That night, I could have beaten Godzilla": Stephen Brunt, *Facing Ali* (Guilford, CT: Lyons Press, 2002), 175.

instead of ducking or blocking them: Ibid., 170.

346 *"Is he now but a relic":* ABC television broadcast, March 31, 1973, www.youtube.com.

"What's wrong with your fighter?": Ibid.

the second knuckle on his right hand: "The Mouth That Nearly Roared," *Sports Illustrated,* April 23, 1973.

347 *"I think he's loosened a tooth":* Ibid.

about things buried deep: Khalilah Camacho-Ali, interview by author, March 4, 2016. In this interview, Khalilah said her outburst was caused in part by the loss and by her discovery that he had slept with prostitutes before the fight, but also by a third factor she declined to discuss.

348 *"I put three cops in the hospital":* Ibid.

"I think you're a jerk": "Norton Stuns Ali, Wants Foreman," *Hayward (CA) Daily Review,* April 1, 1973.

More troublingly, some of the men: Ferdie Pacheco, interview by author, December 30, 2013.

a broken jaw was as serious: "Ali's Stock Plummets, Jaw Aches Too," *Winnipeg Free Press,* April 2, 1973.

"He's no different from Chubby Checker": Lee Winfrey, "Fall of Muhammad: Is It Tragedy or Merely Time?" *Chicago Tribune,* April 15, 1973.

37. A FIGHT TO THE FINISH

351 *gray Rolls-Royce:* "New Act, Same Ali," *Ames (IA) Daily Tribune,* May 4, 1973.

"Best thing ever happened to me": Ibid.

"I needed that": "Wired Jaw Fails to Silence a Humble Ali," *New York Times,* May 4, 1973.

352 *"Losing that fight"*: Ibid.

sit in an old wooden surrey: Richard Hoffer, *Bouts of Mania* (Boston: Da Capo Press, 2014), 118.

353 *"The camp was like a revolving door"*: Bob Goodman, interview by author, December 4, 2014.

"Every guy that shakes hands": Angelo Dundee, transcript of interview with ESPN SportsCentury, n.d., courtesy of ESPN.

paid members of his entourage: "Ali, of Course, Favors Louisville Bout, But . . ." *Louisville Courier-Journal,* March 25, 1975.

354 *Lloyd Wells . . . arranged for women*: Khalilah Camacho-Ali, interview by author, November 21, 2014.

"These people are like a little town": "Ali and His Entourage," *Sports Illustrated,* April 25, 1988.

"They treated her like": Ibid.

"We all loved Ali": Lowell Riley, interview by author, March 14, 2014.

355 *interviews with Ali cost fifty dollars*: Angelo Dundee, transcript of interview with ESPN SportsCentury.

"Ang, we got legs": Ibid.

best shape of his life: "Sights and Sounds from Muhammad Ali," *New York Times,* September 6, 1973.

"Norton don't stand a chance": "Ali Is 'Dancing' on His Mountaintop," *New York Times,* August 26, 1973.

"You the boss with the hot sauce": Ali v. Norton, www.youtube.com.

358 *"That's what he went to the hospital for"*: "Muhammad Ali, Joe Frazier Scuffle in TV Studio," ABC-TV, January 24, 1974, http://abcnews.go.com/WNT/video/muhammad-ali-joe-frazier-scuffle-tv-studio-14906366.

359 *You gotta stop him to win!*: "Once More, from Memory This Time," *New York Times,* January 29, 1974.

Ali rocking from one foot: "Muhammad Ali vs Joe Frazier 2 Full Fight," www.youtube.com.

Red Smith of the New York Times: Daniel Okrent, ed., *American Pastimes: The Very Best of Red Smith* (New York: Literary Classics of the United States, 2013), 418.

360 *"He had me out on my feet twice"*: "Ali Says 'No Bad Feeling between Us,' and Talks of Super Fight III," *New York Times,* January 29, 1974.

"Take a stiff tree branch": "Playboy Interview: Muhammad Ali," *Playboy,* November 1975.

38. HEART OF DARKNESS

361 *walking in circles*: Hank Schwartz, interview by author, July 27, 2016.

marriage had collapsed: Newfield, *Only in America,* 52.

lacked faith in his business managers: George Foreman, *By George: The Autobiography* (New York: Villard Books, 1995), 99–100.

"terrible emptiness . . . meaner by the day": Ibid., 99.

talking nonstop and waving sheets: Hank Schwartz, interview by author, July 27, 2016.

362 *"I know people been screwin' you":* "The Fight's Lone Arranger," *Sports Illustrated,* September 2, 1974.

"This isn't just another fight": Ibid.

an advance of $100,000: Hank Schwartz, interview by author, July 27, 2016.

"This is my promotion": "The Fight's Lone Arranger," *Sports Illustrated,* September 2, 1974.

after two hours of circling: Hank Schwartz, interview by author, July 27, 2016.

363 *They would decide which:* Ibid.

Ali would get $200,000 more: Hank Schwartz, *From the Corners of the Ring to the Corners of the Earth* (Valley Stream, NY: CIVCOM, 2009–10), 155.

364 *"He just repeats the same simplicity":* Victor Bockris, *Muhammad Ali in Fighter's Heaven* (New York: Cooper Square Press, 2000), 125–26.

"If it wasn't for the Nation of Islam": Gene Kilroy, interview by author, May 16, 2014.

organization was running out of money: "Black Muslim Group in Trouble from Financial Problems and Some Crime," *New York Times,* December 6, 1973.

Ali had been dispatched to Libya: Ali and Durham, *The Greatest,* 209.

"Now what do you say, Muhammad Ali?": Kram, *Ghosts of Manila,* 9.

365 *"When Ali came back from exile":* Hauser, with Ali, *Muhammad Ali,* 201.

"hitting a little bit below the belt": Jim Brown, interview by author, June 25, 2014.

366 *$500,000 from an organized crime figure:* FBI memo, March 11, 1975, Herbert Muhammad File, Malcolm X Manning Marable Collection.

Schwartz received a phone call: Hank Schwartz, interview by author, July 27, 2016.

"a walking bank vault": "The Man Who Stole a Country," *Mail and Guardian (Johannesburg),* September 12, 1997.

367 *"I didn't give a shit":* Ibid.

Schwartz and Don King didn't care: "Zaire Prepares with Pride to Become Battleground for Foreman Ali Fight," *New York Times,* July 2, 1974.

39. FIGHTER'S HEAVEN

370 *"One more and I'll be finished":* "Ali Wants Foreman as Finale," *New York Times,* March 5, 1974.

"If you behave like that": "What They Are Saying," *New York Times,* March 31, 1974.

371 *Ali's managers promised:* Gene Kilroy, interview by author, June 10, 2016.

Foreman held a press conference: "Foreman Trains at Pleasanton," *Argus* (Fremont, CA), July 30, 1974.

"I'll just try to beat him": "Foreman Makes Ali Bout 'Official,'" *Long Beach (CA) Press Telegram,* July 30, 1974.

"There's gonna be a rumble": Ibid.

John Ali wound up in a Gabonese prison: Rose Jennings, interview by author, March 10, 2014.

He and Hank Schwartz formed a company: Ibid.

372 *prices starting at $2,100:* "Package Deal Expensive," *Glens Falls (NY) Post-Star,* August 14, 1974.

"this event is like no other": "Zaire: The Toughest Fight Is Just Getting There," *New York Times,* August 13, 1974.

fifty hours and ten thousand miles: "Press Corps Finally Arrives in Zaire," *Chicago Tribune,* September 18, 1974.

most of them clad in bikinis: Bill Caplan, interview by author, August 9, 2016.

"How did we pick the women?": Bill Caplan, interview by author, February 2, 2015.

373 *Mobutu ordered a fleet of buses:* "Zaire Prepares with Pride to Become Battleground for Foreman Ali Fight."

"Zaire's foreign minister said": Rose Jennings, interview by author, March 10, 2014.

"A new emphasis on self-improvement": Tom Borstelmann, *The 1970s: A New Global History from Civil Rights to Economic Inequality* (Princeton, NJ: Princeton University Press, 2012), 12.

374 *"Round One — bing!":* Dave Kindred, "Getting Inside Ali," *Midwest Magazine,* September 1, 1974.

"I wouldn't have said that thing": Ibid.

"The way I feel": "Playboy Interview: Muhammad Ali," *Playboy,* November 1975.

375 *218 pounds:* "The Voice in the Wilderness," *New York Times,* August 17, 1974.

"Ali's had it": Plimpton, *Shadow Box,* 226.

"The time may have come": Kindred, *Sound and Fury,* 198.

"Cosell, you're a phony": Ibid., 199.

376 *"I LOVE HIM BECAUSE HE'S THE GREATEST":* Khalilah Camacho-Ali, interview by author, December 23, 2014.

Belinda loved the movie: Ibid.

377 *"Discreet Lodging:* Maury Z. Levy, "Poor Butterfly," *Philadelphia Magazine,* n.d. (c. 1975), https://mauryzlevy.wordpress.com/2012/06/15/poor-butterfly/.

378 *"It's befitting that I leave the game":* Muhammad Ali press conference, New York City, September 1974, in *When We Were Kings,* Universal Studios, 2005.

"Some people . . . have no imagination": "Does Ali Have a Chance against Foreman?" *Sport,* September 1974.

Ali admitted that he had not: "Penthouse Interview: Muhammad Ali," *Penthouse,* June 1974.

379 *"If you think the world was shook":* "Sports News Briefs," *New York Times,* September 5, 1974.

always knew when her parents: Veronica Porche, interview by author, May 25, 2016.

whispered his approval: Gene Kilroy, interview by author, June 21, 2016.

"That was it": Veronica Porche, interview by author, May 25, 2016.

40. "ALI BOMA YE!"

380 *Ali, his wife, his parents:* "Mirror, Mirror on the Wall, Who Is . . . ?" *New York Times,* September 10, 1974.

"This is strange to the American Negro": Muhammad Ali interview in *When We Were Kings.*

381 *"100,000 new faces every night":* "Getting Inside Ali."

"Then you got the world's greatest fighter": Muhammad Ali interview with David Frost, BBC, n.d., www.youtube.com.

"If he wins, we're slaves": Ibid.

"my country": "Broken Glasses at the Waldorf," *New York Times,* June 24, 1974.

"I'll beat your Christian ass": New York Times used "expletive deleted" instead of "ass," but other news agencies used "tail," which strongly suggests the deleted word was "ass." Ibid.

382 *"If he considers Zaire":* Dave Anderson, "Broken Glasses at the Waldorf," *New York Times,* June 24, 1974.

Ali apologized: "Muhammad Ali's 'Rumble in the Jungle,'" *Louisville Courier-Journal,* September 15, 1974.

entertained notions of joining: George Foreman, interview by author, September 28, 2015.

"I figured if a religion couldn't": Foreman, *By George,* 106.

"our shining black prince": "The Darker Side of Muhammad Ali," *Salon,* http://www.salon.com/2001/06/06/ali_2/.

383 *"Who do these people hate?":* Gene Kilroy, interview by author, May 16, 2014.

He asked a reporter how many people: Ibid.

"I am the greatest!": Ibid.; Jerry Izenberg, interview by author, May 23, 2016.

"the oppressor of all black nations": "Chant of the Holy War: 'Ali, Bomaye,'" *New York Times,* October 28, 1974.

384 *not fond of dogs:* "Cut 'n Run versus the Big Gun," *Sports Illustrated,* October 28, 1974.

"Ali boma ye!": Ali v. Foreman, www.youtube.com.

"He did not look like a man": Norman Mailer, *The Fight* (New York: Vintage Books, 1997), 44.

"Excuse me for not shaking hands": Ibid., 45.

385 *"a stylized mimicry":* Oates, *On Boxing,* 185.

Ali would admit he was worried: Ibid., 391.

"You could actually see and feel": Stokely Carmichael, *Ready for Revolution: The Life and Struggles of Stokely Carmichael* (New York: Scribner, 2003), 707.

they found about thirty-five: "A Lot of Fans Will See Fight — But Not in Zaire," *New York Times,* October 27, 1974.

386 *"Gift from President Mobutu":* "Zaire's $10 Million Bet," *New York Times,* October 27, 1974.

With plenty of plane tickets: Ibid.

because she'd never traveled outside: Veronica Porche, interview by author, December 20, 2016.

387 *speaking mostly about their childhoods:* Ibid.

no kisses, no invitations: Veronica Porche, interview by author, May 25, 2016.

"He just overwhelmed Veronica": Rose Jennings, interview by author, March 10, 2014.

"My babysitter": Kram, *Ghosts of Manila*, 165.

"I remember the moment I fell in love with him": Veronica Porche, interview by author, May 25, 2016.

"the worst thing that could have happened": "Foreman's Eye Is Cut while Sparring, Delaying Title Bout a Week to 30 Days," *New York Times*, September 17, 1974.

388 *persuaded Veronica Porche to take time off*: Veronica Porche, interview by author, May 25, 2016.

Americans called binji: Rose Jennings, interview by author, March 10, 2014.

Ali accused Belinda of sleeping: Khalilah Camacho-Ali, interview by author, November 21, 2014. Veronica Porche, interview by author, May 25, 2016; Gene Kilroy, interview by author, October 22, 2016.

"Ali comes in the room": Khalilah Camacho-Ali, interview by author, November 21, 2014.

confirmed Belinda was hiding two black eyes: Veronica Porche, interview by author, December 20, 2016.

George Foreman button: Kram, *Ghosts of Manila*, 165.

389 *when Ali proposed marriage*. Veronica Porche, interview by author, May 25, 2016.

lay out a metabiche: "The Farther They Are, the Harder They Fall," *Sports Illustrated*, September 2, 1974.

390 *"whoosh went the hair"*: Mailer, *The Fight*, 116.

"Adversity is ugly": Plimpton, *Shadow Box*, 228.

boogie-woogie songs: Veronica Porche, interview by author, May 25, 2016.

ordered meat flown in from Europe: Rose Jennings, interview by author, March 10, 2014.

"I plan to retire as soon as I win": "Ali Says It Will Be Last Fight," *New York Times*, October 22, 1974.

Foreman a three-to-one favorite: "Odds on Foreman to Retain Title Rise to 3–1," *New York Times*, October 27, 1974.

"as remote as Zaire": Red Smith, "Kinshasa Could Be Shelby South," *New York Times*, October 23, 1974.

"Shell him for three days": "Ali's Unique Fame — How It All Began," *Chicago Tribune*, November 3, 1974.

391 *"I have a dream"*: Plimpton, *Shadow Box*, 299.

41. RUMBLE IN THE JUNGLE

392 *"What's wrong around here?"*: George Plimpton, "Breaking a Date for the Dance," *Sports Illustrated*, November 11, 1974.

"Look how much better this one looks": Ibid.

394 *where eight-five dollars bought a ticket*: "A Lot of Fans Will See Fight — But Not in Zaire."

About 50 million: "Foreman 3–1 over Ali in Zaire Tonight," *New York Times*, October 29, 1974.

395 *"Chump!"*: Dundee, *My View from the Corner*, 184.

"You been hearing about how bad I am": Ali and Durham, *The Greatest,* 403.

"Oh, Christ, it's a fix": Plimpton, *Shadow Box,* 324.

Weeks before the fight: Gene Kilroy, interview by author, May 22, 2016.

"traditionally a sort of halfway house": Plimpton, "Breaking a Date for the Dance."

396 *"half-dream room"*: Ali and Durham, *The Greatest,* 405.

398 *"In the entire history of boxing"*: Mike Silver, *The Arc of Boxing* (Jefferson, NC: McFarland, 2008), 123.

"You got eight": Al and Durham, *The Greatest,* 411.

"I got a feeling that George": Ali v. Foreman, www.youtube.com.

399 *"I know it"*: George Foreman, interview by author, September 28, 2015.

400 *Sadler asked him for $25,000*: Ibid.

"That's bullshit!": Gene Kilroy, interview by author, May 22, 2016.

"a military column through": Plimpton, *Shadow Box,* 329.

401 *Low, heavy clouds*: Plimpton, "Breaking a Date for the Dance."

"Bulldogs is falling": Plimpton, *Shadow Box,* 332.

402 *"beating George Foreman and conquering"*: Mailer, *The Fight,* 222.

42. MOVING ON UP

403 *"and my great leader"*: "Champion's Greeting for Ali in Chicago," *New York Times,* November 2, 1974.

For years, there had been rumors: Evanzz, *The Messenger,* 419.

"Let's not talk no more": Ibid., 421.

404 *"My whole life is Elijah Muhammad"*: "Muhammad Ali—Larger Than Life," *Montana Standard,* February 23, 1975.

"I feel real guilty": "Ali to Give Away Profits," *Billings Gazette,* February 11, 1975.

white mink stole: "Ali Challenges Black Men," *Ebony,* January 1975.

"because I'm from here, mainly": "Ali Welcomed by Crowd of Supporters in Hometown, 'Greatest City in World,'" *Middlesboro (KY) Daily News,* November 7, 1974.

white Cadillac limousine: "Ali Challenges Black Men."

"You are the greatest, my man!": Ibid.

405 *"Most were black"*: Ibid.

406 *Ali told them to wait*: Kindred, *Sound and Fury,* 204.

"After hearing of the death": Muhammad Ali, eulogy for Elijah Muhammad, memorial service, February 25, 1975, DVD courtesy of Elijah Muhammad III.

"never leave his side": Kram, *Ghosts of Manila,* 113.

"If every Muslim was killed tomorrow": Muhammad Ali, eulogy for Elijah Muhammad.

407 *"Herbert was not that fond of Don"*: Lloyd Price, interview by author, July 30, 2015.

"Joe Bugner?": Gene Kilroy, interview by author, May 17, 2014.

408 *George Jefferson and his family*: Bruce J. Schulman, *The Seventies* (New York: The Free Press, 2001), 53.

invited white people to join the organization: Evanzz, *The Messenger,* 425.

409 *"Ali has entered folklore"*: Wilfrid Sheed, *Muhammad Ali: A Portrait in Words and Photographs* (New York: Signet, 1975), 161.

more than two hundred stitches: "Chuck Wepner: Boxing's Everyman," *Long Beach (CA) Independent,* January 27, 1975.

"to give the white race a chance": Newfield, *Only in America,* 90.

"a good family man": "Ali-Wepner Fight Part of Twinbill," *Cumberland (NJ) News,* January 25, 1975.

410 *King made monthly cash payments:* Gene Kilroy, interview by author, August 26, 2016.

five hundred dollars a week plus expenses: Abdul Rahman, interview by author, August 19, 2016.

"unsung genius": "Nation of Islam Plans Event," *Chicago Defender,* August 30, 1975.

"The referee was Barney Felix": Chuck Wepner, interview by author, February 26, 2014.

411 *"I'm over-tired and under-trained":* "Ali Says He's Overweight, Unenthused," *Chicago Defender,* March 15, 1975.

Ali sneaking glances at TV monitors: "Tired Ali Scores Knockout in 15th to Retain Crown," *Louisville Courier-Journal,* March 25, 1975.

412 *the first knockdown was real:* "Ali Staggers and 'Fluffs Pillows' for Good Cause," *Louisville Courier-Journal,* May 30, 1975.

"I let my sparring partners beat up on me": "Playboy Interview: Muhammad Ali," *Playboy,* November 1975.

"If you didn't hit Ali": Larry Holmes, interview by author, October 1, 2015.

413 *six packets of sugar:* "King of All Kings," *New York Times,* June 29, 1975.

"For Ali to come out there": Larry Holmes, interview by author, October 1, 2015.

43. IMPULSES

415 *Wilma Rudolph . . . had come to the Alis' house:* Khalilah Camacho-Ali, interview by author, March 1, 2016.

the boxer continued to see Sonji Roi: Leon Muhammad, interview by author, June 6, 2016.

Areatha Swint . . . said she carried on an affair: Jamillah Muhammad, interview by author, December 9, 2014.

Ali met a high-school senior: "Suit Is Filed against Ali for Restoration of Child Support," *Los Angeles Times,* January 18, 1985.

416 *Veronica said she knew about Temica:* Veronica Porche, interview by author, December 20, 2016.

"Ali's weakness was coochie": Leon Muhammad, interview by author, June 6, 2016.

complained of difficulty sleeping: Tim Shanahan, interview by author, January 12, 2014.

"He was automatically stupid and crazy": Khalilah Camacho-Ali, interview by author, December 3, 2014.

"He knew it was wrong": Khalilah Camacho-Ali, interview by author, March 1, 2016.

"I said, yeah, that's true": Khalilah Camacho-Ali, interview by author, November 21, 2014.

417 *"My wife is married":* Michael Phenner, interview by author, January 7, 2014.

"The problem I had": Khalilah Camacho-Ali, interview by author, March 1, 2016.

Black women, white women: Ibid.

special set of coded signals: Larry Kolb, interview by author, May 28, 2016; Lowell Riley, interview by author, March 12, 2016.

Ali took six women back to his room: "Arum, One of Boxing's Most Powerful Promoters, Still Hustling," *Sports Illustrated,* December 5, 2012.

Arum said Ali took three women: Bob Arum, interview by author, November 17, 2015.

"the love I had for him": Khalilah Camacho-Ali, interview by author, March 1, 2016.

418 *crossed paths but never met*: Veronica Porche, interview by author, May 26, 2016.

Herbert Muhammad would keep an office there: Jamillah Ali, interview by author, July 25, 2015.

419 *"She didn't get sick, but I did"*: Veronica Porche, interview by author, December 20, 2016.

"I knew I was going to marry Muhammad": "Greatest Expectations," *New York Times,* April 8, 2012.

420 *"He said Lonnie would be a third wife"*: Veronica Porche, interview by author, December 20, 2016.

"Me, Wheeeee!": "Knockout."

The three of them shared a suite: Veronica Porche, interview by author, May 26, 2016; Khalilah Camacho-Ali, interview by author, March 1, 2016.

"Every two nights": Khalilah Camacho-Ali, interview by author, March 1, 2016.

silver perfume amulet: Veronica Porche, interview by author, May 26, 2016.

"It was totally unfair to": Ibid.

421 *"It's going to be big"*: "King of All Kings."

helped hunt for it: Rahaman Ali, interview by author, November 10, 2014.

422 *holding the medal as late as 1963*: Curt Gunther, photograph, MPTV Images, 1963. Published in Azadeh Ansari, "Previously Unseen Photos Show Young Muhammad Ali at Home," CNN.com, http://www.cnn.com/2016/06/05/us/cnnphotos-muhammad-ali-rare-pictures/index.html?sr=twcnni060616cnnphotos-muhammad-ali-rare-pictures0226AMVODtopLink&linkId=25239242.

"Here's this guy": Peter Bonventre, interview by author, June 2, 2016.

423 *Areatha Swint had made the trip*: Jamillah Muhammad, interview by author, December 9, 2014.

"You couldn't be around a man like that": Ibid.

"Solemn Muslim guards": Peter Bonventre, "The Ali Mystique," *Newsweek,* September 29, 1975.

"You have a beautiful wife": Veronica Porche, interview by author, December 20, 2016.

"No, we ain't gonna go": Dave Anderson, "Magellan to MacArthur to Muhammad," *New York Times,* September 23, 1975.

424 *"I'm not wanted here"*: "Mrs. Ali Leaves Manila, Indicating '3 Is a Crowd,'" *New York Times,* September 27, 1975.

"You really couldn't blame her": Jamillah Muhammad, interview by author, December 9, 2014.

"It ain't no accident": "The Ali Mystique."

"I got three or four lady friends": "Ali Tells Public of His Private Life," *New York Times,* September 24, 1975.

44. ALI-FRAZIER III

425 *"Who'd he ever beat"*: "It Takes Two to Make a Fight," *New York Times,* October 2, 1975.
"He not only looks bad!": Kram, *Ghosts of Manila,* 169.

426 *"I know enough about guns"*: "Ali Tells Public of His Private Life."
"I'm gonna eat this": Kram, *Ghosts of Manila,* 171.
350 arenas and theaters: "Ali-Frazier Gross Likely to Set Mark," *New York Times,* October 2, 1975.
100,000 or so American homeowners: Bill Mesce Jr., *Inside the Rise of HBO* (Jefferson, NC: McFarland, 2015), 79.
transmitter in the Philippines: "TV Notes: Who Jockeyed ABC into First Place?" *New York Times,* November 2, 1975.

428 *"Somebody told you all wrong"*: "Lawdy, Lawdy He's Great," *Sports Illustrated,* October 13, 1975.

429 *"It was like death"*: Ibid.
"The world needs ya": Ibid.
"Lawd have mercy!": Ibid.

430 *thinking of Frazier's kids:* "You Could Trust the Trainer Eddie Futch," *New York Times,* October 14, 2001.
Dundee never confirmed those accounts: Dundee, *My View from the Corner,* 199.
"Why I do this?": Kram, *Ghosts of Manila,* 189.

45. GETTING OLD

431 *"I've changed my mind"*: Muhammad Ali, interview by Howard Cosell, ABC-TV, "Thrilla in Manila with Ali Feedback," n.d. (c. 1975), www.youtube.com.
"I'm not going to break our marriage": "Muhammad and Belinda Ali: Is Their Marriage on the Rocks," *Ebony,* December 1975.
"Well, yes": Muhammad Ali, interview by Howard Cosell.

432 *Ali said he planned:* "Press Conference, 1976 Model," *New York Times,* February 22, 1976.
"I'm so far in my own class": "Wrestler's Chin Withstands Ali's Lip," *New York Times,* March 26, 1976.

433 *"I'm heavy because I need energy"*: "Ali at 230 for Young Tonight," *New York Times,* April 30, 1976.
"I've been eating too much pie": "Young 'Ducks' Away from Title," *Deseret News (Salt Lake City, UT),* May 1, 1976.
"Go to work": "Muhammad Ali v. Jimmy Young," ABC-TV, April 30, 1976, www.youtube.com.

434 *"He was more than just overweight"*: "The Most Subjective Sport," *New York Times,* May 2, 1976.

"The bounce wasn't the same": Angelo Dundee, interview by ESPN Sports Century.
"because I couldn't . . . hear him talk": Ibid.
A reporter asked Ali: "The Most Subjective Sport."
"Six million dollars": Ibid.

46. "THEY MAY NOT LET ME QUIT"

435 *Ali's Trolley:* Photo and caption, *Jet,* January 8, 1976.
    "You're not as dumb as you look": Mike Katz, interview by author, May 17, 2014.
436 *"There isn't any marriage:* "The Ali-Belinda Split Is Made Official — and Mysteri-
    ous Veronica Turns up Pregnant," *People,* April 19, 1976.
    separate apartments: Ibid.
437 *"He was literally"*: Spiros Anthony, interview by author, March 9, 2016.
    earned Ali millions: Ibid.
    "I think he knew he was throwing the money away": Richard W. Skillman, interview
    by author, December 12, 2016.
    "I really want to quit": "Ali Admits Decline, but 'They Won't Let Me Quit,'" *New
    York Times,* May 26, 1976.
439 *"One million dollars a punch"*: "Ali Punches More for Army," *New York Times,* June
    28, 1976.
    By the time he flew back: "Ali Hospitalized," *New York Times,* July 2, 1976.
    Inoki later sued Ali: "Ali Confident in Bout with Norton Tonight," *New York Times,*
    September 28, 1976.
    "extreme and repeated mental cruelty": "Notes on People," *New York Times,* October
    5, 1976.
    drive his Stutz Blackhawk: Tim Shanahan, interview by author, July 15, 2014.
    Harold's Chicken Shack: Tim Shanahan, *Running with the Champ* (New York: Si-
    mon and Schuster, 2016), 98.
440 *"We've got bedspreads and towels"*: "Ali Extends Reach to Sheets," *New York Times,*
    August 4, 1976.
    "Mr. Champ's": "Ali's New Drink: 'Mr. Champs' Soda," *New York Times,* May 9, 1978.
441 *one hundred rounds:* "Ken Spars 225 Rounds; Ali 100," *New York Daily News,* Sep-
    tember 26, 1976.
    "the only thing he does with the same": "Ali Now Talking Comeback on Title Merry-
    Go-Round," *New York Daily News,* September 23, 1976.
    mostly failed: "Ali Is up to Par," *New York Post,* September 23, 1976.
    group of army sergeants: "Busy, Like a Bee," *New York Post,* September 25, 1976.
    "I'm almost twice as better": "How Ali, Dundee United," *New York Post,* September
    22, 1976.
    "I wanna leave him": "Ali Set to Slam in the Rubber Match," *Sports Illustrated,* Sep-
    tember 27, 1976.
    "I want you, nigger!": "The Champ's Show," *New York Post,* September 24, 1976.
442 *The Bronx could be dangerous:* "Police Flout Writ by Blocking Traffic at Ali-Norton
    Fight," *New York Times,* September 29, 1976.

Red Smith . . . got his pocket picked: Mike Katz, interview by author, May 17, 2014.

skins of boa constrictors: "The Fight Crowd Finery," *New York Post,* September 29, 1976.

443 *"I beat you!":* "This Was for Auld Lang Syne," *New York Times,* September 29, 1976.

"I was robbed": "'I Was Robbed,'" *New York Post,* September 29, 1976.

"The judges always like": "Ali Finds Non-Believers in His Dressing Room," *New York Times,* September 29, 1976.

"You think they're going to give Ken the decision": "What's Ali Got Left? Not Much," *New York Post,* September 29, 1976.

"How much longer can you fight": Ibid.

444 *"There is no question now":* Mark Kram, "Not the Greatest Way to Go," *Sports Illustrated,* October 11, 1976.

"At the urging of my leader": "Ali Declares He Is Retiring to Assist 'the Islamic Cause,'" *New York Times,* October 2, 1976.

445 *"If he should lose his wealth":* "Raise New Doubt over Ali's Future," *Manchester (CT) Journal Inquirer,* October 4, 1976.

47. "DO YOU REMEMBER MUHAMMAD ALI?"

446 *"Movie star!":* "Muhammad Ali Tries for a Knockout as a Movie Star," *New York Times,* November 7, 1976.

"This face is worth billions": Ibid.

"I want Foreman": "Ali Sees a Foreman (and Bobick) in Future and Changes His Retirement Plans Again," *New York Times,* November 23, 1976.

447 *"Let's get a Rolls!":* Tim Shanahan, interview by author, January 12, 2014.

five bucks to urinate in a cup: Lowell Riley, interview by author, July 8, 2014.

"You know what the big story": "Spaniard Opposing Ali Is Hardly a Fearsome Name," *New York Times,* May 15, 1977.

"He doesn't look like he can hit too hard": Ibid.

448 *"It's been a vaudeville act":* Ali v. Evangelista, www.youtube.com.

449 *already become a Muslim:* "Ali's New Family," *Jet,* May 5, 1977.

white tails, white gloves. "White Tie and Tails for Ali's Third Marriage," *Los Angeles Times,* June 21, 1977.

brought Howard Bingham along: Hauser, with Ali, *Muhammad Ali,* 343.

knocked him out cold: Earnie Shavers, interview by author, November 28, 2014.

"Me and George Foreman": Ibid.

"make July into June": "The 15 Greatest Composite Punchers of All Time," Boxing. com, http://www.boxing.com/the_15_greatest_composite_punchers_of_all_time. html.

"God didn't make the chin to be punched": "'I Am Still a Pistol,'" *Sports Illustrated,* November 7, 1983.

450 *"an act of criminal negligence":* Ferdie Pacheco, "The Thrilla in Manila," in *The Mammoth Book of Muhammad Ali,* ed. David West (Philadelphia: Running Press, 2012), 359.

estimated 54.4 percent: "Ali Pondering Retirement, but Maybe Not Right Now," *New York Times,* October 1, 1977.

opera singer who fakes the high notes: Ibid.

"Is this guy faking": Earnie Shavers, interview by author, November 28, 2014.

451 *collapsed on a table:* Michael Gaffney, *The Champ: My Year with Muhammad Ali* (New York: Diversion Books, 2012), 49.

His hands hurt: "Ali Pondering Retirement, but Maybe Not Right Now."

"Next to Joe Frazier": Ibid.

if Ali insisted on continuing: Teddy Brenner, *Only the Ring Was Square* (Englewood Cliffs, NJ: Prentice-Hall, 1981), 144.

452 *"Yes, I told him":* Ferdie Pacheco, interview by author, December 30, 2013.

"Quit, son": Gaffney, *The Champ,* 49.

48. STAGGERED

453 *to get Ali $8 million:* "Ali's Not Really 'Bigger Than Boxing,'" *New York Times,* November 7, 1977.

"I am the savior": Red Smith, "Spinks Gets Match with Ali Feb. 15," *New York Times,* November 20, 1977.

"He's about 235, 236": Ibid.

"He lets his sparring partners bang him around": Ibid.

454 *"Hell Has Now Frozen Over":* Red Smith, "Hell Has Now Frozen Over," *New York Times,* January 18, 1978.

"I'm just tired of the press": "Superman a Patsy for Ali, but Spinks Silences Him," *New York Times,* February 1, 1978.

"He's troubled about something": Ibid.

Ali had lost millions: "Ali, Despite Millions Won, Faces Toughest Test, Balancing Budget."

"I spent a lot of it foolishly": "The Rich Man — Poor Man," *Inside Sports,* November 30, 1980.

"Ali's got a costly personality": "Ali, Despite Millions Won, Faces Toughest Test, Balancing Budget."

455 *wake-up call every morning at five:* "He's the Greatest, I'm the Best," *Sports Illustrated,* February 27, 1978.

Veronica and the babies were with Ali: Ibid.

"It was the late 1970s": Kevin Powell, "Ali: Hero to a Young Black Boy," *The Undefeated,* June 8, 2016, https://theundefeated.com.

456 *"I know what I'm doing!":* "Muhammad Ali v. Leon Spinks. 1978 02 15. I," www.youtube.com.

"He was crazy, so I tried": Leon Spinks, interview by author, August 17, 2015.

457 *"Things that you see you wanna do":* Muhammad Ali, interview by Dick Cavett, n.d., www.youtube.com.

Pain ripped through Ali's ribcage: "He's the Greatest, I'm the Best."

"That my round?": Muhammad Ali v. Leon Spinks. 1978 02 15. I."

458 *"we've obviously seen the last of him":* Ibid.

tears in his eyes: "Spinks Defeats Ali to Capture Title," *New York Times,* February 16, 1978.

"I want to be the first man": Ibid.

49. CROWN PRINCE

459 *beige Stutz Blackhawk:* "Ali, at 36, Still Talks the Good Fight," *New York Times,* August 4, 1978.

   "They never saw Jesus, either": Ibid.

   launch an international organization called WORLD: Ibid.

460 *"That happens to people who get hit too much":* Muhammad Ali, interview by Dick Cavett.

   1,100 times: Boxing statistics compiled by CompuBox, Inc.

   "selling their souls": "Spinks Picks Ali as Next Foe; Blacks Oppose South Africa Site," *New York Times,* March 9, 1978.

461 *"He just can't say no":* "Ali, at 36, Still Talks the Good Fight."

   "I asked Ali": Louis Farrakhan, interview by author, August 8, 2015.

   "I know what I'm doing": "Ali, at 36, Still Talks the Good Fight."

462 *"If I fought after this":* Ibid.

   "What can Ali do": "Ali, Spinks, and the Battle of New Orleans," *New York,* October 2, 1978.

   "Muhammad Ali decided one day": Hunter S. Thompson, "Last Tango in Vegas," in Early, ed., *The Muhammad Ali Reader,* 194–95.

463 *running a mile, smoking a joint:* Larry Kolb, interview by author, December 23, 2016.

   "Come on, man, I'm Leon": "Spinks Free on Bond in Drug Case," *New York Times,* April 22, 1978.

   "Spinks got drunk every night": "One More Time to the Top," *Sports Illustrated,* September 25, 1978.

   "a match between a novice": Red Smith, "The Fist Is Courage," *New York Times,* August 7, 1978.

   tried to bribe Spinks: FBI memo, September 6, 1978, FBI Vault.

   "my last day in a training gym": "Ali Winds up Training with a Poem about Spinks," *Syracuse (NY) Post Standard,* September 14, 1978.

   couldn't go on fighting much longer: "The Champ Goes to Muhammad Tonight," *Syracuse Post Standard,* September 15, 1978.

   "I wasn't training to beat": "Ali Winds up Training with a Poem about Spinks."

464 *"The stars were for Ali":* Ishmael Reed, "The Fourth Ali," in Early, ed., *The Muhammad Ali Reader,* 203.

50. OLD

466 *"I'm tired of people telling me":* "Boxing's 'Brown Bomber' Honored," *Altoona (PA) Mirror,* November 10, 1978.

467 *"He was still tickled to death"*: Veronica Porche, interview by author, December 20, 2016.

468 *"Get me a Jewish lawyer!"*: Tim Shanahan, interview by author, January 12, 2014.
"I just thought he was a national treasure": Robert Abboud, interview by author, December 17, 2014.
Richley summarized: Robert Richley, interview by author, December 8, 2014.
"build a fence": Robert Abboud, interview by author, December 17, 2014.

469 *big pay cut*: Michael Phenner, interview by author, January 3, 2017.
"Michael Phenner saved us": Veronica Porche, interview by author, December 20, 2016.
paying medical bills out of pocket: Michael Phenner, interview by author, January 7, 2014.
Ali got $1 million: "Ali in Fast's 'Freedom Road,'" *New York Times*, October 29, 1979.
persuaded by Herbert Muhammad to donate: Veronica Porche, interview by author, May 26, 2016.
donation was arranged: Michael Phenner, interview by author, January 3, 2017.
to endorse Orangina: Michael Phenner, interview by author, January 7, 2014.

470 *"He was extremely naive"*: Barry Frank, interview by author, November 11, 2015.
"the kindest, most pure heart": Veronica Porche, interview by author, May 26, 2016.
heavier the better: Ibid.
"Mike, how much do you think": Michael Phenner, interview by author, January 7, 2014.

471 *$500,000 of Well Fargo's money*: "The Big Boxing Con," *Sports Illustrated*, February 18, 1985.
"A guy used my name": Hauser, with Ali, *Muhammad Ali*, 424.
"And they'll be in the stores": "The Once and Always Champ," *New York Times*, July 1, 1979.
Muhammad Ali Institute of Technology and Theatrics: Ibid.

472 *"It got to the point"*: Michael Phenner, interview by author, January 7, 2014.
Phenner and Frank told Ali: Ibid.
234 pounds: "Alzado Finds a Tarkenton in Ali," *New York Times*, July 15, 1979.
hadn't run one mile: "Ali Is the Same until He Enters Ring," *New York Times*, March 13, 1979.

473 *"What did Abraham Lincoln"*: "Ali Didn't Really Need the Mike," *New York Times*, March 9, 1979; Larry Kolb, interview by author, December 19, 2016.
interview in New Zealand: Muhammad Ali, interview by Bob Jones and Pete Montgomery, n.d., www.youtube.com.
"I'm through boxing": Ibid.
ten more years: "Ali Is the Same until He Enters Ring."
"greatest fighter of all times": Muhammad Ali, interview by Bob Jones and Pete Montgomery.
"The fact is": Red Smith, "This Time Ali Means It, Maybe," *New York Times*, August 8, 1979.

51. HUMPTY DUMPTY

475 *blue plastic chair*: "A Lecture by Muhammad Ali: The Topic Is the Greatest," *New York Times*, November 22, 1979.

"My knowledge": Ibid.

476 *Carter had considered using Ali*: Hauser, with Ali, *Muhammad Ali*, 396.

"Maybe I'm being used to do something": "Ali Re-evaluating Stance on Boycotting Olympics," *Boston Globe*, February 4, 1980.

477 *"I'm not here to push nothing on nobody"*: "Ali Shifts Gears on Tour to Urge Olympic Boycott," *Boston Globe*, February 4, 1980.

never would have undertaken his African campaign: "Muhammad Ali Says African Trip Was a Success," *New York Times*, February 11, 1980.

"the most bizarre": "Diplomacy: Ali's Whipping," *Time*, February 18, 1980.

wanted to fight John Tate: "Ali, in 'Retirement,' Wants to Fight Tate," *New York Times*, March 1, 1980.

"I still don't think": "Ali's Retirement," *New York Times*, March 2, 1980.

"Ali can't fight no more": "Holmes, Ali and a Trainer," *New York Times*, July 7, 1980.

478 *Veronica Ali said she opposed her husband's return*: "Ali Injured by Sparring Partner," *New York Times*, March 9, 1980.

"The last three fights or so": Veronica Porche, interview by author, December 20, 2016.

"twitched a little": Veronica Porche, interview by author, May 26, 2016.

"I thought he wasn't walking good": "Too Many Punches, Too Little Concern," *Sports Illustrated*, April 11, 1983.

"He's only flesh and blood": Rahaman Ali, interview by author, October 19, 2016.

"Ali should not try to come back": "Ali's Comeback," *New York Times*, March 2, 1980.

479 *"It'll be a sad day for boxing"*: "Man Here Wants a $7 Million Payday," *New York Times*, March 7, 1980.

three rounds with . . . Luis Acosta: "Ali Injured by Sparring Partner."

needed ten stitches: "Ali to Fight LeDoux May 30 in Minnesota," *New York Times*, May 6, 1980.

"interview with fourteen-year-old Michael Morris": "14-Year-Old Interviewer Successfully Takes on Ali, 38," *New York Times*, June 29, 1980.

480 *"You think I'd come back now"*: "A Miracle in Las Vegas," *New York Times*, August 22, 1980.

he could get it for them at a discount: "Holmes Goal: Punch away Ali's Shadow," *New York Times*, September 28, 1980.

Everyone liked him: Gene Kilroy, interview by author, September 30, 2015.

build a $500,000 house: "Holmes Goal: Punch Away Ali's Shadow."

if he drove too fast or drank too much: Larry Holmes, interview by author, December 13, 2015.

481 *"fucking freeloaders"*: Ibid.

"would pick Joe Louis out of his wheelchair": "The Impression," *Inside Sports*, November 30, 1980.

"I don't care if he gets hurt": Ibid.

strenuous physical examination: "Ali-Holmes Now Set for Las Vegas," *New York Times,* July 18, 1980.

482 *"Only Allah knows about my brain":* "Ali: Brain Damage Report Is 'Crazy,'" *Reno Gazette-Journal,* June 3, 1980.

"used to be an electrifying speaker": "Ali Showing Some Signs of Brain Damage," *Capital Times* (Madison, WI), June 4, 1980.

"Just about everyone who is": Ibid.

Two reports emerged from the Mayo Clinic: Hauser, with Ali, *Muhammad Ali,* 404–5.

Dr. Howard's memo: Ibid., 405.

483 *dyeing the gray out of his hair:* "Ali: Ready, Willing, but Is He Able," *New York Times,* September 29, 1980.

Witherspoon was excited: Tim Witherspoon, interview by author, August 10, 2015.

484 *"When we were in the ring":* Ibid.

"Ali showing some signs of brain damage": "Ali Showing Some Signs of Brain Damage."

"He's just a shell": "Ali: Ready, Willing, but Is He Able."

"I corrected it": Hauser, with Ali, *Muhammad Ali,* 414.

thyroid drug and a weight-loss drug: Ibid., 489.

485 *thirty different kinds of pills:* Pete Dexter, "The Impression," *Inside Sports,* November 30, 1980.

"As sure as you hear my voice": Ibid.

brick wall at eighty-five miles an hour: "Gary Wells Attempts Caesars Palace Fountain Jump," September 15, 1980, www.youtube.com.

"He's 29 again": "Better Not Sell the Old Man Short," *Sports Illustrated,* September 29, 1980.

"Now that I got my weight down": Ibid.

486 *"He couldn't run":* Hauser, with Ali, *Muhammad Ali,* 410.

Veronica Ali had felt confident: Veronica Ali, interview by author, May 26, 2016.

unable to run a mile: "Muhammad Ali Still Doesn't Know He's 38 Years Old," *New York Times,* October 4, 1980.

collapsed on the side of the road: Larry Kolb, interview by author, November 20, 2015.

"The dumb nigger": Larry Kolb, interview by author, December 10, 2016.

"dehydration" and "thyroid": Tim Witherspoon, interview by author, August 10, 2015.

487 *"Oh, God," he thought:* "Doom in the Desert," *Sports Illustrated,* October 13, 1980.

488 *"You start punching":* "The Event," *Inside Sports,* November 30, 1980.

340 punches to Ali's 42: Statistics compiled by CompuBox, Inc.

"I love you": "The Event."

"I may return": "Muhammad Ali Still Doesn't Know He's 38 Years Old."

52. THE LAST HURRAH

490 *painkillers and antidepressants:* Toxicology report, Southern Nevada Memorial Hospital Pathology Department, October 10, 1980, Nevada State Athlete Commission.

could not be punished: "Ali Retires, but Only in Nevada," *New York Times,* December 30, 1980.

"It would have been an awful precedent": Ibid.

"We rushed it": Sig Rogich, interview by author, December 9, 2015.

491 *paid him only $6.83 million:* Michael Phenner, interview by author, January 7, 2014.

"from any and all monies": Newfield, *Only in America,* 166.

Phenner cried: Michael Phenner, interview by author, January 7, 2014.

492 *"In two or three years":* "Ali's Manager: 'I Don't Think He Should Fight,'" *Santa Fe New Mexican,* October 7, 1980.

"You're my brother!": "Muhammad Ali Talks Man Out of Jumping," *Los Angeles Times,* January 20, 1981.

"held the heavyweight boxing championship": "Joe Louis, 66, Heavyweight King Who Reigned 12 Years, Is Dead," *New York Times,* April 13, 1981.

493 *"Once I happened to walk along":* Louis, "How I Would Have Clobbered Clay."

weighing 249 pounds: "Not with a Bang but a Whisper," *Sports Illustrated,* December 21, 1981.

"Nobody will ever do it five times": "At 39, Ali Has More Points to Prove," *New York Times,* November 29, 1981.

494 *"lethargy, weakness and shortness of breath":* Ibid.

lost his sense of smell: "Too Many Punches, Too Little Concern."

refused to step on a scale: Larry Kolb, interview by author, December 23, 2016.

"sizzle and dance": "Not with a Bang but a Whisper."

495 *"I'll handle him so easy":* "The Greatest Gives Thanks," *New York Times,* November 27, 1981.

"Do I sound like got brain damage to you?": Ibid.

Don King was assaulted: "Dark Clouds over Nassau," *New York Times,* December 9, 1981.

King alleged that the beating: "Berbick First Has a Price to Fight Ali," *New York Times,* December 10, 1981.

convicted felon: "More on Cornelius," *New York Times,* January 15, 1982.

"He's a promoter": "Ali's Mystery Promoter," *New York Times,* December 11, 1981.

Ali seemed unsure: Ibid.

suitcase filled with $1 million cash: Larry Kolb, interview by author, December 23, 2016.

497 *"It was close, it was close":* "Muhammad Ali v. Trevor Berbick. 1981 12 11," www.youtube.com.

"You can't beat Father Time": "Muhammad Ali's Moment of Truth," *New York Times,* December 12, 1981.

498 *"At least I didn't go down":* "Ali Quits the Ring Again," *New York Times,* December 13, 1981.

53. TOO MANY PUNCHES

499 *"We are here"*: Larry Kolb, interview by author, December 31, 2016.
Tallying Angel: Ibid.
500 *sat in the locker room*: "Cobwebs in the Gym," *New York Times*, November 15, 1982.
"clinging together as cobwebs of dust do": Ibid.
"My life just started at forty": Ibid.
punches pounded his headgear: Ibid.
501 *"What does the boxing profession think"*: "Boxing and the Brain," *New York Times*, June 12, 1983.
"the principal purpose of a boxing match": "Boxing Should Be Banned in Civilized Countries," *Journal of the American Medical Association*, January 14, 1983.
"It's possible": "Too Many Punches, Too Little Concern."
"acting depressed of late": Ibid.
Forgotten to whom he was speaking: Hauser, with Ali, *Muhammad Ali*, 430.
502 *"They read this as normal?"*: "Too Many Punches, Too Little Concern."
"It was all consistent with brain damage": Dr. Ira Casson, interview by author, November 23, 2016.
mischievous look crossed Ali's face: Larry Kolb, interview by author, December 22, 2016.
$1,200 "hang-around money": Kindred, *Sound and Fury*, 269.
"He was an old man at forty-one": Ibid., 270.
He drooled at times: Hauser, with Ali, *Muhammad Ali*, 489.
503 *"I've taken about 175,000 hard punches"*: "Muhammad Ali Says He Is Tired of Rumors That He Is Brain Damaged," *Jet*, April 30, 1984.
why his body seemed to be: Hauser, with Ali, *Muhammad Ali*, 489.
Ali displayed a range of symptoms: Dr. Stanley Fahn, interview by author, June 1, 2015.
"He was a little slow": Hauser, with Ali, *Muhammad Ali*, 491.
Floyd Patterson paid a visit: Larry Kolb, interview by author, December 9, 2016.
"At least he didn't call me a nigger *draft-dodger"*: Ibid.
"He's not thinking very fast": "Pendleton Is Right," *Victoria Advocate*, November 26, 1984.
504 *seventh-floor hospital room*: Larry Kolb, interview by author, December 9, 2016.
"I saw so many people": "Hospitalized Ali: 'I'm Not Hurting,'" *Los Angeles Times*, September 21, 1984.
"very possibly": "Ali's Improvement Is Called Impressive," *New York Times*, September 21, 1984.
survey of more than two hundred boxers: "Boxing and the Brain," *British Medical Journal*, January 14, 1989.
as far back as 1975: Dr. Stanley Fahn, interview by author, June 1, 2015.
505 *"My assumption"*: Hauser, with Ali, *Muhammad Ali*, 492.
as clever and intelligent as ever: Dr. Stanley Fahn, interview by author, June 1, 2015.

"I'm lazy and I forget": "Playful Ali Goes the Distance with Reporters," *New York Times,* November 20, 1984.

"I'm more celebrated": Ibid.

506 *"advisers, friends, fans"*: Laila Ali, with David Ritz, *Reach!* (New York: Hyperion, 2002), 20.

"I never heard my parents fight": Ibid., 12.

"I was drawn instead": Ibid., 19–20.

"We had to share him, anyway": Jamillah Ali, interview by author, July 25, 2015.

507 *"That meant more to me"*: "His Gentle Soul," *ESPN Magazine,* June 27, 2016.

feeling like a prisoner: Veronica Ali, interview by author, May 26, 2016.

"I became numb": Ibid.

"He'd bring a woman right in front of you": Veronica Ali, interview by author, December 20, 2016.

selling her plasma: Khalilah Camacho-Ali, interview by author, January 12, 2015.

dined at the Williams's table: "Muhammad Ali Was Her First, and Greatest, Love," *New York Times,* June 9, 2016.

"He was despondent": Hauser, with Ali, *Muhammad Ali,* 469.

508 *"He'd sometimes bring us along"*: Ali, with Ritz, *Reach!* 20.

"You cannot do that": Veronica Ali, interview by author, May 26, 2016.

Ali married Lonnie: "Muhammad Ali Takes Ring Again — Weds 4th Time," *Louisville Courier-Journal,* November 20, 1968.

54. "HE'S HUMAN, LIKE US"

510 *"Larry, get up and go to that line"*: Larry Kolb, interview by author, October 14, 2015.

Robert Sensi, a CIA agent: Larry Kolb, *Overworld* (New York: Riverhead Books, 2004), 205

they suggested Ali go to Lebanon: Ibid., 212.

met with shadowy figures: Ibid., 207–229.

511 *"Dear Gene"*: Muhammad Ali to Gene Kilroy, February 20, 1985, personal collection of Gene Kilroy.

wasn't sure where or when: Kindred, *Sound and Fury,* 272.

512 *"a bad guy"*: Gene Kilroy, interview by author, April 3, 2017.

wondered if the world knew: Ibid.

"Quiet, Drew": Ibid., 278.

513 *"Superman don't need no plane!"*: Larry Kolb, interview by author, December 31, 2016.

"If I had one dollar": Ibid.

wedged his big body through the window: Video from 1987, courtesy of Larry Kolb.

"Black Superman": Ibid.

He heard the song everywhere: Larry Kolb, interview by author, December 31, 2016.

Ali congratulated Afghans: Larry Kolb, interview by author, December 22, 2016.

514 *"Many people in America":* Video from 1987, courtesy of Larry Kolb.
     thin man with a long beard stands out: Ibid.
     told him the man was most likely bin Laden: Larry Kolb, interview by author, December 22, 2016.
     Don King and Donald Trump: Peter Tauber, "Ali: Still Magic," *New York Times,* July 17, 1988.
515 *"I've got Parkinson's syndrome":* Ibid.
     "pleasant back-and-forth conversation": Kindred, *Sound and Fury,* 288.
516 *"I didn't call 'em":* Ibid., 290.
     Hirschfeld had been entertaining friends: "Were Senators Duped by an Ali Impersonator," *St. Petersburg Times,* December 14, 1988.
     "That little Jewish lawyer's": Kindred, *Sound and Fury,* 290.
     Ali . . . knew exactly what Hirschfeld was doing: Larry Kolb, interview by author, January 10, 2016.
517 *"It was a spiritual journey for both of us":* Lonnie Ali, text message to author, January 3, 2017.
     "When Muhammad started to get sick": Thomas Hauser, interview by author, January 5, 2017.
     five thousand dollars for four hours: Brian Bedol, interview by author, April 7, 2014.
     two-thousand-dollar tab: Ibid.
518 *"In my career, everything":* Muhammad Ali interview with David Frost, n.d., www.youtube.com.
     "He was a father": "Father of Muhammad Ali Dies," UPI Archives, http://www.upi.com/Archives/1990/02/09/Father-of-Muhammad-Ali-dies/4127634539600/.
519 *"Book makes me look like a fool":* Robert Lipsyte, "Ali Is Still a Comfort to Many Aging Fans," *New York Times,* June 7, 1991.
     "Shouldn't have done it": Ibid.
     Lonnie was saddened at times: Thomas Hauser, *The Lost Legacy of Muhammad Ali* (Toronto: Sport Classic Books, 2005), 182.
     stepped on his former opponent's foot: Ibid.

55. A TORCH

520 *10:15 one Saturday morning:* Frank Sadlo, interview by author, November 5, 2016.
521 *"Let's go":* Frank Sadlo, interview by author, June 5, 2014.
     "I wanted to do something nice": Ibid.
     gently rubbed her nose: Brenda Bender, interview by author, October 19, 2016.
522 *Sadlo wrote letters:* Copies of letters, multiple dates, from the personal collection of Frank Sadlo.
     "all his oars in the water": Frank Sadlo, interview by author, June 5, 2014.
523 *"Sadlo received a strange phone call":* Ibid.
524 *fighting back tears:* Frank Sadlo, interview by author, October 6, 2016.
     "Ali's lighting of the Olympic flame": "Ali's Return Not Met with Pity, but with Affection," *USA Today,* October 11–13, 1996.
525 *"He's half real":* Seth Abraham, interview by author, June 15, 2015.

56. THE LONG, BLACK CADILLAC

527 *"More and more he is like a soul walking"*: Frank Deford, "You Don't Know Muhammad Ali until You Know His Best Friend," *Sports Illustrated*, July 13, 1998.
"a prophet, a messenger of God": Ezra, *Muhammad Ali*, 183.
"As I watch him eat": Peter Richmond, "Muhammad Ali in Excelsis," *GQ*, April 1998.
"For decades": Ibid.

528 *"I said a lot of things"*: "No Floating, No Stinging: Ali Extends Hand to Frazier," *New York Times*, March 15, 2001.
"God will be the judge": Ibid.

529 *"I am a Muslim"*: "Calm Needed during Time of Anger," *New York Times*, September 19, 2001.
"Tell me what happened again?": George Franklin, interview by author, January 20, 2015.
firefighters wanted to tell Ali: Ibid.
"Islam is not a killing religion": Muhammad Ali interview with David Frost, HBO broadcast, June 25, 2002, www.youtube.com.
Hollywood-produced ad campaign": "Government Hounded Ali," *Syracuse (NY) Post Standard*, January 16, 2002.
The Final Call . . . urged Ali: "Ali, Just Say No," *Final Call*, January 8, 2002, http://www.finalcall.com/columns/akbar/ali01-08-2002.htm.
"I dodge those questions": *Muhammad Ali interview with* David Frost, HBO, June 25, 2002.

531 *$750 per autograph*: Mike Frost, interview by author, December 23, 2014.
"He was a man that never complained": Asaad Ali, interview on the *Today Show*, NBC, June 10, 2016, http://www.today.com/news/muhammad-ali-s-son-opens-about-his-dad-today-he-t97571.
"Speaking as someone": "Muhammad Ali Defends Islam after Trump's Proposal to Bar Foreign Muslims," *New York Times*, December 10, 2015.

532 *"The relationship changes"*: "Caring for the Greatest," *AARP Bulletin*, June 2014.
refrigerator magnet: Khalilah Camacho-Ali, interview by author, December 24, 2014.

533 *"He wasn't no hero"*: Larry Holmes, interview by author, October 1, 2015.
Bender had taken a writer on a tour: Vic Bender, interview by author, October 1, 2015.

534 *"Wasn't it a beautiful night?"*: Rahaman Ali, interview by author, October 1, 2015.
mouth was next to Ali's right ear and other details from hospital: Tom Junod, "The Greatest, At Rest," *ESPN The Magazine*, June 12, 2017.

535 *"'I am America,' he once declared"*: "President Obama's Statement on Muhammad Ali," *New York Times*, June 4, 2016.

536 *"Ali boma ye"*: "In Death, Ali Still Larger than Life," *Louisville Courier-Journal*, June 11, 2016.
"Muhammad fell in love with the masses": Lonnie Ali eulogy, author's recording, June 10, 2016.

537 *"He floated like a butterfly"*: Imam Zaid Shakir eulogy, author's recording, June 10, 2016.

"God is watching me": "Muhammad Ali Talks about His Death," www.youtube.com.

"I had to prove you could be": Remnick, *King of the World*, xiii.

POSTSCRIPT

538 *a political activitist*: Bernardine Dorhn, interview by author, November 9, 2016.

APPENDIX
Career Record

DATE	OPPONENT	LOCATION	OUTCOME	DECISION
10/29/1960	Tunney Hunsaker	Freedom Hall, Louisville, Kentucky, USA	W	UD
12/27/1960	Herb Siler	Auditorium, Miami Beach, Florida, USA	W	TKO
1/17/1961	Tony Esperti	Auditorium, Miami Beach, Florida, USA	W	TKO
2/7/1961	Jimmy Robinson	Convention Center, Miami Beach, Florida, USA	W	KO
2/21/1961	Donnie Fleeman	Auditorium, Miami Beach, Florida, USA	W	RTD
4/19/1961	LaMar Clark	Freedom Hall, Louisville, Kentucky, USA	W	KO
6/26/1961	Duke Sabedong	Convention Center, Las Vegas, Nevada, USA	W	UD
7/22/1961	Alonzo Johnson	Freedom Hall, Louisville, Kentucky, USA	W	UD
10/7/1961	Alex Miteff	Freedom Hall, Louisville, Kentucky, USA	W	TKO
11/29/1961	Willi Besmanoff	Freedom Hall, Louisville, Kentucky, USA	W	TKO
2/10/1962	Sonny Banks	Madison Square Garden, New York, New York, USA	W	TKO
2/28/1962	Don Warner	Convention Center, Miami Beach, Florida, USA	W	TKO
4/23/1962	George Logan	Sports Arena, Los Angeles, California, USA	W	TKO
5/19/1962	Billy Daniels	St. Nicholas Arena, New York, New York, USA	W	TKO
7/20/1962	Alejandro Lavorante	Sports Arena, Los Angeles, California, USA	W	KO
11/15/1962	Archie Moore	Sports Arena, Los Angeles, California, USA	W	TKO
1/24/1963	Charlie Powell	Civic Arena, Pittsburgh, Pennsylvania, USA	W	KO
3/13/1963	Doug Jones	Madison Square Garden, New York, New York, USA	W	UD
6/18/1963	Henry Cooper	Wembley Stadium, Wembley, London, United Kingdom	W	TKO

DATE	OPPONENT	LOCATION	OUTCOME	DECISION
2/25/1964	Sonny Liston	Convention Center, Miami Beach, Florida, USA	W	RTD
5/25/1965	Sonny Liston	Central Maine Civic Center, Lewiston, Maine, USA	W	KO
11/22/1965	Floyd Patterson	Convention Center, Las Vegas, Nevada, USA	W	TKO
3/29/1966	George Chuvalo	Maple Leaf Gardens, Toronto, Ontario, Canada	W	UD
5/21/1966	Henry Cooper	Arsenal Football Stadium, Highbury, London, United Kingdom	W	TKO
8/6/1966	Brian London	Earls Court Arena, Kensington, London, United Kingdom	W	KO
9/10/1966	Karl Mildenberger	Waldstadion/Radrennbahn, Frankfurt, Hessen, Germany	W	TKO
11/14/1966	Cleveland Williams	Astrodome, Houston, Texas, USA	W	TKO
2/6/1967	Ernie Terrell	Astrodome, Houston, Texas, USA	W	UD
3/22/1967	Zora Folley	Madison Square Garden, New York, New York, USA	W	KO
10/26/1970	Jerry Quarry	City Auditorium, Atlanta, Georgia, USA	W	RTD
12/7/1970	Oscar Bonavena	Madison Square Garden, New York, New York, USA	W	TKO
3/8/1971	Joe Frazier	Madison Square Garden, New York, New York, USA	L	UD
7/26/1971	Jimmy Ellis	Astrodome, Houston, Texas, USA	W	TKO
11/17/1971	Buster Mathis	Astrodome, Houston, Texas, USA	W	UD
12/26/1971	Juergen Blin	Hallenstadion, Zurich, Switzerland	W	KO
4/1/1972	Mac Foster	Nippon Budokan, Tokyo, Japan	W	UD
5/1/1972	George Chuvalo	Pacific Coliseum, Vancouver, British Columbia, Canada	W	UD
6/27/1972	Jerry Quarry	Convention Center, Las Vegas, Nevada, USA	W	TKO
7/19/1972	Alvin Blue Lewis	Croke Park, Dublin, Ireland	W	TKO
9/20/1972	Floyd Patterson	Madison Square Garden, New York, New York, USA	W	RTD
11/21/1972	Bob Foster	Sahara-Tahoe Hotel, Stateline, Nevada, USA	W	KO
2/14/1973	Joe Bugner	Convention Center, Las Vegas, Nevada, USA	W	UD
3/31/1973	Ken Norton	Sports Arena, San Diego, California, USA	L	SD

DATE	OPPONENT	LOCATION	OUTCOME	DECISION
9/10/1973	Ken Norton	Forum, Inglewood, California, USA	W	SD
10/20/1973	Rudi Lubbers	Bung Karno Stadium, Jakarta, Indonesia	W	UD
1/28/1974	Joe Frazier	Madison Square Garden, New York, New York, USA	W	UD
10/30/1974	George Foreman	Stade du 20 Mai, Kinshasa, Democratic Republic of the Congo	W	KO
3/24/1975	Chuck Wepner	Richfield Coliseum, Richfield, Ohio, USA	W	TKO
5/16/1975	Ron Lyle	Convention Center, Las Vegas, Nevada, USA	W	TKO
6/30/1975	Joe Bugner	Merdeka Stadium, Kuala Lumpur, Malaysia	W	UD
10/1/1975	Joe Frazier	Araneta Coliseum, Barangay Cubao, Quezon City, Metro Manila, Philippines	W	RTD
2/20/1976	Jean-Pierre Coopman	Coliseo Roberto Clemente, San Juan, Puerto Rico	W	KO
4/30/1976	Jimmy Young	Capital Centre, Landover, Maryland, USA	W	UD
5/24/1976	Richard Dunn	Olympiahalle, Munich, Bayern, Germany	W	TKO
9/28/1976	Ken Norton	Yankee Stadium, Bronx, New York, USA	W	UD
5/16/1977	Alfredo Evangelista	Capital Centre, Landover, Maryland, USA	W	UD
9/29/1977	Earnie Shavers	Madison Square Garden, New York, New York, USA	W	UD
2/15/1978	Leon Spinks	Hilton Hotel, Las Vegas, Nevada, USA	L	SD
9/15/1978	Leon Spinks	Superdome, New Orleans, Louisiana, USA	W	UD
10/2/1980	Larry Holmes	Caesars Palace, Las Vegas, Nevada, USA	L	RTD
12/11/1981	Trevor Berbick	Queen Elizabeth Sports Centre, Nassau, Bahamas	L	UD

KEY

RTD: Retired Between Rounds **UD:** Unanimous Decision **MD:** Majority Decision
TKO: Technical Knockout **KO:** Knockout
Source: Boxrec.com

INDEX